Imprint

Data Engine Thinking
By Roelant Vos and Dirk Lerner

Published by
Vos & Lerner Data Engine Thinking GbR
Astrid-Lindgren-Straße 4
64331 Weiterstadt
Germany

https://dataenginethinking.com
info@dataenginethinking.com

Layout, typesetting, cover
Romi Klockau | linkedin.com/in/romi-klockau

Graphics and illustration
Matthias Seifert | www.matthias-seifert.com

Printing history
First edition, 2025

ISBN 978-3-9827180-0-2
Print softcover edition

ISBN 978-3-9827180-1-9
Kindle Replica-eBook edition

ISBN 978-3-9827180-2-6
PDF edition

ISBN 978-3-9827180-3-3
Print hardcover edition

ISBN 978-3-9827180-4-0
Print hardcover limited edition

Exclusion of liability

About the code examples

We have tried to keep the technical examples as 'human-readable' as possible. This includes using names that follow Title Case[1], which may include spaces. For code samples we follow the same convention, but replace the space with an underscore. In the code samples we prefer to use a readable column name as opposed to using placeholders.

Unless mentioned otherwise we use SQL Server syntax with default highlighting. We intend to conform to ANSI[2] SQL as much as possible.

For instance, technical examples would refer to Inscription Timestamp as one of the standard framework columns. In code, this is depicted as [Inscription_Timestamp].

Testimonials

"This book is a monumental achievement, a classic even before release. I predict this will be as much a landmark of progress and contemporary standards for Data Warehousing as the Kimball series were 20+ years ago. If you are in the business of storing large volumes of data, and need to integrate sources, this book is for you. If you want to make sense of temporal logic in data, this book is for you, too. Great technical insights, but arguably at least as important are the lessons from the trenches on why some DWH projects succeed, and so many of them struggle. Highest praise I can give, arguably most valuable book on Business Intelligence I ever read."

— Tom Breur, VP of Advanced Analytics at Health Advances —

"With the launch of this excellent book, the data warehousing industry will move another step closer to achieving success. Dirk and Roelant, two brilliant thinkers and diligent practitioners, are presenting a vision of a realistic and complete roadmap for an agile business data solution. Any and all data warehouse practitioners, from business analysts to modelers to developers, will benefit greatly from the insights and guidance provided in this book."

— Hans Hultgren, President, Genesee Academy, LLC —

Acknowledgements

We would like to thank everyone who supported us on our journey from the earliest ideas to the finished version of this book. A special thanks to **Tom Breur,** whose invaluable feedback and motivation in the early days pushed us to keep going. Without his continued support, we might never have completed this book.

Our gratitude extends to the thought leaders, experts, and pioneers of Ensemble Modeling, particularly Data Vault: **Hans Hultgren, Remco Broekmans, Dan Linstedt,** and many others. Your tireless efforts to define, discuss, and improve these techniques have been instrumental in driving progress. This includes the excellent work done by the German Data Vault community— **Christian Hädrich, Michael Müller, Olivier Kramer,** and the rest. We've had countless great, constructive, and most of all, friendly discussions on a wide range of topics over the years.

Furthermore, we owe a debt of gratitude to **Ronald Damhof** for his foundational work on the Data Quadrant Model. His innovative classification of data into four quadrants has greatly influenced our approach to managing data.

A special thanks to **Steve Hoberman** for sharing your experience in writing and publishing, and for making data topics engagin—topics that, to some, might seem dry, but which you've brought to life. Anyone who thinks otherwise should definitely check out your work!

We're also incredibly grateful for the support of **Marco Wobben** and **Stephan Volkmann** on FCO-IM. Your patience in answering our many questions on this topic is truly appreciated.

This book wouldn't have been possible without the contributions of **Romi Klockau, Matthias Seifert,** and **Kim de Vries.** Their creative ideas and insights in presenting complex concepts helped bring this book to life in ways we couldn't have done alone. It's not easy to make such concepts not only understandable but also visually appealing, and they succeeded brilliantly. Thank you so much!

We also want to express our gratitude to the many people we've had deep and varied discussions with over the years—at conferences, during projects, and even at bars and campsites. The data community has always been supportive, and we're proud to give back through this book.

Finally, a heartfelt thank you to our families for their unwavering support.

Roelant

Thanks to Jette, Sarah, and Daphne for understanding when I skipped dinner, was absent —mentally or physically— or opened my laptop in the desert at 45 degrees (Celcius). I hope you can now see what all the fuss was about.

And Sarah and Daphne, I haven't given up on making data engineers out of you yet!

And, of course, thank you, Dirk, for this amazing collaboration. These can be complex topics, but our alignment has been remarkable. Your deep knowledge and skill made it possible for us to work through everything so smoothly.

Who would have thought, when we went for whiskey tasting all those years ago, that we'd be here today? We did it!

Dirk

A big thank you to Kerstin for always encouraging me to keep going and for her constant support. And to my daughters —Elisabeth, Catalina, Johanna, and Magdalena— who are already spreading the word at school so everyone can have a copy! Who knows, maybe they or their friends will one day become professionals in our field.

Now that you hold this book in your hands, you can finally see why I spent so many hours at my laptop instead of joining you for shopping trips or kite surfing adventures. You can finally stop asking how many pages are left until the book is finished.

A special thanks to my co-author Roelant. It's been an incredible experience working together, and this book would not have been the same without his expertise and passion.

I know, right? It's amazing to think how far we've come since that whiskey tasting! What a journey — it's been incredible doing this together. We really did it!

Contents

·N'Oonedaatan·
University
City
"Fast Change Co"
"L'Art L'Amande"
"The Dive"
"T-Time"
Football
N
W
S

00 Introduction

Introducing FastChangeCo

FastChangeCo is a fictitious company, but it faces real-world challenges and opportunities that many of you may recognize.

In this book, though imaginary, FastChangeCo provides a realistic use case for our *Engine Thinking* approach to designing and operating data solutions.

With thousands of employees, and hundreds of products across different branches, FastChangeCo has grown into a multi billion-dollar business.

During the 90s, FastChangeCo launched its first Business Intelligence (BI) initiative to better understand its operations and optimize value creation in manufacturing. As years went by, FastChangeCo has built three Data Warehouses, the latest of which is nearing the end of its life cycle.

Due to ever faster changing business needs, FastChangeCo tried to expand the Data Warehouse with modern technologies several times. However, in the end the ambitious goal of having all needs satisfied by the Data Warehouse could not be met.

New requirements constantly arise as business processes evolve, while new operational systems — both developed in-house and acquired externally— are introduced and modified.

All this means that the Data Warehouse must be capable of rapidly adapting to new and changing data sources, as well as shifting delivery and data requirements.

For the BI team at FastChangeCo, these challenges are proving too much to handle. After the senior management becomes aware of this unsatisfactory situation (for all people involved), they decide to hire a new Head of Data Management.

The first task for this new position is to transform the BI function into a modern data competence center, driving the data and reporting strategy, and steering the transition from today's reporting towards a professional system with contemporary visualization capabilities.

After numerous interviews, Michael Mueller emerged as the best candidate to lead FastChangeCo's data management evolution.

Subsequently, Michael was hired as the new Head of Data Management.

The management of FastChangeCo is enthusiastic about embarking on the journey of delivering the best data solution that can possibly be designed. This will be the last one they are going to need.

FastChangeCo disclaimer

All scenarios, projects and persons described here in the book are of a purely fictional nature. However, they are based on real situations and the experiences of the authors. Any similarities with real persons, projects or companies are purely coincidental, and not intended.

The breadcrumbs of human activity

Data is just 'stuff.'

Data is evidence of events frozen in time, which have persisted for us to uncover and analyze at our discretion.

In a way, this process of discovery can be likened to how paleontologists carefully unearth ancient skeletons and imprints, using these artifacts reconstruct what happened at that lost moment in time.

Or, along the same lines, how biologists use the fossil record to refine our understanding of evolution – occasionally redrawing aspects of the tree of life based on new insights.

Closer to home, data can be defined as a byproduct of business processes. These processes themselves can be explained as orchestrated sets of activities designed to reach a specific goal. Or simply put, the things people do day-to-day in their job.

Without understanding these processes, this *context,* truly grasping the significance of the data can be challenging. Without the context, we only have the data. We can use this data to perform forensics and define hypotheses on. But, when we have both the data and the context available, we can have *information* and better understand what happened, how it happened, and why it happened.

Scientists, including the biologists and paleontologists mentioned earlier, know that new evidence and new understanding may mean that what is presently accepted as truth may need be adjusted or rewritten. Fresh findings can have a significant impact on earlier assumptions, and often requires previous artifacts to be reviewed and examined in a different light – potentially resulting in different conclusions.

By following the scientific method, over the years more and more context is provided to support our understanding of what is real, and what is still being clarified.

Working with data in our businesses can be very similar. We often find ways to extract and collect data from what we refer to as 'feeding' or 'source' systems. These are the (IT) applications that support the operation of the business – the operational and transactional systems of an organization.

From the perspective of a data solution, these are the systems that generate events and act as 'source' for data to be collected and analyzed. Feeding systems, operational systems and source systems can be used synonymously, and there are often many in any given organization. Not only are there many, but they come in equally many different types, designs and levels of quality and dependability.

Data is created when business processes are followed by the users of these applications, for example new customers or orders are entered into the system, or refunds are processed.

As mentioned earlier, correctly interpreting this data hinges on understanding the processes that influenced its creation – the context.

In some instances, this is pretty clear, and the subject matter expertise may be readily available. However, in other cases, data may be years old, generated by systems that are no longer in production. Or, the processes have changed over time but the system (and therefore the physical storage of data) has not – which means data that is stored in a given format *may* mean different things depending on the time it was created.

Even worse: the interpretation of the data has changed, but this change in perspective may not be documented.

There can also be instances where subject matter expertise is limited or not available at all. In other cases still, data may not always be consistently available or with questionable quality. And all these factors assume that the established processes are actually followed.

There are numerous reasons why it may not be always immediately clear what the data really means.

01
FastChangeCo – the world of data

Data is just 'stuff.'

Let's go back to the beginnings of FastChangeCo's plans to reinvent its Business Intelligence (BI) and Data Warehouse landscape in pursuit of a contemporary data solution architecture.

Currently, the third iteration of the Data Warehouse is in production. However, this Data Warehouse is now fast approaching its end of life.

And yet, data is mostly still just 'stuff.'

Michael Mueller has frequently encountered this attitude towards data during conversations with BI teams, involved departments, and consumers of the data. The potential value of data is generally recognized, but it is neither consistently promoted nor truly embedded in the corporate culture.

The notion that data should be more than just 'stuff,' but should be the basis for the success of FastChange-Co in the 21st century has yet to take root.

Michael's goals are clear, and he is determined to pursue them from day one.

The first task, and perhaps the most difficult one, is to cultivate a company-wide mindset shift, instilling a culture that treats data as a strategic asset.

Secondly, he intends to dismantle the rigid project structures in favor of a more flexible approach.

And finally, he doesn't want to waste any time starting the FastChangeCo fourth-generation data solution —one that will be able to deal with existing issues as well as future challenges.

The way Michael sees it, there are five major challenges to address.

The number of systems is increasing sharply

Until now, there are only a few operational systems that need to deliver data to the Data Warehouse. This makes the data supply straightforward and convenient. Some areas even rely on a single legacy system, like the decades-old mainframe.

But times they are a changing.

There are many initiatives underway to replace existing systems with one or more modern, state-of-the-art, *independent* and flexible solutions. The objective is always to be able to respond ever faster to the evolving business requirements of today's world.

It is difficult to scale the team

Scaling the BI team has been challenging. A few BI team members hold most of the knowledge about the structure and meaning of the data, and how this is reflected in the Data Warehouse.

This knowledge is not readily available, and documentation is insufficient. As a result, some team members have become single-point dependencies, and it is not easy to distribute their knowledge across the team.

Also, a larger team will likely be needed in the future due to the sheer volume of business requirements that will need to be implemented in a very short timeframe.

Release cycles are long

Today's development and release cycles are long and ponderous. It can take up to six months until new requirements or features have made it to production, even for a relatively small change.

Without shorter and more effective development processes FastChangeCo will not be able to keep up with its competitors.

Demand is increasing

There is a strong need for data consumers to access authored and trusted data from a single source.

No more selecting and copying subsets of data across several systems, laboriously combining them by hand in order to generate a report that ultimately serves to contribute to knowledge and actionable insights, hopefully.

Change is expected to happen faster

It is expected that the pace of change will only increase, and this implies more processes that generate more data and that therefore will generate more questions.

FastChangeCo needs a framework to manage this knowledge gap, which will otherwise continue to widen.

Michael recognizes that data can no longer be just 'stuff'!

This marks the starting point for building an *agile business data solution* that will drive FastChangeCo forward.

Data silos

There are so many data silos at FastChangeCo, and this doesn't seem to be working very well for them.

People at FastChangeCo talk a lot about 'data silos.' But what does this mean? In Michael Mueller's view data silos are disjointed, non-integrated and above all non-comparable places where data is stored.

This is not good at all.

For example, there are complete duplicates of some of the operational systems. In other cases, there are data silos that are ... copies of other data silos! There are also mixtures of both, some containing data of unknown origin.

Each data silo serves its own goals, exists for a specific business reason, and has its own historical legitimacy:

- → Sometimes, the data simply wasn't available in the existing Data Warehouse when it was needed
- → In other instances, IT may not have fully understood the business need, or were either unwilling or unable to deliver the data
- → It may be that the requirements of the business units were not clear or could not be implemented quick enough
- → In some cases, IT and the business units couldn't agree on the costs or timelines for delivery

Occasionally, the reason for existence of a data silo is simply not known. Making assumptions about this can be risky. The reasons and decisions may have been the right ones at the time, with the information that was available back then. But, this context has since been lost.

Either way, decisions were made in the past that created seemingly valid opportunities for standalone island solutions – the data silos.

Michael is convinced there is hardly any reason to argue about why and how the many data silos at FastChangeCo came into being. It is much more relevant to work on a strategy and vision to transfer all these data silos into a new, contemporary data solution.

In most of these data silos there are problems of both a technical and organizational nature, which impacts the reliability of the data they provide. Michael wants to understand these problems and take any learnings from them in order to make the new data solution a success.

He has been collecting a few examples of such problems.

Different historization techniques are used

FastChangeCo's existing BI systems, data silos, and the third Data Warehouse struggle with historization. The BI team currently duplicates entire systems periodically to keep track of history, for example at the end of each month. For other systems they only copy specific tables to keep the state of information as it was at the time of copy.

The BI team calls this 'making snapshots.'

It always takes considerable effort to make these copies at the right point in time. There are no mistakes allowed, and sometimes people have to stay up all night to get the timing right, and to make sure the operation succeeds. It may be obvious that it's not trivial to access this collection of copies and snapshots in order to build meaningful and, above all, reusable reports.

The team is very technology focused

The team is highly skilled, but can sometimes be overly focused on technology. They love keeping up to date with new software features and industry trends.

But most of them hardly think in solutions. Many team members tend to think in terms of 'what can I do with the technology' rather than asking if it's the best approach for the organization as a whole. While it's true that almost anything is possible with the right technology, the broader impact of these decisions is often overlooked.

Lack of consistent architecture

FastChangeCo has several data silos specifically for analysis purposes. However, none of these have been designed to be sustainable and future-proof from 'the ground up.'

In some cases, the data silo was derived directly from the operational system and inherited much of the notation, terminology and rules around data interpretation. Not much care was taken to design this in a way that aligns it to how the business department wants to operate. There hasn't been any transition from the way the operational system describes the data to a more business-focused terminology.

In other cases, the data was changed, bent and summarized on its way to a subject-specific silo in such a way that the data is no longer meaningful nor comprehensible. It simply is unclear how certain transformation were intended and what they are supposed to mean.

Michael is convinced that addressing these challenges is essential for a future-proof data solution that meets FastChangeCo's evolving needs.

What is wrong with our data?

FastChangeCo's management has tolerated this for a long time, but this needs to change. There is simply no alternative, or they are at risk of going out of business.

In short, the answer to the question 'What is wrong with FastChangeCo's data?' is that FastChangeCo cannot get the answers they need out of the data they have. Their data is not *meaningful* enough, not fit for the purpose of helping everyone do their job better.

Michael knows that this should be his focus.

Why? Throughout his career, Michael Mueller has seen firsthand how a well-designed data solution can reduce costs significantly.

For example, in a previous role with a retail company, he led a BI project that uncovered a hidden source of shipping cost discrepancies, which were negatively impacting profitability.

A colleague from accounting noticed that, when a customer ordered particular products, the shipping costs were sometimes incorrectly estimated and invoiced. When such an order was shipped, the actual shipping cost would often turn out to be much higher than originally assumed by the business departments.

When, on the other hand, customers ordered this product together with other products, the phenomenon of excessive incurred shipping costs (as compared to the estimated cost) did *not* occur. In that scenario, the logistics team would ship all products together.

The cause for this mismatch in shipping costs was unclear for a long time, and not transparent for accounting. The weight and dimensions of the product in question matched the specifications of the calculated shipping costs class. So that did not explain why parcels with these particular products slipped into a higher shipping class when they were handed over to the logistics service provider and finally shipped.

The data in the Data Warehouse could not answer the question 'Why are the estimated shipping costs higher for particular products?'

As it turned out, there was an operational process step that was overlooked entirely in the data landscape. Between preparing orders and handing them over to logistics, packages were sometimes reclassified to a higher-cost shipping category.

Needless to say, that fact was not recorded unfortunately. It could happen that the weight and dimensions of the product still fitted the shipping costs class *before* the product was packaged, but when the order was received by the logistics team the weight and/or dimensions of the product might no longer fit in the original shipping costs class.

Apparently, the logistics team would re-evaluate the costs at this stage. This could be an explanation why the costs differ during various stages of the process. Unfortunately, there was no recorded data to analyze this further, and confirm the suspicion.

Progress on this issue can only be achieved by collecting additional data. That would make it possible to discover and confirm the underlying reason, and track it going forward.

After a brainstorming session, Michael's team hypothesized that packaging and filler materials might be adding weight and size, pushing orders into a higher cost bracket. This difference could 'tip the scales' in the most literal sense and push certain product orders into different classifications.

Thankfully, data to support this hypothesis was potentially available, though not yet integrated. When packaging data was integrated into the Data Warehouse, the discrepancies became immediately clear: certain products, when packaged, indeed exceeded their initial shipping class limits.

It was interesting to realize that this question, as well as similar ones, only started to emerge because staff were using the Data Warehouse in the first place. Before that, there was generally no central data available on this, and the problem never came to light.

Armed with this new knowledge, the company managed to reduce costs. Lighter packaging materials were subsequently purchased for these identified products. This new packaging was more expensive than the previous packaging, however, in terms of total costs it was less expensive compared to the additional shipping costs from before.

This experience left a lasting impression on Michael. Experiences like these drove him to start the journey for FastChangeCo to get rid of most, or preferably all, of the data silos and replace them with an effective data solution.

One that everyone can use and collaborate on.

The need for a data initiative

After recognizing the data-related problems at FastChangeCo, the management team announced a new initiative: a next-generation data solution that will address the known issues and deliver meaningful data.

The new data solution will start with a small number of use cases that provide immediate value and visibility to the business.

An important initial objective is to establish a well-defined architecture that addresses the shortcomings of the exiting Data Warehouse and data silos. This architecture must also be flexible enough to incorporate new datasets and technologies without the need for re-engineering.

For now, the project's working title is simply the 'data initiative.'

FastChangeCo's management has mandated Michael to lead the data initiative. This will be a complex and large project, but at the same time it is exactly what the management had in mind when they hired him. Michael, as someone coming from 'the outside,' should be able to bring fresh ideas to FastChangeCo's BI landscape.

Since joining, Michael has already identified several topics he believes should be addressed. These same issues partly led to the launch of the data initiative.

Now, after the announcement, members of the BI team are raising questions such as:

- → "Why another data initiative? The last few didn't deliver significant improvements. So what's the point? Why would this one be any different than the previous ones?"
- → "Should it be a data lake? An area where everything is copied to, so you can start digging into the data with all kinds of software tools once you get access to it?"
- → "Do we need to use existing technologies for this new plan? Or can we use others? What tool should we use?"

Michael quickly realizes that these concerns stem from siloed thinking and a reluctance to change. It's clinging to the old ways, and it must stop.

Given the track record of previous initiatives, Michael knows they must approach this differently. FastChangeCo needs more than just a new data solution. It needs a cultural shift, starting with the BI team and extending across the broader organization!

First and foremost, Michael decides, we should start with a small and motivated team. This team will develop a vision and a strategy based on the management goals, which will be the foundation for any next steps in the coming months.

At this stage, the following guiding principles should definitely be included in the vision and strategy:

- → Data is not just 'stuff.' It must be *meaningful* and allow us to understand, explain, and tell the stories behind why things are the way they are
- → Think big, but start small
- → Develop knowledge *within* the team. Hire consultants sparingly, ensure any knowledge gained is shared across the team
- → Empower small, agile teams that are accountable for outcomes
- → Ensure continuous value creation for the business units
- → Avoid complexity in the early stages
- → Shift towards becoming a profit center instead of a cost center
- → Include marketing as an integral part of the solution roll-out

Michael believes that showcasing early value of the data initiative will lay the foundations for future projects to build on. Like building a house, this foundation must be stable and sustainable.

He is concerned that starting with a large team may lead to a loss of focus on the bigger picture and create unnecessary technological disputes. Too many people early on would likely result in prolonged discussions without quick, tangible results.

A smaller team that can define the frameworks and guidelines for the project may be more effective.

This way, Michael can demonstrate his vision to a larger audience much faster. Having all stakeholders involved is important, of course, but this needs to be done at the right time.

Not just, yet.

Michael's intent is to first focus on the fundamentals of data architecture – independent of specific technologies. The appropriate technology can be selected later.

However, Michael hadn't fully accounted for other departments at FastChangeCo, especially the IT department, which has traditionally viewed BI landscape knowledge as their exclusive domain.

That will need to change.

Starting with the data initiative

More meaning and less stuff! This is the slogan with which Michael would like to kick off the first phase of the data initiative.

But before that, Michael knows he must assemble a carefully selected team. He chooses individuals he had already spoken to and a few who came highly recommended for their expertise and approach.

Since the data initiative would initially mainly deal with business topics, the team should consist mainly of business and BI members. Michael's aim is to create a shared understanding of the business needs that will drive the new data solution. This shared understanding will serve as a foundation for the vision and strategy.

This group will begin by analyzing the requirements already outlined and defining a clear, achievable initial objective. Key questions they must answer include:

→ What data is truly relevant?
→ What use cases should be addressed?
→ How should these use cases be prioritized to deliver the most value?
→ Who are the primary (internal) customers for this data initiative?
→ Which existing systems need to be replaced as a priority?
→ Which current systems are causing the greatest pain?

Michael knows that answering these questions will lay the groundwork for a successful, business-driven data strategy.

Of course Michael knows he must involve people from IT in the initiative. However, IT insists on selecting their own representatives. Even Jeff Jones, Head of IT, has taken a personal interest in the discussions.

Up until now, BI has been part of his remit, and from his perspective, all the necessary systems are basically in place. Jeff believes the real issue lies with the business departments. They just don't know what they want, fail to specify their requirements, and demand to have everything done yesterday. Unfortunately for Michael, the IT representatives Jeff proposes aren't exactly who he had in mind.

One of them is Terence Tindle, a BI architect. In IT terms, this indicates a certain level of seniority, but Terence's experience is mainly based on BI implementations using Enterprise Resource Planning (ERP) vendor tools, such as SAP's Business Warehouse, Oracle's PeopleSoft and Siebel, and Salesforce.

His experience with a solution-oriented approach, on the other hand, is less pronounced. FastChangeCo's previous BI solutions didn't require that level of adaptability.

But it is not just the people in IT that have reservations about the data initiative. Controlling, marketing, and even his own boss, Sylvia Seven, follow Michael's actions cautiously.

Sylvia, in particular, is skeptical about how things will function in the future without FastChangeCo's famous DIN/A3 spreadsheet, a fixture in decision-making for years. She also questions whether IT can really be expected to change.

Despite these reservations, Sylvia supports the project one hundred percent.

The fact is, as CFO, she is tired of hearing different managers present conflicting numbers for the same issues in every meeting. And she no longer wants her controllers to waste time pulling data from disparate silos – instead, she wants them to focus on analyzing and interpreting the data to drive the business forward. That's why she brought Michael on board as Head of Data Management.

Sylvia believes that FastChangeCo's data challenges can only be solved with a fundamentally new approach. And as an ultra-marathon runner, she knows that big achievements don't happen overnight. As long as Michael stays the course and delivers results, she'll have his back.

If the data initiative manages to show early success, Sylvia plans to allocate significant funding to expand it further. To demonstrate support, she agrees with Michael that her top employee in controlling, Yerodin van Dusseldorp, should join the data initiative.

Yerodin spends a great deal of time collecting data from various data silos, but this work does not really satisfy him. He would rather focus on interpreting the data and drawing meaningful conclusions for FastChangeCo.

Yerodin is a person with an optimistic attitude. He motivates both himself and his team to perform at their best. His drive to get things done and see projects through to completion has made him a source of inspiration for many colleagues. He really knows how to create a positive environment to make things happen.

This attitude is the main reason why Sylvia and Michael see him as an ideal candidate for the data initiative team.

Together with a few other colleagues, they begin preparing for the first phase of the data initiative, which involves answering the questions posed by Michael and aligning on the project's goals, vision, and strategy.

After the first meetings, it is clear that there isn't really a solid shared understanding of their own business and its terms. What is important, how do we define core business activities we engage in?

Unfortunately, many available definitions are not fit for purpose. For example, definitions like "The customer is a customer of FastChangeCo" are circular and need to be defined much better. One potential definition might be: "A customer of FastChangeCo is a natural person of legal age who has made at least one purchase from FastChangeCo, regardless of whether the customer is currently active or inactive."

To address these issues, the team decides that one important deliverable should be an information model of the business that can be used as a foundation for future discussions and decisions.

As the first phase unfolds, the group realizes that they might need some external input. That's why Michael leverages his network to collect a number of lectures from a wide variety of domain experts.

Throughout these weeks, the team members start to listening to these presentations. They listen to the vision of 'Engine Thinking,' and to Ronald Damhof and Martijn Evers on the Data Quadrant, and thought leaders like Dan Linstedt, Hans Hultgren, and Steve Hoberman on data modeling. The team also explores fact-oriented modeling (FOM), as explained by Marco Wobben, to better understand how to accurately define information models using natural language.

These talks are refreshing, and help the team gain understanding about various data modeling techniques such as conceptual and logical models, entity relationship (ER) and ensemble logical modeling (ELM). They also become more familiar with physical models and implementation, particularly Data Vault methodology.

To avoid past mistakes, they need a flexible approach and the 'Engine Thinking' concept fits with what they have in mind. They intend to define an architecture that is centered around data and information hubs, making sure that incremental additions can be delivered with ample flexibility in order to revisit past decisions. They are ready to get started.

Vision and strategy

The first priority for Michael's team is to deliver a clear vision and strategy.

This will be the framework for FastChangeCo's journey towards a new data solution. All future decisions must be measured against this vision and strategy. If a decision conflicts with the vision and strategy, it will be discarded, except in rare cases where adjustments to the vision or strategy are necessary.

What is the goal behind all this? Why does FastChangeCo actually need this new data solution? What value will it create for the company?

Every member of the data initiative team must be able to answer these questions confidently and without hesitation. However, not all recipients of the vision and strategy paper will have the full context or background behind it. That's why it's crucial for the team to define the vision and strategy in simple, clear terms.

Terms that emphasize why each statement is important and how it benefits FastChangeCo.

The road to a common vision and strategy for the new data solution at FastChangeCo was not always easy.

Despite his optimistic nature, Yerodin developed a certain level of cynicism during the process. Especially when IT dismissed requirements from business departments due to supposed 'challenges,' or insisted that existing approaches and infrastructure are more than sufficient. He was particularly frustrated by the suggestion that all problems will be solved simply by buying a new tool. As if that would solve all problems.

Yerodin wants to focus first and foremost on fast, targeted value creation and sees the new data solutions as a strategic imperative. For FastChangeCo itself, and for the people that work there.

For him, the need for the data solution is obvious. "Why are we even discussing this? It's clear this is the way to create value for FastChangeCo!" he often remarks.

Terence, on the other hand, holds the opposite view. He is not too keen on the new ideas, approaches and methods that the team is investigating. He is firmly rooted in tradition and loyal to FastChangeCo's existing IT tools and processes.

"We don't need this new stuff. Everything we need can be done with the tools we already have," Terence often argues. "And if not, we should get a new tool."

He insists that better tools would eliminate the need for a new data solution altogether.

Michael has a difficult job reconciling these two extremes. Managing Yerodin's enthusiasm and cynicism, while convincing Terence to consider new approaches and soften his resistance is a true balancing act.

He is well aware that this dynamic is not sustainable in the long term. Nevertheless, conflicts like these in the team reflect the overall situation at FastChangeCo.

Through long discussions, Michael works to minimize the conflicts. He listened carefully to concerns, demands, objections and wishes, while patiently explaining the rationale behind the data initiative's plans. After this difficult phase, the data initiative team finally comes together to develop a common vision and strategy.

The Data Vision

As FastChangeCo, we must consistently promote awareness of the value that data brings to our business. Data is not 'stuff,' but the foundation our success in the 21st century. Data literacy must become part of our corporate culture. Together, we must make sure we understand our data — so that we can react quickly to the fast pace of change in today's world. By building this capability, we will drive FastChangeCo's success in innovative, economic, ecological, ethical and social ways.

The Data Strategy

To achieve the data vision, the strategy is based on the following key pillars, which are all interrelated.

1) Operate as a data management center of excellence

An interdisciplinary Data Management Center of Excellence (DMCE) will bundle, coordinate, and largely implement all activities. The DMCE will play a key role in identifying (data) synergies between future projects and simplifying data exchange between parties that need it. The DMCE will consistently focus on embedding data as a core part of FastChangeCo's company culture. Over time, the aim is to formalize these responsibilities into a Data Office, with sufficient mandate to execute on this vision and help FastChangeCo manage their data in line with their goals.

2) Design business-driven

Design solutions that are business-driven, and not technology driven. The entities to be described in the data solution are fundamental and existentially important business objects. They are described by business requirements and processes, and not led by technical implementations in operational systems. The DMCE will maintain a central metadata repository, with the goal of technically defining and describing all critical business objects and their associated attributes.

3) Focus on results

Every use case must contribute to the company's success and align with the overall vision. A use case must have a solid, logical and comprehensible justification and must deliver clear value. This includes evaluating both risks and opportunities, with a focus on professional and business impact.

All work will be assessed based on how it contributes to FastChangeCo's success, including innovation, economic impact, environmental sustainability, ethics, and social responsibility. Business representatives should be involved as much as possible — it will go faster[3]. Value should be delivered at the shortest possible intervals.

4) Leverage data models

Being data model driven leads to high data quality, which goes hand in hand with a good data model.

FastChangeCo will adopt Fact-Oriented Modeling (FOM), describing fundamental business objects unambiguously using natural language. This knowledge will not only be available to the DMCE but to all projects in the company that use data, establishing company-wide standards.

Business logics and rules should be transparent, clearly comprehensible, and traceable (with data lineage). While these rules primarily serve the current use case, they must also be flexible enough to adapt to future needs.

A Data Vault physical data model, derived from the FOM model, should:

- → Be incrementally extended by data sources and processes over time
- → Be easily extensible to accommodate additional areas of the organization and their requirements at a later stage
- → Respond flexibly to changes in the FOM model, business logic, or rules as business requirements evolve
- → Support full historization of all data (uni-, bi-, and multi-temporal)
- → Be fully auditable

5) Embrace agile

Agile, at FastChangeCo, means embracing change and managing uncertainty in the world of data.

As a team, this means that:

→ Responding to change is more important than adhering to a plan. Nothing is set in stone, every prior commitment is re-negotiable
→ 'We'll cross that bridge when we come to it,' addressing challenges as they arise, instead of over-engineering solutions for potential issues. Just-in-time problem-solving is key
→ We keep (data) scopes as small as possible, and focused on the value it will bring
→ We don't stubbornly follow a single way of working, but regularly question our actions to see whether adjustments are necessary or desirable
→ We use Kanban and time-boxing, and tailor these methods to fit our needs and our culture, so that we take the uncertainties in new data projects in stride

6) Be inherently scalable

Solutions must work well regardless if they are small or large, and gracefully allow for growth over time. This is achieved by using design metadata to deliver on the previous mentioned pillars. Manual development or configuration other than working on the solution frameworks should be the exception.

Scalability can be built-in by adhering to principles such as:

→ Infrastructure as code; environments must be able to be scripted and deployed automatically – as opposed to manually created and configured
→ Adopt a DevOps mindset, by making sure that all design, code and deployment is repeatable and can be automated
→ Standardize and automate processes in the data solution to enable efficient data integration, and so that reusable or recurring logic can be generated
→ Work in frameworks, everything from documentation, design, infrastructure and development can be forward engineered through good design
→ Be capable of loading and analyzing data with low latency, and ultimately as a goal in near real time, and be able to handle data streams
→ Be ready to accept diverse data sources and structures, and scale with high data volumes

This vision and strategy will be the foundation the coming months. This journey, toward a new, visionary data solution, is being named 'The Resurrection' by the data initiative team.

The Resurrection – The revival of data with meaning!

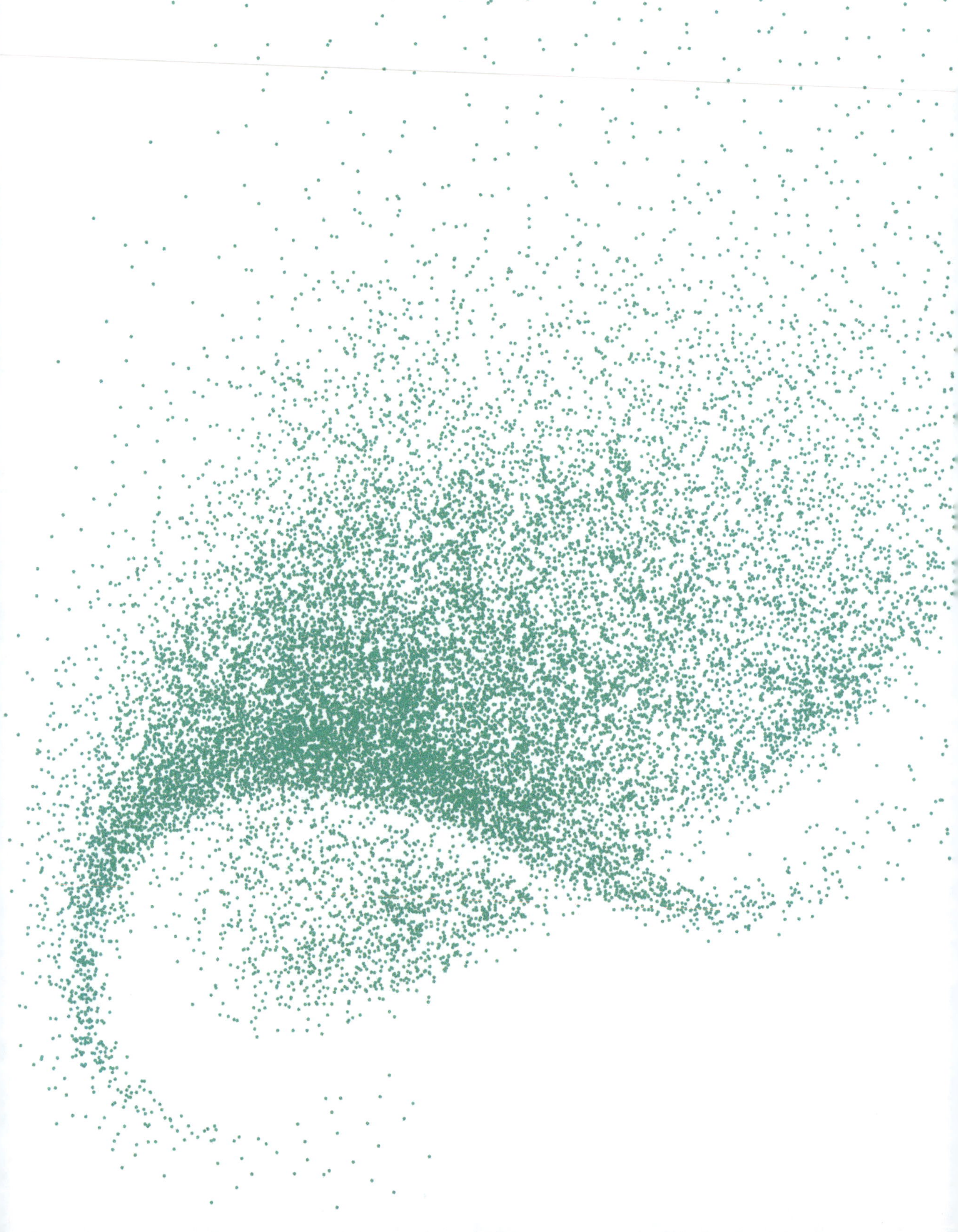

02 the world of data

It's no surprise that 'data' sits at the heart of data solutions, particularly within Data Warehouse ecosystems. Data shapes the fundamental capabilities that a data solution must deliver.

To truly understand this, let's take a closer look at what data actually is and how it behaves within our systems and processes.

Fundamental assumptions when dealing with data

When working with data, it is often helpful to make assume that —at least for the purposes of designing a data solution— any initial requirement may be 'wrong.' Instead, business requirements and questions are better viewed as starting points for a deeper process of data discovery, clarification, and understanding in collaboration with subject matter experts.

This cautious approach applies not only to requirements but also to the data itself, which should be approached as potentially unreliable.

In short, when interpreting data, we assume that the questions that we're asked may be wrong, the data we have available may be unreliable, and the operational systems that captured data are inherently imperfect.

We believe that a data solution that is designed to *solely* to meet an upfront requirement is unlikely to achieve the intended business outcome.

This may sound somewhat negative, but it simply reflects a commitment to building flexibility in the data solution, so that we can adapt when the results don't align with expectations.

This flexibility enables gradual testing, learning from the available data, improving data quality, and building a knowledge base together with subject matter experts.

We assume that individuals work to the best of their abilities, and with the right intentions, but that no single person has a 'full picture' of the complete history of systems, processes, and workarounds across the entire organization.

Over time, organizations may accumulate considerable 'technical debt' from implementing workarounds that were never fully corrected. Sometimes, the original reasons for these fixes may even be lost entirely. These past decisions are still reflected in data, and are often considered 'data quality' issues.

Data teams often have limited control over the operational systems, and may not be fully across the history and evolution of these systems and their data. Fixes to data which have been applied in the past may not have been recorded, or changes were allowed through backend access or APIs that should not have been allowed.

Sometimes, all that remains is the trace left in the data itself, and it's up to us to make sense of it.

Given this complexity, we consider it a best practice to design for repeatability in data clarification until a shared understanding is reached. And, as in scientific fields, this understanding may evolve as new evidence or perspectives emerge.

However, and this is a key guiding principle, the data itself—the events that happened and were recorded in the data solution— remains *immutable.* The data will never change. It is just our perception and understanding of them that shifts.

By embracing this, we can design data solutions that support ongoing data clarification, continuous learning, and an adaptive approach to data management.

A machine designed for change

The data solution defined in this book is fundamentally different from what traditional data solutions were perceived to be.

Because of the nature of data and the need to progressively understand it, we can't define the data solution by its reporting, Data Warehouse, Business Intelligence, or Advanced Analytics requirements alone. Rather, to be successful, the data solution needs to be able to adjust constantly to facilitate continuous clarification of these requirements.

For example, take the first iteration of a given reporting requirement. As per our fundamental principles, we will assume that both the question itself as well as the data we have to answer it are not fit for purpose. Of course, we do our best to assist the consumer in question, but always keep the possibility open that adjustments will be required.

The solution may deliver an initial data set based on what is available in the various relevant operational systems, but without any interpretation applied. When this initial report is presented to a subject matter expert, he or she is likely to respond with feedback that highlights issues and proposals for adjustments with some sort of business rule.

Thank you for your requirement!

This feedback then can be incorporated into a subsequent version — as a new interpretation on the raw data.

And so the process continues.

The dynamics of data are so varied that, without this continuous *feedback loop,* it will remain unclear if a given finding may simply be a data quality issue, or a genuine insight. The ability to reprocess the original data —the immutable events— with different interpretations, or lenses, is a key capability that we believe the data solution must have.

This can be achieved by separating the data *ingestion* from its *interpretation.*

This is an aspect of *separating concerns,* something that will be covered in-depth later.

Reprocessing of data when new understanding becomes available —supported by code-generation and automation— is a powerful way to assist organizations in their journey of improving their knowledge of the data and the involved business processes.

But, it is not only the capability for reprocessing of *data* when new clarifications emerge that is essential. Systems and infrastructure often change over time as well, both for the data solution itself and for the organization as a whole.

A successful data solution is adaptable at a technical level as well. New technologies and concepts become available all the time — the only constant is change. These may change the way data can be managed. It pays off to be adaptable and scalable to be able to make the most of these opportunities when they arise.

For example, being able to scale out to different technical architectures for the components where this makes sense. Or switching out loading technologies (i.e., Extract-Transform-Load, or ETL, platforms) for different approaches.

In these cases, it is just the technology that may change. As we will see in this book — the design, concepts and metadata will remain.

Lastly, the organization itself is not static either. Many organizations are continuously evolving, conquering new markets, introducing new products and business models — divesting or sun-setting other parts of the business. This too has an effect on the data that is available, and the way it is used.

In a way, an organization can be seen as an organism that is continuously adapting, and a data solution should try to match the pace and agility of these changes as much as possible. This means that the intent, direction, goals and delivery of the solution may change often, and fast.

The closer the data solution can stay to this ever-moving goalpost, the more successful it is likely to be.

Many products, regardless if they are consumer goods or software products, are designed for a specific purpose and created exactly as per the design. If you design a dining table, the specifications are usually very clearly defined. You would expect the finished product to be exactly as was intended – the dining table may be returned to the store if not!

Designing a data solution following the practices explained in this book is done with a very different mindset. The data solution is not designed for a specific deliverable, it is a machine that is designed for change.

The role of a data solution

The previous sections highlighted many of the challenges in working with data and emphasized that data interpretation is often a gradu-al, iterative process, typically undertaken with subject matter experts. With each iteration, our understanding of what the data means and how it behaves becomes clearer.

When these understandings are established, there's a natural tendency to solidify them in the data solution as 'business logic,' using calculations or code to apply specific transformations. However, it can be helpful to consider how much of this complexity the data solution should absorb.

What issues can, and should, the data solution address? Where should architectural decisions be made to make data fit for its intended purpose? To what extent must the data solution implement complexities to address shortcomings in the system landscape?

These can be important considerations, but they are often influenced by specific contexts and personal preferences. Regardless, decisions must be made with a full understanding of their potential ramifications.

The Data Management Association (DAMA) offers helpful guidance here through its Data Management Body of Knowledge (DMBoK).

This reference provides various definitions and context around common terms related to 'data.' From the perspective of the data solution, it is often good to remember the context we work in, and what the relationships and roles are to related areas of expertise.

Inspired by the 'DAMA Wheel,' the illustration below shows these areas:

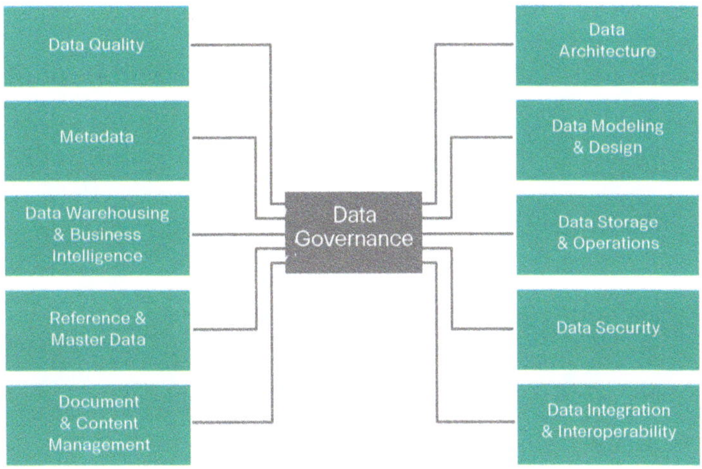

Here, the implementation of the data solution falls under the data governance umbrella as part of 'Data Warehousing and Business Intelligence.' This can be a sobering realization for many professionals involved in these disciplines, but it is also a very helpful one: not every data problem need to be solved by the data solution.

Consider, for example, the varying definitions of a 'customer,' 'policy,' or 'premium' in different parts of a business. Such disparities can be challenging for traditional Data Warehouse solutions, especially if the goal is to deliver a *single version of the truth.*

This objective often requires extensive upfront alignment on interpretations. These outcomes are subsequently cemented into the information model, and data must be mapped or transformed to this definition – a heavy and onerous upfront design and development effort.

When interpretations change or disagreement occurs at a later stage, the efforts to accommodate these changes can be significant.

An alternative approach is to acknowledge that different business areas may have different requirements, and that it may not be immediately needed to align or agree on interpretation. It might be better to 'agree to disagree' initially. As long as the data solution accurately represents the *facts* –the raw events as they occurred– interpretations can be adjusted iteratively over time.

Often, shared definitions for common business entities emerge only after prolonged exploration, and a process of 'guided democracy' where senior leadership, perhaps even a Chief Data Officer, strives to align all stakeholders.

Rather than placing the burden on the data solution to find a common solution, it should be able to accommodate and even report on competing interpretations, providing a basis for further discussion rather than forcing a single interpretation upfront. This way, the burden of finding a common definition shifts from the data solution to the data governance process.

It may be possible that there are even multiple definitions of information that are considered 'core' such as revenue or customer. This can be an eye-opener to: how is it possible that there are so many different views on revenue?

When agreement is reached, the updated interpretation can be reported back to the data solution and addressed in future iterations.

Thank you, again, for your business requirement.

One key advantage of this approach is that it both increases the speed to value, as well as engagement of the stakeholders. The approach can be made fully transparent.

While the goal of achieving a single version of the truth is noble and should remain part of the long-term strategy, it may not be the responsibility of the data solution to deliver this. Instead, it is better suited as an objective for a comprehensive data governance program.

This is why a fundamental design decision is that the data solution is *not* designed to be the source of truth. Rather, it is designed to be the source of facts as they occurred, without any specific interpretation.

Throughout this book, we refer to this as the *single version of the facts.*

Data represents the events created by systems when certain processes occur. It is the core purpose of the data solution to record this correctly, timely, and completely.

Resolving differences in interpretation, however, is ultimately a task for data governance.

Solutions for ongoing data interpretation

A data solution, such as a Data Warehouse, can be considered to be a necessary evil.

In an ideal world, there would be no need for it. Ideally, optimal data governance and near real-time multi-directional data harmonization would have created an environment where it is easy to consume data across systems without any ambiguity. The same applies to business logic – if everything is neatly organized in an all-encompassing data architecture, how many transformation rules would still be required?

This ideal scenario remains beyond reach for most organizations and, more broadly, for the data industry as a whole.

However, treating data solutions as mechanisms to facilitate communication can help move an organization closer to this ideal. Achieving this is yet another reason that a data solution needs to be flexible, quick to adapt, and easy to manage.

Herein lies a paradox, which will be a recurring theme.

To make a data solution sufficiently flexible, easy to manage, and able to adjust at the speed the business operates, the solution requires multiple well-defined layers, areas of design, and frameworks.

At first glance this may appear to be a complex configuration.

A paradox of complexity

The flexibility required for a data solution often introduces complexity, typically manifesting as distinct 'layers' and 'frameworks' within the solution design, each focused on implementing specific concepts.

A common question that arises is whether it's worth investing time and effort upfront in what might appear to be a complex system involving various layers and concepts.

Wouldn't it be simpler to just query the raw data directly, without the hassle of managing multiple data management and interpretation layers? How can we strike the right balance between necessary complexity and desired functionality?

It is our opinion that a necessary baseline of functionality needs to be in place to ensure efficient and effective management of a data solution – including the *refactoring* necessary to adapt to changing data interpretation.

We will refer frequently to the term 'refactoring.' In this context, refactoring involves redesigning parts of the solution to optimize it for a given scenario. It's a concept borrowed from software development, where it typically refers to improving existing code without necessarily adding new features.

Refactoring may not always yield visible changes to the end user, but it often results in code that is more flexible, maintainable, and robust. We believe that refactoring is a fitting term for the restructuring of the data solution, aimed at delivering the intended optimization outcomes.

Our goal is to define and standardize this necessary complexity upfront, so that it becomes a natural part of the solution rather than a barrier to implementation.

This foundational baseline, with its well-defined layers, design areas, and supporting frameworks, is critical for making the data solution easy to operate and maintain. It facilitates refactoring –even automated– and supports quick adaptation.

While these concepts may add complexity, they can be standardized and integrated into automated code generation and delivery. By establishing this baseline, we believe that data solutions can become a machine designed for change, capable of evolving alongside business needs.

We will explain our approach using the concept of *separating concerns,* the mindset of *data solution virtualization,* and the implementation framework of *Engine Thinking.*

Together, these three concepts form the specification of the data solution we propose.

Separation of concerns

A key concept to ensure that the inherent complexity of data solutions can be managed in a simple way is the *separation of concerns.* Separating concerns means breaking down the tasks that a data solution must perform into smaller, modular, and atomic processes, each with a defined role within the overall data and IT architecture.

This approach stands in stark contrast to traditional methods, which often feature complex, monolithic data logistics processes. These processes typically perform numerous functional steps in a single operation.

For example, typical two-layered solution designs approaches (e.g., dimensional models or Kimball-style Data Warehousing) load data into a staging area (layer 1) that resembles the target model (layer 2). Data is then merged with the already existing information.

The data logistic processes that execute this logic have to support a broad variety of functions, including but not limited to:

→ Implementing a variety of business rules
→ Integrating multiple data sources
→ Managing changes over time
→ Key distribution
→ Defining structure and hierarchies
→ Balancing performance requirements
→ Handling granularity and aggregation
→ Detecting data changes

This may result in solutions that can be difficult to extend, and tend to suffer from increasingly complex interdependencies. The resulting effort to implement changes pushes out delivery time, and creates a gap between the required functionality of the solution and the degree that these requirements have been implemented.

This can lead to critical issues and the emergence of alternative solutions that may eventually render the data solution obsolete, especially as requirements evolve over time and become harder to keep pace with.

The larger the system grows, the wider this gap tends to become.

'Hybrid[4]' modeling approaches, which combine elements of normalized and dimensional modeling, tackle these challenges by separating the fundamental housekeeping of data solutions from business logic, maximizing flexibility and ease of maintenance.

Unlike more traditional forms of dimensional modeling, where a single process often handles multiple functions, hybrid modeling techniques decompose these tasks into distinct, atomic operations.

For instance, key distribution is managed by core business concept entities representing the central business keys, and historization is embedded in context entities. Additionally, relationships between business concepts are modeled separately using natural business relationship entities.

Business rules —or the interpretation of data— are layered on top of the raw data, but only after it has been safely recorded — rather than applied when the data is loaded *into* the data solution. This approach preserves the integrity of the original data while enabling flexible interpretation.

Requirements inevitably change over time, especially during the early phases of data projects and more generally as business needs evolve. By separating the delivery of information (via business rules) from the storage and management of raw data, hybrid modeling techniques —supported by a matching solution architecture— make it easier to accommodate different perspectives and reduce the complex interdependencies often seen in traditional approaches.

Hybrid modeling techniques acknowledge that the 'truth' is subjective and may differ across consumers of data, even within the same organization. While there may not be a single version of the *truth,* there is always a single version of the *facts* — the immutable transactions that serve as a reliable foundation for delivering multiple interpretations.

This approach forms a core part of our methodology, and we will explore it in detail throughout the following chapters.

Data solution virtualization

In the data modeling community, discussions often focus on specific, technical topics closely tied to the physical implementation of data solutions.

For instance, in Data Vault methodology, questions like 'Do we still need Hubs?,' 'Should we create separate tables for each attribute?,' or 'Is this transaction better modeled as a Hub or a Link?' tend to center around physical implementation details.

While these are interesting considerations, it can be much more valuable to separate the principles and concepts from their technical implementation choices – and use these to agree on how to best create value for a business using data.

Physical data modeling concepts and methodologies are subject to evolution themselves, it's not just the business, models, and technology that evolves. Newer, sometimes better, ideas emerge regularly, and it is essential to periodically reassess and adapt existing approaches. It's also perfectly acceptable to experience a form of atavism –where certain practices resurface after a period of absence– if they provide a good solution for today's problems.

How do we keep the things that work in the current environments, and move away from what doesn't make as much sense anymore?

Inevitably, there will be some tension between adhering to prescribed standards and this evolutionary mindset. Rigidly following an implementation standard may lead to dead ends. Some ideas lose relevance, don't work as well using certain technology, or prove less effective than anticipated. Methodologies must evolve to remain practical; otherwise, they risk becoming obsolete – along with any solution that strictly follows them. However, by adopting a mindset of continuous improvement, where designs are iteratively adjusted, the likelihood of long-term success and relevance increases significantly.

This is where the concept of *data solution virtualization* comes into play.

Data solution virtualization is a mindset where changes in data models, concepts, patterns, and business logic are directly and automatically translated into the implementation and deployment of the data solution. It's refactoring taken to the extreme: when you update your model or design, the data solution adjusts itself automatically.

The *virtualization* aspect alludes to the idea that –given sufficient resources– any interpretation of data can be generated at runtime. In essence, the entire data solution could be ephemeral, recreated as needed. However, in the real world, resource constraints mean that the actual implementation may vary. This could involve recreating views, dropping and rebuilding database tables, or regenerating and executing the data logistics processes needed to repopulate tables with up-to-date data.

Regardless of the specific implementation, the outcome remains the same. Even if development and deployment follow a controlled, gated approach –which is often the case– this method allows for previewing a design before formally committing to it. It enables direct examination of the data outputs resulting from data modeling and interpretation logic, without needing to fully develop the entire solution first.

This can be particularly helpful during the early stages of development, where there typically is more volatility in the design.

A paradox

At first glance, data solution virtualization may give the impression that a physical data solution is unnecessary, which presents another paradox. If you can represent your target data model as a set of views and automatically allocate infrastructure resources for optimal runtime performance, does it still make sense to implement the solution using physical tables and corresponding data logistics processes?

The answer, in most cases, is still *yes* – at least for now. This is due to various factors, such as the available technical infrastructure, software capabilities, performance considerations, and the size of data sets.

However, the purpose of data solution virtualization is not necessarily to render traditional data logistics obsolete. Instead, it serves as a litmus test to verify that all the necessary capabilities of the data solution are in place, and properly configured.

A useful way to think about this is: if you can generate and deploy your entire data solution using queries or views based on metadata, then you can *also* use the same metadata to deploy the solution with physical tables and data logistics processes.

A core concept here is the ability to process data *deterministically.* Deterministic processes always produce the same outcome when given the same input values. In databases, deterministic queries consistently yield the same results when run against the same data set.

When your data solution is guaranteed to be deterministic, it provides flexibility in choosing *how* the results are delivered. In essence, when processes are deterministic, data solution virtualization treats the main functionality of the data solution as a commodity that can be deployed into a specific physical design and supporting data logistics. The physical implementation becomes a parameter.

Returning to the vision of data solution virtualization, what seems realistic is that many functions of the data solution will increasingly move into the background. The exact specifications of the physical model become less relevant, as these are driven (and automatically refactored) by defined optimization rules. For example, automated refactoring might eliminate the need for manual decisions about splitting Satellites due to high change rates in a few attributes. The engine might decide to create multiple physical tables for a single context of a business key—or not—depending on the data dynamics at the time.

Instead, the focus can shift towards the information model, including the definition and interpretation of data entities, with everything else derived automatically.

Data solution virtualization, as a test of fundamental capabilities, demonstrates that the data solution can evolve alongside the business, continuously bridging the gap between raw data and its consumption. The exact requirements for achieving this make up the core of the engine, which will be detailed in the Engine Thinking section.

Engine Thinking

To implement the vision of data solution virtualization, and fully embrace flexibility through automation, we can integrate the necessary components for delivering a reliable and adaptive data solution into a cohesive system capable of operating autonomously.

This capability—to treat the data solution as a dynamic communication asset while maintaining principles like layered design and separation of concerns— is what we refer to as *Engine Thinking.*

The engine concept acknowledges that many technical implementations share a common foundation in terms of their information (e.g., conceptual and logical) models and essential components. The resulting physical data model and data logistics processes can be viewed as by-products — outcomes driven by the *optimization* needs of the solution.

Consider the analogy of a database optimizer, which uses statistics and parameters to determine the most efficient way to execute a query. The engine operates in a similar manner, but at the application level. It continuously refines the physical model based on usage patterns and performance considerations, optimizing the implementation automatically in the background.

Imagine the utility of embedding these optimization decisions as parameters, letting the engine drive the creation of the most suitable physical structures. Or even better, allowing an intelligent optimizer to decide the optimal approach. If we elevate the data models (and corresponding design choices) to a higher, abstract level, many low-level physical model implementation decisions can be streamlined, or even eliminated.

Do we really need to worry about how relationships are modeled physically when we agree on their existence at a conceptual level? Is it necessary to physically instantiate key tables if they are rarely used in queries? Could we generate them only on demand?

Does it matter to the information model if certain columns are moved into separate objects for performance reasons?

Should relationships always be represented as unique instances (e.g., core business concepts or key tables), or can they be managed as many-to-many tables? Should we select a specific hashing approach across all tables, or can we balance out necessity and performance versus risk appetite for collisions in the algorithm?

These questions, and many others like them, can be addressed through the engine concept. The key lies in connecting the components required to build the data solution effectively from the outset.

The engine combines a suite of related capabilities that facilitate a flexible approach to designing and managing data solutions. The diagram below outlines the core components of the engine. Each concept is explored in-depth in subsequent chapters.

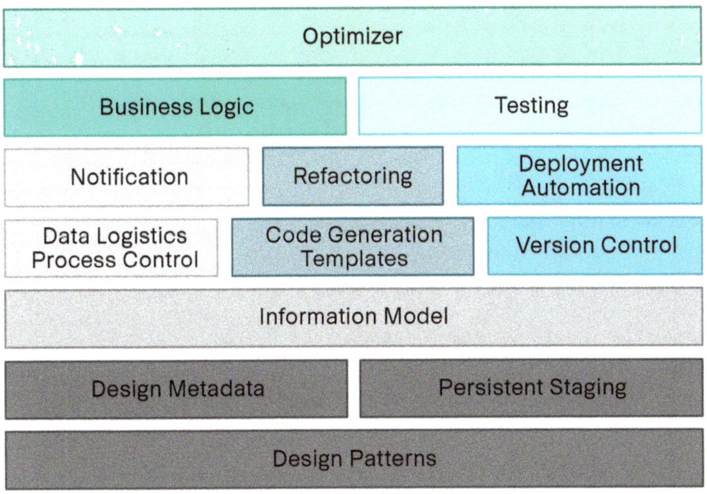

The engine is governed by a combination of *design* metadata and *environmental* metadata that decides and manages how the physical models and corresponding data logistics processes are generated, deployed, and maintained.

The core premise of Engine Thinking is to establish a mechanism that enables (re)modeling of data, while the technical solution is automatically refactored in the background to accommodate new or revised designs. Technically, this includes capabilities like automatically redefining physical tables and reloading them with data using dynamically generated data logistics processes — and more.

Now, let's begin constructing our own engine by diving deeper into these concepts and aligning them with the right technologies and frameworks.

Design patterns

The foundation of any code generation or automation efforts is a clear understanding of what needs to be accomplished. Design patterns offer a structured framework for documenting the core concepts of the solution, including data logistics processes.

They serve as a 'what' and 'how-to' guide, detailing these concepts while remaining technology agnostic — independent of any specific implementation. Design patterns are explored in depth in the ⚐ data solution architecture sections.

For now, it's important to emphasize that any key decision made by the engine should be grounded in a well-documented design pattern. Code generation templates, in turn, act as the practical implementations of these design patterns, translating the documented concept into executable artifacts.

Design metadata

Design metadata is software and platform agnostic, and focuses on conventions and source-to-target mappings — including data definitions and transformation rules.

An example of design metadata is the definition of the core business concepts and their relationships (a convention), or a transformation to conform a specific data set to a defined target (a lineage, business rule, or source-to-target mapping).

This type of metadata is closely tied to the concept of design patterns. These essentially guide the delivery of the data solution by using design metadata as input.

Design metadata defines how many data logistics processes are expected, captures how data is transformed, and determines what data needs to go where. In the ⚐ code generation chapter, we will introduce a standard format to record design metadata.

Design metadata encompasses all metadata necessary for deploying a solution, including:

→ Process and data logistics details, recorded as 'mappings' or lineage information capturing where data is moved to – or interpreted from

→ Storage metadata, describing objects such as tables, views, formats, domains. These can either be derived using conventions, or specified directly

Managing design metadata is the cornerstone of the engine, particularly defining the source and target models (structure metadata) and establishing source-to-target mappings (process or data logistics metadata).

Each organization has its own systems and processes, and mapping these to a data model is always tailored and specific. This is why design metadata is the true intellectual property (IP) of the data solution. It encapsulates the unique and custom interpretations of data specific to an organization.

When combined with code generation templates and guided by design patterns, design metadata drives the automated creation of data logistics processes. Design metadata defines the *what,* while the code generation templates provide the *how.* Together, they form the essential components that fuel the engine.

At this stage of the engine, a *standardized framework for recording design metadata* is in place. This repository will serve as a foundation, gradually enriched as additional components of the design are finalized – particularly the definition of the *information model.*

As the design evolves, the metadata will capture and reflect these developments.

Persistent staging

A *persistent staging area (PSA)* forms the backbone of a flexible data solution. It acts as an immutable archive, capturing all original transactions that have been presented to the data solution *before* any transformation or interpretation is applied, including data modeling.

Often referred to by other names like 'history zone,' the PSA can be broadly defined as an insert-only, time-stamped log of all transactions (events) received by the data solution and organized by arrival time. The PSA can be implemented using databases, tables, logs, streams, files, or a combination of these technologies.

Because the transactions stored in the PSA are original and immutable, the PSA enables deterministic (re)processing of data. Reprocessing simply means running the input data through updated logic, recalculating the output. This capability is essential for replaying historical transactions against an revised target data model or modified transformation rules.

The main purpose of the PSA is to store raw, unaltered transactions for potential reprocessing when design metadata changes. This includes changes to the target model itself, which may evolve as details are refined and reconsidered.

This aligns with the iterative approach of clarifying data meaning over time. Even with the best intent and skills, initial models may not fully capture all nuances, and are therefore subject to change.

The PSA provides a reliable foundation for reconsidering raw transactions from different perspectives. It allows an organization to solve the inherent overall complexity of its business incrementally.

An application-readable log

A helpful way to think about a PSA is as an event-based system — an application-readable 'log' that is similar to a transaction log in a relational database[5].

In database systems, a transaction log is an insert-only, time-ordered sequence of data events (inserts, updates, deletes). It is central to how databases work. Data events are first written to the transaction log and then propagated to (potentially) various data structures such as tables or indexes, which serve as *representations* of these events. Events can even be forwarded to other systems through techniques like log shipping or transaction log-based replication.

For a database, the log is the ultimate source of truth — the main record of all changes. It is also essential for implementing the ACID[6] principles. In a mature system, this is handled almost autonomously in the background — but it remains a fundamental mechanism for ensuring data consistency and reliability.

Pub/Sub

A PSA operates as a 'Write Once, Read Many' (WORM) system, where multiple data logistics processes can independently 'read' from the log. Each consumer can track its own processing state using pointers like inscription timestamps, which indicate the time of the event's arrival in the PSA. This way, consuming data flows, selections or streams manage their own load window and can therefore operate completely independently.

The PSA does not need to 'know' which processes use the log, or how up to date they are in their processing.

This independence aligns with the principles of the publish-subscribe (pub/sub) pattern, where producers (data sources) and consumers (data processes) operate independently without direct knowledge of each other.

This approach even makes it possible to support applications that only require to be online from time to time, and allow them to sync their data when required. Applications control the way they consume data. It is only necessary to track the event up to which processing is completed.

For the data logistics processes of the data solution, this works the same way. Essentially, every data logistics process can be independent and maintain their own state and consistency. In a sense, they are all individual consumers of the application-readable log. This supports an almost endless degree of parallelism and flexibility in data processing, something that will be explored throughout this book.

Implementing the PSA

A PSA can be implemented using a wide range of technologies. Regardless of using database tables, files, or streams, the core concept remains the same: an insert-only, time-stamped sequence of events.

In databases, this may involve physical tables, while other implementations might use formats like Parquet, Avro, Iceberg, JSON, or HDFS.

Contemporary technologies support this concept, including bridging solutions like PolyBase and distributed commit log systems such as Apache Kafka, Azure Event Hub, Amazon Kinesis, and Google Pub/Sub. These are just some of the technologies available at the time this book was written. In the future, different tools and techniques are likely to be available. However, the concept is expected to remain the same.

These tools offer scalability, high throughput, fault tolerance, and features like log retention and partitioning. They allow consuming applications to subscribe via APIs or services. This way, the PSA effectively becomes a 'stream' with potentially infinite retention (Time to Live, TTL) — an institutional memory.

We have explored the role of the PSA within the context of a data solution, where it acts as a central repository capturing transactions from various operational systems. However, the possibilities of the PSA extend beyond just supporting the data solution.

Besides supporting the myriad of automatically generated atomic data logistics processes that consume data from the PSA into the data solution, the PSA can also serve as a subscription source for any information-consuming system.

This positions the PSA as a central 'data hub' that provides the infrastructure to provide raw data change events to *any other* system that requires it – often an early win in data projects. Downstream processes can consume events independently and at their own pace, and as supported by the available technology.

Information model

The information model serves as the brain of the data solution, shaping how data flows through the system, and ultimately unambiguously describing what the data represents.

At this stage of the engine, design patterns detail how concepts need to be managed, an approach for capturing design metadata is available to start documenting what objects exist and what data needs to be mapped to them, and the PSA has begun recording transactions from the connected operational systems.

However, it has not yet been determined how all of this should be applied. This is the role of the model. It is the model that defines what the data should look like at every stage of the solution.

Levels of abstraction

There is a distinction to make between different levels of modeling abstraction. Without going into too much detail, these can be classified as more conceptual, more logical, or more physical.

Conceptual models focus on high-level representations of terms and concepts, their definition, and their interactions. A logical level is more focused on clearly-specified entities, their types, attributes, and relationships. The physical model covers the technical implementation tailored to a specific database or technology.

The relationships between these different levels of abstraction can be recorded in design metadata – for example as a mapping between a logical model entity and a physical model table. These mappings can then be used to generate physical model structures using code generation templates. The physical model is often convention-based and can be derived from its more abstract logical version.

In the context of the engine, this distinction is important. We often experience discussions that focus on differences of opinion at the physical level (e.g., table structures, specific columns), when there is sufficient agreement at the logical level.

Using the engine, the focus is placed more on the logical level and above – the physical level can be automatically generated, and is subject to improvements as determined by the optimizer and its directives.

We will predominantly use the term 'information model' (or simply 'model'), particularly when contrasting certain design decisions with the physical model. We'll leave the exact level of abstraction intentionally flexible, as this is subject to different opinions and does not materially affect how the engine operates.

Developers can choose to work directly with physical models, apply these to design metadata, and generate the solution accordingly. Alternatively, they can define a more abstract, business driven representation –what we refer to as the information model– and use conventions to derive a physical version.

Mapping data to the model

An important piece of design metadata to capture is the relationship between data sources and model objects. What data needs to go where? This relationship often becomes apparent during the data modeling efforts, but can also be added later. This key piece of information is required to generate the data logistics processes that populate the model.

When the model is complete, it effectively has become part of the design metadata. In other words, the design metadata contains a representation of the model.

When the model changes, these changes must be reflected in the design metadata as well, so that the solution can be automatically adjusted to reflect this updated definition of data.

Code generation templates

Code generation automates the production of data solution components.

To generate the necessary code, both code generation templates and design metadata are required as inputs. Together, these inputs can be compiled into executable data logistics processes or object artifacts tailored to a specific platform or environment.

A design pattern defines the goals and outcomes for a concept or component, and the code generation template specifies the corresponding technical implementation. Templates are typically described using a *Domain Specific Language,* making them interpretable by a compiler or runtime engine.

The outputs of this process can include programming code, SQL scripts, or proprietary objects for various data technologies. They cover all aspects of the data solution, including data objects (tables, views, files), data logistics processes, scripts, and even infrastructure and connectivity.

We refer to this as *model-driven* code generation. The model, as encapsulated in the design metadata, drives the output based on the selected code generation templates.

The challenges of manual development

Historically, developing data logistics processes has been a manual and resource-intensive task. This made it one of the most time-consuming aspects of data solution development. The overhead caused by manual (re)development, maintenance, and testing of the many involved data logistics processes has traditionally been a major barrier for refactoring.

Pattern-based approaches, combined with code generation, can mitigate many of these issues.

Manual development also often imposed restrictions on developing truly scalable data solutions. For instance, in modeling techniques such as Data Vault or Anchor Modeling, each data set associated with a context table and its corresponding core business concept table typically requires its own independent data logistics process. These processes, while following the same pattern, are unique and may number in the hundreds or thousands.

With manual development, the trade-off between creating potentially hundreds of seemingly redundant data logistics processes for long term scalability and short term delivery would usually favor the latter. However, code generation shifts this paradigm. By automating the production of these repetitive processes, code generation enables the scalability and high degree of parallelism in data processing that manual approaches struggle to achieve.

Following evolution

Defining a collection of well-structured design patterns and code generation templates to deliver the data solution is essential for achieving flexibility in delivery. Patterns and templates evolve over time, and this can sometimes lead to a desire to refactoring part, or even the entire data solution.

Investing in code generation supports a continuous evolution of the data solution. It allows you to easily incorporate and test new ideas and improvements.

This reduces the time to value because the output data logistics processes can be delivered faster, and more consistently. Code generation also helps to dramatically reduce technical debt when tweaks to the patterns are applied, since updates can automatically propagate throughout the solution.

It is a best practice to ensure the *entire* solution can be generated to effectively combat the inevitable accumulation of technical debt.

Lastly, one of the most important benefits is the consistency in delivery both in terms of time and quality. In our experience, businesses value consistent quality and reliable delivery timelines over speed with variability (though speed is still important).

By automating the generation of data logistics processes, teams can ensure predictable results while maintaining flexibility and short delivery timelines.

Data logistics process control

A data logistics process control framework (or simply, 'control framework') is a structured set of procedures designed to govern the execution, orchestration, monitoring, and logging of individual data processing and integration tasks.

A robust control framework is an essential requirement of any data solution, and intends to:
→ Orchestrate data logistics process executions
→ Provide logging and audit capabilities
→ Simplify the management of the data solution
→ Enforce application-level transaction control (based on ACID principles)
→ Enable recovery and restart in the event of failures

This section outlines the core requirements of a control framework. Further implementation details are covered in the ⚐ data logistics control framework section.

Orchestration of process execution

In some scenarios, it may be necessary to define dependencies between processes. Some processes have to run before others. While the approach outlined in this book aims to minimize dependencies where possible, you may find cases where dependencies between data logistics processes are still required. This may be due to interface wait-states (e.g., waiting for call-response), performance reasons, interdependent business rules, or specific pattern design (e.g., key lookups).

For example, a separate delta-detection process might be required to capture data changes in a staging area before subsequent transformations can proceed.

Beyond managing execution order, orchestration and understanding dependencies can also be used to detect and prevent issues such as race conditions, cache staleness, and referential integrity violations.

A good example is populating core business concept (key) tables in a parallel environment. Potentially many data integration processes can insert new keys in these central tables, but if two or more processes attempt to insert the same key at the same time a constraint violation may occur. A smart control framework can temporarily suspend conflicting processes such as these.

Logging and audit capabilities

Regardless of whether the solution delivers data via views, functions, scripts or materialized objects (e.g., tables, indexed views, files), the control framework must record all activity for transparency and accountability.

The control framework tracks every unique process execution in a log or repository, and issues a unique execution instance identifier. The data, processed via a data logistics process execution, will be stored with this unique identifier so that it is always traceable which data was handled by which process, and when.

This attribute is called the *Audit Trail Id.*

Using the Audit Trail Id, all materialized data is 'tagged' with a pointer corresponding to the unique process execution that inserted or modified the records.

For example, if a data logistics process inserts 100 records into a target table, the control framework logs the start and end times of this unique process execution, records the number of rows processed, and assigns a unique Audit Trail Id to those 100 records. As a result, the 100 records that have been inserted will all have the same Audit Trail Id.

In virtualized environments, the control framework logs view and function executions, recording the user who issued the query and the exact version of the object accessed. This enables precise auditing and tracking of all interactions with the data solution.

Application-level transaction control

This 'link' between the control framework and the data will also become important in preparing the data for downstream processing, including delivering data for consumption.

At various stages, it will be necessary to assert which data is consistent and available for next steps. Since the control framework 'knows' what data is still being processed and what data is ready for further use, it supports the implementation of transaction control at the 'application level.'

This is similar to the ACID principles as mentioned in the previous PSA section. ACID encompasses a set of properties of database transactions intended to guarantee validity in events such as errors, outages and power failures. The control framework is used to apply similar concepts across the data solution.

This can be used to prevent 'dirty reads' from the solution, and to implement associated locking strategies for data integration. Dirty reads occur when data can be accessed that has not been fully committed by the solution – when data logistics processes have not yet completed successfully.

Another use case is the ability to report on data latency, providing insights on data freshness – an important metric for managing data solutions.

Simplifying data solution management

Ideally, a process control framework is designed to be *idempotent.* In this context this means that the system remembers which tasks were run successfully, and re-runs only the failed tasks. To support this, the control framework captures the state of a process; whether it is running or completed, and if failures were encountered that require attention or can be reprocessed automatically.

For example, imagine a workflow running five tasks in a certain order. When a failure is encountered while running the fourth task, both the failing process as well as the workflow will report failure. Upon rerun, the first three tasks –which succeeded previously– can be skipped. The fourth task will then retry and, if successful, the fifth task will be executed.

This mechanic helps in simplifying day-to-day management and monitoring, but is also important for protecting the consistency of the overall solution. For example, if the first process in the above workflow detects and loads change data delta (differential) from an operational system using a truncate & load pattern, then this data delta must be *fully committed* to all targets before it can be rerun. Otherwise, the data delta might be lost forever.

Version control

With the fundamental components now in place, the engine is able to run on its own. However, in order to adjust independently, additional 'operations[7]' components should to be added – the first of which is versioning.

Versioning is the practice of tracking and saving changes made to solution artifacts. If you save something, the previous versions should be retrievable.

There are many versioning tools, plug-ins, and concepts available, and they should be used in the context of release management – where a defined group of changes can be grouped, tested and deployed as a 'release.'

With the engine concept, we take versioning a step further.

In the engine, versioning goes beyond standard version control for individual artifacts. Instead, it manages snapshots across the design metadata including the information model, the code generation templates *and* the data itself as an integrated unit.

This holistic approach captures the state of the entire data solution —including data integration logic and data— at any given point in time.

Engine versioning is based on two core premises:

→ We can version all our design metadata and code generation templates together
→ We can generate all our code, and rebuild the entire data delivery using the PSA concept

If both are true, then we can always (re)deploy the entire solution as it existed at a particular point in time.

In many cases, it is not even necessary to version-control the *outputs* of the code generation templates. After all, artifacts like data logistics processes can always be re-created as they were in a given version. Versioning only the design metadata and code generation templates suffices.

This capability even allows the solution to host multiple versions simultaneously. These versions can be compared, tested, and optimized to determine which performs best or meets current requirements most effectively.

This approach transforms the data solution into a time-machine, enabling not just point-in-time restoration of the solution's structure and logic, but also facilitating dynamic experimentation and validation across different solution versions. Unlike traditional bitemporal data systems, this versioning component applies to the *entire* solution, offering unparalleled flexibility in managing both design and operations.

Refactoring

Imagine you start capturing transactions (events, records) early in the development process using a PSA, but finalize your overall data solution design and model some time later.

In such cases, the ability to 'replay' these transactions *as if they were processed at the time of their initial capture* would be incredibly valuable.

After all, these transactions have already existed in the PSA for some time and represent the 'transaction log' of what happened.

Loading this historical data into the data solution requires that the involved data logistics processes have the capability to process data *deterministically.* A deterministic process is one that, when executed, consistently produces the same result given the same input values.

For a data solution, this means processing the same raw data will always yield the same result in the target table. Adding this capability introduces some complexity to the pattern. However, while the pattern becomes more complex, this is offset by the ability to generate the code automatically.

Having a PSA is essential to do this. It drives the ability to *refactor* the solution in a deterministic way — a controlled process of restructuring existing code or design.

Re-initialization

The ability to replay history is referred to *re-initialization.* This involves truncating parts of the model and reloading the corresponding data from the PSA. If the process is deterministic and nothing has changed, the results will be identical to the original output. If the code or model *has* been modified, the historical transactions will be applied to the new version. With proper version control in place, it is even possible to revert to an earlier state and reproduce the data exactly as it was.

To support re-initialization, data logistics processes must be able to handle multiple data changes in a single processing pass. This is one of the fundamental principles of data logistics that underpin the data solution.

The ability to refactor and re-initialize is essential for iterative development. Solution designers can refine models and definitions over time, knowing they can refactor and reload the environment, or parts thereof, as needed.

Following the mindset of this book, change is inevitable and must be anticipated. Over time, we are likely to find flaws in our approach, our patterns, our understanding of a given technology and let's face it – our models and definitions of business terms as well. This is simply human nature, and goes back to the fundamental assumptions when dealing with data. Over time, our understanding of this complex matter will increase, and imperfections will be addressed while further developing and testing the system.

Embracing refactoring, supported by re-initialization, means you can afford some flexibility while designing use cases. You always have the option to change your mind and refactor the design whenever it makes sense to do so.

The myth of a perfect model

Some argue that refactoring simply means you didn't get it right the first time. There seems to be a deeply rooted mindset in the data community that a data model should be 100% correct after the initial design phase. Indeed, many data solution architectures rely on this, and choose not to have fallback mechanisms –like a PSA– in place.

In reality, interpretations of data change often and few, if any, data solutions are perfect from the start. Have you ever encountered a data solution that was 100% correct on the first attempt, with the perfect data model and interpretations? In hindsight, haven't you looked at past models and realized a different approach would have been better?

In some cases, a data solution can be refactored even after interpretations have been applied, but this can be complex and cumbersome. In other cases, refactoring may be impossible if the required original data is not available anymore. This can happen when calculations or aggregations have transformed the original values into a new data element, but one that cannot be reversed into the original values – a 'destructive' transformation.

Contemporary modeling techniques aim to delay business logic application until later in the architecture, after raw data integration and closer to the consumption of the data. These techniques advocate that, while it takes time to deliver the single version of the truth, there is at least the notion of the 'single version of the facts.' Pushing business logic to delivery layers allows iterative exploration and refinement of requirements.

However, even the core model and its corresponding data integration patterns can contain design flaws. For instance, a raw Data Vault model might have decisions around business concepts or business keys that, in hindsight, could have been better. Modeling data requires making interpretative decisions at every stage. This is why a PSA serves as the ultimate safety net.

In essence, downstream layers of the data solution become a form of schema-on-read applied to the raw data in the PSA. While data can still be persisted in various layers, the tools now in place allow teams to evolve their thinking and adapt designs as the organization grows and changes.

Shifting the mindset

This shift requires modelers to embrace the idea that mistakes will happen, and designing for change is better than attempting to achieve a perfect model upfront. The reality is that in every business there is diverging and often limited understanding of what data means, and it 'is a process' to get clarity and understanding how data should be accurately represented in models.

This perspective applies to design patterns and code generation templates as well. Models, concepts, technologies, and *even methodologies* evolve. Based on our own experience, we can say that even after working for decades in the field, we still find the occasional bug or encounter progressive thinking that would make us want to reload the environment in a slightly modified version.

In our opinion, refactoring is not a failure but an acknowledgment of progress — a way to adapt to new insights and evolving needs.

At this stage in the engine, the foundation is set for tweaking models, design patterns, or code generation templates to deliver updated versions of the data solution — even at runtime.

Notification

In addition to the data logistics process control framework, a monitoring framework is essential for *pro-actively* informing developers and support teams about the integrity of the system. Building a data solution requires to create trust in the available data for its users, and a robust monitoring framework is a powerful way to *do* so.

Functional and technical errors such as missing data, duplicates, large delays etc., will erode trust in the system and hinder its adoption and overall effectiveness. This problem becomes worse when users themselves have to identify and report these issues.

A monitoring framework assists in preventing many of these issues from happening, and also fosters trust when issues are pro-actively investigated when they do occur.

The framework involves detection mechanisms to flag specific behavior based on predefined rules. When issues are detected, the notification feature delivers these results to users and administrators for timely awareness and actioning.

The monitoring framework consists of a number of exception checks on the solution, as defined in the ⚐ testing framework. For example, asserting referential integrity or consistency for logical groups of data.

The data logistics control framework also plays a central role in enabling this functionality. It schedules and executes the tests and processes responsible for monitoring the system.

Monitoring tasks

Monitoring tasks are designed as standalone executables that can run independently, either manually or via the data logistics control framework. These tasks:

- → Collect outcomes from various test cases
- → Report on the health and quality of the environment
- → Provide proactive insights into the solution's state

Monitoring outcomes can also feed back into the engine as *environmental metadata*. These results can direct the engine to refactor parts of the solution automatically, based on predefined directives. For example, system information such as CPU usage, memory pressure and disk use can inform the optimizer to adjust settings or processes dynamically.

Notification rules, as part of the monitoring tasks, can address a wide range of scenarios related to data solution integrity and performance, including but not limited to:

Adherence to conventions

- → Are table names consistently prefixed or suffixed according to agreed conventions?
- → Do core business concept tables include key attributes but exclude context attributes?
- → Are all names in lower case?
- → Are file names appropriately structured, such as including a timestamp indicator?

Infrastructure and environment information

- → Do tables have the correct compression settings?
- → Is index fragmentation exceeding acceptable thresholds?
- → Are query wait states increasing?
- → Does the I/O subsystem work as expected? Is disk space, latency, or read/write performance within expected parameters?

Latency and availability

- → How long does it take to complete one full refresh cycle across the data solution, where all involved processes have run at least once?
- → What is the current latency between receiving data deltas and making them available for reporting?
- → Are there any data logistics processes defined but inactive for over a month?

Data consistency

- To what point in time can referential integrity be assured in a continuously loading environment?
- Are there any orphan tables?
- In case of 1:M relationships, does a relationship really change or was it a case of 'ghost hunting?'
- In case of N:M relationships, is this valid, or should it be a 1:M?

Data platform optimization

- Are there full row duplicate records across the system?
- Are certain areas experiencing a 'flip-flopping' effect (e.g., repeated inserts and logical deletes)?

Any functional checks on data content

- Does every invoice have an associated customer?
- Are daily sales figures within 10 % of yesterday's values at the same time?

An effective approach for notification is establishing a common schema, and publishing events to a centrally accessible location. Examples of these could be the data logistics control framework event log, a database table exposed via a web page, dashboards, Slack, MS Teams, or Kafka topics.

Interested parties can then subscribe to these events, and treat these notifications with high priority.

Deployment automation

At this stage, the engine can confidently deliver specific versions of the data solution, including change or releases, ensuring that the entire solution can be generated and processed.

The next step is managing these releases in a deployment operations framework, ultimately aimed at achieving continuous deployment. By incorporating a workflow that is able to operate autonomously, the solution's day-to-day deployment can be handed over to the engine, reducing human error.

A typical workflow might look like this:

- Commit changes to a central repository, using a feature branch
- Build and test the changes in a development environment
- Initiate a deployment to a pre-production or integration environment to detect any unforeseen conflicts
- Release to production once validations are complete

This process can range from manual to semi-automated (e.g., trigger by commits) or fully automated (optimized by the engine). Implementation details are covered in the later sections on ⚐automating deployment.

Continuous deployment

So far, this is a fairly straightforward 'DevOps' approach. But using the engine and its available metadata, we can further automate the development and refactoring efforts.

The design metadata 'knows' which upstream tables are impacted by changes. With this information, the engine is able to automatically generate the necessary code, update or truncate associated target tables, and adapt the solution accordingly.

This requires a robust, automated deployment mechanism that can perform the following actions:

- Deploy physical model changes
- Generate and execute data logistics code
- Run test cases, log results and notify interested parties of exceptions
- Perform rollback in case of failure

The engine can trigger these 'builds' based on certain events. This can be a commit to a specific feature or release branch, or as a result of rules captured in the ⚐optimizer. For instance, the monitoring framework may detect a high demand for certain datasets and refactor the code to optimize against these usage patterns.

'Ops' in the engine concept

Deployment automation aims to shorten the delivery cycle and produce higher quality results. But it is also intended to foster collaboration between data professionals and consumers. Most importantly, it intends to facilitate communication between involved parties about the process of data design, integration and delivery.

It is about understanding deployment practices and see how these can be applied to data, for example:

- → Finding a suitable deployment frequency that meets business expectations
- → Involving stakeholders in the release process, by defining tests, performing post-implementation reviews and monitoring the outputs over time
- → Enabling stakeholders to contribute to the information model and corresponding design metadata, supported by versioning
- → Discuss directives for ongoing optimization of the data solution, for instance analyzing usage patterns to spot new opportunities and support decision making on prioritization

An automated deployment mindset helps engaging stakeholders early in data design, involving process owners and operational systems administrator to work towards a full end-to-end data management approach that is running smoothly.

For example, you could define two alternative designs for a subject area to see what works best. You could prototype different approaches for surrogate key distribution, and evaluate what works best in a given technical environment or concept. Or, you could consider table elimination from the model based on usage patterns. It is also possible to assert what physical delivery of your data solution has a better outcome for compute cost or I/O.

The engine can then automatically generate and deploy these improvements.

By embedding deployment automation within the engine, the data solution becomes a living, evolving system capable of adapting to new requirements. The engine not only streamlines deployment but also supports iterative experimentation, enabling teams to explore alternative approaches and optimize for performance, cost, or specific business needs.

Testing

Traditional data solutions often adopt the principle of *judging data on the way in,* requiring data to meet strict quality standards before being accepted. This contrasts sharply with the philosophy of this book.

In our vision, all data is welcome. We don't judge. In fact, we go to great lengths to make sure *all* data has a place, including data that can be considered 'bad' quality. We may not have the right context (at the right time) to make an upfront call on what is considered 'bad' and 'good' for the consumers of the data.

And, what may be 'bad' for one consumer may be 'good enough' for another. In exceptional cases it may exactly be the 'bad' data that turns out to hold golden nuggets of value.

This is why we separate the collection of raw facts (e.g., via the PSA and the ⚐ back room concept) from their interpretation, and it's also where testing comes in. Testing, especially related to data validation and asserting if the data conforms to specific requirements, is a form of business logic – an interpretation of data.

However, the testing mechanism in the engine does *not* judge data and then bars it from entering the solution. Rather, it provides a framework to monitor and understand the state of the data across multiple perspectives.

The role of testing in the engine

Testing in the engine serves two primary purposes:

1) Tests capture the knowledge gained during design and implementation, and store this in a shared repository so that this can be reused during unit- and regression testing

2) Tests are reused as ongoing controls to verify that the data solution continues to behave as expected in the monitoring framework

Both purposes share in an important feature; a central repository to which tests can be added. Test can be developed during the development process as unit tests or in response to issues, and act as a permanent record of requirements and expectations.

As a guideline, a test should be created every time an exception has been encountered to make sure this specific scenario can be monitored in the future. Developing the test also ensures that you properly understand the violation in requirements encountered.

In this sense, the terms 'test' and 'control' are used interchangeably. While testing is used more in a unit-testing context, and typically focuses more on correct business interpretation, the same artifact (test case) is used as a control (check) to ensure ongoing consistency of the data solution.

There is no hard and fast rule on what should be tested, but it pays off to embed any understanding accumulated during development in the testing framework. At design and development time, a lot of business understanding is gained in a relatively short amount of time, and capturing this knowledge in a test case that outlines the expected behavior is a powerful way to embed this knowledge in the solution. This aligns with Gojko Adzic's 'Specification by Example' (2011), where examples are used to define and validate system behavior.

Tests can be developed for a wide variety of scenarios, including but not limited to:
- → Validating data against domain values
- → Detecting uniqueness constraint violations
- → Ensuring completeness of timelines in temporal data
- → Identifying outliers in sales or volume data using statistical thresholds (e.g., two standard deviations from the mean)
- → Verifying referential integrity

Testing framework

A testing framework, of which many are available either as open source or as part of commercial software, at a minimum has the following functionality:
- → A repository to store test cases
- → A standardize format for writing test cases
- → A set of evaluation functions (e.g., assertions, range checks, binary checks)
- → A mechanism execute tests and display the results

Simply put, a functional testing framework allows one or more tests to be executed and the results of the performed tests to be returned. This allows tests to integrate with deployment automation for regression testing and with the monitoring framework.

The testing framework can be combined with the event log of the data logistics process control framework, providing a unified monitoring point for the entire data solution.

Labeling data

Validating data is not the same as rejecting it. So how then should we act when the tests inform us of issues?

The solution is to 'label' the data that does not pass certain tests. This allows the data solution to manage data both in the incoming layers ('back room' in the data solution design) as well as the delivery layers (interpretation, 'front room') without physically filtering or removing the data.

This process, also known as 'flagging,' allows flexibility in routing data to specific delivery areas, such as data marts, depending on specific demands in these areas. Labeling can be used as a filter to allow only data that meets certain criteria in any specific data mart, without impacting others which may have different use cases and requirements.

The implementation of labeling is explained in detail in the ⚐ exception bitmap section.

Business logic

Not all transformations and data flows can easily be captured using standard patterns. For these cases, the engine provides a facility to record design metadata that specifies complex interpretations, calculations, aggregations, and other types of transformations.

This *business logic* —or data interpretation— is captured independently in a dedicated area of the engine and applied automatically during the generation or refactoring of the solution.

By separating business logic, the engine allows transformations to be overlaid on raw data, providing additional context without altering the underlying immutable events.

There are many ways to implement this. For instance, a dedicated directory could be polled by the engine at runtime, containing instructions that can be understood by the compiler (e.g., SQL views). Another option is to store a separate set of design metadata artifacts that contain complex logic.

This separation of business logic from raw event data is both intentional and critical. It allows the data solution to remain adaptable by enabling adjustments to business logic without requiring changes to the underlying design.

Detailed implementation strategies for managing business logic within the engine will be explored in the ⚐ getting the data out chapter.

Optimizer

Using the engine, we can now automatically generate and deploy the entire data solution. The combination of versioned design metadata, complex business logic, and code generation templates allows us to create and deploy different perspectives at runtime.

If needed, we could delete the entire solution downstream of the PSA and rebuild it exactly as it was before — a like-for-like restoration. This also means that we can consider deploying the solution in different technical ways.

For instance, we could 'virtualize' the data solution using the PSA and deploy the solution as a series of database views, replacing tables and data logistics processes. We could also generate a set of tables and matching data logistics processes — or a combination of both.

We could consider implementing the PSA as a file storage layer and use parallel file parsing techniques to generate the data solution objects, loading processes, and data marts. Once data consumption areas are populated (e.g., BI tools), the nodes can be powered down.

This flexibility allows the engine to adapt the design of the data solution over time, opening up numerous technical implementation possibilities.

However, these are still decisions made by the data solution designers. The next step is to delegate some of these decisions to the engine itself.

Optimizing using environmental metadata

As the system operates, *environmental metadata* is created. While design metadata drives the logical structure of the solution, environmental metadata records system performance, such as available resources, processes execution times, memory and disk space.

Environmental metadata functions like a 'sensor,' monitoring system performance and apply this to determine the optimal physical implementation for a given directive or use case.

This is the final component of the engine, the *optimizer*.

Through the optimizer, the engine is made aware of technological constraints and directives (parameters). By interpreting the environmental metadata, and taking into account the directives, the engine can automatically refactor data structures and data logistics processes to make the most efficient use of the available technical environment.

Examples of this are:

→ Normalize or denormalize data structures
→ Select optimal aggregation strategies
→ Choose the best key distribution technique

For example, the engine might assess whether hash keys, sequence values, or natural business keys are best fit for a Data Vault implementation. Depending on the data profile, hash keys can be costly to store and retrieve. A typical hash key quickly requires 16 or 20 bytes storage per key, whereas integer sequence keys typically only require 4 or 8 bytes.

However, sequence keys introduce dependencies which may impact overall data delivery requirements. A 'middle' option of using natural business keys can also be considered. This might require less storage space and does not incur processing dependencies.

Based on environmental metadata, the engine can dynamically select or even combine these methods for optimal performance.

Unless specific overrides are in place, decisions are driven by data profiles and optimization directives (e.g., cost, compute, storage) rather than subjective preferences.

This is possible by interpreting the statistics and execution times from the data logistics control framework, as well as outputs received from the monitoring framework. With this, the code can be re-generated using a different template, and the updated solution can be automatically deployed and re-initialized.

This process modifies the physical delivery while maintaining consistency in the design metadata — automated refactoring.

Directives

The optimizer applies rules, *directives,* to determine how the data solution should operate. These optimization goals can be set by the administrator, and may include:

→ Reducing compute or storage costs
→ Achieving specific data latency thresholds (data freshness, availability)
→ Achieving specific data latency thresholds
→ Balancing I/O, storage, or compute utilization
→ Improving query performance for selected domains

The optimization process can be a fun and engaging way to manage the data solution.

Different implementation approaches can be simulated and compared (e.g., hash keys versus sequence keys) to determine the most effective approach for the environment. The optimization outputs also provide transparency that can be used to manage the environment — for the data team as well as the consumers of the data.

After all, delivering data solutions often involves a careful balance between resource (cost) constraints and business requirements.

Finite resources can be applied for specific outcomes, but it also makes the point that the sky is not always the limit, and that restricting certain resources will have an impact on important data solution metrics, such as latency.

Starting the engine

When the engine components are fully configured, the data solution becomes an active system capable of rapid, reliable delivery. While information models and project plans still need thoughtful design, we know that the engine can deliver fast and consistent results and supports our journey in uncovering the meaning behind the data.

From the moment the first data is processed, we can start understanding the effects the patterns have on the data. We can immediately see the initial results of our modeling decisions. Environmental metadata begins flowing in, allowing the optimizer to suggest or trigger refinements.

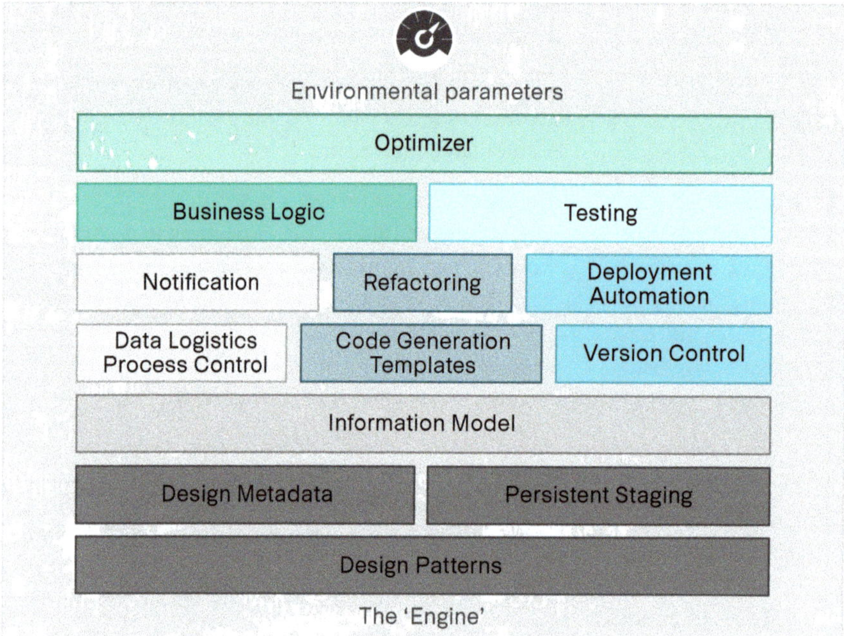

With the engine, data professionals no longer need to focus on low-level physical data model decisions. Instead, methodologies and best practices are embedded into the engine as conventions, freeing teams to focus on higher-level goals such as innovation, collaboration, and alignment with business objectives.

03
FastChangeCo – Understanding the landscape

"As FastChangeCo, we must consistently promote awareness of the value that data has to our business. Data is not 'stuff,' but ..."

The Vision.

Michael is impressed with his temporary team's performance during the initial phase of the data initiative. The team has truly come together to tackle this challenge, and Michael recognizes the progress they've made in such a short time.

Still, there is a long way to go.

The presentation of their vision and strategy has surprised the management – in a positive sense. The board's feedback is that a solid foundation has been created in a remarkably short time.

Michael suspects this probably doesn't happen too often at FastChangeCo.

The initial hurdle on the path towards *The Resurrection* of the data landscape has been taken.

The birth of the DMCE

Presenting the vision and strategy to the board has been a milestone, and its effects are immediately visible in Sylvia's support for the project. Based on a successful pitch and broad support by the top management she had promised Michael the necessary funding.

So now it's time to make good on this promise.

With these funds, the initial steps can be taken to deliver data management foundations that will ultimately operate as a profit center.

Jeff still argues that FastChangeCo already has all the IT systems required to analyze the company's data. Sylvia, however, is not convinced. The data initiative team, on the other hand, seems to be on the right track.

Sylvia thinks: "Jeff has been around for such a long time. He just doesn't like to change anything. He just wants to keep things steady until retirement, and then go down in the annals of FastChangeCo managers as a successful 'Head of IT.' Unfortunately, we can't afford to wait any longer!"

She ponders if there's any way she can persuade Jeff. She doesn't want to corner him into a position where he pushes back against the plans for the next few years – someone with whom she has to fight again and again over any obstacles that arise. None of that should be necessary.

Sylvia knows she needs to devise a strategy for this in the coming weeks. But first, let's focus on the current situation and make sure that Michael can continue.

The first point of the data initiative's vision and strategy –Operate as a Data Management Center of Excellence– already outlines that all future data management activities should be concentrated in a *Data Management Center of Excellence (DMCE).*

By announcing the DMCE, the cornerstone for the new data management approach will be laid. Formal organizational changes always take longer at FastChangeCo, and further discussions on accountability, reporting lines, and operations in general still need to take place.

Sylvia's second important action is to officially name the project that will build the new, cutting-edge, and visionary data solution:

The Resurrection – the revival of data with meaning!

The team and Michael feel proud to be part of the founding of the DMCE.

This calls for a celebration!

Celebrations

While celebrating the birth of the DMCE, the team reflects on the presentations they have attended over the past weeks. They discuss what they found useful, what didn't resonate, and what they, as a team, would like to understand better.

The concept of 'Engine Thinking' made a lasting impression. The team is fascinated by this vision.

So, during their laid-back gathering, the newly minted DMCE team decides to adopt a flexible approach for *The Resurrection* that aligns with the principles of Engine Thinking.

This way, they can avoid repeating the mistakes of the past.

They aim to establish a solution architecture and data landscape that supports incremental delivery of future additions and requirements, while maintaining the flexibility to revisit and adjust prior decisions as needed.

Good ideas often emerge during celebrations, when there is a brief respite from work pressures.

The following day, with these ideas and the insights from the presentations fresh in their minds, the DMCE team kicks off their work, armed with a clear vision and strategy.

The data landscape draft

During several brainstorming sessions and coffee rounds, the DMCE team sketches an initial outline of the new data landscape.

The team wants to make it clear that it is a *draft,* and that the final data solution architecture may look very different. And that is fine. Evolving from idea to implementation takes time.

The stakeholders on the steering committee still have different views on how the new data landscape should work. Some expect the first reports for the departments to be available in the very near future.

That would be a tall order!

Michael isn't fazed by this. He's seen it all before in previous projects. Together with Sylvia, he will manage these external pressures. Both he and Sylvia are committed to shielding the team from such distractions.

Sylvia informs the team, explaining how she addressed the steering committee. She compares a big project, like the new data solution, to her preparation for the '100 Miles of Temptation City' — a familiar analogy that makes the team smile.

She takes a long-term approach to both work and sports, knowing that planning is measured in months, or even years.

The ensuing discussion was an opportunity to explain why a completely new data solution involves more than just generating a new report.

The team hopes that Michael and Sylvia have bought them somewhat of a breather. Past experience at FastChangeCo has shown that decision makers tend to forget these reasons, and short-term thinking often takes over.

Learning from past mistakes

"Learning from past mistakes," Michael writes on the whiteboard. "At our first meeting, we all agreed this was important. But can we pinpoint what often goes wrong at the start of projects? Can we make this more specific, so we can avoid repeating those mistakes going forward?"

Michael scans the room.

Terence, not fully paying attention, looks up from his laptop. "By the way, did you know GOOF[8] visited us last week? They showed us that we can implement these data initiative requirements quite easily and *goof-proof* with their new database, *SPEEDY.* Shouldn't we take a look at that first, instead of spending all this time and effort inventing something that is already done by a vendor who actually specializes in these things?"

Yerodin sighs "Please, not another tool! Can we please first focus on the solution and outcomes we are trying to achieve, instead of jumping straight into technology? If you ask me, that's exactly one of those things that has gone wrong in the past."

"Both are valid points." Michael muses. He asks Terence to explore the technology further. That way, the topic isn't completely dismissed and doesn't immediately provoke another conflict. Who knows? Maybe SPEEDY could be a good fit for the future. It doesn't hurt to keep ones eyes open.

Terence sees the value in this approach, and is please that there is an option to investigate SPEEDY. At least he managed to bring it into the conversation, and now he can continue to look into it.

With that settled, the team agrees to leave the topic of 'technology' off the agenda for now — at least for the first draft of the data landscape. This way, they can have meaningful discussions without the distraction of tools and technologies before fully understanding the objectives of the solution.

To make sure that there is a record of important events, the team decides to document all key decisions and agreements in a decision register. This is to ensure that, once they have been made, decisions are recorded and transparent for all involved.

Not everyone may always agree with a certain decision, but once a decision has been made, every team member *must* commit to this decision – even if they did not fully agree with it at the time.

Meanwhile, the discussions about what exactly went wrong in the past continue.

Yerodin sighs again: "Oh man, we were always so deeply involved with everything. It's hard not to get bogged down in the details. Can we take a break and take a step back, so we can look at everything again with hopefully some new perspectives?"

"That's a great idea Yerodin. In fact, I could use another pot of green tea for my sanity. Let's go to the kitchen!" Michael says as he heads over to prepare his tea.

In the kitchen, Michael carefully measures a few grams of tea into his Japanese teapot, heats the water, and lets it cool to the desired temperature. He pours the water into his teacup to cool down, then into the teapot. Minutes pass as Michael quietly monitors the infusion, ensuring he empties the pot completely, knowing the second infusion won't taste right if he doesn't. Yerodin watches in silence, not wanting to interfere with this ritual.

While Michael is meticulously preparing his green tea, Terence approaches him. "Michael, something's been on my mind during the discussion. We haven't really talked about where we're going to put the business logic yet."

Moving business logic downstream

Xuefang Kaya overhears the conversation. She has just joined the DMCE team as a newcomer. This is her first 'real' job after completing her studies and several internships. Full of energy and eager to learn everything about data modeling, Xuefang joined the team specifically to work with Michael and the DMCE.

She approaches Michael and Yerodin, excited to contribute. "I heard something about this at the data modeling presentations when we investigated what the world of data means to us. Let me check my notes. One moment."

Xuefang quickly pulls out her small notebook and flips through it. "Ah, here it is. A common theme among the presenters was that, in a modern Data Warehouse, business logic should be applied *downstream.*"

"What exactly do they mean by that?" Michael asks, while Terence, looking slightly irritated, listens. "What the speakers meant," Xuefang explains, "is that business logic shouldn't be applied when loading data into the Data Warehouse. Instead, it should be applied only after the raw data is safely stored."

Terence begins to object, "Yes, but..." before Michael cuts in, suggesting they revisit the topic after the break.

For now, all Michael wants is to enjoy his green tea.

As he sips, Michael reflects, "Could that have been a mistake we made in the past? Applying all the logic upfront when loading data? Maybe that's what made previous solutions so complex."

Once everyone returns from the break, Terence immediately brings the discussion back. "We really need to talk about how we implement business logic."

As usual, it's a back-and-forth of opinions, views, and emotions. But gradually, as Xuefang and Michael introduce the ideas they've gathered from the presentations, the team starts to recognize the potential benefits of applying business logic downstream:

→ It reduces the complexity of the initial data loading process
→ Separating the application of business logic from loading raw data ingestion helps break up the process in smaller, more manageable, steps that are easier to understand. The business logic can run after the collection of the raw data
→ It can enable faster delivery of data, especially for data marts that require little or no business logic
→ Raw data is available in its original form for minimum viable products (MVPs), prototypes or research. There is no need for additional provision of data in its unaltered form, as was the case previously
→ Data consumers can engage with the data earlier, as it becomes available more quickly for testing and validation

Reluctantly, Terence agrees to see how implementing business logic after the initial loading phase could work out.

"Why hasn't anyone at FastChangeCo come up with such an obvious idea before?" Yerodin wonders aloud. Meanwhile, Xuefang feels a quiet satisfaction, knowing she has made a valuable contribution.

However, the team would like to explicitly state that the business logic is not less complex because of this. Not that there is any misunderstanding here. And some complexity cannot be resolved without modifications to existing IT systems.

With this in mind, the team moves forward with the understanding that separating business logic from the initial data loading will reduce the overall complexity of the solution.

Each individual transformation can be implemented independently, on demand, and without the need to adjust existing processes.

Marbles, data, and hubs

"Now, how do we translate this idea into a design? How can we sketch it out? The team contemplates."

Yerodin recalls a term from one of Martijn Evers' talks: "I liked the idea of a 'data hub.' We could define something around that, perhaps?"

"Maybe we should draw up the 'data hubs' as boxes?" Xuefang suggests, thinking aloud.

"Yeah, that's a good idea. Once at an event for controllers, one of the presenters depicted data as marbles. Why not use different colors for each major data domain and fill the boxes with those marbles? It'll give us a nice visual to explain what each 'data hub' contains." Yerodin looks around the room for feedback.

Michael notices how Terrence is about to say something, which is usually a sign he disagrees with the direction. To keep the momentum positive, Michael quickly steps in: "Yerodin, I think that's a brilliant idea. We're here to try new things. If it doesn't work, we can always go back to the old way of designing with tons of documentation."

"Let me draw something," Xuefang says, moving to the whiteboard.

The marbles illustrate how data might flow through the new data landscape:

→ Unsorted data is landed in a dedicated data hub — the blue, green, orange, gray and black marbles. Let's call this a log data hub

→ Data is then organized into well-defined structures in a raw data hub, where business-driven data modeling gives it clear meaning – the same blue, green, orange, gray, and black marbles, but better organized

→ The raw data hub can be extended into an information data hub, which stores the outcomes of applying business logic — represented by the yellow marbles

→ The innovation and research data hubs pull data from the log data hub, and if needed, from the raw and information data hubs. These hubs also allow users to load and experiment with external data as required

→ The presentation data hubs, there can be as many as required, make up the presentation layer. On the way to each presentation data hub additional business logic can be applied — these are the additional red marbles. But this is ideally already prepared in the information data hub

The team decides that Xuefang's idea is a solid first step to think about the new data landscape, and they are satisfied with adopting it as the first draft.

A first draft

The team's draft of the data landscape begins to takes shape as a structured approach to organizing data.

Data hubs will be defined for specific roles and purposes, supported by a set of guidelines that govern how to data is organized into types ('marbles'), how data passes through these hubs, and what rules apply when moving data from one hub to another.

It is expected that this would help to avoid at least the following past mistakes:

→ High complexity of loading processes on the way into to the data solution. Going forward, business-specific transformations that are necessary for specific data interpretations will be implemented later in the overall flow of data

→ Too much focus on technology, at the expense of solution design. The new approach will prioritize definition and classification of data (modeling) over technology choices

→ Involving the consumers of the data too late. Consumers and stakeholders will now be involved earlier, helping categorize the 'marbles' and shape the data from the start

→ Long data delivery times. Data will be made available more quickly, even in raw form, offering different quality levels instead of waiting for it to be 100 % correct

- → Writing lengthy requirement documents. The focus will now be on smaller, iterative, initiatives that can incrementally clarify how data should be used, in collaboration with the consumers of the data
- → This approach is expected to streamline data processes and align better with the needs of the business, and at the same time reduce unnecessary complexity and improve stakeholder engagement.

The team adds these principles to the decision register. The first draft of the data landscape seems to be a good concept.

Aligning the data landscape to the vision and strategy

"But, does this data landscape approach align to our vision and strategy?" Michael wonders. "We should review this first. After all, the vision and strategy are meant to provide the foundation for all DMCE activities, and everyone should understand how our next actions are derived from it."

With that, Michael invites the team to a meeting to review the concept of the data landscape in relation to the vision and strategy.

Over the past few months, he has learned that shared decision-making and careful deliberation have been uncommon at FastChangeCo. Traditionally, the company has been very hierarchic in its decision-making.

There was always someone in the hierarchy who felt the need to formally confirm or reject important team decisions. Often, that person was not fully aware of the context and, in the worst case, completely ignorant of the background and the considerations made.

Reviewing things like these as a team is just not part of the company culture. As a result, the question "Why must we review this together?" is evident on the faces of the team.

Michael explains his intent: "Only by reviewing our data landscape ideas against the vision and strategy as a team we will be able to truly internalize them. I would like for us to deliver these ideas together and ensure that everyone is on board. To make this work, we need robust and inclusive discussions, capture the outcomes, learn from them, commit to the decisions made, and move forward."

"In my view," Michael continues, "this way we can empower us, the team, to make the right calls when faced with design decisions in the future. We know that any decision made must fit within the framework we are defining now, and this all starts with aligning with the vision and strategy."

The initial investigation

Motivated by the prospect of ongoing collaboration and Michael's vision, the team sets out to compare the draft data landscape with the vision and strategy. Together, they work through each aspect, challenging how it applies to their draft.

Operate as a Data Management Center of Excellence

"That one's easy," Yerodin remarks. "We've already started this. We still need to make sure our team secures a formal place in the company structure, though."

Design business-driven

"We'll learn more about the data when we start 'sorting the marbles' by color, and organize them into data domains," Michael explains. "This begins in the raw data hub but will require input from subject matter experts to get it right."

"We'll use the presentation hubs to make data accessible and with the right level of quality," Xuefang adds.

The team notes, however, that while domain-oriented data modeling is an excellent goal, the draft data landscape still lacks this focus. "We need to work out *how* we'll model domains in a practical way," says Yerodin.

Amal Leyla Qasim, a recent addition to the DMCE team, remarks, "I attended a talk by Ronald Damhof that might help with this. He introduced a model that guides when certain data modeling methods are appropriate." Like Terence, she is 'borrowed' from IT and doesn't formally report to Michael, but to Jeff.

She has worked in FastChangeCo IT's department for many years. In her spare time, she likes to educate herself on various topics that pique her interest – especially data topics. This is how she came across Ronald Damhof's Data Quadrant Model – the DQM.

However, learning new ways of doing things is one thing, but introducing them in IT —with its rigid structures— is quite another. The DMCE sounded like an ideal way to drive real change.

"The key message is," Amal continues, "that different modeling methods are appropriate for certain situations, but that there's no one-size-fits-all approach. He has created a model to explain this, and help figure out when a certain approach might make sense, and when it might not. Give me a moment to check my notes on this. It might help us in our understanding of the data landscape. Especially 'why it works the way we think it works.'"

"Oh, Amal, please spare us the philosophical views right now," Terence grumbles. "It's hard enough drafting the data landscape without sidetracking into 'data management' theories."

Ignoring Terence, Michael replies, "Amal, this is great! Could you prepare an overview of the quadrant model for us? For now, though, let's get back to the review."

Focus on results

The team feels confident that even as a draft, this data landscape approach can deliver results faster.

"For the research and innovation hub, we can provide raw data for experimentation quickly," Yerodin explains. And, when requirements are clearly defined, we can deliver this data through a presentation hub."

"We're in a good position here," Yerodin continues, "but involving business departments and subject matter experts early in testing might take some time."

Around the room, everyone nods in agreement.

Leverage data models

"Our draft doesn't specify which types of data models we'll use," Amal notes. "Michael, I recall you mentioned this could be explored in a master's thesis. Do you think that could work here?"

"Yes, let's follow up on that!" Michael replies, seeing the positive responses around the room. "For now, let's assume we have enough suitable options to design a good data model. One thing is certain though, whatever we decide, we'll need to ensure full historization of the data for auditability."

Embrace Agile principles

Michael opens the discussion on the way of working, "I think we're already in a good position here too. Our small-scale, use-case-driven approach supports an agile way of working. We can narrow the scope for our data solution to a minimum. Does everyone agree?"

Once again, the team agrees, though Yerodin adds a final point: "I think that, as a team, we should work on being open for change. The way I see it, sometimes we hold on to predefined requirements too long, and only adapt when the pressure's really on. If we had been more flexible, we could've saved a lot of time. I think that involving a Kanban coach might help us follow the strategy more effectively. How many times have we thought we could 'pick it up as we went?'"

Michael nods, appreciating Yerodin's self-awareness. Just then, Terence interjects, "Wait! Every time we make a change, downstream applications have to pause for weeks —sometimes even three months— while we are adjusting the data structures the applications depend on. How are we supposed to stay agile like that?"

The team exchanges a few eye rolls, but Michael listens carefully, noting that Terence's point about scalability has some merit. He's learned that resistant feedback often highlights real challenges. "Good point Terence, we need to address this, and I have an idea on how we can," Michael responds.

Terence, seems pleased, likely already planning to tell Jeff about his 'counter' to all this 'modern agile stuff' over a beer.

Be inherently scalable

The team moves on to discuss scalability goals for the data landscape.

"Loading processes should be able to 'transport' individual marbles independently, and as quickly as possible – ideally operating continuously," someone suggests. But the team acknowledges that the current draft doesn't clarify *how* this point of the vision and strategy can be achieved.

Creating many independent loading processes could require substantial development and technical infrastructure. Which frameworks should they use? Could parts of the data landscape be automated?

They acknowledge that creating a vision and strategy is one thing; implementing it is quite another. Recognizing the work ahead, they add these ideas and challenges to a backlog, ensuring that none of this hard work is lost. For now, they agree that the approach is feasible but requires detailed planning.

There is general agreement that it *can* be done, it's just a matter of agreeing how – and doing it.

Moving forward

Turning to the team, Michael asks, "How else can we improve?" He writes down the feedback during the ensuing discussion:

- → The implementation of the metadata repository is still unclear in the data landscape design
- → The data log hub might need to be subdivided. Otherwise, how can we land *and* hold data at the same time?

These are the comments so far, but Michael is confident that more points will arise in the future. As the project progresses, more and more details will need to be clarified. Overall, though, the team seems satisfied with how the design of the data landscape aligns with the vision and strategy.

Michael reflects on how differently things could have gone. With some discomfort, he recalls a former project where objective discussions were almost impossible. Team members were highly protective of 'their' tools, and even the smallest demand led to defiant reactions or outright refusal. He hopes this project won't be like that.

A green tea would be really good right about now.

At the end of the meeting, Sylvia joins the team. Michael has let her know that they are talking about how the draft data landscape supports the vision and strategy. While the team present their results she, like Michael, feels proud of her team's commitment to *The Resurrection.*

But, the feeling is short-lived.

"By the way," remarks Terence, "I spoke with the GOOF guys again. They said SPEEDY could be used to solve all this stuff quickly and with little effort. Wouldn't that be something? Everything would be faster to implement, and we don't have to define all of these things we're discussing now. They've already done that for us. What do you think, Sylvia? Michael?"

Michael feels his agitation rise. First, he can't enjoy his tea after the lengthy meeting, and now here's that familiar refrain again: "A new tool will solve all our problems!" How often has that worked out?

Michael sighs inwardly "Didn't we agree to keep tooling out of the picture in this phase of the project?" Silvia steps in, turning to Terence, "It might be useful to prepare a general proof of concept (PoC) that includes all our technical and, especially, business requirements. What do you think?"

"I still have to look into SPEEDY a bit more first." Terence deflects. A PoC like Sylvia suggested sounds like a lot of work. "I'll think about it."

Back in the kitchen, Michael is finally enjoying his tea when Amal approaches him. "Michael, what Terence said about IT's change deployments doesn't sit well with me. It can't be that our plans will fail because of this. Is there a way we can solve it? Because it does sound like we'd have to test everything —interfaces, downstream applications, data content— constantly. That doesn't feel very agile, does it?"

"No no, we'll approach that differently. We could add an additional version of the outgoing interface, which would incorporate the changes we'd want to make." interjects Xuefang.

Michael thinks it's worthwhile encouraging the team to attend conferences; how many great ideas have come from them already? "Xuefang, Amal, sounds like a solid idea. Let's add it to the backlog. Do you two want to explore it further?" They agree, moving away to continue brainstorming.

Carrying his tea, Michael strolls over to Silvia, who is using the informal setting as an opportunity to get to know the team better.

"Silvia, 'little birds' told me a few things that might help us get Jeff on board." A smile lights up his face. Sylvia appreciates how Michael tackles challenges at FastChangeCo. Overall, she's pleased with Michael's work; hiring him was a stroke of luck for her and for FastChangeCo. "Let's hear it, Michael. What did you find out?"

"Well, Jeff successfully upgraded a completely outdated IT infrastructure. Wasn't that a huge career boost? He moved up quickly after that. But since then, he's become more of a guardian of his past achievements rather than a driver for change. At least, that's what I've heard. And Sylvia, you know what that means: in reality, doing nothing is like taking a step backwards."

"That's pretty much what's happened," Sylvia says. "How about we frame this initiative as an opportunity to solidify Jeff's legacy during his final years here? Perhaps we can reignite his ambition with a chance to repeat his success."

"That's a great idea, Sylvia." Michael nods, relieved that she already has a plan to get Jeff on board.

Assess data?

Later that evening, Terence joins Jeff for a beer at *The Dive,* their favorite pub. He recounts in detail how he pushed back against the agile approach during the DMCE meeting and voiced his overall frustrations with this new way of working.

"We need at least three to six months for a deployment. Faster is just not feasible for us," he insists.

"You are so right, Terence. Another round?" Jeff doesn't wait for an answer, ordering another round of drinks – at Terence's expense.

Terence then describes the data landscape design the team is working on, as well as the approach of handling business logic downstream. Jeff is visibly appalled by this idea.

"That's just nonsense! They'll drive the project into a wall with those harebrained ideas. Everyone knows that you design the database for exactly what you need, then clean and prepare the data so it fits. The departments don't want raw data – they can't handle that! It's IT's job to prep everything, give them the right data, end of story."

"Exactly, Jeff!" Terence says, nodding. "I guess I got caught up in the moment during the meeting. But I'll bring up my concerns and challenge this approach."

Jeff looks at him, a hint of a smirk playing on his lips. "How will you do that? Michael Mueller's the one setting the course, isn't he?"

"Well ... yes," Terence concedes. "But we usually make our decisions as a team."

Jeff snorts. "We, or more specifically I, have always made these decisions. How am I supposed to be responsible for something if I can't control it directly?"

For the next half-hour, Jeff shares his frustrations about FastChangeCo's management changes, with Terence nodding in agreement. Before they part, Terence promises to raise his concerns about the business logic approach and, if possible, prevent it from going forward.

A few days later, Terence does just that in a team meeting.

"Michael, we really need to talk again about implementing business rules on the way into the data solution. I keep thinking about this idea, and it just doesn't sit right. I'm not convinced we can do it that way."

Michael looks up. "Why not?"

"Well, without a clear way to implement these rules, how can we be sure everything's tested, accepted, and bug-free for each release? Our deployment cycle is every three to six months for a reason. If we don't carefully plan each release, we'll never deliver on time. And IT will be the ones shouldering the blame! We're just not set up to work differently as a company."

"And besides," he continues, "the people in the business, they want *good* data. They can't work with raw data. It's always been IT's job to clean and prepare it. They can't do a damn thing..."

"Stop!" Michael interjects firmly, cutting Terence short. "What do you mean by they? Who are *they?* Maybe we should actually ask what *they* want – or what they're capable of handling. Right?"

The tension that has been building up in the team over the last few days finally reaches its breaking point. Voices rise, and the room soon fills with a flurry of tangled, overlapping remarks. Xuefang, Amal, Terence, Yerodin, and the rest weigh in on the issue.

Terence argues for assessing data quality on the way into the solution, insisting that IT —or at least their team— should be the gatekeepers. Yerodin strongly disagrees, advocating to preserve the 'facts' as they come in. After all, he argues, when data is loaded, it's not always clear if it's 'good' or 'bad.'

One by one, the others start gravitating towards either Terence's or Yerodin's perspective. Meanwhile, Michael stands back, observing, and wondering why these divisions are suddenly surfacing. Wasn't this issue settled in earlier discussions? Hadn't they already documented their approach in the data solution landscape?

Lost in thought, Michael heads to the kitchen, leaving the team to hash things out among themselves. He puts on the kettle and considers how he might clarify the benefits of handling business rules downstream, maybe even using real-life examples to illustrate the point.

A few minutes later, Amal joins him, picking up on his frustration. "Everything all right?" she asks gently.

"Yes, for sure," Michael replies, stirring his tea thoughtfully. "I'm just wondering how we can move forward. Would practical examples help?"

Amal takes a moment to think it over. *Would* that help? She's cautious of anything that might seem like management pushing a decision. She's seen plenty of projects go wrong that way, particularly when Jeff was involved.

Finally, Amal reaches a conclusion. "I think that's a great idea. A 'forced' decision —by you or anyone else— wouldn't be the way to go here. Let's reconvene later this afternoon. Meanwhile, I can talk with a few people privately, to try to ease some of the emotions."

"Thanks Amal," Michael says, feeling a bit lighter. "I'll pick up some biscuits for later."

Nothing is as it seems

Later in the afternoon, the team gathers in the kitchen for tartelettes. Michael has brought these from his favorite pâtisserie, *L'art L'amande,* right beside *The Dive,* as he's done so many times before.

Sometimes it's the little things that motivate people.

One by one, the team members trickle in. Michael's tartelettes are renowned for their taste, and everyone in the team likes them.

The tension from this morning has lifted; everyone seems relaxed and is standing together. Michael notices how well Amal has managed things. Seizing the moment, he begins to speak.

"This morning, we passionately discussed the pros and cons of our data solution. I think it's a great sign that you're all so engaged and that we, as a team, can challenge ideas and decisions. This kind of dynamic will be valuable during *The Resurrection.*"

He continues, "I had a similar experience in a past project when we were decommissioning a so-called 'legacy Data Warehouse' and building a new solution from scratch. We called the project 'ShiftX.' The team followed agile principles and used Data Vault[9] as the physical modeling approach for a column-oriented database." Michael omits the political squabbles, the technical challenges, and other details that might distract from his story.

"Our ShiftX team collaborated closely with the subject matter experts involved, and in retrospect, that collaboration was one of the project's biggest success factors. A key goal of ShiftX was to make a small amount of raw data available to the subject matter experts as soon as possible, so they could begin testing. The result was a small star schema in an access layer, with one fact table and one dimension table."

Michael takes a bite of his strawberry tartelette, then resumes. "And then something surprising happened: the raw data was completely different from what the subject matter experts had expected. Not only did the data content not match the business' expectations, but it was also drastically different from the data in the legacy Data Warehouse."

After another bite, he explains, "The ShiftX project was based here in Temptation City, just like FastChangeCo. Many companies in our city work almost exclusively with data; it's why Temptation City is also nicknamed 'Sin datos, no hay paraíso,' which means 'without data, there is no paradise.' If there were no data, there'd be no revenue, and therefore, no paradise." Michael adds with a grin, "But I'm sure you all know that already!"

Settling into a chair, he continues his story. "One of the key metrics we worked with was the *ratio of students to the total population of a city.* This metric was essential for the company's daily operations. When we ran tests, this ratio differed significantly between the legacy Data Warehouse and the new data solution."

"At first, we assumed the error was in our new data solution. Errors can happen in new implementations, and we thought we might have made incorrect assumptions about the operational systems, leading to downstream issues." He pauses to assess the team's reactions before continuing. "But that wasn't the case. The raw data we collected in the new data solution was 100 % consistent with the data in the operational system. What was surprising, however, was that this operational system delivered identical raw data to the legacy Data Warehouse."

After a sip of green tea, Michael adds, "Working with the subject matter experts, we soon discovered why the data was so different in the legacy Data Warehouse. Do you have an idea what the problem was?" He looks around, but no one answers.

"The issue came down to how address data was managed. Temptation City has several districts, each with its own zip code. However, address data was entered manually into the operational system without validation. As a result, the 'City' column, which should have contained only the city name, also included parts of the address like zip codes and even typos. We saw entries like 'Templetion City of 69,' '4711 Temptation City,' 'City of Temptations,' or even 'Temptation Kitty.' It should, of course, all just have been 'Temptation City.'"

The team murmurs in acknowledgment of the all-too-common data quality challenges.

"With these variations alone," Michael explains, "the metric we needed —students as a percentage of total city population— returned multiple results (six different results: the correct value and five incorrect ones) instead of just one, resulting in major inconsistencies when we compared the new data solution to the legacy Data Warehouse."

"But why wasn't that the case in the legacy Data Warehouse?" Xuefang asks.

"Yes, that was our question too. How could that be?" Michael pauses. "It turned out that the developers were already attempting to 'fix' data quality issues during the legacy Data Warehouse loading process. They had implemented steps like stripping out zip codes, 'which is relatively simple to program. Any issues they couldn't solve were later also attempted to be fixed by report and dashboard developers — again, to the best of their ability."

Terence interjects, "That seems like a smart approach. We should probably do that too. This way, we don't end up with poor-quality data in our data solution, which would just be useless anyway. I've been through enough conversations with the business about data quality; best to avoid those!"

"Hold on, Terence," Michael says with a smile, "it's not over yet. For the subject matter experts, this turned out to be a huge problem. They had assumed the data in the legacy Data Warehouse was identical to the data in the operational systems. Unfortunately, these metrics weren't only for analysis — they were critical to operations and drove decisions. This poor data quality prevented the company from achieving optimal margins, as they were working with distorted baseline figures."

Michael sees the surprised expressions around him and continues, "The experts were understandably appalled. They quickly addressed the issue in the operational system, implementing changes to prevent future errors and cleaning up the existing data. As a result, the added value of the new data solution had already become apparent after the very first implementation step."

After another sip of his tea, he concludes, "The moral of this story is that raw data had value, regardless of whether it was 'good' or 'bad' from our perspective. The discrepancies helped us uncover issues in the operational system, which we might not have noticed otherwise. This experience taught me that our own knowledge of data management can sometimes lead us astray. We might make assumptions and decisions that end up counterproductive. Today, I believe it's our responsibility to discuss even small data transformation decisions with subject matter experts."

Yerodin chuckles and rolls his eyes. "Will we ever learn?" he says, clearly recognizing a familiar theme.

"Nothing is as it seems," Amal notes thoughtfully.

Michael nods. "That's exactly what we felt. We could only explain the situation and support the quickest possible fix. For the project, this incident was a stroke of luck. It gave us credibility and the green light to continue loading raw data first and only applying transformations afterward, as needed."

He glances at the team. "As the project continued, we saw further advantages to this approach, especially when we got to implementing complex business rules. But that's a story for another day."

He finishes the last sip of his green tea and, with a grin, says, "Now, time for a refill. I just discovered a new green tea, Japan Sencha, at *T-Time,* my favorite tea shop really close to *L'art L'amande."*

Through knowledge one attains humanity

While Michael sips his tea, he eyes the last tartelette – the one with mango. But Terence snatches it before he can reach for it.

Michael clears his throat and begins, "Let me share a second example."

"I used to work at a company called MOOSE[10]. They're still around. Not as old as FastChangeCo, but they've been running for a few decades. One of my projects there involved implementing a Data Warehouse – a large one for its time. Some doubted it could even be done. The departments were so siloed; getting everything integrated seemed unrealistic.

"It would still be a big project today, when I think about it. We implemented hundreds of business rules, and many were added right into the data loading processes for the warehouse. That meant some data was transformed as soon as it entered the system."

"Michael, is this story similar to the last one? If it is, maybe we could cut it short," Terence suggests, looking around for support.

"Why don't you let Michael tell it his way?" Xuefang responds. "Even if it's similar, it wouldn't hurt." Terence falls silent.

Michael continues: "Since the late 1950s, MOOSE had used a mainframe computer as its operating system. Each night, it ran a batch process that calculated transactions, overwriting the previous day's data. So fresh data was made available just once a day, and no history was recorded. Storage was a luxury back then. That's one reason the Data Warehouse project got underway – it would finally provide a historical archive."

"That mainframe was still around many years later when I joined the project. For a subsidiary, we had to adjust values for an existing business key to match a standardized, company-wide definition. Unfortunately, using only the raw data to achieve this wasn't possible. Duplicates and ambiguities were commonplace. The department in charge gave us a business rule to handle these quality issues, and after countless tests, we put it into production."

"At first, everyone thought we'd done a great job. But after a few months had passed, a subject matter expert noticed that we'd overlooked a small, but very important part, of the business rule design." Michael pauses briefly.

"Today we would say that the implemented business rule was 'destructive.' That is, we wouldn't be able to recreate the original data from the processed results. In fact, the raw data was permanently lost, because we only stored the business rule outcomes. Sure, we should have kept the raw data, but at the time, no one thought of it. Everyone was confident in the solution."

"Through knowledge, the human being attains humanity," says Amal.

Michael smiles, "That's from Hāfez (Hāfez), isn't it? And it was precisely this that led the whole team to face a huge problem: we needed to update the business rule and rerun it. But we no longer had the original data."

"It's like trying to calculate a quotient, for instance $A/B = C$ and $B/A = D$, and then using the result, $C/D = C^{new}$ and $D/C = D^{new}$, again as the initial value. A and B don't exist in the system, only C and D do."

"But surely, there were backups?" Yerodin asks.

"Yes, there were mainframe backups, even eight months back. But they were meant for system recovery, not data restoration for third parties. To retrieve our data, operators would need to restore backups day by day, with us extracting what we needed as fast as possible. Meanwhile, they couldn't interrupt regular operations. It just wasn't feasible within an acceptable timeframe. Our Data Warehouse had backups too, but they didn't go back far enough. Too much time had passed since the rule roll-out."

"That's not a good position to be in," Amal observes.

"You're absolutely right. Despite huge efforts and a maze of new rules, we couldn't get the data back to where we needed it. The costs and time spent were staggering."

"What a bummer; that was the worst luck possible!" remarks Terence, but his tone lacks genuine sympathy.

"I wouldn't wish that experience on anyone; it was a complete disaster," Michael says. "But it wasn't bad luck, Terence. It was self-inflicted because..." "Because you didn't keep the original data!" Xuefang finishes.

Separation of concerns

"Always the raw data. What about *high quality* data? Isn't that what we want to provide to our customers, the business?" Terence complains. "If we're not going to improve the data anyway, we might as well leave every-thing in the data lake. So what's the point of building another data solution?"

Amal remembers an analogy that might help, so she tries to illustrate it for her IT colleague. "Terence, think of the data like a Rubik's Cube. Each colored square represents a data source. Red is for customer data, yellow for sales, blue for products, and so forth."

She continues, "Imagine the data lake as an unsolved Rubik's Cube — everything's mixed. Now, let's say you're a subject matter expert who wants to analyze sales data. You'd have to examine each side of the cube to find all the yellow squares. And to link sales with products, you'd repeat the process for the blue squares. That's a lot of work, isn't it? Wouldn't a solved Rubik's Cube, where each color is sorted to its own side, make things easier?"

Terence pictures a solved Rubik's Cube, nodding slowly. "Alright, that makes sense so far," he says, "but I still don't see how it solves the need for clear data rules."

Amal and Terence continue to discuss the Rubik's Cube analogy in more depth. Meanwhile, Michael's thoughts drift to a broader question. "Why does the disorder —the 'chaos'— in the data bother the team so much?" He considers how deep the team's instinct to organize and clean data runs.

In past projects, he's noticed this same urge. Why is this quest to sort out 'bad data,' to clean it up, so deeply embedded in the data community? Where does this need to define everything down to the smallest detail upfront come from?

Is it just company culture, where mistakes are punished, so everyone aims to protect themselves with precise specifications? Or is it politics, where rigid documentation is a shield in case projects don't go as planned?

Michael's head swirls with questions. *Maybe I need some green tea,* he thinks, deciding he'll consult Amal on these thoughts later.

One thing is clear to Michael: past projects that have tried to define all requirements upfront all have struggled.

He recalls a coaching session with Diego Pasión on these topics: *big bang Data Warehouses often fail due to long release cycles, delayed value, inconsistent requirements, and unmet expectations.*

Diego is an external advisor recently brought in to help the team tackle some of their more complex challenges. His philosophy is straightforward: he aims to make the team self-sufficient by offering multiple pragmatic options tailored to their needs. The team then makes the final decision, with Diego's ultimate goal being to impart enough knowledge that his presence eventually becomes unnecessary.

Diego had emphasized that BI requirements are never fixed. New data inevitably drives new understanding and change, which, in turn, drives new requirements. Requirements change often, the Data Warehouse should keep pace with them.

Michael remembers hearing about 'separation of concerns' at a recent conference, though the details are fuzzy. As he's lost in thought, Yerodin's excited shout jolts him back to the present.

"Eureka! What if we turned the Rubik's Cube into a Rubik's Polyhedron?" Yerodin exclaims. Michael, still catching up, gives him a puzzled look. "A polyhedron?"

Amused, Terence mutters, "Controllers and their quirky ideas…"

Unfazed, Yerodin explains, "A polyhedron is a geometric shape with many faces. The Rubik's Cube is one form, with six faces. But imagine expanding it! You could have shapes with twelve or even more sides, like the dodecahedrons in Dungeons & Dragons."

Yerodin presses on. "So if the cube's colors represent business objects, and each square represents raw data from an operational system, then surely we could add new faces for things like business rules, validation, or enrichment."

Yerodin continues that the Rubik's Cube could be extended by more sides until, for example, the Rubik's Dodecahedron is formed.

"Six more sides – for business rules, new IT source systems, and space for validating, classifying, and testing raw data," Yerodin says, smiling as he imagines even more surfaces to add.

Terence looks around and notices that the Rubik's Cube metaphor seems to resonate with everyone. He considers mentioning the connections to the marbles, data and hubs idea, but decides to hold back for now.

Staring out the kitchen window, Terence says thoughtfully, "I think I get it now. We start with an unsolved Rubik's Cube – the raw data mixed together. Then we solve the it by sorting the data by the business objects. After this, we add can additional surfaces to address data quality issues, validation, and testing – using the previously sorted raw data as the base for it. The finished cube, I mean dodecahedron, would be ready for subject matter experts to analyze."

"Glad to see you're all caught up, too." Yerodin remarks, flashing a grin.

Despite the usual back-and-forth between Terence and Yerodin, Michael is pleased with how the discussion is evolving.

It's clear that the team is beginning to grasp the importance of 'separation of concerns.' The concept of isolating individual components in the data solution aligns perfectly with the project's vision: load raw data, organize it by business object, then use business rules to validate and enrich.

Michael decides to recap. "So, are we all agreed that separation of concerns is the way forward? Here's what I've gathered from today's discussion."

Michael ticks off points on his fingers. "First: decoupling keeps solutions simpler. Trying to 'take care of everything' on the way into the data solution requires far too much effort and can cause issues."

He raises a second finger, "A flexible implementation of business rules is possible. We can add business rules as needed, without having to redo everything from scratch."

"And finally," he continues, "integrating new data sources is much easier, as we won't need to refactor the data logistics processes each time we load new data sources into the solution."

"I'm sure we can think of more ways separation of concerns could benefit us," Michael concludes, signaling the end of the session. He really does need that break.

As the group wraps up, Yerodin contemplates Michael's *'nothing is as it seems'* example. Could one of the extra cube surfaces be a layer where he could add tests on the fly without modifying the data logistics processes? This thought intrigues him. It could mean less manual work in the long run. He'll have to explore the idea with Michael sometime.

With a sense of accomplishment, Michael wraps up the gathering. He starts preparing his tea, and the group begins to disperse.

The tartelettes are no longer there.

Exploring reality

What are facts, and what is truth? Amal contemplates how context shapes truth, noting that in business, different definitions can lead to vastly different interpretations.

Data, as a byproduct of business activities, faces similar conflicts as you would experience in information modeling. These can be —including, but not limi-ted to— objective conflicts, context con-flicts, or time conflicts. These can never be entirely resolved in the pursuit of a 'single point of truth.'

Even 'facts,' the raw data from the IT systems, are contextual in a way. These are still only representations of what happened.

Amal mind wanders to movies like 'The Matrix' or 'Men in Black.'[11] "Until you're aware of another reality," she muses, "everything you know feels like the truth." Although, she admits, that might be a stretch.

Each IT system stores data in its unique context, understandable only with the knowledge of the subject matter experts familiar with this context.

It's a striking realization. Data, even at its rawest form, isn't immune to subjectivity. "Source data is often said to 'suck,'" she thinks, "but is it the data itself, or simply our misinterpretation of because we're missing the right context?"

Xuefang interrupts her thoughts. "You look lost, Amal. What's on your mind?"

"Hey Xuefang, yes, I was deep in thought. After discussing the Rubik's Cube analogy, I started thinking about what 'facts' and 'truth' actually mean for data. I was about to email my former philosophy professor with some questions – want to join?"

"Definitely!" says Xuefang eagerly, grabbing her notebook.

The call with Amal's professor at Albert Fast University stretches over an hour, with Xuefang furiously taking notes. The professor explains that understanding data is about layering context – how, where, and when the data originated reveal its underlying meaning.

Xuefang summarizes her notes:

- → The questions asked of data (our requirements) may be flawed
- → The data itself may be inaccurate
- → The systems capturing data are imperfect

Initially, this sounds a bit pessimistic, but Amal reassures her: "It's not negative. Armed with this understanding, we can approach data differently, questioning everything to deliver the most accurate version of the truth."

"In an ideal world, we'd have optimal data management, with near real-time multi-directional data harmonization and a flawless IT landscape where data flows without ambiguity. Business rules wouldn't even be necessary in such an environment."

"Yeah, I suppose if all that is in place, combining data would be much easier!" Xuefang agrees.

"But for FastChangeCo, that ideal is a long way off," Amal continues. "We have plenty of systems we can't properly fix for various reasons. That's why, at our company, a data solution is, shall we say, a necessary evil to transform the available data into something more useful. Even if that 'truth' remains somewhat subjective."

"Maybe we should present these ideas to the team," Xuefang suggests. "I could put together a short presentation."

"Great idea, Xuefang. I think this will spark some interesting discussions about our data solution."

A few days later, the two present their ideas in a presentation titled *Facts, Truth, and the Resurrection!* Sylvia joins, intrigued by Amal and Xuefang's initiative.

Using the mainframe as an example, Amal explains how data can be difficult to interpret without context. "I once encountered a mainframe program where not all of the digits in a number field were used.

Say only 1 to 7 were used for a given field A, leaving 8, 9, and 10 unused. Another field B did use these additional digits. To optimize storage, a rule was implemented that if a 10 appeared in field B, and 8, 9, or 10 appeared in field A, the values of both fields were added and subtracted by 7. This made it possible to extend field B's range to 1–13 without using up additional storage space. Without this context, the data in A and B would certainly have been misinterpreted."

They close with a few takeaways:

- → Data is not just stuff
- → We should value raw data as much as its processed forms
- → Truth is subjective

Afterwards, the team agrees: data should *not* be judged prematurely on the way into the data solution.

As the meeting wraps up, Sylvia pulls Michael aside. "That was excellent, Michael. It really sheds light on why 'good data' is such a challenge here. We should adapt this for a management presentation."

Meanwhile, Terence mutters on his way home, "If only we had SPEEDY and its AI modules we wouldn't need all this. It would've been perfect."

Preparing to start the engine

For Michael, these discussions reveal that it is possible to avoid repeating the mistakes of the past, and he feels optimistic about this. Still, a flexible approach is necessary to safeguard what has been achieved so far.

The concept of Engine Thinking, which the team embraced early in the project, continues to align well with their approach. Michael considers that one of the next steps toward Engine Thinking is defining an architecture centered around data and information hubs, ensuring incremental additions can be delivered with the needed flexibility.

"Inherently scalable," Michael mutters to himself, then adds, "we already have that in the vision and strategy."

Amal interrupts his thoughts. She overheard him. "And to achieve this, our data solution needs to be flexible, quickly adaptable, and manageable. But there's a paradox: for our solution to be flexible enough to keep pace with the speed of the business, it needs well-defined layers — the data hubs. And having many layers doesn't exactly sound flexible." Amal pauses briefly. "The goal now has to be designing a solid, technology-independent solution architecture."

"And what I'd like to avoid," Michael continues, "is diving into another debate on the specifics of loading data into these hubs. We've hopefully clarified the purpose of evaluating the data. But we haven't yet addressed how and where data should be stored in the data solution."

"And then there's also the technology aspect — a topic we really need keep out of the conversation a little bit longer" adds Amal.

"We can't answer all of this yet — we're still some distance from that stage. Before technical details come into play, we need to continue discussing the conceptual aspects of our data solution. Otherwise, we risk repeating the mistakes of the past."

Bringing Jeff on board

Sylvia Seven stands on her office terrace, gazing out over the Temptation City skyline. The setting sun bathes the skyline in a special light. Sylvia treasures these moments of tranquility when she's working late, as she is today.

Her mind drifts. She's contemplating how to get Jeff on board with data management, hoping they won't be at odds. A collaborative relationship is important to her. Hearing Jeff argue that FastChangeCo already has all the necessary IT systems and doesn't need anything new makes her realize that there's work to do.

Sylvia suspects Jeff may also be influencing Terence, who, according to Michael, has been disrupting the project's progress with his stubborn opposition. While she contemplates, her thoughts shift to the upcoming long-distance run she's preparing for: The 100 Miles of Temptation City.

"I should get back to doing more of my running meetings," she thinks. "Wait, maybe that's actually a good way to talk to Jeff. Should I call him now and set up a running meeting?"

It's Thursday, Jeff's soccer night. He once told her that after playing, he always feels motivated to consider more exercise. Watching the sun set, Sylvia decides to wait a bit longer before calling him.

A little later, Sylvia reaches Jeff on his mobile. He's relaxing with a beer, celebrating a rare win with his team. Jeff is in a great mood, and has no intention to let Sylvia spoil it. He quickly agrees to join her for a running meeting the following day, feeling uncharacteristically athletic and eager to get back to his drinks.

The next day, Jeff quickly regrets agreeing to one of Sylvia's notorious running meetings. Despite his weekly soccer games, he's out of breath almost immediately. "Maybe I should start exercising more," Jeff thinks as he struggles to keep up with Sylvia. "But I'll think about that later – with a cigar and a bag of chips," he mutters, only half-listening as Sylvia says, "... your reputation as an IT leader."

"Excuse me ... puff ... what did you ... gasp ... just say?" Sylvia's running meetings always give her an advantage — she can talk while the others struggle to keep up.

"Jeff, your reputation as an IT leader is legendary!" She slows her pace to let him focus. Gasping, Jeff nods.

"When you joined FastChangeCo after your management consulting years, you did some sensational things. You brought our IT systems up to date. Not only purchased new software, but re-imagined our entire IT infrastructure and IT architecture."

"Yes ... gasp ..., all new ... gasp ... from scratch!" Jeff can't help but feel flattered how well Sylvia values his past work. "If we had you advising us on implementing our new data solution, everything would be easier."

Jeff isn't sure if he wants to return to the challenges of transformation, with all the resistance, politics, and hostility. He plans to spend his final years before retirement at FastChangeCo without stirring things up. But something Sylvia says resonates. And she isn't slowing down.

Completely out of breath, he interrupts her, "Hold on. You're saying ... gasp ... the DMCE team wants me ... gasp ... as an advisor?"

"Yes, your experience and your knowledge of our IT systems would be invaluable. You know these things so well — their relationships, interactions, the frameworks you helped implement, like the auto-optimizer, the logging, and alarm framework."

Somewhat skeptical, Jeff sits down on a bench, considering her suggestion. "All these new methods you're using aren't for me. Your approach is so different from what we've done at FastChangeCo. What's worked has worked. Why change it?"

Sylvia, cooling down and stretching, explains the DMCE team's methods and the benefits they offer. As Jeff's pulse steadies, he can think clearly again. Their back-and-forth continues for a while, and slowly, he warms to the idea of an advisory role.

He's not ready to commit but is intrigued enough to consider it.

Still, Sylvia manages to secure a promise from him: he'll put together what he considers the most important success factors for the DMCE team.

"The biggest challenge I see is where to automate — and how," he tells Sylvia, before saying goodbye and heading toward the FastChangeCo locker rooms. He's beat, and in need of a break. And a cigarette. And maybe a stop at the vending machine.

The DMCE engine

Amal and Michael continued their conversation about data solution architecture —a blend of solution and data architecture— and the principles of Engine Thinking. Not wanting to define the data solution's direction alone, they invite the whole team to join the discussion.

Together, they tackle a central question: *What should the engine look like?* Amal summarizes the essential components of *Engine Thinking* on the whiteboard.

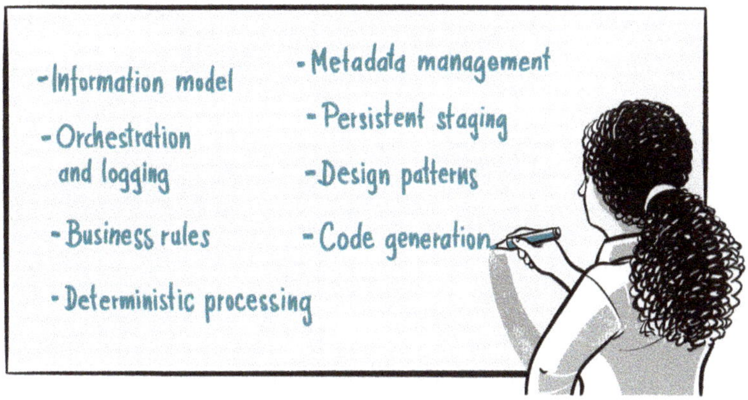

The team wants to develop an engine that achieves these goals. It will be the centerpiece of the new data solution. Their discussions lead to increasingly bold ideas about what might be possible.

For instance, the team considers: *Where should the design metadata be stored?* Initially, they assume all metadata should naturally reside in a relational database. But as the topic of continuous integration and continuous delivery (CI/CD) comes to the fore of the discussion, the idea of storing the design metadata in a file format, such as JSON[12], no longer seems so far-fetched. JSON files, or similar, would be more technology independent, avoiding lock-in.

Or, the matter of: *The engine must preserve the facts as they are.* As presented by Amal and Xuefang in their ' *Facts, Truth and the Resurrection!'* presentation, the design must ensure that data is not modified on the way into the data solution. Current truths, or later ones, that emerge during the project due to new requirements can thus always be added – a 'single version of the facts.'

The team's ideas also extends to virtualization. They imagine that, with sufficiently fast hardware, the entire data solution could be virtualized. That is, without having to build data persistence or data logistics processes right in the core layers of the solution – at least during the development process. How cool would that be?

In the meantime, Jeff shares the key success factors from his IT projects – at least the ones he could recall on short notice. Unfortunately, due to his busy schedule he can't attend the meetings in person, but his top tips are:

→ Testing and data validation – implement a way to not only test the quality of data, but also whether the data logistics processes are working as expected
→ Notification – make sure you can inform operators and users when system events, such as delays and errors, occur
→ Optimizer – using logs to optimize the implementation on an ongoing basis

For the team, Jeff's tips are an invaluable addition. Sylvia is quietly pleased to see her 'Jeff strategy' succeeding: Jeff, once a skeptic, is now actively advising the team, albeit still somewhat reluctantly.

Jeff's last tip –optimization– intrigues the team. Imagine handing over tasks like refactoring or splitting data sets to the engine itself. They envision an engine capable of building new physical data models from internal and external metadata, even adjusting based on feedback from subject matter experts while ensuring raw data remains intact.

It's a wild vision. Could this engine even incorporate artificial intelligence? The team resolves to work toward this ambitious goal.

The important thing here is that the design, concepts and metadata always remain the same due to the abstraction provided by data models. This would make virtualization together with the supporting frameworks the cornerstones of an adaptive data solution – a system that can adjust to internal and external disruptions.

The team imagines an adaptive data solution where the engine can perform internal optimizations, such as refactoring data logistics processes and data storage structures. External changes, detected via monitoring, alerting, and testing frameworks, could trigger the engine to respond accordingly.

The team feels confident that nothing like this has been attempted before, certainly not at FastChangeCo. And speaking of bold ideas, there's also talk of a 'time machine': the ability to restore the data solution to a previous version from months prior.

Michael feels a surge of pride reviewing the team's progress. Engine Thinking represents an inspiring vision for the new data solution at FastChangeCo, and he couldn't be more satisfied with 'his' team.

Marketing

Michael brings up the subject of marketing for their new data solution when he meets Sylvia for tea for the first time in a long time.

"Sylvia, we haven't really thought about marketing *The Resurrection* yet. I think it's going to be important for us, though. From past projects, I've seen that if there's no marketing, people in the company can perceive the project negatively. It can seem like it's just creating more work without a clear benefit."

"But when there was marketing that highlighted the positive impact —especially once we showed some real financial wins— it made a huge difference."

"I agree," Sylvia replies. "Let's make this a priority. I'll take on the task of building a foundation for a 'brand strategy' so you don't have to worry about it on top of everything else. Right now, it's much more important that you focus on the engine!"

With that, Sylvia leaves Michael to his thoughts. But as she walks away, a phrase from their conversation keeps running through her mind:

The engine must be designed for change
– Design for change!

"That could be our brand message: *Engine Thinking – Designed for Change!"* she reflects with a smile.

Introducing the Data Quadrant Model

When *aligning the data landscape to the vision and strategy,* Amal suggested Ronald Damhof's Data Quadrant Model (DQM) as a way to cultivate a shared understanding of the data landscape.

Following her presentation, *Facts, Truth, and the Resurrection!,* Michael and Sylvia complimented the content, saying it was excellent but suggesting that the team focus on simplifying the presentation of ideas.

The rationale is clear: top management is often pressed for time and may not be able to engage with detailed discussions. To convey the message, it's worth investing effort into capturing key points as succinctly as possible.

So, Michael asks Amal to prioritize preparing a presentation on the DQM. He also encourages her to find a student to help develop a knowledge base on the topic, which can serve as long-term documentation as the project progresses.

Lost in thought, Amal flips through her notes, organizing an initial outline for the DQM presentation. She has a student in mind for this assignment – someone with promise, enthusiasm, and a keen interest in working on this project as a research topic.

Her name is Zalika Okoro.

"If Zalika does well, perhaps she could also take on her thesis with us later," Amal considers, recalling that they also wanted a student to work on fact-oriented modeling.

Zalika, currently studying computer science at Albert Fast University in Temptation City, had seen Amal's notice about opportunities for a student research project, bachelor's, or master's thesis with the DMCE team. After discussing the assignment with Amal, she knew this was the right fit: the DQM sounded exciting, and its connection to data modeling piqued her interest even further.

Data modeling is one of Zalika's favorite subjects. And the DMCE team seems great, too. Everyone was incredibly nice to her and made her feel at home.

Over the next few weeks, Amal and Zalika work intensively on their *Data Quadrant Model in a nutshell* paper. They both enjoy exploring the DQM's potential, uncovering opportunities it could bring to the project.

Impressed with Zalika's progress, Amal proposes her as a candidate for a master's thesis with the DMCE team. Zalika, delighted by Amal's confidence in her, readily accepts and is especially intrigued when Amal suggests FOM as a possible thesis topic.

Together, they present a summary of the DQM to the team.

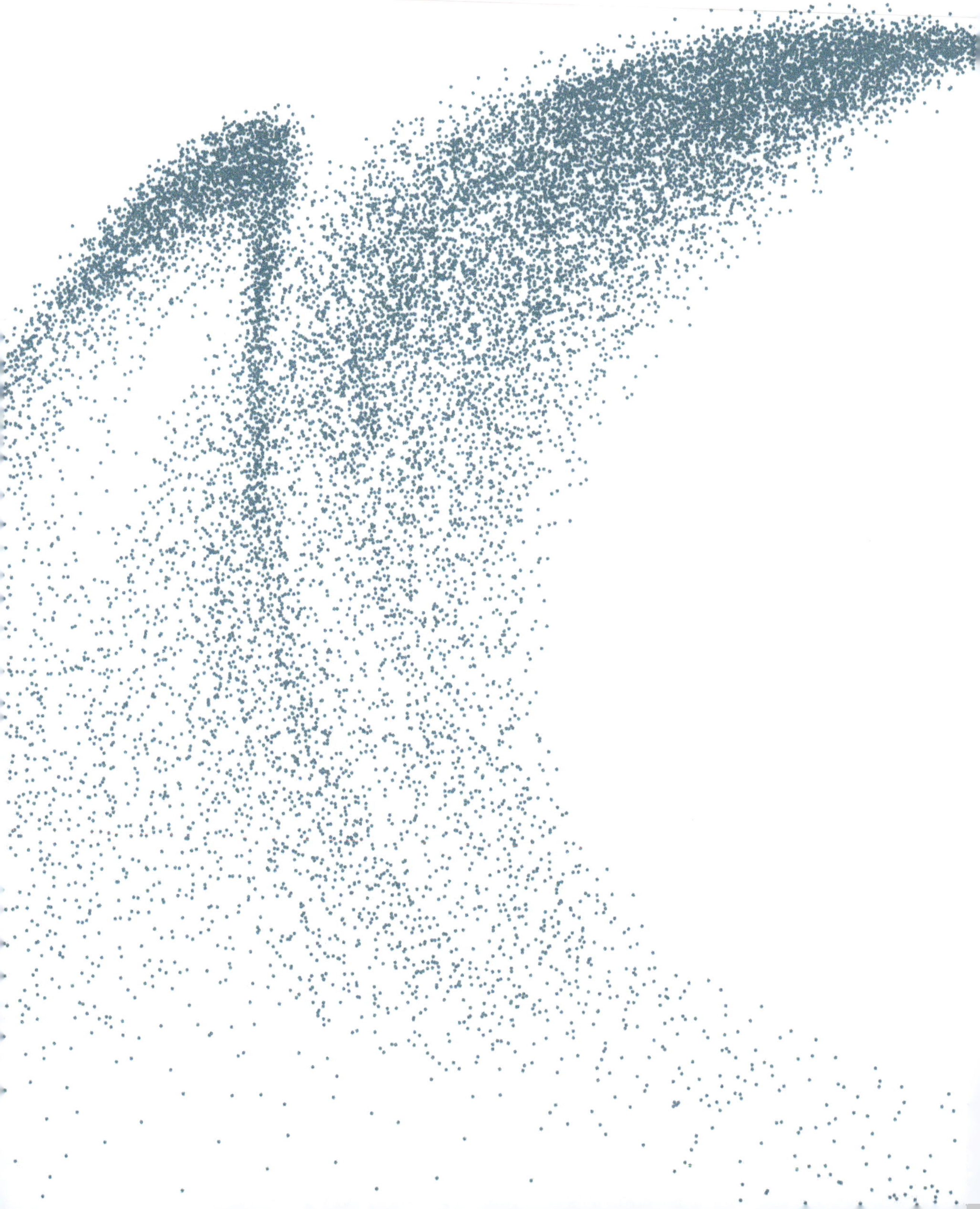

04
The Data Quadrant Model

↗ The Data Quadrant Model, published by Ronald Damhof in 2013, is a methodology designed to manage data effectively within the enterprise — a managerial perspective on data.

In projects where the objective is to get a company's data under control, and make it widely available and usable, there often is a plethora of people and sometimes conflicting interests involved.

The Data Quadrant Model (DQM) is a framework that can help resolve the challenges of bringing stakeholders on the same page with regards to data management. This framework provides a structure for individuals to connect their understanding and experiences, so that potentially divergent experiences and perspectives can be resolved in a common context.

It provides a way to position one's views on a particular topic in the context of how others might experience these. It's a way to 'get on the same page.'

Usually, the majority of stakeholders share a common goal. However, they may not have a common understanding of the *journey* to achieve this. Therefore, it is helpful for all parties involved to create a common ground —a shared understanding— for the planning, design, execution, control and management of data across the organization. At the same time, they need to take their different responsibilities into account, their mutual expertise, and intended use of the data.

This is not an easy task.

The larger the project, the greater its complexity. Communication is a key factor in creating common ground for a successful project.

To facilitate adequate communication between parties involved, the DQM provides an abstraction of the complexities involved with data management. The intention is for the majority of people involved to be able to at least identify the quadrants in the DQM and understand the underlying ideas and principles.

The DQM defines four quadrants, based on two axes. Each axis represents a high-level principle that describes how data management might be approached. These are:

→ The way data supply and demand interact (x-axis), and
→ The development style (y-axis)

Supply and demand

Push and pull principle

The DQM adopts the *push* and *pull* concepts from industrial manufacturing, and applies it to the way data is processed. Push and pull production or manufacturing are two forms of production control. These are opposite ways to describe how demand influences the production process.

↗ The x-axis of the DQM describes how supply and demand of data interact, and which factors are involved.

In *push production* (the push principle), a central unit controls the production and flow of materials. Materials, parts, and products are 'pushed' through the logistics production chain in accordance with a fixed, predetermined plan. Throughout this process, the quality of the products is strictly controlled. Push systems aim to achieve economies of scale to provide an acceptable price point for the customer based on volume and demand. This is also known as a *supply-driven* process.

For a highly 'commoditized' product, this could be something you buy off the shelf in a supermarket. A toothbrush, or a bar of soap, for example. There is low variability in demand and no personalization of the product.

A customer does not have to order or specify any requirements for these products. They are either available, or not. For products like these, the *decoupling point* is all the way at the end of the production process – when the customer can browse and purchase the available products.

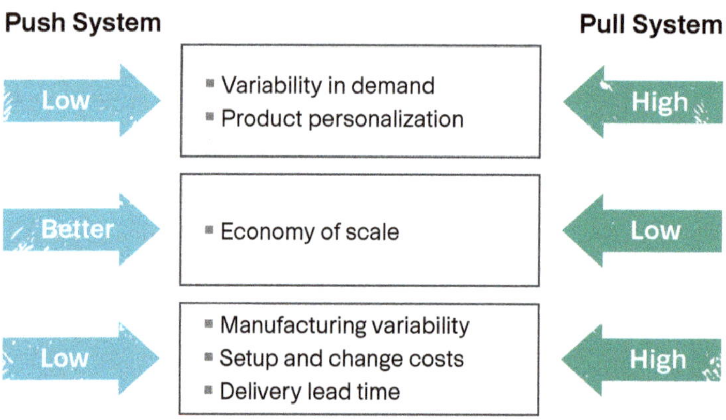

Pull production (the pull principle), in its extreme form, operates without a central planning and control unit. Production begins with a customer order. It is a demand-driven process. From the perspective of the customer, the product is 'pulled' through the production process. The product typically experiences high variability in demand, and tends to be more personalized. Because of this, production times are usually longer.

In this scenario, the decoupling point is at the start of the production process. The production for a custom-made grandfather clock doesn't start before the order is received and paid for.

Push-pull point

The decoupling point 'splits' the production process in a push and pull side. In the examples so far, the decoupling point was placed at the extreme ends of the production process, but depending on the product this can be anywhere in between.

Depending on the degree of *how* the production process is aligned to customer demand and requirements, the decoupling point shifts between push and pull production. For a given product it is defined as the *push-pull point.* This is also how it is referred to in the DQM.

Meanwhile, many products exist where the push-pull point is closer to the middle of the production process. Lifestyle footwear production is one of these. Footwear production has evolved from mass production, a pure push principle, to semi-customized production based on individual orders. In this scenario, customers can modify their shoe design online.

Even though there are limits with regards to the general shoe model that the customer needs to adhere to, within those confines the customer is free to apply any kind of color scheme and has access to a large number of possible fabrics and materials. The footwear is not produced until the order has been completed, an example of a pull principle implementation.

Because the available selection of shoe models is known upfront, the production process can still use ample standard parts (push principle) for the production of each individual shoe. For example, the shoe sole and inner lining.

The x-axis

The DQM applies these principles to the world of data. The production of dashboards and reports, for example, is similar to the production of customized footwear. The push-pull point lies somewhere in the middle between preparing the data in the data solution and delivering the report.

In data architecture, the push- or supply-driven domain should be highly standardized, as it is in manufacturing. It is the only way automation can succeed. All 'product-specific' features should be avoided.

The situation is quite different in the pull domain. This is where users may seek to develop *their* unique products using data, creating their truth based on their experience, context, and knowledge.

The inherent conflict between push-driven commoditization —and automation of data processing—, and pull-driven customization leads to a fundamental concept in the DQM: that data must be separated into facts and context.

The x-axis of the DQM therefore displays the push pull point as the decoupling point between the push- and pull processes.

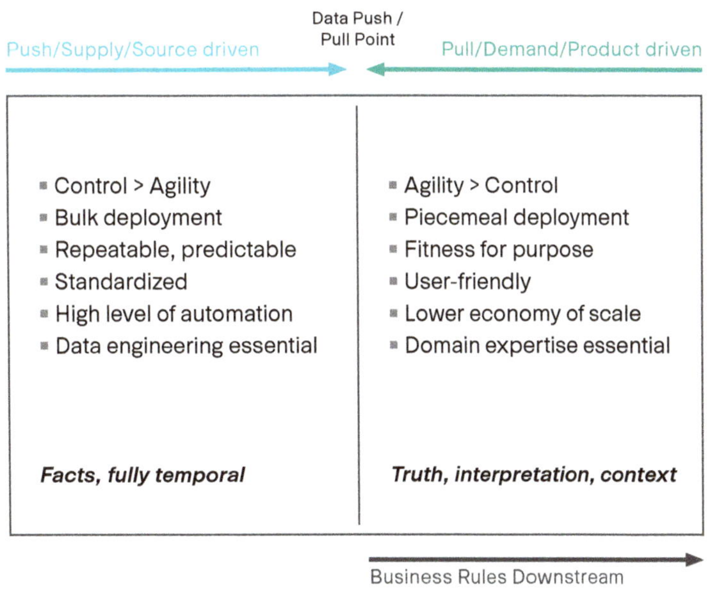

From a data perspective, push systems focus on accurately recording and time-stamping transactions. Data is immutable, and stored in a way that is not necessarily intended for immediate consumption.

In the ⚐ Engine Thinking section we introduced the concept of a PSA. This concept sits squarely in the push area when mapped onto the DQM.

Development style

↗ The second perspective, and y-axis, of the DQM, concerns the development style. How are data products created? Who is involved, and how are roles, responsibilities, and governance processes implemented?

DQM defines the development style as *systematic* on the one end, and *opportunistic* on the other. As with the push-pull point, this is a somewhat gradual scale with both styles represented as the extreme endpoints.

Systematic development

Systematic development has strong governance, focused on control and compliance with internal and external rules and regulations. Everything that is involved in controlling the process of creating and quality-controlling a product is in place. As a result, the processes involved can be highly structured, formalized, and therefore automated.

This is referred to as *defensive* governance. Roles and responsibilities are clearly defined, and usually assigned to specific people.

A systematic development style is often applied to large projects that involve people from different departments, and with different skill sets. For example, in a project that implements data delivery to regulators, the users and developers typically are different people.

This allows for a more controlled and traceable process. Individual process steps may require approvals by people who have management responsibility for specific parts of the process. If an organization does not provide sufficient evidence with regards to the transparency of data collection and processing, or produces incorrect data, fines could be applied by regulators.

Systematic development corresponds to the classic educational background for a data or information engineer, using structured project management techniques and waterfall approaches for delivery. For example, Prince2 or Structured Development Methodology (SDM).

Opportunistic development

Opportunistic development lies at the other end of the spectrum. This often applies to smaller and more innovative projects. The consumer and developer may be the same person, a data analyst for example. The focus is on the flexibility and adaptability of the product that is being developed.

In this case, the governance model is *offensive*. Analysis is done, hypotheses are created and tested, and the product is tweaked, tested, discussed and modified in a more iterative fashion.

The y-axis

The systematic and opportunistic approaches constitute the y-axis of the DQM. The following diagram contains a summary of the properties of each approach.

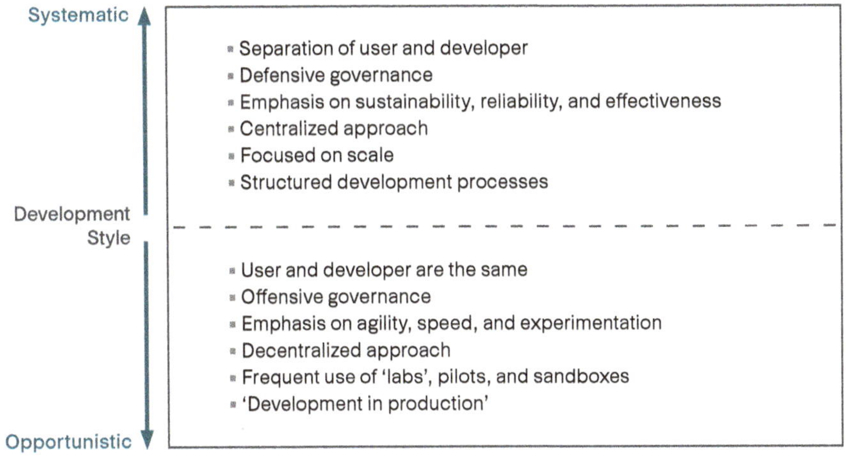

Some data solutions require the rigor and scalability of systematic development, while others benefit from the agility and creativity of opportunistic approaches, and some leverage both. Understanding where your project or organization falls on this spectrum is key to aligning development practices with business needs and objectives.

The Data Quadrant Model

When the x-axis (push-pull principle) and the y-axis (development style) are combined, the DQM emerges as four distinct quadrants:

→ Data quadrant I — systematic push
→ Data quadrant II — systematic pull
→ Data quadrant III — opportunistic push
→ Data quadrant IV — opportunistic pull

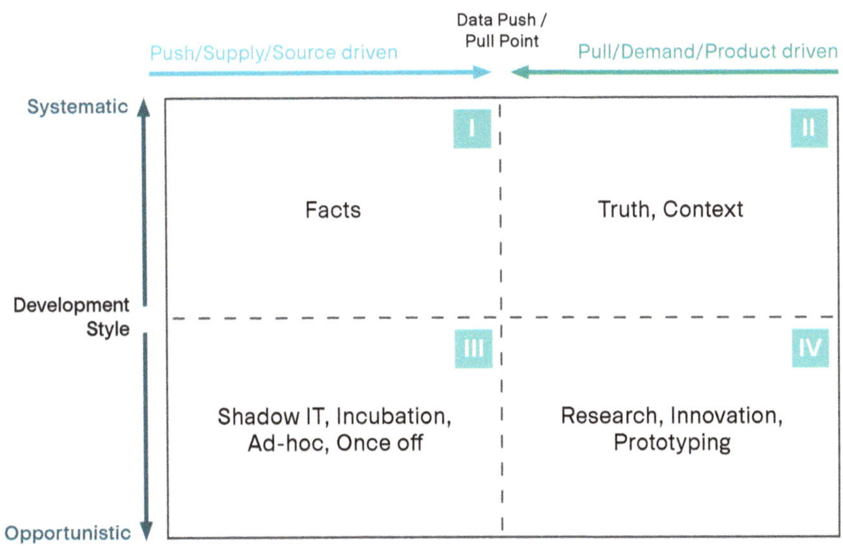

These quadrants represent different combinations of supply-demand interactions and development styles, offering a structured view of how data is managed and consumed.

The DQM rests on four additional fundamental assumptions about data solutions:

1) Every data solution begins with raw data —the 'raw materials' of the data world— and aims to deliver a data product. This journey requires multiple processes, such as data logistics, design, and quality assurance, working well together
2) A successful data solution must balance two often competing demands: reliability and flexibility. While reliability ensures consistency and trust, flexibility accommodates evolving business needs and exploration
3) Every data solution includes a push-pull point: the boundary where standardized processes (push) transition to more customized or user-driven processes (pull). This decoupling ensures efficiency in data preparation while also enabling tailored data consumption
4) Data solutions must separate facts (immutable raw data) from context (interpretations or transformations). This separation supports flexibility in how data is consumed and repurposed, catering to diverse use cases without compromising the underlying data

Data quadrant I

Data quadrant I, or DQ-I, contains the immutable facts of the data solution. All data in this quadrant is processed through standardized, automated data logistics processes.

Automation of these processes and data structures can deliver extremely high reliability, stability, predictability, and repeatability.

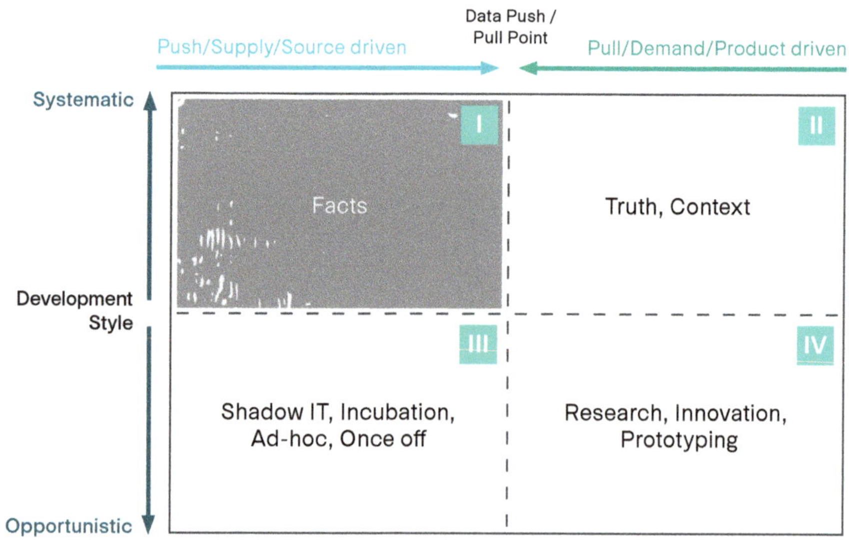

DQ-I is both systematic in its development style, as well as focused on push-driven supply of data. This combination fosters a more centralized governance style that allows for strong control over the management, processing order, and adherence to data standards and conventions. Typically, the people working in DQ-I are data or information engineers.

Reliability is the cornerstone of DQ-I, and this always takes precedence over flexibility. There is an 'urge' to constantly optimize to become more efficient.

As part of data management, DQ-I also focuses on *consolidation* of the data. All data must be processed following the same principles, standards, and conventions. Even though the data may not necessarily be stored in a single technical environment, it is processed the same way. For example, all data is subject to the same time-stamping processes or standard data type conversions. Data is made available in DQ-I 'as-is,' reflecting the transactions as they were received.

In DQ-I, it is important to make sure that data is compliant with company-wide data standards and conventions. For example, if a certain allowed range of domain values are agreed, the incoming data is evaluated whether it falls into this range. This approach will surface issues around completeness, reliability, and basic quality early in the process.

When enterprise data standards include agreed-upon definitions and validations, incoming data is measured against these benchmarks.

Data quadrant II

In data quadrant II, or DQ-II, data is enriched based using context that is provided by subject matter experts.

While DQ-I only stores the raw, unmodified data representing the so-called 'single version of the facts,' DQ-II transforms this data to create meaningful interpretations that align with user-defined needs.

The data products are created according to the wishes and needs of the users.

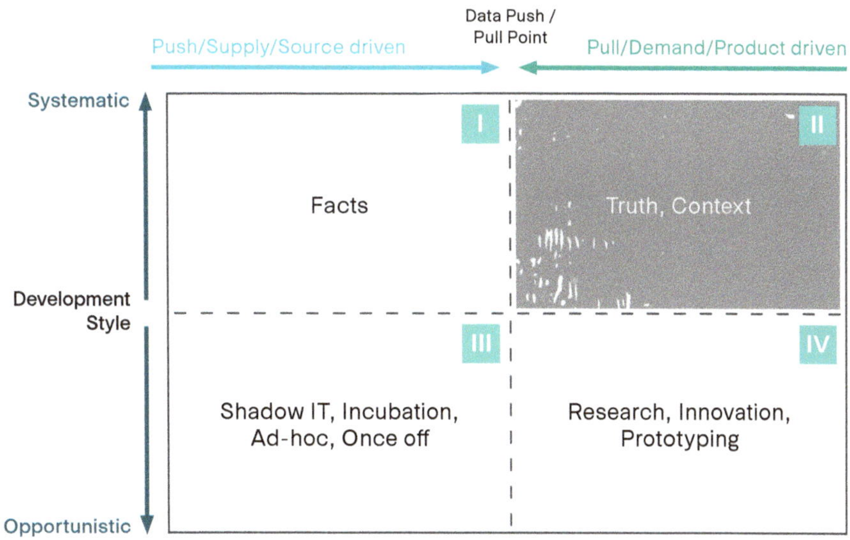

This data quadrant sits in the pull area, to the right of the push pull point. The systematic development style indicates that strong governance is still place, driven by requirements. This reflects a more traditional way of development, where requirements are gathered first and development starts when these are sufficiently clarified.

The requirements dictate the development. In DQ-II, flexibility takes precedence over reliability.

Typically, individuals with a deep technical understanding of their domain and analytical skills work in this quadrant.

Because of individual context, background knowledge and expertise, several and potentially different truths may emerge over time. They are truths from the user's point of view, but, they are all based on the same facts — *multiple versions of the truth.*

Data quadrant III

Data quadrant III, or DQ-III, encompasses data sources that have not yet been brought under governance.

These can be Excel documents, publicly available data, or a 'found' memory stick with data. In other words, the data that users may use gathered from downloads, data stores in the company, or obtained from somewhere else.

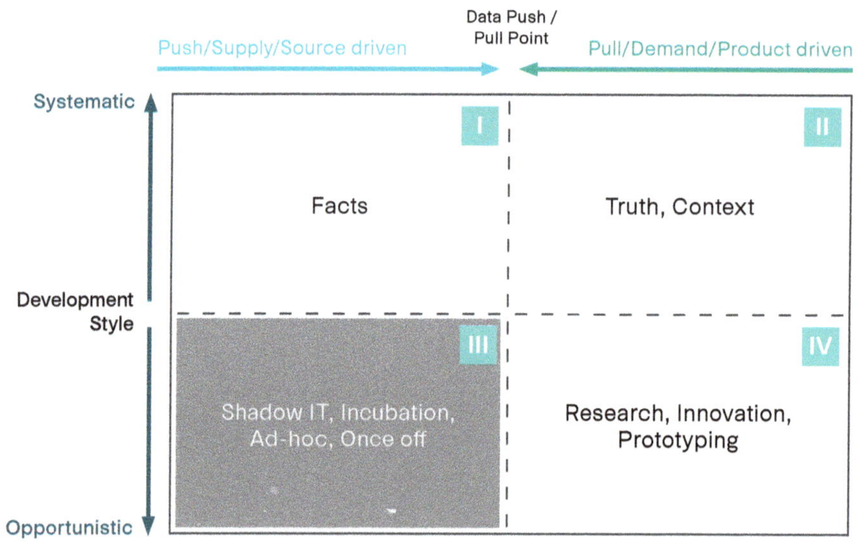

DQ-III adopts an opportunistic development style, and is push-driven. The value of DQ-III is that it defines an place for data that may not be governed, but still may have its use.

This quadrant implicitly exists in every organization. This data exists mostly unnoticed, away from any form of governance. A good way to think about this is a place to store temporary, or in-the-moment data that needs somewhere to stay.

Data classified as DQ-III can be used in combination with data from other data quadrants, for example during prototyping in DQ-IV. If, however, the resulting designs in DQ-IV are considered meaningful enough to implement in a more structured way —for example making the data available company-wide— then the DQM recommends additional efforts to bring the DQ-III data under governance first. For example, by first formalizing the data source and integrating this into DQ-I.

Therefore, DQ-III is no less important or useful than the other data quadrants.

Data quadrant IV

Data quadrant IV, or DQ-IV, is diagonally opposite to DQ-I. This quadrant is designed to encourage ideation and the development of new data products, fostering a culture of creativity within the organization.

It is a space dedicated to innovation, experimentation, and prototyping, where flexibility takes precedence over reliability.

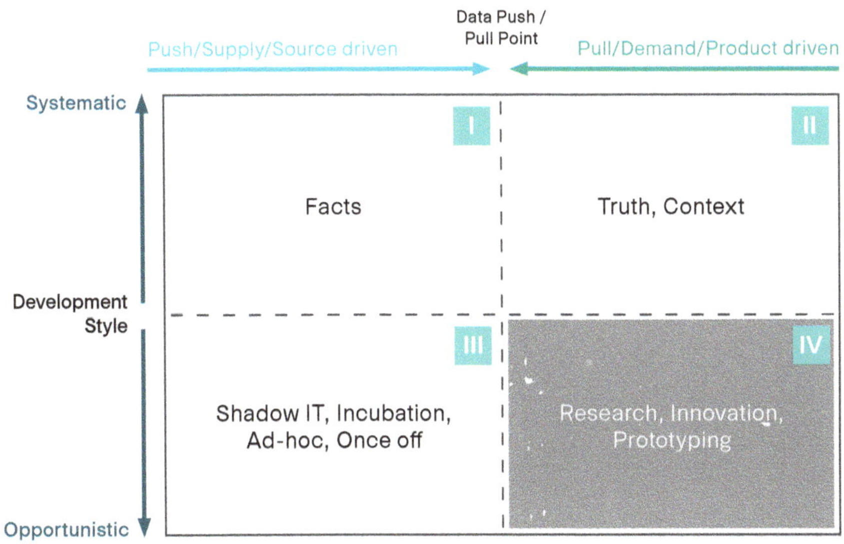

DQ-IV is characterized by a more offensive governance style, which removes barriers to allow for new ideas and experimentation — supported with data evidence and testing.

It is an incubator for new ideas, where data from various places can be combined and explored. Reliable foundational data from DQ-I, enriched data from DQ-II, and ungoverned data from DQ-III can all play a role in supporting the work conducted in DQ-IV.

This data quadrant is typically staffed by knowledge workers, data scientists, or analysts with strong technical and analytical skills.

Ideally, the aim is to develop new data products for the company and evaluate these for market readiness. When a prototype is deemed successful or promising, the organization may seek to bring this to market, or make this more widely available internally. In this scenario, the DQM suggests that the prototype must be transferred to DQ-II for long-term, managed, use.

This enables economies of scale for an economically viable and company-wide deployment of the data products.

Applications of the Data Quadrant Model

The following sections outline some of the applications of the DQM from different perspectives:
→ How data is produced
→ How accountability can be organized
→ How governance can be applied
→ How people and skills are considered
→ Where technology fits in
→ How and where data modeling is applied
→ How development can be automated

None of these configurations are necessarily 'set in stone.' Rather, they serve as a discussion framework to clarify how each organization chooses to operate when it comes to data management.And, most importantly, align this across the stakeholders involved in data management.

Data production

In the DQM, you can define different production pathways for data, each serving a specific purpose in the data solution. This section explores these pathways and their implications for governance, flexibility, and reliability.

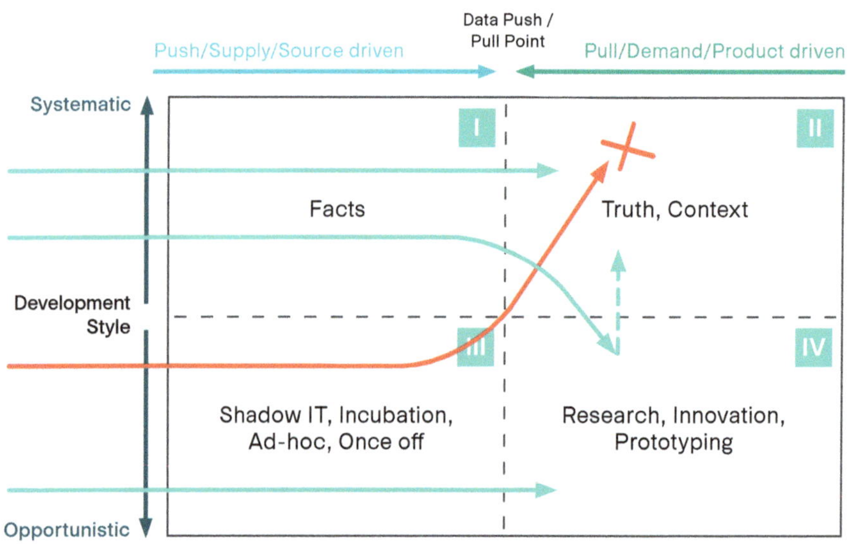

From DQ-I to DQ-II, DQ-IV and onwards

Data from DQ-I can be provided to DQ-II and/or DQ-IV for further processing. DQ-I provides a consistent and repeatable foundation to (re)apply further transformations to, and these two downstream quadrants benefit significantly from the governance and predictability of the data made available there.

This is a typical scenario for Data Warehouse and Business Intelligence use cases.

When data from either DQ-I or DQ-II is used for prototyping and research in DQ-IV, the results may need to be integrated into DQ-II if they prove meaningful for production use. Since DQ-I already provides the foundational data, this process primarily involves implementing specific interpretations in DQ-II. This relationship is represented by the dotted line in the diagram.

From DQ-III to DQ-IV

Data from DQ-III can flow into DQ-IV to support innovation, research, and prototyping efforts. Flexibility in accessing all kinds of data can be beneficial for innovation, and DQ-III exists to ensure that this is considered.

Using data from DQ-III for prototyping and research in DQ-IV must come with the understanding that if the research proves to be promising, the necessary data sources that are in DQ-III —and therefore not under governance— must be formally integrated into DQ-I.

From DQ-III to DQ-II (anti pattern)

Data from DQ-III should *never* flow directly into DQ-II.

If this were the case, the resulting data products in DQ-II would use data that may not be subject to adequate governance.

An example would be a compliance report intended for a regulatory agency that uses comparison data downloaded from an external source. Because this data source is not formally tracked, integrated and timestamped the outputs may not be repeatable.

This can result in fines that can be many times higher than the cost of integrating the data from DQ-III into DQ-I.

If DQ-III data is necessary for DQ-II, it should first be formally integrated into DQ-I, where it can be governed and standardized before being used to create data products.

Accountability

A meaningful perspective offered by the DQM is how accountability can be organized.

Who is responsible for the data, its quality, timeliness and general management is often a contentious topic in many organizations. While it is not a fully-fledged data governance methodology, the DQM offers interesting insights on high-level governance that can help align some of the roles and responsibilities.

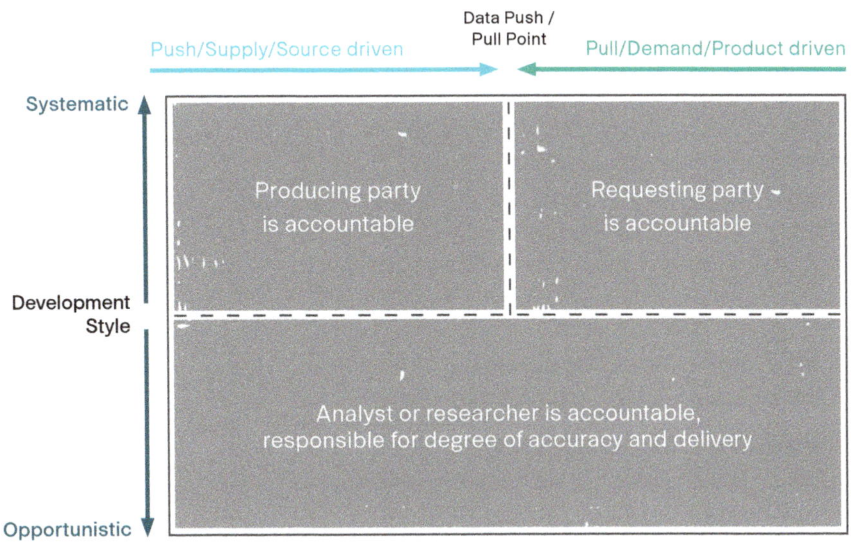

The assignment of accountability ties into data ownership, including the responsibility to look after the data being available, on time, and conform expectations. This links back to our introduction in the ⚐ world of data chapter on how technical teams cannot magically deliver 'meaning' from data.

To elaborate on this a bit more: an engineering team should not be held accountable for data results —such as in DQ-I or DQ-III— if the business teams do not engage in clarifying requirements. The DQM quadrants provide a framework to discuss these kinds of issues between the involved parties.

DQ-I — the producing party is accountable

In DQ-I, the party responsible for making data available must ensure it meets expectations regarding completeness, accuracy, and timeliness. This includes managing the data logistics related to receiving data from operational systems (incoming interfaces) and ensuring that a PSA is in place, for example by making sure incoming data can be stored as time-stamped transactions.

Expectations that should be managed typically revolve about robustness, timeliness and managing of any exceptions (errors) that may occur during the involved data logistics processes. In short: the producing party is responsible for keeping commitments for data refresh and availability.

DQ-II — the requesting party is responsible

For DQ-II, the requesting party is accountable for ensuring that the data is 'correct.' This goes back to the earlier statement about engineering teams not being responsible for the correct definition (though still for the execution). It is up to the subject matter expert or domain expert to work with the engineering teams to produce data that meets requirements. This also includes testing, quality monitoring and sign-off.

The technical teams can still be responsible for the general maintenance and monitoring of the data solution overall, but not for the output.

DQ-III and DQ-IV — the analyst is responsible

In DQ-III and DQ-IV, with their opportunistic development style, the developer and consumer are often the same person — such as an analyst or data scientist. It is up to each individual or small team to make sure process is followed and data is fit for purpose.

The accountability lies with these teams.

As outlined in the ⚐ how data is produced section, elevating certain initiatives to an enterprise-wide or market deployment means 'moving' the solution through the other quadrants. This means that accountability shifts along the way.

Once a prototype is in production, it is no longer the responsibility of a data scientist to make sure it is correct. This responsibility has moved to a responsible business stakeholder, who may still request other experience from time to time to make sure the solution continues to work as expected.

Governance

The DQM can be applied not only to data processing and accountability, but also to the implementation of data governance for each data quadrant.

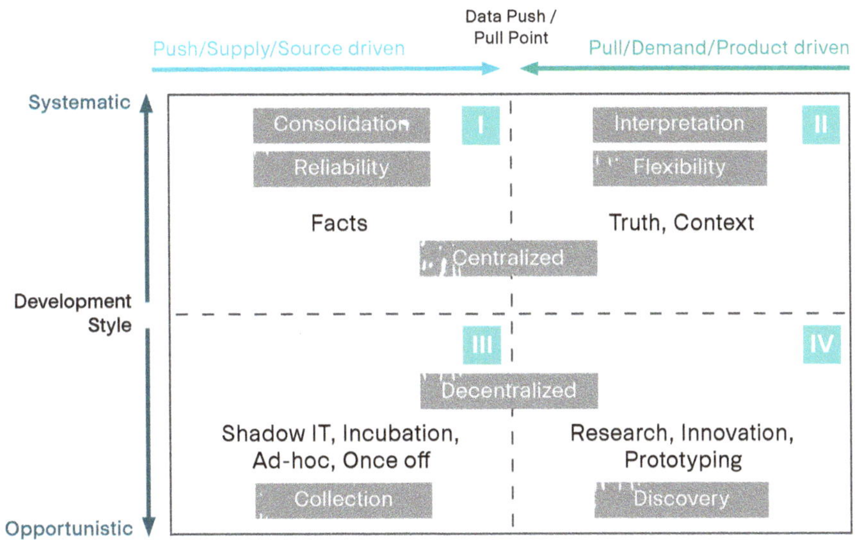

In DQ-I, governance focused on operational quality, and resulting predictability both in terms of delivery as well as applications of conventions. This is achieved through a high level of standardization, reliability, historization, and auditability. To achieve this, all data processing in DQ-I is subject to a high level of regulation. This is a *defensive governance* attitude, aimed at protecting the reliability of the data provision. Because of the focus on standardization, the implementation of this governance model is typically centralized.

In DQ-II, the governance shifts to managing the administration of business logic, such as transformations, aggregations or similar types of derivations, that are applied to deliver the resulting data products. DQ-II governance is less about managing the properties of the data, that is the task of DQ-I, but more about seeking shared understanding of definitions and terms, and how these can be consistently applied.

This can be achieved through standardization of modeling and taxonomy approaches. The governance attitude that is applied to DQ-II can also be classified as defensive, aimed at safeguarding the quality of the data products.

In contrast, DQ-III involves minimal governance. From the perspective of the data solution, the incoming data is of an unknown status. The data sets have little or no formal definition — there is not (yet) enough information about the data. The only governance that does apply here is to ensure DQ-III data is not used for formal data products in DQ-II. Unless this data has been formally investigated and 'promoted' to DQ-I first.

DQ-IV adopts a more offensive governance model for data management. The intent is to allow for a greater degree of freedom to prototype and investigate the data. Where governance is applied in DQ-IV, the focus is very narrow, designed for a limited number of scenarios. This is mostly for regulatory reasons.

The following illustration shows the decreasing governance in a clockwise direction:

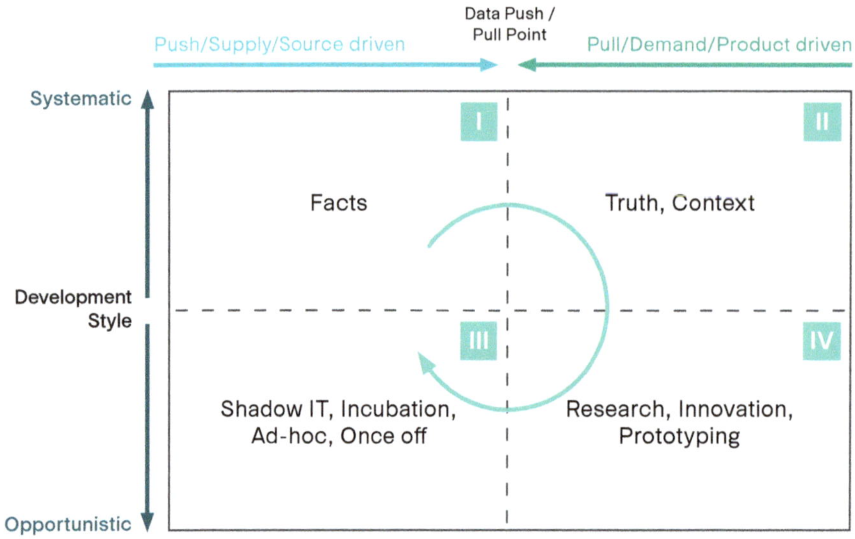

An example of this is data protection in the context of GDPR, or specific rules around using sensitive data for research purposes. Apart from these specific aspects, DQ-IV data management generally relies on self-regulating development or discovery processes, conforming in broad lines to the company's wider data management strategy.

In today's world, more and more departments are being set up as dedicated 'innovation labs,' where data scientists have more freedom to use data for experimentation and analysis with the goal of innovation and discovery.

Applying governance to promotions

The governance model also guides decisions for promoting data or prototypes between quadrants.
When certain ideas (from DQ-IV) or data sets (from DQ-III) prove successful, they may require the more formal approaches of DQ-I and DQ-II.

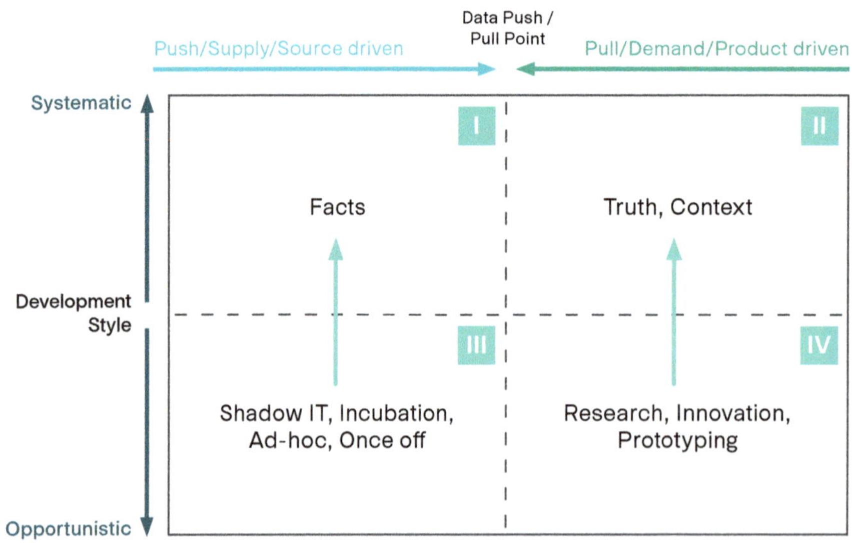

If a prototype in DQ-IV works, it must be lifted out of DQ-IV into DQ-II. This is because you can only achieve economies of scale and production-level reliability with data if you can generate, evaluate and govern it systematically. This way, the data product can be used throughout the company and will be sufficiently reliable for use in a production context.

It is the process of moving an experiment into a robust, scalable, solution.

The situation is similar with data from DQ-III that is considered important to use in formal data products. These, too, must be lifted — in this instance into DQ-I. This promotion applies the defensive governance to the data, by applying the fundamental tracking, identification and processing. Without these foundations, the data products may not be reliable enough to use.

The efforts to promote data to different quadrants should not be underestimated. Upgrading data (DQ-III to DQ-I) or products (DQ-IV to DQ-II) can be costly and time consuming.

If you would ask various data scientists what takes up most of their time, many of them will answer that it is the task of getting the data to the right, dependable, level of quality — into DQ-I.

People and skills

The structured nature of the data processing in DQ-I, with its standardized data processing patterns, conventions and rules, demands a data engineering mindset to implement effectively.

An engineering focus is a key asset for DQ-I data management, which prioritizes robust, deterministic, and repeatable processes. The primary challenges often involve interfacing, networking, and general connectivity.

It is about making sure different systems can be connected to, and data can be brought into the environment for further use.

Teams managing DQ-I data take pride in ensuring reliable and timely access to data, and monitor metrics such as latency, availability and uptime. While they are open to requirements for modifications, it is the responsibility of data consumers to provide these or implement them themselves.

The mindset in DQ-II is more usage-focused. The emphasis is on creating data products that deliver business value. This requires skills in analysis, Business Intelligence, and subject matter expertise — all with a decent amount of technical proficiency in, for example, SQL or scripting.

People working on DQ-II data benefit from the structure and standardization that has already been applied in DQ-I, and continue to build further on this foundation. A large amount of effort goes into clarification, and correct administration of, business definitions and terms.

DQ-III and DQ-IV, by their nature, are more free-format and require a wider spectrum of skills — typically analyst and data science focused. These people are working with any data available, usually through direct access such as using SQL or programming languages.

Technology

The DQM can help organizations identify the types of technologies best suited to various data scenarios.

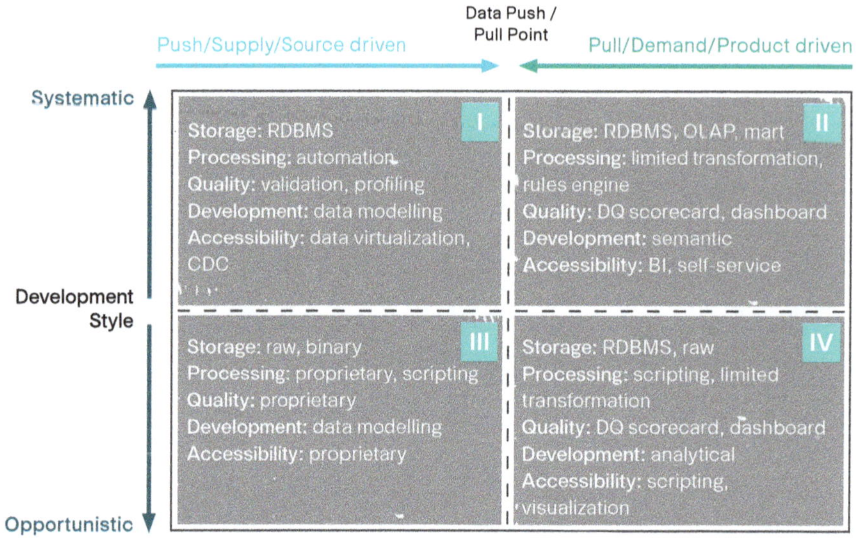

For example, a typical technical use case for DQ-I is the storage of raw data, transactions. This can be implemented as a data lake or similar (file) storage environment.

Alternatively, it could be a relational database supporting the staging layer of a data solution, including both the landing area and the PSA. The staging layer applies the various standardizations in line with DQ-I principles.

Remember, we are talking about the *technology* that can be applied in DQM, not about data modeling or governance — separations of concerns.

From a technical perspective, DQ-III could also be a data lake. It could be the same environment as is used for DQ-I, but without the standard processing. It would be a separate area of the data lake where data can be (temporarily) stored as-is. It is uncommon to see database technology used for DQ-III data, although key-value databases can serve a purpose here since there is no requirement to define the meaning of the data upfront as there is in relational databases.

DQ-II usually is defined by one or more databases that allow for data manipulation, but it can also be a designated area of a data lake. OLAP technologies also fall in this quadrant.

Data modeling

The DQM can provide valuable insights into how different approaches towards data modeling can be applied across a data solution. Different quadrants work better with certain styles, approaches, and methodologies. The DQM can help position a certain modeling technique for a given area of the data solution.

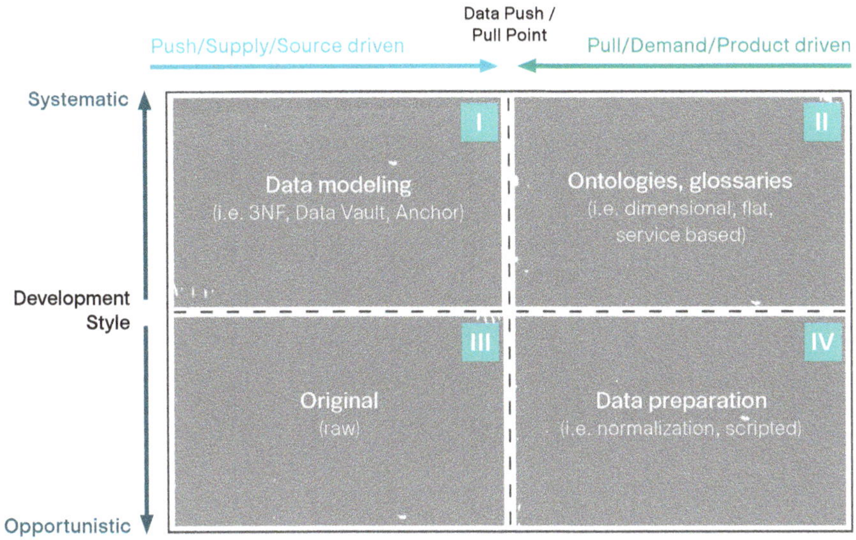

As a systematic and push-driven area, DQ-I aligns well with structured, well-defined approaches to data modeling. Even though most of the physical data modeling approaches allow for some degree of flexibility, they can sometimes be prescriptive in how data logistics and data structures should be organized.

Approaches such as Data Vault, Anchor Modeling, and similar techniques tend to have robust and repeatable patterns that allow for consistent consolidation of data. These techniques usually cater for flexible ways to incorporate interpretations, and may occasionally overlap somewhat into DQ-II.

A PSA also falls in DQ-I.

DQ-II is still systematic, but shifts to a requirement-driven focus. The modeling approaches are tailored for data delivery, ensuring that structure and meaning conform to well-defined requirements. Dimensional modeling is a good example, but services and glossaries fall in the same category.

The physical modeling techniques are only one part of the modeling considerations for DQ-I and DQ-II. Generally speaking, the focus in both quadrants should be placed on detailed, precise, and domain-specific information modeling.

The translation from an information model into a physical data model in this context can be seen as the instantiation of a domain-specific data model for a particular technology.

Which brings us to the Fact-Oriented Modeling (FOM) family, which facilitates and supports communication between the data modeler and the domain expert through natural language based information modeling methods — which includes traditional conceptual and logical modeling.

FOM expresses concrete examples in the (natural) language of the business expert, and provides a guided design process for creating models with a focus on elementary facts when capturing business requirements.

Automatically generated documentation of the models in natural language makes it much easier for the subject matter expert to validate them —unlike other information modeling methods— and ultimately leads to a better, high quality information model. And therefore also to a better derived physical data model.

The most popular FOM modeling methods today are *Second Generation Object Role Modeling (ORM 2)* and *Fully Communication Oriented Information Modeling (FCO-IM).*

In contrast, DQ-III and DQ-IV emphasize opportunistic development. These quadrants prioritize short-term results and iterative processes, often foregoing formal modeling methodologies. Instead, the focus shifts to use case-driven physical modeling tailored to immediate needs.

Although structured methodologies may occasionally be applied opportunistically within DQ-III and DQ-IV, they are typically not used consistently across initiatives. This flexibility allows for experimentation and rapid prototyping, but with less emphasis on long-term standardization.

Development

Finally, the DQM can be used to understand where automation and code generation can be adopted. Unsurprisingly, the degree of automation aligns closely with the levels of standardization and governance associated with each quadrant.

DQ-I allows for a high degree of automation and code generation. Standard templates and processes mean that most, if not all, of the data logistics and structures can be generated from design metadata. The outcomes can then be subject to standard deployment automation ('DevOps') processes for testing, approval, and deployment. Investing in code generation and automation for DQ-I is a powerful way to quickly provide data for consumers, as well as ensuring existing processes continue to work as expected.

To a large extent, this applies to DQ-II as well because there still is ample opportunity to use standard templates for code generation. As with DQ-I, formal deployment processes support a controlled way of delivering the outputs to the production environment.

Compared to DQ-I, there is a greater opportunity to combine deployment workflows with unit- and regression testing, so that specific data interpretations can be validated when changes are made to the solution. In DQ-I the validation would focus on ensuring consistent application of standards and conventions. In DQ-II this validation can also include a library of tests that validate specific transformations and scenarios.

DQ-I and DQ-II, with their focus on defensive governance and repeatable patterns, benefit greatly from code generation and automation. For DQ-III, however, this is the opposite. Since the data is not subject strict governance, and varies in origin, structure, and intent, there can be very little to automate. Automation and code generation will start to apply when certain DQ-III datasets are 'promoted' to DQ-I.

DQ-IV data could see bespoke automation for individual projects and initiatives but this depends on the analyst or data scientist working with the data. Code generation is therefore limited. However, automation for deployment processes may still play a role.

05 FastChangeCo –Finalizing the data landscape

After an engaging presentation covering the *Data Quadrant Model in a nutshell* by Amal and Zalika, the DMCE team feels confident that the initial sketch of the data landscape fits well with the DQM.

But *why, and in what specific ways,* should the data —the marbles— be mapped onto the data landscape?

This question has come up repeatedly as the team has delved deeper into DQM. It highlights the importance of not only presenting the future data landscape in a tangible way to create shared understanding among stakeholders but also of offering a well-reasoned explanation for the chosen approach.

Until now, the approach to the data landscape has largely relied on experience and intuition. Now, they aim to build a solid foundation that supports their decisions with rationale and clarity.

The Data Quadrant Model

Even before Amal and Xuefang's presentation, the team already understood the importance of explaining data management in general, and especially the plans for the data initiative in particular.

Discussions with Jeff had also left Sylvia and Michael with a key takeaway: project decisions must be made accessible and transparent for all stakeholders, with well-founded reasoning.

To address the 'why, and in what way' question, Amal explains: "Remember that the DQM is a 'sense-making,' or positioning framework. It is intended to classify different types of data accurately and align the potentially varied perspectives of data management stakeholders."

Zalika adds, "The essential principle of the DQM is that none of the four quadrants is more valuable than the others. Unlike the Eisenhower quadrants[13], for example, there's no scoring. Each quadrant is essential for a company aiming to become more data-centric, adaptable, and innovative."

"In other words," Amal summarizes, "exactly what we set out to do with our vision and strategy! The DQM isn't meant as a *blueprint* for implementing our data solution. But it can serve as a guide for organizing ourselves as a team and company. It can guide us how we develop things, how and where, and to what extent, we apply governance. Or inform our technology decisions. It can even shape our hiring priorities."

An analogy

The challenge, as often, is to explain an abstract framework like the DQM in a way everyone can grasp. The team discusses if one of FastChangeCo's long-standing manufacturing practices could serve as a relatable example.

Amal summarizes their conversation: "Of the various value chains at FastChangeCo, the evolution of our shoe business could be a good example. This is a wellknown product in the company that people connect with."

"With industrialization, FastChangeCo began to move shoe production to an assembly line. Until then, shoes were mostly handcrafted. Automation made it possible to produce larger quantities of shoes in less time, reducing production costs, and ultimately offering customers a reliable, affordable product," she continues.

"The trade-off, however, was a loss of personalization, as shoes became more of a mass-produced item."

"But over the past few years, this has changed again significantly. Customers now expect 'their brand' to meet their individual preferences, and FastChange-Co has responded. Today, customers have far more options to personalize their shoes," Amal explains. "Our production has shifted from mass production —a purely push-driven model— to semi-individualized production based on personalized orders. The share of the pull principle has increased," Amal says, linking the example to the DQM.

"A customer can now customize the design of their shoe online," Amal points out. "Though customization has its limits — they can select colors and choose from a wide range of fabrics and materials, but not an unlimited palette. The production only begins once the order is received, which corresponds to the pull principle. And since we know the standard customizable shoe models in advance, we can still incorporate standardized parts in production, like the sole or inner lining, maintaining some aspects of the push principle."

"But what does that have to do with our data solution?" Terence interjects.

"Terence, let's finish the example, and we'll get to the data quadrants (DQs) shortly," Amal says, gently steering him back.

She continues, "We can think of the standard parts in shoe production as equivalent to DQ-I. A high level of automation, along with clear rules and guidelines, supports an fully automated production line. The same is true for our data solution. In the same way, data created for DQ-I follows strict rules, standards, and adopts automation. This data represents the unaltered facts as received from the operational systems."

Zalika adds, "The individualized aspect of shoe production aligns with DQ-II. DQ-II provides the enriched context that provides the individual truth of a thing, product, or topic. This is like when customers select colors, fabrics, and additional details that transform a standard shoe into their customized product."

"In our data solution, it's similar," Amal elaborates. "By adding additional context such as reference data, rule sets, and other specifics, we create unique truth for individual 'data products.' For example, revenue for shoes could be defined differently depending on the department, perhaps at order placement or at the time of a return."

The team begins to understand the ideas behind the push-pull principle better and better. They engage in a lively discussion about the importance of making DQM and the concepts behind their data solution understandable to anyone interested.

They take note that a high degree of automation is possible —necessary even— in the push area of the DQM to achieve the required standardization, while use case-specific requirements are deliberately excluded.

In contrast, these specific requirements are implemented in the pull area (DQ-II). The push-pull point —between DQ-I and DQ-II— represents a decoupling from an architecture point of view.

Terence, still skeptical, interrupts, "But why? I still don't get it. What do shoes have to do with our data solution?"

Yerodin, growing visibly frustrated, holds back his irritation, while Sylvia recalls Jeff's comment during a recent meeting: *sometimes FastChangeCo has implemented projects without understanding why they succeeded or failed.*

"We're at a crossroads here," Sylvia says thoughtfully. "We can either make sure everyone understands the DQM now, or risk another project where we don't know why things work, or not. And that could have serious consequences."

"Terence," she continues, "the challenges in our data solution are similar to those in our shoe production. External demands and adaptability expectations have changed dramatically in recent years. It's no longer enough to 'just' provide a data set. Just like FastChangeCo can no longer 'just' produce shoes to sell off the shelf."

"We have to be ready to meet our customers' needs, just as FastChangeCo did by introducing customizable shoes. This means building a robust, well-thought-out architecture that can handle these challenges, and the foundation for that is the DQM."

The four data quadrants

Sylvia suggests that the team delve into each data quadrant to clarify how the DQM benefits the data solution.

"Amal and Zalika, is that something you can look into? Unfortunately, I have to leave now. I'm running later for another meeting."

"Yes, we do. Let's start."

Amal turns to Terence, explaining, "The push-pull point helps us better evaluate where to apply governance in our data solution. At this point, we assess what our customers need in terms of raw data. After this point, we can ease governance, implementing specific requirements as defined by business experts as business logic or rule sets. Let's call this the 'vertical decoupling point.'"

Zalika continues, "Another fundamental concept is *horizontal decoupling* — the development style."

Michael interrupts. "That's interesting. I often wonder why, despite having solid strategies and talented people, some projects still led to disengaged employees, dissatisfied users, budget overruns, and stress. It seems to me that not enough consideration was given to choosing the right development and management styles. Without this, people with specific skills could end up being assigned to unsuitable tasks, leading to the very symptoms we want to avoid."

"Exactly," Amal agrees, picking up on Michael's point. "Often there's a lack of communication or common understanding among all involved parties, or simply not enough alignment."

Amal then returns to development style. "Above the horizontal line, we apply what's called a systematic development style. Here, well-defined roles, responsibilities, development processes, rules, and conventions are essential to producing high-quality, consistent results. Below the line, on the other hand, is what we call an unstable or volatile development style. This approach is less structured, allowing users —often analysts— more freedom to explore ideas or try out things as prototypes."

Michael interjects, "This opens up interesting possibilities since there's always a demand from users to 'try something out quickly.' In my experience, project teams have often struggled to meet this request."

"Absolutely," Amal confirms. "We'll dive deeper into DQ-IV shortly, where this approach truly shines. But first, let's return to the basics. The combination of vertical and horizontal decoupling results in the four quadrants. These help define the design, development, implementation, and management the data solution."

“Shall we start with the first data quadrant?” Zalika suggests.

“But only after a quick break,” Michael says with a smile. “I need a green tea – how about everyone else?” The team, grateful for the pause, heads toward the kitchen together, chatting along the way.

Data Quadrant I — the quadrant of the order

After the short break, Amal and Zalika begin to explain the first data quadrant, or DQ-I, in more detail.

“The overarching goal of DQ-I is to focus on completeness, consistency, availability, reliability, and traceability of data within a well-defined data architecture,” Amal explains.

“How do we make these ambitious goals a reality?” Yerodin asks. “We’ve set intentions like this before. Good ideas that never quite materialized.”

Amal nods thoughtfully, while Terence begins, “Well, it would work if you applied the business logic right from the beginning of the ...”

The team collectively cuts him off, already more than familiar with his views on this topic. Terence quiets down, gazing out the window, sulking.

Amal tactfully redirects the conversation back to Yerodin’s comment: “To achieve these goals, we need to start referring to FastChangeCo’s information models – even for DQ-I. Among other things, we’ll be organizing the raw data around business concepts. These models might not be complete, and we probably won’t fully implement them in DQ-I, but they’ll serve as a starting point and guideline. And if no models exist, we should start defining them.”

These models should be independent of the technologies used in the data solution, making them more future-proof. Ideally, we coordinate them with the company’s data models and glossaries to the extent they’re available ...”

“And if nothing is available, perhaps we should create a glossary as part of our project. Set up a kind of data stewardship team to manage the definitions of business terms in a way that fits FastChangeCo. I’ll have to discuss this with Sylvia,” Michael murmurs, sipping his green tea.

“... And that ultimately means the consistent implementation of information models – by that, I mean convention-based physical data modeling and integration. It also requires temporal consistency, so that all data is historized uniformly.”

“Let’s see how far we get. I really hope we can achieve this.”

“It’s part of our vision,” Michael replies. “What Amal and Zalika are describing is the ideal state. Let’s work together to get as close to it as we can, one small step at a time.”

While Amal continues speaking, Zalika shows which data hubs are assigned to DQ-I in the data landscape:

- The log data hub, where unsorted data –both structured and unstructured– is recorded in chronological order
- The raw data hub, where data is structured around core business concepts, organizing related data into clearly defined groups

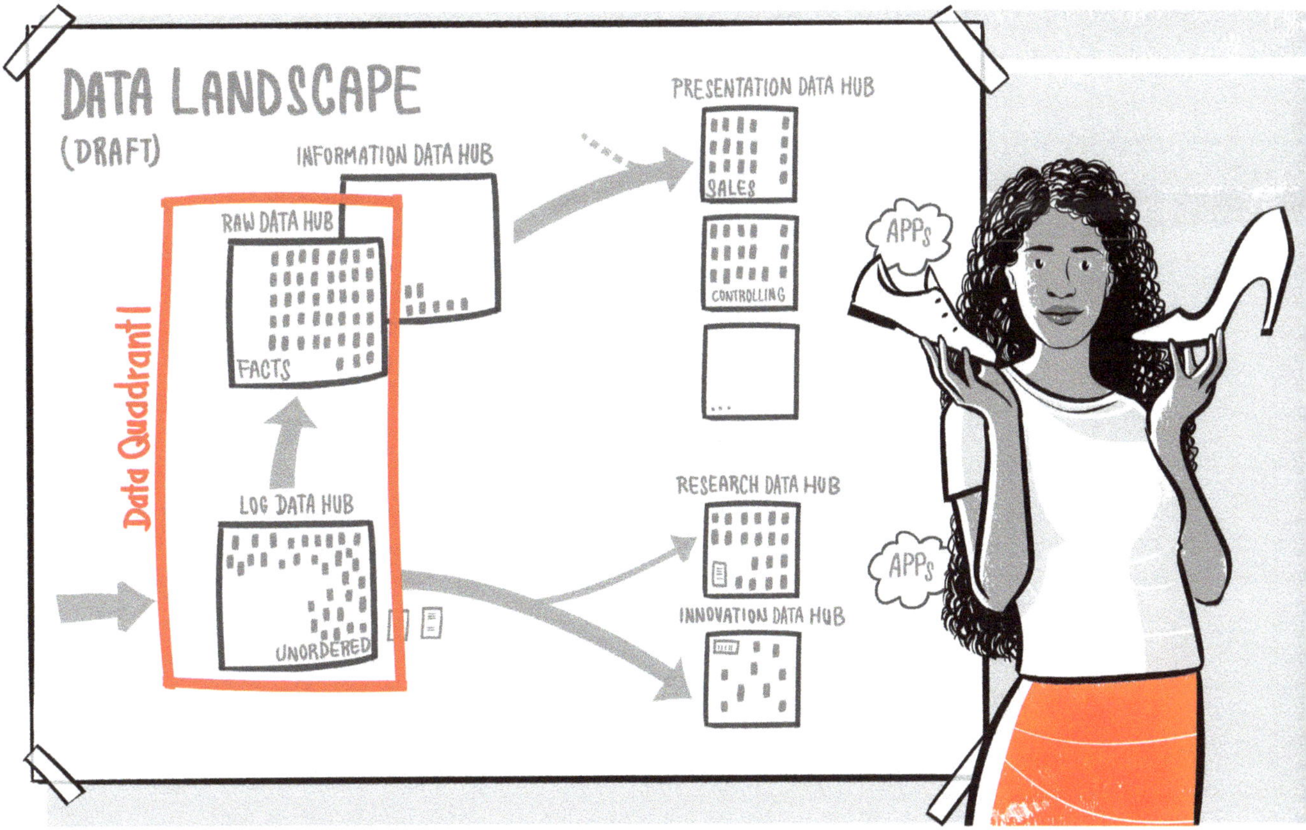

Amal adds that governance is crucial in DQ-I. This means strict implementation rules, such as naming conventions, data architecture specifications, structural standards, continuous quality control, role assignments, and procedures for handling technical debt.

After some discussion of the pros and cons, the team agrees to regulate (or govern) the data solution's implementation much more strictly than in previous projects, consistently following the philosophy of the DQM.

This governance will allow the team to standardize the structures (data model) and data logistics as much as possible, set development rules, and automate them. Ultimately, DQ-I will store the raw data, the 'facts.'"

This way, data will be automatically 'pushed' into the data solution and made available for further use. The strict rules and specifications of DQ-I support a high degree of automation.

Data Quadrant II — the quadrant of the context

The next day, Amal and Zalika start by summarizing the first data quadrant.

"DQ-I serves as the 'single point of facts,' where we store unaltered data straight from the sources. Each original data point is captured exactly as generated," Amal explains.

"If stopped at DQ-I, our customers would only have access to raw data, 'take it or leave it,' so to speak," she continues. "It's like our early days in shoe production when customers could only buy from a very limited selection."

"But we don't want that anymore, do we?" Zalika adds. "We want to give our customers data tailored to their needs. Just like a customer choosing colors and designs for their shoes, our data customers should be able to add their customizations, their 'secret sauce,' to get their desired data product.

This happens in the second data quadrant, or DQ-II."

Terence interjects, "But where's our 'single point of truth?' How will we ever achieve that if everyone does something different? Without it, no one will get useful data. I went over this with Jeff again, and he agrees we should implement clear business logic to get us there."

"Terence, we covered this already. Remember the Rubik's Cube?" Yerodin reminds him. "It's not like we don't want a single point of truth, but we have to accept that it may take a long time to get there."

Michael steps in, hoping to clarify things with a different example. "Here's something Diego shared with me recently. Imagine DQ-I as ice blocks. Originally, these water molecules were in a puddle somewhere, which is akin to DQ-III. The water is then pumped up, filtered, and carefully frozen into clear ice. This is DQ-I: data is neatly sorted, stacked, and stored on shelves – structured, governed, and following repeatable processes."

He continues, "But to make a soft drink, we break up the ice, melt it a little, and add syrup. This is DQ-II. The ice-water is still pure, but we create a unique 'soft drink truth' by adding context and flavor. It's similar to working with data – DQ-II is where 'meaningful' data is created, where we can work with data to create value and answer future questions."

"Interesting example, Michael," Terence concedes. "But does that mean we're letting people create their own versions of sales figures? If each department defines 'sales' differently, how will we compare?"

"You have a point," Amal says. "In our solution, we'd store each definition of sales separately —with different names— to make clear they're distinct.

"It's like cola from different brands," Zalika adds. "Take Roka Rola's and Repsi, for example. Both are 'cola,' but made with different recipes. Each product has its own 'truth.' That's why in *The Resurrection* we also speak of 'multiple versions of truth' alongside a single version of fact."

Terence stands and sighs, "I think I get it…" before stepping out of the room.

Meanwhile, Zalika has assigned the data hubs to DQ-II:
→ The information data hub stores the outcomes of the applied business logic and rule sets
→ The presentation data hub —of which there may be several— form the presentation layer

Data Quadrant III — the quadrant of unorder

"Data Quadrant III, or DQ-III, is often called the *unordered* area of the DQM. And it's probably the most misunderstood quadrant" Amal continues.

"For *The Resurrection,* DQ-III isn't meant to encompass all data within or outside the organization. It's specifically for temporary or ad-hoc data, the kind of data you might use for 'what does it actually look like' profiling."

Amal and Zalika argue that this data can be quickly connected to the data solution, because no governance or historization is needed. This makes it more readily available for DQ-IV, where it can be used for experimentation and research, swiftly providing prototypes for the experts to evaluate.

Michael summarizes: "In plain language, from a governance perspective, it would be 'unordered.'"

"Almost, but not entirely," Amal responds. "We still provide a managed, regulated technical infrastructure for DQ-III to facilitate controlled experimentation."

Amal and Zalika emphasize that a key advantage of DQ-III is the ability to incorporate new data quickly, even if it hasn't been formally integrated into the data solution. This data remains under minimal governance, providing a safe space for testing.

"This is meaningful," Zalika adds, "because experimenting with the data can reveal whether it's valuable. If it's not, we avoid the time and effort of full integration. If it is useful, we can choose to integrate it fully through DQ-I, applying the necessary controls. However, there is a risk: some solutions may start relaying on DQ-III data even if it hasn't gone through formal integration and production deployment."

Moving to the other side of the room, Zalika states, "Our governance processes need to ensure that when data is identified, through experimentation, as necessary for a specific 'data product,' it *must* first be integrated in DQ-I. As a team, we need to be vigilant about this and learn from past mistakes."

Michael adds, "To continue the water analogy, imagine sampling different lakes to see if the water is suitable for making ice cubes. If the sample passes, ice cubes are later produced in DQ-I."

Meanwhile, Zalika overlays DQ-III on the data landscape, explaining that this isn't about structured data hubs but about artifacts like CSV[14] files or open data.

Data Quadrant IV — the quadrant of innovation

"DQ-IV, is intended to foster research, innovation, and prototyping with data, and support the 'I want everything, but don't know why yet' questions we sometimes get," Zalika begins, introducing the fourth, and final, data quadrant.

Michael adds: "True to the motto 'everything can, nothing must,' this quadrant could reveal interesting possibilities. The desire of our users and developers to 'try things out quickly' won't go away."

A lively discussion emerges around maintaining control in DQ-IV – what level of governance make sense, and to what degree data should be 'ordered.'

The team quickly recognizes it's too early to impose stringent rules here. They need to learn to 'loosen the reins' to support the highly specialized 'creatives' in their innovative work. A certain amount of disorder must be possible.

"It's not easy," Michael notes, "especially after agreeing on strict governance for DQ-I and DQ-II." He offers an analogy: "It's like a child's bedroom. Just when it's finally tidy, the 'unorder' of toys begins. Presumably, this happens because creative play works better when there is a certain amount of disorder in an otherwise tidy space."

After a sip of his green tea he continuous: "Kids grab items from orderly shelves (DQ-I), use something made before (DQ-II), and perhaps drag a box that is left over from a recent delivery (DQ-III) to create something entirely new (DQ-IV). Sometimes, a new 'prototype product' emerges from this creative play that no one could have imagined."

Some team members nod in agreement as Zalika continues, "Similarly, in DQ-IV, we need to allow some disorder in the data solution so new ideas can emerge, innovations can develop, and ultimately, FastChangeCo can move forward."

Amal adds, "But, as in DQ-III, there's a big challenge: bringing innovations and prototypes from DQ-IV into production as 'data products' in DQ-II isn't easy. Have you heard the term 'sandbox?' For those unfamiliar, a sandbox is an environment where experiments and prototypes can be developed. These spaces are common in our existing Data Warehouses and typically aren't subject to strict controls."

Amal pauses, then asks, "Does anyone remember how many issues we've faced when trying to move successful prototypes from our sandboxes to production?"

Everyone reflects and nods, recognizing the challenge. Using the DQM, the team understands the need for a structured process to transition into production and why stakeholders often question the additional resources required to turn a prototype into a stable production solution.

Michael adds, "Where possible, we need examples to demonstrate the value in moving these innovations to DQ-II to stakeholders."

"Or, they can stay in DQ-IV – that's an option too. But then we must be strict to avoid supporting them as 'product zombies' in DQ-IV," Amal clarifies. "Using a prototype in DQ-IV as a production 'data product' can create long-term issues. Since it was developed opportunistically and possibly without sufficient regulation, it might be found during the transition to DQ-II that a product doesn't fully meet regulatory requirements, needs more work."

"This could be due to GDPR[15] or other compliance requirements, including internal company guidelines. These issues may not be noticeable in DQ-IV but could have serious consequences in production."

By this point, Zalika has mapped the data hubs to DQ-IV. The innovation and research data hubs access data from the log data hub and, if needed, processed data from the raw data and information hubs. Users can also add internal and external data into these hubs as necessary.

Maturity of data management

Reflecting on the outcomes of the DQM investigations, Sylvia says: "This requires specific skills, knowledge, and experience within the team. Our data management may still be somewhat disorganized, so it's crucial to recognize this and outline improvement plans."

"I suggest we focus on the 'data solution architecture,'" Michael replies. "That will establish a solid foundation for DQ-I and DQ-II. If gaps are found later, or if the other quadrants aren't fully adopted or defined yet, we can address those challenges one at a time, using the DQM as our guide."

Currently, there are no analysts involved in the project, and this is not planned for the first phase. For now, they agree that setting up sandboxes as 'innovation labs' would be valuable. The DMCE will formally establish this concept to support users in prototyping, providing a space for ideas to develop free from the usual constraints of the data solution.

For now, Michael's team will be responsible for implementing and maintaining DQ-I and DQ-II, and the remaining topics that Amal and Zalika described in the ⚐ Data Quadrant Model in a nutshell presentation will be addressed gradually.

Data governance practices, including standards and rules, will also play a significant role in developing the data solution. A shared understanding of the business terms at FastChangeCo will be essential for the data modelers during the modeling efforts. This also includes definitions, business logic, and their conversion into runnable code.

There's a lot of work ahead for the DMCE team. Sylvia underscores the importance of reserving time and budget for integrating innovations and prototypes from DQ-III and DQ-IV into production, which means aligning the required data with DQ-I and DQ-II standards.

Setting these expectations for a future innovation lab is essential.

Research the solution architecture

Sylvia, speaking also on behalf of Michael, thanks the DMCE team for their excellent presentation of the DQM. She is excited about how effectively the DQM illustrates the vision and future of the data solution in an engaging way for executives, stakeholders, and project funders.

The way the team mapped the data hubs from the draft data landscape to the various data quadrants has been especially helpful, making it easy for both Sylvia and Michael to understand and appreciate the structure.

Sylvia and Michael then share the final data landscape diagram with Jeff, to make sure he feels engaged but also to get some feedback from him if possible. After Michael provides an overview of the DQM, Jeff is fully 'on board' with the current state of the data landscape. He finally recognizes the advantages of the 'single point of facts' concept and is pleased to see how the data landscape will evolve into a tangible architecture.

The finalized data landscape now serves as a starting point for the DMCE to explore a suitable solution architecture. For this purpose, the team retreats to the quiet and isolated research area that FastChangeCo provides.

During this relatively quiet, undisturbed phase, the team works on the important next steps for the data solution:

→ Defining objectives and principles of the architecture
→ Creating an overview of potential architectures, including examples

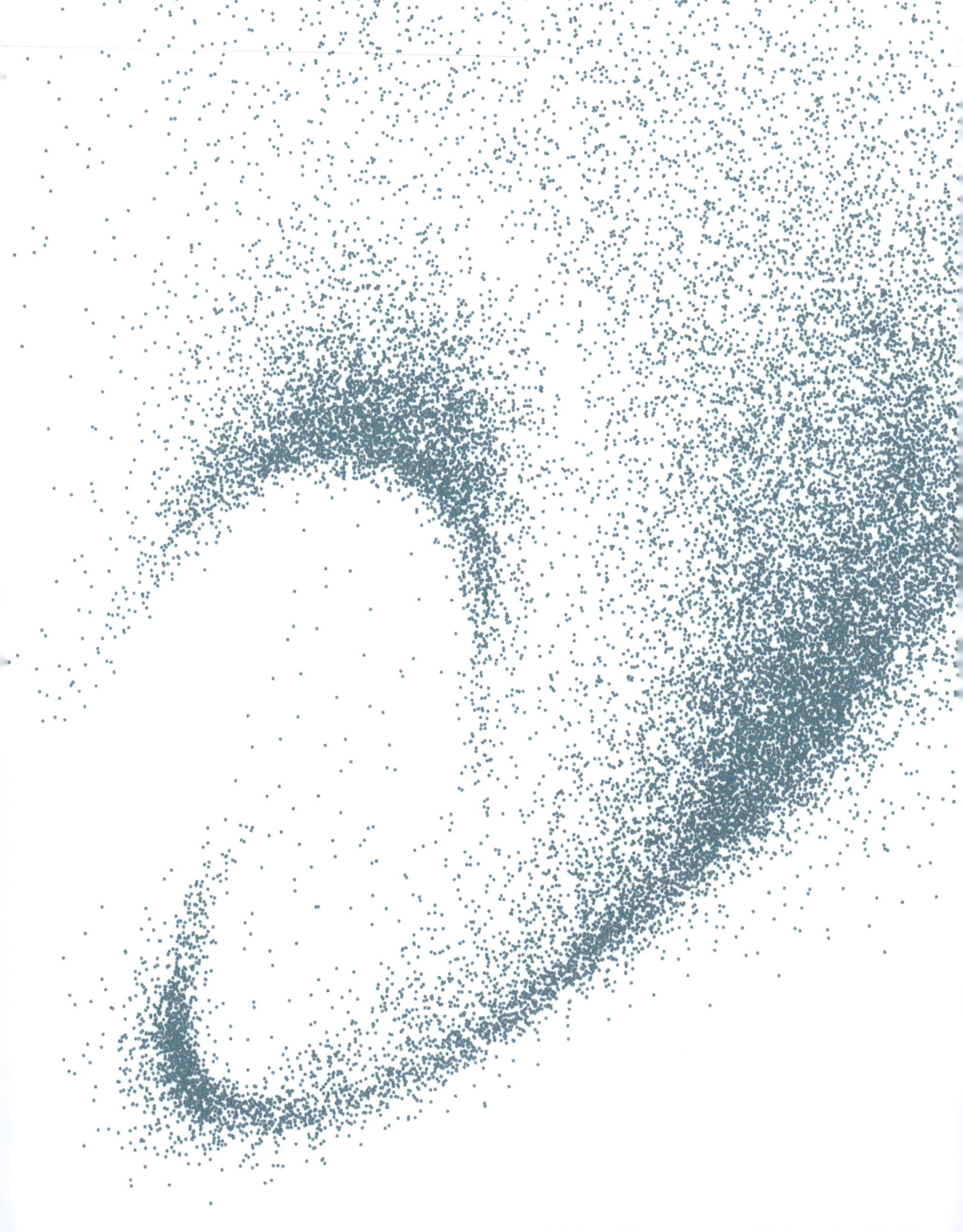

06 Data solution architecture

This chapter provides an overview of the reference data solution architecture we advocate. Often referred to simply as the solution architecture or 'architecture,' it offers an end-to-end perspective on how the various building blocks fit together. It is designed to deliver a platform-independent, flexible, and manageable data solution — a machine built for change.

Purposes of a data solution

Before delving into the design of a data solution, we must first understand what we're trying to build. Equally important, we should start with the outcomes we seek to deliver in mind.

When we design a data solution, these goals should permeate every aspect of the design. This requires that they have been considered upfront, and that we do not forget them along the way. This section provides an overview of the main purpose of the data solution. In subsequent sections, we will apply this to specific approaches, methodologies, and concepts.

So, let's break it down, align our understanding, and then design to deliver this.

Making data accessible

Almost every company these days relies on computer systems, and the data being processes by them. Many companies would grind to an immediate halt if a critical system suddenly stopped functioning.

These systems are typically designed with a specific purpose in mind, such as:

- → HR management systems keep track of employee details, manage leave balances, generate pay slips, track corporate health insurance payments, and calculate a multitude of ever-changing tax components and retirement benefits
- → University student enrollment systems keep track of student details, which courses they enrolled in, their grades, who taught them and when
- → General ledger systems manage financial transactions
- → Fast-moving consumer goods (FMCG) logistics systems track that goods are picked up from the warehouse and arrive at a location on time, and in the right order
- → Warehouse logistics systems monitor exactly what is in store at this moment, where it is located, and in which quantities

These systems, known as operational systems or online transactional processing (OLTP) applications, are designed to excel at their intended functions. However, they are often decidedly *not* designed to support anything outside of that core purpose. From the perspective of the data solution, they are the 'source' or 'feeding' systems.

There will inevitably come a point when an organization will want to use its data for more than what the system was originally built for. And it is not always easy to access, integrate or otherwise use this data. Sleek front-end user screens and out-of-the-box reports often hide the complexity of the average operational system 'under the hood.'

While these systems tend to maintain large behind-the-scenes databases to store the data they need to operate, they are usually not intended to be accessed directly for non-standard data requests (relative to the purpose of the system).

This simple posit presents a host of challenges once those types of questions, data requests, are inevitably getting asked to the operational system.

Impact on system performance

Querying or retrieving data from an operational system can be troublesome. This is especially the case when large (bulk) data sets are requested. The reason for this is the way the data is stored, optimized for the support of the core function of the system – which typically has a transaction focus.

Operational systems can be ill-equipped for retrieving (potentially very) large data sets such as –for example– all sales of the last year for a specific region, aggregated by sales channel.

Data requests may negatively impact the performance, or uptime, of the system and even prevent its users from interacting with it for periods of time. Data requests may cause an *operational impact.* Effects such as these may lead to a variety of downstream impacts including, but not limited to, loss of productivity, not meeting SLAs, outages, and loss of revenue.

Systems administrators are understandably wary of anything that has the potential to cause the system itself to slow down or even grind to a halt; especially during peak operational hours.

Complex data access

Many operational systems have underlying databases that are not designed for easy retrieval of data. Anyone who has ever attempted to look into the data structures of SAP for instance, the data model of which is vast, in German, with table and field names abbreviated beyond recognition (which even Germans themselves don't necessarily understand), will have quickly realized that.

This is not to say the design is bad, just that it was not made for the purpose of simplifying data requests. The data may also be redundant, that is to say, stored multiple times in the system or otherwise stored in a way that may mask its true intent. We have seen many examples where the underlying structure of systems was adapted to facilitate shortcuts in processes or functions. While this may benefit functionality, it complicates retrieving the right data.

Not all data may be retrievable

This is somewhat of a contradiction in terms, but operational systems may not necessarily record *all* data in databases. Systems may store data (in databases) in certain ways but subsequently apply interpretation that is coded in the application when certain functionality is called.

We refer to this as *application logic,* and is a way of explaining otherwise inconsistent results between the user interface and the data that can be found inside the system's databases.

Another variation is that operational systems may not require certain data to function properly, even if it might seem logical that it would exist from a business perspective. These systems might not be configured to capture or store such data explicitly.

For example, a sales region important for analysis might not exist as a distinct data point. Instead, users infer it by convention, such as considering the region as the sum of areas 1, 2, and 3. This type of context often resides solely in the collective memory of employees, making it difficult to formalize or retrieve systematically.

Data retention

Operational systems may not always retain certain data points beyond their immediate use, whether related to a current event or past activity. Some systems delete data once its purpose has been served, or overwrite it when updates are made.

For instance, when a customer updates their address, previous addresses might be overwritten, leaving no record of past changes.

The design and implementation of operational systems vary greatly, and their maturity in terms of system design and controls can range from basic to highly sophisticated. It is not always possible for data teams to influence this.

A data solution makes data accessible

The challenges mentioned here make it difficult, and sometimes simply not feasible, to access or retrieve data directly from operational systems.

This is where data solutions come in.

One of the main purposes of the data solution is *making data accessible.* The data solution can do so by providing the data in a way that is optimized for data retrieval, and in a way that is not impacting the performance of the systems that provided the data.

In addition, data solutions can be repositories of data for eternity, even when the original systems themselves do not have the data anymore. The data solution intends not to remove data – unless for compliance or regulatory reasons.

The data solution can become a *corporate memory* for data, so to speak.

Integrating data

'Integration' is one of the oldest and most fundamental concepts in the world of data solutions. At its core, integration involves making disparate data sets function together in a meaningful way, typically by combining them on a common key. When making data from various operational systems centrally accessible, some level of integration is always required.

In the data space, integration is arguably best known as a collection of processes that manipulate data from its source location into a defined target structure – the traditional ETL processes.

Transformations can be applied to make sure that the meaning and structure of data are compatible with data from other locations. This is how we position integration as well: a term that describes how the data solution combines data from different systems and aligns its meaning, so that all data can be compared and used for a broad variety of use cases.

However, traditional ETL is just oneway to achieve integration. Alternatives can, for example, rely on database views, queries or procedures to display the original data in a certain way. This can even include data virtualization approaches where the data is never physically moved at all.

In all cases, integration for a data solution, means applying a set of rules that cast data into a defined target structure, and align its meaning.

More broadly, integration extends to the concept of 'data integration,' which often involves the way systems exchange data (or 'talk to each other') through interfaces or APIs. Data integration, in the sense of system interoperability, applies to a data solution as it does to any IT system. This is part of the data management and data governance domain, which also intents to ensure that systems have the same understanding of data elements, definitions, and so on.

Data solutions may be integrated into processes or systems and provide data to support their tasks as an 'operational' data hub. However, whether this is the right thing to do is very use case specific.

Mapping the data to the information model

Models can be a means to understand the matter at hand, because some of the complexities can be presented in a way that is easier to understand – or abstracted away for the purpose of highlighting the most important features. A model is an abstract version of reality, whether it's a information model or a physical data model.

The information model defines how the business operates. It captures the many processes that sustain the business, their definitions, and their inputs and outputs.

In the ⚐ world of data chapter, we outlined the view that data can often be seen as the byproduct of processes running in a given business. The activities people perform –whether as part of formalized workflows or informal tasks– generate data as outputs.

Business processes not only produce data, but also require it as *input.* In fact, in many companies the flow of data is what enables them to function.

When mapping data to the information model, the goal is to define data structures in ways that align to business terminology. The information model takes precedence in defining terminology here, because many operational systems are likely to follow a different implementation — at least at the data level.

The data must therefore be translated from its technical implementation in operational systems to the more holistic definition and meaning of the information model.

We believe that the vision of the *machine designed for change* also applies to information models. Our understanding of how a business operates may be incomplete at any given time. Improving the information model, and our understanding of it, is an iterative process too. This evolution goes hand in hand with improvements to the data solution.

Fortunately, there are some well-established modeling templates and methodologies available that provide great starting points and direction. Approaches such as Ensemble Logical Modeling —including Data Vault and Anchor Modeling— can be used to define the core business concepts, or themes, in a way that allows for refinement over time.

We will explore this in more detail in the implementation chapters. For now, it suffices to say that a key purpose of the data solution is be organic, adaptable to its environment, and flexible in how data is stored and used — so that it evolves alongside the information model.

Architecture objectives and principles

In the previous section, we have outlined some of the key reasons for implementing a data solution. Here, we will detail the fundamental principles and objectives that a data solution should be designed for — in the way we would define it.

These objectives will appear on multiple occasions throughout the definition of the solution architecture, where we will reference them as needed. They are therefore worth explaining upfront.

Establish trust

A primary focus of any data solution should be to *establish and protect trust* in the data it provides to its consumers.

To achieve this, the architecture must have a strong focus on auditing and reliability. Data solutions often lose the trust of their consumers when the data fails to meet expectations. And as they say in the Netherlands: "Trust comes on foot, but leaves on horseback."

Trust is hard-earned but easily lost, and regaining it can be challenging.

Trust can erode when data cannot be reconciled with what is visible in the operational systems or when data is not made available at expected times.

Trust is gained when data is both reliable and correct — or at least auditable since what constitutes 'correct' may be subjective.

When designing a data solution, care must be taken to implement auditability, consistency and durability principles at both technical level and application (consumer) level.

At the technical level, this means looking after data consistency by implementing principles such as ACID[16] and transaction isolation. How this is done may vary between platforms, and much of this functionality is often already managed by the underlying database system.

At the application level, this can be as straightforward as pro-actively notifying consumers in case of delays, but also covers more complex use cases such as delivering bitemporal data — something we will cover later in detail.

In all cases a robust data logistics framework is essential to support all of this. This framework plays a central role in our reference solution architecture.

Be unbreakable

To establish trust, the data solution must be as robust and resilient —unbreakable— as possible.

Achieving this involves a collection of carefully designed components, each contributing to the system's overall resilience and its ability to maintain trust with its consumers.

A robust solution also makes the life of its administrators easier. After all, who wants to be paged at 3 a.m. for a system issue? We would like everyone to enjoy a good night's sleep.

Resilience is achieved through a multifaceted approach, with small but impactful features implemented across the entire solution architecture.

The decision to not judge data 'on the way in' but instead to apply business logic on the way out of the system reinforces resilience.

For example, if a certain interpretation fails due to a division by zero error it should only impact that particular data delivery, while others can continue.

An example at a more technical level is using large enough data types, so that impacts caused by data type changes in the operational systems are minimized. If the data type changes from 3 to 4 characters in the originating system, this will have no impact if your data type can already accept 100 characters.

Another example is implementing retry mechanisms in the data logistics processes, and making sure these can run independently. If one fails, others aren't blocked, and data deliveries that don't rely on this failed process can continue as normal.

Designing data logistics processes to be truly independent is one of the best ways to increase the overall reliability of the data solution. Independent processes can be run in any order, and as often as necessary. This can be achieved by combining the features of the data logistics control framework, and through careful template design.

No single feature can prevent *all* possible issues, but as a *collection* of features they significantly reduce the chance of failure.

The result is a more resilient and reliable system with higher uptime, reinforcing trust for all stakeholders.

Enable flexibility in orchestration

A data solution must continuously adapt to remain in sync with the business. This may require certain sets of data to be made available more (or less) frequently on short notice.

Changing the frequency of data processing, or the data refresh rate, can be a major problem for data solutions. This is because data logistics processes are often designed in a way that depends on fixed loading schedules. This is often fundamental to the design, and changing the data refresh rates may well require an end-to-end refactoring of the solution.

In batch-style processes, where a number of processes run as a workflow, dependencies between individual data logistics processes are often implemented simply by executing them sequentially. For instance, a dependency might exist in the form of a key lookup, which requires the parent table to be loaded before the child table.

Similarly, dependencies can also arise from timestamp generation – for example, when a 'load timestamp' is created in the initial step of a batch process and reused across subsequent processes within the same batch.

Design decisions such as these can have substantial implications on how data is delivered, as it effects the technical timeline and influences the audit trail – something we will spend time on later in the book.

In our reference solution architecture, we aim to ensure that changes in data refresh frequency *never* impact the design of the solution. Or in other words, the scheduling is independent from the design of the data logistics processes.

Instead, increasing data refresh rates should be as simple as running data logistics processes more frequently, constrained only by available resources.

Be an institutional memory

The data solution should always accurately record and track (changes in) data as it provided by the operational systems. Furthermore, the data solution must never physically remove data. This is, of course, within the boundaries of regulatory frameworks and compliance — such as the GDPR.

This implies that the data solution 'remembers' that certain data points were 'current' in the operational system at some point in the past, even if no trace of this data remains in the operational system itself.

It may happen that data is updated or removed in the operational system, either because the application allows this, or because of changes made directly in the back-end database. As a result, data might be overwritten or removed entirely in the operational system. However, the historical 'state' of the data, at any given point in time, remains available in the data solution.

We have seen this behavior in operational systems many times, even with commercial software that claims it is 'not possible.' Transactions/records collected in the data platform contain evidence on the contrary though, and in some cases may even uncover fraudulent activities.

For our solution architecture, this means we will prevent records to be physically deleted from the data solution. Instead, we implement *logical deletes* at all times.

A logical delete involves adding an 'is deleted' flag or indicator to a record, instead of physically removing it from the data solution.

Respond to changing business requirements

To deliver value, a data solution architecture should ensure that its design can be updated quickly to respond to changing business requirements.

The architecture aims to separate concerns by allocating distinct functionality to defined layers and areas. In addition, the way the solution is designed should facilitate metadata driven development practices (e.g., code generation, deployment automation).

Being able to respond quickly to changing requirements requires various components to work well together. It is not achieved through a single feature.

The choice of (physical) data modeling technique(s) is one of these factors. Is the data model easily extensible? For example, not every technique is able to ingest data when the (nature of the) relationship changes. Many hybrid data modeling techniques define relati-onship entities as many-to-many for this reason, even though the data itself may represent a one-to-many relationship at design time.

In our solution architecture this challenge is addressed by ensuring raw data is carefully recorded and separated from its interpretation — the application of business logic. Business logic is applied as late in the architecture as possible, typically just before information is delivered to consumers. This way, multiple versions of the data interpretation can be provided simultaneously in case there is misalignment on definitions across the organization.

Another aspect is the deployment process itself. How easy is it to apply the changes to the environment? Is it possible to reload part of the data solution when requirements change? How is release management configured?

In our solution architecture, we seek to implement the engine concept as outlined in the world of data chapter to facilitate efficient responses to changing business requirements.

Refactor without impacting consumers

Related to the objective of quickly responding to business requirements, the data solution architecture must also support refactoring with minimal impact on its consumers – or ideally, no impact at all.

By decoupling data storage, data modeling and business logic, our solution architecture enables the delivery of multiple versions or interpretations of data to consumers.

This design allows consumers to update their interfaces to the data solution at their own pace, and not necessarily at the same time the data solution changes its structures.

In a multi-layered solution design, there are many options available for modifying the structure of a given layer while adapting the data delivery in a way that is not noticeable by consumers – regardless whether all layers are implemented as physical data stores, or not.

Manage data quality and interpretation

Assessing 'data quality' is a special kind of data interpretation, or *judgment*. What is good and bad is often subjective, open to debate.

It is for this reason that data quality rules are treated the same way as transformations or business logic. In our solution architecture, these data quality rules are viewed as interpretations that should be applied *after* recording the data as it was provided, rather than during the initial recording process.

We recommend designing against the rejection of erroneous records early in the architecture.

Ideally, data quality concerns are handled by the operational systems and through data governance processes. The data solution can support these efforts by providing exception reporting.

In our solution architecture, we recommend asserting data quality rules by 'flagging' or 'labeling' records rather than rejecting them. We will introduce the *exception bitmap* concept for this purpose.

After all, what may be considered 'bad' for one group of consumers might still be valuable for another. Consequently, 'bad' data from the perspective of one delivery should not delay or hinder the delivery to others.

Implement a modular design

Many techniques exist for every aspect of a data solution, and some work better than others for specific technical environments.

To be able to modify certain aspects of the data solution without impacting others, the solution architecture aims for a modular design. This applies to both implementation and concepts, which evolve over time as well.

For example, key distribution, historization, transformations, and relationship management are separated into distinct processes. This is opposed to 'big bang' data logistics processes that sometimes attempt to perform all of these functions at once.

At a broader level, modular design aims to isolate the frameworks and components used within the solution, making it easier to replace or modify them as needed. For instance, a component such as the data logistics process control is independent from the rest of the solution – only referenced by the *Audit Trail Id* column.

Architecture overview

↗ In the solution architecture, a layer is a container for functionality that shares the same characteristics and intent. An area is a more specific division within a layer, dedicated to a particular role or function.

The reference architecture we advocate is designed to deliver a platform-independent, flexible, and manageable data solution – a machine designed for change.

This is achieved by embracing two core principles: *designing for change* and *separating concerns.* These principles, introduced in the ⚐ world of data chapter, serve as guiding directives for the data solution architecture.

Layers and areas

In practical terms, these principles are implemented by methodically separating functionality (decoupling) within the data platform, and organizing this into *layers* and *areas.*

A 'layer' is a high level container for functionality that shares the same characteristics and intent. For example, a layer defines entities that follow the same data modeling patterns.

Data logistics processes always operate from one layer to the next. This is referred to as 'downstream' direction of data logistics. Data should not flow backward from a higher-level layer to an earlier one. This convention simplifies and structures the solution, and results in in clearer data logistics patterns.

The differences between layers are most evident in the data modeling techniques used, and not necessarily the technical components. It is perfectly possible for a single layer to span different technical environments.

An 'area' is a more specific division within a layer, dedicated to a particular role or function. Areas within a layer share the same modeling approach, patterns, and techniques as directed by the layer, but they fulfill distinct purposes.

An example for this can be taken from Data Vault methodology: the difference between a 'raw' Data Vault and a 'business' Data Vault. These two areas both implement the Data Vault modeling technique, but perform different functions in the overall design.

The raw Data Vault focuses on ensuring correct ingestion of data is provided to the data solution by the operational systems. The business Data Vault on the other hand, focuses on implementing transformations to align the raw data to shared definitions and implement business logic.

Both areas belong to the integration layer and collectively form the data model. This supports incorporating new or changed requirements without major impacts to the data solution foundations. There is no need to copy all data in both models, they work together.

Aside from providing a structured overview of the architecture, this approach of defining layers and areas assists in establishing a decoupling of logic that is used to prepare data for integration and 'business' transformations. In addition, it makes it easier to configure each data integration process to run independently, in parallel, and with built-in recovery mechanisms.

Layers often mean complexity, so adding layers (and areas within layers) should be a careful consideration. We define what we believe to be the least amount of layers to achieve functional separation of concerns — while supporting the purposes and objectives of the data solution as we have outlined this in the previous chapter.

Defining a data solution architecture

↗ A design pattern explains a concept in detail, but remains implementation-agnostic. The solution pattern defines the actual code, technique and detailed data logistics process.

Architectures should be customized for specific situations. Every company, team, and combination of factors —such as technical environments, regulatory frameworks, and budgets— is unique.

In line with Engine Thinking, the solution architecture is designed to allow individual components to be selected or replaced as needed to fit these specific circumstances. We recommend documenting these decisions in a *data solution architecture* artifact, which records the reasons why certain components from the reference architecture were chosen for a given initiative.

A good way to think about this is that a given data solution architecture is an *instance* of the reference solution architecture described in this book.

A collection of design decisions

We see the solution architecture as a collection of design decisions, made based on the best available information at the time. To effectively manage and document these decisions, the *options and considerations,* we define two key types of pattern: design patterns and solution patterns.

These are collectively referred to as 'patterns' and follow a standard format to facilitate structured documentation of key design decisions, at both conceptual and technical level.

A design pattern or 'design decision' explains a concept in detail, but remains implementation-agnostic.

The solution pattern defines the actual code, technique and/or detailed data logistics process. It is therefore technology-specific by definition. Both the design and solution patterns will be covered in more detail in the next sections.

High level overview

Our reference solution architecture contains three layers, each hosting two areas. This layered design ensures abstraction and functional separation that assist in managing the solution as it changes over time. The solution architecture describes each layer and its areas, and refers to the (more detailed) design patterns for further explanation of the concepts selected, and options considered.

Documenting the reasoning behind these decisions is as valuable as documenting how the solution is implemented. This rationale allows others to understand the original designers' thought processes — providing transparency in why certain options were selected or omitted, and what considerations were made as part of this process.

By using design and solution patterns to document key decisions, the resulting solution architecture artifact provides principles and guidelines to help the delivery team create a scalable, maintainable, and durable data solution.

The sum of the parts

We tend to position data solutions as being *complex, but not difficult* – provided they are broken up into sufficiently modular, atomic components. But, decisions made for one component often interact with other components – another reason for careful upfront planning of the data solution architecture.

A solution architecture, as a collection of patterns, can be thought of as a series of interlocking cogs in a machine. Changing an individual cog may have an impact on how others start behaving.

Individually, the modular functions performed by each pattern are often straightforward and clear. However, the full scope of these components, and the way they interact with each other can be complex to fully appreciate – one of the reasons to separate concerns.

Consider the example of setting load timestamps, and where and how this can be done. Should this be done in the staging layer, or in the integration layer? Will the load timestamp be linked to a batch-style process (e.g., a 'daily run?'), or is this simply the moment the record is committed to the database independent of when the loading process started?

A batch-style process, which sets a timestamp once when the process starts and propagates this it to all processes in the workflow, might make it easy to understand how data relates together. After all, all processed data shares the same load timestamp. However, a downside of this approach is that a tight coupling between the scheduling (part of the data logistics framework) and the data logistics processes themselves is established.

To make this work, the *complete* workflow needs to run successfully, which in turn may impact scalability when intra-day data refreshes are required. The loading frequency is limited by the time it takes for the entire workflow to complete.

How long does it take for the full workflow to finish? Is there sufficient window for scalability? How much reengineering will be required to be able to support intra-day processing if scalability *does* become an issue?

For example, in the aforementioned batch-style process, the timestamp that is propagated may be a 'day' value that captures the data that is processed for that day, assuming only a single daily process run. The original requirements might only have required a daily data delivery, but the efforts to modify this to a timestamp may be prohibitive later on.

Good design patterns capture considerations such as these.

Solution architecture contents

At a high level, the solution architecture describes:

→ The layers and areas that have been considered and included
→ The sequence of high-level steps for data integration and their intended processing order
→ The options and considerations for each of these steps, and the decisions made
→ How data logistics process control data is used and linked to the layers and areas
→ How exception handling is applied to the layers and areas

The intent of the pattern-based approach towards documentation is to emphasize and encourage recording the reasoning behind decisions made, rather than solely focusing on technical details. Technical platforms often serve as the best source of truth for implementation specifics, but the rationale for certain choices often goes undocumented.

This way, pattern documents can make it easier to focus on the 'thinking' behind decisions and place focus on documenting the essentials. At implementation time, the focus will be on automation, forward-engineering as much as possible following the patterns. This means many of the low-level technical details do not require explicit documentation, since these are embedded in the code generation templates.

The idea is that design and solution patterns are continuously updated and expanded, resulting in an ever-evolving solution architecture artifact — the complete set of directives the solution follows.

Design patterns

A design pattern is a detailed description of a concept. It is a 'what' and 'how-to' guide explaining concepts in detail. They are the starting point for the solution design as well as the primary tool for the data solution architect to manage and maintain the system.

Design patterns focus on how to use the concept, provide the best-practice approaches, and document the options, considerations, and decisions.

Every layer in the architecture specifies the concepts and steps to be carried out. Design patterns then define *how* these concepts and steps are implemented. As such, design patterns have a huge impact on the implementation of the solution.

Design patterns are, in principle, technology-agnostic. This way they will remain relevant when the technical implementation or software changes. In some cases, however, it may be necessary to include specific technical details, depending on the nature of the concept being explained. It is advisable to keep the design patterns as detailed as possible without introducing technology dependencies where possible.

Examples of design patterns are the listing of essential data logistics requirements, handling logical deletes, key distribution, and managing temporal or time-variant information. Design patterns can also apply to specific methodologies, for instance loading contextual data in a Data Vault solution.

Solution patterns

Solution patterns provide highly detailed implementation-specific documentation. They are software and environment specific by their nature.

If design patterns explain the purpose and general operation of a concept, solution patterns focus on the execution for a given technical environment. A single design pattern may be implemented in multiple ways, each documented as a solution pattern. As such, solution patterns detail the precise 'how' for implementing a concept within a particular technology stack or infrastructure configuration.

The underlying reason is that specific implementation choices may be necessary to get the best results for certain software or infrastructure configurations.

What may work well for one database, may require a different approach in another. This may be because of functional limitations, or because certain applications have certain strengths and weaknesses that can be catered to.

We don't advocate a single approach for everything, but instead suggest this separation between the 'what' (design patterns) and the 'how' (solution patterns), so that each investment in technology can be leveraged to the fullest extent possible.

Pattern structure

The structure for both design and solution patterns follows a standardized format:
- → A title, the name of the pattern
- → The purpose of the pattern, containing a concise statement what the pattern aims to achieve or explain. What is the intent?
- → The motivation, a brief overview of the background and relevance of the pattern. Why is there a need to document this pattern? This complements the purpose, which is more holistic in nature, by providing practical context
- → The applicability of the pattern, providing an outline of scenarios where this pattern can be expected to play a role
- → The structure, the main section with the pattern details
- → Implementation guidelines, highlighting any references or considerations to how to apply this pattern. Note that the solution pattern is intended to explain the specifics in a technical context. For design patterns this is meant to capture any general topics worth mentioning
- → Considerations made, and consequences discussed, as part of the pattern definition. This is meant to offer some alternative views and experiences as to what it means to take a certain decision, as well as providing transparency in decision making for future designers
- → Related patterns, any references towards further reading and related content

We would like to explore our website for a freely available set of design patterns and solution patterns: https://dtng.link/squmh.

An overview of the data solution design

When describing the architecture for the data solution following the principles and objectives outlined earlier, the first point to note is the division into three distinct layers that define the solution at a high level of abstraction.

These are the *staging layer*, the 'core' or *integration layer*, and the 'access' or *presentation layer*.

When data flows through the solution, it will always pass through these layers. This could be in the form of a physical data copy from one layer to another, or an interpretation or transformation thereof (virtual).

Having multiple layers is generally associated with increased complexity in the data solution. The more layers are defined, the more data, the more objects, and the more metadata is usually required to manage the solution.

Multiple configurations can be defined in which some layers and areas can be considered optional. When we position our reference architecture, we will explain which combinations of layers can be implemented to minimize the overall complexity in relation to the functionality they provide — options and considerations.

The basic direction of data is as follows:
1) Data is loaded to the staging layer with the purpose of bringing the data into the data solution environment. This layer focuses on connecting to the data sources, accurately replicating the data, managing data differentials (deltas), and archiving. The staging layer can be deployed independently of the other layers
2) Data is modeled and integrated in the integration layer. This layer focuses on mapping the data against the information model, and correctly storing the history, relationships, and context
3) Data is prepared for consumption as part of the presentation layer. In the presentation layer, the information is optimized for upstream use cases, such as reporting or analytics software

Any mention of 'data movement' can both mean physical moving or copying of data, or a virtual interpretation or calculation used to present data in a certain way.

Each layer is sub-divided into two distinct *areas,* displayed in the diagram below.

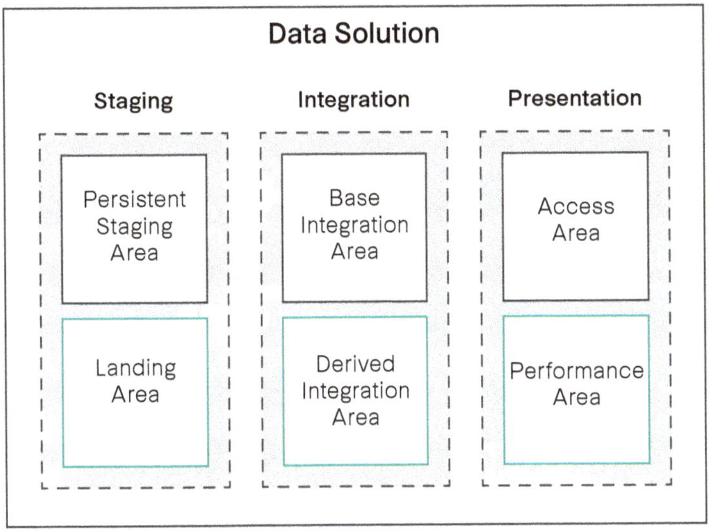

We will outline the details, functionality and purpose of these layers and areas further in this chapter.

Rooms

One of the main reasons to adopt a collection of layers and areas is to separate concerns, and to provide a logical organization of functionality within the data solution.

It can be helpful to think of the data solution as having 'rooms' which focus on a specific capability.

Using this metaphor, the data solution has a 'back room' where the intent is to ensure robust ingestion of data and safekeeping for further processing. *Everything* in this room is geared towards ensuring that everything 'just works.'

This focus on reliability is reflected in many aspects in this part of the solution, for example by using large (accommodating) data types, removing constraints such as foreign keys, and prevention of NULL values.

The way the back room is intended, data is not judged on the way in to the system. This will happen later – in the 'front room' of the solution.

The front room is where interpretation, transformation and (preparation for) delivery takes place. This is the consumer-facing part of the solution, with the intent of making fit-for-purpose data available in downstream applications, such as Business Intelligence platforms.

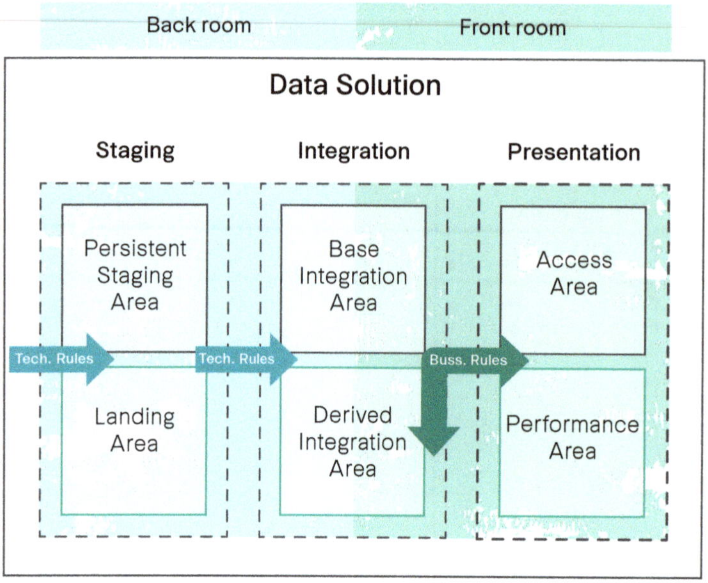

As shown in the diagram, the division between the back room and the front room runs through the middle of the integration layer.

The staging layer is entirely part of the back room, and therefore plays a role largely focused on making sure data reliably enters the data solution environment.

The integration layer spans both rooms, and looks after both safely reorganizing data, as well as applying 'business rules' to apply interpretations.

Lastly, the presentation layer is entirely part of the front room — fully focused on fit-for-purpose delivery of data, and generally making this accessible to downstream processes.

Technical and business rules

The diagram also introduces the terms technical rules and business rules, which ultimately define the split between the back room and the front room.

Technical rules are non-destructive transformations, which means that applying these does not fundamentally change the essence of the data. It is possible to revert back to the previous state of the data when a technical rule has been applied.

Examples include renaming attributes (columns), or changing data types to a larger format. Technical rules are often applied to reorganize the way data is stored in the data solution without altering the contents. Another example is changing data into a (standardized) target domain format, such as changing data from integer to decimal.

A common design pattern involves restructuring data around defined objects, types, or subject areas. Depending on the selected data modeling technique, these can referred to as for example 'core business concepts' in the integration layer, and 'facts and dimensions' in the presentation layer.

Technical rules can act as a router in this sense, since data from a given staging layer object may be directed to multiple target objects. In these cases, it is possible to reconstruct the original data set assuming the lineage is still available, which is usually the case when automation and code generation have been implemented.

Business rules, on the other hand, are considered *destructive* transformations — albeit in a positive sense. Once applied, it is not possible to revert the data to its original state, as these rules fundamentally alter the data.

Examples of business rules include aggregations of values and similar (complex) calculations. For instance, after calculating and storing a total (sum), the individual values contributing to that result are no longer accessible unless they are explicitly retained.

This only applies when the original values, as received from the operational system, are no longer available in the underlying data. In our architecture, we recommend to always maintain the original values so that business rules can be re-applied when understanding progresses or requirements dictate this. One of the reasons to define the 'split' between the front- and back room right in the middle of the integration layer is to highlight that both the original values as well as the calculated values can coexist in the same solution.

An overview of common technical and business rules is provided in the below image.

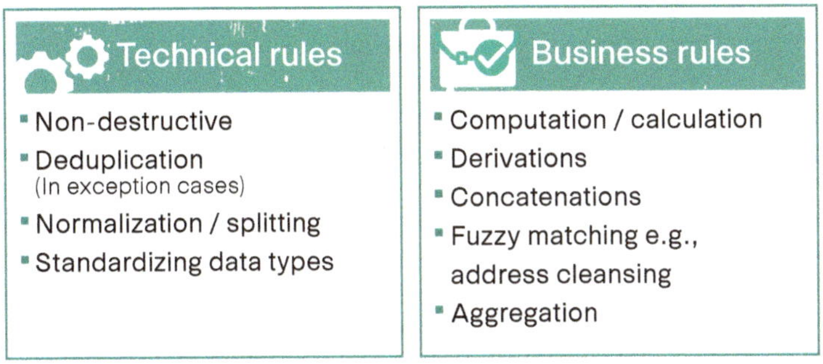

Note that the implementation of deduplication as a technical rule requires special consideration. Deduplication is the process of eliminating rows where there is no difference across all values —the entire record— compared to the next record in a certain order. Typically, this evaluation is performed in the order records are received from the operational system.

Applying deduplication should be treated with care, because the reason duplicate records occur can either be of a technical or functional nature.

For example, the data solution could receive duplicate rows because of suboptimal interfaces or change data capture processes. For this technical reason, implementing deduplication logic can be a way to remove redundant rows early which were erroneously created, and have no business value.

However, receiving duplicate records may also highlight flaws in the underlying systems and processes, which *could* be valuable to be aware of and track.

These are decisions that are primarily made in the staging layer, when defining the interfaces that make data available to the data solution.

A first full overview

Before we explore the staging layer in more detail, we would like to provide a preliminary overview of the reference architecture, so that we can call out specific features when we cover each layer in the subsequent sections.

In the diagram, the flow of data is visible from left to right, from various data sources into the data solution.

On the left side of the diagram, the interfaces between the operational systems and the data solution are depicted. The delivery of information for various downstream use cases is visible on the right side of the diagram.

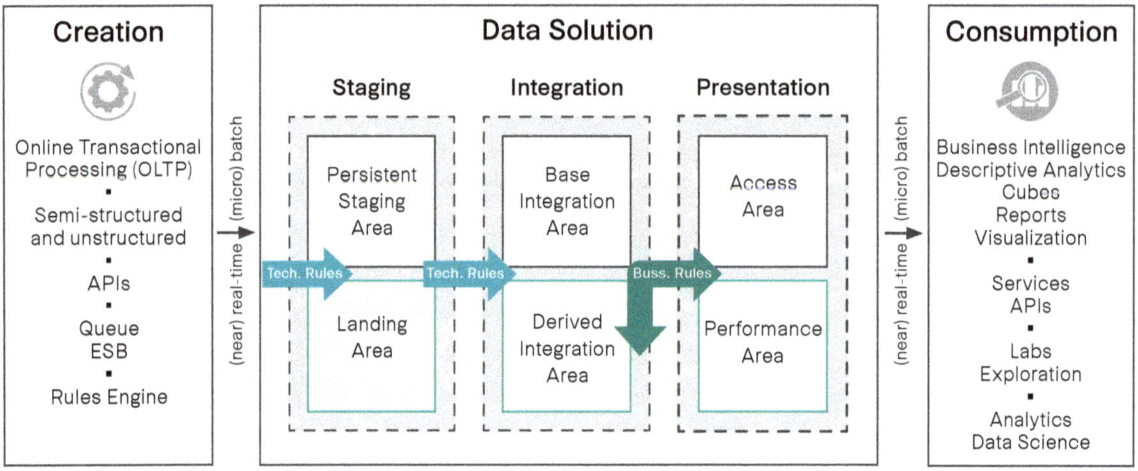

Making the most of the infrastructure

A last, but important, note is that the definition of areas and layers does not limit the use of available technical infrastructure. Different technologies can be used interchangeably across all layers and areas of the architecture when it make sense to do so.

You could implement a staging layer using a file storage configuration, use a database implementation of the integration layer, and subsequently deliver the data using views in the presentation layer.

Or, you could develop the staging and integration layers in a file-based parallel compute setup, and only deliver the presentation layer in a database. Different technologies can be even used *within* a layer or area.

The rationale is to make the most out of available infrastructure, and focus on the management of the data solution metadata and data logistics patterns to facilitate automation and code generation.

We are convinced that the real intellectual property of the data solution does not necessarily lie in the implementation of the data logistics processes, but in the design metadata required to generate these — so that it is possible to generate similar outputs for different technical environments if and when this becomes appropriate.

This is the topic of the ⚐ metadata, automation and code generation chapter later in this book. For now, we will keep the option open to use different technologies and platforms knowing that we will be able to replace these at some point in the future — when necessary or desirable.

The staging layer

↗ The purpose of the staging layer, which contains the landing area and the persistent staging area, is to collect the data from the various operational systems into the data solution environment, and prepare it for further processing.

The first layer in our reference architecture is the staging layer, which is divided into the *landing area* (LDA) and the *persistent staging area* (PSA).

The purpose of the staging layer is to collect the data from the various operational systems into the data solution environment, and prepare it for further processing. In other words, the staging layer is responsible for the physical movement of data from any external platform onto the data solution platform.

This may sound somewhat mundane, but this layer provides some important building blocks that are needed to ultimately deliver the objectives of the data solution.

The staging layer is possibly the most challenging layer to implement. The reason for this is because here the interfaces between the —often many— operational systems are defined, and each system is likely to have specific options and limitations to consider. These interfaces make the data available to the data platform.

Because of this, the staging layer is most likely to require scenario-specific implementation decisions. In contrast, the integration and presentation layer are fully under the control of the data solution, which means that there are far fewer external factors to consider.

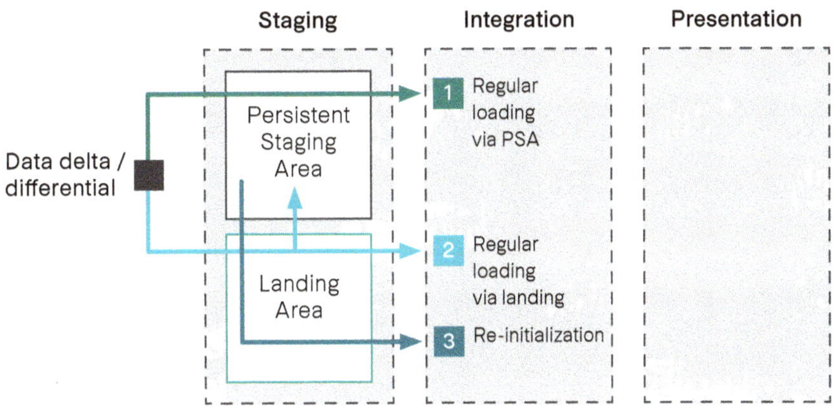

The above diagram provides an overview of the staging layer, highlighting that data can be loaded into this layer in a few configurations depending on how the LDA or PSA are implemented.

First, we will outline the objectives and requirements that shape the staging layer design. We will finish this chapter explaining the options and considerations when it comes to moving data through the solution.

Areas of the staging layer

The staging layer consists of two distinct areas: the LDA and the PSA. However, it is not always necessary to explicitly implement both areas.

For instance, you could design the solution to load data into a PSA directly, or, omit the PSA altogether and 'stage' data in an LDA first before loading it into the next layer. The decision should be part of the tailored solution architecture.

Later in this book, we will explore examples of these configurations —including their advantages and disadvantages— in the ⚐ example architectures section.

Landing area

The LDA is non-persistent and volatile, meaning that data is only retained until it has been successfully processed downstream. Therefore, the LDA is continuously emptied and reloaded with a new data delta – it is *transient.*

This is often referred to as a *truncate & insert* mechanism.

In many data solution designs, the LDA is the first step in the overall process of data logistics. In this configuration, this is where the 'source' data is loaded into the data solution environment. Having an LDA often can be convenient to prepare batch files for further processing, and to assist in deriving delta data —for example by implementing a snapshot comparison mechanism— so that inserting this into the PSA and upstream processes becomes easier.

If an LDA is not implemented, data is either directly loaded into a PSA, or even the integration layer.

Persistent staging area

A PSA can loosely be defined as an insert-only time-stamped administration of all original transactions that have been presented to the data solution by interfacing with operational systems, ordered by time of arrival.

The PSA is an optional area within the staging layer, but strongly recommended.

Being an *insert-only* area, no information is ever deleted or updated. This is how the PSA provides an historical record of all data that was ever presented to the data solution in its raw form.

Having a PSA allows you to refactor your downstream designs by being able to reprocess the events (transactions) and 'replay history' in a deterministic way. Reprocessing events —reinitialization— simply means running the input through the (updated) logic again, in order to recalculate the output.

The PSA is an important component in virtualization, disaster recovery and re-initializations if parts of the data solution have to be reloaded.

It often is a relatively easy concept to implement. After all, it is only a matter of making sure received data is stored as-is for further processing.

Generally speaking there are two ways to approach PSA design, regardless of the choice for the technical platform.

These approaches are:

→ Stacking – receiving and storing snapshots
→ Delta based (transactional) – receiving or deriving the data differential

In our reference solution design, the delta-based PSA is our recommended approach as this offer the most flexibility and scalability. By designing the PSA with this delta based transactional view, we are closely aligned to the concept of the application-readable (transaction) log as introduced in the ⚐ world of data chapter.

This approach will enable a data solution that can operate fully in parallel, where each data logistics process can run continuously and independently. This is easy to manage, flexible and still guarantees data that is consistently delivered – a concept we refer to as *eventual consistency.* This is covered in detail in the ⚐ getting the data in chapter.

There are many ways to develop a PSA from a technical perspective. A PSA does not need to be implemented as a set of database tables. A PSA could just as well be a streaming technology topic, or subscription, or an archive of files – or any mix thereof. Due to the relatively simple structure of the PSA it is often straightforward to migrate the PSA to a different platform – such as from file based to a database or vice-versa.

Objectives and requirements for the staging layer

The work to deliver this begins in the staging layer. In our reference design, the staging layer supports the following functionality:

→ Agreeing on data interfaces
→ Determination of the data delta
→ Recording the data origins
→ Setting the inscription timestamp
→ Logging the record order
→ Setting the source timestamp
→ Evaluating logical deletes
→ Streamlining data types

↗ In the staging layer, the goal is to ensure that all data that enters the data platform is *sequenced, time-stamped[25], time-ordered, and identifiable with respect to its origin.* This is important for a deterministic, flexible and reliable data solution.

These features are intended to be implemented in the *first point of entry* in the data solution. This is typically either the LDA or the PSA, depending on the exact configuration of the solution (see example architectures for the most common use cases).

This means that if an LDA is used, the associated data logistics processes and interfaces must implement the functionality outlined in this section. And, if an LDA is *not* implemented but the PSA *is,* then this applies to the data logistics processes that populate the PSA. It is also possible that the entire staging layer is omitted, in which case the same applies from the interface to the integration layer (or even presentation layer).

As with all layers and areas, all data logistics processes should be integrated to the data logistics control framework through the Audit Trail Id.

To facilitate this the physical staging layer structures are designed with the following properties below:

→ There are no constraints. Data is disconnected, meaning that *no RI is enforced* in the staging layer. Any foreign keys, unique constraints or similar, exist in the data these are recommended to be removed. This is yet another 'back room' feature designed to enhance reliability, as any constraints in place will risk preventing data from entering the data solution. This also means that all attributes are in principle *nullable*
→ The staging layer contains the raw data, the original transactions as they occurred with no business logic is applied

This applies to both the LDA and the PSA.

These features are designed with the back room concept in mind. There is no judging of the data, and everything is aimed at making sure data can be captured with the least possible amount of risk that something goes wrong.

We want the data solution to be as welcome to new data as possible.

Agreeing on data interfaces

An important objective of the staging layer is defining *how* data will enterthe data solution environment.

Often, the options for developing a data solution are limited by external factors. These can be organizational or technical in nature, but all complicate the delivery.

Nowhere in the solution design will this become more apparent than in the staging layer, because we will have to deal with potentially many systems, platforms, organizations, and technology – all of which are external to the data solution, and on which we are dependent to receive the data.

Creating interfaces between operational systems and the data solution is often the first time these limitations become apparent – especially when the operational systems deliver data to the data solution (a 'push interface').

Operational systems may not be forthcoming on clarity when it comes to the data they can provide. Imagine an operational system delivering this data:

820152	320	10000	2024-01-12	T

This is not very helpful because this lacks any context. Ideally this data is (at least) supported by a header which shows the names of the columns that label each data element.

Person	Processing Run	Amount	Date	Status
820152	320	10000	2024-01-12	T

Column names give us a bit more information, but can still be ambiguous.
Is this the monthly pay run for employees?
But what happens when the following data is added:

Person	Processing Run	Amount	Date	Status
820152	320	10000	2024-01-12	T
820152	320	9000	2024-01-12	R

Is this a correction, or an adjustment? Should both values be added to each other? How come they share the same date, if this is indeed a correction? Or maybe the time-stamp isn't precise enough to include a different time? What do these statuses mean?

What if the column names are slightly different, does this change our interpretation? Would we look at this data differently?

Convict	Processing Run	Commissary Balance	Date	Status
820152	320	10000	2024-01-12	T
820152	320	9000	2024-01-12	R

To avoid misalignment on expectations, it is helpful to agree on the details of the data interfaces for each individual operational system. This can be done in the form of a data interface schema.

Data interface schema

Part of the data interface is the schema definition, or simply 'schema.' A schema provides a description for the data that is transferred for the data set as a whole and each component in particular. For example, when a database table is described, the schema would include the table and its columns.

↗ A data interface is a contract, an agreement between the data solution and each individual operational system. Its purpose is to understand and clarify options, limitations, and ways of organizing physical data access and transfer upfront.

To clarify, the term schema is adopted from the application development and integration world. A schema contains the specifications of the data elements. This includes the constraints and structure, so that this can be used by other systems to exchange information – by adhering to the schema definition. This is not the database term 'schema' which can mean different things depending on which database technology you use.

For the purposes of this section, data access and data transfer are used interchangeably. Physical movement of data is an option, but so is transforming data in streams or through direct access. For the purposes of agreeing on an interface, these can be considered similar.

The template for a data interface schema is one of the design patterns that comprises the solution design. This means that every interface should be considered and documented the same way.

A data interface should contain the following elements:

→ An explanation of how data transfer is initiated, and by which party. Is this an interface where the operational system 'pushes' the data, or does the data solution 'pull' the data?

→ A schema of the data and its definition. This should contribute to better mutual understanding, avoiding potential misinterpretation

→ The definition of the delivery techniques used. Is data provided as flat files? Is an API or endpoint available to connect to? Is there a direct database connection? Is change data capture middleware an option?

→ An explanation of how a *range* of data can be selected. For example, can both data delta be accessed as well as the full history if required? Can a date range be specified? Is an identifier available that can be relied on for delta selection – *guaranteed* to be reliably incremental and immutable?

→ An understanding of the granularity of data that is exposed. What is the unique identifier for a record? Is this aggregated information or are the raw values made available as they are available in the operational system database?
→ An explanation of how logical deletes can be evaluated
→ A definition of the expected frequency and schedules
→ A definition of the source timestamp. What information can be used to assert the moment of change in the data?
→ Any expectations on delivery service levels. What are the availability expectations and what happens when something goes wrong?

To sufficiently understand the data, a logical model of the interface data can make all the difference in the world. As the previous example shows, a file itself may not mean much in isolation.

Data interfacing mechanisms

Data interfaces can be incoming or outgoing, and this is true for interfaces related to the data solution as well. In the context of the staging layer, we specifically cover *incoming* data interfaces. These interfaces make data available in the staging layer.

A key component of an incoming data interface schema is defining the mechanism for actual data access and exchange between the operational system and the data solution.

How can data be retrieved or received?

Making data available for further processing in the data solution is limited to committing data in the staging layer. Any further processing, including the definition of data delta, is not in scope for now.

There are many ways for systems to interface. At the end of the day, data is either made available somewhere by the operational system (pushed) or actively selected by the data solution (pulled) — which is where the 'push' or 'pull' terminology originates from. Within these generic terms there are various variations, some of these very subtle.

The next section highlights some of the most common interfacing mechanisms — serving as options to consider when agreeing on how to obtain the data for further processing.

These can be seen as variations of either push or pull mechanisms, and in some cases can be implemented both ways.

Push mechanism

A push interface is viewed from the perspective of the operational system, where data is 'pushed' out of the system towards a location accessible by both the operational system and the data solution.

The advantage of this approach is that (performance) impacts of the extraction process can be managed by the operational system itself. The data solution can't access the data directly, so will not be able to negatively impact the day-to-day operation of the operational system. Also, the responsibility of making sure the interface *keeps* working when the underlying system is modified is clear: this lies with the operational system.

Many push mechanisms do not cater for logical deletes, although this is in principle something that can be developed with the right combination of technology, time, budget, and mindset. It is worth making sure this is covered when defining the data interface schema.

When implementing push interfaces, our recommendation is to implement a separation between the output of the operational system and the ingestion into the data solution database tables, such as in the LDA. This means that the data files can be stored on disk (i.e., using flat files as intermediary), following the schedule implemented by the operational system. The data solution can then ingest these files on its own schedule.

This way, the data solution can control when new data delta is loaded into the solution. Flat files are often used for this type of separation and isolation, because they can be archived or simply added to a directory without immediately impacting the data available in the data solution. This is one of the reasons why flat file exports, such as comma separated value (CSV) files are ubiquitous for this type of interface.

Using flat files provides an opportunity to (securely) archive the received files. This can provide additional auditability to the data solution, as well as the ability to reload the original data. It is also possible to use the archive itself as LDA. The LDA is not limited to a single technology, and can be a mix of tables and files, depending on the interfaces used.

Various file storage systems provide features to add new files to an existing container, and access this for further processes — effectively making this a staging layer.

A key downside of using flat files is the loss of metadata that occurs, especially if data is exported from a database only to be imported into another database later. However, this also depends on the technical implementation because some (compressed) file storage technologies also incorporate the 'mask' — the column names and types.

While it is possible for a push mechanism to write data directly into the data solution LDA (if this is implemented using database tables), this is not recommended. This is because the data solution needs to ensure that the received data delta is fully processed, and allowing external systems to write to the LDA tables creates a risk of losing a data delta due to timing issues. If the operational system writes the next delta before the previous delta has been successfully processed, it may overwrite the earlier delta.

There are alternatives to work around these issues, such as ensuring that the interface can only insert rows (and not update and/or delete), and managing the deletion of already processed data delta from the LDA. Having an operational system add snapshots to the data solution's LDA is an example of this — where the data solution archives snapshots that have been processed correctly. However, this adds a layer of complexity that may not always be desirable.

Pull mechanism

A pull interface is driven by the data solution, as it 'pulls' data from the operational system at will, or following an agreed upon schedule.

Using this mechanism, the data solution has direct access to certain tables, views or similar in the operational system. This could be achieved by implementing a database link, direct access using a connection string, or using an open database connectivity (ODBC) connection.

This allows for a certain degree of flexibility for the data solution to self-select the appropriate data.

The main advantage of this approach is that it is usually easier for the data solution to select either a data delta, or a full extract. Moreover, the data solution can direct the frequency of when data is received. And, it is possible to do so without involving the operational system.

Since the data solution directs the interface, it can also control how, when, and where the data is handled. This can be an advantage compared to the push mechanism.

The potential performance impact associated with direct access to the operational systems needs to be considered. Sometimes, ongoing data retrieval may prevent users of the operational system to properly access the system. This is because a data pull may lock certain data sets until the transaction is completed. In other cases, the process may consume an amount of resources (i.e., CPU, I/O) that could be noticeable —even prohibitive— for users of the operational systems. A lot of this depends on the operational system's technical infrastructure, including the transaction isolation configuration of the underlying database and available resources.

It is for this reason that resource governance restrictions are typically agreed when adopting a pull mechanism. For instance, by only allowing the data solution to pull data outside office hours or only a limited amount of times a day. Alternatively, it may be possible to agree on a 'hot stand-by,' a live copy of the operational system for data interfacing purposes.

Because a hot stand-by is not used normally by users there often are fewer restrictions on data access for data extraction and integration purposes.

In all cases, we recommend recording this as an agreement in the data interface schema definition.

Another disadvantage of a pull mechanism is that making an adequate selection of data requires a good understanding of the operational systems, and its inner workings.

For example, it may be possible to select a data delta based on an incrementing value in the source such as a timestamp field or sequence. However, it should be ensured that these values are indeed incremental, and cannot (easily) be modified. It is rare to find a data point that is *reliably* immutable and sequential. And even then, this mechanism will not detect records that were deleted – an issue to meet the evaluating logical deletes objective. To work around this, both push- and pull mechanisms often implement a full outer join equivalent that runs periodically to 'mop up' any data changes that were missed by the regular interface.

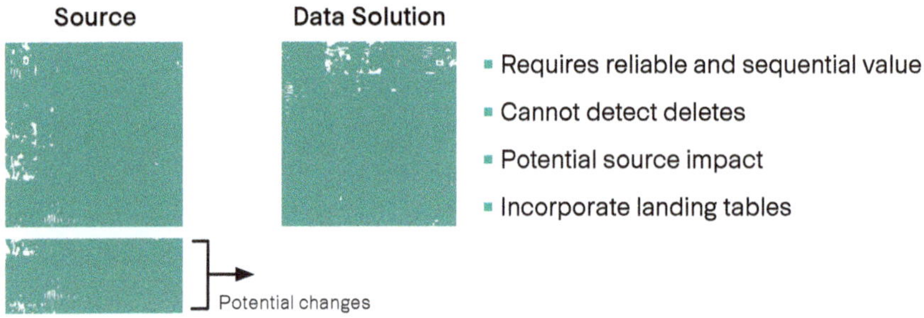

As this kind of interface is operated by the data solution, the ownership to ensure correct functioning lies here. This introduces a risk when the underlying operational system introduces changes, for example by modifying the table structure, but neglects to inform downstream consumers of their data in a timely manner.

Full outer join

The full outer join (FOJ), or full comparison, is the 'brute force' of data interfaces. This mechanism can be thought of as a specialized 'pull' process, because this is driven by the data solution. This can be applied to a specific object, a group of objects, or the system as a whole.

Using this mechanism, a full comparison between *all* data in the operational system, and the most recent state in the data solution is performed, to evaluate the change rows.

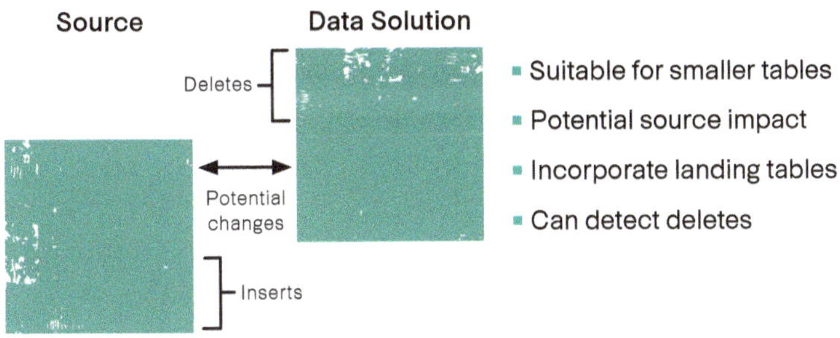

The most recent state is usually the order of arrival, so 'most recent' is according to the time of arrival – which is the inscription timestamp. Technically speaking, this is the record for a given key which has the most recent (highest, max) inscription timestamp.

In most cases such a comparison is performed against a PSA, but it is also possible to keep the previous snapshot of data in the LDA when a PSA is not part of the solution.

The resulting data delta can be saved in the landing area for further processing, or directly committed to the PSA.

From here, the data —now a data delta— can be used for downstream processes. Performing this comparison once in the staging layer prevents executing this (performance expensive) comparison operation multiple times when loading data into various integration layer target objects.

Application Programming Interface

An Application Programming Interface (API) is a set of rules and protocols that allow one system to interact with another, enabling the exchange of data or functionality. It provides the language that let you interact with other services from your own environment.

APIs can be accessed programmatically, or through special-purpose adapters to receive data in a pre-defined, often well-structured format.

From a data solution perspective, APIs can be considered a special form of a pull mechanism. Although it is also possible to develop APIs as push mechanisms, this is uncommon. Most APIs are designed to support interoperability with multiple consumers without requiring the operational system hosting the API to track or manage individual consumers.

Many larger software vendors provide APIs that allow consumers —including data solutions— to interface with operational data, and integrate it into various processes. Although APIs can support a wide range of functions, for a data solution, data retrieval is the primary focus. If the option is available, accessing data through APIs is often a desirable approach.

One of the benefits of using APIs is that the schedule can be dictated by the consumer. Calls to an API can be made often, and as needed.

APIs also provide an abstraction layer between the operational system and external consumers, which means some of the complexity that may exists in the system can be 'hidden' by the API. For example, by standardizing data types, choosing user-friendly naming conventions, or combining data from various locations.

This way, logic that otherwise would need to be implemented in a data solution is often already addressed in an API. This can be very helpful – even if it only saves joining a few data sets together.

The abstraction layer also provide additional guarantees that changes made in the operational system won't directly impact the consuming applications – including the data solution.

APIs are often developed in a way that supports backwards compatibility, by offering more than one concurrent version of the same API. This gives consuming applications time to switch over to the new version.

Despite their advantages, there are potential limitations to consider for using APIs as well. APIs are often not particularly flexible when they need to be extended, and often require IT development to do so. Missing from the API data exchange format —such as reference codes needed for linking data sets— may become a blocker.

Another point to clarify is whether the API allows you to select a range of data, and to what extent this process is deterministic. Especially initial loads can be difficult to implement, and may require multiple calls with prohibitively limited data ranges — even requiring custom coding (pagination) to handle this.

Change Data Capture

Change data capture, or CDC, can at times be a contentious topic.

In this book, we distinguish between 'technical' CDC and 'logical' CDC. Technical CDC focuses on detecting changes in data records, whereas logical CDC is more concerned about correctly asserting the state of a business concept — is it active or not?

Logical CDC is covered later in this book. In this section, we refer to technical CDC whenever 'CDC' is mentioned.

For the staging layer, CDC is most relevant, as this concerns correctly interfacing with operational systems to receive data delta.

In its most basic form, CDC is a mechanism to detect if a record has been inserted, updated (changed), or removed (deleted). Typically this is provided as the record at the time of detection (i.e., with all the values present at the time of detection), and an additional attribute ('flag') containing the CDC event — indicating an insert, update or delete.

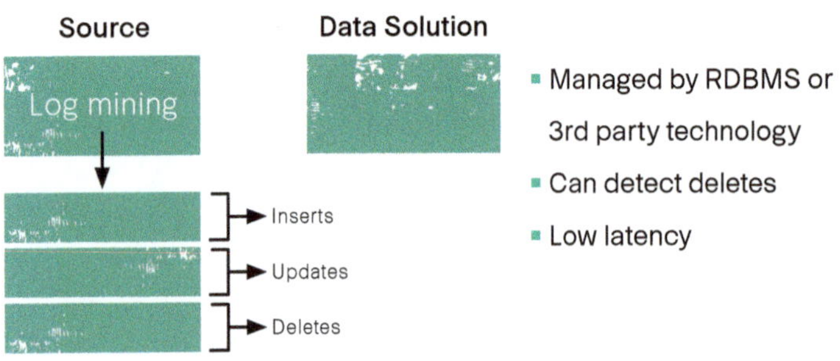

CDC technology is available natively in some relational database management systems (RDBMS), and also available as middleware software. The term CDC can be interpreted differently depending on the context, as it covers a wide variety of techniques, concepts and solutions.

CDC can be implemented both as a push- or pull mechanism, but the pull variant is more common. In this configuration, native CDC detection is applied on the operational system, or a production-like copy (e.g., hot stand-by, near real time synchronized version etc.). Detected changes are recorded in tables that are made accessible to consuming systems, including the data solution. Change data can be selected from there as needed.

An example of push CDC is often found using specialized middleware, as agents that operated autonomously of the operational system and data solution.

These agents detect changes in systems (usually by monitoring system transaction logs) and can push them to various subscribers — including the data solution. In slightly different configurations, changes can also be buffered for central access — effectively transforming the mechanism into a pull solution again.

Subscription

Subscription-style interfaces include the more traditional service-bus or message queueing solutions. They also include native (database) technologies, that enable replication of transactions. Examples of this are real-time transactional replication features, or asynchronous functionality such as log shipping.

In these solutions, events are published by operational systems and 'sent' to a message bus (or equivalent infrastructure). Depending on the configuration, the message bus delivers the message to all subscribed consumers. These consumers will then translate the message to the proprietary format using their own adapters.

The concept of 'replication' can be classified as a subscription mechanism in this sense. Replication allows certain records to be 'sent' to subscribers when certain events are triggered.

Replication is often implemented in tandem with CDC, with replication being in place in a hot stand-by instance of the operational system, and CDC being the listener for data changes.

Many service bus/message queue solutions, offer 'inbox' functionality (buffers) to record messages, even though the processing of these is delayed or organized in a batch fashion.

The data solution can implement its own adapter that receives messages from the message bus. The main consideration to make is how to receive the initial load of data. Messages are often transactional and typical have shorter 'time-to-live' (TTL) before being removed. It is recommended to consider functionality to manage latency issue — as well as catch-up processes in case events are missed.

This may sound somewhat over-engineered but we have seen many cases where transactions were missed due to network problems or otherwise. It is our recommendation to periodically run reconciliation (full compare) processes to understand any divergences between the operational system(s) and the data solution that may appear.

Streams and pub/sub

Publication/subscription (pub/sub) mechanisms, including streams, are specialized adapters or middleware solutions with similarities to APIs and traditional messaging subscriptions. The key difference is that a pub/sub mechanism will continuously 'stream' events to an endpoint that can be accessed asynchronously.

Much like an overview of banking transactions, events are continuously added to a list that can be viewed by authorized consumers.

Events are transactional and immutable. Once an event is generated, it is never updated. Any changes made in the operational system trigger the creation of a new event rather than modifying an existing one.

For the data solution, this means that events can be accessed for further processing in various ways, and on schedules driven entirely by the data solution. Because event streams operate in near real-time data can be pushed into downstream processes directly, or managed by batch processes.

Pub/sub mechanisms are often implemented as middleware to allow different systems to connect, modify, combine and re-publish data. The data solution can be one of these consumers, and will have to implement a specific connector for this which is managed by the data solution itself.

The TTL for each pub/sub stream or topic is usually configurable by the platform, but is rarely infinite. This means that data must be accessed within a certain time period, or it will no longer be available for processing.

Incorporating business logic in interfaces

When integrating data across systems, one approach to consider is implementing the complexities of joins and business logic in the operational system and its (outgoing) interfaces, rather than handling them within the data solution – or any other consuming party for that matter.

This concept aligns with the principles of API design, since an API natively provide an abstraction from the operational system, and may include transformation logic so that the operational system can provide data in a predefined way – though not necessarily so. This approach can be applied more broadly: by ensuring that the operational system takes ownership of complexity in its data provisioning, the downstream usage of the data can often be greatly simplified.

In this configuration, the operational system manages the implementation of the necessary logic, and the data solution simply ingests the prepared data.

The data, as it is stored in the operational system, can be difficult to access. It might be 'spread out' across many objects and could require many joins and interpretation to piece together. This kind of complexity is often implemented as 'application logic' in the operational system: internal procedures that combine the data into what users see on their screens. When accessing the raw data, these are all tasks that must be preformed by the data solution.

This is the difference between accessing data directly from the operational system's data stores and asking the system to provide dedicated export tables, files, or APIs that perform the initial 'heavy lifting.'

Not only is this much easier for data consumers –including the data solution– but it also clarifies ownership. The export feature becomes an extension of the operational system, and should be managed by its support team – as opposed to leaving the responsibility for data integration with its consumers.

These export objects can be interfaced with any of the mechanisms that have been covered in the previous sections. And any meaningful preparation can be included in these interfaces, including complex business logic.

However, if any changes are required these must be requested to the operational system, which might result in delays depending on how changes are prioritized. This can be significant, because any implemented business logic may contain interpretation issues and might need to be adjusted over time.

Additionally, for many systems it is simply not an option to provide a feature like this. It might be not technically possible, not allowed, or may involve IT development that is either too costly or takes too long to complete.

We believe that, where possible, this conversation should be had to ensure that operational systems take as much ownership as possible to provide 'the right data' and complexity is implemented where it makes the most sense to do so.

Determination of the data delta

No matter how data is provided by, or received from, the operational systems, the staging layer aims to derive a data delta, or differential. This is the distinct set of changes compared to what is already available in the data solution, also referred to as change records. The defined data delta can be temporarily stored (staged) in the LDA until fully processed and/or committed to the PSA.

As outlined in the ⚐ data interface mechanisms section, the way data is made available to the data solution highly depends on context and capabilities of the operational system.

Irrespective of the interface used, the intent of the staging layer is to record whatever data is made available as-is, without alteration.

Depending on how the data is obtained a delta may either be already available, or must be derived.

For example, if the operational system provides a full extract of a data set each time then it is possible to calculate the differential by comparing the incoming data set with the most recent state available in the data solution.

This comparison is usually performed by using a technical CDC pattern. This may be a FOJ against the PSA, because this area typically has the same structure as the incoming data set. But this can also be implemented by various other technical CDC solutions.

In the former approach, an LDA table may be used to stage the full data set to facilitate comparison with the PSA. This comparison can have the following outcomes:

1) If a record exists in the incoming data set, and not in the PSA, it is considered a new record ('insert')
2) If the record exists in both the incoming data set and the PSA, and the contents are different, it is considered a change record ('update')
3) If the record does not exist in the incoming data set, but it does exist in the PSA it is evaluated as a record that has been removed from the operational system ('delete')
4) If the record exists in both the incoming data set as well as the PSA, but the contents are the same, there is no change and the record can be disregarded

An advantage of this approach is that it is possible to determine deletes from the operational system. Scalability may be an issue, however, depending on the volume of the data.

When using a pull style interface, a direct comparison between the operational system and the PSA will achieve the same outcome – but may not be feasible due to performance impacts these queries may have on the operational system.

When operational systems support a CDC-capable interface, the delta of transactions that have occurred are already available – including logical deletes. In this case, these records can be processed directly to the PSA and upstream layers.

In a delta-based approach, only the changes that have occurred in the operational system are persisted. This means that every incoming transaction is appended to the existing data, which usually is in the PSA.

This approach is closer to the original concept of a transaction log, or application-readable log, that records every mutation and thus allows representation of the state of each object by following the transaction over time (replaying history).

In all cases, the determination of the data delta is something that is implemented in the interface and part of the data interface schema documentation.

As a note, if the interface allows for it, it is also an option to store the full data set as received by the operational system as-is. This is referred to as a *snapshot*.

Snapshots and deltas are variations of the same theme – two sides of the same coin. As approaches they are conceptually interchangeable and it is possible to derive a snapshot from an existing (history of) data delta and vice-versa.

Receiving and storing snapshots

Snapshots are full copies taken from a data set, such as a file or database table, at a given moment in time – usually the current state when the data set is prepared or extracted. This moment in time is referred to as the *snapshot time-stamp*. The snapshot contains everything from this table as per the snapshot time-stamp, including any historical data that may still be present.

This snapshot can then be appended in its entirety to the corresponding PSA table or file, and remain identifiable from earlier snapshots by the snapshot timestamp. We refer to this mechanism as *stacking*, as it essentially comes down to piling full copies of the data sets on top of each other.

It is advisable to separate the snapshot date from the inscription timestamp, and store these as separate attributes. This enables having a fine-grained audit trail that distinguishes between the timestamp for *receiving* the data, from the point in time this snapshot represents.

This is important because with larger data sets there may be a noticeable timing or latency difference between the snapshot timestamp, and the moment when the data has been committed to the PSA, the load timestamp.

And, worst case, if the same data would be committed multiple times then both copies can be conveniently distinguished this way. This could happen when issues in the orchestration happen, if the process has been run out of order, or simply twice or more.

Considerations to make regarding which snapshot approach to choose are with regards to weighing scalability versus convenience. Copying and committing the full data sets each 'run' may not be feasible or scalable when it comes to larger data sets. Potential demands for an increase the overall data refresh rate can trigger a (partial) redesign further down the line.

Another point to be mindful of is that snapshots do not manifestly capture logical deletes. However, these can still be derived by comparing each snapshot to its previous one.

An advantage the snapshot approach does offer, is that it is a relatively simple way to represent the state of data at distinct points in time —the snapshot timestamp— during processing and delivery.

This is because for the same snapshot timestamp all data across all tables is available for easy joining. This may negate the need for complex timeline math to join the right data at the right points in time, or at least dramatically simplify this. Timeline math is something that will be covered in depth in the integration layer and presentation layer implementation chapters, but applies here as well.

The downside of this approach is that there is a limit on how often the data can be refreshed, as this needs to be done for all data sources across the data solution. The typical use case for this approach is to implement a daily data refresh this way, or possibly a few times per day.

Storing the data differential

Regardless of whether a data delta is directly available or a snapshot is implemented, the data needs to be stored for further use. Referring to the overview of the staging layer functionality, this can either be done in the LDA or the PSA.

The LDA is typically used to derive data delta for the interfaces that require this, and then subsequently commit the change records to the PSA. This is a delta-based PSA implementation that relies on the LDA to guarantee a flow of transactions.

Downstream processes, such as data logistics towards the integration layer, can either be supported from the LDA or the PSA. Our recommendation is to use the PSA as the source for these processes because this simplifies scheduling and timing later on. This will be explored in detail in the getting the data in chapter.

Recording the data origins

As part of the audit trail, a reference to the originating operational system and table or file needs to be stored with each change record. This means that every record in the data solution can be identified as to where it originated from.

Recording the origins of the source data is part of establishing an audit trail, and this begins in the staging layer of the data solution.

The objective is to make sure that *every* data set or record is identifiable as to which operational system made the data available to the data solution.

In many implementations, the record origins are managed as part of the data logistics control framework. This can be helpful to optimize resources (space) and also to reduce complexity. In these implementations, each record will contain a pointer to supporting metadata managed in the data logistics control framework. This metadata typically includes interface and run-time details, but can also include the record origins.

Since each record should contain a pointer for the full audit trail anyway, it often makes the most sense to record the record origins as part of the control framework metadata. This way, only a single attribute is required to satisfy these requirements.

Other approaches may include storing a string value identifying the operational system in each record, or its numeric equivalent.

Record origin details can later be used to identify certain patterns in natural/business key behavior, and are part of the audit trail that ultimately contributes to establishing trust in the data.

Setting the inscription timestamp

In our reference solution design, a 'current' timestamp value is added to each record when it is initially committed to the data solution. This will become the foundation for the *assertion timeline* during data delivery.

Setting the inscription timestamp means that a timestamp (date and time) value is added to each record the *very first time* this record enters, and is committed to, the data solution environment.

When implementing an LDA as part of the data solution design, this is the place where the timestamp value is added to ('stamped on') each record as it comes in. If a PSA is implemented without an LDA, then the PSA is where this functionality is implemented.

An inscription timestamp is simply a value containing a timestamp that logs when the record was first detected in the data solution environment. This is often implemented by a default value, such as a system-generated timestamp value of the current coordinated universal time (UTC).

Because records are written into the environment in an essentially sequential (though not deterministic) manner, the inscription timestamp value will always be incremental. We recommend implementing the inscription timestamp attribute with the highest precision settings for the data type, so that a very specific time of arrival of the data can be recorded.

The inscription timestamp is *not* the start of the data logistics process. This process metadata can be retrieved from the data logistics process control subsystem, if required.

If it is desirable to record the start timestamp of a process (either individual or workflow/batch) for each record, we recommend also storing the per-record inscription timestamp as well, so that a unique timestamp value for every single record remains available.

The resulting inscription timestamp provides a detailed audit trail of when data was received by the data solution, and it enables deterministic refactoring of the data solution.

Logging the record order

In addition to time-stamping the moment of entry in the data solution, a sequence number is added to each record in order of arrival. This is necessary for enforcing deterministic behavior and *uniquification* later on.

The *inscription record id* is an additional framework attribute in the staging layer that records the order of arrival in a continuous stream, or within a process. The purpose of the inscription record id is to log the order in which records arrive in the data solution.

The loading of records into the data solution is incremental in nature, and always unique – at least theoretically. However, this may not always be visible in the inscription timestamp values alone. Many systems have limitations in the precision of the data type that is used to store the inscription timestamp, and if it's too course some details may be lost. The speed at which records arrive can be so high that even high precision data types —such as DATETIME2(7)— may not be able to distinguish between subsequent records, and multiple records for the same key may occasionally receive the exact same inscription timestamp. In this scenario, the inscription timestamp values in neighboring records (i.e., that arrived one after another) may be identical.

It may be a good problem to have: loading data too quickly. So quickly that, even at high precision, multiple changes for the same key are recorded with the same inscription timestamp.

In these cases, the inscription timestamp values provide a rough indication of the order of arrival. This can be made more granular by adding the inscription record id.

The inscription record id is an incremental (sequence) integer value, that can be set as a default value or provided by a sequencing object or data integration function. In data logistics processes with a distinct start and end, e.g., transactions or batch processes, the sequence is reset each time the process ends. In this case, the inscription record id will provide information of the order of record arrival within a specific process execution, always starting at 1.

In a continuous or stream process the sequence value must be reset at given intervals.

Adding an inscription record id ensures deterministic processing to downstream targets, which is a key requirement for refactoring and reloading of (parts of) the data solution. This attribute will play a critical role in supporting uniquification in case of inscription timestamp values being so close that the difference gets obfuscated because of insufficient precision.

For instance, by adding this inscription record id to the primary key of context entities, this order of loading can still be retained even when there is no difference in the inscription timestamp — guaranteeing deterministic data retrieval and processing.

The Structured Query Language (SQL) —the most widely used language to query data— is not deterministic by design. It is up to the data solution to maintain the order of data and guarantee deterministic outcomes.

Whether this scenario might occur depends on the interfaces that load data into the staging layer. Some interfaces, such as a FOJ approach, can't deliver multiple changes each time the interface is run. Other interfaces, however, would.

Many transaction-log based Change Data Capture (CDC) technologies, for instance, create a 'buffer' of change records which can be periodically retrieved and committed into the data solution.

Changes accumulate over time in this buffer, and when the data solution retrieves these change records they could be inserted into the staging layer in bulk. In this scenario, multiple changes for the same key may be loaded back-to-back in a short timeframe, even if they originally occurred at different times in the source system.

Extending the primary key to include the inscription record id is our recommended approach to manage the 'fast loading' issues.

Setting the source timestamp

The source timestamp is an additional metadata attribute which *may* be required in later steps. The source timestamp captures the moment the change record was altered and committed in the operational system — if this information is available. This is a very specific attribute, because it is not factually part of the data set received from the operational system. Instead, it is defined in the interface agreement and may need to be derived as part of the CDC mechanism. An example is the timestamp in a file header, or the modified or created timestamp. Another example is the point of snapshot comparison using a full outer join process.

The source timestamp is the moment a change occurred in the operational system, or the closest proxy to this if the exact moment in time is not available.

For instance, native transaction log mining CDC —as available in some database platforms— can provide a very accurate timestamp for the moment a user changes a value and commits the change to the database.

This is because the timestamp that this type of CDC provides is the transaction log entry timestamp itself! As soon as the value is committed the very entry into the database is recorded, by the RDBMS, and available through the transaction log. This is as accurate as it gets.

In contrast, most push and pull mechanisms only provide the moment when the extract is run e.g., the time of extraction or evaluation. There can be a significant time gap between the moment the change was committed in the operational system and the time of extraction, but in some cases this simply is the best option available. Each interface mechanism has options and limitations when it comes to asserting the source timestamp.

When it comes to defining incoming interfaces in the staging layer, the goal is to pick a reliable source timestamp which is as close to the 'real' moment of change as the interface mechanism allows.

Reliable often means 'system generated,' or in other words, a timestamp value that is not likely to be influenced by human operators.

The inscription timestamp and the source timestamp are two essential pieces of metadata that should be added to the data solution. Both of these points in time have an important role to play later in the delivery of data, and its interpretation.

These timestamps are added to each record in the data solution, and it is important to note that all other attributes —including any timestamp attributes— are considered regular data (context) and should be loaded as-is.

Evaluating logical deletes

In the staging layer, the data solution should try to identify if a change record was triggered by a *removal* of the record in the operational system. This information is added to the record as an identifier or flag such as 'delete.'

If a record has been deleted in the operational system, it is possible to detect this, i.e., the event of deletion, and mark this with a special attribute – a deleted record indicator. In the data solution this value identifies that a record has been deleted from the originating operational system.

This is referred to as a *logical delete.* The 'logical' wording stems from the fact that the resulting record is technically an *insert* in the data solution, derived by SQL logic (or equivalent), one that captures that a delete event has occurred in the source.

In other words, the record is available in the data solution in its most current state, but classified as a deleted record. This means that the data solution contains a history of events even when any of the original data may no longer be available.

Logical deletes and Change Data Capture

A deleted flag can be stored as a separate attribute, which is added to the record it refers to. However, in most cases this data is stored in a CDC attribute.

This is because the mechanisms necessary to detect if a record has been physically deleted are typically built-in, or at least part of, CDC functionality. A change to a record can be an 'insert,' 'update,' or a 'delete,' and this evaluation can be stored in a single CDC attribute – making a separate 'logical delete' flag superfluous.

There are many ways how CDC can be implemented e.g., how inserts, updates or deletes can be detected.

A CDC flag refers to the *full* record, as it was in the originating operational system, 'full' as identified by its primary key. This is an important note to consider in the integration layer, because if the original record is remodeled into potentially various other tables, the CDC data cannot always be applied without further context.

This is covered in detail in the ⚐ getting the data in chapter.

This view of defining CDC as a mechanism to detect new, changed or deleted records based on their original structure is a fairly narrow —though useful— technical view. This technical perspective on CDC typically is how CDC is implemented in the staging layer, including the PSA.

In most cases, native CDC technologies provide the state of the record (i.e., all the values) at the time of delete so this creates a clear state of up to which point certain values were active.

CDC can also be defined as part of a broader, more complex, approach to evaluate the correct context of business concepts or business keys in an information model. The terms 'business concept' and 'business key' have not been introduced yet in this book as they are part of the integration layer, and in the context of CDC these can be used interchangeably. This concerns the logic to define the correct state of a business concept (e.g., 'customer' or 'product'), including whether it should be considered active or not at any given point in time.

This line of thinking we've introduced as 'logical' CDC earlier in this book, as opposed to the aforementioned 'technical' CDC. Logical CDC is usually implemented in the integration layer.

Why is recording logical deletes helpful?

Recording logical deletes helps to guarantee that the data solution will remain in sync with the operational systems from which the data was received. If we can't detect that data is removed from operational systems, how can we ensure that the information the data solution delivers is an accurate representation?

A key acceptance criterion for a data solution is its ability to audit and represent information as it appears, or appeared at some point in time, in the operational systems that provided the data. If you open up a screen in the operational system and view current clients, sales or customer details you would expect to see this information the same way in the reporting figures the data solution supports.

Recording CDC data, including logical deletes, supports the ability to do this. Another interesting use case is low level monitoring and even fraud detection.

The PSA records all incoming transactions ordered by their time of arrival in the data solution. By storing the technical CDC information it is possible to query if certain records (keys and their context to be precise) are removed from the system, or even (re)added and removed multiple times.

Operational systems may claim that data is never deleted, so it can be interesting to investigate why in some cases this somehow *does* happen.

Streamlining data types

As one of the many features to improve reliability, data types can be defined to be more accommodating storage-wise. For example, using larger data types (for text) or higher precision (for decimal values).

Operational systems can be different in many ways. Some of these differences may be related to the utilization of specific technology, or are simply due to specific design choices that were made when the operational system was developed.

Because of reasons such as these, there is likely to be a large variety of data types and formats in which data is presented to the data solution. For instance, numeric values may be presented in sometimes exotic data types such as 'money,' 'real,' or 'float.'

In the staging layer, we intend to streamline these data types to a limited set of options. This means that the data from the operational system is mapped to standard data types and formats.

Not only are the possible data types limited in the staging layer, they are also configured as large data types. A *large* data type or format includes making sure that timestamp information is stored in a high precision format, numeric values can contain large numbers, and textual data is stored in large text fields.

This design decision is in the spirit of the back room concept, because this makes the staging layer as accommodating to new data as possible. This way, the data solution is more isolated from change; certain changes in the operational system do not impact the data solution.

For example, if the data in the operational system is defined as a VARCHAR(3) and the format in the data solution is also VARCHAR(3) for this attribute then a change to VARCHAR(4) will directly impact the data solution. Instead, if the data solution defines a VARCHAR(MAX) for this data it will not make a difference[17].

The standardization of data types facilitates easier management of further data processing, for example towards the integration layer, simply because it provides standards that can be relied on. This itself also contributes to the reliability of the overall solution.

These are examples of *technical rules.* While the data is loaded into a potentially different data type or format in the staging layer, no alterations or transformations to the data contents are performed. It will be possible to reverse this step, if necessary.

The attributes that are directly controlled by the data solution, such as the *Audit Trail Id,* the *inscription timestamp,* and the *source timestamp,* can be treated differently. There is no external way to modify these values, so full accountability to configure this properly lies with the data solution.

Code pages and character sets

A separate topic on standardizing incoming data is the decision how to physically store and encode the data. To reduce the chance of technical errors and, again, to make sure the data solution is as welcoming to new data as possible, it is recommended to consider a Unicode character set such as *UTF-8* or *UTF-16.*

UTF-8 will be sufficient for most applications, and reduces the overall storage (by half) compared to UTF-16.

This can be a pitfall for early revisions for the data solution, as the operational systems that are connected first may not require this. However, it will become a problem when an operational system is integrated that *does* utilize Unicode. This is why, as a reference architecture, we adopt Unicode as default.

The same line of thinking applies to collation as well, with *case-sensitive* and *accent-sensitive* configurations recommended. This is yet another component of future-proofing the data solution.

Some operational systems may not be configured as case-sensitive, but some are, and this can become a problem if the data solution is not configured to support this.

In these systems, the value 'Abc' may mean something different than 'ABC' and it is important that the data solution can distinguish between these values. Imagine if this is your business key!

Streamlining the data types, formats, and means of storage, provides many options to make sure data from existing and future operational systems can find a good, flexible, and welcoming home in the data solution.

The integration layer

↗ The integration layer manages the complexities involving transforming data into an integrated system of record. It consists of the base integration area and the derived integration area.

Where the staging layer is all about providing a robust foundation for the data solution, the core purpose of second layer of the reference architecture —the *integration layer*— is to manage the complexities involving transforming data into an integrated system of record.

The integration layer is sometimes referred to in different ways, for example as the 'core' model, the 'central transaction repository,' the 'system of record,' the 'Data Vault,' or any combination or variation thereof.

In all cases, the purpose is combining incoming data into an integrated model and manage the many complexities involved in doing so. This is achieved by providing distinct and modular features for important processes within the data solution — separation of concerns.

The staging layer has leveled the playing field for data processing through standardization and looked after the hard part of getting the data into the solution, and it is the job of the integration layer to combine these disparate data sets into an information model.

Without an integration layer, all tasks required for data delivery in the presentation layer must be handled by a few large and complex processes. The integration layer simplifies this by serving as an intermediate step, resolving complexities in a generic and efficient manner. Key concepts include the generation and assignment of surrogate keys, managing history, and defining relationships between data sets.

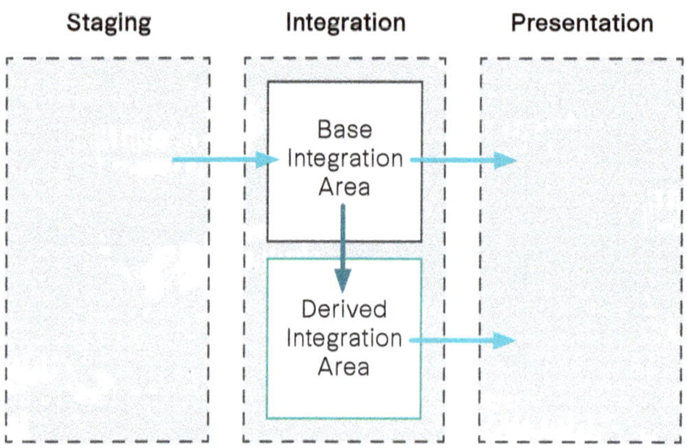

This layer consists of the base *integration area* and the *derived integration area.*

The delineation between these two areas is also the separator, or handover, between the front room and the back room of the architecture.

Areas of the integration layer

The *base integration area* still contains the 'raw' data, but now mapped against the business entities that make up the intended, target, information model. This is still considered a back room process.

The *derived integration area,* however, contains interpreted data to which business logic —including destructive transformations— have been applied. Together, the base- and derived integration areas form the information model.

For example, it is common to have both a raw and derived data set describing the same object or event. If the object is a 'product,' then the raw context for this product could contain attributes or properties such as 'name,' 'color,' and 'production period.'

The derived information, which can be drawn from various sources, could add additional context to the product such as for example 'variable gross margin,' 'classification,' or 'lifetime value.'

A key feature of having an integration layer is that these derived interpretations can be re-created using the available raw data. This combination of the base- and derived integration areas provides the data solution with a flexible mechanism to apply common business logic without losing the ability to change the interpretation. The 'raw' data will always be available in the base integration area (and the PSA, if adopted).

The derived integration area is not necessarily a full copy of the base integration area's data. Typically, derived integration tables will *contribute* to existing base integration area entities tables and provide an alternative perspective.

In many implementations, the ratio of base versus derived integration is approximately three to one. This is because often the remodeling of the data to the target model removes the need for further transformation, simply by aligning data that logically belongs together.

This often referred to as *passive integration,* and is covered in more detail in various sections that cover business keys.

Base integration area

The *base integration area* is the place where data from the staging layer is first remodeled into a data model intended to represent the organization in a holistic way – the information model. The data in this area remains largely in its original raw form and no destructive transformation are applied. No content is irreversibly altered.

This is done by assigning data sets to information model entities, such as the previously mentioned 'product,' that is not specific to any of the operational systems. The source-to-target mapping from the incoming staging layer data to the information model creates a first build of the core data solution.

This area sits firmly in the back room of the solution. It offers the flexibility of presenting the data in more than one way while the original data remains unchanged. Because the original data is retained, and therefore traceable, this approach also facilitates a high degree of auditability.

Derived integration area

In the base integration area, the data is mapped to the information model to the extent this is feasible without fundamentally changing the data. This provides a 'raw' view of the data in the shape of the target model without any transformations applied.

While this is a big step towards completion of the data solution, in many cases specific interpretation is necessary to properly align the data to the information model. To a large extent this is done in the *derived integration area.*

The derived integration area implements logic that is necessary to finalize the information model, and may irreversibly change the nature of the data by doing so. It is an augmentation to represent data in a way that is not readily available in the operational systems, by applying specific interpretations – referred to as transformations or 'business' logic.

These are typically destructive transformations, because only the result of the transformation is recorded in the derived integration area.

An example is an aggregation of values. If you summarize a series of value and store the outcome, it is not possible to derive the original atomic values just from the sum.

By design, the original values are still available in the base integration area and, if implemented, in the PSA but conceptually the transformations of data are part of the derived integration area. Because of this, the derived integration area is the first area that is part of the front room of the solution design.

The intention of the derived integration layer is to avoid replicating transformation logic downstream. For instance, formatting of addresses where abbreviations such as 'st' or 'rd' get expanded to 'street' and 'road,' or the validation of phone numbers.

In separating the state of the data into two physical forms (original and modified), it provides the flexibility of applying multiple sets of rules to a specific data set, in order to suit specific needs.

Examples of reasons to do so are:
→ Data cleansing
→ Data enrichment
→ Data standardization
→ Deduplication
→ Validation
→ Exception handling

Where is business logic applied?

The intent to simplify data management by reducing replication of logic does not mean that *all* business logic is implemented in the derived integration area. This can also be implemented in presentation layer processes.

There is an art to this more so than a science, but a guideline is that business logic in the derived integration area is often *organization wide.* This means that the outputs are used in *many* downstream processes (as opposed to just a specific data mart).

Essentially, the derived integration layer implements that what is necessary to represent the main parts of the intended information model in the best possible way. The presentation layer can facilitate deliveries of information that are specific for the intended consumer.

The main integration layer entity types

There are three main types of entities[18] that make up the integration layer model:

- A core business concept (CBC), which is an entity that identifies the data. A CBC has a clear and unique name that covers the subject, and is identified by its *organization-wide business key*
- A natural business relationship (NBR), that describes the relationship between CBCs
- A contextual entity, that describes the CBC or the NBR. The context entities contain the descriptive information (attributes) and store the historical data

Data is organized against CBCs, NBRs, and context that describes these in the integration layer. These same entity types are used in both the base- as well as the derived integration area.

In the next sections we will provide a brief overview of the most important features of these entities. In the getting the data in chapter we will go into more detail on the specific ways these entities can be used and implemented.

This initial overview will be provided at a *logical level.* Most technical details will be abstracted away so that the focus can remain on the concepts and their purpose, instead of the physical implementation.

The physical implementation of the integration layer can be done in many ways, and using various techniques. We will provide details on implementation decisions later on, in fact, they will cover a substantial part of this book in later chapters.

In some cases, this may mean that the main three entity archetypes as described here are either *combined* (in a 3NF-based or similar deployment), *remain separate* (e.g., Data Vault, Head and Version), or are implemented in the third style as *many smaller physical tables* (Anchor, Focal Point).

Core business concept

Core business concepts (CBCs) embody the 'things' or 'concepts' that are most important for the organization. **Examples of CBCs are:**

- Vehicle
- Customer
- Product
- Shipment
- Pageview
- Location
- Student
- Bike

A CBC is based on an organization-wide business key (referred to simply as 'business key' from here on) defined by business terminology and use – how it interacts with business processes.

The intent is to define a *single* unique business key for each *unique instance* of the CBC. Good business keys are therefore agnostic of the operational systems they are implemented in.

For example, a product can be stored in a given operational system using the 'product id' as primary key. However, the 'product code' could be the term that is used across systems —by the business— to define a unique product.

Selecting the right CBC and business key can be a difficult process. In many cases there are strong similarities in the definition of CBCs across similar organizations, and this is a place where a link can be made to reference, or 'industry,' information models and archetypes such as the involved party, arrangement, item etc.

Regardless of the similarities in CBCs between some organizations —which become stronger the higher the level of abstraction becomes— each individual implementation requires mapping of the data generated by business processes and recorded in operational systems to the CBC entities.

This invariably is a tailored activity, which is different for most organizations. In other words, while similar companies may use similar CBCs, the mapping of their systems and processes to these CBCs will vary significantly.

Identifying core business concepts

The *involved party* has an *arrangement* with *our involved party* regarding a *resource item.*

A statement like this is likely too vague, too ambiguous, to be meaningful for clear communication. What are we really trying to say?

Using very broad or abstract terms as CBCs will not make for a model that is easily understood.

At the same time, saying that the *EFTSL supervisor* has a *preliminary conditional approval* with *AU procurement* regarding a *3-year running FDR,* is probably too specific.

It might be easier to just say that a *supervisor* has an *approval* by *the procurement department* for a *research grant.*

Part of the difficulty in finding the right CBCs is to establish the right level of detail. This is not a trivial question, as finding the right level of detail is essential to build a data solution appropriate for the task at hand.

The 'right level' varies between organizations and use cases.

This becomes apparent when considering how to describe a certain thing or event. Should we define a customer as it's own CBC entity, or should we define an involved party entity which can encompass many types of customers, other individuals (such as employees) and even companies?

One useful approach can be to take stock of how often certain terms are used during the various meetings and workshops, assuming there is an adequate representation of the business to avoid overly technical terminology.

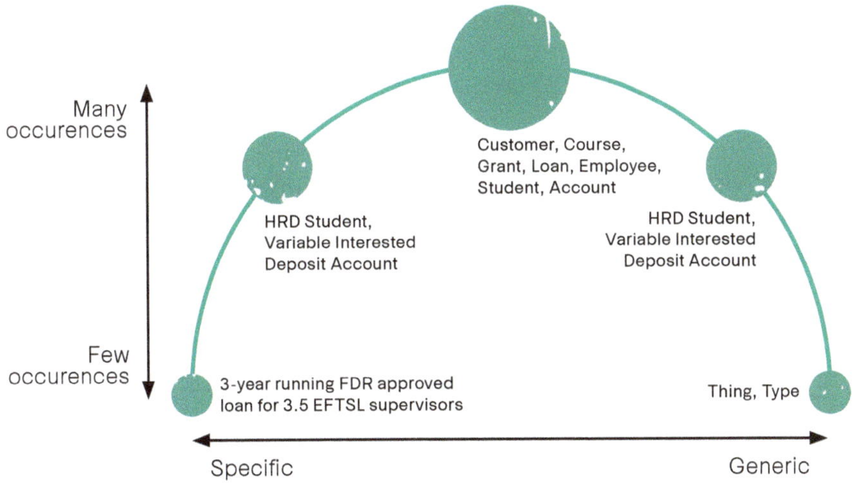

Is the term seldom used, except in a very specific context? If so, it may not be a suitable CBC candidate. The key to success lies in finding a representation of subject matter experts who understand the business well enough to ensure effective implementation. After all, modeling is primarily about communication. If discussions become overly technical, it's important to assess the model in relation to other areas of the organization.

Abstraction — subtyping and supertyping

In the previous example, the term *involved party* is a supertype of a customer. The abstract concept of involved party can cover many (sub)types for various people and organizations.

Whatever the outcome is, a certain level of abstraction or detail is established as a result of defining the CBCs. Consider the image below. Will we define a 'thing,' an 'account,' or both 'credit account' and 'savings account' as specific account types?

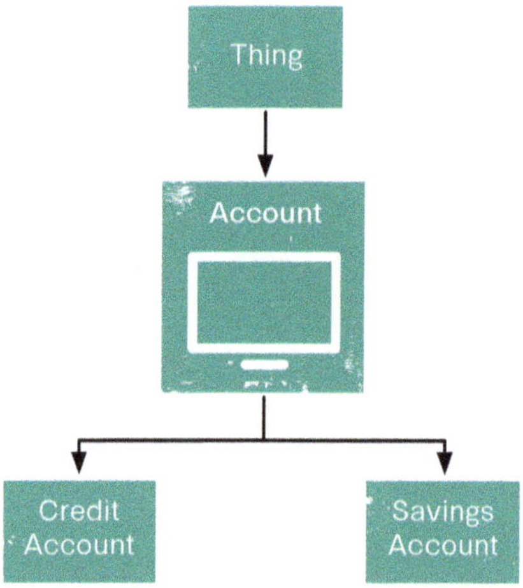

Deciding on the right level of abstraction is often an interesting and engaging conversation with subject matter experts, facilitated by 'whiteboard sessions' and similar workshops. Countless post-its have been used in workshops for this!

For the purpose of defining an integration layer model, we recommend *avoiding* sub- and supertyping in the physical model, and instead being as precise as possible in the definitions.

This means that only the chosen level of abstraction is added to the model. Sub- and supertyping can still be used in conceptual and logical models so that the meaning of data can be explained at a higher level.

One of the reasons we include a PSA in our architecture is that selecting the right CBC and business key is often so difficult and ambiguous. With the PSA, decisions can be reverted into a new and updated version of the model when understanding evolves – possibly with new or modified CBCs and business keys.

The business key

The (organization-wide) business key is the fundamental tenet at the center of the CBC. They are the central 'hubs' around which descriptive or contextual data is gathered.

A good business key:

- → Must have business meaning, and will have this independently of other objects (stand-alone)
- → Allows everyone to talk about the same thing, in the same way
- → Is the ideal identifier for systems and processes across the organization, even though this ideal may not be fully implemented
- → Can be used in natural conversation with stakeholders
- → Is persistent through time e.g., does not change meaning, or is reused
- → Is used in, or interacts with, business processes and is used when describing business events
- → Is based around a common code or term, where it uniquely identifies the CBC across multiple business areas

A business key is known and understood by business stakeholders in the organization. It is not a technical value that is hidden inside operational systems, but a value that is exposed to users in their day-to-day work.

This is why they are sometimes referred to as 'organization-wide' business keys. This is to really drive home the point that these are not technical keys (e.g., system-specific surrogate keys or sequence values), but values that can be found in multiple systems and processes.

Isolating business keys

It can be helpful to consider CBCs and their business keys as independent constructs or entities. This is regardless of physical implementation, though many implementation techniques create a dedicated key table for each CBC, such as the Data Vault *Hub* table.

Having an independent CBC construct makes it easy to add additional data regardless of any existing objects. If a CBC has relationships to other CBCs as well as some descriptive information (context) it is straightforward to 'plug-in' additional context to this CBC – usually from other data sources or derived logic. This is shown in the image below.

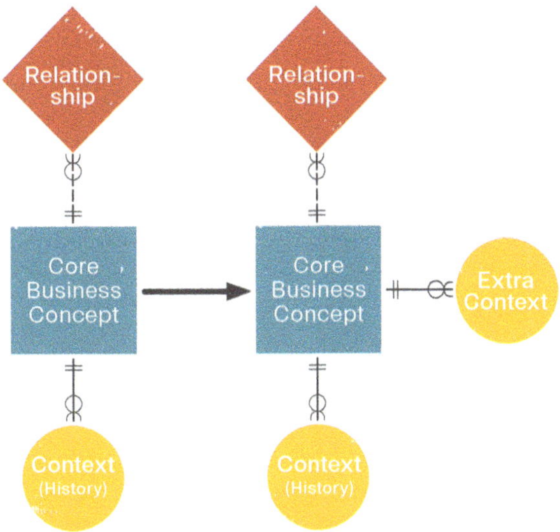

Adding the extra context does not alter the already available context and relationships in any way. This approach is referred to as *decoupling*, and significantly contributes to a reduction of maintenance of the data solution as well as making it easier to refactor.

Another benefit of this approach is that the business keys are identified very early in the data solution, and propagated from there. This make it easier to trace related data throughout the data solution, because all data can be identified by its business key.

This section provided a conceptual overview of CBCs and business keys, but there is much more to cover. This will predominantly be done in the getting the data in chapter.

Business keys and integration, an example

From a more practical point of view, business keys serve as *integration points*. When data from various operational systems is mapped to CBCs and their associated business keys, it implies that the data shares the same meaning.

After all, the data is mapped to the same 'thing.' In such cases, the data modeling itself is a form of interpretation. Consider the following example for a Fast-Moving Consumer Goods company, which involves three operational systems:

1) A Human Resources (HR) application that organizes employee records for each store using *employee IDs*. The central concept here is the *store*, around which the HR team structures its operations and terminology
2) An operations Asset Management System (AMS) application that is focused on building maintenance including lease and general upkeep. Operations staff reference uniquely numbered brick-and-mortar *branches* for delivery and maintenance purposes
3) A finance system to manage the General Ledger (GL). The Finance team uses *account codes* to track expenses and budgets

When it is time for resource planning, the HR team provides operations with an Excel sheet listing the employees and stores related to each branch. This list is not recorded in the AMS system, and is not maintained in the HR system either. This mapping data only exists in the Excel file. HR owns this process, and it may not be widely known.

There is also a daily system interface between finance and operations, developed by IT. This interface ensures that each account can be mapped to a branch. These details are recorded in the operations system as a free-format notes field for reference during cost-attribution discussions with the finance team.

There is no way to relate accounts to stores directly between the finance and HR systems, which makes it hard to manage expenses at a more detailed level.

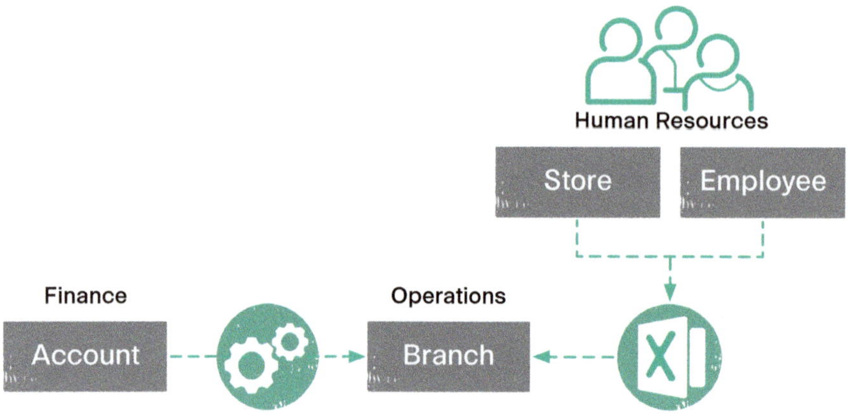

Defining the core business concepts

Depending on the level of analysis, discussions, and workshops, the resulting model can vary significantly – even at a higher level. When systems and processes are considered in isolation, without full awareness of both formal and informal data integrations between them, an initial definition of the CBCs might look like this:

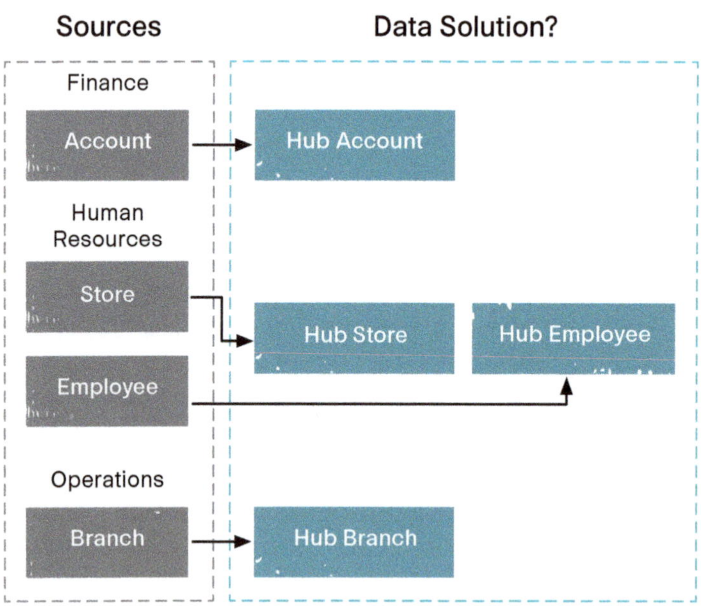

This often happens when a model is automatically generated based on the structure of the operational systems. A technical, 'source-based,' bottom-up approach can profile the available data, including primary keys and foreign key references between the data sets to derive a model for a specific target methodology.

However, this model is created from a technical perspective.

As discussed extensively by experts, the true value of a model lies in defining the key elements of the business —the business keys— and using these to integrate the various disparate data sets.

Investigating the business key

In this simple example, further investigation of the data and interfaces between the systems reveals that the terms 'store,' 'account,' and 'branch' are, in fact, identical in meaning. They are simply different names for the same 'thing.'

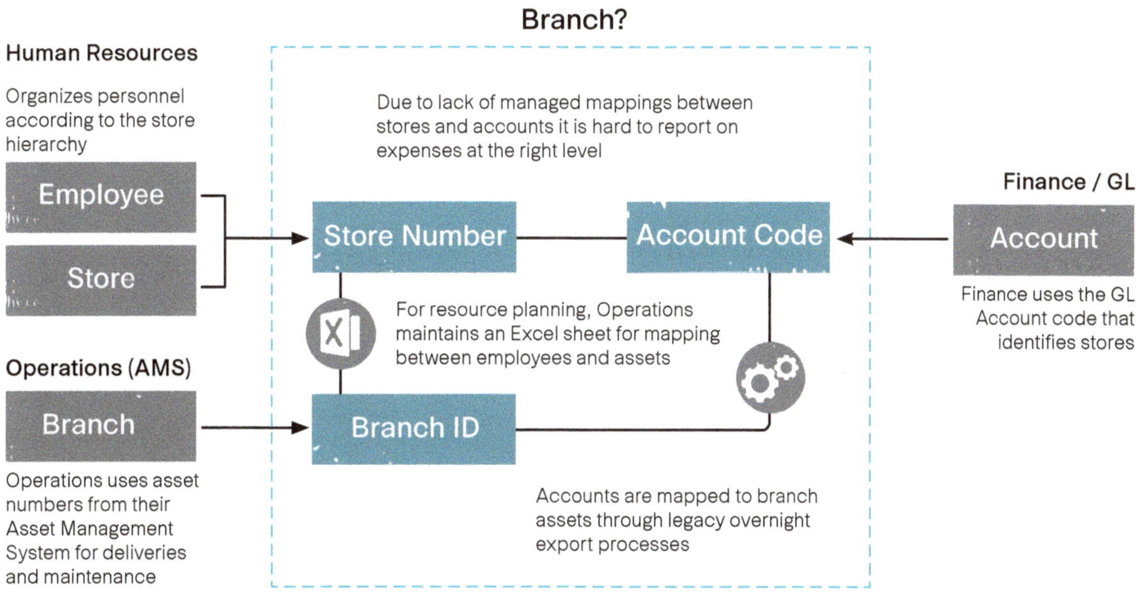

Because these different data points identify the same thing, a more appropriate and generally agreed-upon name can be established. The key values, along with their descriptive context, can then be safely consolidated.

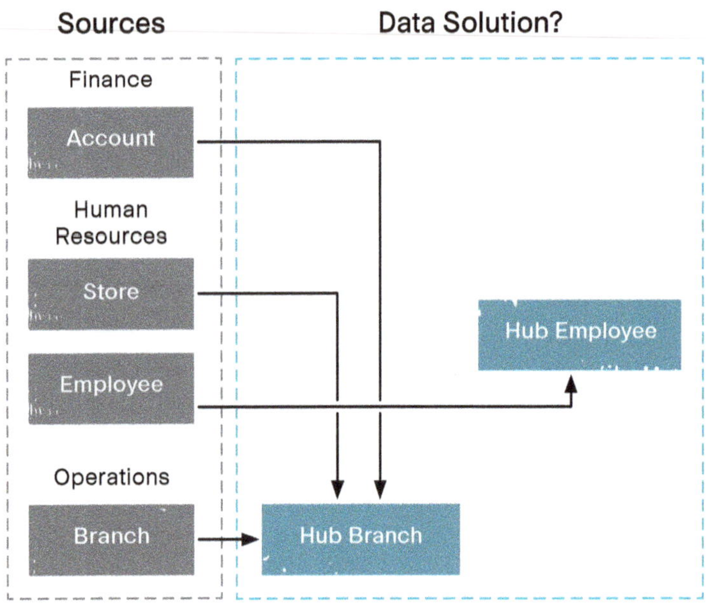

This is called *passive integration.* When data from different sources is mapped to the same CBC, it results in a de facto integration of the involved data sets.

Integration is implied.

In this example, data management has ensured that each system uses the same codes instead of relying on system-specific technical keys. As a result, we have direct access to the business key rather than having to use an internal technical key, which would only exist in one system. Other organizations may have varying degrees of consistency in their data management.

In some cases, additional integration logic may be necessary to connect the data to the business key. This is further covered in the ⚐ getting the data in chapter.

For now, from a modeling perspective, we can assume that the 'account code' from the general ledger system can also be mapped to the 'branch' CBC.

Natural business relationship

A natural business relationship (NBR) represents a connection, a relationship, between CBCs. It tracks interactions between CBCs and by extent the business keys themselves.

A relationship can be established between two or more CBCs, but it can also be a reference from a CBC to itself. In case of a self-reference, the NBR indicates a recursive hierarchy, a chain or similarity, internal to the CBC.

More than one relationship can be established between two (or more) of the *same* CBCs. This is referred to as ⚐ role playing, where each individual relationship between the same CBCs determines a specific role for the relationship.

Similar to how CBCs are essentially distinct lists of business keys and their data solution surrogate key counterpart, NBRs are distinct *groups* of surrogate keys of the involved CBCs. Similar to CBCs, the NBR aligns to business process and business terminology.

NBRs cover relationships only without putting a value judgment on that relationship. It is also independent of time. The intent is to avoid any preconceived interpretation of the nature of the relationship, other than that there is one.

Technically, this implies that these are *many-to-many* (intersection, or, associative) entities.

As with CBCs, data in the NBR is created once, and subsequently never altered.

For example, it may be the case today that an employee only has one manager as part of the organization's reporting line approach. But, in a few months' time, the organization may adopt a matrix-style reporting structure where employees might have multiple managers to report to.

For an NBR, this does not matter. All that is relevant is that there is a relationship between an 'employee' CBC and a 'manager' CBC. For contrast, in a normalized (e.g., 3NF) model this would require a modification of the physical data model.

Examples of relationships in data are:

- Events, transactions (e.g., sale, call, incident)
- Relationships (e.g., product-component, employee-manager, area-region)

There is an important note to make that the distinction between what constitutes a CBC and an NBR is not always clear in the physical model.

For example, a *sale* conceptually is a transaction — a moment in time where different things come together such as 'customer,' 'product,' and 'shop.' Logically, the sale is the business relationship between these concepts.

When it comes to physical data modeling though, there are considerations to make whether this transaction should be created as a stand-alone (core business) concept, or as a separate relationship that binds these concepts together.

This section provided a conceptual overview of NBRs for the purpose of introducing the entity type and its place in the reference architecture. As before, further details will be provided in the getting the data in chapter.

Granularity

The NBR defines the granularity (grain) of the relationship, the level of detail. A key factor to understand the relationships between CBCs and its correct grain is what is called the *unit of work* in ELM.

The unit of work can be defined as a correlated set of data that is designed to keep the data together at the right granularity. Breaking the unit of work into smaller components, multiple NBRs, can cause retrieved data sets to no longer match their original data.

Consider the following example, where products, suppliers, and a categorization are provided together:

Original data

Product	Category	Supplier
Data Design Patterns	Training	Dirk
Data Design Patterns	Training	Roelant
DIY Meetup	Workshop	EngineCorp
Data Design Patterns	In-company	Roelant

NBR - Product by Category

Product	Category
Data Design Patterns	Training
DIY Meetup	Workshop
Data Design Patterns	In-company

NBR - Product by Supplier

Product	Supplier
Data Design Patterns	Dirk
DIY Meetup	EngineCorp
Data Design Patterns	Roelant

When the original data is broken up into two separate NBRs, how can you reconstruct the original data set?

That's no longer possible. By recombining the data, a record will be created that didn't exist in the original data set.

NBR - Product by Category

Product	Category
Data Design Patterns	Training
DIY Meetup	Workshop
Data Design Patterns	In-company

NBR - Product by Supplier

Product	Supplier
Data Design Patterns	Dirk
DIY Meetup	EngineCorp
Data Design Patterns	Roelant

Recombined 'Original data'

Product	Category	Supplier
Data Design Patterns	Training	Dirk
Data Design Patterns	Training	Roelant
DIY Meetup	Workshop	EngineCorp
Data Design Patterns	In-company	Roelant
Data Design Patterns	In-company	Dirk

When implementing NBRs, the goal is to enable reproduction of the original grain. Designing the right granularity, and capturing what the relationship exactly represents is the main challenge when designing the NBRs.

In this example, the data set should not have been broken up, as shown in the below example.

Original data unit of work

Product	Category	Supplier
Data Design Patterns	Training	Dirk
Data Design Patterns	Training	Roelant
DIY Meetup	Workshop	EngineCorp
Data Design Patterns	In-company	Roelant

Link Product by Category by Supplier

Product	Category	Supplier
Data Design Patterns	Training	Dirk
Data Design Patterns	Training	Roelant
DIY Meetup	Workshop	EngineCorp
Data Design Patterns	In-company	Roelant

Role playing

When modeling NBRs, it is often found that multiple types of relationships can exist between the same CBCs. For instance, the relationships between a ‘vehicle’ and a ‘person’ CBC.

A person can have a ‘driver’ relationship with a vehicle, but there can also be an ‘owner’ relationship, among others. The person who drives the vehicle is not necessarily the one who owns it.

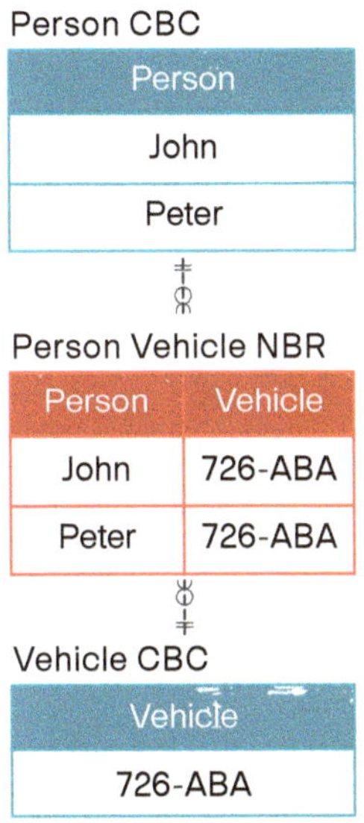

Defining a NBR that connects the vehicle and the person may not be sufficient to accurately describe these scenarios. There needs to be a indication of the relationship *type* in some form.

When a relationship can perform multiple roles, this is referred to as *role-playing.*

To illustrate this, let’s assume that John owns a car (with identifier ‘762-ABA’), but Peter is driving it.

There are two unique relationships between the person and the vehicle, but they mean different things. This model does not provide details on the type(s) of the relationships between the person and the vehicle. Therefore, we must find a way to add the relationship type to the model.

One possible approach —though not recommended by us— is to use dedicated context entities to independently track the state of each relationship type. Assuming that only one person can drive the car at a time, and only one person can own it at a time, this could be implemented like the diagram below.

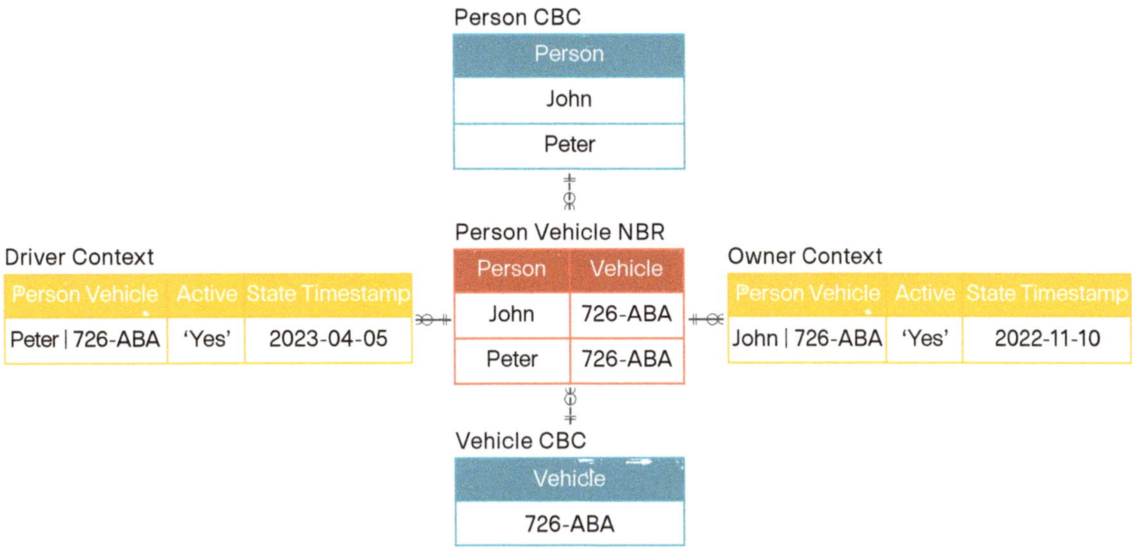

These assumptions are modeling decisions and, depending on the specific situation, this model might be adequate or too limiting. Perhaps it's possible to have multiple owners (or drivers) simultaneously? For this example, let's proceed on the basis that these initial assumptions are valid.

The context entities implement the validity period of each driver or owner relationship state. When a new driver or owner becomes active, the previous state is closed. The details of this mechanism are further explained in the driving keys section.

After a while, Peter decides to buy the car and therefore becomes the owner. This scenario can play out in in various ways. The list of unique relationships is still the same, but the owner context has changed.

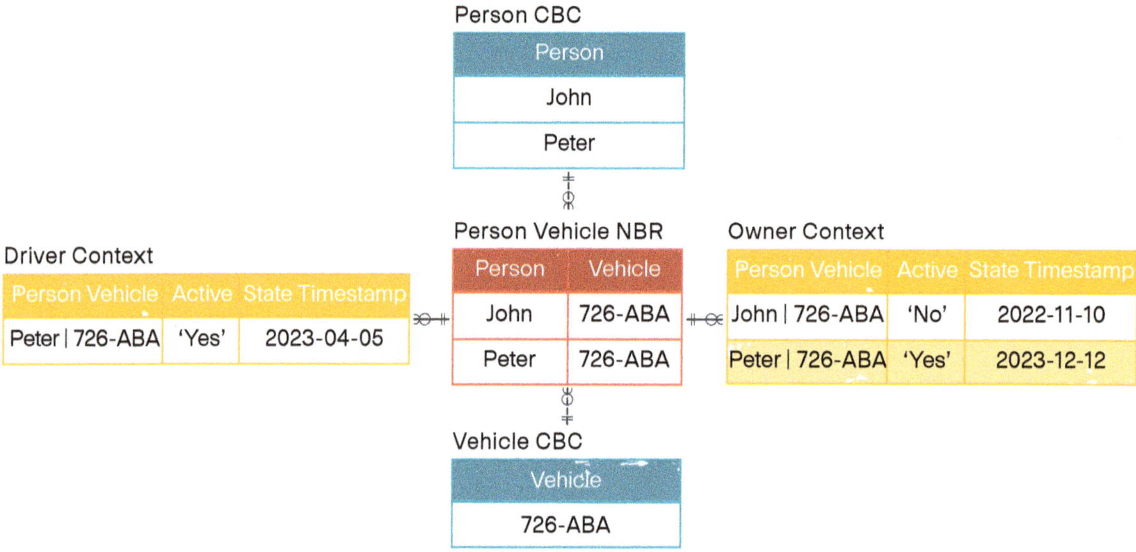

The record where John is the owner is no longer valid from 2023-12-12 onwards. To illustrate this —for the purpose of the example only— the active status is updated to 'no.' In practice, the state would be determined by evaluating which relationship exists for a given point in time instead of physically updating superseded records.

There are various other ways to implement this. For example, we could add a 'type' property to the model, possibly as a degenerate column. The same information is available, just in yet another way.

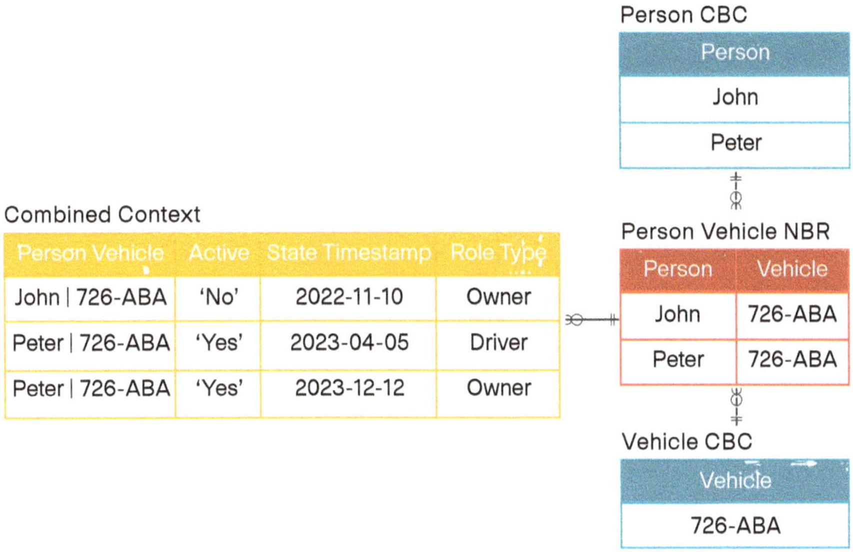

In this approach it's arguably harder to 'read' the model. It is impossible to understand what kind of relationships exist without looking at the data. For this reason, we don't recommend this approach either.

Our preferred solution is to model the relationships as separate objects so that the model clearly describes the available relationship types.

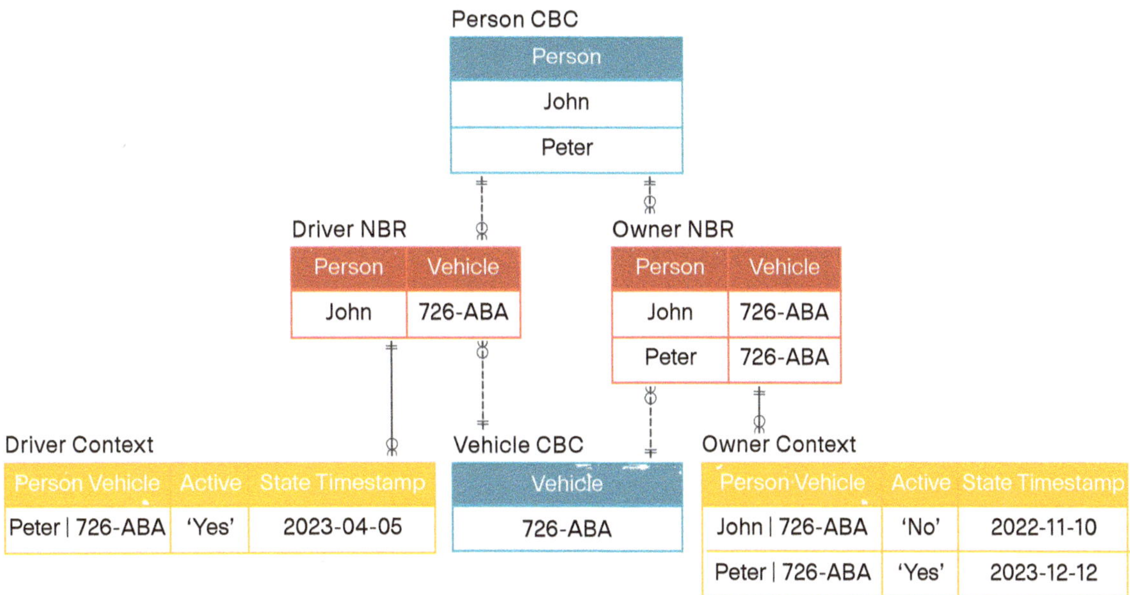

An initial observation is that the overall record count may be higher with this approach. Both NBRs contain some of the records, and there might be cases where the same relationship exists in both NBRs — the relationship between 'John' and '726-ABA' in this example. In the earlier example, a single object would contain all relationship records without redundancy.

However, separating relationships into distinct objects often avoids complicated (and costly) filtering required to select the 'right' relationship. If some relationships are more sparse than others, as is the case with the Driver NBR in this example, this also means that there is a smaller set to work with independent of other relationship objects — which may contain many records.

More importantly, it is immediately clear what types of relationships are available *without* looking into the data. When information modeling is done correctly, the result should steer in this direction.

It can be a directive set in the engine to generate tables in this way, and we recommend doing so.

Recursive structures and hierarchies

NBRs provide multiple ways to implement recursive structures and hierarchies, and this can be designed in a variety of ways.

The first example represents a recursive relationship. In this situation there isn't a relationship between different CBCs, but a relationship that references the *same* CBC twice. This design can capture a hierarchy, or order, among different instances of the same thing. For example, in an organizational structure, both the 'manager' and 'employee' are employees.

The manager may report to another person, creating a recursive structure.

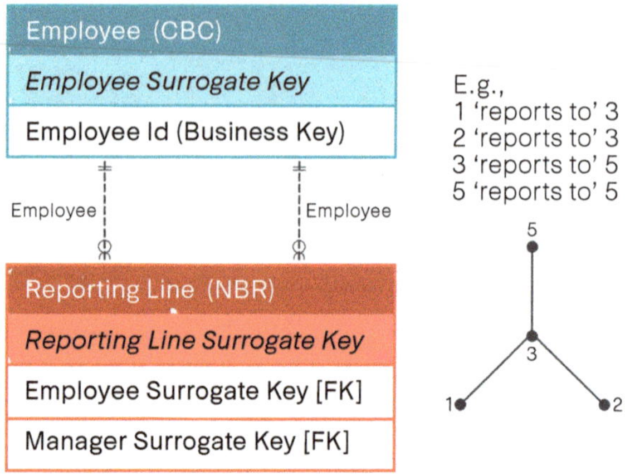

In this construct, the hierarchy can take various forms: asymmetric, ragged, balanced, skip-level, etc., depending on the data. Often, a recursive structure is already present in the original data and can be mapped as-is.

In this example, a 'top level' can be identified by a relationship where the item relates to itself. Depending on how the data is originally organized, this may be available or be derived as a business rule, if required.

Of course, reporting lines change over time, and this time-variant aspect will be covered in the ⚐ time-variance in relationships section.

Implementing a recursive structure is often convenient for data ingestion due to its flexibility. However, it is less prescriptive and understandable as a model. The organizational structure cannot be directly inferred from the model, only by querying the data.

Alternatively, these relationships can be explicitly modeled to make the structure more easily understandable.

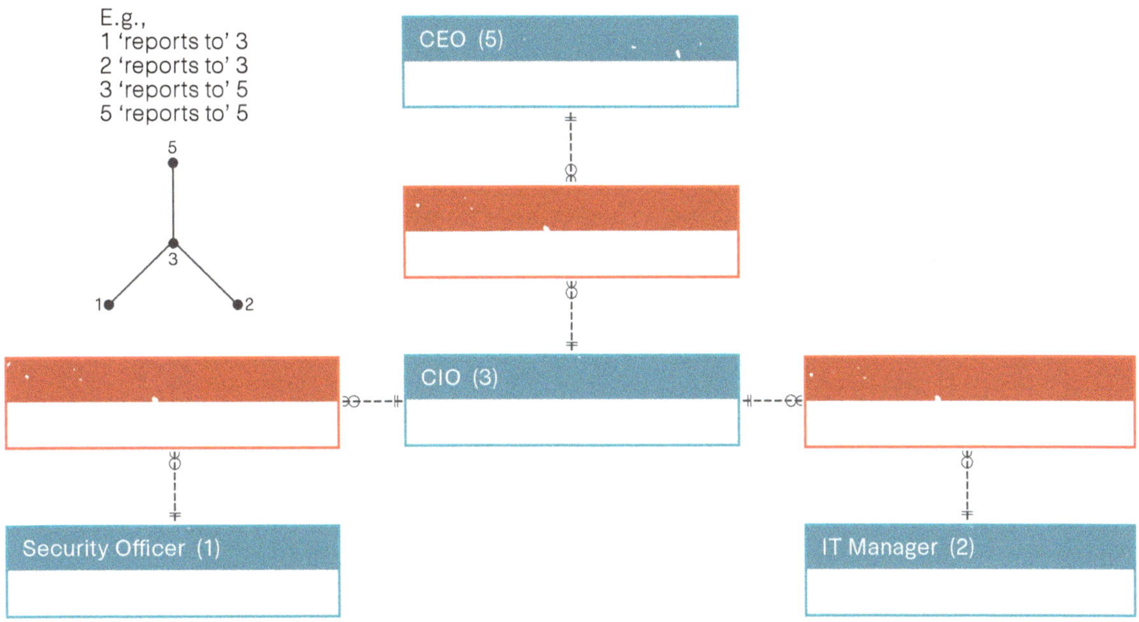

This is a different representation of the same data. Both approaches are variations on the same theme. Arguably, the second alternative is easier to 'read' since you can look at the model and understand the types of relationships that exist.

The downside? In large organizations, this approach can result in having *many* objects in the model. Moreover, if job positions change regularly, it may require frequent refactoring to keep up. For the recursive structure, none of this matters, as it will always stay the same.

The goal is to find the right level of detail for the business and its requirements. This was discussed earlier in the section on identifying the CBCs and is critically important.

The information model will be your guide here. For a small selection of subtypes that are not expected to change much, the 'modeling out' approach might make sense. For a completely fluid, ragged, and skip-level hierarchy, a recursive structure might work better.

Most importantly, it depends on whether these objects are truly core business concepts. This varies by organization. As an example, for an airline, separating a 'pilot' employee as its own concept might make sense due to regulatory requirements. In this case, modeling the pilot and 'other employees' separately could be effective. In other scenarios, this might apply specifically to contact center agents or ground staff.

The information model should capture these distinctions and provide direction.

As a last note, we have focused on the representation of a functional hierarchy. But this concept applies to a number of similar use cases, including *networks*. Certain types of the same item may be related to other items of the same type in various ways. Examples of this are geographical regions, or a bill of materials involving a product defined by a number of smaller components.

Context entity

If the CBCs and NBRs form the 'skeleton' of the model, then CBCs are the joints and NBRs are the bones. By themselves, these entities do not provide anything more than just the 'things' and their relationships. There is no other data to describe them.

This is where context entities come in. Context entities contain *descriptive, non-identifying* data related to a CBC or an NBR. This data may be subject to change over time.

Context entities contain all descriptive properties (attributes) that describe the entity they are associated with. And continuing the earlier metaphor, the context entities are the muscles and skin.

For example, a context entity for a 'customer' CBC might include the customer's name, address, and account details. Likewise, a context entity for an NBR —such as a relationship between a 'vehicle' and a 'person'— could store data specific to that relationship, like the 'time behind the wheel.'

This is data that specifically applies to the *relationship* and not to either of the involved CBCs.

Context entities depend on the CBC or NBR they describe. Technically, the context entity references the surrogate key of its 'parent' CBC or NBR. In database terms, this means the context entity has a foreign key[19] reference to the parent's primary key —the CBC or NBR surrogate key— although it is typically not enforced.

In many cases it will suffice to design context as a single entity that describes its parent CBC or NBR. However, there is no limit to how many descriptive tables you can have. At the logical level, a single entity might represent all descriptive properties, while at the physical level, multiple tables or objects could be employed to optimize performance or meet other objectives.

Deciding how many context entities makes sense depends on the goals, which are different for the logical level and the physical level. At the logical level, it may make sense to organize certain values in the same context entity (e.g., all personal details separate from sensitive data), while at the physical level better performance outcome may drive a different structure.

Either way, as many context entities can be defined as is fit for purpose.

Tracking changes over time

Part of the context entity definition is that its data is subject to change over time. This deserves more explanation, however the definition of 'time' in a data solution is such a broad topic that this warrants its own section.

The concept of 'time' will be covered in the ⚐ getting the data in chapter, especially the section ⚐ struggling with time.

In short, context entities record the changes in data for the attributes they contain. This way, context entities manage the state of the descriptive data — for a given point in time.

As an example, a 'person' CBC can have a context entity that contains the attribute 'height' – as in the length of a person in centimeters. At various stages of life, this height value will differ:

Person Identifier	Measurement Date	Height	Date of Birth
20315	1975	109.2	1970-03-05
20315	1980	138.3	1970-03-05
20315	2000	175.7	1970-03-05
20315	2055	172.0	1970-03-05

Note that the height changes over time, a measure recorded at different points in life. By contrast, the date of birth value remains constant. It is expected that this is the case, unless data corrections are made.

For a context entity, this does not matter. *All* descriptive properties are tracked over time, which means that a new record version is created if a value changes in one of the properties.

The new record will contain a new (inscription) timestamp value, and will be the latest received record version from that moment onwards. At least, that is, until a newer record is created – because an event occurred that led to newer change record being inserted.

It is the job of the context entity to manage this, including if a given key is no longer valid or even deleted from the operational system (but never from the data solution unless for compliance reasons) – see the section on evaluating logical deletes.

As a note, which will be covered in the struggling with time. section, the notion of changes over time implies that a time value is selected. This will be referred to as a *timeline* in this book.

In a data solution, recording changes over time really means recording changes against a *selected timeline*. For now, it is sufficient to state that the purpose of a context entity is to facilitate this.

Objectives and requirements for the integration layer

In our reference architecture, the following concepts are supported to deliver this:

→ Mapping data to the information model
→ Defining core business concepts
→ Distributing surrogate keys
→ Managing history
→ Managing relationships
→ Preparing the assertion and state timelines
→ Handling changes in data structures
→ Implementing organization-wide business logic

↗ The overarching goal of the integration layer is to ensure that all data is re-organized and aligned to the target information model.

The integration layer includes both back and front room objects and processes. The goal is to ensure all data is mapped to the intended business entities. This is predominantly implemented in the base integration area and is regarded a back room activity. The derived integration area can then use this data to apply any transformations as needed – which is a front-room process.

The shift from the base to the derived integration area marks the boundary between the front room and the back room of the overall solution.

Whether a process is considered back or front room also informs the way constraints should be applied. Back room processes are geared towards avoiding any kind of failure. However, in the derived integration area –the front room– processes can be implemented in a way that can be fully controlled by the data solution. For this reason, additional checks can be considered here, and these can be implemented in such a way that the process will not hinder the movement of data further into the data solution.

Following this line of thought, by default referential integrity (RI) between the main entity types in the integration layer is implied, but not enforced. Maintenance checks (see section ⚐ monitoring framework) can be implemented to validate if the solution is behaving as expected – a form of *lazy referential integrity* where the validation is performed *after* the data is inserted.

This allows for maximum flexibility for the data logistics process orchestration, and is covered in more detail in the ⚐ about referential integrity section.

Mapping data to the information model

The integration layer represents the information model in a way that is both system and delivery agnostic. The model focuses on what is *core* to the business, and provides a holistic representation of it.

This is a model in the purest sense, an abstract and simplified portrayal of the business it covers and describes.

Being agnostic of operational systems means that the information is almost certainly a *different* model. After all, the operational systems represent a part of the business in a way that make sense for the specific functional area it supports while the integration layer covers *everything* – across the entire business.

Mapping data from the operational systems to the target integration layer model is one of the main objectives of the integration layer. These data mappings are called *source-to-target mappings* (referred to just as 'mappings' from here). Mappings are essential design metadata required to deploy the solution, and a key ingredient for data logistics (code) generation.

Organizations in the same domain may find that they share similar integration layer models, but the mappings to these models will invariably differ between them. This is one of the reasons why mappings are one of the main areas of intellectual property to safeguard.

Details on technical platforms and models can often be (re)construed relatively quickly, but the correct data mapping from the particular operational system to the integration layer requires deep understanding of the application involved, its processes, and ultimately the data that they generate as a result.

Mappings are often recorded in specialist software or a metadata repository that is part of the design and development framework, platform, or automation solution.

The mapping schema

This chapter intends to provide an overview of everything that is required to deliver an effective and efficient data solution. It is not yet the intent to go into the detail of *how* to deliver this.

This becomes especially obvious when covering mappings, which are essential design metadata elements and warrant careful administration.

The chapter on ⚐ metadata, automation and code generation contains in-depth content and examples on *how* to define and record mappings, and we refer there for more details.

At this stage, it is important to note that one of the integration layer objectives is to do the modeling exercise and define the resulting mappings. For now, we would like to introduce two terms that we believe are useful to describe mappings at a conceptual level.

These are the *data object* and the *data item.*

The data object is a data set, such as a database table, file or object. The data item is an individual column or element that belongs to a data object.

A mapping essentially consists of a 'source,' a 'target,' and a 'relationship' between the two at both the data object as well as the data item level. This means that a data object maps to another data object and, as part of this, the data items that belong to the data objects can also be mapped accordingly.

An interpretation of reality

It is an interesting thought that the very act of modeling is an interpretation in itself. This refers back to the message of the ⚐ world of data chapter: we can only create the best model based on the information we have, and this will change over time because of our evolving understanding of the subject matter.

We may look back at earlier modeling decisions, interpretations, and consider we would do things differently based on today's understanding. This is a strong use case to consider the PSA concept.

When we replay the history captured in the PSA with an updated set of mappings —now mapped to different targets— we are effectively delivering a different integration layer model.

Defining core business concepts

Earlier in this chapter, we touched on the concept of the CBC. An objective of the integration layer is to define the CBCs, so that it is clear what things are important to the organization – and consequently what integration points for data will be available.

Defining CBCs is first and foremost a data modeling exercise, and it's somewhat of an art and not necessarily a science – something we will provide approaches for in the ⚐ CBC implementation sections.

Once defined, CBCs become target objects for mappings as outlined in the previous section. This includes the relationship between the 'source' object and the CBC as well as the mapping from *the business key as it is known in the operational system* to the (standardized) business key attribute in the CBC – the business key mapping.

These mappings truly give meaning to the CBC. Until data is mapped they only exist as concepts – expressions of intent on what would be ideal. The reality of data mapped to the CBC, the business key definition, defines what a CBC *really* is.

Many *data objects* from operational systems can potentially be mapped to a single CBC and its business key. This indicates that the mapped data carries the same meaning – an interpretation and design decision.

The fact that a mapping shares a target with another mapping is referred to as *passive integration.*

After all, the data is all mapped to the same thing.

An example of this is provided below, where three different data objects from three different operational systems are all mapped to the 'customer' CBC.

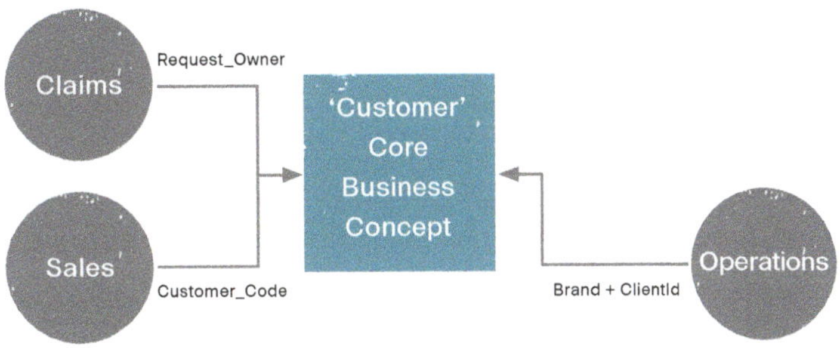

The business key from 'operations' to 'customer' in this example is created from two attributes: 'brand' and 'client id.' This highlights that a business key can be as complex as it needs to be to accurately describe the CBC. For this purpose, a business key definition can consist of many attributes, transformations, and hard-coded values.

Distributing surrogate keys

Surrogate key distribution covers the creation of keys that are specific to, and fully controlled by, the data solution. They are used internally to combine data sets. Surrogate keys simplify the solution and further insulate the data solution from the operational systems – providing additional reliability.

A surrogate key is directly related to the business key, so conceptually the key distribution can be considered a feature of the core business concept.

As with (correct) business keys, surrogate keys must be unique. The mapping between the surrogate key and the business key is one-to-one.

However, business keys can be complex, consisting of multiple attributes (composite), concatenated values, hard-coded values, or a combination thereof. A business key is not necessarily a single value.

The surrogate key maps (and decouples) this potential complexity into a *single (column) value* that can be used throughout the data solution. This makes it far more straightforward to combine data sets – without having to manage complex and composite keys throughout the solution. Additionally, surrogate keys provide a standardized way to manage exceptions, such as missing values in parts of the business key.

In many implementations, CBC entities are just that: a distinct list of business keys (in all their complexity) mapped to their corresponding surrogate keys.

Traditionally, surrogate keys in data solutions used integer values for space and performance reasons. There are, however, various alternative approaches available for key distribution – each with their own pros and cons.

The main mechanisms for surrogate key distribution are:

→ Integer sequence keys
→ Natural business keys
→ Hash keys

These will be covered in detail in the getting the data in chapter.

Managing relationships

In the integration layer, relationships between CBCs are established and maintained as NRBs. Relationships may have their own descriptive properties that provide details not about any of the involved CBCs, but about the relationship between them.

Relationships change over time, and in some cases may become invalid or obsolete. A special objective of the integration layer is to manage and record the changes in *validity* of a relationship over time.

This is sometimes referred to as 'effective-dating' or 'end-dating' – two sides of the same coin. In both cases timestamp values are attached to a relationship as context, as well as any other necessary details to correctly identify the state of a relationship at a point in time.

The objective is to be able to accurately represent the relationships as they were at a given (historical) point in time.

Imagine that, in a sales organization, each *customer* has a designated *account manager*. Both the customer as well as the account manager are CBCs, and in this organization a customer can only be assigned *one* account manager at a time.

To correctly interpret sales figures, performance, complaints, and anything else, it is of interest to understand current and past relationships.

Over time, a customer may be appointed a new account manager. When this becomes in effect in this scenario, the relationship between the customer and the previous account manager ceases to be active. If this is not managed well, historical sales or complaints might be attributed to the wrong person!

The information to correctly interpret this pattern may, or may not be, available in the operational system. For instance, the operational system may just update the account manager to a new one, or could use an internal effective-dating mechanism.

Either way, it is the job of the integration layer to record these relationship changes, so that correct representations of data over time can be delivered.

The details on how to implement this are covered in the getting the data in chapter.

Managing history

The integration layer delivers a deterministic representation of the state of data, at any (historical) point in time. *Context entities* are the mechanism to do so.

Their feature to track changes over time is the centerpiece here, as it is all about making sure each change record is correctly recorded against the corresponding CBC (or NBR).

Context entities contain an additional timestamp component in the primary key to facilitate this. Each new change record is inserted with this timestamp, and added 'on top of' any existing (earlier) records for the surrogate key.

A best-practice is to use the inscription timestamp as part of the context entity's primary key. This concept was introduced in the PSA, and records the arrival time in the data solution. The inscription timestamp value is copied as-is, unmodified, from the staging layer when the change record is inserted. In other words, it is inherited from the staging layer.

This means that the history is recorded against the time of arrival in the data solution – the *assertion timeline.* Data is 'historized' in the order that it arrives in the data solution environment, irrespective (for now) of functional meaning.

This is a back-room feature, and as with all back-room features it is intended to boost the data solution's reliability. Because the inscription timestamp values are managed by the data solution, and are always incremental, there is almost no risk of creating duplicate keys (primary key constraint violation).

Note that the source timestamp should *not* be used for historization, even though this may appear to be a good alternative. This value is dependent on the interface, and not always (typically not) under full control of the data solution.

The following example shows how the context entity, and associated concepts, come together.

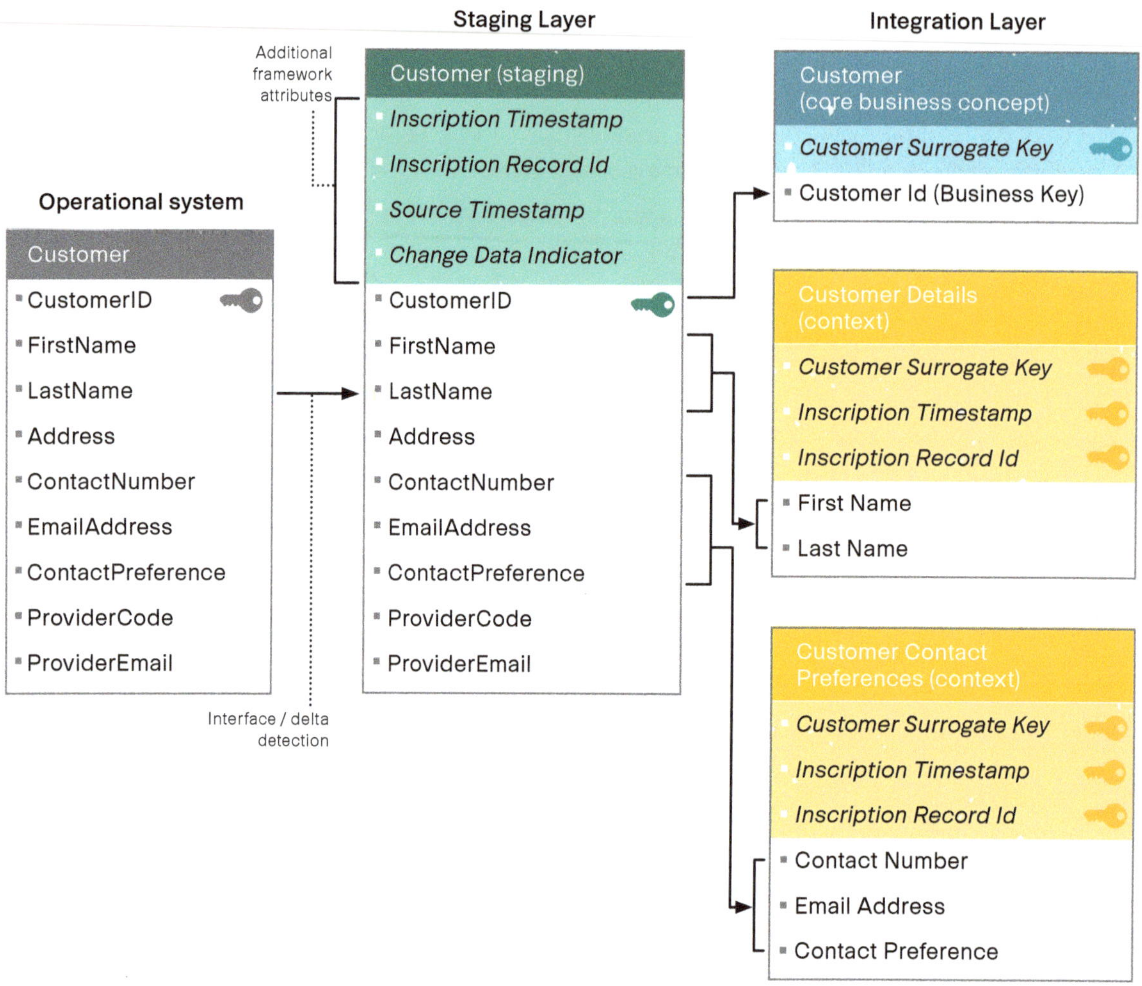

This example displays a data flow from a 'customer' object in an operational system, through the staging layer, and into the CBC and context entities.

This touches on the following objectives and concepts:

→ The interface between the operational system and the staging layer only processes change records (determination of the data delta)
→ The inscription timestamp is set as soon as the record arrives in the staging layer (setting the inscription timestamp)
→ The interface records the time of change of the record in the operational system (setting the source timestamp)
→ The interface evaluates if a change record is inserted, updated, or deleted in the change data indicator attribute (evaluating logical deletes)
→ Attributes are mapped to various integration layer objects (mapping data to the information model)
→ A business key has been identified—'Customer Id' in this case— and mapped to the CBC (defining CBCs)
→ The business key has been matched with a surrogate key, the 'customer surrogate key' in this case (surrogate key distribution)

The diagram also highlights the option of having *multiple* context entities, as well as the additional key components required to track changes over time.

Every time a value changes for one of the in-scope attributes —the attributes used in the context tables— an insert in one of the context entities will occur, with a higher load timestamp.

Also note the use of the 'inscription record id' column. Its purpose is to ensure uniqueness of the data in situations where the inscription timestamp is not sufficient for this. It is a technical trick to uniquefy the inscription timestamp. More detail on this is provided in the inscription record id section.

Prepare the assertion and state timelines

Managing time in a data solution can be complex, but the integration layer provides features to help with this.

Essentially, there are two main concepts of time to consider and both are configured in the integration layer. These are the *assertion timeline* (also referred to as technical timeline) and the *state timeline* (also referred to as 'business' timeline)[20]. They are the main levers used to organize data for delivery, and fundamental for the implementation of data marts and related concepts such as slowly changing dimensions.

The assertion timeline

The assertion timeline is embodied by the inscription timestamp. This timeline represents the —always sequential— order of events, or transactions, in which data was received by the data solution. The assertion timeline provides the *time traveling* feature that allows the data solution to deliver results based on when data was *available.*

Following the axis of the assertion timeline, you can go 'back in time' to understand when certain transactions were received and 'go forward in time' up to the present day to understand the impacts of any transactions that arrived later — and even replay the transactions with a potentially different representation of the data.

The assertion timeline is intended to be used for filtering only — selecting the (scope of) transactions that should be considered for processing, e.g., up to a certain timestamp.

For example, if you seek to understand the sales at month-end, then the assertion timeline will inform you what data was available in the data solution up to that point.

There is no concept of late-arriving data for the assertion timeline. The order in which data is received always progresses sequentially forward in time. It may happen that, after month-end, data arrives that applies to a historical period such as the month that just ended. You may receive data now that applies to one or two months ago, for instance as a backdated adjustment or correction. From the perspective of the assertion timeline, however, you received this data now.

New data may include a correction of a sales figure that was meant to apply months ago, but it was received whenever it was received.

When we go back in time along the assertion timeline axis, we can demonstrate to the consumers that the figures in today's reporting might differ from the figures that were reported originally — because corrections hadn't yet arrived when the original report was created. When go forward in time, we can show that the sales figures have changed due to these later transactions.

In other words, we can provide a perspective of as-was and as-is — and switch between them. This is especially important when operational systems do not track the history of events themselves, which means only the latest update (state) is available. For system such as these, the historical information will always be up to date — because the history is updated.

From their perspective of 'now' the sales data from two months ago looks all right. So why did the data solution provide the 'wrong data' earlier?

Answering questions such as these is the purpose of having an assertion timeline, since changes of data can be demonstrated over the period they are received by the data solution. Being able to do this is a significant boost to achieving trust in the data solution.

The state timeline

For the assertion timeline, there is no such thing as late-arriving data. This simply cannot exist, because this timeline is fully controlled by the data solution. After all, the inscription timestamp —the attribute representing the assertion timeline— is set *by* the data solution when the data enters the environment for the first time.

Late-arriving data is only relevant for the *state timeline.* The state timeline reflects the events as understood, and expected by, the consumers of the data – the 'business users.'

The order of events as they were received may not align with the users' expectations. A helpful way to think about this is to consider what users see on their screens when working with an operational system. What does the operational system report as 'current?'

Can the data solution represent this?

The state timeline is represented by a value that exists in the data provided to the data solution. The exact 'right' value for this varies for every organization. It is possible that an operational system uses its own internal effective dating, which can be used to construct the state timeline. If nothing is available the data solution source timestamp (set in the staging layer) can be used.

In all cases, this timeline is intended to represent the validity of data as expected by the users in the real world.

In practical terms, the state timeline is used to join data sets together. The assertion timeline should *not* be used for this – that is for filtering only. So, data is combined across the state timelines as per the scope of the assertion timelines.

Returning to the sales figures example: to retrieve last month's sales figures *as per the end of last month,* the data is joined using the state timeline but the involved data sets are capped as per the end of last month assertion timeline timestamp. Any data that arrived later is not considered for this query, and doing so also ensures that the results are always deterministic. If you want to allow any backdated adjustments to be part of the result, you increase the range of data along the assertion timeline to incorporate these later-arriving transactions.

This approach of applying both timelines for data analysis or delivery is called *bitemporal analysis,* and will be the main topic of the ⚐ struggling with time section.

There are potentially many state timeline data points to consider, and one of the objectives of the integration layer is to solve this by standardizing on one of them so that further processing can be simplified. If the state timeline is a standard attribute, many presentation layer data logistics can leverage standard patterns.

Standardization of the state timeline

Note that standardizing on the state timeline can be done in various places in the data solution. Some methodologies suggest helper constructs that map data to a certain timeline, such as the point-in-time (PIT) table in Data Vault. Standardization on this can also be done in the PSA, by adding a derived attribute that is consistently used as the state timeline in all subsequent steps.

Conceptually though, we consider this a feature of the integration layer. Even within this layer this can be done in two ways:

→ As a mapping from the staging layer to the base integration area
→ As a transformation or interpretation in the derived integration area

Both approaches effectively provide a single timeline against which data can be aligned and reordered to, so that delivery can be simplified.

Handling changes in data structures

The integration layer provides an elegant solution for mitigating the impact of changes to data structures. Because of the main entities' hub-and-spoke nature, it is relatively easy to incorporate new data into the data solution. We have already seen examples of this, for instance by implementing multiple context entities that describe the same CBC or NBR.

Adding new CBCs and NBRs can also be done without impacting any existing logic and structures.

The integration layer facilitates this by providing the means to 'plug in' new data sets without downstream impacts. This way, new data can be integrated piecemeal and be refactored over time.

In the diagram below, building on the example from the ⚐ defining the core business concepts section, the integration layer is extended to include additional data.

Specifically, customer context is added to the existing 'customer' CBC, a new 'provider' CBC is introduced, and an NBR between customer and provider is established.

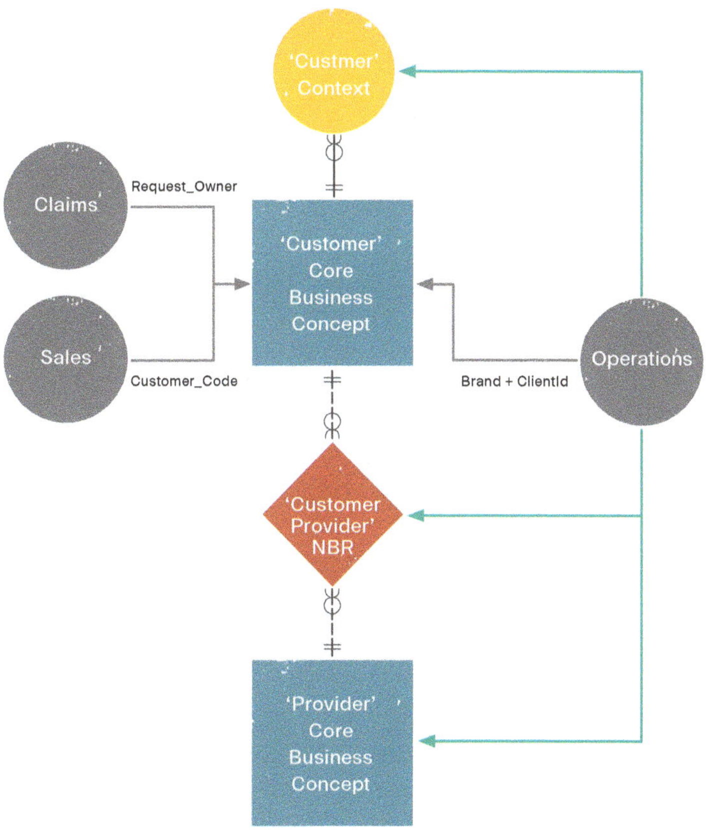

No changes whatsoever to existing structures are necessary.

This does not mean that this added data always needs to remain in this structure. It is perfectly doable to combine, and further integrate, this data into existing structures over time.

Implementing organization-wide business logic

Organization-wide business logic, first introduced in the ⚐ the derived integration area section, is meant to finalize the information model – or at least get the data as close to this as possible.

A distinction is made between 'organization-wide' and 'data mart only' to emphasize that logic implemented in the derived integration area is meant to be more general in nature.

The specific transformations applied depend on the implementation, but they typically address the following:

→ Deduplication
→ Cleansing and scrubbing data to manage data quality issues
→ Introducing CBCs that are not directly present in operational systems
→ Determining additional relationships, such as creating a single customer view

The presentation layer

↗ The focus of the presentation layer is to compile the data available in the integration layer into a format that is fit-for-purpose for consumption. It is composed of two areas: the *access area* and the *performance area*.

The third layer of the architecture is the *presentation layer,* also known as the 'data access layer.'

In this layer, the focus is to compile the data available in the integration layer into a format that is fit-for-purpose for consumption. This means transforming the data from the organization's holistic the information model into specific deliveries depending on their use case.

In the section ⚐ the staging layer, the term *incoming interfaces* was introduced. In the data solution, we speak of *outgoing interfaces* due to the variety of delivery formats. What is considered the required delivery format varies from case to case. It is very dependent on the type of data consumers.

Common consumers include front-end reporting and analysis software, APIs, export files, or data sets that are otherwise exposed. Of course, consumers are also people versed in data interrogation languages via a wide variety of coding approaches — most notably using Structured Query Language, or SQL.

Usually, the goal is to limit and simplify data access. A typical presentation layer model has a limited number of relationships between data sets so that the user does not have to implement complex (join) logic to access the data.

This is the case for data delivery in a dimensional model[21] — fact and dimension tables. Reportable metrics are combined in fact tables which reference various dimensions tables containing the descriptive information for a certain fact.

Data can be provided in one or more data marts, typically organized around one or more fact tables with their supporting dimensions. Data marts are often specific to a certain *subject area* which scopes a specific domain or function in the organization, e.g., finance, HR, sales, or operations.

Fact tables may or may not share (conformed) dimensions. Ideally, the constellation of fact and dimension tables represent the information model for delivery, but data access can also be provided using *independent* data marts which are essentially stand-alone.

Dimensional modeling is still one of the most common approaches, though not the only one, for making data available for reporting and analysis.

The presentation layer can contain any number of models, and modeling approaches. While typical delivery is often done using a dimensional model format, this can also include snowflake data models, disparate data marts, completely denormalized joined data sets and anything in between.

These outgoing interfaces may, or may not, have certain types of historical data for delivery purposes, depending on the requirements.

There are many approaches for all of this, and specific mechanisms work better for certain use cases or technical and performance challenges than others.

As a simple example, you can define a product dimension which is linked to a sales fact table. But, the same data can also be represented in a single interface in a fully denormalized form. In this case, all the elements that would otherwise be split across the product and sales tables are delivered in a single data set. Either way, the results will be the same but the data logistics and performance impacts will be different.

The getting the data out chapter will go into more detail on which options and considerations are available.

There are many.

For now, the message is that the presentation layer is *all about organizing the data for delivery* – including any remaining transformations or interpretations that apply.

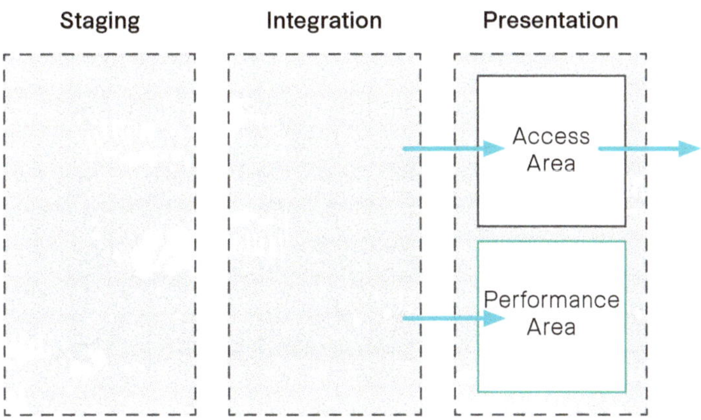

Areas of the presentation layer

The presentation layer is composed of two areas: the *access area* and the *performance area*.

The access area is the final area of the architecture, where the prepared data leaves the data solution for further use. This is where the consumers can access the data.

An optional performance area can be added to assist in this final data preparation step, and to simplify the data processing into its final delivery format. The performance area is not intended to be accessible to the consumers.

Performance area

The performance area is an optional area which focuses on ensuring that the presentation layer can be delivered in a performant and efficient way.

Having good performance for data processing is important throughout the data solution, but it is in the presentation layer where this usually matters most. In previous layers, transformations were often specific and relatively isolated. Also, transformations tend to be more generic (pattern-based) and can be thoroughly optimized.

However, in the presentation layer everything comes together – and for reporting purposes this often is in a denormalized way.

This is where the performance area comes in.

To keep data logistics running smoothly, it may be necessary to create temporary result sets or (semi-)aggregates, which can be physically optimized, e.g., indexed or partitioned, and reused by more than one process.

Especially when *multiple* data logistics processes need to run the same calculation or transformation it may be more effective and efficient to implement the required data set once at the start of a processing schedule, after which it can be reused many times.

This applies to both performance optimization as well as implementation of business logic. The presentation area implements specific transformations that are not covered by the integration layer. It may be that these transformations also need to be implemented by multiple data logistics processes. What is considered generic versus specific business logic will be covered in the ⚐ implementing specific business logic section.

Examples of helper processes are:
→ Aggregations, preparing data for a target level of detail
→ Pivoting data to suit a certain interface
→ Combining multiple integration layer objects to reduce the number of joins
→ Reduce code duplication for often-used calculations
→ Date math, the logic to combine data sets that use different date ranges into a single data set

In cases such as these it can help to limit code duplication by combining functionality that is shared by more than one process.

Access area

The access area is the final stage of the architecture. This is where data is made available to consumers through outgoing interfaces.

The notion of the 'single version of the truth' is often part of conversations about structuring the access area, and it is the best place within the architecture to have these discussions – even if the truth only applies for a specific use case or subject area.

Typical implementations in the access area include applying specific business logic for data delivery, to the extent this hasn't been already addressed in the integration layer.

Common use cases also involve implementing aggregation and organizing data into hierarchies.

In all cases, the access area captures the target delivery model for the data.

Further decoupling

The access area often introduces a decoupling mechanism to isolate data consumers from changes in the structure of the data solution.

An example of this is the creation of database views on top of access area objects. The semantic layer references these views, and not the underlying objects directly.

This way, changes in the objects can be applied while using the view for backwards compatibility purposes until such time the consumers have updated their interfaces.

Another consideration is to keep the data marts as small as possible to decouple the marts from each other. This way, changes in one data mart do not affect other data marts and their applications.

Objectives and requirements for the presentation layer

In the presentation layer, data is prepared for consumption.

For this, the following concepts are implemented:
→ Transforming data to the delivery format, the outgoing interface
→ Granularity; establishing the right level of detail for data delivery
→ Implementing specific business logic not yet covered by earlier layers
→ Calculation of timelines and 'date math,' in order to deliver information in the expected order
→ Displaying data changes over time

Transform data to the delivery format

When all is said and done, all that really matters for consumers is that their data solution provides data in a fit-for-purpose way.

All the concepts, technology and smarts built into the solution are null and void if nobody can access the data in a way that aligns with their purposes.

Making sure that data *is* transformed into the format of the outgoing interface is therefore one of the main objectives of the presentation layer – and for the data solution as a whole.

A single data solution can encompass multiple delivery formats for potentially different consumers, often logically grouped into different subject areas or data marts.

In all cases, data is mapped to a final delivery, target model that makes sense for the consumer use case.

One of the most common delivery formats is the dimensional model, which has been mentioned a few times already. In this example format for data delivery, the corresponding data from the integration layer needs to be mapped to this model.

Hierarchies

Certain data elements have an intrinsic relationship to other data elements. A relationship of two or more data elements can form a *hierarchy* which can determine a pathway to navigate through the data.

Hierarchies can exist in many variations, and can even contain circular references. Hierarchy types that occur frequently are *balanced* and *unbalanced.*

A balanced hierarchy has a defined number of levels, and all branches within the hierarchy reach this level.

A unbalanced hierarchy however will have branches with varying levels within the hierarchy. This means that one part of the hierarchy can be 5 levels 'deep' for example, while another part stops at 2 levels.

To complicate things further, both hierarchy types can potentially skip levels (ragged). For example, by navigating from 'country' level straight to 'postal code,' without having data points for the 'region' level.

Data can also be stored as a *recursive structure,* a parent-child hierarchy type that only captures the immediate relationship between two data points. Hierarchies can be navigated by using, most time complex, query code without having the need to persist the hierarchy or commit to a target form just yet.

The target delivery model commonly has hierarchies defined, and the data from the integration layer must be mapped to these as part of the overall presentation layer efforts.

In many cases, the levels in a hierarchy correspond to CBCs in the integration layer —the information model— but this is not always the case.

Note that the use of the term hierarchy is in a data modeling sense, and not in an OLAP context. In traditional Business Intelligence data delivery solutions OLAP processes read a dimensional model and calculate some, most or all cross-sections between the dimensions and facts into an OLAP cube.

Hierarchies are defined also here, and they follow the data structures of the model but also provide additional features to improve user experience in data navigation – built on the OLAP cube.

Performance

For now, the focus is on establishing the right combination of concepts in the form of a reference architecture. This focus is still predominantly software-agnostic at this stage.

However, even though we are not yet diving into the world of physical optimization it is relevant to mention that performance must be considered throughout the solution – and particularly for the presentation layer.

Performance must be fit for purpose for the users, and what this means must be considered a business requirement. It is then up to the data solution to deliver an efficient solution that can optimize data delivery for these requirements.

An effective approach for this is to define a *data latency* metric. Data latency informs consumers of the 'delay' between the moment that data is received by the data solution (in the staging layer) and the moment this is visible to consumers in the presentation layer.

Using the Engine Thinking concepts, this latency requirement can be used to optimize (prioritize processing of) certain data logistics to meet the given requirements – often at the expense of other areas of data logistics.

Being able to direct data logistics will also assist in building a case for additional compute resources, if required.

The implementation of this concept will be covered in detail in the getting the data in chapter.

Granularity

The objective of transforming data to the delivery format covers the mapping to the target model and specific use cases — such as hierarchies.

Defining the granularity —the 'right' level of detail to be fit for purpose— can be viewed as a special case of transforming data into the designated delivery format.

This is important because underlying data (in the integration layer) may not be available directly at the level of detail required for data delivery.

In the integration layer, data is stored as detailed as possible so that the greatest number of use cases can be supported. However, certain data deliveries only need data aggregated to a certain time period, geographical region, numeric precision, or otherwise.

Defining the granularity then becomes a requirement to aggregate the data when loading the data into, or interpreting the data against, the target information model.

Implementing specific business logic

The topic of 'business logic,' specific transformations that are needed to deliver the data in the desired way and with the intended meaning, has been covered in the ⚐ integration layer section — to an extent.

In the integration layer, the aim is to apply relevant transformations to make sure the data matches the information model. This is agnostic of any specific use cases, but should match with the holistic view of how the business operates.

The business logic, or business rule transformations, applied in the integration layer are organization-wide. They are more generic in nature.

The presentation layer provides an opportunity to apply business logic that is *specific* for a consumer, use case, or data mart. These data interpretations do not apply to any other area, but are just needed to deliver the data specifically for a given use case.

An example is providing support for legacy applications via the data solution. Usually, the data models for the legacy applications are not compatible with the organization-wide information model as is implemented in the integration layer. Still, there may be good reasons why data needs to be provided in a specific format and with business logic that may contradict, is inconsistent with, the integration layer. Connecting the data solution to a standard 3rd party API is another example — for instance for open data sharing initiatives.

In these examples, attempting to fit these requirements in the integration layer would mean making concessions in the information model. As an alternative, these specific scenarios can be supported as specific business logic to be implemented in targeted outgoing interfaces — such as a stand-alone data mart.

Why is there a need for specific logic at all?

When using the term specific in this context, you may wonder what exactly falls into this category. What constitutes specific business logic, as opposed to organization-wide?

In the ideal world, no specific logic would need to be implemented in the presentation layer at all. This is because in the ideal world the integration layer truly provides the holistic view of information that every consumer aligns to. All data will then be mapped to this model, so that consumers can access it without further interpretation — albeit still via the presentation layer for the purposes described in this objectives section.

In this case, there would be no need for any further —specific— interpretation.

To summarize, all interpretation, or at least as much as feasible, should be implemented in the integration layer. If there are any strong reasons a deviation in interpretation is necessary for a *small number of consumers,* we can consider this specific logic and implement this in the presentation layer.

Calculation of timelines and 'date math'

In our reference architecture, one of the integration layer objectives is to prepare the assertion and state timelines.

This step standardizes the available timelines for data delivery.

It is now up to the presentation layer to deliver the data against the selected timelines in a way that is fit for consumption.

For this, we refer to two main timelines against which data is organized. The assertion timeline represents the order of data arrival, so that data can be shown exactly as how it was received at any point in the past.

The state timeline represents the way data can be combined (joined) because this is the correct 'business' validity period.

For example, let's assume a sales discount period was 'current' from 2018 to 2019 but we only receive a record for this today in 2022 – a substantial time after 2019 for the purpose of this example.

In this case, we should not match recent orders or sales events to this sales discount period even though the information of the discount period was also recently received. Functionally, the data applies to a time in the past even though it was received today.

The assertion timeline will show this sales discount period as 'current,' and this is correct from this perspective. But to join the sales discount to the orders or sales events we should not use this information, but the state timeline instead.

In other words, we can only join orders or sales events to their discount period based on the state timeline i.e., making sure the sale transaction timestamp falls between the discount period start and end timestamp.

The preparation done by the integration layer has already standardized these timelines, the data elements are already mapped to standard fields. This makes it easier for the presentation layer to take the next step.

Date math

From the integration layer to the presentation layer, various historized data sets will be combined together into data sets that match the delivery model.

For example, attributes selected from multiple context entities describing a CBC may be merged into a single dimension.

The process for doing so involves many joins using both the assertion timeline as well as the state timeline. These joins are often range joins which assert if a value (timestamp) falls within a certain (validity) time period.

This process can be referred to as *date math,* it is about merging two or more time-variant data sets together into a single historical view.

To discuss date math we would like to introduce some new terms, the first of which is a *timeline.* In essence, a timeline captures the changes over time for a designated value (e.g., identifier, business concept, or 'thing').

Change over time are arranged against a timeline. Conceptually, only the moment of change is essential because the data value will be *valid* from this point until a new change is encountered.

Each part of the timeline is referred to as a *time period* because it can show the state of the record at a given point in time. The data elements are valid for any points in time between the start and the end of the time period. There are many nuances at time periods which we cover in the section struggling with time.

In other words, the 'expiry' of the time period is the change timestamp of the next record along the timeline. Because this is a derived value, this is portrayed as a separate column in the example below.

The time period is also frequently referred to as 'effective period' and the start timestamp as 'effective timestamp.' Consequently, the end timestamp value is often called the 'expiry timestamp' of the time period.

The records in the following example can be visualized as changes for a horizontal timeline arrow.

'Zero record'

Person Key	Colour	Change Timestamp	Expiry Timestamp
25	Unknown	1900-01-01	2022-06-05
25	Red	2022-06-05	2022-07-23
25	Blue	2022-07-23	2023-03-16
25	Green	2023-03-16	9999-12-31

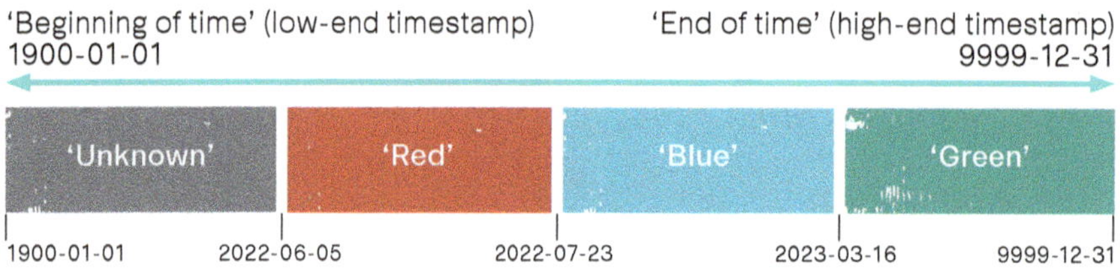

The first time period does not actually hold any data, but enables data logistics to query this date range and return information that states no information is available (as opposed to returning nothing at all) which is usually helpful to simplify the code.

This first time period, or rather the first record in the data set, is called the *zero record.* Having a zero record initiates the timeline for a given key, and enables the evaluation of the initial 'unknown' time period.

Consider the example below. Three separate data sets are displayed that each capture a data change at a point in time.

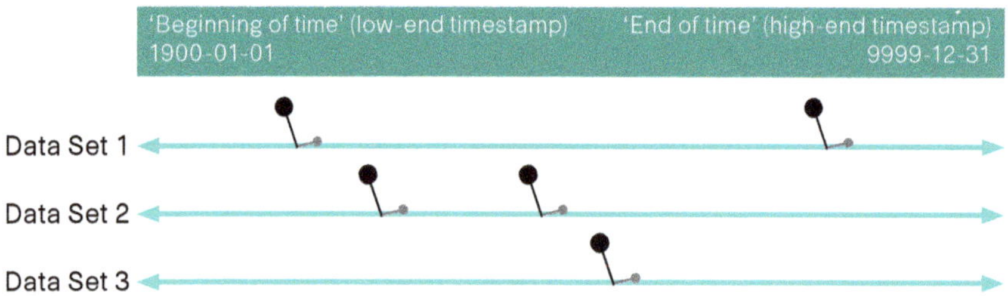

The first data set contains two changes (records), identified by the pins on the timeline. The second data set also contains two changes, but they happened at different points in time compared to the first set.

The third set only contains one change record. It occurred on yet another point in time.

If we were to combine these three data sets, how many records would the combined data set have? For this, we can assume we define an arbitrary start of the timeline; 1900-01-01 in this example – the 'low-end' timestamp.

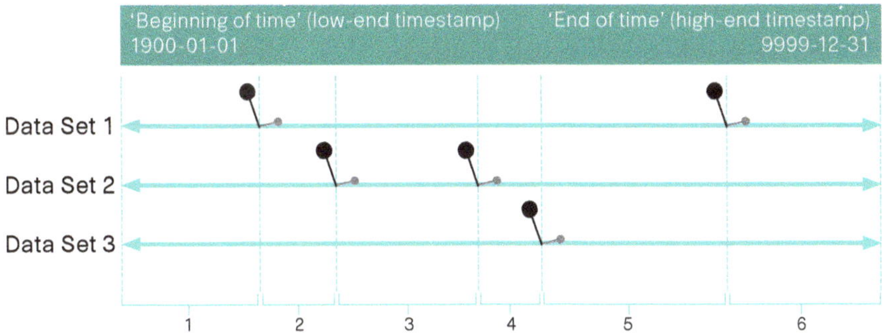

The resulting data set will contain six rows, covering the combined changes over time in a single data set.

The first time period starts at the beginning of the timeline (1900-01-01) and ends when the first change is encountered from data set 1.

In addition to this, the timelines for each individual data sets all start at the exact same point in time (1900-01-01) so this is collapsed into a single change timestamp. All timelines start at the same low-end timestamp.

Time period 2 up to and including time period 6 contains regular data elements that highlight the change in data.

This is the concept of date math in simple terms. If we were to apply sample data to this example, it would look like this:

Data Set 1

Change date	Colour
2022-06-05	Green
2024-03-05	Emerald

Data Set 2

Change date	Smell
2023-02-15	Apple
2023-04-02	Fruity

Data Set 3

Change date	Size
2023-12-03	Regular

Change date	Colour	Smell	Size
1900-01-01	NULL	NULL	NULL
2022-06-05	Green	NULL	NULL
2023-02-15	Green	Apple	NULL
2023-04-02	Green	Fruity	NULL
2023-12-03	Green	Fruity	Regular
2024-03-03	Emerald	Fruity	Regular

This example corresponds with the time periods of the earlier example, but now includes some sample data. The resulting data shows a single timeline containing the changes across all data sets.

With this new timeline, it becomes possible to pinpoint the value for a specific state time period. For example, if we were to query the data (state) for 2023-06-01, the resulting values would be 'green,' 'fruity,' and NULL respectively.

At this point in time, the 'newer' values of 'green,' 'fruity,' and 'regular' have not yet appeared so the most recent data is returned.

Conceptually, date math can be implemented by using join logic that evaluates the (lack of) overlap between validity periods.

When combining two data sets, there is an overlap if the greatest of the two effective timestamps (change timestamp) is smaller than the smallest of the two expiry dates.

The technical approach for this will be discussed in the ⚐ getting the data out chapter.

Displaying data changes over time

As one of the final stages in the data delivery, decisions must be made how the data can be *presented* over time.

The date math algorithm has made a historical view of data available using at least two timelines (the assertion timeline and state timeline). This data set contains the changes over time for the selected (in-scope) data elements.

Using this historized data set, data can be presented in various ways. To begin with, there are two generic ways historized data can be looked at. These are *as-was* and *as-is*.

As-was

As-was considers the data as it was valid for a given moment in time. This means looking at the data from that moment's perspective and context – as if the future were still an unknown.

From the perspective of today, later data may, of course, be available for the selected historical point in time. For an as-was view this is just not considered. It is filtered out using the assertion timeline.

If we use the example of an organizational structure, which consists of (a hierarchy of) regions, countries, states, and areas, we could have a history of sales that are attributed to certain areas and aggregated from there.

An as-was view of sales for each geographical grouping would represent the sales as per the organizational structure at that time. This means that even though at a later stage the 'states' were removed from the hierarchy and areas have been reorganized, the as-was view would still represent the sales in their original context.

As-is

As-is presents the historical data from a later point in time's perspective, which usually is 'today' or 'now.' This means that the available (historical) data is perceived with all the knowledge we have gained since the time the data being queried was originally recorded.

We look at the history from today's perspective.

Creating an as-is perspective on data does not necessarily have to be 'today,' but this is usually the clearest way to illustrate the concept. The same algorithm can also be applied to any point in time later than the data period being investigated.

Returning to the previous example of reporting sales against the organizational structure, the as-is view would display the historical sales against the organizational structure as it is *today*. This means that newly-formed areas 'inherit' the historical sales of the areas to which the sales were originally attributed.

As-was and as-is perspectives are not incompatible, and many reporting engines are capable of showing these perspectives side-by-side.

After all, the data is still the same. The original transactions are immutable. These are the facts that occurred in the past, and are recorded as they were.

The as-was and as-is perspectives can represent these transactions in a way that allows analysis of the (same underlying) data from different perspectives.

Data changes over time

Even though the date-math algorithm has provided a full view of historical events, this does not mean all history is required to be presented.

For example, even though a full history is available it may not be necessary or desired to provide all previous (historical) data states. In these cases, only the *most recent state* (as-is) may be sufficient.

In many cases, a more granular definition of 'changes over time' is adopted and the concepts are well documented in the dimensional modeling methodology – so called slowly changing dimensions (SCDs).[22]

It is important to note that the representation of historical data is configured, defined, at attribute level – so for each individual data element.

In a typical dimension table, each attribute can have a different historization setting that encapsulates an as-is view, and as-was view, or a combination of those two.

These are the many 'types' of history as per dimensional modeling techniques.

There are many good resources available on this, and we won't go into much detail here other than stating that the configuration of the historization is conceptually applied at an attribute level.

For example, within a dimension table some attributes may be defined as 'SCD 2' (full history) and others as 'SCD 1.' If *all* attributes are of the same type, we generally refer to the whole table as of this type.

As part of the presentation layer data logistics, the data (prepared through the date-math process) is subsequently converted to match the attribute-level requirements governing how data changes over time are made available.

Supporting frameworks

The previous section concludes the overview of the reference architecture and its main layers. However, in most cases it is essential to implement supporting frameworks to truly achieve the levels of flexibility of Engine Thinking.

These are the:

→ Data logistics control framework
→ Orchestration framework
→ Testing framework
→ Monitoring framework

With these in place, the diagram of the solution design can be completed:

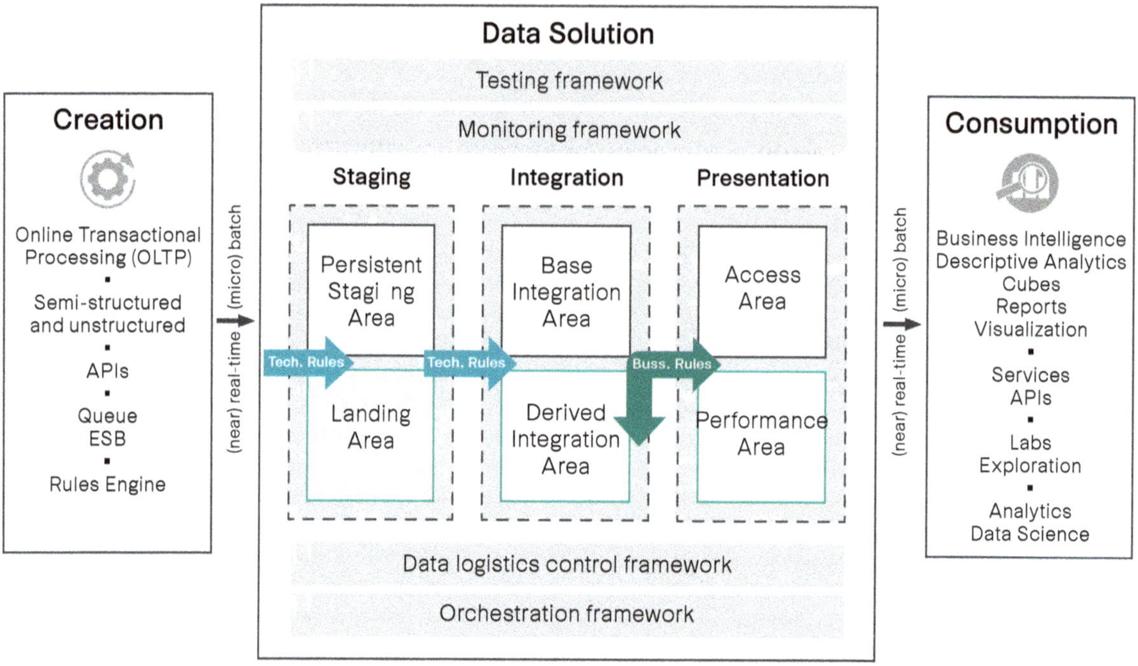

Data logistics control

↗ The control framework manages the runtime execution, logging, and monitoring of data logistics processes.

The *data logistics control framework* ('control framework') is an essential component of the data solution.

Through the Audit Trail Id, the control framework links to *all* data logistics processes in the solution design – irrespective of their parent area or layer. Every individual process interfaces with this framework.

A control framework:

→ Defines the orchestration of process execution
→ Provides logging and audit capabilities
→ Enforces idempotence and transaction control at the data logistics process level
→ Simplifies management of the data solution

There are many control frameworks available, as part of off-the-shelf products, as open source, and as designed on-site by project teams. Most of these frameworks share the same core mechanics, and in this section we would like to highlight the purpose of this essential functionality.

For links to robust control frameworks, please refer to our website: https://dtng.link/xucf2.

Elements of data processing

↗ A module is an individual, atomic, data logistics process. A batch is typically used to implement dependencies or group modules together.

While the physical components involved in the end-to-end data logistics process can vary in scope, and can employ a range of technologies, the control framework provides a logical layer of abstraction so that a consistent and software-agnostic view of the data logistics workflow can be visualized, maintained, and reported on.

At the center of the control framework, there is a logical model for describing data logistics units of work.

All data logistics processes that run as part of the data solution environment conform to this basic two-level hierarchy, consisting of the following two types:
→ Module — the smallest executable unit
→ Batch — a group of executable units (modules)

A module is an individual, atomic, data logistics process. A module may only apply to a single area of the solution architecture, and encapsulates a single executable process.

Modules are designed to run autonomously and independently, but can also be called from a batch as part of an orchestrated workflow.

A batch can be defined to fit any purpose by incorporating the corresponding modules but is typically used to implement dependencies or group modules together. For example, a batch can be defined to move (or interpret) data from one layer to the next by executing a collection of modules. Batches can also be nested, to implement additional logical groupings and dependencies — all the way up to a single 'main batch' executable.

In practical terms, a batch equates to a data logistics workflow, and a module is an individual data logistics process in the form of an executable, script, procedure call, or other form of code.

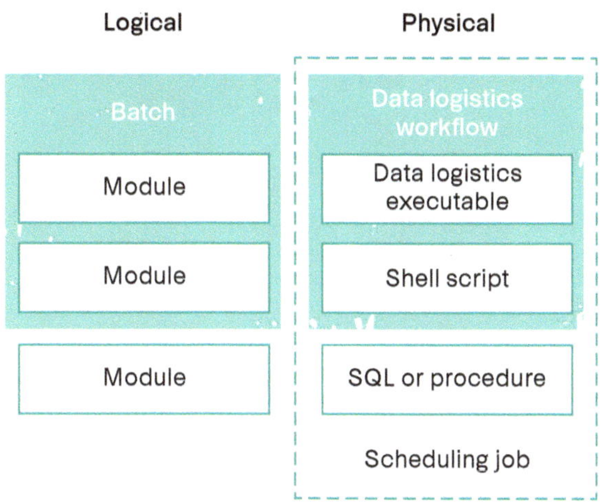

The modules assigned to a batch are not necessarily processed sequentially by default, but this is configurable. The batch acts as a 'container' for a group of related modules for which dependencies can be defined, if required. As part of the batch, the associated modules can be run in parallel, or configured so that certain modules are run before others.

Both batches and modules are executable objects. A batch simply calls modules or other batches. Modules can be executed independently, or by other batches as well. A module does not necessarily require a batch to run.

Overview of the control framework

The control framework administers the static (definition) of batches and modules. When a batch or module is invoked, the runtime *instances* are created and stored with the data that each batch or module processes as the Audit Trail Id. This is so that each data record or set is directly associated with the data logistics process that handled it.

This is the core of the control framework, but it is possible to add various properties to this administration that can be used to further drive and manage the data logistics.

The administration of the control framework is typically implemented as a *repository,* a database, or set of files that define batches and modules and record the events associated with them.

The logical view of this constellation that we subscribe to is as follows:

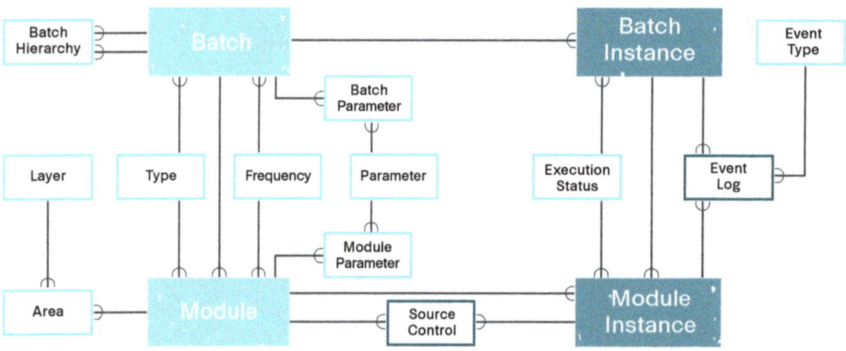

This model shows how the control framework covers both administrative data (light rectangles) – the configuration of the framework– as well as the runtime event data (dark rectangles).

As part of the administration, certain properties can be linked to both batches and modules. For example, it may be possible to add parameters to modules and/or batches to drive specific behavior or disable certain processes from running.

Another example is configuring the frequency that processes are *allowed* to run. Can certain modules or batches be executed more than once an hour? Or are they only supposed to process elements for a specific layer of the architecture?

Registration and instantiation

Batches and modules are logical concepts that are registered in the control framework during implementation.

'Registration' in this context means that there is an entry in the control framework that uniquely defines a batch and/or module including any relationships and properties that apply.

This creates a register of all batches and modules involved with the data solution. Data logistics processes can access this administration at runtime, during execution. Every time a process is invoked, it will request a unique process execution identifier from the control framework that is connected to the module or batch.

This is the *Audit Trail Id.*

The generation of a new unique identifier at execution time is referred to as *instantiation.* When executed, a batch or module is instantiated – and thus given its unique Audit Trail Id.

In the control framework this is recorded as a batch or module *instance* – a record of the individual unique execution transaction.

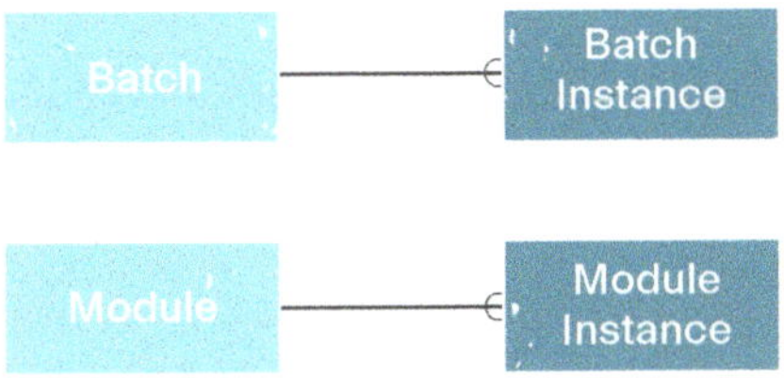

The module instance is saved as an Audit Trail Id with each individual record that is part of the processed data set. This way, it is always known exactly which unique process execution handled which record.

The following image shows how instantiation works in practice. The static view represents the registration of batches and modules in the control framework. The runtime view represents the instan-ces created when, in this case, a batch is executed.

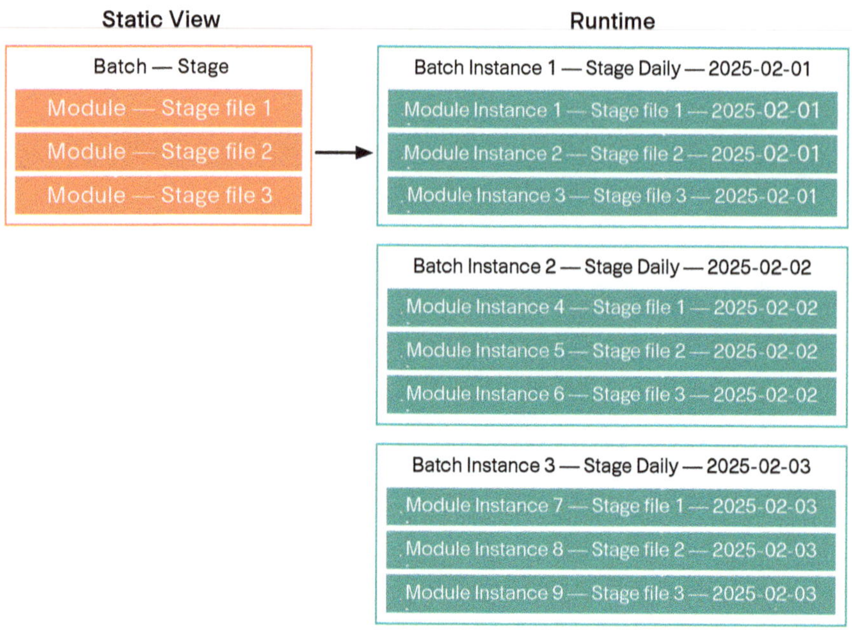

In this example, a batch runs three times – once every day. Each of these batch-level executions will start the modules associated with the batch.

The image below shows the interactions with the repository, including an example when modules are executed independently (i.e., not called from a batch).

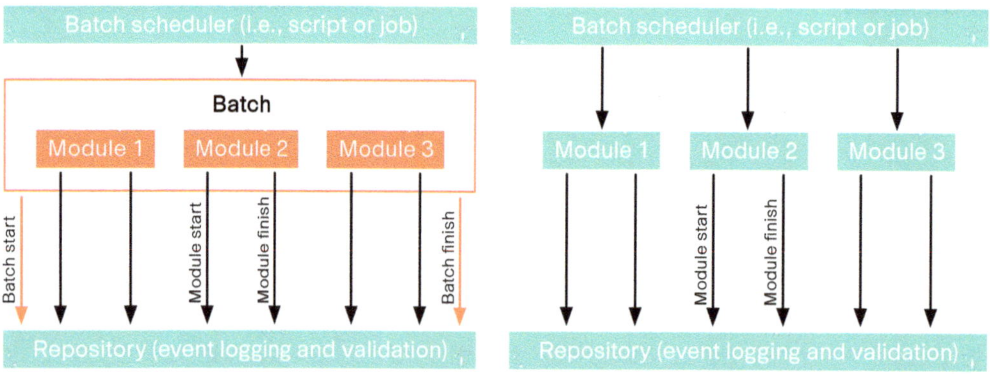

This is an example of how workflows can be defined using the batch concept, but it is important to make sure the modules themselves remain components that can be executed independently. This principle improves the overall scalability of the data solution.

Consider the following scenarios that benefit from the ability of modules to run independently:

→ You want to call some (generic) modules from multiple different batches
→ You don't always want to implement the batch concept. Batches should not become mandatory. If a module can run independently, the option to *not* use batch processing remains available
→ You prefer to implement data logistics orchestration that allows for continuous parallel processing of data, where all data is processed continuously without any dependencies

The ability to operate without batches allows for continuous parallel processing of data with minimum overhead. While it is still possible to implement the batch concept, this is not a necessity when all modules run in a fully parallel orchestration. In this configuration, implementing batches may incur unnecessary overheads. For more details on this approach please refer to the ⚐ continuous parallel processing sections.

About batch processing

Even though a scheduled data refresh, such as a 'daily load,' may be enough to meet (current) business requirements, the control framework and reference data solution architecture have been designed for *any* processing frequency. This is a fundamental design principle, which intends to guarantee scaling of data logistics by not depending on batch processing alone.

This is the concept of continuous parallel processing and *eventual consistency,* which allows all data to be processed continuously and without dependencies or constraints. During parallel processing, there will be an ever-increasing point in time when consistency of data can be asserted.

By using the data collected by the control framework, this moment can be calculated and used for further processing or reporting purposes. This concept, and the mechanisms to implement it, will be covered in more detail in the ⚐ getting the data in section.

Creating the audit trail

↗ Each time a process is run, a uniquely generated Audit Trail Id is saved with the data.

The control framework supports the ability to record ('log') what data has been loaded, when, and in what way, for every individual data logistics process.

This means that the following information must be available (with an accompanying timestamp):

→ When a record was inserted
→ What module processed the data
→ What the operational system was where the record originated from
→ Which interface has loaded the data
→ Which batch has loaded the data, if any
→ On which platform the process took place
→ Any notifications, warnings, or errors that may have been raised
→ How many records were read, inserted, updated, or deleted

The control framework records these details when batches or modules are instantiated, joined via the Audit Trail Id. Each time a process is run, the unique generated Audit Trail Id is saved *with* the data.

This way, for every individual record you can trace what process (instance) inserted or otherwise modified the record, when this happened, and what the context was.

Consider the example below. This diagram contains administrative (static) details on batch and module definitions. This is the *registration,* where each batch and module receives an unique identifier from the control framework – the 'batch id' and 'module id' in this example. This represents the administrative view of the control framework.

Batch Administration

Batch Id	Batch Name	Batch Description
500	Load Customer Details from Source A.	Example of a batch that calls three separate modules.
600	Refresh Data Delivery for Sales.	Example of a batch that only calls a single module.

Module Administration

Module Id	Module Name	Module Description	Data Target	Area
7500	Module 1	POS_XREF_CS	NBR_CUSTOMER_SALE	Integration Area
7501	Module 2	POS_XREF_CS	CUSTOMER	Integration Area
7502	Module 3	POS_XREF_CS	PRODUCT	Integration Area
8000	Module 10	POS_Demo	CUSTOMER_DETAILS	Integration Area
9000	Module 1000	HR_EMPLOYE	DIM_EMPLOYEE	Access Area

Batch / Module Relationship

Module Id	Batch Id
7500	500
7501	500
7502	500
7500	750
8000	600

Modules can optionally be assigned to a batch to implement a container or workflow. In the diagram this concept is shown as the 'batch/module relationship' table:

→ Batch 500 contains modules 7500, 7501 and 7502
→ Batch 600 only contains a single module – module 8000
→ Module 7500 is called by multiple batches – 500 and 750

There is also a module that is *not* allocated to a batch – module 9000. This serves as an example that defining batches should not be mandatory.

The next diagram contains example runtime details that are generated by the control framework during instantiation – the batch and module processing. These are the Audit Trail Ids that are ultimately linked to the data.

Batch Instance

Audit Trail Id	Batch Id	Batch Execution System Id	Start Timestamp	End Timestamp	Execution Satus
26397	500	0x425	2024-01-05 16:32	2024-01-05 16:59	Succeeded
27001	600	0xF43	2024-01-05 17:12		Running

Module Instance

Audit Trail Id	Module Id	Batch Audit Trail Id	Module Execution System Id	Start Timestamp	End Timestamp	Execution Status	#Selected	#Inserted	#Updated	#Deleted	#Discarded	#Rejected
26911	7500	26397	0xA23	2024-01-05 16:32	2024-01-05 16:35	Succeeded	4555	2050	0	0	2505	0
26912	7501	26397	0x262	2024-01-05 16:35	2024-01-05 16:45	Succeeded	1000	1000	0	0	0	0
26913	7502	26397	0x8B3	2024-01-05 16:45	2024-01-05 16:59	Succeeded	500	500	0	0	0	0
27029	8000	27001	0x9FE	2024-01-05 17:12		Running						
27031	9000	0	0x15D	2024-01-05 17:13		Running						

Target data set

Surrogate Key	Inscription Timestamp	<payload>	Audit Trail Id	<other framework attributes>
10	2024-01-05 : 16:33: 01	<data>	26911	<other framework attributes>
15	2024-01-05 : 16:33: 02	<data>	26911	<other framework attributes>

Even if we wouldn't have access to the static control framework data, the example shows that using the runtime information it's possible to derive which module was called by which batch.

In the 'batch instance' and 'module instance' data, we can see that batch 500 (Audit Trail Id 26397) has spawned three module processes related to the modules 7500, 7501 and 7502. Because these are instances —unique executions— each will receive its own unique Audit Trail Id (26911, 26912, and 26913).

The 'module instance' Audit Trail Id represents a singular data logistics process which may perform a copy, transformation, or similar, across a data set potentially containing many records. The runtime details are tracked by the control framework, as visible in the number of records selected or inserted.

Module 7500 is defined in the static control framework 'module administration' as a process that loads data from the 'POS_XREF_CS' source data object to the 'NBR_CUSTOMER_SALE' target data object. Judging from the runtime details in the module instance object, this process selected 4555 records and inserted 2050 records, while (gracefully) discarding 2505 records.

As a note, the difference between discarding and rejecting records in our view is that discarding is by design and rejecting is related to system errors – but this distinction can be implemented as desired.

The 'target data set' in this example really is the 'NBR_CUSTOMER_SALE' table or file. After all, this is where module 7500 is writing data into according to the administration. The example displays two records (of an expected total of 2050) to demonstrate how the link between the Audit Trail Id and the data is established.

If, at some point in the future, it's necessary to understand how the data found its way to a table or file it is always possible to query what process was responsible for the data change.

Similarly, most data integration platforms also use internal execution runtime values that can be written back to the control framework. In the examples used, this is represented as the 'batch execution system id' and 'module execution system id' – both represented as GUIDs (binary values) which refer to values managed by the data integration platform.

By querying the control framework it is possible to find out when this process ran, what the process was meant to do, and if there are any events associated with this unique module execution.

Recording events

The logical view we introduced in the overview section of the control framework contains an *event log* that can be reference by both the module and the batch instance. Any events worth capturing can be logged against an Audit Trail Id at both the batch and/or module level.

Depending on the implementation, these events can be verbose or capture only essential information that can't be retrieved from the instance tables themselves – for example technical errors. Many data integration platforms provide features to catch error messages and –through *event handling*– write these back to the data logistics control framework.

The implementation of event handling and error detection is custom development that will be different for each technical environment (data integration platform). A common way to manage this is to create an API that passes the Audit Trail Id and error message back to the control framework.

Idempotence and data logistics process transaction control

In the world of data chapter we wrote that, ideally, a process control framework is designed to be *idempotent*. The framework must be able to remember which tasks completed successfully, and re-run only tasks that failed.

We also mentioned that one of the functions of the control framework is to protect the consistency of the overall data solution, similar to how ACID principles guarantee data consistency for compliant database systems.

The control framework applies similar concepts across the data solution – at the 'application level.' It provides information that can be used to only select data that is *fully committed* to the data solution when delivering information to downstream processes or consumers.

To be able to meet these requirements, the control framework has to capture the process state; whether it is running or completed and if failures were encountered.

To show how this can be done, we can use a modified version of the example used in the creating the audit trail section.

Batch Instance

Audit Trail Id	Batch Id	Batch Execution System Id	Start Timestamp	End Timestamp	Execution Satus
26397	500	0x425	2024-01-05 16:32	2024-01-05 16:59	Succeeded
27030	500	0x76C	2024-01-05 17:15		Running

Module Instance

Audit Trail Id	Module Id	Batch Audit Trail Id	Module Execution System Id	Start Timestamp	End Timestamp	Execution Status	#Selected	#Inserted	#Updated	#Deleted	#Discarded	#Rejected
26911	7500	26397	0xA23	2024-01-05 16:32	2024-01-05 16:35	Succeeded	4555	2050	0	0	2505	0
26912	7501	26397	0x262	2024-01-05 16:35	2024-01-05 16:45	Succeeded	1000	1000	0	0	0	0
26913	7502	26397	0x8B3	2024-01-05 16:45	2024-01-05 16:59	Succeeded	500	500	0	0	0	0
27035	7500	27030	0x18A	2024-01-05 17:15		Running						

Target data set

Surrogate Key	Inscription Timestamp	<payload>	Audit Trail Id	<other framework attributes>
10	2024-01-05 : 16:33: 01	<data>	26911	<other framework attributes>
15	2024-01-05 : 16:33: 02	<data>	26911	<other framework attributes>
25	2024-01-05 : 17:15: 01	<data>	27035	<other framework attributes>

Instead of using this information for audit trail purposes, as we have done previously, we now focus on the execution status.

After successfully completing earlier, batch 500 has now restarted. This new run has been issued with batch Audit Trail Id 27030 and has the execution status 'running.' It will remain in this state until all of its modules are completed, or when failures are encountered.

The modules invoked by batch 500 will also start as a result of the batch execution. Since these have been implemented with a sequential dependency only module 7500 has begun processing. This module instance —with Audit Trail Id 27035— is also in running state.

What does this mean for the data in our target? We can see that there is already data associated with module Audit Trail Id 27035, because this data is currently being processed.

However, at this point in time we can not be certain of the outcome of the process. There may be a technical error that will require a *roll-back* of the data to its original state. Until the process associated with, in this case, Audit Trail Id 27035, is successfully completed we should not use this data yet.

If we do, it could be considered a *dirty read.* Since the data can potentially be reverted, a query against the same table at a different point in time may yield different results. This is because the data in the table may have been related to a failure in the processing and has since been removed, and will not be available until reprocessing — and even then it is not guaranteed that the content will be exactly the same.

The similarity between ACID implementation at the database level are striking, and because of this we refer to these mechanisms as application-level transaction control. The information in the control framework, the execution status for each process, will inform us what data we can query and what data to exclude for now.

Now, imagine that the running instance of batch 500 (27030) fails at the second of three planned module instances:

Batch Instance

Audit Trail Id	Batch Id	Batch Execution System Id	Start Timestamp	End Timestamp	Execution Satus
26397	500	0x425	2024-01-05 16:32	2024-01-05 16:59	Succeeded
27030	500	0x76C	2024-01-05 17:15	2024-01-05 17:18	Failed

Module Instance

Audit Trail Id	Module Id	Batch Audit Trail Id	Module Execution System Id	Start Timestamp	End Timestamp	Execution Status	#Selected	#Inserted	#Updated	#Deleted	#Discarded	#Rejected
26911	7500	26397	0xA23	2024-01-05 16:32	2024-01-05 16:35	Succeeded	4555	2050	0	0	2505	0
26912	7501	26397	0x262	2024-01-05 16:35	2024-01-05 16:45	Succeeded	1000	1000	0	0	0	0
26913	7502	26397	0x8B3	2024-01-05 16:45	2024-01-05 16:59	Succeeded	500	500	0	0	0	0
27035	7500	27030	0x18A	2024-01-05 17:15	2024-01-05 17:17	Succeeded	125	124	0	0	1	0
27036	7501	27030	0xACB	2024-01-05 17:17	024-01-05 17:18	Failed	1000					

When a failure is encountered while running the second module instance, both the failing process as well as the batch instance will report failure.

The next time the batch runs again, the first module (that previously completed successfully) will have to be skipped in order to be idempotent.

The second module should then retry and, if successful, the subsequent and final (third) module will be executed. Until this time, the data should not be used even if it's *technically* committed to the data platform.

This example shows how a batch configuration can help manage the unit of work, and recovery processes thereof. If modules are executed independently the application-level ACID still applies to the data that is intended to be processed by the module.

This mechanism helps to simplify day-to-day management and monitoring, but is also important to protect the consistency of the overall solution.

Consider, for example, what would happen if the modules part of batch 500 would detect and load change delta (differential) from an operational system using a truncate & load pattern? To guarantee consistency (prevent data loss) it is critical that this data delta needs to be *fully committed* to all downstream targets before it can be released.

Orchestration

The orchestration framework is closely related to the control framework. However, they are not the same. While the control framework focuses on logging and status control, the orchestration framework looks after the *scheduling, execution* and *dependencies.*

To function properly, the orchestration framework uses design metadata that is stored in the data logistics control framework — such as any constraints in the order of execution.

A core tenet of the orchestration approach is that every data logistics process can be executed independently. The ability to do so depends both on the design of the data logistics processes (the 'patterns') as well as the way these are configured in the control framework — as individual processes.

If it is possible to execute each process independently, at any time and in any order, it is also possible to create containers or groups of processes that control the overall data flow.

For instance, you can group all processes related to a specific operational system, and load all its data into the data solution by running the single batch.

The fact that processes can be executed independently does not mean that you have to, just that you have that option. It provides flexibility.

At this stage, the only things to do for the orchestration framework is to schedule the data logistics processes either completely separately or in a workflow. This typically requires a 'wrapper' that allows the data logistics process to be run, and a scheduler to run them in.

If we use the batch and module definitions from the control framework, this involves creating an executable that can invoke a batch or module. This executable can then be scheduled.

Specific orchestration concepts are covered in each of the main layer chapters that are part of the ⚐ getting the data in chapter.

Testing

A *testing framework* can be used at both development and test time, as well as part of notification checks that monitor the health of the data solution at runtime.

Test definitions and implementations are handled by the ⚐ testing component, whereas pro-active monitoring is covered by the ⚐ notification component.

The testing framework allows for the definition of test cases that specify the expected outputs for a set of given (test) inputs.

Tests can be run to evaluate if the returned outputs are in line with the pre-defined expectations, and thus assert that the process works as intended.

Most testing frameworks, both open source as well as commercial, offer a variety of features to define many types of test cases. Included functionality, for example, is to generate test data for record counts or mock-up copies of existing tables and/or data that are created when the test is executed — allowing tests to run without touching live data.

Range checks are also typically supported, and can be used to evaluate if outcomes are within an expected range (numeric or statistical) when exact outcomes may not be expected.

Overview of the testing framework

The testing framework is typically implemented as a repository separate from the data platform. This repository can be a database (or schema) or a set of files.

An overview of the testing framework at a high level is illustrated below:

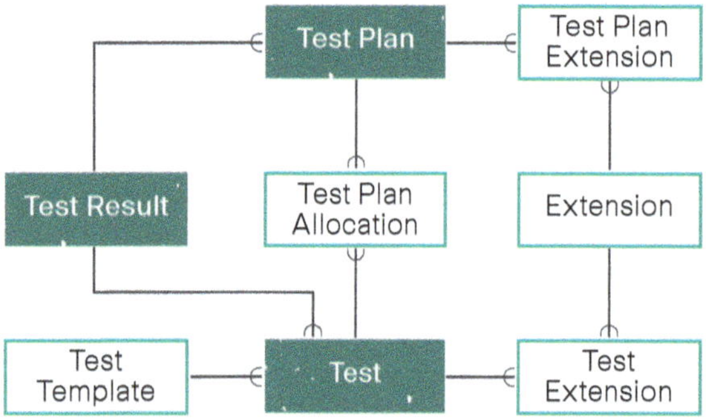

The testing framework defines *tests.* Tests are independent executables that return a 'pass' or 'fail' response when executed. This binary result, along with additional details to assist in troubleshooting or clarification, is recorded in the *test results.*

Each test is ideally created based on a *test template,* which links to a design pattern outlining the test's purpose and approach. This can be the blueprint for further automation and code generation. Examples of these include 'asserting referential integrity' or 'ensure temporal completeness.'

The template also serves as a grouping of tests, because a test is essentially an instance of the template which applies to a specific data object. A typical testing framework contains many tests for a given template.

Tests can also be organized into a *test plan.* This is a collection of tests intended to be run together, potentially with dependencies and sequencing.

Furthermore, both tests and test plans can be extended with custom properties to accommodate specific requirements.

Running tests

A test is an independent executable tailored to the target platform, designed to return a pass or fail result. Tests can be run directly from the testing framework or registered in the control framework using modules and batches.

By registering tests as modules, they can be included in orchestration and executed through the control framework, providing additional logging and visibility.

Similarly, batches offer an alternative way to implement the test plan concept. Alternatively, it is also possible to wrap the entire test plan in a module, as this is an executable —generated from design metadata— as well.

Applying the testing framework for development and testing

When working with data, there rarely is a better time to fully understand the underlying logic and reasoning than during the creation of a data logistics process. During development time, the expected outputs of a given process are the most clear.

This is the perfect time to capture this understanding in test cases.

Not only does this deliver a (re-testable) artifact that can act as documented 'evidence' of unit-testing, the same test can be added to the testing framework repository and executed each time a change in the solution is made.

DevOps pipelines can be configured to run all tests when a new change (build) is created, and the build can be configured to fail if one or more tests report an issue.

Applying the testing framework for monitoring

Beyond the DevOps or development context, some tests can be meaningful to run against the live environment as monitoring tasks from time to time. This guarantees that the system continues to behave in accordance with the design, even after deployment.

A typical approach is to schedule these test cases independently of other data logistics tasks. The reason for this is that not every test necessarily requires to be run as often as regular data logistics processes do, and performance and other impacts can be a factor too. But it's equally possible to embed these tests in the main data logistics process execution workflows. Scheduling can be customized for the environment.

Running tests as maintenance tasks can be a very powerful feature for the data solution, and one that contributes to establishing trust in data with the stakeholders – especially the data consumers. It demonstrates to all involved that the solution is under tight control.

To enable this, the tests can be added to the monitoring framework. This concept, which is covered in the next section, essentially schedules logic execution (tests or otherwise) and informs the administrators depending on certain conditions. For instance when certain tests fail or are not run.

Tests can be specifically developed for the purpose of pro-actively monitoring the system and its data. For instance, to periodically evaluate certain key figures like total revenue, produced items, number of claims, or customer sales.

If a test triggers a notification, for example because the produced items are more than 20 % lower week by week, this may not necessarily be an issue that is caused by incorrect configuration of the data solution. It may be correct purely looking at the data. However, being able to pro-actively reach out to stakeholders with this kind of information can be another major contributor to fostering trust in and, by extension, the acceptance of the data solution.

Another use case is testing the control framework itself:

- → Are there any data logistics processes that are were expected to run, but didn't?
- → Are there any processes that did run, but shouldn't?
- → Are they running longer than usual?
- → Are there any flags that were inadvertently changed?

Having test cases to monitor the control framework can be a powerful maintenance tool and often highlights issues in its configuration.

Similarly, the same concept can be applied to the technical environment as well:

- → Is there a high degree of index fragmentation?
- → Are all indexes available?
- → Are there any constraints enforced when they shouldn't be?
- → Are any conventions violated?

Some test cases are created specifically for monitoring purposes, some are only for unit testing, and some can be used for both scenarios. In all cases the same testing framework can be leveraged.

Monitoring

The monitoring framework includes tracking process status (monitoring), alerting, notification, maintenance, and logging. The framework is closely aligned to, and dependent on, both the control framework and the testing framework.

This supporting framework serves to ensure that the data solution asserts if known issues do no (re)appear on an ongoing basis, and that administrators are notified when this is the case.

A monitoring framework is a combination of several closely related concepts, including a mechanism for notification —when certain events are raised— as well as routine maintenance and the collection of internal data for management of the data solution itself.

Notification

Notification tasks can run on their own schedule, or as part of the data logistics framework. The only difference is that a notification is issued based on certain conditions (e.g., test outcome not as expected, values out of expected bounds).

Maintenance

A special category are *maintenance tasks.*

Maintenance tasks carry out specific actions at a specified frequency, or when certain events occur. The difference between test cases and maintenance tasks is that maintenance tasks actively address certain issues or execute code for optimization purposes.

Examples are defragmentation processes for indexes, when the fragmentation levels reach a certain threshold. Or evaluation of compression configurations, when it is detected that certain areas of the solution do not meet specifications.

We have seen maintenance tasks that evaluate to what extent a data solution does not meet (design and development) conventions, and fix any inconsistencies encountered. The more stringent the standards are, the better these options will fit the solution.

The available options often depend on the technical environment to some degree, as certain platforms offer different features – or not suffer from certain problems at all.

Logging

A related concept to both notification and maintenance is logging.

A data solution potentially uses various technical components, such as a data logistics technology, a data store (file storage or database) and data delivery components – and possibly multiple of these in various combinations.

Each of these systems provide, or can be configure to provide, operational data on usage, state and (depending on the technology) many statistics on the health of the technical component.

This operational data, as is relevant for the performance and reliability of the data solution, can be collected and made available. This is what the logging concept intends to ensure.

Logging information can be exposed and integrated into the maintenance and notification tasks. For example, when disk space is getting low or when CPU utilization is above certain thresholds.

A common use case is understanding data query patterns across the data solution. What are users querying the data for? How much data is returned, and how long does this take? How often are these queries run?

This information can be fed back into the engine to automatically optimize the data solution for the most common use cases – or to guarantee certain service level agreements.

The monitoring framework overall, and the logging component in particular, enable this. Having said that, this information can also be a powerful design tool. After all, if it is clear that users are more interested in some data rather than other, this can be a sign that more of this kind of data might be beneficial.

Example architectures

Up to this point, this chapter provided an overview of the concepts that define the data solution. As a *reference* architecture we have organized these into three layers, with each layer having two areas. The reference architecture also incorporates various supporting frameworks.

This does not mean that every data solution should be designed this way. In fact, there are *many* possible configurations that can be defined using the outlined concepts.

In this section, we provide a number of the commonly used configurations. It is important to note that this is a conceptual view, not relating to any technology or platforms. In many cases, different technologies can be considered even *within* an area. Please note that the supporting frameworks are not displayed in these diagrams for brevity.

There are additional possible configurations than the ones mentioned, and there is no right or wrong. There are only options and considerations.

Layers and areas mean complexity, so it is important to make sure the functionality this brings is worth it.

The reference

The 'reference' configuration is simply our complete reference solution architecture. This configuration utilizes all layers and areas.

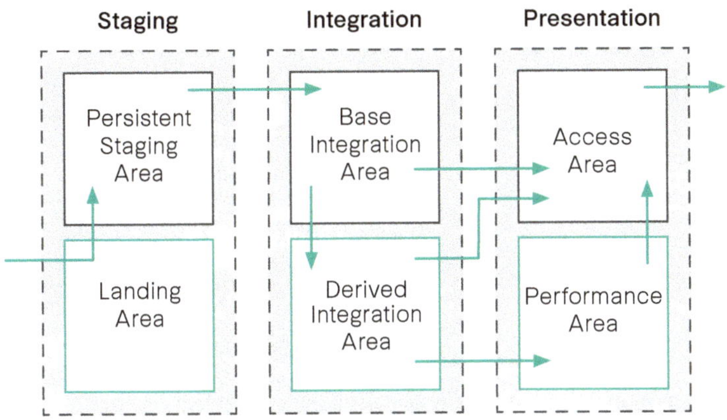

The data received from the operational systems is first committed to a PSA, using an LDA where necessary—for example when requiring a full compare to derive data delta.

The PSA is the foundation of the solution, and the data is mapped to the information (business) data model from here. If additional transformations are necessary these are done in the derived integration area.

Data is loaded into the target delivery structure from both the base integration area and the derived integration area. The performance area may be used for performance efficiencies and to prevent duplication of logic.

The consumers receive their data from the access area.

The traditional

The 'traditional' configuration essentially is the reference architecture without a PSA.

Because of this, there is typically more emphasis on the LDA. Data may be first staged in the LDA to perform data delta detection —technical CDC— where necessary and, for example, to standardize data types.

There is also a slightly different version of this approach where data is *directly* loaded into the base integration area. This is an option for where this is possible, for instance if data deltas can be reliably received.

Whether this is possible depends on the way the data can be delivered to the data solution, the interfacing approach, which is sometimes limited by the operational systems in place. This is not always something that can be controlled by the data solution, and implementing different ways of interfacing for operational systems may take a long time to implement, or may not be feasible at all.

If data is loaded directly into the base integration area, the data logistics process needs to incorporate the features of the staging layer because it is essentially omitted.

Many solutions that adopt this configuration have an LDA for some data sources, and load the data directly into the base integration area for others. This decision depends on how the data can be delivered. For data that is already in a transactional structure, such as event streams or CDC the data can be directly loaded into the integration layer. This is because there is no need to derive data delta.

For other sources, such as complete flat file ('full file dumps') the data delta first needs to be evaluated to understand logical deletes – for which the LDA can be applied.

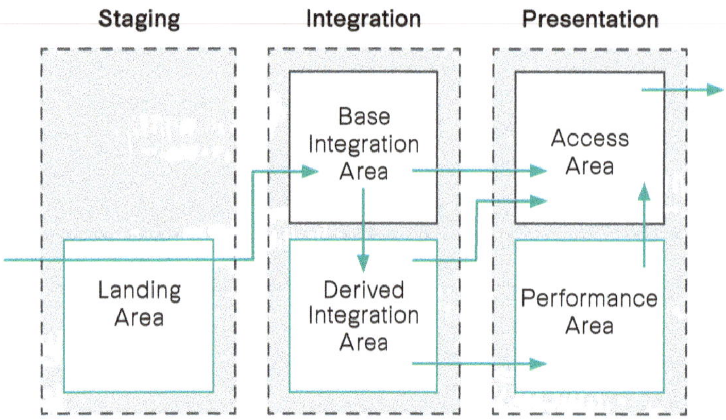

This configuration offers a limited ability to modify and refactor the information data model over time.

Conceptually, it is possible to refactor the information data model by reusing the data in the base integration area. However, in practice this can be complicated because the new model is created from data that has been distributed all over the integration layer.

Custom data logistics processes need to be created to load the refactored entities. While this is not impossible, there is a reasonable chance of running into unforeseen issues which can render the solution into an unstable state (data loss) – so care must be taken.

Also, this implies that *all* data is available in the integration layer which may not be the case – simply because the development of the solution has not yet progressed to this stage.

A last consideration is that this approach is geared towards a more traditional view of first loading raw data into the integration layer, and deriving all other interpretations afterwards – in the derived integration layer.

The better safe than sorry

Adding a PSA to the *traditional* configuration, but not making this an integral part of the data flow creates a 'better safe than sorry' approach.

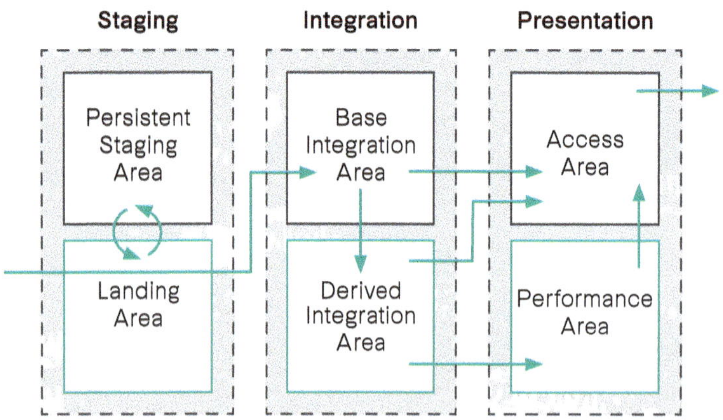

In most aspects, the same features from the traditional configuration apply. However, because the PSA is configured as supporting area an LDA becomes all but necessary. The reason for this is that an incoming data (delta) set must be committed to two targets: to the PSA as well as the base integration area.

It is typically easier to stage the data in the LDA first, wait for *both* downstream processes to complete and then start the next fetch of data.

The PSA can still support refactoring of the integration and presentation layers through re-initialization. However, in this configuration this involves copying the PSA contents to the LDA, and then restarting the downstream data logistics from there.

When regular operation resumes, the regular processes that process data from the operational systems to the LDA will truncate the LDA again, and insert the new data (delta).

Data solution initiatives that adopt this approach often do this with the intent to use a PSA in the early, more volatile, phases of the data solution – while the information model is still 'settling.' The idea is that once the model is sufficiently stable, the PSA can be dropped to reduce the data storage footprint.

The judger

The 'judger' configuration uses the same concepts in yet a different way. It adopts an approach that loads data into an information data model that is as complete and correct as it possibly can be. Applying transformations *into* the integration layer is supported in this line of thinking as it places emphasis on getting the model right upfront. It's just the data that needs to fit.

Because interpretations are done 'on the way in' to the solution, a derived integration area is usually not necessary and therefore not displayed in the diagram. After all, why need a derived version if the original is already complete?

However, configurations can be defined that still include this.

As a safety measure, a PSA is typically included in the design because this allows reloading the integration layer when changes to interpretations are made.

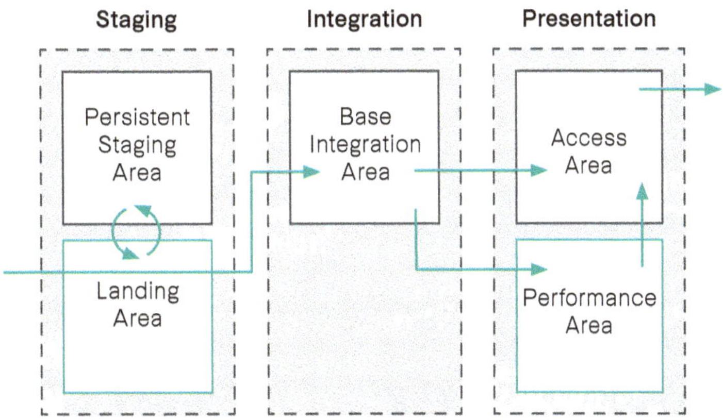

Note that the PSA itself can be configured in two ways, as an optional supporting area with a re-initialization process, or as the area that populates the integration layer directly.

The go for broke

The 'going for broke' approach is an example of a *two-tiered* architecture. There is no integration layer, only a staging and presentation layer. The presentation layer represents the data in a way that is fit for consumption. Because of this, data is judged on the way in to the solution.

This is an example of how the dimensional bus architecture[23] can be implemented. In most cases, the landing area is already shaped to the structure of the presentation layer. The staging layer serves to prepare the data so that it can easily be merged with the data already available in the presentation layer.

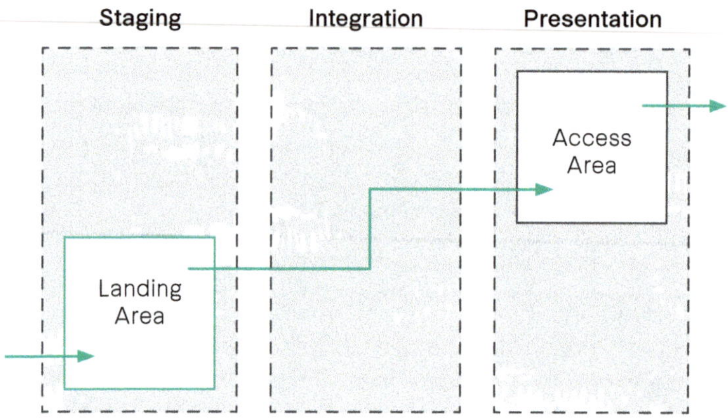

This approach often defines data marts, centered around fact tables supported by dimension tables containing the descriptive attributes.

In some cases, data marts may share dimension tables. These are called *conformed dimensions*[24]. In such cases, the same dimension table is referred to by more than one fact table.

In a two-tiered architecture, the presentation layer usually embodies the organization-wide information data model. In previous configurations, this was managed in the integration layer.

The minimalist

An even more basic version of a two-tiered architecture is the 'minimalist.' This approach populates the presentation layer *directly* from the operational systems.

This is also known as an *operational data mart.* The design of the presentation layer is typically related to the structure of the operational system it receives the data from. For example, the naming of columns and tables is often similar.

There often is no organization-wide holistic information model, or, if there is the presentation layer is not integrated in it. It is of course also possible to incorporate a more holistic information model in this configuration, but this is uncommon.

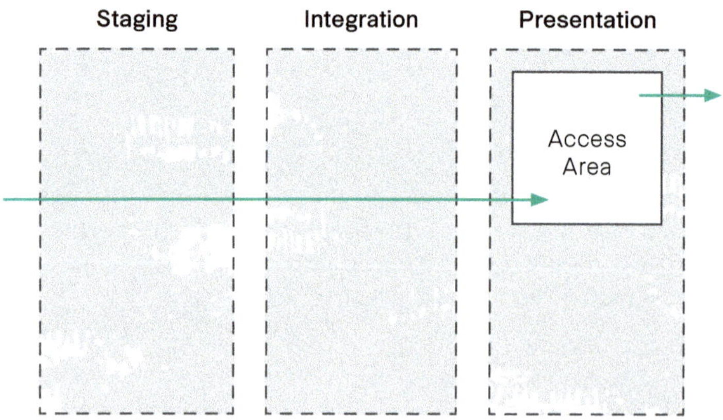

There can be many independent data marts that follow this configuration. An operational system can 'spawn' multiple data marts – either connected or independent.

The hedger

A special version of the two-tiered solution design is the 'hedger.' This essentially is a data mart-centric design that incorporates a PSA.

Similar to the previous two examples, the information model is represented through the presentation layer. However, because a PSA is available the data marts can be re-initialized to facilitate new requirements and address known issues.

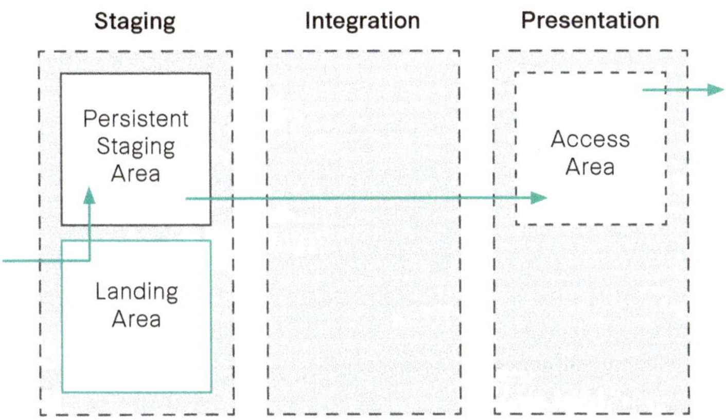

It is common for organizations to start with this approach, and build a solid foundation and show some early results, while keeping options open for a more extensive design that incorporates the additional components from the reference architecture over time.

The virtual delivery

There is a different way to look at data logistics, and the role they play in the solution design, by considering 'virtual delivery.'

'Virtual,' in this context, means that data is not physically 'moved' from one place to another. Instead, it is *interpreted* without actually instantiating the result to disk. The outcome is identical to physically loading data.

Conceptually, this is similar to a database view or query. You look at the data in its intended state —as per the target model— but don't store the data in a physical object.

Virtual designs can be applied to almost all areas of the solution, and can be thought of as an implementation alternative. From an architecture perspective, it is important to mention that the ability to 'virtualize' parts of the design requires a reliable underlying persisted data store.

In most cases, this persisted data store —the one that enables virtualization— will be the base integration area or the PSA.

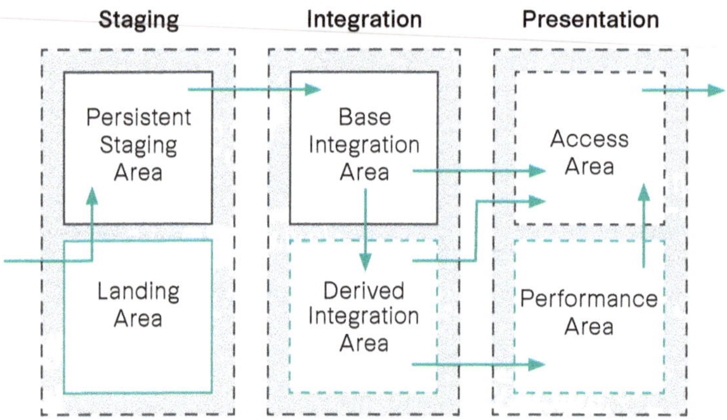

This diagram shows a possible configuration that focuses on virtualizing the delivery — the presentation layer. In this approach, the data marts are virtualized and therefore easy to modify, and can host multiple versions.

Virtualizing the derived integration area is also an option. This results in a base integration area containing physical objects, and (derived) interpretations accessible as views or APIs.

Performance is a major consideration for virtualization. Can the data be delivered in an acceptable timeframe? Are there costs associated with running the code (compute)? Considerations such as these are an important driver when deciding for a virtual delivery. In some cases, this may result in solutions where parts of the system are virtual while other parts are persisted.

The dynamics at play involve balancing (acceptable) performance with cost, speed of development, and ease of maintenance. Requirements for this may change over time, throughout the lifecycle of the data initiative. The resulting 'mix' of physical and virtual components may change over time as well.

The all-in virtual

For an extreme virtual delivery, you can go 'all-in virtual.' For some, this is the dream of managing data solutions, because all functionality in the data solution is derived at runtime from the original transactions in the PSA.

In this solution design, the PSA is the only persisted area.

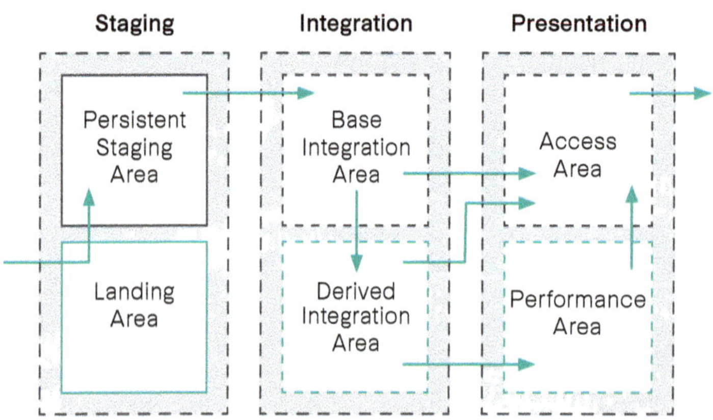

This approach provides maximum flexibility at the expense of requiring more performance from the underlying technical platform. It can be thought of as 'layers of views,' and the performance cost may be prohibitive even for medium-sized systems.

However, as with the other example architectures, components from the design can be modified when it makes sense. For the all-in virtual approach this may mean that, over time, parts of the solution are persisted if performance demands this. The areas in the presentation layer are good first candidates for this.

All-in virtual provides an easy way to look at the results of your design and metadata without physically creating tables, files, and data logistics processes that copy and transform data.

For this reason, it is often used for prototyping and workshops. Once the design is agreed on, the corresponding design metadata can be used to generate physical data logistics processes as easy as they can be used to generate views or queries.

The Lambda

The 'Lambda' architecture is the first example of incorporating streaming concepts in the data solution architecture. In previous examples, data is delivered with a certain frequency. This might be often but is not continuous – even if the recurrence is *very* frequent (i.e., 'micro-batch').

When data sources stream data, transactions arrive in the data solution *all the time.*

Describing streaming concepts crosses into technology to an extent, but for our reference architecture we try to keep a conceptual view on the application of this technology.

In some cases, there may be a requirement to expose the incoming data *near real-time* in the presentation layer or in reports. It is possible to support this without delay, as well as integrating the data into the information data model following the reference architecture (which will be slower).

This is what Lambda architecture intends; to have a 'fast lane' where data is immediately made available for consumption (reporting) purposes, and a 'slow lane' where the *same data* is processed and integrated following batch-focused processing.

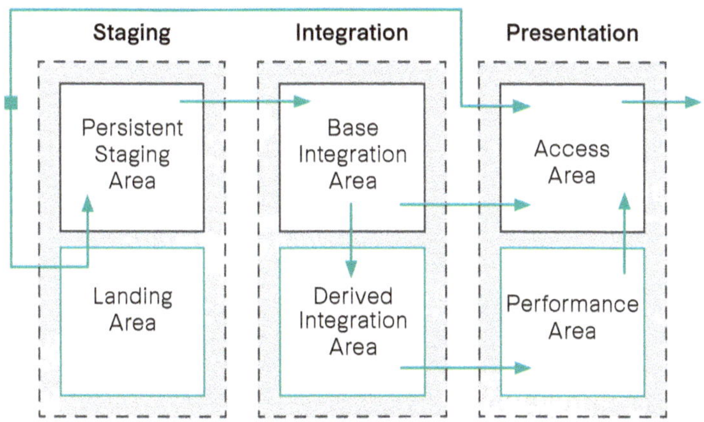

Working with stream data processing can be different than using traditional data stores, not easier or harder – just (slightly) different. It may be helpful to think of streaming technology as a PSA built in different technology – one you can also query directly.

In this context it is worthwhile to mention that event streaming technology uses a concept referred to as time to live (TTL), which is the time historical transactions remain available. Depending on the TTL settings, historical transactions are either compacted (deduplicated), or removed outright after a certain amount of time – or never if this is configured.

For reasons such as this, it can still beneficial to keep a 'local' PSA for the data solution. The streaming platform may not be in full control of the data solution.

The Kappa

The 'Kappa' is the second example of using streaming technology for the data solution. *Kappa* stems from the Kappa architecture concept. The main difference compared to Lambda architecture is that, in Kappa architecture, you use the *same* technology to (re)build the data interpretation. In Lambda architecture you need different approaches for real-time and batch.

In other words, both batch and streaming are handled by the same technology.

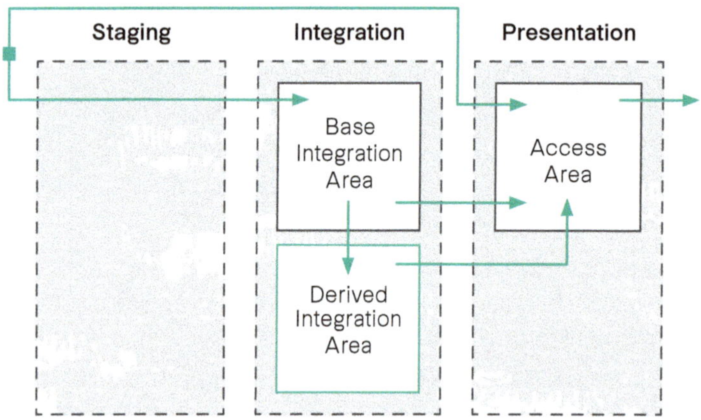

If you have a complete event streaming middleware solution such as a distributed log pub/sub platform (e.g., Kafka) with an infinite TTL, the PSA as a separate area becomes superfluous. The pub/sub already contains all transactions (events) and it is up to the consumer to manage to what extent the consumption of these events needs to be up to date.

Every consumer manages their own interpretation, and reads from the log from the offset (e.g., pointer, timestamp) that applies to them individually.

The data solution is one of the consumers and can provide various independent representations of data –in the form of the information data model or through the access area– which can be made available to yet other consumers (such as the semantic layer).

In this approach, this all happens on a single platform. There are variations of this approach that can be considered, such as deploying the presentation area first and adding an integration layer concept when complexity increases. The pub/sub platform provides the same functionality as the PSA otherwise would.

This is assuming that the pub/sub platform provides a generous, ideally infinite, TTL. This can be essential for the data solution because this ultimately determines the window to replay historical transactions for refactoring and virtualization.

A PSA can potentially be added to the design if a longer timespan of historical transactions is required then, or when it is accepted that certain states of interpretation cannot be refactored when the data reaches a certain age – because transactions have exceeded their TTL.

Closing notes on the solution architecture

We have come to the end of the overview of our standard reference architecture. In some cases, we have taken a position on what we consider the default approach for certain concepts, but this does not mean this is the *only* correct solution.

In most cases, making sure certain aspects are considered –and a decision is made– is more important than a specific implementation. In other words, it is more important to make sure *that* certain concepts are implemented than *how* they are implemented.

Specific details on how to do certain things best, for a given situation, is the domain of the solution pattern. And these can evolve, along with their technical implementation.

In these closing notes we would like to provide some additional background, so that this hopefully contributes to decision-making in your data solution architecture.

Fundamental principles for data logistics

↗ The fundamental principles for data logistics processes enable them to be run and re-run at any point in time to support flexible scheduling and implementation.

In this chapter we have provided a comprehensive overview of the reference architecture. These rules and guidelines provide the foundation for a successful data solution.

But every data solution ultimately is about the data. And data is moved around, or interpreted, by the many data logistics processes that feed into the data solution. Data logistics processes are the heart of the data solution because, together, they provide the data in a meaningful way – molded into the target information data model.

Regardless of its place in the architecture or purpose, every data logistics process should be created to follow a concise set of basic rules.

The overarching motivation is to develop data logistics processes that won't cause errors due to unplanned or unwanted execution. Essentially, data logistics processes must be able to be run and re-run at *any point in time* to support flexible scheduling and implementation.

These essential concepts, such as making sure data logistics processes check if they have already run before inserting duplicates or corrupting data, will simplify testing, maintenance, and troubleshooting.

Because of this importance, we would like to summarize the essential features any individual data logistics process should have.

Atomic

Data integration processes are designed to contain transformation logic *for a single, specific purpose.*

This approach focuses on creating many processes that are modular, where each one will address a specific function, as opposed to few larger processes that perform a wide range of activities.

Each single data logistics process focuses on its own separate concern. It executes atomic functionality, such as key distribution, detecting changes and performing date math.

These atomic processes are typically easier to define, document, and implement as reusable, recurring patterns — something that is often not feasible with larger, monolithic processes.

Target-centric

As a convention, a data logistics process can read from one or more sources, but *only writes to a single target.* This rule further supports enabling data logistics processes to be atomic.

Forward-only

The direction of data processing and selection is always aimed *towards the next (target) area or layer.* In other words, it is always 'downstream.' The typical processing of data is from an operational system to a staging layer, integration layer, and then to a presentation layer.

No data logistics process should write data back to an earlier layer. This implies that the data required to continue processing is always available in the same layer.

Idempotent

Related to the previous principle, *idempotence* is a key feature of a robust data logistic process. By implementing this guideline, data logistics processes can be run many times without inadvertently altering any outcomes and can to be *rerun without the need to manually change settings.*

Each process should be able to run, and be rerun, without causing data loss or requiring manual intervention. If you run a single process multiple times in a row, it should not lead to any errors.

A great test is to run a process twice.
Does this cause issues?

Deterministic

Data logistics processes must be deterministic, consistently producing the same outcome when given the same input values. This dependable-by-design behavior simplifies solution maintenance, and ensures greater predictability and reliability in the overall system.

Independent

Data logistics processes should be able to run in any order, without any dependencies to other processes. This is related to the atomicity principle and corresponding modular design. By ensuring that data logistics processes can be run independently, any constraints on scheduling can be addressed.

Independent processes do not *have* to run independently, they can still be organized in workflows (batches). However, it is much harder to redesign a batch process into fully independent components *unless* they are independent. Designing data logistics processes to be independent provides a great degree of flexibility when requirements regarding data latency and availability change.

Auditable

Processed data can always be tied to the data logistics process that modified it, and the origins of data across processes are always available. This is the audit trail for data – represented by the *Audit Trail Id.*

This is covered by a correct implementation of a data logistics control framework and concepts such as the PSA.

Scalable

Data logistics processes must be able to *process multiple intervals* (data changes) in one run. Every time a data logistics process runs, it needs to process *all* available data.

This is an important requirement for data logistics processes to be able to be run at any point in time and to support near real-time processing.

A process should not just be able to load a single snapshot or change for a single key, but to correctly handle multiple changes in a single data set (for potentially the same key). For instance, if the address of an employee changes multiple times during a day and the process is run daily, all changes are still captured and correctly processed in a single run of the process. This guideline also prevents processes to be run many times for catch-up processing and makes it possible to easily change loading frequencies.

Failure-tolerant

Data logistics processes detect whether they should insert data or not. They should not fail on constraints. This design decision ensures that data logistics processes manage referential integrity and constraints regardless of the capabilities of the underlying technical environment or platform. They are self-sufficient.

An example is the distribution of surrogate keys by checking if keys are already present *before* they are inserted. Another example is performing checksum comparisons to avoid inadvertently inserting data that has not changed compared to earlier runs, and may even be duplicate.

Not only does this requirement make testing and maintenance easier, it also ensures that no data is corrupted when a process is run by accident.

Data logistics processes should also *automatically recover from failure.* This means that if an error has been detected, the process automatically rolls back the transaction or protects it until fully committed.

About referential integrity

In the sections covering the ⚐ integration layer it was mentioned that, by default, referential integrity (RI) is not enforced. Instead, we recommend implementing maintenance checks that can be run from time to time to assert that the solution is (still) behaving as expected.

We call this *lazy referential integrity,* because validation is performed *after* the data is inserted. It only exists to highlight something really gone awry, typically caused by incorrectly configured patterns or when certain data logistics processes are missed in the scheduling entirely.

Issues with RI should not exist. And of course, they still do happen – which is why having validation certainly is useful.

The thinking behind this approach is twofold:

→ Defining a solution without enforced RI is the most scalable by design, because this allows parallel loading and makes it possible to process data without any loading dependencies whatsoever (the eventual consistency concept)

→ As a back-room process, the intent is to avoid any technical errors so that data logistics processes always 'work.' Any issues with data (quality) can be solved in the front-room, or addressed by reloading or otherwise managing inconsistencies

Even though this is our preferred approach, it is more important *that* RI is addressed than *how* this is done.

It is perfectly feasible to start a project using a batch-oriented loading approach in which RI is managed by the database, and switch off the database-enforced RI at a later stage to facilitate a higher degree of parallel loading.

However, it is also true that being able to deliver a consistent solution without having the database enforce RI means that your patterns can do everything, and do it well.

This also indicates that the patterns can be adapted to other technical environments more easily. In some cases, the technical infrastructure in use may not even provide RI features. In others, having RI constraints defined can assist the internal query optimizers to deliver better performance.

Additionally, it is sometimes possible to define RI constraints but not enforce them — which benefits the optimizer without sacrificing parallel or independent loading of data.

We recommend considering these options and commit the decisions into a solution pattern for your data solution.

Exception handling

Fundamentally, exception handling is applicable to every process in the architecture. However, *how* this is managed is different for each individual layer.

For this, we can refer to the 'back room' and 'front room' concept again.

Exception handling in the back room

In the back room, everything imaginable is done to *prevent* any exceptions from ever occurring.

The back room, which covers the staging layer and a large portion of the integration layer, is designed to be as accommodating to the incoming data as possible.

Exception handling mechanisms in this part of the data solution are therefore designed to not reject data that does not fit requirements.

There is no judgment.

They are however, designed to *recover from technical errors,* with a focus on reload mechanisms, fault-tolerance, and reconciliation.

In terms of implementation, this means that the concept of exception handling —for the back room— becomes part of the requirement and design of the interfaces and standard data logistics controls.

For example, our recommendation is to make sure any interface to an operational system can periodically perform a reconciliation. In a reconciliation, the complete data set from the operational system is compared against the most current state of the data solution. The current state is defined as per the assertion timeline, when the data was inscribed — e.g., the most recently received data.

From an exception handling point of view, this means that you can recover from any outages, whenever a reconciliation is run. If for whatever reason some data was missed, this will be detected and inserted with the inscription timestamp of 'now.'

Being able to implement a reconciliation mechanism may not always be feasible, because it is part of the interfacing between the operational system and the data solution and this is not always something that can be controlled.

But if it can be done, it is worth the effort. We have seen many cases where data was found to be missing, which may happen for many reasons and often goes undetected. It seems that, unless a ⚐ full outer join approach for delta detection is used, it is almost certain that at some point the data between the operational system and data solution will drift apart.

This creates a risk of losing credibility for the data solution, even though the reasons for it may be out of its control.

Another example of back room exception handling is the configuration of retry mechanisms. If a data logistics process —or even a connection or lookup process— fails then this activity can be retried a number of times.

Ideally, the control framework will log events such as these.

If the data logistics process fails altogether then this is also recorded in the control framework. This also provides the safeguard that the —now uncommitted— data set is restarted or reprocessed and that no new data is processed unless the pending process is successfully completed. If not, there is a risk of overwriting this data set and losing data which was not yet fully processed downstream as a result.

This way, the control framework —with its focus of ensuring the data solution ACID implementation— is the exception handling approach for the back room.

Exception handling in the front room

In the front room, data *is* judged. However, judging and rejecting are not necessarily the same.

A guiding principle in the front room is that what is considered 'unfit for purpose' for one user may not apply to others. In other words, what is considered bad data for a specific perspective or delivery, should not necessarily be rejected because it may still be meaningful and useful to others.

The front room implements exception handling via *flagging*. In flagging, records or record sets are updated with an indicator that can contain one or more classifications, usually exceptions. These classifications can identify certain scenarios, and can be used as filter criteria for downstream processes, such as towards the presentation layer.

These flags are set as either as part of data logistics processes, or implemented as a separate data logistics process that is dedicated to evaluating data (and flagging records) for a specific object. Even though there can be overlaps and synergies, this is different than the testing framework, which is primarily focused on running many checks against many objects and reporting the outcomes separately – in the testing framework. In front-room exception handling, the results are added to each record directly as part of each data logistics process module.

This way, the same base data can be delivered to various consumers based on their criteria. An exception management process can also be implemented here, for example using an *error data mart* – as a specific presentation layer construct created to report on any exceptions that may have been detected.

Exceptions are interpretations, and evaluating these is typically done in the derived integration area. However, evaluating data and adding classifications can be implemented as a standalone process that runs completely independently of regular processing. Exception classifications can for example run on a maintenance schedule.

These are non-destructive transformations, and can also be applied to data in the base integration area.

A good, and arguably more objective data quality check is to validate data against the logical data model and domain classifications.

The mechanism we recommended to apply more than one classification to the *same* data value in a single element (attribute) is the *exception bitmap*. This implementation will be covered in the ⚐ getting the data in chapter.

The semantic layer

The reference architecture includes the ⚐ staging layer, the ⚐ integration layer, and the ⚐ presentation layer. Another layer may be the semantic, or abstraction layer.

However, the semantic layer is somewhat out of scope for the data solution itself. Nevertheless it is an important part of the broader data delivery to users.

Put simply, this is typically the layer that ingests the data into a BI or reporting software model. The concept of a semantic layer originates from the BI world, but a BI solution certainly isn't the only way to consume data.

For the purposes of this book, we define the semantic layer as the *business data representation*. It is created for analysis and reporting purposes, and it is meant to support users to work with the data even if they are not necessarily trained technically (e.g., proficient using SQL).

This is the layer which ultimately is used by most consumers of the data to make decisions. As mentioned earlier, even though the original concept stems from the BI domain, conceptually this covers many approaches for consumption – including APIs, streaming solutions and database views. We call these outgoing interfaces.

A business data representation is about making sure that data elements can be presented well, for example by using proper casing of attribute names and values, so that the content makes sense to reporting users.

As part of this, the semantic layer also configures the data relationships that allow BI algorithms to function properly. Examples of this are the definition of hierarchies, similarities and relationships between metrics and descriptive features. A semantic layer also often governs join paths to allow or disallow certain navigation routes through the data and the way information can be aggregated (or not).

A semantic layer can also support preparation and pre-processing of complex questions, that may take a long time to answer in SQL. This is the traditional domain of Online Analytical Processing (OLAP) – often referred to as 'cubes.'

Without going into too much detail on this, OLAP allows for calculations of cross-sections of data so that some or all (this is often configurable) combinations are already available (precomputed) when users interact with the data. In all cases, data is intended to be easily understood by the intended users.

The *access area* aims to provide data in a way that is easy to ingest into a semantic layer, if one is available.

The structure of the access area and the intended consumer (semantic layer) are therefore largely the same. The main difference is that, in the access area, the required data is made available 'as is' at the intended level of detail but without the polish of how to navigate it.

In other words, the access area delivers the data with defined structure, content and context but it is up to the semantic layer to add a veneer of user-friendliness to it.

07 FastChangeCo – Setting up the project

Sylvia and Michael are impressed by the work that Amal and Yerodin have done developing the ⚐data solution architecture. It took Sylvia, Michael, and the other team members, a few days to internalize the results and prepare for further discussion.

Terence was not part of the team this time. He preferred to investigate of SPOOF's new database technology SPEEDY. Sylvia had even suggested that he create a PoC.

"As a BI architect in IT, I have to stay up to date with the latest technologies. To prepare the PoC, I need to understand SPEEDY in detail and try it out. I also discussed this with Jeff."

A few days earlier, Terence had met Jeff at *The Dive,* where they enjoyed several rounds of beers. Somehow, Jeff always managed to order another round and leave Terence to pay. Terence had grumbled repeatedly that good technology is all you really need to solve your problems – that's what SPOOF says too.

Growing weary of Terence's negativity, Jeff considered that having him look into SPEEDY might not be a bad idea – at least it'll keep him occupied. Jeff had finally said, "Just leave them alone; in the end, we'll probably buy a good tool. At the last dinner hosted by SPOOF, their SPEEDY database sounded pretty convincing. Why don't you dive a bit deeper into SPEEDY?"

"That's exactly what I'm doing. I've been working with the SPEEDY database for some time now. Honestly, I figured that was more important than focusing on this new 'data solution architecture.' We already *have* concepts that work, right, Jeff? It's like soccer – you stick to tried-and-true values. A new ball or shoes here and there, but the rest..."

Terence's musings are interrupted when Amal and Yerodin begin their presentation, drawing him back to the present. They introduce a rough outline of their work, clarifying that various architecture decisions are still open, though they have some clear preferences.

Amal starts, "We've approached the architecture conceptually, focusing on creating a data solution optimized for data retrieval without affecting the performance of FastChangeCo's operational systems."

"We can only achieve this if the architecture is technology-agnostic." adds Yerodin.

Michael and Sylvia are particularly excited by the architecture's goal of making the data solution ⚐unbreakable and ⚐modular. They are confident that many current concerns will fade over time.

The team's approach to documentation –using information models, design and solution patterns, and inline code documentation– will also make the data solution sustainable and future-proof.

While the concept paper paints a promising picture, some implementation details remain unclear. For instance, the team is still figuring out the differences between handling technical CDC in the PSA versus logical CDC in the integration layer. Other concepts, like streamlining data types, handling logical deletes, and implementing 'date math,' have been well-received and should help avoid previous issues loading data into the staging layer.

In the past, FastChangeCo struggled to explicitly define data types for each column – a time-consuming process that often fell short.

At the end of the meeting, Michael concludes, "The development of this data solution architecture aligns well with our vision and strategy. It's well-documented, and we can build on it moving forward. Any questions?"

"Yes, I do," Xuefang says, reaching for her notebook. She flips through a few pages and asks, "I learned in my studies that ensuring referential integrity –and having foreign keys in the schema– is critical. Are we leaving that out? I'm not quite clear on this."

She pauses, then adds, "And why the Audit Trail Id? According to Data Vault standards, we should always use the 'LDTS' and 'RSRC' columns."

Enforcing referential integrity?

"You probably learned in your studies that referential integrity, or RI, implemented using foreign keys is important in schema design." Yerodin begins, addressing Xuefang's question. "That was the same for me."

"But it is important to not lose sight of the data solution goals – all data should be welcome and loadable without issues."

"I remember the frustrations with many Data Warehouses only too well," he continues. "Data was often unavailable on time because there were constant loading issues. And in most cases, it wasn't even the data we needed for reports that caused the issues; it was something else – a failed lookup for a transaction key, for instance. This would halt the *entire* data logistics process, sometimes after it had been running for hours. As a result, no new data from the operational systems would be loaded at all. In this case, one RI check could prevent everything from updating."

"What's more, the operations team wouldn't notice these errors until 9 a.m., when the office day started. I'm exaggerating a bit, but it wasn't unusual for us to have important data delayed until the afternoon – data we really needed in the morning. Suboptimal, to say the least."

"That makes sense; I hadn't considered that," Xuefang nods. "At university, we were taught that this is how it's always been done, and that it's a good practice."

"Yes, and it still is in many cases, especially for applications and operational systems where data consistency is critical," Yerodin says. "The same goes for normalization. But data solutions have different purposes and goals, so these concepts don't always apply – or they apply in different ways. Applications and Data Warehouses have traditionally used the same database technology, so it's an easy leap to apply similar constraints to Data Warehouses. That's probably why we've been doing it this way for 30 years," Yerodin sighs.

"One more example. Sometimes, data from operational systems would be held back because the corresponding records were missing in a parent table due to an RI violation. These records stayed 'parked' until the parent table data finally loaded."

He pauses, then continues, "This delay once caused our controlling department's risk report to show all risks as 'green,' even though some were edging into 'red' territory – a real threat to the company."

"Was that because of data being held back for further processing?" Xuefang asks.

"Yes. Those on-hold records would have alerted us to the rising risks. Fortunately, a few experienced controllers caught it in time. Luckily, not all processes had been fully automated yet, so it didn't turn into a crisis. But it was a close call, and it should never happen."

"These are some of the reasons why we decided not to use RI, at least not in the back-end of the solution," Michael explains. "RI can still be useful to verify that data logistics processes are working correctly, but it's more of an after-the-fact check rather than a constraint that prevents data loading. Plus, we want the data solution to support parallel data logistics processes, and RI isn't ideal for that – it would prevent exactly that."

"I'm currently testing SPEEDY," Terence interjects, "and one of the main things they recommend is always using foreign keys. With foreign keys enabled, the database optimizer can generate better access paths. So, I disagree with the comments on referential integrity in the closing notes. This is true for other databases I know as well. As an IT architect, I need to know this because…"

"Terence," Yerodin interrupts, "since we haven't decided on the technology for the data solution yet, we can't determine whether RI will be necessary for performance. We're focusing on where and how the concept of RI applies."

"We want to integrate data from FastChangeCo's various systems. We have to account for differences in content, which I'd call data quality problems."

"It's clear we'll need a supporting framework to ensure data quality, one that checks RI after the fact. We call this approach 'lazy RI,'" Michael adds.

"As Yerodin mentioned, in other systems, you absolutely need RI, and it's highly recommended. But those systems serve a different purpose and have different goals."

Benefits of the Audit Trail Id

Yerodin addresses Xuefang's second question, explaining why they prefer to use the Audit Trail Id instead of the LDTS and RSRC columns.

"First, the LDTS isn't exactly *replaced* by the Audit Trail Id," Yerodin begins. "We simply propose a different column —the 'inscription timestamp'— which adds a current timestamp to each record when it's first submitted to the data solution."

Twisting his pencil around his thumb, he continues, "As Diego explained, the goal of the data solution is to be idempotent."

"That means the data solution must recognize which processes are still running or have been successfully completed. In case of an issue, the data solution must 'know' which processes haven't yet been run when processes are restarted. Depending on the type of error, this could even happen without manual intervention. Also, we want to ensure that only complete and consistent data is made available for evaluation."

"And how exactly does the *Audit Trail Id* helps us with this?" Terence grumbles.

"Getting to that, hold on," Yerodin replies. "The Audit Trail Id, combined with the ⚐ control framework provides the option of informing our data consumers if a data logistics process is delayed or has failed. Completed modules can be identified using data in the control framework, allowing us to present a consistent status up to a specific point in time."

"The more transparent we are, the more confidence users will have in our data solution. In our existing Data Warehouses, it's not uncommon for data to be unavailable for reporting, and since daily changes in key metrics aren't always obvious, we might not even notice immediately. And even if we do, it's hard to know if the processes are still running or stalled entirely. Like we saw in the referential integrity example."

"The control framework," Yerodin continues, "links each module's execution to the data records written to target objects, using the Audit Trail Id. This way, we can always present the current status of the data solution to our users."

"So each record will contain an Audit Trail Id that links back to the control framework, to a module definition," he explains. "This module already 'knows' what source and target data objects associated with it, so we don't need a separate record source column, the RSRC, for that."

"So we're just moving RSRC somewhere else. Sounds like extra work," Terence interrupts again.

"I see, we can use it to collect more information." Xuefang's understanding of the control framework starts to take shape.

"That's right. Without the Audit Trail Id, we'd only have minimal 'meta' information about target data objects, and the transparency we aim for would be very challenging to achieve. In the control framework, we can add more information if needed. Initially, we want to start with these basics:

→ Module start and end timestamps
→ The number of records read, written, updated, or deleted
→ Module status, like 'running,' 'finished successfully,' or 'error'
→ Error details including an error number and message
→ Module restarts

"But if we do this, we're changing the standards," Terence objects.

"You're right Terence, standards are there for a reason. They're useful as guidelines. But we also want to evolve with this data solution, breaking new ground to create the best, most visionary (and hopefully last) data solution for FastChangeCo – one truly built for change." Terence is really getting on Yerodin's nerves today.

"We didn't name this project 'The Resurrection' for nothing," Amal reminds everyone.

Xuefang, jotting notes, asks, "Could we start with a small, minimal control framework and expand it gradually? Or do we have to implement the entire framework right away?"

Amal smiles, "No, a basic implementation is enough for now. We can expand step by step. But we should define the fundamentals before starting – like how a module gets an Audit Trail Id and how data is written back to the control framework. That might even be an API."

"This is very different from how we've operated so far." Terence interjects. "In our existing Data Warehouses, data would just be ready at some point, and IT would send an email saying everything was OK. Or, if there were issues, an error message would go to the operations team."

"Yes, I know those emails. But when there are dozens every day saying everything is fine, no one reads them. Fewer alerts would be better – just a notification when something's wrong. But let's get back on topic." Michael says, bringing the conversation back.

Yerodin describes an example where log data showed that the system was no longer 'healthy.' Statistics based on deviations from the median revealed a drop in processed data due to a change in the operational system, which altered how data deltas were identified.

Another metric tracked the number of records processed per second, showing exactly when system load slowed the process. Load balancing eventually solved the problem.

The team agrees to break new ground by proactively notifying users when processes in the data solution are delayed, keeping data users informed if something is amiss. They imagine a central dashboard to access all this information.

"Great idea, Yerodin," Michael says, wrapping up the discussion. "Let's add that as a feature for the data solution. Terence, I understand your concerns, but we agreed to rethink our past approaches and avoid repeating mistakes. This approach aligns much more closely with our vision and strategy than previous ones."

Later, over a cup of green tea, Michael and Sylvia decide to proceed with the data solution architecture proposal as it stands, even though a few details still need clarification.

MVP or PoC?

As Michael and Sylvia stand together after deciding on the data solution architecture, Sylvia suddenly asks, “What exactly is the difference between a minimum viable product (MVP), a prototype, and a proof of concept (PoC)?”

“Good question, Sylvia. A PoC, prototype, and MVP might seem similar at first glance, and they’re often used interchangeably in projects, but they’re actually quite distinct,” Michael explains. “Each has a specific focus and purpose.”

“A PoC is used to test the feasibility of an idea or technology. The outcome of a PoC isn’t meant for a broad audience — it’s usually just for the team, to verify if the technology or concept ‘works.’ For example, testing the appropriate streaming technology was a PoC. It’s crucial to define success criteria beforehand to decide if the concept has been ‘proven.’”

"A prototype, on the other hand, is typically used to demonstrate an idea or vision without fully implementing it. It might only have the basic, necessary, features in a functional state. Think of it like a mock-up of a dashboard interface – enough to visualize the idea, but not a working product."

"Unlike both the PoC and prototype, an MVP is geared toward production release. It's a working product, though with limited features. Those included features are fully functional, so the MVP can deliver early value and evolve over time with new features."

"Thanks, Michael, that's really helpful," Sylvia says. "In the past, we never clearly defined these for data products. We usually just started working and adjusted as we went."

Michael nods, having seen this approach many times. "Exactly. We realized in our draft data landscape that we could implement an MVP using raw data without building all the business logic first. That previous approach was partly why new use cases took so long to deliver."

"Wouldn't the logical next step be to start with one of these to kick off the project and begin implementing the data solution architecture?" Sylvia muses. "An MVP, probably."

"That way, we'd have a first product much faster and could show results for the initial investments," she adds, ever the CFO. "Yes, I think starting with an MVP makes the most sense. We just need to find a suitable use case."

"We'll make it happen, Sylvia. I'm sure we'll find some good use cases to get the project off the ground," Michael promises, placing his teacup in the dishwasher.

Defining an MVP

Based on Sylvia's suggestion, the team plans to define an initial MVP to ensure the solution can be implemented in a way that delivers early business value. It's a chance to prove the approach works – after all, how else can they be certain they're on the right track?

If the MVP proves successful, it can serve as a stable foundation for incrementally deploying new additions.

What is the best use case?

Michael opens the *MVP Best Use Case Meeting* with a small surprise: he has once again bought tartelettes from his favorite café, *L'Art L'Amande.* The team is really looking forward to these treats!

Michael quickly emphasizes that the new data solution should begin with one –or at most, a few– use cases that deliver immediate value and visibility. They're looking for an MVP that will showcase the potential of the data solution architecture.

"I love that we're going with an MVP approach! It feels so startup-like," says a delighted Xuefang, while Terence mutters his usual doubts about the necessity of change.

Before Yerodin can comment on that, Michael swiftly asks Xuefang to give the team a quick explanation of what an MVP is.

"With an MVP, a very small but fully functional product is delivered in a short timeframe. It can be internal or external – that doesn't really matter. It could be an app with a few core functions or a dashboard displaying key metrics. The MVP is then developed further, often with user feedback. In line with the KISS[26] principle, the goal is to bring a product to market as quickly as possible."

"Thanks, Xuefang, for this concise summary of what an MVP is," Michael says. "In our vision and strategy –focus on results– we've already recognized the importance of this approach. We want to think big but start small, always remembering that data isn't just 'stuff.'"

Reflecting on the ⚐ world of data, Michael has been considering existing reports that could serve as ideal first projects for the new data solution. He asks the team, "With this in mind, what could be a suitable existing report or function to replace, or something that's causing a lot of data pain? Something small enough to deliver results quickly, but valuable enough to make an impact?"

The DMCE team dives into a lively brainstorming session. Many existing reports and solutions come up as potential candidates, along with some new use cases. But as they evaluate each option, many are discarded for being too large, too complex, or unlikely to deliver the desired value.

After a few days of brainstorming, the team narrows it down to two potential use cases for the MVP. They present their ideas to Michael, who has taken a step back to let the team drive the process.

Together, they'll decide which of these two options will be the most suitable MVP.

The 'Wearables' use case

Amal presents the first use case: "We found a prototype that had 'accidentally' gone into production."

"Let's call it the *Wearables* use case!"

"In simple terms, 'Wearables' covers the biosensors FastChangeCo has developed to attach to clothing and integrate into accessories as wearable devices. Each device generates a large amount of —often sensitive— data, both about the person wearing the device and the environment around them."

Amal pauses briefly.

"Just a moment." Michael says. " Amal, what exactly do you mean by 'accidentally?' I'd like to know who created this prototype, who's responsible for it now, and what problems it's facing. If the IT department is already managing it in some kind of operational state, it may not be suitable for us."

"Michael, the background is quite interesting. I didn't want to 'bore' you with details, but since you're asking: the prototype was built alongside the biosensors to experiment with sensor data and explore potential 'data products' — that's what they called them."

"These data products turned out to be so useful," Amal continues, "that they gradually became part of daily operations. But at the end of the project, the prototype wasn't formally handed over to IT. The external developers have moved on, and many of FastChangeCo's developers involved in it are either on other projects, working elsewhere, or even retired."

"Oh my!" Michael exclaims.

"This means that the code is no longer up to date, resulting in security vulnerabilities and a increased risk of losing the entire distribution channel if something fails. This, in turn, could have major financial and reputational consequences for FastChangeCo."

"Some things you'd rather not know, but now we understand your choice better," says Michael. "Thank you, Amal."

Amal smiles and continues with the presentation: "We want to use this data to improve our marketing, making it more specific and relevant to individual customers — more targeted communication, more customer-centric strategies, and so on. But we're also looking to improve product quality and use this data as a foundation for developing future products."

"For example, data collected on a customer's running behavior —gathered from their running shoes— can help determine when a customer might need a new pair. Or, at least, when FastChangeCo believes they should consider it. This data also allows us to give customers personalized recommendations based on their sports profiles and to offer additional services."

"We could redevelop this current approach within our new data solution, building it with the frameworks we've identified. This would allow us to test our concepts, technical implementations, and DevOps processes in a real-world setting."

The 'ReCol' use case

"We'd also be able to apply robust data governance, effectively moving this prototype from DQ-III to DQ-I, and from DQ-IV to DQ-III."

"Thank you, Amal, for presenting the Wearables use case," says Michael, turning to Yerodin. "You're presenting the second MVP use case, right?"

"Yes, that's right," replies Yerodin. "Our second suggestion for an MVP use case is to replace the report for supplier quality monitoring, currently used by the controlling team."

"About 10 years ago," Yerodin begins, "our controlling department noticed an interesting trend with some of our products, shoes to be precise. Every now and then, there'd be an unusually high number of complaints and returns, but only for short periods. Outside those periods, everything was normal, with complaints and returns within the expected range."

"Controlling suspected the spike in complaints and returns might be linked to our strategy of using multiple suppliers per product. Often, a single supplier doesn't have the capacity to produce the desired quantities, so we split orders across multiple suppliers, all under the same quality requirements."

Taking a deep breath, he continues, "Back then, we suspected that some suppliers were intermittently failing to meet our quality standards, which led to increased complaints and returns. This is an expensive issue for the company."

"At the time, supplier data wasn't available in the Data Warehouse, so we requested it be added. Once it was, we were able to confirm our suspicions: a specific supplier wasn't always meeting quality requirements, and we took corrective action. The IT team was a huge help on this project!"

"Finally, a positive comment about IT," Terence mutters.

"This project was a success. We saved a lot of money on complaints and returns management, and supplier quality monitoring became an essential control for the organization. But now it needs an update if we're to continue monitoring our suppliers effectively. Over the years, the data logistics processes for this report have been misused and have grown overly complicated. Modifying the existing Data Warehouse has become too difficult and costly," Yerodin explains.

"We could implement these changes in the current solution. But instead of modifying the existing Data Warehouse, we could address these needs within the new data solution

He adds, "There are still anomalies in the complaints data, but we can't manage them as well as we used to due to these data issues. Implementing this use case in the new data solution would allow us to prove the effectiveness of our new approach while also improving our supplier monitoring."

"I call this use case *ReCol*, short for returns controlling," Yerodin concludes.

Return
Return
Return
Return
Return
Return
Return

Deciding on a use case

"Thanks team, these are two excellent use cases for our first MVP. We know we can't do them both at the same time," says Michael. "Now we have to pick one …"

"I have an idea!" Xuefang interrupts, flipping excitedly through her notebook. The others –Zalika, Yerodin, Amal, Terence, and Michael– smile as they watch her in action.

"Since I'm still relatively new to the team and FastChangeCo, I make it a habit to take notes," Xuefang begins. "For ReCol, the core business objects 'customer,' 'product,' 'order,' 'returns,' and 'supplier' seem to form the basis for the report. These same core business objects also form part of the foundation for Wearables, along with a few additional objects like 'recommendation' and 'measure.'

"So, wouldn't it make sense to implement ReCol first and use it as a base for Wearables? Doesn't this naturally determine the order of implementation?"

"Absolutely, Xuefang!" Michael agrees, biting into the last tartelette and taking a sip of his tea. "This approach offers several benefits right away. We can replace the existing report *and* work towards reducing duplicate data storage – data silos. An issue for both use cases."

"Does anyone else have ideas or suggestions to add to this? If not, it seems Xuefang has solved our MVP selection." Michael concludes.

After some further discussion, the DMCE team agrees that the Wearables use case, though valuable, might still be too complex for an MVP. It's better suited as a feature to add once the ReCol report is implemented.

One of the main reasons for holding off on Wearables is the large volume and high velocity of incoming data. This would add technical complexity, potentially drawing focus away from establishing the foundational concepts and frameworks quickly.

Yerodin suggests that Wearables would be useful for demonstrating the concept and explaining the data quadrant approach. However, Michael notes that processing fast-arriving data brings challenges that require specific technical solutions, which are not essential to the core concept and approach.

"I think we all agree it's safer to start with an improved ReCol report for the new platform," Michael summarizes. "This will allow us to demonstrate the data solution's functionality and provide usable features more quickly, especially since users can easily compare the numbers from the old platform to the new one."

"Wearables could also be useful as a PoC for streaming data and the technologies required for that," Michael adds.

Migrating an existing report

As Xuefang and Yerodin wrap up the outline of the proposed use cases for the first MVP, Michael recalls a story from one of his past projects.

"I have to share this," Michael begins. "Picture a report on an old mainframe: monochrome screen, all text-based. You could navigate with the keyboard cursor – no mouse support whatsoever."

"This 'dashboard,'" he continuous, "was to be replaced by a new version, powered by a Data Warehouse, with additional functions and –according to the project managers– a modern graphical interface."

"That was not well received at all."

The team listens intently as Michael continues, "The sudden aversion to the new interface came as a shock. The employees were so used to the old text-based system that the mouse-dependent, graphical interface felt slow and cumbersome."

"Would you have expected that reaction?" Michael asks the group. They shake their heads, and he adds, "Neither did the project leads. They assumed users would be thrilled with a new, modern interface. But they hadn't considered that the old text-based interface was optimized for speed with cursor keys. Plus, people are generally resistant to change, especially when they've become highly efficient with the current solution."

"Did you manage to get everyone on board? Or did the project fail because of this?" Yerodin asks. "We've had projects fail due to resistance to change."

"Well, as you can imagine, it wasn't easy," Michael replies. "Replacing the old dashboard, getting employees used to the new system, and finding a solution that worked for everyone wasn't straightforward."

"The first step," he continues, pausing to sip his tea, "was to create an exact replica of the old text-based dashboard with the new technology and database. This allowed users to compare the data side-by-side and maintain the familiar look-and-feel to build trust in the new platform."

"That's a smart move!" notes Zalika as she sips her maté. She has only recently discovered maté, but already likes it better than the coffee she used to drink.

"Yes," Michael smiles, "it worked. Users found it much easier to transition to the new platform. Almost everything looked and functioned just as they were used to."

"As the project progressed, new features were gradually and *indirectly* integrated into the dashboard. To put it in terms of our data solution, the updates were made in the integration layer, and the necessary data was reloaded from the PSA."

"We had also added various data objects to the staging layer beforehand, especially those we didn't need immediately but knew we'd need soon."

"What do you mean by 'new functions were integrated indirectly?'" Yerodin asks.

"We kept the original star schema for the old dashboard as-is," Michael explains. "New features were built into a separate star schema for an upcoming version of the dashboard. In the emulated old dashboard, we simply added 'links' to these new features. This way, users could gradually explore the new dashboard. Over time, requests for new features sped up the transition. In the end, no one used the old dashboard anymore, and we were able to phase it out."

"We should definitely keep that in mind for our MVP," says Yerodin, and everyone nods in agreement.

Decide for a solution architecture

"We've decided to start developing an improved ReCol report using the new platform," Michael announces. "This will allow us to demonstrate that the data solution works, and that we can quickly deliver usable functions. Now my question to you is: What do we do first?"

"What would be the next relevant steps for us to implement the ReCol MVP?"

Xuefang and Zalika turn to Amal and Yerodin, comparing notes and discussing briefly. Soon, they reach a consensus and share their proposed steps, aligned with the vision and strategy:

- → Capture the requirements to ensure that the use case is designed from a business perspective
- → Create a data model for the use case
- → Formalize the DMCE as a department in the organization
- → Define the approach for brining data into the data solution
- → Investigate and document the approach for making the data available to users

"Wait, don't we need a solution architecture to support all this?" Xuefang asks. "We haven't chosen one of the architectures from our 'defining a data solution architecture' concept yet, have we? It'd be helpful to start capturing our approaches and learnings in a consistent format."

"That's a good point," Michael responds. "So far, we've only provided an overview of the concepts in our data solution definition. The reference architecture we described divides the data solution into three layers, with each layer consisting of two areas, and includes the various supporting frameworks we've outlined. But we haven't made an explicit decision."

"I suggest we implement our data solution based on the reference architecture. Calling it the 'reference architecture' in our documentation reflects that it's our preferred choice. What does everyone think?"

"There are more configurations for a solution architecture than we've documented, and there's no absolute right or wrong," Amal replies. "But we recommend the reference architecture because its layers and areas strike a good balance between complexity and functionality for us."

With that, the DMCE team quickly agrees to move forward with the reference architecture.

Normally, a decision of this magnitude would take much longer at FastChangeCo.

Data hub, or not?

The decision to adopt the reference architecture keeps Xuefang thinking. How does the reference architecture fit within the data landscape? And how does it align with the DQM concepts?

She recalls that Amal and Zalika had already mapped the data hubs to the data quadrants in their DQM overview.

But somehow, the link to the architecture itself still feels incomplete.

As she flips through her notes, she picks up the diagram of the data landscape, considering how to map the data hubs to the layers and areas of the reference architecture.

Letting her mind wander, Xuefang gazes out at the clouds drifting over the nearby mountain range.

Log data hub

We have mapped the log data hub to DQ-I, Xuefang reflects. The data there is unsorted, but fundamentally already structured.

In the reference architecture, the log data hub aligns most closely with the staging layer, particularly the PSA, as it's intended to store data as a like-for-like copy of the operational system data. This means that the structures in the PSA could change over time.

However, depending on the technology, the log data hub might also partially belong in DQ-III. With certain technologies, the format in which the data is provided can be unpredictable, sometimes varying in structure or 'schema.' In these cases, the data is typically interpreted with a schema-on-read approach, where the structure is applied during processing rather than storage.

In such scenarios, the data remains timestamped upon arrival, but its contents, or 'payload,' are otherwise unstructured. This could still align with the PSA in our reference architecture, Xuefang concludes, but conceptually, it might fit better in DQ-I.

Raw data hub

We've also mapped the raw data hub to DQ-I, Xuefang notes. This is where data is organized into clearly defined structures without fundamentally altering it.

In the reference architecture, the raw data hub would therefore correspond to the base integration area, she concludes.

Information data hub

The information data hub is where the results of business logic and rules are stored, thereby completing the data for the information model.

In our reference architecture, this aligns clearly with the derived integration area. Here, additional context is added to the data from the raw data hub, transforming 'facts' into specific 'truths.'

Presentation data hubs

The presentation data hubs collectively form the presentation layer, or the so-called outgoing interface. "Yes, that makes sense," Xuefang thinks. This aligns the presentation data hubs with DQ-II. There can (theoretically) be any number of presentation data hubs in our data solution, depending on requirements.

Xuefang has also noted that individual presentation data hubs can be implemented in a variety of technologies, based on specific needs.

With this in mind, she concludes that the location of the presentation data hubs within the reference architecture is also clear: the access area.

Innovation and research data hubs

Xuefang reflects on the innovation and research data hubs, which are part of DQ-IV. Data for these hubs usually comes from the log data hub, and sometimes from already-prepared data in the raw data and information hubs. Additionally, developers working on the innovation and research data hubs can load and use external data, wsuch as data from DQ-III, if needed.

However, she realizes that there's no suitable area or layer for this in the reference architecture. As she ponders this, flipping through her notes, she comes across Amal's explanation of 'sandboxes,' which she had found clever at the time. "It's a good thing I take so many notes," Xuefang thinks.

"Why not include an optional area for sandboxes in the reference architecture, where these two types of data hubs can be accommodated?" she muses. Liking the idea, she sketches it out in her notebook.

After some time, Xuefang has combined all her thoughts on mapping the data landscape, the DQM, and the reference architecture in a new diagram.

She presents her idea of an optional sandbox area and asks the team for other ideas on how to incorporate the innovation and research hubs —and DQ-IV— within the reference architecture.

The team decides to go with Xuefang's idea of adding an optional sandbox area for now. No one else has a better idea, and it sounds like a good idea. The team updates the decision register one more time.

Missing data hubs

Looking at the diagram she designed, Xuefang notices that there are no corresponding data hubs for the LDA and the performance area.

"Have we overlooked something when defining our data landscape? Misunderstood something?" she wonders. The innovation and research hubs are mapped to DQ-IV, but they don't fit neatly into the reference architecture either.

The following day, she explains her challenges to the team. She points out that she hasn't found a way to map the LDA and performance area to the data landscape and is struggling to align the data landscape, reference architecture, and DQM into a single cohesive design.

Xuefang's questions spark a lively discussion. Should two data hubs be added to the staging layer – a log data hub (or PSA) and a volatile data hub (or LDA)? And what exactly defines a data hub? Are data hubs and areas essentially the same?

After much back and forth, the DMCE team reaches some initial conclusions. They decide to *not* define a separate data hub for the LDA. They recall from their data solution architecture definition that the LDA is transient, not persistent – it exists only to temporarily hold data until it has been successfully processed downstream.

Creating a data hub for a transient area would contradict the team's original vision that data hubs are meant for longer-term data storage. This clarification hadn't been formally documented, so the team updates their decision register to reflect the LDA's transient nature and explain why it won't be designated as a data hub.

Similarly, they decide against mapping a data hub to the performance area. This optional area focuses on delivering data in the presentation layer efficiently and effectively.

According to the team's definition, data in the performance area is neither consistently available nor directly accessible to the user. If this 'data' exists at all, it remains mostly in the background. This decision is also added to the log.

For now, the team agrees to revisit the (supposed) contradiction between the terms data hub and area as they continue refining the architecture.

Either, or both?

Should the DMCE team stick with the term 'data hub,' or would it be better to align with the terms in the reference architecture? This question arises for the team after their recent discussions.

Yerodin notes that while 'data hubs' is a useful term, it's challenging to introduce new concepts at FastChangeCo. "You probably have to explain them constantly," he says.

Terence, meanwhile, prefers SPEEDY's terminology, which refers to 'plateaus.' "What do you mean by plateaus?" Yerodin asks. "Does the data just stagnate on each plateau, like when you hit a plateau and stop improving?"

"No," Terence responds, "SPEEDY's plateaus refer to storing data at specific stages for a particular purpose or intermediate step. And then there are a few additional plateaus for processing…"

Amal interrupts, pointing out that she and Yerodin have based the reference architecture terminology (areas and layers) on a de facto standard within the data community. She proposes sticking to this standard to avoid misunderstandings, especially given their recent experience.

These terms are well-recognized in the data community, make it easier to on-board new team members, and generally reduce the risk of misunderstandings.

After listening to the discussion, Michael finally weighs in. "Let's consider this from different perspectives. On the one hand, we need a data solution architecture for the project and our MVPs. But on the other, we have stakeholders who already find the reference architecture too 'technical' — not because of the technology, but the terminology."

"The data hubs in our data landscape have always been a great help for Sylvia and me in explaining our project to the business departments, users, and other stakeholders," continues Michael. "Combining this with the DQM has only improved communication and understanding."

"Maybe we don't have to choose just one approach. Why not use all of them to support communication as needed?" Amal muses aloud. "It's a bit like epistemology. We think everyone should perceive the data solution as we do, but perspectives shift depending on the angle…"

Lost in thought, Amal doesn't notice the ongoing discussion until Xuefang brings her back to reality. "Amal, are you with us?"

Amal takes a moment to gather her thoughts, then turns to Michael. "I think you've found the answer. We should use all three models —the data landscape, the reference architecture, and the DQM— in our communications. Each serves a unique purpose for knowledge sharing and engagement. It's not an either/or situation. Rather, these are complementary views of our data solution."

"Exactly," adds Yerodin. "The reference architecture for implementing the solution, the data landscape for communicating with subject matter experts and stakeholders, and the DQM for contextualizing data management roles and responsibilities."

After further discussion, the team agrees on this multi-perspective approach and documents the decision in their decision register. They decide to revisit the topic of sandboxes later, when discussing data retrieval methods, and add this item to their backlog.

Taking Xuefang aside, Michael says, "That was impressive. You objectively analyzed the implications of adopting the reference architecture and paved the way for this solution with your diagram. Great work!"

How to resolve architecture dependencies?

Michael arrives at the office early the next day, his mind preoccupied. Reflecting on the previous day's decisions about the data landscape and reference architecture, he realizes the outcome was positive. The team even managed to integrate the DQM into the overall picture, creating a cohesive framework. So why does he still feel unsettled?

As he prepares a cup of tea to clear his thoughts, it dawns on him: Terence had highlighted the challenges of managing dependencies between the layers of a Data Warehouse and with downstream applications during release roll-outs. This also contributes to the lengthy release cycles that Terence often mentions.

Now is the right time to revisit the topic of dependencies, Michael thinks. In his opinion, potential dependencies should be clarified upfront rather than waiting for them to cause issues in daily operations.

He decides to discuss this with Xuefang and Amal. Xuefang has already suggested an idea for decoupling the access layer from data consumers, and Amal always has valuable insights — especially on solution architecture.

Michael promptly schedules a workshop, aiming to brainstorm solutions together.

Decoupling source systems and staging layer

In the workshop, Xuefang, Amal, and Michael explore the decoupling between a 'source' operational system and the staging layer.

By defining the PSA as a structural copy of a data source, where all transactions (inserts, updates, and deletes) are recorded as inserts —similar to a log— they effectively decouple the data solution from the operational systems.

A key advantage of this approach is that even if the data source no longer exists, the data remains available in the PSA with its complete history. If the integration layer's data model changes and data needs to be reloaded, it can be done directly from the PSA instead of re-extracting from the source, which may no longer be available.

This setup allows downstream data logistics modules to read data from the PSA independently of the original source data set and source-to-staging processes. For example, modules can track up to what point they've already processed data by using the inscription timestamp as a reference.

Amal points out that this approach supports all types of incoming data interfaces, whether push or pull, full or delta. The three agree that this will enable a new, flexible way of orchestrating modules.

They also discuss potential challenges, such as structural changes in the operational system – for example, if a column's data type changes from CHAR(10) to CHAR(12), or if columns are added or removed. Possible solutions include defining large-enough data types in the staging layer, using NULL values for removed columns, or simply adding new columns.

To avoid getting too deep into technical details, they agree to add this issue to their backlog for future resolution. For now, their main goal is ensuring the staging layer can be developed independently of downstream processes.

This means the MVP can be started without knowing the exact columns required from the source or the final integration layer data model – only the essential objects.

They all agree this is a great foundation for the project.

Decoupling the integration layer

Later in the workshop, Xuefang, Amal, and Michael continue discussing the decoupling of the staging layer from the integration layer. They realize that the fully historized PSA is key to achieving this separation.

By using the PSA, a data logistics module loading data into the integration layer can identify records in the PSA that haven't yet been processed. This means there's no need to synchronize orchestration between staging and integration modules – a major simplification.

This wasn't always the case. In some current solutions, *all* data logistics processes must complete successfully before the next data delta can be loaded. If any step fails, data changes can be permanently lost.

With the PSA, however, flexibility is improved, since a landing area module can be re-executed *before* integration layer processing is complete.

Another benefit of the PSA is that it allows the MVP to be developed in smaller increments. This means the team can reduce the initial scope –driven by time constraints or a limited set of requirements– to a minimum. For example, an integration layer MVP can be built quickly by loading just a few columns from a PSA table.

"As the MVP progresses, we could add more columns from the same PSA table –and even additional tables– without losing any history or requiring costly extractions from the operational system," Xuefang says aloud, leafing through her notebook.

"Exactly," agrees Amal. "This also makes it straightforward to make corrections or enhancements to the physical data model in the integration layer. With the data always available in the PSA, loading it into the integration layer is straightforward."

"And," Michael adds, turning to Amal, "this approach allows us to refactor and develop the integration layer independently of both the operational systems and the staging layer. The only dependency is that the objects already exist in the PSA."

Michael stands, taking his tea to the window. As he looks out at the mountains, he begins to share a story.

"I wish we'd known this in my earlier projects. It would have made things so much easier. We'd load billions of records from the same operational system, over and over, with only minor changes each time. It took hours — days, even."

"Why is that?" Xuefang asks.

"Because we didn't have a PSA back then," Michael explains, sipping his tea. "We only had an LDA, and we always loaded data directly into the integration layer target objects. This meant we had to fetch the data from the operational system repeatedly whenever new columns were needed."

"In hindsight, it made everything much harder. Modeling took longer, as we had to accommodate extra columns we didn't even need yet. And once they were there, they added complexity and sometimes caused issues we had to fix. Limiting scope to necessary columns would have saved so much time."

Amal joins him at the window. "And when you had to refactor the integration layer, how did you handle that?"

"It was a massive effort every time. We had to perform a fresh, full extract from the operational system, which took considerable time. It also meant losing a large part of our historical data. Although past years' data still existed in the operational system, it was only available in its current state. Earlier changes, updates, and deletions were lost," Michael says, realizing his tea cup is empty once again.

"Was the approach flawed back then? From today's perspective, with the knowledge we have now – yes, I think so. But at the time, we did the best we could with what we knew."

The three of them look out of the window in silence. Each of them reflects on past projects, and how many things could have been easier with the insights they now have.

Decoupling the presentation layer

After a short break and a fresh green tea for Michael, the three of them reconvene to discuss how to design the outgoing interfaces so they're as decoupled as possible from the integration layer.

They quickly agree to use virtual objects (views) wherever possible to decouple the access area from the integration layer. This approach means that if the data structures in the integration layer –which the views are based on– change, only the impacted views need adjustment. From their perspective, this could be a quick and efficient solution, at least until performance or costs become limiting factors.

Additionally, data in a modified view can be compared with its previous version before the change, making testing easier.

Michael turns to Xuefang. "You mentioned there are better ways to handle changes to an outgoing interface than directly updating it, right?"

"Yes," Xuefang replies. "To make outgoing interface changes as seamless as possible for consumers, I think we should treat them like APIs in software development."

She stands and walks around the room. "By that, I mean creating a new version of the interface rather than modifying the existing one. This allows for a transition period, giving consuming applications time to migrate to the new version."

"I see," Michael says as he gets up and walks over to Xuefang. "This gives the downstream applications the opportunity to create their own roadmap for transitioning to the new interface version. This way, we don't have to organize one big, coordinated roll-out for everyone to make the changes at the same time."

"To get the best of both ideas," Amal adds, "we could avoid one big, allencompassing data mart and instead build several smaller data marts."

Xuefang and Michael look at her with curiosity.

"If we do that, we not only decouple the entire access area from the integration layer but also allow each data mart to operate independently. This means changes to one interface wouldn't impact others that don't rely on it."

"That's fantastic," says Michael. "One of the biggest challenges is getting customers to understand why they need to test their application when they didn't even request a change."

As he organizes his thoughts, Michael gazes out the window. "Let me make sure I've got this right. Say we have three downstream applications – A, B, and C. With one big data mart, if we make a change for application A, then applications B and C also need to test for any unintended impacts."

"Exactly," Amal confirms.

"But if we create separate data marts –one each for A, B, and C– then only application A would need testing, since it's the only interface affected."

"Exactly!"

"Makes perfect sense, and it should definitely help with the overall acceptance of the data solution."

The three agree that these strategies are the right path to minimizing dependencies within the data solution.

Decoupling decision

Amal, Xuefang, and Michael present the results of their workshop to the team.

With the exception of Terence, the team is enthusiastic about the ideas presented, and after a brief discussion of the pros and cons, they agree to add the decoupling approach to the data solution decision register. The team plans a more detailed investigation to determine implementation specifics and adds several items to the backlog to outline the next steps.

Now we just need the team to get it all done, Michael thinks to himself.

Later that evening, Terence meets Jeff at The Dive, sharing his growing discomfort with the team's direction. He confides that he feels compelled to support the team's decisions but no longer feels comfortable with so many methodological changes. He'd rather be doing something different.

"You know, Jeff, I'd like to work with a new technology, but I'm not comfortable with all these changes. Things were fine before I joined DMCE – I actually preferred the way it was back then."

Jeff peers into his beer glass, pondering how to help Terence. Change can be challenging, and he empathizes with Terence. Still, adapting to new circumstances is inevitable, as Sylvia reminded him recently. He wonders if Terence's skills might be better suited elsewhere and takes a long sip from his glass, weighing his options.

"Terence, I'll see if there's anything I can do, but I can't promise anything. Now let's leave work aside – how's football going?"

They chat over a few more beers (which Terence ends up paying for, as usual), discussing everything but work.

The need for automation

While Terence and Jeff enjoy their beers, Michael is preoccupied by a single thought.

To achieve all this, we really need to automate our development. We can't expect to build everything by hand and still meet the demands and goals of this project, he thinks.

Michael recalls the final pillar of their strategy: automation. But what does that truly mean? Should we be investing in an automation tool right now?

He considers a different approach. Perhaps it's better to understand how the new data solution works with the architecture we've designed first. This way, we keep our focus on the design itself, separate from the automation of its development. It's in line with our principle of separating concerns in other areas.

This would mean developing the MVP with their existing technologies, proving the concept's value before getting 'bogged down' in selecting a tool. We can demonstrate value first, then look at automation. But automation *must* be part of the next steps once the MVP has proven to be a success.

However, this approach also signals that now is the right time to decide on a solid information and data modeling method – one that creates real value for FastChangeCo, regardless of technology. After all, the team knows one thing for certain: whatever form automation eventually takes, it will require metadata. And the best foundation for that is a robust data model.

Satisfied with the direction his thoughts have taken, Michael decides to call it a day and rest up for tomorrow.

How to data model

The next day, Michael presents his decision to the team: for now, design and development automation will remain separate in the project. The selection of a development automation tool will be postponed until after the MVP has demonstrated its value to FastChangeCo.

As expected, this decision –made independently of the team– sparks a lively discussion. Terence, in particular, is clearly displeased, especially since he had hoped SPEEDY would be the tool of choice.

However, this time Michael stands firm. In addition to advancing the data solution's design, he emphasizes that the team's focus should now be on selecting a robust modeling approach.

Leveraging data models

Terence, visibly disgruntled that his preferred tool, SPEEDY, isn't being considered for the MVP, asks, "What benefits do data models actually bring us?"

Yerodin responds promptly, "Well, they provide a shared understanding between business and technical teams. They facilitate communication, document requirements, and clarify use cases."

As Xuefang reviews her notes in her ever-present notebook, she adds, "Data models are also invaluable for transferring knowledge within the team. They help new members quickly understand the information landscape."

"For me," Michael interjects, "it's essential that information isn't 'buried' in any one person's head but accessible to everyone."

"Why do we need a data model ...?" Yerodin repeats Terence's question, thoughtfully. "In the past, so many changes were made directly in the database without documenting them in a data model – sometimes even undone later, accidentally. This has created a lot of technical debt that still lingers today. And the worst part is, no one's really sure why certain changes were made, if they're still relevant, or what impact it would have to change them now. If these had been documented in data models, we wouldn't need to dig through data 'archeology' to understand processes and relationships."

"As far as I'm concerned, we never used data models and we got along just fine. This feels like an unnecessary waste of time," Terence grumbles.

"No, Terence," Amal explains patiently. "It might seem that way initially, but, as Diego emphasized in our recent coaching session, you'll be more efficient overall. Good data modeling clarifies requirements, narrows the scope, and ultimately reduces rework."

"And," she continues, "we need a lot of metadata for our new data solution. A solid data model is the best foundation for that. That's where 'data model-driven development' comes from."

Terence listens, but his frustration remains. Annoyed, he leaves the room to clear his head with a walk before his youth football training. At least there, he thinks, everything stays as it should.

Sensing the need to recharge, the team decides it's time for a break and grab some refreshments to clear their heads.

The information model

After the break, the team gathers again, though without Terence and Zalika. Terence is at youth football training, and Zalika is spending the day at the university.

With everyone else settled in with coffee or tea, Michael starts a recap of the project's vision and strategy.

"As we decided earlier, we're adopting Fact-Oriented Modeling (FOM) as the approach for our information model. This means our data model should describe all essential business concepts in natural language."

"From what I understand of FOM," he continues, "the knowledge embedded in these information models could be accessible to anyone, perhaps through a portal. It wouldn't just benefit us but could support many projects – like establishing clear, well-defined interfaces between systems."

Just then, Sylvia enters with a surprise: tartelettes from L'Art L'Amande. The team is overjoyed.

Sylvia asks for a quick project status update, and once she's up to speed, she adds, "I think everything you're discussing sounds very promising. From what I understand, we need information models to maintain long-term data and information quality. But we also need it right now to improve communication with subject matter experts and different departments. Maybe this way, I won't have to hear anyone defining a customer as, 'The customer is a customer of FastChangeCo.' That would certainly be progress!"

Michael, Amal, and the others agree, recognizing that a more structured understanding of data *will* help make it more than just 'stuff' at FastChangeCo.

"Have you decided which variant of FOM you'll use? I remember we discussed a few during the vision and strategy sessions," Sylvia asks.

"Yes," Amal replies, "there are a few options, like ORM2 or FCO-IM…"

"Wait a minute," Sylvia interrupts, "what happened with the invitation to tender for a Master's thesis at the university? The idea was to evaluate which FOM variant best suits our needs, right?"

"Yes, but we don't need to go forward with that," Amal explains. "I already spoke with Zalika about it while we were preparing the DQM presentation, and she's enthusiastic about exploring FOM for her upcoming Master's thesis. She's discussing it with her professor today."

"Thanks! That's great to hear. I'll leave that in your hands, then?" Sylvia asks.

"Absolutely. I've got it covered," Amal confirms.

The team leaves it to Amal to oversee Zalika's new assignment, confident that it's in good hands.

The physical data model

Meanwhile, Xuefang leafs through her notebook, pausing on her notes about Data Vault. She studies them thoughtfully.

"Is Data Vault, as mentioned in our vision and strategy, still the right approach for the physical data model?" she wonders aloud. "Modeling the Data Vault will take effort, and if we're already putting so much work into information modeling, can't we just access the PSA directly? Maybe using Python or something similar?"

Xuefang feels a thrill in openly questioning aspects of the strategy. "And I think I read somewhere that refactoring Data Vault isn't always easy, especially when it comes to 'rebuilding' raw data due to incorrect assumptions made during initial modeling. Wouldn't that contradict our 'design for change' principle?"

"These are valid questions," Amal replies. "With our information modeling approach, we aim to minimize false assumptions as much as possible – though maybe not entirely. Ideally, we uncover these through discussions with subject matter experts."

"But you're right: starting with Data Vault modeling without considering the information landscape could make fixing mistakes costly. Of course, incorrect assumptions can be made when creating information models too."

Xuefang, reassured, says, "Thanks to the information model, we have a solid basis for modeling the Data Vault. But isn't that still a lot of work?"

"I don't believe so. Zalika, who's working on her Master's thesis on FOM, suggested that we could potentially derive the physical Data Vault model directly from the information model. If this works as we expect, the effort could be minimal."

Michael sips his green tea, listening intently. "Wouldn't that mean that if we make changes to the information model, we'd only need to regenerate parts of the Data Vault? And then reload data from the PSA?"

"Exactly," Amal confirms. "'Designing for change' would be *implemented* in the information model, so updating the Data Vault would involve minimal effort.

Most of the work lies in profiling source data, mapping operational systems to the information model, and implementing the necessary business logic."

"And that's also a reason to stick with Data Vault," Amal continues. "It provides a clear, structured physical model that's aligned with the information model. This means developers can usually navigate the data more easily than they could in the unstructured PSA."

The team agrees that Data Vault remains the right choice for the physical model, at least as a starting point. Over time, the 'data engine' could explore alternative physical modeling techniques as they become relevant. But for now, Data Vault seems best suited to the technical provisioning of data in the solution, rather than as a method for designing data models.

Data Vault seems more destined to take a place in the technical provision of data in the data solution, rather than as a method for designing data models.

Importantly, Data Vault has proven capable of supporting the key requirements in the vision and strategy:

- → Incremental integration of data sources
- → Extensibility for additional business areas and evolving requirements
- → Flexibility for changes in the information model, business logic, or rules
- → Complete historization of data (uni-, bi-, and multi-temporal)
- → Fully auditable

These requirements wouldn't be fully met if everyone just wrote queries on the PSA.

Data Vault, the team agrees, offers a robust foundation for the physical model that links well with the information model. However, they conclude that the data solution should focus on information modeling and management, with Data Vault serving as a secondary, physical design technique.

Formalizing the department

The following week, Sylvia gathers the team. She has news to share.

"As you all know, the DMCE has only existed as a virtual team. Transforming it into a formal department —which has always been our goal— takes time, as is typical here at FastChangeCo. But, we've made a big leap forward. Later this week, it will be announced that we're officially creating a new DMCE department!"

The team is pleasantly surprised and exchanges excited glances. What changes lie ahead?

Sylvia quickly refocuses the conversation. "For now, Michael will remain your manager, and your tasks won't change. The first to officially report to Michael will be Yerodin — we'll talk to you and your current manager later this week."

"One advantage of having a dedicated DMCE department is that we've been promised additional permanent positions – more than we currently have on the team. In the coming days, we'll meet with each of you to discuss whether you'd like to formally transfer to the DMCE or stay in your current role."

The team buzzes with excitement. This news represents a huge milestone.

Over the next few days, Michael and Sylvia plan to sit down to define the skill mix the department needs and consider ways to organize the team for the future.

With this formalization, Michael is well on his way to solving one of the core challenges he identified early on – the ability to expand the team to meet future requirements.

Movers and shakers

Michael has brewed himself a special green tea for today's meeting with Sylvia, which will focus on the required team skills. He is looking forward to this new flavor because he only recently discovered it in his tea store *T-Time* but hasn't tried it yet. It is a green tea with the name Feng Huang Dan Cong.

"In preparation for our meeting, I spoke with Diego about how we can avoid reverting to our old behavioral patterns where most people work in a technology-driven manner, as opposed to a data model-driven way." Michael gets up briefly and switches on the light. Outside, storm clouds are gathering, darkening the day.

"He recommends that we develop a training pathway to cultivate these skills internally. Among other things, this would allow us to incorporate our standards into the training plan, as well as additional necessary skills, such as communication and requirement gathering."

After some back and forth, the two draft an initial outline of the skills and corresponding modules to include in the training concept.

As Michael looks thoughtfully out of the window, he says: "Sylvia, there is this quote[27] from Niklaus Wirth that I love. It goes something like this: *'A primary effort must be education toward a sense of quality. Programmers must become committed crusaders against home-made complexity. Complexity is not a thing to be admired; it must be fought wherever possible.'*"

Sylvia smiles, and nods in agreement.

"We should definitely include that as a team guideline. We already have more than enough complexity today."

Both are satisfied with what has been achieved and decide that the creation of this training pathway should from now on be called *DMCE Academy* and will be implemented swiftly.

After a short break, Michael mentions that the creation of the DMCE department will also bring further changes.

One of these changes is that Zalika will be leaving the team to complete her Master's thesis. She has become a valuable part of the team over the last few months, and her presence will be missed. "But, I hope that she will return after her Master's thesis. I know that she really wants to be part of the team in the future, and we made her a job offer."

Michael continues "Also, Amal has indicated that she wants to change departments. She is very ambitious and wants to be part of this new direction."

"At the same time, Terence has repeatedly signaled to me that he would prefer to work with SPEEDY and basically go back to IT. Do you think you could talk to Jeff and work this out? It would be perfect to get Amal into DMCE, and ensure that Terence has a spot in IT."

Michael takes a break and thinks about what to say next. He decides to be open with Sylvia.

"To be brutally honest, I expected more from a BI architect. Terence has been reluctant to support the decisions for our data solution, decisions that were made as a team. He often opposes them just for the sake of argument. His objections are, how shall I put it, backward-looking. They don't align with our vision and strategy, and it impacts the team's morale."

Sylvia is not surprised. She anticipated something like this.

"Fortunately, we had Diego supporting us. He played a key role in the solution design and has been a valuable architect for us where Terence fell short. To cut a long story short, Terence doesn't really fit into our team."

"I get it Michael, it's not really a surprise. He would be better of supporting Jeff with SPEEDY. I'll talk to Jeff and I'm sure we'll find a way."

Michael is relieved to hear that, and they conclude their discussion about the future team.

As luck would have it, Sylvia has her monthly running meeting with Jeff later in the afternoon. I wonder if Jeff now regrets having agreed to a monthly, informal running meeting.

Sylvia takes things slowly at the running meeting this time, intending to convince Jeff of her plans. But Jeff beats her to the punch.

"It's good that we're going slowly today. I need to talk to you. SPEEDY seems to be really promising and I would like to roll it out for a pilot project and perhaps more, but I don't have any people for it. I have enough people in my department, but in reality they're mostly working for some other team, like Amal and Terence are doing for you."

Although they are walking slowly, at least from Sylvia's point of view, Jeff is out of breath and soon they take a break.

"Jeff, you have assured us that you would not suddenly withdraw Amal and Terence. You also support us as a mentor and you know how important the project is for FastChangeCo. Are you alright? Shall we continue?"

Jeff nods silently.

"That's why I want to help you. What if Terence could support SPEEDY for you? As far as I've heard, he's very enthusiastic about it. Amal could then join the DCME department, freeing up budget for you. That way, you would have support for SPEEDY right now *and* could hire someone new for your longer term plans."

Jeff realizes that this couldn't have come at a better time for him. He wanted to make Sylvia a similar offer —Terence had asked him to— with the only difference being that he now has an extra vacancy to fill with a suitable person for SPEEDY.

After a few more laps, they agree.

Since Jeff knows that Terence will be going to The Dive after soccer practice, he waits for Terence there to tell him the good news. After all, Jeff thinks to himself, this way he will pay for my beers without hesitation.

And anyway, Jeff thinks, he deserves it after the long running meeting. Why is it always so exhausting!

Researching how to get the data in

A few weeks later, the DMCE department has become a reality. Zalika is already writing her Master's thesis, and Terence is more than happy that he can now finally focus solely on SPEEDY.

Michael, Xuefang and Amal —who is now working in the DMCE department— are interviewing candidates to expand the team.

But The Resurrection itself also needs to move forward. It is time to research a feasible implementation of how data can be loaded into the data solution. To this end, the 'new' DMCE team is retreating back to its quiet research and development area.

In this relatively quiet, undisturbed phase, the team is working on the critical next steps of the data solution:

- → Metadata, the DNA for the data solution
- → Automation, and the basics of code generation
- → Loading the data into the staging layer
- → Further processing of the data from the staging layer into the integration layer

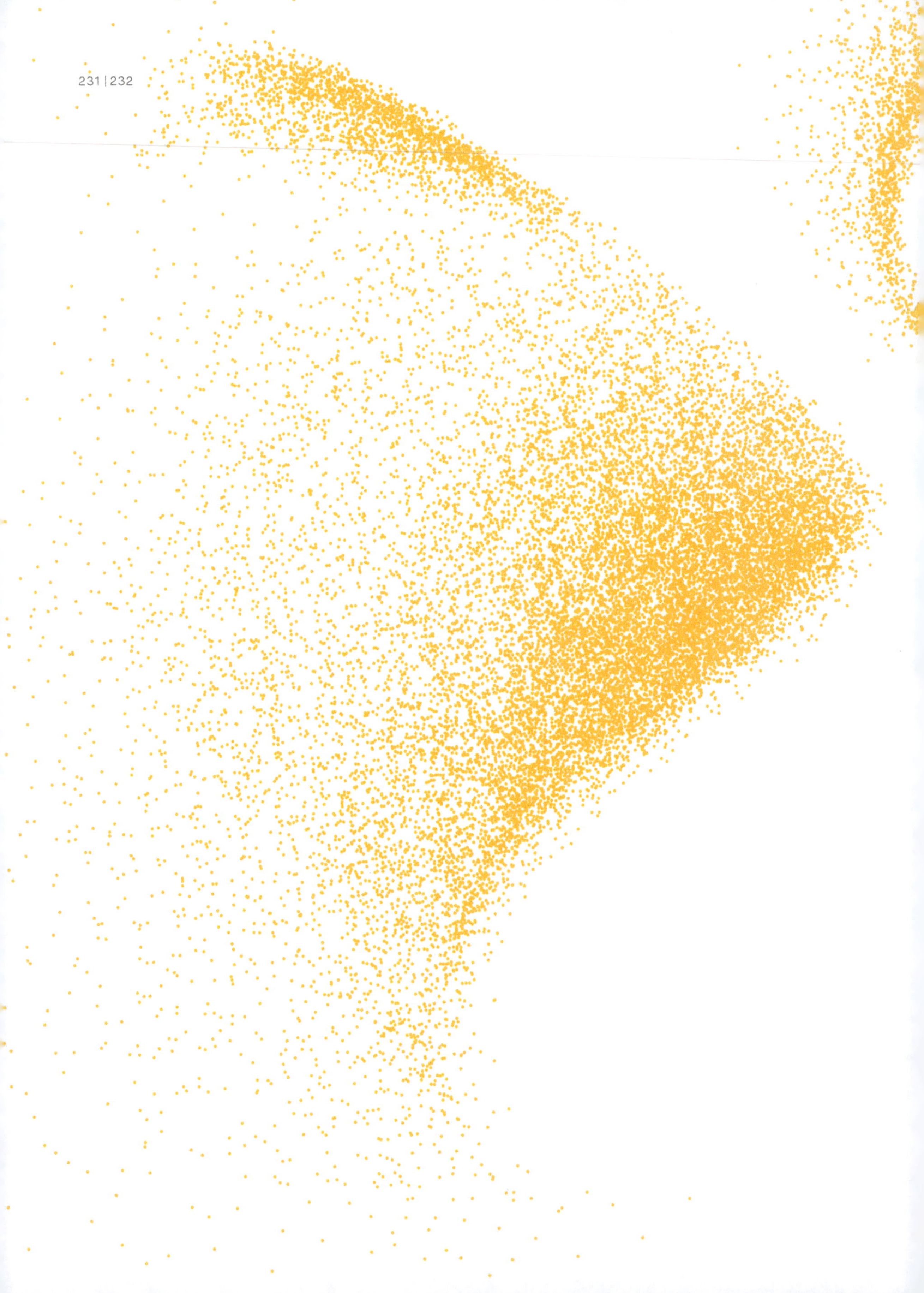

08 Metadata, automation, and code generation

Engine Thinking advocates seamless and automated refactoring of the solution when things change. With the architecture in place, and the (initial) information model defined, it's time to 'populate' the model with data. Guided by design patterns, it is clear what needs to be done. The next step is creating the actual processes or interpretations that morph the data into its intended mold.

Seamless and automated refactoring requires a strong and dependable administration of the data solution's design metadata, so that this can be used to (automatically) generate the code to process the data.

↗ Design metadata is a succinct and technology-agnostic collection of conventions, definitions, and instructions about which data elements need to be mapped, where they are mapped to, and how they need to be used.

The DNA of a data solution

For the creation and management of the data solution, design metadata is everything.

The data lineage, the physical model, the data logistics processes — these are all governed by a relatively small amount of content that can describe how the data is meant to be used.

Design metadata is a succinct and technology-agnostic collection of conventions, definitions, and instructions about which data elements need to be mapped, where they are mapped to, and how they need to be used.

This design metadata, further referred to as just 'metadata,' can be seen as the DNA[28] of the data solution, because it holds the essential instruction to fully (re)build the data solution into its physical form. Using strands of metadata, parts —or all— of the solution can be completely regenerated.

In practical terms, metadata is the ingredient that fuels deployment workflows, infrastructure, physical models, and the creation of data logistics processes. Together, these allow for the data solution to be automatically generated, tested, and deployed.

For instance, if you retain the history of transactions in a PSA, you can rebuild the entire solution exactly as it was by re-applying the metadata. Or in a slightly evolved form, if preferable or required.

How this works, and what is needed to make this work is this chapter's topic.

Perhaps surprisingly, the amount of metadata needed to manage even large data solutions is relatively small. Solutions typically have metadata sets containing no more than a few hundred data logistics processes, with a few really large ones having maybe a few thousands.

However small this data volume may seem in the scheme of things, this metadata represents the output of huge amounts of design effort – often exceeding thousands of working hours. The data modeling, the analysis, and mapping of data elements, the data logistics patterns and design conventions are all captured here in their essence.

Because of this, design metadata is important *intellectual property* (IP) that warrants careful management and safekeeping.

Automating the delivery of data logistics processes

In a modern data solution, almost every data logistics process —from a simple file copy to a complex transformation— is *generated* from metadata and deployed using deployment automation (e.g., 'DevOps') workflows.

A well thought-out approach for metadata-driven automation enables multiple teams to work together on the same data solution, even though they may be separated by geography and time.

To make this possible, we would like to introduce an approach for consistently recording design metadata and applying this to code generation templates. By involving source control for versioning, branching, merging, test automation, build workflows, and automated deployment, the level of sophistication to truly start the engine can be achieved.

It is not our intent to explain concepts such as Git[29] or specific DevOps and process automation frameworks in technical detail. Rather, we aim to cover how these approaches are used in unison to automate the delivery of the data solution.

In many ways, this is similar to software development processes for regular application development. This follows what appears to be a general trend: aligning data development with software development best practices.

We referred to this as 'deployment automation' in earlier sections, and the requirements to validate a data solution go beyond what is required for a typical software product that can be compiled and run. For data solution development, the produced (compiled) outputs also need to be applied to data to review the end result. We will go into this in detail in the following sections.

Time to put it all together.

What do we need?

To automate the end-to-end delivery of the data solution, we can combine the following components into a single assembly line:

- → A definition for *metadata* storage, for which we use the schema for data solution automation
- → A *version control* approach that manages changes in design metadata, and supports branching and merging to enable multiple areas of concurrent development
- → A set of *code generation templates* to apply to the design metadata
- → A *compiler* that can merge the metadata with the code generation templates, so that output can be generated. This includes, but is not limited to, infrastructure, physical model structures, data logistics processes, and orchestration wrappers
- → Testing mechanisms that ensure new additions or modifications do not impact existing parts of the data solution
- → An *automation engine* to coordinate (orchestrate) the various steps in the build process, for instance in a DevOps workflow

A schema for data solution automation

To generate outputs using metadata, there must be a defined structure or format available to record the metadata, so that code generation techniques can reliably access it for further processing.

This format is referred to as a *schema,* a term borrowed from software development where this means 'the agreed format in which data can be exchanged.' For example, for an API call/response.

Many APIs publish their schema so that consumers know how to access its services and data. The metadata schema for data solution development and automation has the same purpose: it facilitates interoperability between potentially various software products, code generation approaches, and APIs that tools and ecosystems offer.

The intent is to define a sufficiently generic format that can be used to record and share details about data platform automation metadata.

Using repositories

In many cases, metadata is stored in *repositories.* A repository essentially means a location where (meta)data is stored so that it can be accessed later. This can be in any kind of technology.

In practical terms, and in the context of data solution development, this is often implemented as a database that is managed by the data solution team.

In our solutions, we prefer to avoid this approach in favor of implementing the repository as a collection of text files conforming to the metadata schema.

One advantage of this approach is that files are natively easier to incorporate in version control, and subsequent deployment automation workflows. Files also facilitate decentral development, because each file —containing a single metadata object— can be created or modified independently of others. This means that different teams can work on different metadata in parallel, and by proxy on the data solution as a whole.

In a way, a metadata file is akin to a record when using a database repository.

A metadata database repository is often harder to accurately version control, because version control is managed independently from database *record* management. Using a database repository, a proprietary versioning approach often needs to be developed *in* the database to integrate well with 3rd party version control solutions.

Another common issue concerns locking and transaction isolation issues. These can occur when multiple people or teams access the same metadata database tables or records.

In this scenario, changes could get overwritten – something that is natively resolved using text-based version control using concepts such as Git. Following the same example, the earlier change would be visible by the person committing the later one using basic Git usage.

In our reference solution, we adopt a schema for data solution automation where each file represents a target data object. The collection of files is then connected to version control, and subsequently used as input for compiling data logistics and physical model output using deployment automation workflows.

Being implementation agnostic

True to the engine way of thinking, metadata management should be implementation-agnostic. Metadata, the design, is likely to change independently and at a different pace than the involved technologies do.

Metadata will slowly adjust to cater for changes in the business, and to accommodate new and changing data sources. But this is independent of technical infrastructure or data logistics software that is used to support the data solution.

One of the engine goals is to allow rapid adoption of new technologies when there is a good opportunity to do so. To leverage new features, or change technologies altogether, all that is needed in principle is to redeploy the *existing* metadata into a *different* format.

At least, that is the concept. In reality, applying existing metadata to new formats does require more than just defining a new compiler. Typically, new templates are defined to make the most out of the new technology, infrastructure must be configured, and it must be investigated how to connect to automation features in the new tool.

However, a key message here is that this can be done gradually, over time, as part of regular data solution development and independent of the solution's data model and architecture.

Not a black box

Code generation can sometimes be presented as a 'black box' process where metadata goes in, and data logistics processes come out.

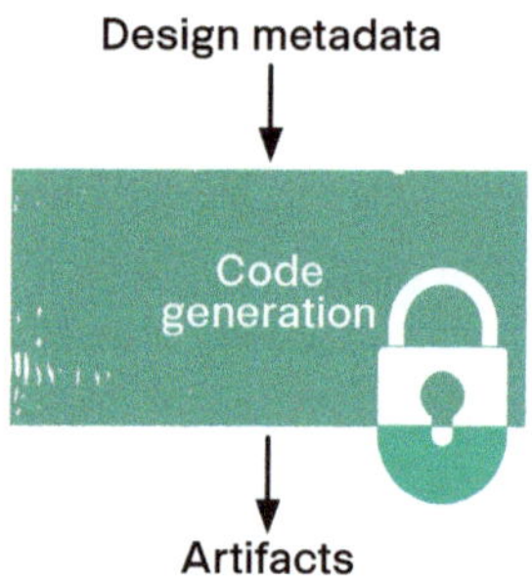

Developing a code generation solution as a closed tool, or purchasing an automation product with limited integration features, can prevent automation of the complete data solution at a later stage. In many cases, metadata management and code generation templates are combined in the software's 'secret sauce' which makes it harder to change technologies.

We advocate *separating concerns* on what is required for automation as the following image shows.

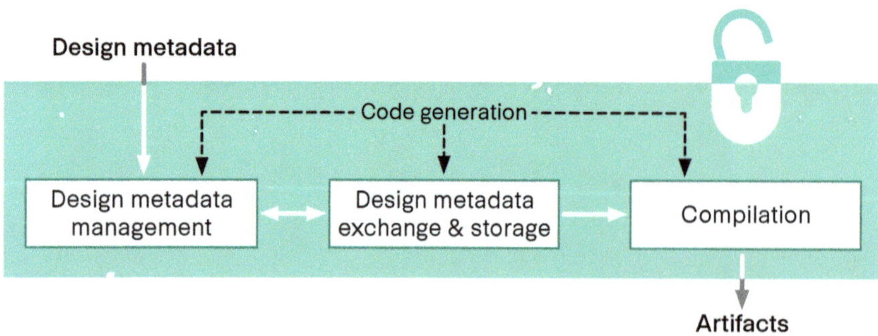

We believe that the recording and management of the metadata should be as independent from its application —the compilation process— as possible.

During compilation, a code generation template is applied to the metadata to generate the desired outputs. There are many possible techniques and software to perform the compilation, which will be further covered in the ⚐ compilation and generation section.

We advocate a separation between the *management* of the metadata and its *application*. This means an interface is needed that the compiler can access to retrieve the metadata, and this is one of the reasons for our schema for data solution automation.

This approach both separates the management of the metadata and it provides a descriptive interface format that can be interpreted by various compilers.

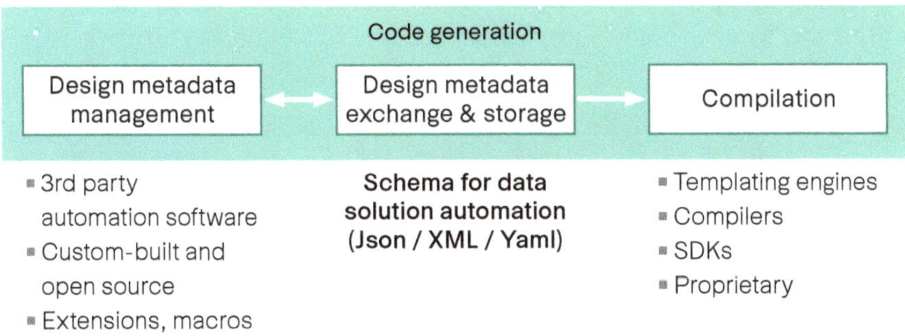

A separation of concerns such as this makes it possible to introduce new technologies, something that is not always possible with black-box software products that combine these features into a single tool — unless an interface is made available to do so.

Another advantage is that these separate activities can be implemented as individual steps in deployment automation workflows, a best-of-breed approach.

In the engine way of thinking, implementing *builds* this way means that the data logistics processes themselves can be considered ephemeral. They can always be generated anew, and it is perfectly doable to generate them 'on-the-fly.' There is no need to specifically version-control the data logistics processes themselves — only the metadata and code generation templates used require this.

The metadata itself, together with the templates, provides everything that is needed. As mentioned before — this is the true intellectual property of the data solution.

Introducing data objects, items and mappings

At its core, the schema for data solution automation metadata captures the direction of data movement or interpretation between two data sets. It is a vector that identifies a selection, transformation, copy, or other type of interpretation from a given data set as well as a definition of the target.

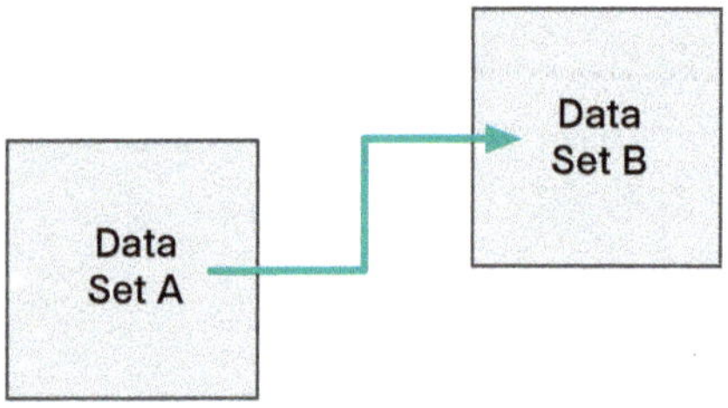

In simple terms: data goes from A to B.

However, *how* this happens is up to the code generation templates that are applied to this metadata. This means that the same metadata can be used to deploy different data logistics approaches, and for different technologies.

For example, the same metadata can as easily be used to generate a data logistics process to copy data from one database table to another as it can produce a python script, procedure, function, or database view.

In this and the following sections, we will focus on what design metadata needs to be available in the schema.

From A to B, but what is A and what is B?

Each data set can be defined as an object, a blueprint with properties, similar to how classes are defined and instantiated in object-oriented programming.

This blueprint of a data set is reusable. Both sources and targets are an instance of a data set definition sharing the same properties.

To emphasize the different possible use cases and formats of data, we refer to these generic data sets as *data objects*. A data object can be a table, file, query, procedure or anything you define it to be in the metadata schema.

Properties of a data object, at data object level, are typically identifying details such as name and identifier, applied filters, and connection information such as connection strings or tokens.

The direction of data interpretation, the vector, is the mapping between data objects. This is its own object in the metadata schema, a *data object mapping*. This mapping at data object level has its own properties, such as for example the name of the data logistics process.

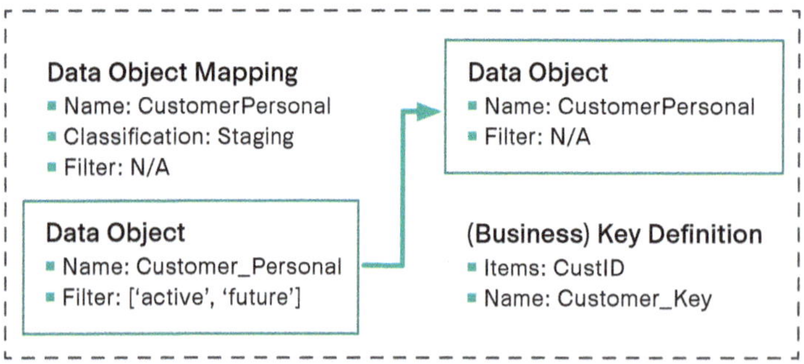

In this simple example, a data object mapping is defined and given the 'name' and 'classification' properties. The data object mapping contains two data objects, each also with some example properties.

This is the direction of data logistics (or interpretation) at data object level.

In addition to this, we can identify a lower-level mapping with a similar nature —between attributes or columns— that we refer to as a mapping at *data item level.*

Similar to a data object, a *data item* is a construct that can have various properties to describe its purpose. A data item can be a column, so that it can be mapped to a column in a different target data object. Alternatively, a data item can capture a specific bit of code, query logic, or other form of transformation.

To summarize, there are two concepts that form the core of a data object:

→ Data object, which defines the source(s) and target of the data object mapping. A data object can optionally have a connection defined as a string or token, and can be a query, file, or table

→ Data item, which belongs to a data object and represents an individual column or calculation (query) at column level and is also used to in data item mappings

A data object can have zero or more data items. A data item has to belong to a data object, but can belong to multiple data objects.

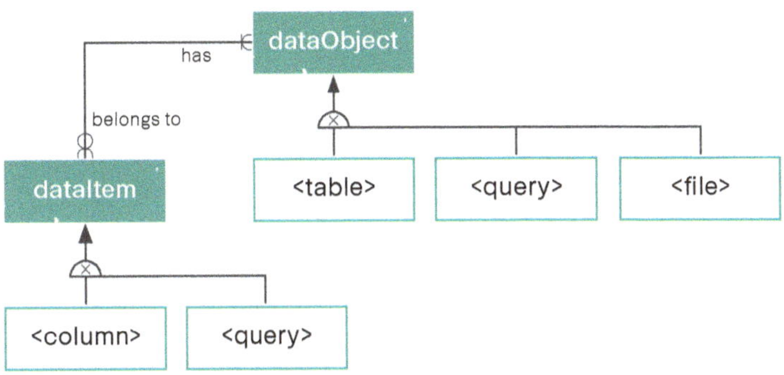

Schema definition

Data objects and data items, and their mappings, are the main concepts for the schema definition. But they are not the only ones.

↗ The schema for data solution automation provides a descriptive and flexible mechanism to record design metadata.

The relationship between these various objects are shown in the diagram below, except *extensions* as these can apply to every component. This overview presents a logical view describing how the various components conceptually relate to each other.

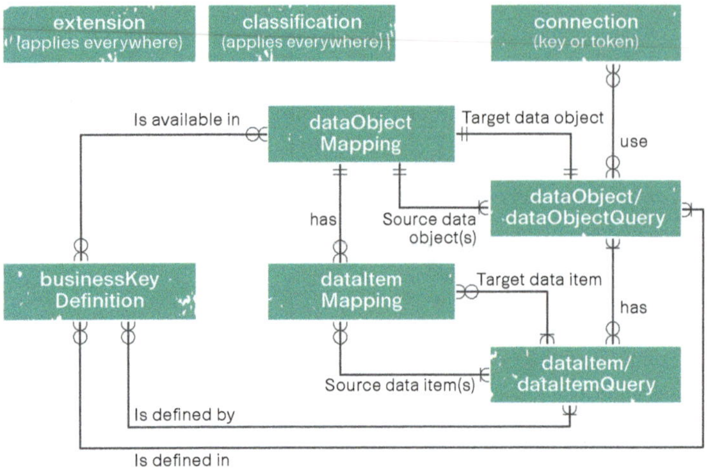

In the next sections, we will outline the configuration and purpose of these objects.

We will begin by providing an overview of the supporting objects, including connections, classifications, and business key definitions. These will then be used to formally define the structure of the data objects, data items, and their mappings.

For brevity, only the essential properties of each schema object are documented in the following sections. Generic properties such as identifier, classifications, extensions, and notes are omitted from the diagrams.

Please refer to our website for up-to-date details on the schema definition and practical examples on how to apply it: https://dtng.link/viwz0.

Data objects, items and queries

Data objects

↗ Data objects, data items, and data queries are the fundamental building blocks of the schema. These can act as sources and targets in data item and data object mappings.

Data objects are used as the sources and targets for data logistics processes. A data object that acts as target in one mapping, can be a source in another mapping, establishing a data logistics lineage.

Data Object		
Name	String	mandatory
Data Items	List<DataItem/DataItemQuery>	optional
Connection	Connection	optional
Business Key Definitions	List<Tuple<int, BusinessKeyDefinition>>	optional
Relationships	List<Tuple<int, Relationship>>	optional

Except for the 'name,' none of the data object properties are mandatory. This is because the use of this metadata varies depending on the intended template, and a high degree of flexibility is necessary to accommodate different interpretations and opinions.

For example, the same data object metadata can be used to generate both the physical model (data definition language – DDL) and data manipulation logic (DML) scripts by applying different templates.

Data objects contain the following other notable properties:

→ A list of data items. This captures which data elements, columns, or attributes belong to the data object. Conceptually, each data item can be either a true data item (column), or a data item *query* (logic)

→ A *connection,* to identify the intended location of the data object

→ An ordered list of *business key definitions.* A data object can host various different business key definitions, which can be used to define keys and map these data to potentially many targets. Even though the business key definition is mostly used in the data object mapping, the business key definition and its order in the list can optionally be recorded against the data object for reusability across potentially various data object mappings

→ An ordered list of *relationships,* which indicates associations from one data object to another – for instance if there is a one-to-many cardinality, or if the data object has a lineage relationship in some form

Data items

Data items belong to data objects or data object queries. This means that a data item always has a parent object. They describe individual elements, such as the columns in a table, or headers in a file.

The data item itself is identified by name, and can have various descriptive properties covering model details.

Data Item		
Name	String	mandatory
Data Object	DataObject/DataObjectQuery	optional
Data Type	String	optional
Character Length	Integer	optional
Numeric Precision	Integer	optional
Numeric Scale	Integer	optional
Ordinal Position	Integer	optional
Primary Key Indicator	Boolean	optional

These properties contain specifics on the individual data item, such as the data type, length, precision and order (ordinal position). It is also possible to set a flag on a data item to see if it is part of the data object's primary key, if this is relevant.

Using a data object and its child data items, the essential information covering model objects is available for generation purposes.

The (parent) data object or data object query itself is also an optional property of the data item. In most cases, this is redundant but –depending on the use of the metadata and templates– it is sometimes required to uniquely identify the data item when multiple data items from multiple data objects are brought together.

Using the data object property, a *fully qualified name* can be constructed. This is typically done by combining the data object name with the data object schema (from the data object's connection property) and the data item name.

Data queries

A data query is a bespoke code element that is scoped for a specific function or purpose, and can act as a 'source' in a source-target mapping.

This applies to both data object and data item level.

When acting as the data object, the data query replaces the source data object in the mapping. This is a *data object query,* which could be a view, script, or procedure that provides the data in the mapping instead of a table or file.

When used at data item level, the query is a *data item query.* This can be an individual expression, or combination of expressions, that is mapped to a target data item.

Data Object Query		
Name	String	optional
Query Code	String	mandatory
Query Language	String	optional
Connection	<Connection>	optional
Business Key Definition	List<Tuple<int, BusinessKeyDefinition>>	optional
Relationships	List<Tuple<int, Relationship>>	optional

Data object queries and data item queries are very similar, but have slightly different properties.

Data Item Query		
Name	String	optional
Query Code	String	mandatory
Query Language	String	optional
Data Type	String	optional
Character Length	Integer	optional
Numeric Precision	Integer	optional
Numeric Scale	Integer	optional
Ordinal	Integer	optional
Primary Key Indicator	Boolean	optional

For example, a connection does not apply to a data item query, but it does to a data object query. Similarly, ordinal position and data type details are not relevant for a data object query, but can be defined for a data item query.

In all cases, the core properties that document the code and language are shared.

The only mandatory property for the data query is the code, but optional descriptive properties can be added such as the name of the code snippet and the language it is written in.

Additionally, a dedicated connection property can be set to allow different sources to use different connections – as would be the case when connecting to different data objects.

By using a combination of one or more data queries, data objects, and data items, complex transformation can be defined in metadata.

Supporting objects

In this section, the additional descriptive properties commonly used in schema for data solution automation are covered.

These are:
→ Connections
→ Classifications
→ Business key definitions
→ Relationships (including cardinality)

Connections

Connections are used to 'access' data objects as they are available in the technical environment. For example, a connection can be a database connection string if the data object is a database table. Or, it can be a file path if the data object is defined as a file.

↗ A connection is an optional property of a data object or data object query, and can be reused across data objects.

The name property holds the key identifying details for the connection. This can be a connection string, or API token.

It is often not advisable to store sensitive information such as user name and password in a local file, such as a text file that is part of the data solution — even if it is encrypted. In these cases, it is often necessary to connect to the data using a uniquely identifiable label, which itself refers to connectivity information such as a connection string.

This is how the name property can also be seen as a *reference* to a connection object that has already been defined in the data logistics environment. A data object, through its connection property, can use the name as a 'key,' 'token,' or 'secret' that refers to this object in the data logistics environment.

In this approach, the sensitive connection details are managed in the target platform, and only its reference is stored in the metadata file.

Connection		
Name	String	mandatory

Using a connection name reference is often preferable because no sensitive information needs to be stored with the design metadata.

Classifications

Classifications can be used for a variety of purposes. Examples are to organize the metadata in a front-end environment (Graphical User Interface — or GUI), or to direct the behavior of the compiler.

↗ Classifications are labels that describe data objects, data items, business key definitions, connections, or data object mappings. They are meant to be defined using conventions, so that these can be consistently used across the metadata.

Classification		
Classification	String	mandatory

A common use case is to add template classifications so that the compiler can select the matching code generation template. This can be done, for example, by adding a classification 'PSA' to a data object mapping so that only PSA code is generated.

Data objects, data object mappings, data items, and business key definitions can have more than one classification. In technical terms, an array of classification (objects) is a property of the parent object.

Business key definition

↗ A business key definition is a special object that is defined as an optional property of a data object mapping, data object, or data object query. The business key definition can be a part of describing the relationship between a source data object and a target data object.

A business key *definition* is not the same as the business key *concept* that was introduced in the data solution architecture, but the two are related.

The business key concept itself represents a unique instance of a core business concept, and is an attribute in integration layer entities. The business key definition represents one or more data items from the source data object that are required to create the (target) business key.

It is the way the business key is defined in the source data object.

Business Key Definition		
Name	String	optional
Business Key Components	List<Tuple<int, DataItem/DataItemQuery>>	mandatory
Surrogate Key	String	optional

The business key definition is a collection of data items, where each individual data item represents a component of the business key. Each component can be a data item, or it can be a query and even include constant values – or any combination thereof.

Although this allows to capture complex business key definitions in metadata, in most cases one or more source data items suffice to generate a target business key.

Lastly, the business key definition has properties that record the business key definition name and surrogate key name. Potentially, a business key definition is a construct involving many data items. Having a single name allows the result to be referenced by an alias, and this simplifies generating code for the business key.

When a concatenation of various data items is intended to generate a surrogate key, it is important to maintain the order of data items. This is why the order is stored with each data item. Where the business key definition is used in other objects, the order of the business key definition *itself* is stored alongside the business key definition as well.

The ordinal position of a key in a list of keys can be significant. A different order of keys may have significant impacts on the output, for example when checksums are applied.

Relationship, type, and cardinality

↗ A data object and/or data object mapping may optionally include an ordered list of relationships, which can capture various associations between data objects.

Relationship		
Name	String	optional
Related Data Object	DataObject	mandatory
Data Item Mappings	List<DataItemMapping>	optional
Type	String	optional
Cardinality	Cardinality	optional

The relationship holds the data object it relates *to*. This is represented by the *related data object* property, which is of type 'data object.' Conceptually, a relationship is expected to specify at least the data object as a target. That is the only mandatory property.

The nature of a relationship can vary widely and is defined flexibly. Here are a few examples:

→ A data object might be a parent or child to another data object in the data lineage
→ A data object may have a reference or association, such as a foreign key, to another object
→ A data object is intended to be used as a lookup by another data object in a data logistics process
→ Similarity between objects may need to be defined

To accommodate this broad range of use cases without imposing restrictions, a relationship can be defined by the custom *type* property and the more precise definition of the *cardinality* property.

Type is a free-form label that can categorize a relationship for specific purposes. For example, a data object might have a 'lookup' relationship to a parent data object that can be used in data logistics. The 'type' can be used when there is a need to associate objects without explicitly modeling their relationship.

For data modeling scenarios, cardinality can be defined. Cardinality can be very specific, and is defined as a separate object due to its relative complexity.

Cardinality		
Name	String	optional
FromRange	String (min),String (max)	mandatory
ToRange	String (min),String (max)	mandatory

Cardinality in database design refers to the uniqueness of data values contained in a column of a database table. It specifically defines the number of occurrences of one entity that are associated with the number of occurrences of another entity through a relationship.

Common examples include:

- →One-to-many, where one instance of an entity (e.g., a parent) can be associated with many instances of another entity (e.g., children), but each child belongs to only one parent
- →One-to-one, where each instance of an entity is associated with exactly one instance of another entity
- →Many-to-many: where multiple instances of one entity can be associated with multiple instances of another entity

Cardinality can further specify a *range,* indicating the minimum and maximum number of occurrences allowed on each 'side' of the relationship. For instance:

- →Zero or one (0..1), where an entity instance may optionally be associated with one instance of another entity, or none at all
- →One or more (1..*), where an entity instance must be associated with at least one instance of another entity, but can have many
- →Zero or more (0..*), where an entity instance may have zero or more associations with instances of another entity.

This supports definitions such the ones in the below diagram:

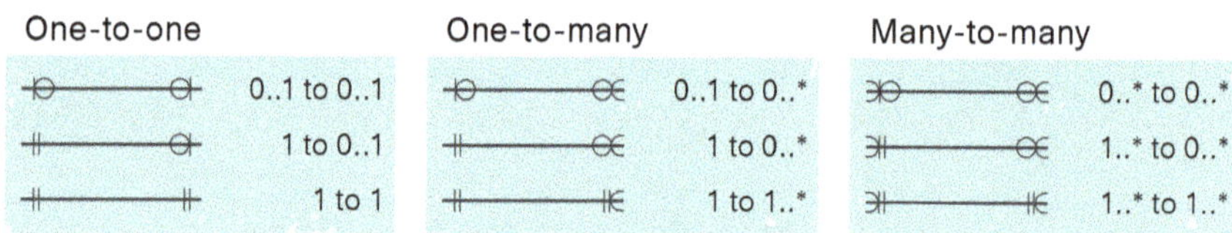

As a final notable property, a list of data items can be defined for specific elements that play a role in the relationship. For example, this list can include the names of foreign key columns, or similar references.

This property allows for the explicit identification of key components that facilitate the relationship between objects.

Mapping objects

Now the supporting objects are covered, we can complete the definition of the schema. For this, we will revisit the mappings themselves.

Data object mappings

↗ In the schema definition, a mapping between sources and targets is a data object mapping.

By convention, a data object mapping always contains a mapping between *one or more* source data objects and a *single* target data object. In addition to this, a data object mapping can contain a list of data item mappings —representing column-level mappings or transformations— and additional properties such as a business key definition.

This is shown in the following diagram:

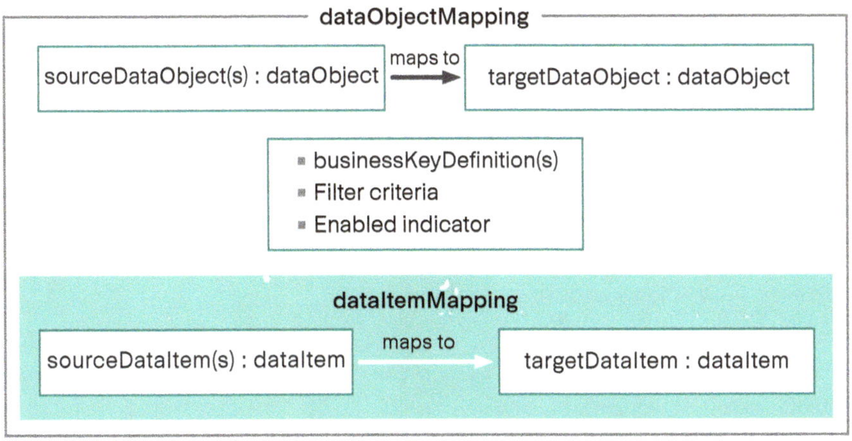

This shows that conceptually, a data object mapping contains at least a source instance of the type data object called 'sourceDataObject' and a corresponding target instance 'targetDataObject.'

The mapping between data objects is defined by the business key definition. That is to say, the business definition object 'links' the data objects together, by mapping the source data object components to the standard target key. This definition, and the complexity thereof, depends on the layer in the architecture it is applied.

In the staging layer, the key definition may be a simple data item mapping but in the integration layer —when multiple data sources are mapped to the central information model— this can become relatively complex. Either way, the mechanism to record the relationship between data objects is the same.

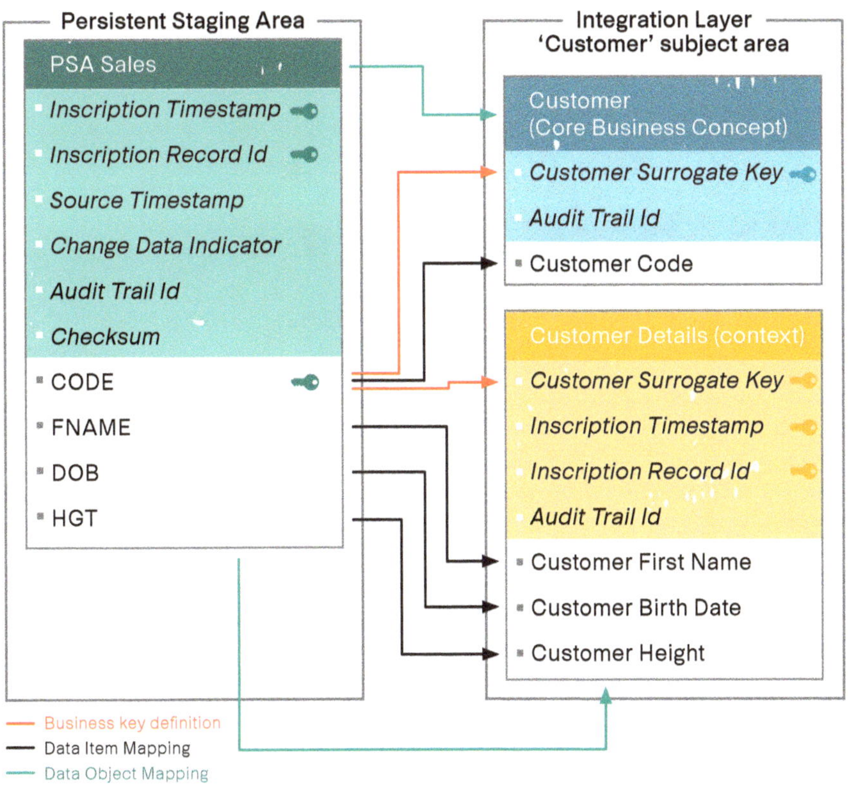

The previous image shows an example data object mapping, with the 'PSA Sales' source data object mapped to the 'Customer Details' target data object in the integration layer. As part of this data object mapping, three data item mappings are also defined.

The business key definition, as a special data item mapping is displayed as both the connecting element between the data objects as well as its special function as a data item mapping.

If we consider the more detailed overview of the data object mapping below, a number of things stand out.

Data Object Mapping		
Name	String	mandatory
Source Data Objects	List<DataObject/DataObjectQuery>	mandatory
Target Data Object	DataObject	mandatory
Relationship	List<Tuple<int, Relationship>>	optional
Data Item Mappings	List<DataItemMapping>	optional
Business Keys	List<Tuple<int, BusinessKeyDefinition>>	optional
Filter Criterion	String	optional
Enabled Indicator	Boolean	optional

First, the collection of source data objects is defined as a list that can contain data objects and data queries. This indicates that the definition of the 'source' in this mapping can be one or more data objects, but that it can also be a query (or set of queries) that is interpreted by the target data object.

This way, complex transformations can be mapped to target data objects at this level—for instance by using stored procedures, common table expressions, or similar scripts and mechanisms in an available compatible language.

Another special property for a data object mapping is the list of *relationships*—the data objects that are involved with the mapping in some form. Using this property, any number of relevant data objects can be added as additional context for the data object mapping. Use cases are many and include key or value look-ups, joins, or unions for generation of data logistics processes. A list of relationships can also link mappings to higher levels of abstraction such as conceptual and physical model entities, which can be useful in graph representation of metadata, design and lineage tracking.

The *filter criterion* property can be used to capture any global filters that should be applied when compiling the metadata into executable code. For example, this could be interpreted by the compiler to create a WHERE clause in SQL, or a filter object in a data integration platform.

It is common to apply filtering at data object mapping level, because this can direct data logistics to different targets based on data content. For example, if a given source data object contains a certain classification that should be routed to a specific target, a data object mapping with the corresponding filter can be defined. Multiple data object mappings can 'split' a source data object into various targets this way.

Lastly, the *enabled indicator* can be used to 'switch' a certain data object mapping on or off. In our experience, being able to control the output using a metadata indicator is often useful —for example during testing and development.

The collection of all data object mappings represents the full scope of design metadata.

Data item mappings

↗ In the schema definition, a mapping between sources and targets is a data object mapping.

Data item mappings represent column-level *mappings, and* are a property of a data object mapping.

A data object mapping can optionally have a data item mapping, and this often is the case. When data item mappings are necessary —for example when loading descriptive data— then this requires a data object mapping parent to be in place. In practical terms: if you map a source column to a target column, you also need to capture the parent tables or files to which these columns belong.

Data Item Mapping		
Source Data Items	List<DataItem/DataItemQuery>	mandatory
Target Data Item	<DataItem>	mandatory

The structure of the data item mapping object is similar to the data object mapping. One or more source data items are mapped to a single target data item, and similar to the data object concept, a source can be defined as a (combination of) data items and data queries.

This means that at column-level it is also possible to define potentially complex logic, and map this to a data item target.

Extensions

A suitable schema definition for data solution automation is prescriptive enough on the details it records, but also flexible to allow for differences in usage.

To maximize flexibility, and to allow for edge-cases and local customizations, we have defined *extensions* throughout the schema.

Extension		
Key	String	mandatory
Value	String	optional

↗ Extensions are key-value pairs with an optional supporting description. They are applicable to any object in the schema definition.

When extensions are added to an object as a property they are defined as a *list of extension objects* (list<extension>) so that any number of key-value pairs can be added.

The purpose of extensions is to add definitions to objects that are not directly supported by the schema. Using extensions, the compiler can be directed to support specific configurations that are otherwise difficult to record, or very specific.

The below is an example of an extension in JSON format, in this case for a data object.

```
{
 "dataObjectMappings": [
  {
   "name": "MyDataObjectMapping",
   "sourceDataObjects": [ { "name": "products_src" } ],
   "targetDataObject": {
    "name": "Products",
    "extensions": [
     {
      "key": "color",
      "value": "green",
      "notes": "The color of the object."
     },
     {
      "key": "taste",
      "value": "questionable",
      "notes": "The taste of the object."
     }
    ]
   }
  }
 ]
}
```

In this example, the data object called 'Products' is a target data object that is part of the 'MyDataObjectMapping' data object mapping. The extensions 'color' and 'taste' have been added specifically to this data object.

In reality, adding 'color' and 'taste' as properties to a data object wouldn't make much sense – but it shows that anything is possible!

Data object mapping lists

In the previous section we have defined a data object mapping as the intended data logistics from one or more source data object(s) to a target data object.

↗ The data object mapping represents a unique data logistics definition that moves, or interprets, data from one or more source(s) to a destination.

Conceptually, there is a higher level of abstraction that we can define in the schema. This is the *list* of related data object mappings – a *data object mapping list.*

Data Object Mappings		
Data Object Mappings	List<DataObjectMapping>	mandatory

The data object mapping list is an array of individual data object mappings. It is the top level object in the schema, every data object mapping definition file that conforms to this schema starts with an array containing potentially (but not necessarily) multiple data object mappings.

In other words, even though there may be only one data object mapping defined, it is still placed in a data object mapping list.

The decision to start the schema format with an array/list that contains potentially multiple data object mappings provides additional flexibility to support different ways of technical deliver later on.

By grouping related data object mappings together based on their shared target data object, it is possible to generate these as individual data logistics modules as well as a full representation of the target data object in a virtualized context.

As an example, consider the loading of a single table (the target data object) from multiple data sources. If the corresponding data object mappings are treated independently, each would typically lead to a single generated data logistics process that targets the same table.

However, if you are seeking to generate a database view that represents the target table you would need to access the collection (list) of all data object mappings that are mapped to this target table. The same applies if you want to generate a single data logistics process that uses a series of UNION statements, instead of separate data logistics modules.

In cases such as these it is easier to process a list of (related) data object mappings because this supports all use cases.

Lineage and graphs

Data object mappings are a great fit for graph representation. Together, all data object mappings can be visualized as a (directed) graph model. The complete set of mappings provides a lineage graph showing exactly how data moves, and is transformed, throughout the data solution every step of the way.

Data objects represent where data is queried from, or where data is committed to. A data object can be the 'target' in one mapping, but the 'source' in another.

By connecting these data object *instances* across data object mappings, a graph model is created.

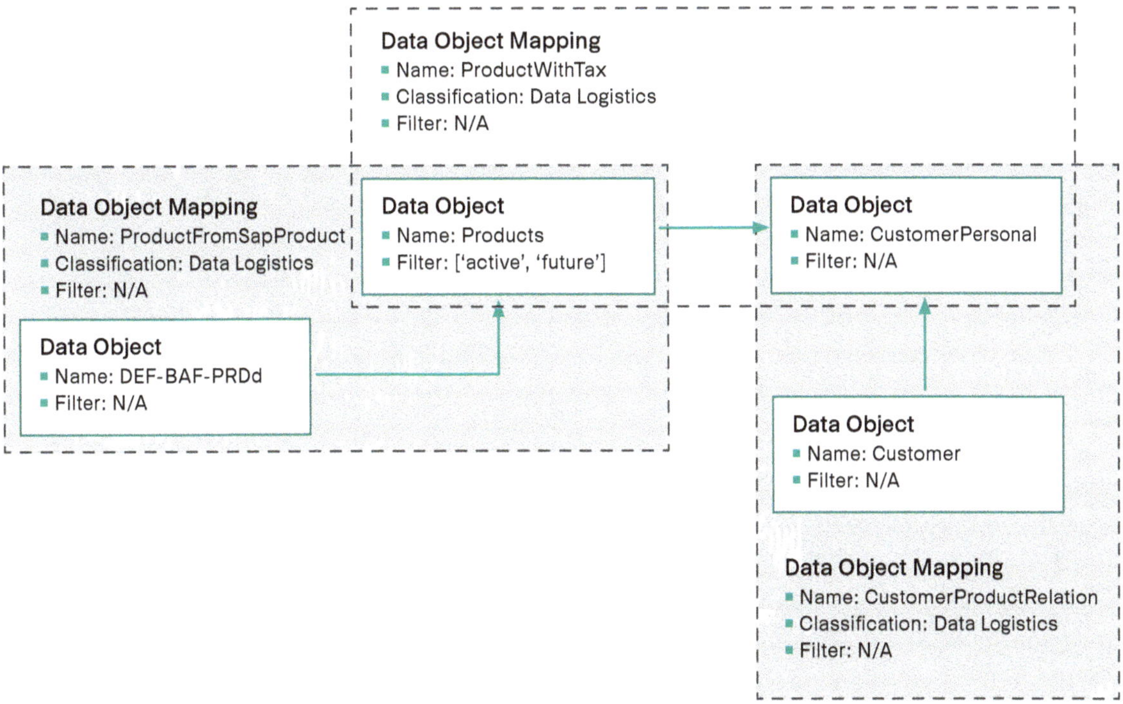

In graph terminology, the data object mappings create a *directed graph* model. There is a direction defined by nature of defining a 'source' and a 'target' data object.

Each element in the data object mapping, at both data object as well as data item level, is a graph node, and every relationship is a graph edge. The information in the mapping, data object mapping properties, becomes a property of the edge. This applies, for instance, to the business key definition at data object level and the transformation or copy at data item level.

Moreover, the relationship between a data item mapping and its parent data object mapping is also an edge — which translates into a graph that shows which attributes belong to which entity.

The example below contains two individual data object mappings. The 'PSA Sales' table —a source data object— is mapped to both the 'Customer' CBC and its supporting context entity.

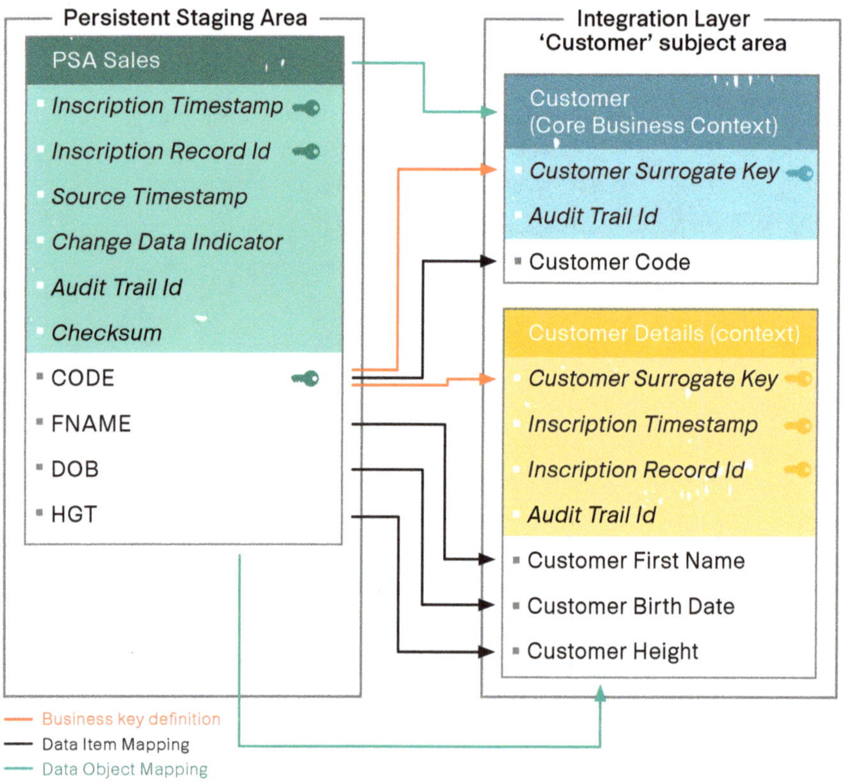

The source business key is defined as 'CODE.' This means that as a result of analysis and modeling, it was decided that this value represents a 'Customer' in the information model for this particular data source. The CODE column is mapped to the standard customer target surrogate key, but for other source data sets it is likely that a different column is selected to represent the customer.

Descriptive data such as 'first name,' 'date of birth,' and 'height' are mapped to the context entity. The data item mapping for this connects the values to a target data item with a more standardized name.

Visualizing levels of abstraction

A powerful feature of graph models is the ability to abstract ('zoom out,' or 'collapse') and display the —often complex— collection of all mappings in a more simplified way.

The previous example looks like this when some of the details are abstracted away:

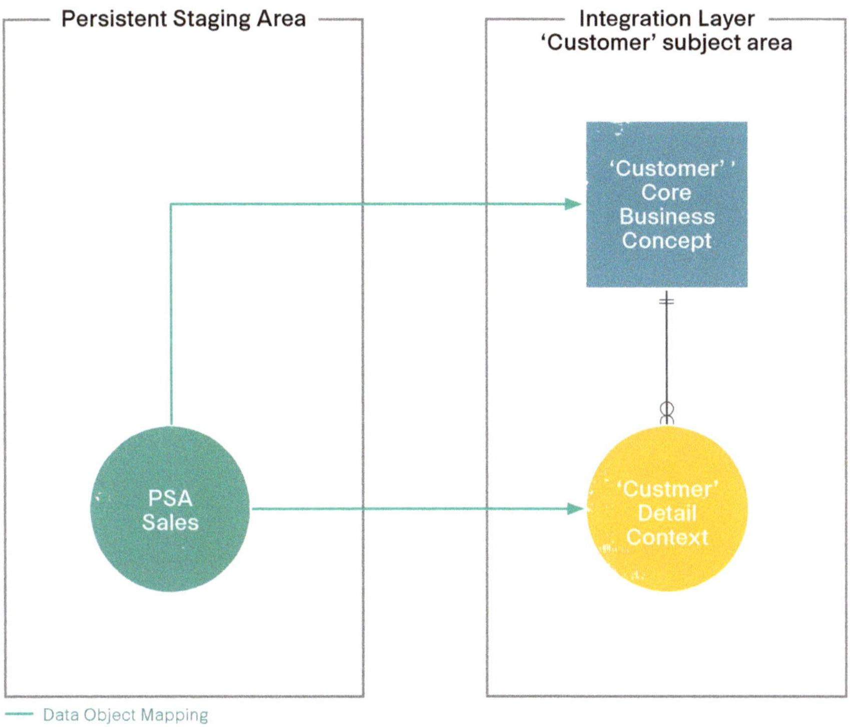

Similarly, the relationship between the data object and the system or subject area it belongs to *also* is an edge. You get the idea.

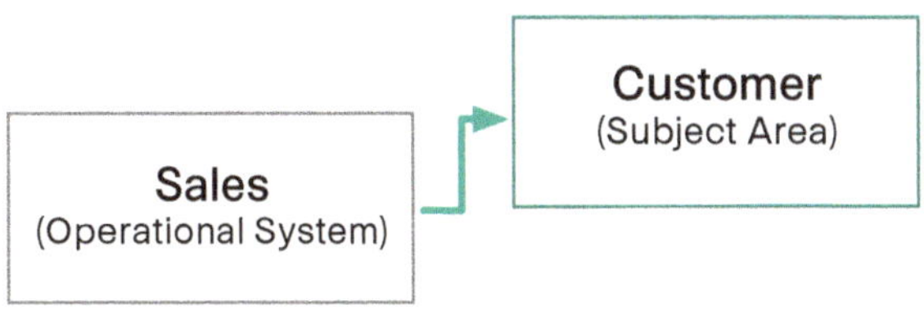

These higher level abstractions contain all objects in these categories. The Sales container would contain all data objects belonging to this operational system.

We believe this is a more natural approach for documenting data logistics, as opposed to creating separate documentation to specify data logistics so that these can be developed by others. It is common that, over time, documentation and the reality in code diverge. Worst case, differences between documentation and reality exacerbate until the documentation becomes meaningless.

By using the same base artifact, the design metadata schema, for both documentation as well as implementation —through code generation— both will stay in sync. The documented data lineage always accurately explains the 'route' data follows through the various data logistics components to deliver the data.

Data lineage

This approach for defining design metadata also enables visualization of the full data lineage. Data lineage describes the journey of a given data set or column throughout the solution. It is possible to start with a given data object or item and follow the graph to see where it is used, or trace the steps backwards to understand where it originates from.

Because both the physical model as well as the data logistics themselves can be generated from this format, it represents not only the documentation of the data solution but also the actual implementation.

More than just a representation

The combined metadata defines the graph. Conversely, a graph model can also be a highly effective way of defining the metadata. It is a powerful design and development tool.

Data object mappings are technology-agnostic and able to define relationships at more abstract levels of design. The same mechanism can be applied for a conceptual or logical mode – or to define a relationship between objects in a logical model and their physical model counterpart(s). For instance, a mapping between a conceptual object and a physical model object can be a data object mapping too.

Storage considerations

The schema for data solution automation is designed to be concise, flexible, and to capture the essential requirements for recording design metadata.

Flexibility is important, and as part of this consideration only the minimum of constraints are applied. It is up to individual teams to agree on *how* the schema will be populated, what the approach will be to interface with the design metadata.

For example, it is possible to manually create or modify data object mapping files using a text editor. However, manually editing formats such as JSON can be frustrating, and if certain broadly used properties —such as object prefixes or special column names— are changed, then all files need to be updated.

For this reason, many organizations choose to develop their own custom application or invest in third-party software to simplify the interaction with design metadata. There are many ways to easily create a front-end, a user interface, that can consume, create, and modify these files – ranging from Excel applications to simple proprietary forms applications and simple websites or database solutions.

These applications have the added benefit to store and apply central configurations on conventions, such as the aforementioned table prefixes or column names. From a central location, standards and conventions can be validated across the files and updated if and when necessary.

The collection of files is still the de facto metadata repository, but any tools that are able to read and write to these files can serve as management tool for the design metadata.

The thinking behind this is that different individuals, teams, or companies can use their own preferred front-end tools without being locked into specific technologies.

Compilation and code generation

The actual generation of data platform components, such as data logistics, is performed by a dedicated process that is independent from design metadata, patterns, and templates.

This is the engine's *compilation* process. Compilation merges the design metadata with the code generation patterns, and produces output for the target infrastructure.

The compiler is able to understand the template and applies the design metadata to produce executable code – data logistics processes in this case. The exact format depends on the target infrastructure and selected data logistics technology.

If design metadata, recorded using the schema for data solution automation, is the *what* for code generation then the code generation templates are the *how*.

In the compilation process, both ingredients are used to produce the data structures and the data logistics processes to interface with them.

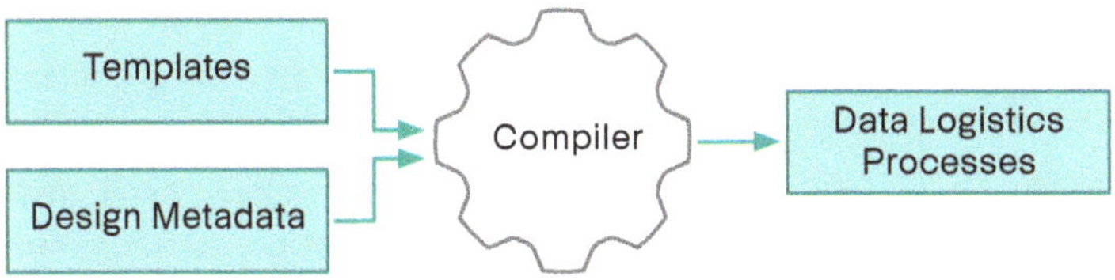

For example, a compiler may create various types of SQL-based data logistics components, such as queries or stored procedures in the dialect (syntax) of a specific target database. Alternatively, it could connect to APIs or use software development kits (SDKs) provided by data logistics software vendors. It could even use Domain-Specific Languages (DSLs) for code generation.

In all cases, the compilation output is delivered in a format native to the target data logistics technology.

Styles of code generation

↗ A brute force approach for code generation creates many individual physical data logistics processes.

Broadly speaking, styles for code generation for data logistics can be divided into two categories: *brute force* and *metadata injection*.

Brute force

In a brute force approach, each data object mapping is compiled as a single, *individual* executable artifact in a format that is native to the target platform.

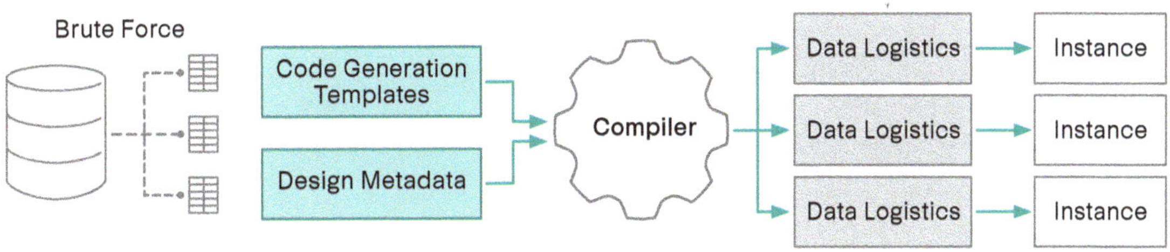

Brute force code generation typically uses an API or SDK that is provided by the data logistics software, so that the data logistics processes are created specifically for the target technology.

This means that the templates themselves are specifically codified for this target environment – describing the intended data logistics structure in a way the native platform understands, and operates with. The templates and compiler may even be combined in the same code base, as they tend to be strongly related.

An execution instance is created each time an individual generated data logistics process is run – creating a log in the control framework accordingly.

Each tool has its own name for their data logistics process object type. Common names for data logistics objects are mappings, jobs, data flows, agents, packages, sessions, or processes. Some SQL queries, stored procedures, and views also fall in this category – assuming a separate object is created for each data object mapping.

An advantage of brute force code generation for data logistics is that output can be generated in the target environment's native format. The generated artifacts will be indistinguishable from manually created data logistics processes.

Metadata injection

↗ A metadata injection approach for code generation defines a small set of standard and generic physical data logistics processes.

The metadata injection approach is in many ways the opposite of the brute force style of code generation. Instead of creating multiple individual data logistics objects (executables) for the target environment, only a small set of standard and generic physical data logistics processes are defined. They act as templates themselves and are highly parameterized so that they can accept variable inputs – parameters.

These generic processes are often manually created and maintained, although they can usually be scripted so that they can be deployed as part of the overall infrastructure configuration ('infrastructure as code'). They can be run multiple times, and in parallel. Each time the process is executed with a given set of inputs (parameters), a runtime instance is spawned.

The instance is the unique execution of the 'real' data logistics process and integrates into the control framework as usual.

The parameter inputs are usually provided as *parameter files,* and are provided in a structure that is specific to the target data logistics platform[30], so that they can be interpreted as individual data logistics processes at runtime.

The parameter files simply contain a concise list of parameters in a way the generic data logistics process can read them. In some cases, the data logistics software can even be configured to read data object mappings defined as per the schema for data solution automation format directly.

Metadata Injection

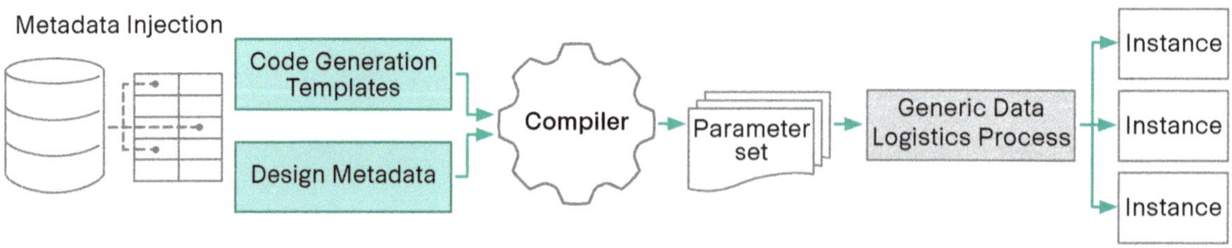

When using a metadata injection approach, the emphasis on code generation is on creating the input parameters and not the physical data logistics object itself. Parameters can be configured in many ways, depending on the capabilities of the available technical environment. However, they are typically defined as text-based files. The format of these files can vary, but includes many popular text-based formats such as plain text, JSON, XML, and Comma-Separated-Value (CSV) files.

To summarize: the compiler generates many parameters —one entry for each data object mapping— and these are made accessible to the data logistics template for execution as a parameter file, or set of files.

Since the compiler only needs to create text files with a small amount of properties, the required template and code are relatively simple — at least compared to the brute force approach. There is no need to produce output that is compatible with the native target format, or to adopt APIs or SDKs as the generic processes do all of the heavy lifting.

The feasibility of adopting the metadata injection style for code generation depends on the features available in the technical infrastructure. Not every data logistics platform supports parameterization to the same extent. Some technology simply works better if every data logistics process is its own physical object. Other platforms, however, are developed with parameterization in mind, or support both approaches.

The main advantage of metadata injection is that it is often easier to generate code, because the compiler and templates are less complicated as compared to the brute force approach. The compiler only needs to produce text files, which is often easier than interacting with an API, SDK, or DSL.

Examples of metadata injection can be found in the data logistics capabilities offered in various cloud platforms such as Amazon Web Services and Microsoft Azure, but stored procedures can also be defined as a dynamic object — in a way that accepts input parameters and evaluates these at runtime to produce and run dynamic SQL statements.

Either one of these two approaches may be the better fit for a given technical environment. This depends on the features and capabilities of the technology used.

Ways of code generation

Regardless of the code generation style, many techniques are available to automate development.

Common techniques include templating engines, APIs, software development kits (SDKs), and domain-specific languages (DSLs)

Templating engines

Data logistics processes can be generated by using a variety of available templating engines[31]. Templating engines provide capabilities to apply an input, or series of inputs, to a predefined template. Many templating engines find their origins in the world of web development where they are often used to dynamically generate HTML pages for web applications.

They are best suited to produce text-based outputs, such SQL files, which can then be executed by the target technology.

Text-based outputs are not limited to only SQL or HTML code. In fact, many data logistics technologies store their artifacts, such as data logistics processes or table definitions, using text-based formats such as XML, JSON, or similar. In these cases, a design and development environment can render (interpret, visualize) these XML or JSON files as a visual data logistics process.

In other words, the user interacts with the data logistics in a visual way but the artifact itself is often saved as a text file.

Many data logistics technologies fall into this category, and as such provide opportunities for code generation using templating engines.

For instance, SQL Server Integration Services (SSIS) data logistics artifacts (packages) are XML files. However, they are rendered as visual process workflows when opened in Visual Studio. The same applies to Azure Data Factory (ADF): the various components are essentially JSON files that are visually represented as workflows or linked services in the portal. Azure Resource Management files work the same way, and can be used by Azure to create infrastructure.

In all of these cases, the underlying artifact is text-based. And for these, generating code using templating engines can, and probably should, be considered.

Templating engines require two elements to produce the output: an input design metadata object, and a template. The input object can be defined in many ways, and this depends entirely on how the developer prefers to organize the design metadata. It can be an Excel sheet, a text file with a list of values, a database connection, or a more complex object model.

In our approach, the schema for data solution automation is used as input object model. Most templating engines can easily consume design metadata in JSON format or similar, for example as a data object mapping List (List<DataObjectMapping>).

The second element is the template itself. The template contains a set of instructions to apply to an input metadata object. The syntax of these instructions vary between templating engines, but typically include iterations (loops), conditions, and features to interpret arrays.

Code generation templates

The code generation templates, 'templates' for short, direct what needs to be done with the design metadata – how metadata is applied. For instance, how sources and targets are defined, how joins, filters, unions, and transformations are implemented.

Consider the following data object mapping:

```
{
 "dataObjectMappings": [
  {
   "name": "MyDataObjectMapping",
   "sourceDataObjects": [ { "name": "products_src" } ],
   "targetDataObject": { "name": "Products" },
   "dataItemMappings": [
    {
     "sourceDataItems": [ { "name": "PrdNm" } ],
     "targetDataItem": { "name": "ProductName" }
    },
    {
     "sourceDataItems"": [ { "name": "PrdValue" } ],
     "targetDataItem": {"name": "SalePrice" }
    }
   ]
  }
 ]
}
```

This mapping contains a single source data object that is mapped to a target data object, as well as two data item mappings.

As a mapping, it contains the direction of data logistics or interpretation but not its application. You can use this design metadata for many things, for example by only focusing on the source and specifying a SELECT statement as the template such as:

```
SELECT * FROM [products_src]
```

This simple template can be expressed[32] as:

```
SELECT * FROM [{{sourceDataObjects.0.name}}]
```

In this template, the first entry in the sourceDataObjects collection (array) will be passed onto the resulting query statement. The first position in the array is '0,' so the first available sourceDataObject will be inserted when compiling this template.

The exact syntax may vary depending on the selected technology and compiler. This is explained in more detail in the ⚐ compilation and generation section.

Alternatively, you can focus on the target and use a TRUNCATE TABLE template:

```
TRUNCATE TABLE [Products]
```

This can be expressed as a template as follows (note the added square brackets):

```
TRUNCATE TABLE [{{targetDataObject.name}}]
```

Since a targetDataObject is a single object, not an array, the value can be selected directly.

The following two queries are variations on the same theme. Both queries will return the same result set, but the preferred one might depend on available technology and opinions on what is considered 'the best way.'

```
INSERT INTO Products (ProductName, SalePrice)
SELECT PrdNm, PrdValue
FROM products src
WHERE NOT EXISTS
 (
  SELECT NULL FROM ProductMaster tgt WHERE src.PrdNm = tgt.ProductName
 )
```

```
INSERT INTO ProductMaster (ProductName, SalePrice)
SELECT PrdNm, PrdValue
FROM products src
LEFT OUTER JOIN ProductMaster tgt ON src.PrdNm = tgt.ProductName
WHERE tgt.ProductName IS NULL
```

Both queries use the same values from the metadata, but apply them in a different way. This is the power of using templates independent from the design metadata. It allows for gradual design changes and incremental improvements, without impacting the data model and design of the data logistics overall.

As a template, this can look like the example below. Only one template is shown because the same values are used.

```
INSERT INTO {{targetDataObject.name}} ({{#each dataItemMappings}}{{targetDataItem.name}}{{/each}})
SELECT ({{#each dataItemMappings}}{{sourceDataItems.0.name}}{{/each}})
FROM {{sourceDataObjects.0.name}} src
WHERE NOT EXISTS
 (
  SELECT NULL FROM {{targetDataObject.name}} tgt
  WHERE src.{{dataItemMappings.0.SourceDataItems.0.name}} =
     tgt.{{dataItemMappings.0.targetDataItem.name}}
 )
```

This example contains iterations to list all the source and target column names, captured as data item mappings. The EXISTS predicate requires a key value, and for this the first available data item mapping is used.

In this example, the template uses the order of data item mappings as a convention to provide the join key details. Another approach would be to define the key as part of the design metadata, for example using the business key definition or extension properties.

These template examples are relatively straightforward, and therefore limited in their application. What would happen if composite keys need to be supported? Templates can be complex, and include many iterations over the available metadata to achieve the intended outcome.

Examples of production-ready templates can be found on our website: https://dtng.link/hb2ay.

The template descriptions in this book are less technical and more descriptive on purpose, because technology continues to evolve at a steady pace. We have chosen to document the template intent and reasoning, and provide additional code examples on our website: https://dtng.link/.

A simple example

A simple example of a template using Handlebars syntax, and using the schema for data solution automation, is provided below:

```
{{#each dataObjectMappings}}
--Working on {{name}}.
SELECT
{{#each dataItemMappings}}
{{#each sourceDataItems}} [{{name}}] AS [{{../targetDataItem.name}}]{{/each}}{{#unless @last}},{{/unless}}
{{/each}}
INTO [{{targetDataObject.name}}]
FROM [{{sourceDataObjects.0.name}}]
WHERE [{{dataItemMappings.0.sourceDataItems.0.name}}] != NULL
{{/each}}
```

This example implements a simple iteration over the elements in the dataObjectMappings collection – creating a SQL statement for each. Note that a comma is added to the column names in the SELECT statement, unless it is the last one in the list (@last).

When run, the templating engine code loads the JSON design metadata and maps this to an internal object (class) model. Next, it will load the template and merge this with the design metadata. The templating engine acts as the compiler.

For each segment in the metadata, the content will be applied to the template.

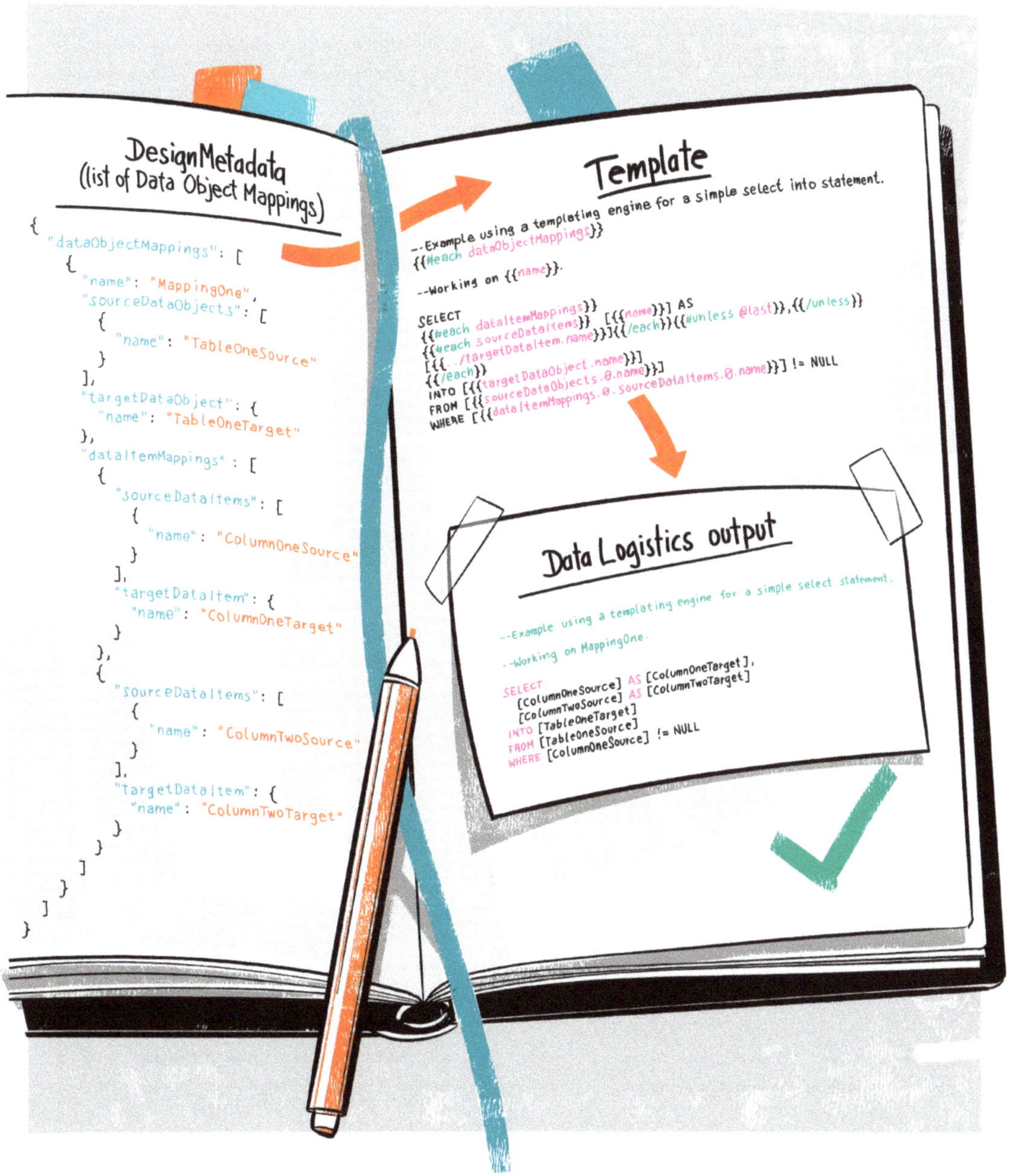

Alternatives to templating engines

There are various alternatives to templating engines that follow the same way of thinking, but don't require a templating engine library.

In most common programming languages, it is possible to generate text-based data logistics output by *deserializing* the design metadata —loading the design metadata into memory— and progressively constructing the output by iterating over the segments.

As with the earlier example, the design metadata input can be a data object mapping list that is loaded into a matching object model (class structure) so that it can be accessed from memory by the program.

By iterating over this metadata, output can be defined using string building and/or interpolation mechanisms. The resulting string output, in the form of a SQL statement or similar, can then be written to a defined target location.

This approach for generating data logistics can be implemented using many widely used programming languages such as C#, Python or Java. It is also possible to achieve the same result via macros in popular software such as MS Excel or data modeling tools. The same outcomes can even be achieved using SQL directly, for instance by using a cursor to iterate over design metadata segments.

The key difference between this approach and templating engine libraries, is that templating engines natively separate design metadata and templates. This means that an effective solution can be developed in a relatively short amount of time, while automatically enforcing best practices. And, arguably, time is saved developing functionality that is already available.

While it is also possible to achieve this by developing a similar solution in code, it often results in templates being less accessible by others, unless they have a coding background and access to the necessary technology — whereas templates are usually text-based and more easy to read.

Templating engines offer a lot of flexibility, and require only a bare minimum of coding expertise.

In this ever-changing landscape, we refer to our website for additional resources about implementing your own data logistics using templating engines: https://dtng.link/feww1.

Using APIs and SDKs

A final common approach for generating data logistics is using APIs or SDKs.

For our purposes, although definitions may vary, these are largely synonymous. At a high level, an API is a library, or a set of libraries, that provide the coding language that allows you to interact with other services from your own environment. The SDK is often a more broader set of tools, components, instructions, and code samples that are provided to make it easier to connect to the intended environment.

Both are ways to interface with, and control, resources provided by a different software platform — such as the data logistics software or service.

In this approach, the templates are coded in a local development environment that uses the API or SDK to program — creating data logistics.

These technologies typically contain authentication features that allow access to a third-party service from a local development environment. The local development environment can contain the design metadata, which can be presented to the third-party services so that data logistics output can be created there.

APIs and SDKs are often proprietary, which means that a certain degree of vendor lock-in is involved when committing to this approach. The benefit is often better support, and access to specific features related to the selective (native) technology.

Domain-Specific Languages

Various open source and commercial data logistics software products[33] offer an alternative to developing your own compiler by providing a simplified way to specify templates using a DSL.

A DSL provides a set of standardized terms for objects and operations to define the data logistics processes. DSLs offer a compiler that is developed specifically to interpret these standardized terms into a native delivery format. It's a special-purpose language, as opposed to the more general purpose of software development (coding) languages.

This can be an effective way to describe some of the more complex transformations in the data solution. By contrast, templating engines often require complex logic to be codified into either a proprietary DSL, or by using an existing one – such as SQL. This means the design metadata must contain the SQL statements as input, which are then injected as-is by the templating engine.

Third party DSLs are often rich in features, and allow defining this complexity using simplified, often less technical, language.

In terms of development, the design metadata is used to produce output in the DSL format so that this resulting (higher level) code can then be generated into the target data logistics format by the DSL-compatible compiler.

In almost all cases, this requires a simple iteration over the design metadata to produce the initial DSL output – which acts as the template. In other words, the template is described in the DSL format, and it is created as many times as it is specified by the design metadata.

This implies that templating engines can also be used to generate the DSL-specific output, so that the compiler can then use this to produce the end result.

As an example, a popular format in the Microsoft space is BI Markup Language, or Biml. Biml uses XML tags to describe data logistics operations such as selecting, joining, merging, manipulating, filtering, and writing data.

The Biml compiler can interpret these standardized names and translate these into Microsoft native data logistics components such as for example SSIS and SQL Server Analysis Services (SSAS), or various Microsoft Azure formats including ADF and Mapping Data Flows (MDF).

The advantage of this approach is that developers don't need to define templates that specifically apply to the target technologies. In this example this means that they don't need to understand the specific Azure syntax to describe these components – in this case using JSON.

The output of the development work is delivered in the DSL format, and the delivery into the target data logistics format (e.g., ADF, MDF, SSIS) is a compiler setting. The compiler manages the translation to the target syntax.

This means that the DSL format that describes the template can theoretically be done in a relatively technology agnostic way – although in practice it still tends to be fairly implementation-specific.

This is illustrated in the diagram below:

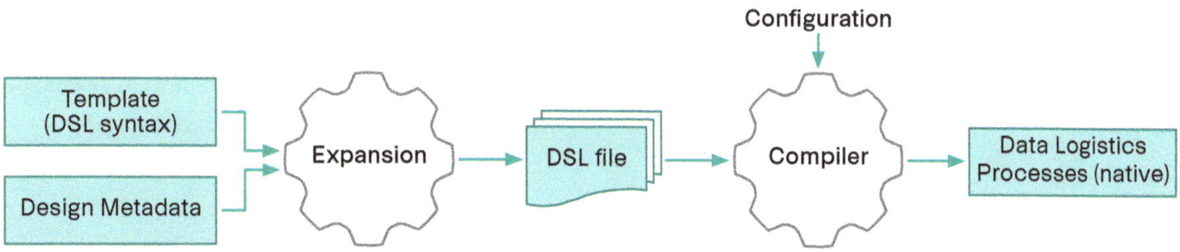

The metadata, which again can be in the (JSON) format of the schema for data solution automation, can be consumed by code that applies the DSL syntax. This creates a number of objects or files in the DSL format – a process that is often referred to as *expansion.*

Note that the exact form in which the DSL is presented to the compiler is not relevant. Whether you process one large file or a series of small files, the process remains the same. As an example, a number of files are shown in the diagram, but the message is that there is a separate step (expansion) in which the design metadata is prepared in the DSL format before the compiler processes these.

This separation allows the compiler to accept settings, or configurations, that direct the intended output format – allowing the same metadata to be generated into different data logistics outputs.

A DSL example

We provide a sample template script that uses the Biml DSL —a mixture of C# and Biml (XML) syntax— on our website: https://dtng.link/emlz8.

This sample code deserializes the schema JSON files into memory, and adds each data object mapping to a list. This in-memory object model follows the same structure as the schema, and is part of an open-source class library.

When the JSON files have been added to the list, the code iterates over this list to produce output in Biml DSL format – the expansion. This reflects the true template which can be subsequently compiled into native objects. Every DSL element can be recognized as an XML tag. For example, the <Package> tag is the Biml wording for an individual data logistics process, and <Dataflow> is a function container inside a data logistics object that holds sources and targets.

It is not the intent of this book to go into detail on the Biml language any deeper, as there are many good resources for this. The message here is that DSL syntax, such as the <Package> and <Dataflow> tags in Biml, can be recognized by the compiler.

The result of this code produces an expanded output that only contains DSL syntax, and no longer anything else such as C#. A single element is provided as an example below, but there can be as many as there is input design metadata for.

```
<Package Name="HUB_INCENTIVE_OFFER1">
  <Tasks>
   <Dataflow Name="DF - HUB_INCENTIVE_OFFER1 - 1">
   </Dataflow>
   <Dataflow Name="DF - HUB_INCENTIVE_OFFER1 - 2">
     <PrecedenceConstraints>
       <Inputs>
         <Input OutputPathName="DF - HUB_INCENTIVE_OFFER1 - 1.Output" />
       </Inputs>
     </PrecedenceConstraints>
   </Dataflow>
  </Tasks>
</Package>
```

This snippet contains the results of merging the design metadata and template, as per the first piece of example code. It is a pure DSL text that the compiler can use to produce data logistics processes, such as for SSIS or ADF in this case.

Version control

Versioning, also referred to as source control, is an essential component of the engine. Versioning looks after the saving, safeguarding, and tracking of design changes of the data solution, and in particular its design metadata.

An effective implementation of versioning allows for transparency across the history of changes. It should be possible to find out who made what change, and when.

Git, in a nutshell

↗ Git is a distributed version control system that enables decentralized development for projects of any size.

There are many approaches for versioning, but we will use Git[34] as a reference because of its broad industry adoption. In Git, as in many other approaches, changes to files are stored in code *repositories.*

The concept is that every developer works independently, using a local repository version. This is why Git is often referred to as a *distributed* version control system. Each local copy, known as a *clone,* is a complete and self-contained version control repository.

When changes are saved to the repository this is called a *commit.* A commit represents a snapshot of all code/files at a point in time which then can be *pushed* (uploaded) to a *branch* (development line) that is accessible by other team members.

Branches represent a copy of the code which can be used to develop a specific feature or implement a change. During *branching,* an existing branch is 'copied.' The branch from which the 'copy' is made is referred to as the *origin.*

A branch is ideally created from a stable origin, such as the *main* branch. The main branch usually represents the version of the code that is in production. A branch that specifically intends to deliver a specific feature is often called a *feature branch.*

When the necessary code changes have been committed, and testing of the branch has been completed, it is time to merge the changes back into the main code base. The developer can announce this by creating a *pull request (PR).*

Depending on the workflow —there are many variations— a PR can be reviewed by others, and hopefully approved, after which it is merged into the target branch. After merging, the feature branch is usually archived or deleted.

When code is merged back into the target branch this way, all the commits that were part of the branch and PR are added to the target branch and will become visible to others.

Each commit represents one or more changes in the code, and the history of commits makes it possible to see exactly who made a certain change in the past, and when.

What code to version?

So far, we have outlined the versioning concepts that are relevant for the data solution. It is equally important to clarify *what* code should be versioned.

The essential artifacts that require versioning are:
→ Design metadata, ideally as a collection of files conforming to the schema for data solution automation
→ Code generation templates

Our recommendation is to manage the versioning of the design metadata *in the same repository* as the templates, so that a direct relationship between the two artifacts is established.

This is necessary to be able to reproduce the data solution exactly as it was at a point in time – the topic of the ⚐ data solution versioning section.

In many projects, physical data logistics processes and data structures are versioned, instead of the metadata and templates. This is a viable approach. However, we perceive data structures and data logistics processes as *output* of the design metadata and templates. In this sense, they are ephemeral and do not need to be versioned.

The deployment automation workflow will generate and deploy them as needed.

For this reason, we advocate generating the structures and data logistics as part of a deployment automation workflow because this brings us one step closer to the goal of running the engine.

Versioning the data model

It is also highly recommended to version the data model, ideally in the same repository as the design metadata and templates. If this is not possible, it is usually possible to add a reference to the design metadata to link it back to the logical or conceptual models. In the schema for data solution automation, this can be done using classifications and/or extensions.

At the time of writing, many data modeling software products manage their content (i.e. data models) in a proprietary format, and using an internal version control solution. Version control often is a cost option of these tools that allows users to store versions of the models in a proprietary repository. This approach is not always compatible with Git, and results in the data models being managed in a different version control solution than the design metadata and templates.

While it is sometimes possible to extract data models, these are often saved in a binary or proprietary format that does not work well with text-based differential tracking as used in Git. In other words, it is not always straightforward to understand what has changed between model versions by looking at the text differences.

Versioning applies predominantly to the conceptual and logical models rather than the physical models. In Engine Thinking, the physical model (and changes thereof) can be generated using templates, similar to how data logistics processes are created.

The physical data model is typically expressed as data definition language (DDL), which uses SQL syntax to describe data structures. These structures can include elements such as keys, indexes, partitioning, constraints etc.

Producing DDL simply involves using a specific code generation template. Or to pivot this perspective: data logistics processes and DDL can be generated from the same design metadata.

This approach to managing the physical model ties back to the intent of the engine: realizing a self-optimizing data solution. By interpreting usage statistics and defining an optimization configuration, it is possible to automatically implement physical model variations that are closer to the intended optimization goal.

This can include, for example, adding or removing indexes, adjusting co-location and hash distribution, or vertical or horizontal splitting of data sets. The data is not altered in a way that changes its meaning, but the physical way it is stored is automatically optimized.

To bring this back to the data model and its versioning: the conceptual and logical models might not change but its physical model counterpart can. And these changes are forward-engineered/generated from the design metadata using code generation templates.

To summarize, in Engine Thinking we derive the physical model from the design metadata. As such, it is not necessary to specifically version-control DDL files.

Data solution versioning

↗ Data solution versioning provides a 'time machine' for the entire data solution. By versioning the design metadata, data, and templates together the solution can be rebuild as it was at any moment in its history.

There is a different, broader, way to think about versioning: that of the *complete* data solution.

You can rebuild your full data solution —as it was at any moment in its history— if you version the design metadata and templates in the same repository *and* maintain a snapshot of your original data (transactions) at a point in time.

Versioning design metadata has now been covered, this is the collection of files that conform to the schema for data solution automation under version control. The code generation templates are versioned in the same repository.

The second component, the original transactions, is supported by PSA. Data in the PSA is already time-stamped and transactional, and therefore provides a technical timeline that can be aligned to the design metadata version.

By combining the metadata version with the PSA the full data solution can be rebuild to represent any point in time – including all data structures and data logistics processes downstream of the PSA.

This provides a the 'time machine' for the *entire* solution, not just for data in a bitemporal context. A temporal analysis of data is in principle bound to the data structures, at least practically speaking.

Full data solution versioning, however, allows for *time-travel* to review the complete data solution and its deliverables as they were at a point in time – further complementing multi temporal capabilities.

Given sufficient resources, it is possible to even host different versions of the data solution concurrently.

Limiting PSA data access

A topic that has surfaced a few times when reproducing historical data, is to prevent involving data that is 'ahead.' This is data that has been recorded *later* than the moment in time for which the data is meant to be reproduced.

This applies as well when reproducing a data solution as an earlier version. The solution may display data for time periods that would not have happened yet. That is, from the perspective of the selected point in time.

When required, these can be filtered out in the data delivery.

This is already managed if the correct patterns have been applied, at least for the periods *prior* to the selected point in time. If all is well, recorded data changes that arrive later, but apply to an earlier time period, will already be covered by the bitemporal perspectives.

Consider the example below:

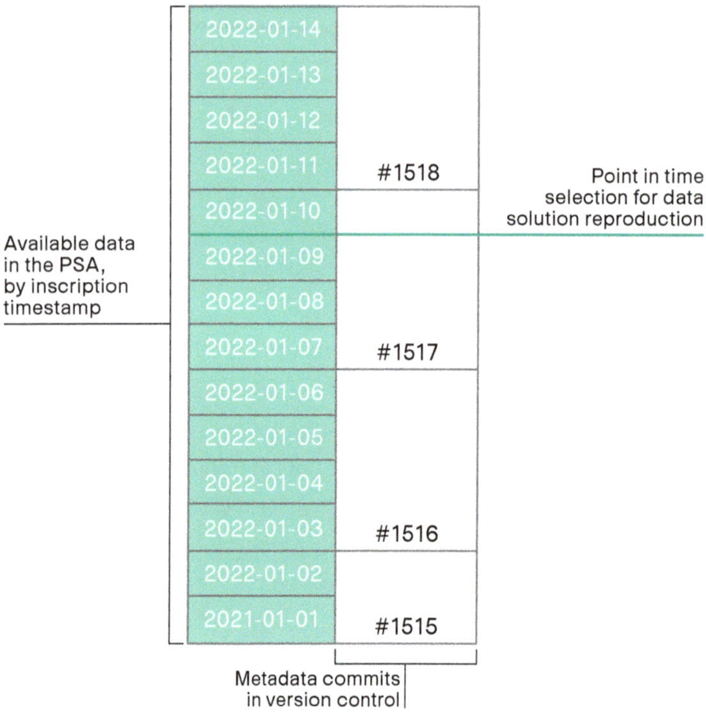

This example shows the two involved components: the PSA and the version control of the design metadata and templates. The line represents the point in time that has been chosen to rebuild the data solution as it was.

This means, to deliver the solution, that the code is generated using the templates and metadata as per commit #1517, and used to process the data up to and including the 9th of January 2022 – excluding anything after this commit and timestamp.

Data from the 10th of January 2022 onwards must be excluded if a true historic representation is intended.

Deployment automation

The components we have covered so far are required to fully automate the delivery of data logistics processes and data structures. They come together in deployment automation workflows ('workflows') – often referred to as 'DevOps.' These workflows use the available metadata and components and apply these in an executable workflow – a *pipeline.*

The idea is that after running a number of *build steps* –the individual steps in the workflow– something completed comes out on the other end: a *build.*

A large number of concepts converge in this workflow, starting with the configuration of individual development environments, ways of working, testing, and ultimately deployment.

Builds for a data solution

An interesting difference exists between using deployment automation workflows for software development and for data solutions.

When developing an application, code changes directly apply to the (whole) product that is under development. When you compile and run a version of the code, a *build* will be created that allows you to interact with the resulting software at that version.

The build process provides you with the final result.

But for data solutions, code changes apply to data structures and transformations that in turn *still must be applied to data.* The build process essentially takes you halfway there — it provides the code outputs such as data logistics processes, but these still need to be validated against the data to ensure the changes have the intended results.

Therefore, a deployment automation workflow for the data solution must not only build the outputs, but also execute the processes to ensure end-to-end validation can be done.

Environments

Organizations tend to employ standard approaches for development, testing, and production deployment. These approaches may use a varying number of *environments* depending on their standards and philosophy. Each environment is a distinct configuration of frameworks, tools, data, and settings that is designed to support a specific purpose in the change lifecycle.

The exact number, and intended usage, of these environments is a balance between the degree of control of the change process and its complexity and flexibility. Additional environments provide dedicated spaces for review and validation, but there is also benefit in reducing the number of environments because of overheads related to promoting changes and, of course, maintenance of the environments themselves.

An example is the 'DTAP' approach of having separate development, testing, acceptance, and production environments through which changes will be propagated.

We define (at least) three separate environments for the deployment workflow: development, integration, and production. More (or less) environments can be implemented to suit specific scenarios.

Production

At the very least, there is a production environment. This is the *live* environment that is accessed by data consumers. It must be protected from any service interruptions at all costs, and is typically subject to service level agreements that stipulate data availability and latency.

While it's not uncommon for changes to be applied directly to the production environment, we don't recommend this and will propose alternatives in the subsequent sections.

Development

An important concept for Git is that each developer works using their local code repository. By extent, we recommend that —where possible— each developer has access to an individual development environment to apply and test their changes in.

By individual, we mean that the environment is only used by an single developer or at most a very small team working on the same feature. It is not shared by others. This provides an isolated environment for the developer to change and test in without impacting anyone else, and without being impacted by others as well. Any potential clashes due to changes made by other developers will be resolved through pull requests and *continuous integration.*

This may be different compared to the somewhat more traditional approach of having centralized shared environments that the entire team is working on. Having a centralized development environment is still a suitable option, and in some cases it simply is the most practical or cost-effective one. Beyond the risk of impacting each others' work, attention must be given to periodically resetting the environment so that it remains sufficiently similar to the production environment. Abandoned work, accidental data changes, and testing, tend to 'clog up' the development environment over time – an issue that can largely be avoided using individual environments that are created to deliver specific features. Ideally, they are short-lived.

Having a separate environment for each developer may sound unrealistic. But in many cases there are options to support this, and these can be automated (e.g., scripted). Some technologies even provide features for this out of the box, often in ways far more efficient than simply copying all the data.

In most cases it is relatively straightforward to provide individual databases for each developer even though the approach for this varies between technical platforms.

Local databases can be automatically deployed using build tools, scripting or local workflows. Cloud databases can be automatically cloned or provisioned, and removed. And in other cases it is usually possible to create a logical separation on the same database, server, or instance – for example using schemas or instances.

Integration

The nature of working with version control —Git in particular— and the specific requirement for data solution to run and validate the data outputs *after* applying code changes shape the environments that are involved in the deployment approach.

To validate data results in a way that is not impacted by ongoing development, it is recommended to do so in an dedicated environment that is separate from both the development environment(s) and the production environment: an integration environment.

The role of the integration environment is to make sure changes don't have unforeseen consequences or impact data output in an adverse way – especially when combined with other changes. It can be seen as a parking area for the promotion of changes to the production environment.

The integration environment helps to ensure that the data behaves as expected after data logistics processes have run, and ideally have been running correctly for a period of time. Changes from various developers may be combined in this environment to understand if there are any unexpected consequences when bringing these changes together.

These changes can be promoted to the production environment as part of a release when the team is confident that they don't have unforeseen impacts.

Environment considerations

We advocate a setup that includes an individual development environment for each developer, and at least a centralized integration and production environment. Any additional environments can be added if and when required.

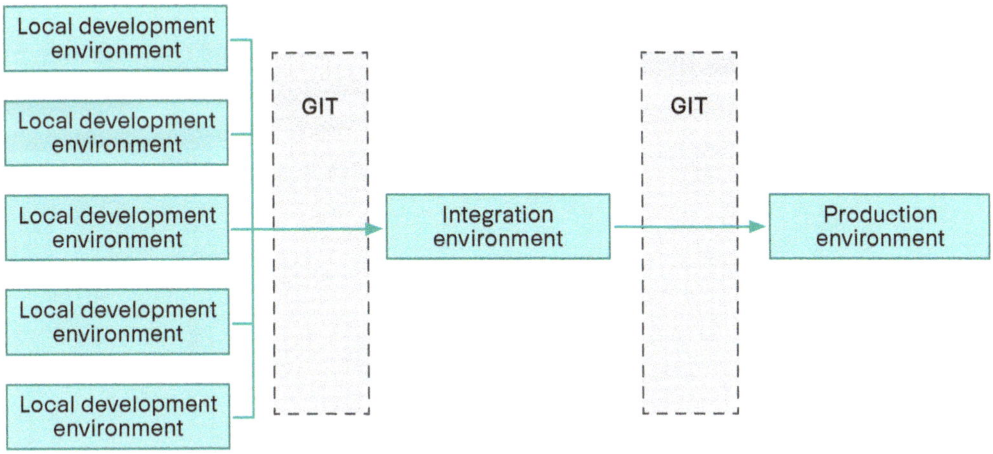

The integration environment is in some ways similar to the traditional 'acceptance' environment, but it is not the same. The reason to use a different name is to place emphasis on the integration of potentially various changes —from different developers— so that mutual impacts can be understood. It is not necessarily meant to assert the overall correct data outcomes, although it can also be used for this.

The integration environment is a closed environment, which means that developers have no, or read-only, access. It is treated as a production environment with the exception that there are no service level requirements.

The integration environment ideally contains a copy of production data, and access must therefore be tightly controlled for compliance reasons. In some organizations this is simply not allowed because this would violate data management policies which stipulate that production data may not be used in non-production environments.

When this scenario applies, it may be necessary to implement additional measures to either obfuscate sensitive data or define a representative, production-like, data set for the integration environment.

Using production, or production-like, data for development and integration streamlines the development process.

It simply is easier if realistic data can be used for development.

This way, developers encounter issues, which can then be clarified early in the process and resolved faster. Production data can be provided automatically when an environment is copied or cloned from the production environment. By contrast, a production-like data set can be time-consuming to prepare and maintain.

Alternatively, there are several ways to make sure production data can be made available for the integration environment. Depending on local circumstances some are more feasible than others. For example:

→ Implementing an interface from operational systems to both the integration and production environments
→ Synchronizing data from the production PSA to the integration PSA
→ Implementing one-way synchronization techniques, such as log shipping or transactional replication

Whichever approach is chosen, if at all possible, the ideal outcome is to configure development and integration environments that mirrors the production environment.

Many variations on this approach can be conceived, and there may be strong reasons why adding additional environments is needed. The concept we describe here is what we consider essential, but of course this does not mean other environments can be added whenever it makes sense to do so.

Reasons to add or remove environments may be related to budgetary constraint to provide the adequate number of software licenses, or limitations from a technical resourcing perspective.

But, at the end of the day, it is about finding a balance between compliance, company policy, maintenance overheads, and managing risks and expectations associated with delivering the data.

The deployment way of working

So far, the focus has been on defining the environments to develop, test, and deploy changes.

But what does this mean for the development *process?*

In the ⚐ version control section, we stipulated that the most important files to version (together) include the design metadata and code generation templates.

When new changes are made, these must be updated in the version-control repository and then applied to the environments. For instance, to define new data logistics processes the developer creates new metadata files containing data object mappings, generates the outputs, and executes these so that the data outputs can be reviewed.

Changes to one, or more, of these files, including removals or additions, are either committed directly to repository or merged via a pull request.

Deployment automation, including its code generation component, depend on a standardized way of working for implementing, testing, approving, and ultimately deploying changes.

In addition to selecting the environments, a *branching strategy* is required.

Branching strategy

↗ Branches represent a copy of the code which can be used to develop a specific feature or implement a change. During *branching,* an existing branch is 'copied.' The branch from which the 'copy' is made is referred to as the *origin.*

There are many ways to define a Git way of working. Some projects use feature branches in combination with one or more standard branches. Others don't use any separate branches whatsoever, and everyone commits directly to the main branch.

The workflow, and its steps, outlined here are not the only options. They are based on what we consider a good mix between complexity and standardization for data solutions. The necessary steps also depend on which environments have been selected.

Each team must define a workflow that fits, taking into account skills, technology, the intended degree of automation, and the involved environments. The overarching goal is to automate everything, and limit human interaction as much as possible.

Another objective is to ensure that the code in the central 'main' branch remains in sync with the (deployed) reality in the production environment.

As might be gleaned from this section, for data solution development we prefer a more *trunk-based* Git style where developers commit changes to a central branch via short-lived feature branches. The key to success for this is to restrict scope where possible – the quicker the changes are made, the less merge conflicts there are and the easier these can be resolved.

And always remember: commit early, and often!

To define the Git workflow, we introduce three standard branches:
→ A development branch
→ An integration branch
→ A main branch

In addition to these standard branches, feature branches are used to implement specific changes or sets of changes. Feature branches are short-lived and are merged back into the appropriate standard branch once the work is completed and approved.

Last, a hot fix process can be considered as part of the branching strategy. We'll mention it in some detail, but haven't included it in our standard branching strategy for reasons outlined in the corresponding section.

Main branch

↗ The main branch contains all code that has been successfully tested and deployed to the production environment.

The branch name 'main' is a well-established convention, so we stick to this term instead of calling it the production branch. Its code is always in a deployable state, and doesn't include code that has yet to be deployed to the target infrastructure.

In software development, the production version of the software is represented in the main branch. When the build completes successfully, there is a working software available for that version.

Due to the unique requirements for data solution versioning —the changes still have to be applied to data after the build— the main branch is updated *after* production deployment has completed in our proposal. This way, any failed releases will not yet appear in main.

This differs from regular software development, but it is the only way for data solutions to guarantee that only tested, approved, and successfully deployed changes are merged into main.

The main branch is protected. Commits and merges to the main branch are tightly controlled, and are subject typically to various policies to avoid out-of-process changes which may cause misalignment between the production environment and the code base in main.

Development branch

↗ The development branch serves as the main workspace for integrating new changes, features, and fixes.

Since the main branch never includes code that has yet to be deployed to the production environment, a separate branch must be used to develop against.

This is the 'development' branch.

This serves as the main workspace for integrating new changes, features, and fixes. All active development feature branches converges here. After changes have been incorporated back into the development branch, a release can be defined and scheduled for (automated) testing and deployment.

As is the case for the development environment, over time abandoned work will accumulate due to its role in active development. For this reason, a separate integration branch is required – which is the topic of the next section.

From time to time, it is necessary to update or recreate the development branch from main to remove any changes that never made it to production.

Integration branch

↗ The integration branch acts as a staging area for final testing and quality assurance before changes are deployed to the production environment and promoted to the main branch.

The integration branch is primarily to the integration environment. It's the branch where deployments ('releases') are standardized and consolidated – acting as a staging area for final testing and quality assurance before changes are deployed to the production environment and promoted to the main branch.

This branch ensures that only thoroughly validated code reaches production.

Other names for this branch could be 'release' or 'deployment,' but we believe integration is the best-fitting name because of its role in asserting that sets of changes have no adverse impacts on each other or the data solution as a whole.

'Release' is often also a reserved word, which prevents it from being used in certain technologies. However, the intent is to (automatically) deploy the *same* code to the production environment after the deployment and validation have been successful in the integration environment.

Feature branches

↗ A feature branch is created for the purpose of completing a specific task or scope.

The standard branches are never removed, but every other branch is intended to be short-lived. These are *feature branches.*

Feature branches are meant to exist only during development, and are usually removed when the changes are merged back into the origin – the development branch in this case.

Each developer can contribute to the development branch this way. The developer can create a new feature branch from the development branch, make the changes, and merge these back into the origin branch by means of a pull request.

The development process

The development process as outlined in this, and subsequent, sections intents to describe a way of working suitable for data solutions. As always, and especially when it comes to Git, there are many approaches that can be considered.

We will close these sections with further considerations on this topic, but would like to start with a reference development workflow intended to cover the most important aspects of Git workflows for a data solution.

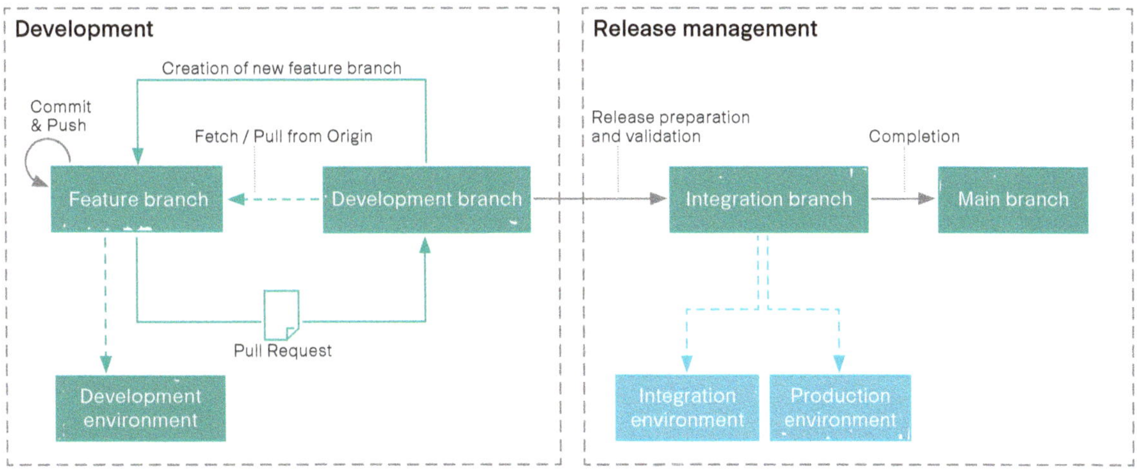

In this approach, development is done using feature branches that originate from the development branch. Changes —either developed individually or by a small team— are implemented and tested in this local branch and merged back into the development branch (origin) when completed and approved.

Developers regularly *pull from origin* to integrate any completed work by other developers into their local branch so that conflicts can be managed early in the process – continuous integration.

When completed, and a last pull is done, the changes are merged back into the development branch using a pull request. If everything is as expected from here on, the work of the developer is done and the release manager takes over.

The resulting commit point can be selected as a release for deployment and testing in the integration branch.

Finally, if the changes continue to behave as expected in the integration environment they can be deployed to the production environment. If this deployment is successful —which it should if the process is configured and managed correctly— the code can finally be promoted to main.

To ensure correct synchronization between version control and reality it is important to focus on deployment automation, avoiding any manual steps during the promotion of changes to downstream environments where possible.

In this approach, the promotion of changes to main is the last step in the process – performed *after* production deployment. The reason for this is to ensure that the *exact same code* can be (automatically) deployed using automation workflows.

Every time code 'moves' from one branch to another this requires a pull request, and with it the potential to modify aspects of the code. Deploying to production from the *same* branch, the integration branch in this case, guarantees that code as per the same commit point is applied to the production environment. This is also arguably easier to automate since most deployment automation technologies support the concept of 'stages' (also referred to as releases or phases) where the same artifact be reused for different environments in the same pipeline instance. But for this, the same branch must typically be used.

This does mean that the changes are in production before they are moved to the main branch. A downside of promoting changes to main *after* deployment to the production environment is that this becomes an administrative task which requires process rigor to adhere to. When forgotten, the main branch will be 'behind' the integration branch. Thankfully, most DevOps environments make this visible, and easy to keep track of.

As mentioned earlier, there are many possible –and viable– approaches for working with Git, and it is equally possible to promote the changes to main first, and deploy to production from there. However, this requires the creation of a pull request from integration to main, and this introduces a risk that code can be modified in this step.

This means the version used for production deployment *may* be slightly different from what was tested –if not in code then at least in the administrative sense– which introduces the possibility that deployment may fail into production after all.

This approach is also less intuitive to automate, as most DevOps platforms don't allow the automated creation and approval of a pull request without additional coding efforts. By contrast, running the same release (commit point) against other environments as stages is often natively supported.

Creating a new feature branch

New development starts with the creation of a new feature branch from the development branch. The feature branch contains a complete 'copy' of all design metadata and code generation templates up to and including the commit point when it was branched from its origin.

Feature branches serve as the local Git working environments for the developer, or (small) group of developers.

Ideally, the project uses a task management system that uniquely numbers each feature, task, or activity, and is actively used by the team. The branch can then be named to correspond to the number of the task or user story that is intended to be delivered.

This way, the team commits to a specific scope of work that is detailed into discrete tasks, and which will be reflected in the branch. Each developer accepts one or more tasks and uses this to create a feature branch using the development branch as origin.

When created remotely, the new feature branch can be *pulled* (synchronized, or downloaded) to the developer's workspace so that changes can be made there.

Any changes the developer makes –including modifications and removal of existing files and adding new files– will be committed (updated) to this branch and deployed to the (individual) development environment.

One of the mantras for this approach is to *commit early, and commit often.* This way, it is easy to revert to an earlier local version if mistakes are made.

It's a great way to keep track of what you're working on.

Periodically, at least daily, it is recommended to *push* the commits to the feature branch on the Git service. Doing this protects the developer from losing commits in case there is a serious issue on the local environment. A hardware failure on the working computer or a lost laptop, for example.

By pushing commits to the feature branch, these are saved to the central environment – often a server that is maintained with backup plans, or a cloud service.

Another reason to push commits to the feature branch applies when working on the same branch with multiple developers. Pushing the commits makes them available for the other developers so they can integrate their changes in the ongoing collaborative effort.

This helps with detecting merge conflicts early, making them easier to resolve.

If only a single developer is working on a branch it is only necessary to pull the branch at the start of the process so that the files are available on the local environment. However, when working on a branch with multiple developers it is important to pull from the branch more often to make sure the latest code base is available on the local environment.

This is part of ⚐ continuous integration, which is covered in more detail in the next sections.

What needs to be in a change?

How long is a piece of string? It's a common phrase used to indicate something is impossible to specify. This, too, fits an overview of what a change should cover. After all, it can be anything.

There are, however, a few artifacts we believe can be meaningful to include in a standard approach. These are the manifest, a readme, recovery instructions, unit test cases, and of course the change code itself.

So how long *is* a piece of string?

It's twice as long as half it's length.

Manifest

Ideally, the change includes a *manifest* that includes all the components that comprise the change so that these can be included in automated deployment, and in the right order.

That's all a manifest is: a list of components and the order in which they should be run to implement the change.

After all, the changes themselves are only half the story. For data solutions, the changes still need to be run to evaluate the final outputs. In these cases, making sure the identifier of the work package or user story is clearly visible often makes it easier to keep track of things.

Readme

Another useful artifact is a standard set of instructions and notes in text format. For example, a 'readme' file in MarkDown (md extension) or plain text (txt extension) containing any relevant notes and considerations.

Ideally, this covers the thinking –the rationale– of the changes as well as the driver to implement these in the first place. The readme can also include links to relevant other documentation, for instance the user story.

Recovery instructions

One aspect that differentiates data solutions from regular software development is that deployment may still fail even though the changes can be technically merged in the target branch. After all, the changes still need to be deployed to a database and execute – and things might fail in this step.

To manage this, it can be helpful to include recover instructions in the change. A rollback script, for instance.

Ideally, this is a script that the release manager can execute to revert any modifications – bringing the environment back to it's pre-deployment state.

Knowing what to do when deployment fails can save time bringing the integration environment back online, or minimize downtime in production environments if deployed against directly.

Deterministic scripting

The changes themselves, for data solutions, typically include scripts that represent data objects. SQL files, for example.

We believe it's worth to ensure that every script, always, is idempotent. All references in the manifest should be able to be run multiple times without technical errors and continue from failures.

This makes it possible to 'execute' the manifest multiple times, and use it as a 'deployment script.'

There are many ways to implement this, but for SQL scripting this may include logic such as IF EXISTS or ALTER statements.

Testing and validation

As part of the working agreements across the team, it is common for developers to perform a certain degree of *unit testing* on their own development efforts.

The exact definition of the scope, requirements, and intent of unit testing may vary from team to team. However, in most cases testing focuses on ensuring that each developer has validated their own work, and that the functional intent can be (re)produced without error.

This applies to both technical errors that may be found when running data logistics processes as well as issues related to the data outcomes. In other words, the resulting data needs to match expectations.

Not experiencing technical errors is insufficient to complete testing.

Aligned to Data Engine thinking, specifically the testing and ⚐ data validation component, we recommended to record these scenarios in a testing framework.

A testing framework record tests in a way that is agreed and understood by the team. Each test case contains standard functions to assert the correct outcome by comparing the results with the provide 'correct' data set.

Providing unit test scripts or test cases with a change demonstrates that the developer has verified the desired outcome, and that no errors are detected. This validation can later be used by the release manager to confirm that the changes continue to deliver the correct outcomes during deployment to the integration and production environments.

The deployment itself might be without technical errors, but performing post-deployment validation by means of testings provides the final confidence that everything behaves as expected. The execution, and approval, of these testing scenarios can be further automated as part of the deployment automation workflow —when the changes are promoted to the integration and production environments— or as part of wider regression testing.

Pull requests

↗ A pull request is a formal request to merge changes from one branch into another.

When the changes are implemented and unit testing has been completed, the developer can create a pull request. This is the formal request to merge changes from one branch into another.

Ideally, any change is associated to a task, work package, or user story, depending on the adopted project management approach.

We recommend including this in the pull request name and description, so that the pull request can be easily linked to a work package.

Depending on how the team agrees to operate, pull requests can be reviewed by other members of the team. Reviewing pull requests can be implemented as optional or mandatory, depending on the team's agreement on the way of working.

When the pull request is approved, or simply completed, the commits will be added to the development branch, and the feature branch can be removed.

Reviews

A pull request provides an excellent opportunity to review the work done. This is often referred to as a *peer review,* indicating that other developers (peers) can review each other's work and thus nurture a collaborative environment. Of course, the reviewer can be a true peer, or hold a position of seniority such as a technical lead or architect.

DevOps platforms usually support various way of configuring this process, including how many people and roles are involved and any specific policies that may apply. This is a flexible concept which must be discussed with, and tailored to, the team.

In any case, if concerns are found, the code can be updated and committed again. These commits can be added to the existing rejected pull request for re-approval or presented as a new pull request.

This, again, depends on the team's agreements.

To facilitate further automation, pull requests can be used as 'trigger' for next steps in automation workflow. For instance, when a pull request has been approved it can be automatically move to the next step in the process.

It is important to keep in mind that, using Git, a pull requests always contains all code up to the point of the last commit. This means any other changes from the development branch *may* come across when completing a pull request from development to integration. For data solutions, this is often not an issue since changes require to be deployed consciously using follow-up deployment scripts.

Continuous integration

While the developers are working on their code in their feature branch, it is likely that new commits will be added to the origin —the development branch— by other developers. They follow the same process with their own feature branches, but as soon as their pull requests are completed their code will become available in the development branch.

To stay up to date with the other developers' changes it is recommended to frequently, at least daily, check if new commits have been added to the origin branch. This can be done by *fetching* and *pulling* from the origin branch.

Fetching will check the origin branch and notify the developer if code changes are available, and pulling will add these changes to your local repository.

The same applies for the feature branch as well, when multiple developer work on it at the same time.

If code has been updated in a way that conflicts with the local version, i.e. the same files have been updated in a way that clashes, the developer needs to carefully merge the code into a new combined version. It is the developer's responsibility to make sure this is adequately tested and merged back into the origin branch as soon as possible.

Keeping these cycles short, merging branches often through pull requests, and regularly pulling from origin is what *continuous integration* is about.

The practices of continuous integration help to solve problems early, so that it is easy to understand what is happening, and how to resolve it. It is a mindset that everyone in team needs to endorse, because success is dependent on keeping iterations (branches, scope) small.

The intent is to integrate code often, resolve and version conflicts, and release as often as possible.

Releases

When the pull request into the development branch is completed, the changes can be planned for release. The goal is to test out the deployment of the selected code version on the integration environment, and then —when everything is as expected— automatically deploy the same code version to the production environment.

Ideally, no developer should touch the code between integration and production.

DevOps environments often provide a feature to define a release by selecting multiple commits. In other cases specific commits can be selected and others left, a process referred to as *cherry picking*. For this, the release manager selects (e.g., cherry-picks) the commit point representing the code-to-be-deployed, and creates a pull request to promote the changes to the integration branch.

This defines a release, which technically is a code snapshot up to, and including, the selected commit point. Often however, multiple sets of changes are bundled into a *release*. Reason for this is that the integration environment accumulates changes provided by multiple developers, and these usually arrive in the integration environment at different points in time.

A release may incorporate multiple sets of changes, depending on which branches were completed prior to the selected commit point. Most DevOps platforms provide features that guarantee this code snapshot is kept safe as a release artifact, so that it is no longer possible to modify the code during the process.

Approvals can be configured at any of these stages, for instance ensure that post-deployment verification has been successfully executed. The entire process can also be fully automated, letting the engine decide based on directives.

The most important approval is the one to deploy the release to production. The timing for this varies based on team processes and risk appetite, but it can take a few days to be fully satisfied all post-deployment verification testing has been completed on the integration environment, and that the outputs do not clash with other processes.

This means that, if a commit has not caused issues running for a few days, the approval can be given. The code is then (automatically) deployed to production, and ultimately promoted to main. This will *always* be done from the integration branch.

Release schedules

Releases should be done as often possible. Multiple smaller releases are often easier to manage than a few large 'big bang' releases that impact many parts of the system.

Many organizations agree on a *release schedule* that helps to manage the expectations around when new features become available. This schedule often aligns with the organization's project management practices, for instance by following the sprint cadence, or linking releases to project phases.

For most organizations, planning a release every two weeks is a realistic goal, and a weekly release (or even more frequently) is aspirational.

When urgent changes are required between planned releases, an out-of-schedule release process can be implemented. These ad hoc releases typically require higher-level management approvals, and a sound justification.

Ideally, development for out-of-schedule releases should follow the regular development workflow – though ⚐ hot fixes are an option too.

What happens when deployment fails?

No one, and nothing, is perfect. Mistakes happen, and unexpected results can occur. In short, deployment can fail during any step of the process.

When a release is created, it marks a commit point for the repository code – a snapshot of the code at a point in time. And if this code fails post-deployment validation and testing, it highlights a need for additional modifications, and therefore new commits in the development branch.

When deployment fails, approval is withheld and the release is therefore rejected. The development team is then notified that additional work is required to complete the change. When necessary, the recovery instructions provided with the change can be followed to revert any changes (in structures *and* data) made by executing the code – again due to the special characteristics of data platforms versus regular software development.

DevOps platforms typically provide visualizations to monitor these processes – often implemented in deployment or release pipelines. These visualizations highlight the individual process steps and approval stages that are completed, and where the release encountered issues.

When a release fails, the work is returned to the developers. When the necessary updates are done and merged back in the development branch, a *new* release is defined and taken through the process. It could happen that subsequent work has been committed to the development branch in the meantime. This is taken in stride as part of ongoing continuous integration, and will become part of the update.

In this forward-only approach, in line with Git principles, each update is represented by a newer commit point.

The forward-only approach means that the failed code remains available in the commit history, and the failed release remains visible in the logging. This provides helpful auditing details on the deployment processes.

Automating deployment

The development workflow outlines the environments, process steps, and concepts involved in developing data solutions. This workflow can be operated manually, semi-automated, and even in a fully automated way. Automation can take over when the developer's pull request has been accepted, and move the change through the entire process.

Deployment automation workflows –often referred to as DevOps, or even DataOps– are flexible in how they can be configured, including which approval stages apply, if any.

The technical landscape for deployment automation changes continuously. In essence, however, automation workflows ('pipelines') are simply steps containing activities that are executed in a defined order. They can contain decision trees that use outputs from earlier steps to determine what needs to be done in the next ones. Deployment workflows also can respond to certain events, such as completion of other workflows, or commits in the Git environment.

Deployment automation in the engine is used to automatically deploy changes following the steps outlined in the previous sections, and in some cases even the changes themselves and their approvals. A fully automated workflow only requires a design change, for instance a modification of the model, to be committed. Technically, this commit represents a modification of design metadata – the schema for data solution automation.

Pending full end-to-end automation as per the engine approach, a common use case is to start a workflow automatically whenever a pull request to the development branch is completed, as this indicates the intent to release.

The workflow can be *triggered* to start when a commit is detected in the development branch, or during any of the subsequent steps.

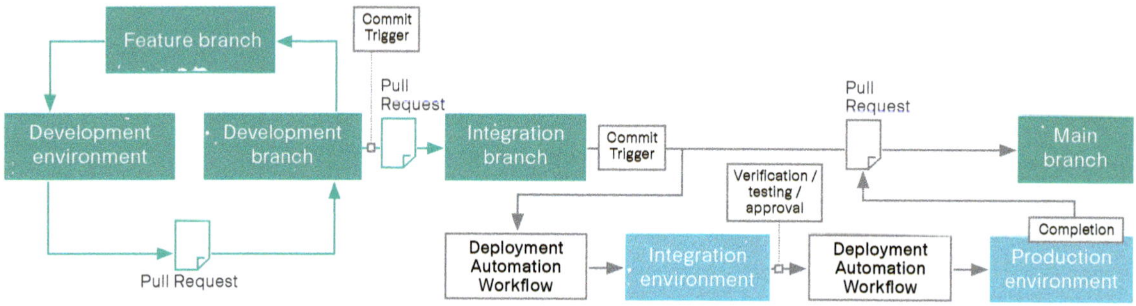

The deployment automation workflow will then run the following steps in sequence, first for the integration environment, and for the production environment after this.

1) Pause the data logistics processes
2) Generate and deploy the data structures
3) Generate and deploy the data logistics
4) Start the data logistics processes
5) Run system and regression testing

An approval point can be added at the completion of the integration workflow, for instance to authorize the execution of the production deployment workflow. Alternatively, this step can be evaluated programmatically – when testing identifies no issues and the processes run successfully for a predefined period.

Pausing the data logistics processes

To avoid conflicts when applying changes to data structures and data logistics processes, it is recommended that running processes are allowed to complete gracefully, and new processes are prevented to start. This 'pauses' the data logistics processes so that changes can be safely implemented.

This can be as straightforward as disabling the processes in the data logistics control framework (e.g., modules and batches) so that they don't start when they are due according to their schedule. Alternatively, if you are orchestrating your data logistics processes in a continuous fashion, the state machine can be paused. Lastly, in many solutions, 'main' batches run on set schedules, and in this approach it's simply ensuring the process is not running and paused in the orchestration so that it doesn't start during deployment.

In all cases, the deployment automation workflow waits until all processes have completed.

In a fully automated engine deployment, the metadata 'knows' which data logistics processes are impacted because this can be derived from the design metadata, facilitating full automation of this process step.

Generating and deploying the data structures

The data structures are generated by applying the corresponding code generation template against the design metadata – the full set of data object mapping files. The format is dependent on the target platform but usually contains a number of table, view and/or file definitions – for example using SQL.

Data structures, including the differential between the model and the data solution reality, can be generated from design metadata. In fact, we prefer to generate both the structures and data logistics processes from the *same* design metadata, as this 'single point of truth' helps preventing inconsistencies between the data structures and data logistics processes that interact with them.

If data modeling software is adopted —which has numerous productivity benefits in general— it's ideally intended for the design process and not for code generation or deployment even though features may be available for this.

We prefer to use modeling tools for visualizing the design, and applying this to design metadata. This way, data modeling software can be integrated with the approach for creating and managing the metadata files. It can even *be* the software to do this, if configured this way.

In this approach, the data modeling software creates or modifies the metadata files, which are then versioned and used for downstream code generation and deployment.

Differential

Code generation typically creates output that represents the *new* (updated) state of the data solution. It is not necessarily aware of the current state, the reality that still exists in the data platform environment. This new version of the structure can be compared with the current structure to create a *differential*.

The differential shows where, and how, data structures are impacted by the changes, and typically represent the code that is actually deployed. Unless, that is, when a full virtualization approach is adopted. In this scenario, the view (or similar) object can directly be replaced with the newer version.

There are various approaches for this, and not every platform supports all of these. Some vendors provide features and command line utilities to perform the compare automatically, and export a list of changes for subsequent deployment.

With this list of changes, the differential, a number of options become available — which are:

- → Forward-only deployment
- → Differential merge deployment
- → Impact-rebuild deployment

Using a forward-only deployment approach

In a forward-only approach, changes in data structures are applied as a new objects in the target environment. Generally speaking, a forward-only deployment makes sure that only the latest state is available.

For example, when the structure of a database table changes, the forward-only approach will create a new table and copy the data here from the old version. This is as opposed to updating the table in place.

An advantage of this approach is that the existing structures remain available until the new ones are ready to be used. Many parallel databases favor this deployment approach, because of the overhead involved with physical data updates.

Using a differential merge deployment approach

The differential merge applies the differential to the data platform's current state, modifying existing structures and data to accommodate the changes. The existing objects are updated, new objects are created, and obsolete objects are removed.

This approach requires scripting containing logic to modify the structures, for example using a SQL 'ALTER TABLE' statement. Various software tools exist to generate this differential automatically, which can then be run from a command line — making it easy to incorporate into a deployment automation workflow.

Using an impact-rebuild deployment approach

This deployment approach removes ('DROPs') impacted structures from the solution entirely, and redeploys these as new structures. This means that any data that was part of the structure is also removed.

Once the impacted structures have been (re)created, and the updated data logistics processes are available, they can be reinitialized to repopulate the created data structures with data.

The data used for this is sourced from the history of original transactions — the PSA.

For example, let's assume that changes are made in the design for one particular table. This table has now been 'split' into two separate tables. The impact-rebuild approach will drop the existing table, deploy the two new ones and load the data from the PSA.

If, at some point, the two tables are merged again into the original single one this is supported as well. In this scenario, the two tables are dropped and the singular table is (re)created again. The corresponding data logistics process can then populate the table using PSA data.

The impact-rebuild deployment approach is often the easiest way to manage deployment, but only if the time it takes to reprocess the original data is acceptable for the data consumers. This is because in principle all data from the PSA is applied again to the new structure, and this may take minutes or hours during which the data is not available for consumers.

An effective way to implement this is by using the *eventual consistency* concept as explained earlier in this book. Every data logistics process maintains its own technical timeline for loading the target data structure. If this structure does not contain data, because it has been dropped and re-created by the deployment process, the timeline is reset and the data will be reloaded from the PSA.

This approach leverages various concepts that are necessary for the *engine,* is a powerful way to implement it.

Combining deployment approaches

It is also possible to combine the forward-only and impact-rebuild deployment approaches. This way, you can (re)build one or more data structures while the existing objects remain available.

Both versions will be part of the data solution for a limited amount of time. Access to any of these objects can be controlled using an interface layer such as for example using database views.

As soon as the new area has been completed, these interfacing views can be updated to refer to the new structures, and the old structures can be decommissioned.

This is an approach that is similar to the *partition switching* technique that is sometimes used to load data sets into separate physical objects until these are ready to be accessed.

Generating and deploying the data logistics

As with the data structures, data logistics processes are generated by applying the corresponding code generation template to the design metadata.

If required, the generated artifacts can be moved to a location from where they can be deployed. This is often a simpler process compared to the deployment of the data structures, because existing artifacts can usually be simply overwritten. There is no risk of data loss, and no need for a differential upgrade.

The exact method for this differs between data logistics technology. For example, some platforms support a scripted replace, or update, of objects that can be performed using command line utilities. Many databases support this, and this applies to objects such as stored procedures, views, and functions.

In other cases, proprietary upload tools are provided for deployment so that data logistics artifacts can be moved to a dedicated server, repository, or framework.

In other cases, a simple file replace is sufficient. For instance when the data logistics platform uses services such as agents or daemons that consume parameter files. In this scenario the template is built into the service, and this is updated separately from the data logistics inputs – the parameter files.

In all scenarios, this deploying data logistics processes relies on the features and syntax that the data logistics platform offers.

Starting the data logistics processes

When code generation and deployments are successfully completed, the next step is to re-enable the data logistics processes. This is typically done by enabling the processes in the control framework, schedule, or state machine, depending on the orchestration in place.

If everything goes smoothly, the data logistics processes will execute without errors. After a few successful completions of all processes, schedules, or queue cycles —and assuming automated regression testing has not identified any issues— the changes can be promoted to production. If errors are detected, however, the process fails and the release is returned to the developer for further investigation and fixing.

The timing of this promotion depends on the team's and business stakeholders' risk appetite, as well as any established conventions for release planning. Releases are often scheduled weekly or fortnightly, though release cadences can vary significantly. Some organizations release multiple times a day, while others prefer a cadence of once every couple of weeks.

In some companies, Friday is blocked for release to avoid potential issues from occurring over the weekend.

System- and regression testing

System testing and regression testing for data solutions are two sides of the same coin.

Available test cases from the testing framework —either provided as part of unit testing, or created specifically for the integration environment— can be executed within the deployment automation workflow.

The expectation is that these tests not only run successfully from a technical perspective but also produce the correct expected outcomes.

System testing ensures the technical execution is correct, while regression testing revalidates known scenarios automatically as part of the workflow. Together, these tests confirm that both the system operates as intended and the expected results are achieved.

The testing framework captures the developer's understanding of the intended result in a way that this will be automatically verified for future changes. The repository of test cases are the embodiment of the team's understanding of how the solution is supposed to work.

The degree of remaining testing and validation depends on the organization's risk appetite. Since the integration environment is representative of production, it is reasonable to regularly invite business users to review the data at a higher level.

This is particularly valuable when a feature has been requested by a particular individual. Enabling the requester to validate the results upfront is a great way to build trust and commitment, and provides another great opportunity to record tests for posterity.

Production release

If no issues have been encountered in the integration environment for the agreed amount of time, the changes are ready to be promoted to the production environment.

The promotion of changes from the integration environment to the production one is the same for the deployment automation workflow. The same process is followed, with the same code version and tests—only now with the production environment as target.

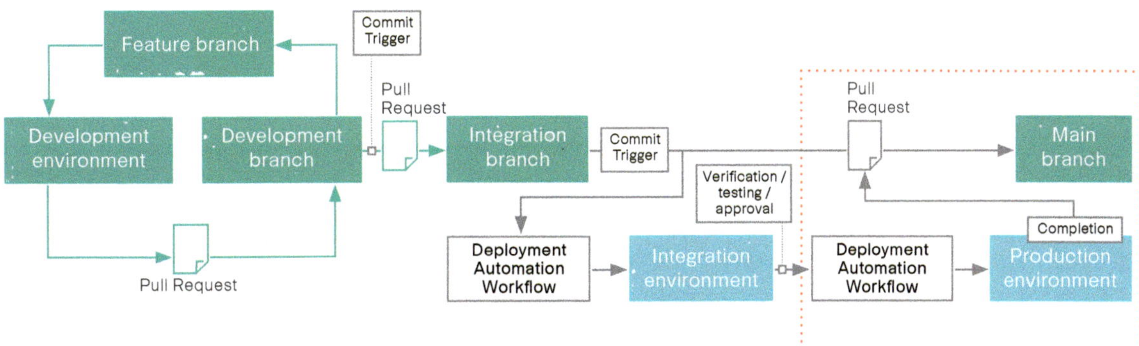

There is no need for human intervention. The *same changes* that were deployed to the integration environment are applied to the production environment *the same way.* In fact, any manual steps or otherwise required human interaction poses a risk to the stability of the production environment.

The only thing left to do is to select a formal moment to schedule production downtime or (limited) service interruption. This is also a perfect time to inform the consumers of what has changed.

It is possible to automatically commit the changes to the production version control repository – the main branch. This merge can be automatically triggered after production environment conditions have been met – at this stage this typically refers to the completion of the deployment without technical errors.

Further considerations

Many philosophies on working with Git exist, and certain combinations of technologies provide opportunities and limitations. Our reference approach for the development way of working is only one of these options, but one we believe and experience shows works well for data solutions.

In the next sections, we would like to provide some additional considerations to further tweak this approach so that it suits specific requirements.

Refreshing development

The development branch may need to be refreshed at regular intervals, similar to how the development environment is replaced from time to time with a production clone.

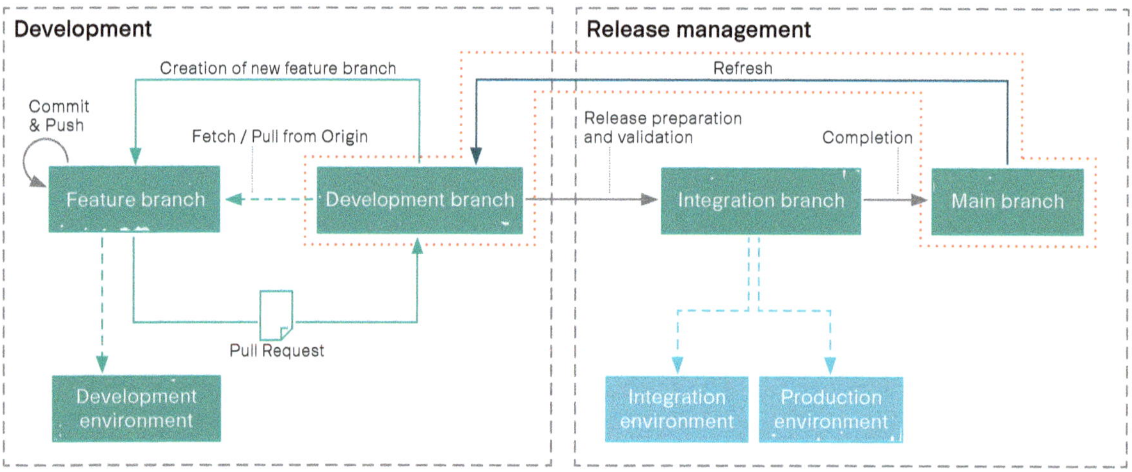

Work that has been added to the development branch may not always be selected for deployment. Every project experiences abandoned work every now and then, and this accumulates over time. A refresh addresses this by aligning the development branch to the contents in main.

This can be implemented in various ways, for instance by recreating the development branch from main or by performing a force push. In all cases, work might be overwritten so it's important to carefully organize this with all involved developers.

A useful approach is to synchronize the refresh of the development environment with the branches: when the environment is replaced, it might be time to refresh the development branch as well.

Hot fixes

When there is no time to follow regular development processes, 'hot fixes' can be considered as an approach to remediate critical production issues.

A hot fix is a branch that is created from, and merged back into, the main branch. While it is also possible to configure the main branch to allow direct commits, it is widely considered a best practice to restrict this option – which means changes have to be applied via a separate branch.

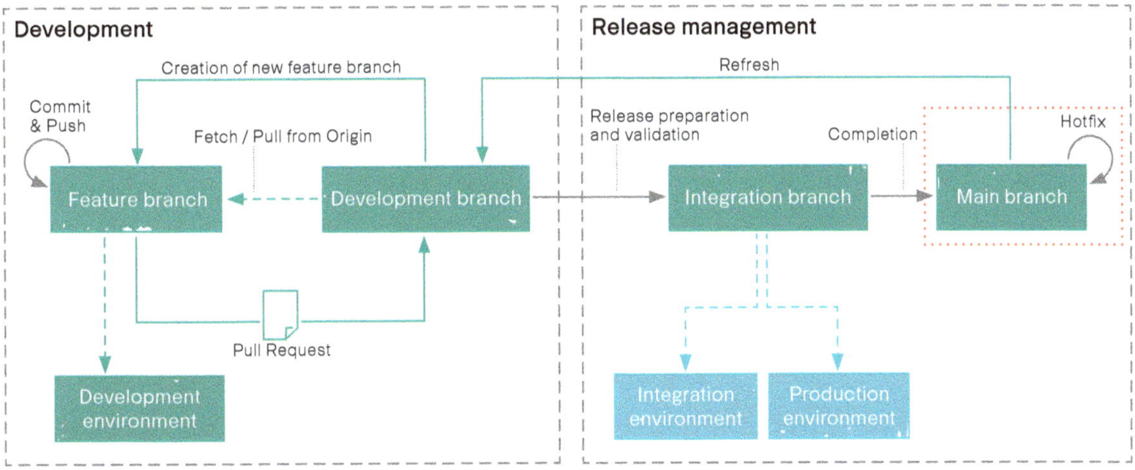

It is possible to avoid a hot fix mechanism altogether when the development process is sufficiently streamlined. Urgent changes can also be created as a feature branch from development and follow the regular process. This is ideal: defects and patches can be implemented quickly simply by prioritizing the review and deployment of changes made in development feature branches.

Data solution virtualization

↗ Virtualization, as introduced in the 'world of data,' focuses on generating and deploying the data solution in such a way that the resulting outcomes are *immediately* visible.

This section explores a very specific approach to data solution implementation and deployment: data solution virtualization.

It uses the same concepts and mindset around metadata management, code generation, and automation – but the deployment, considerations, and usage are slightly different compared to physically generating and executing data logistics processes.

Reducing barriers

To allow ideas to grow, creators need an immediate connection to what they are creating[35]. This means that, as a creator, you would like to be able to directly see the effects your changes have on what you're working on. But often, this is not easily achieved.

If you take the example of coding, for instance, you first need to write code in a specific language, and then compile the code to see the result of your work. The link to the code itself and the result can be hard to make if you don't compile the code. It's not always easy to imagine the outcome just by looking at the code. And, it goes without saying that a certain amount of technical expertise is required to code and compile in the first place.

Coding is a creative process. How amazing is it, for any coder, to immediately see the impacts of their work on their application or website? How many ideas have been missed because this direct connection was not available? How many concepts never materialized because there were too many technical barriers?

More and more development environments allow for this kind of direct connection, so that you can directly see the effect of code changes. This means that, as a creator, you can see what feels right as an outcome while you are working through different options.

You can immediately see what effects your changes have – like painting a canvas.

'Data' is also an area that potentially holds many new ideas waiting to fulfill their promise. And similarly, these ideas often do not materialize because data cannot be adequately made available.

This is what data solution virtualization, as a turbo-charged version of the engine, intends to enable: providing a *direct connection to data* to facilitate exploration while still working in a defined architecture.

It is about finding ways to seek simplification, to keep working on removing barriers to deliver meaningful data and actionable information. It's about enabling ideas to flourish because data can be made available for any kind of discovery or assertion.

Layers of views

Data solution virtualization, simply referred to as 'virtualization' here, removes the need to first generate data logistics processes, and then apply (run) these against the data to analyze the results. Instead, the data logistics output is generated as a form of compute that provides the result *directly*, without persisting data in any of the data solutions's involved layers and areas.

Although different implementations are possible, a good example of a virtual data solution is a series of database views that run on the PSA. The views provide the same data as if you would create tables, and then run the data logistics processes to populate these.

The reference architecture still applies, it's just that the data is not persisted anywhere except in the PSA. The PSA is mandatory because all original transactions are maintained here.

This way, the virtual data solution can be implemented as (multiple layers of) views that ultimately source data from the PSA. Each view represents an object in the data solution that works as it had been materialized (defined as an object and loaded with data).

Using database views to deploy a virtual data solution is only one of the alternatives. Similar results can be achieved using compute clusters (e.g., Spark), streaming technologies (e.g., Kafka, ksqlDB,) or coding approaches (e.g., Python).

Virtualization has its caveats, most importantly performance concerns. However, it also is a litmus test to assert if the Engine Thinking approach is implemented correctly. For virtualization to work, all engine components, metadata, and templates must be in place and work optimally.

At various times throughout this book, we highlighted that deterministic data processing is essential to make the engine work. A database view is a quintessential representation of deterministic data processing, because *every time* a view is called, you would expect the same result – assuming no changes occurred in the underlying data.

Performance permitting, a virtual data solution can be used to verify the results in a proof of concept setting or as part of initial development – potentially before deploying the full solution using deployment automation. For a virtual data solution, no workflows are needed. This makes it ideal for prototyping.

As we covered in the ⚐ world of data chapter, working with data can be complex. Often the 'right' answer is the result of a series of iterations where subject matter experts and data professionals collaborate. Defining the correct business logic requires ongoing clarification before it can be considered fit-for-purpose, and the data model may also evolve as a result.

Having the ability to prototype these designs, and immediately review the results can be a significant boost to the design process of the data solution.

In a production context, the engine may decide to virtualize parts of the data solution based on data usage patterns. In this sense, a database view or similar form of on-demand compute is just another data logistics process that 'moves' data through the architecture. The engine would simply select a different template to generate the data logistics – a view in this case.

In many data solutions, it is already considered a best practice to be able to 'virtualize' the data delivery (presentation layer) in a similar way, and when performance considerations allow for it.

Applying a virtual delivery in the presentation layer is widely used. The 'virtual data mart' is often also a database view that represents one or more fact or dimension tables. The principle is the same: to allow faster delivery, and tighter interaction between the business and engineering teams.

Data solution virtualization takes this approach one step further by allowing the *entire* data solution to be refactored based on the original transactions in the PSA.

This allows the design teams to test out new concepts, patterns, and technical tweaks to get the best possible results. It is even possible to test out different methodologies, or modifications of existing ones.

Do you prefer natural business keys, hash keys or integer values as your data solution key distribution approach? This can be changed at the click of a button.

We believe a data solution model is not always something you can get right in one go. In fact, it can take a long time for a model to stabilize, and in the current fast-paced environments this may even never be the case.

Data solution virtualization helps maintain both the mindset and capability for a data solution to continue to evolve with the business, and to reduce technical debt. After all, when a data solution is immediately generated on the fly, there are no parts of the solution that do not conform to the latest approach, standard, technology, or convention.

Not the same as data virtualization

A virtual data solution is not the same as data virtualization. These two concepts are fundamentally different. Data virtualization, by most definitions, is the provision of unified direct access to data across many (disparate) data stores.

It is a way to access and combine data without having to physically move the data across environments. Data virtualization, however, does not focus on data logistics patterns, data architecture, and data modeling.

The virtual data solution on the other hand is a flexible approach to deliver data outcomes following a defined architecture, essentially providing a deterministic schema-on-read.

The two concepts can work together. Data virtualization can be a technique to access to (raw) data in the form of an interface. It can serve as a common access layer for consumption of data by the data solution – virtualized or otherwise.

Either way, a virtual data solution requires a transaction-based data archive, such as a PSA, to operate on. Data virtualization techniques do not provide this, at least not at the time of writing. Consequently, even if a data virtualization technique is adopted any data changes still require to be recorded in the PSA to support a virtual data solution.

Performance considerations

What about performance? Surely users don't want to wait for hours to see results?

At the time of writing, if you process billions of rows of data every second, data solution virtualization will not work. Even though modern cloud infrastructures provide amazing abilities to scale, the degree of compute required to process the data through all layers may still be too demanding.

However, when it comes to performance considerations in general, and data solution virtualization in particular, it is important to remember three things. These are the balance between performance and complexity, the realistic data volumes, and the degree of flexibility your are looking to achieve.

Performance versus complexity

When considering performance requirements, it can be helpful to think of these in the context of balancing 'performance' with 'complexity.'

Generally speaking, the more performance is tuned, the more complex the data solution tends to become.

Additional complexity tends to also brings additional maintenance overhead with it, as well as a degree of brittleness.

Sometimes it may work out better overall to sacrifice performance in favor or simpler, easier manageable, solutions — especially when there are no urgent demands for 'more faster.'

Data solution virtualization, as an alternative of using physical tables and data logistics processes, is a prime example of this consideration.

Data volume

Data solutions come in all kinds of shapes and sizes. And with very different data volumes.

The success a data solution has is unrelated to the volume of data it holds and processes. A solution may be relatively modest in terms of data volume, but can still have significant business impact.

As such, it wouldn't be correct to judge the performance impacts for all data solutions only from the perspective of the few really big deployments.

Scalability is important to understand and consider, but not everyone needs to adopt techniques to scale out to massive data volumes. Or, in different words, tweaking the right balance between performance and complexity can also be done progressively.

The degree of flexibility

As the above two sections allude to, it's really all about balancing the flexibility with the performance considerations.

Being able to prototype the data solution can increase the rate in which data interpretation can be clarified. An immediate view of the intended solution is an effective way to reduce the time for each iteration of this process.

Using a PSA that provides data to virtual layers, so that the data can be represented according to the design metadata allows to try out different approaches — and see which one works best.

From there, conversations can be started on performance requirements, so that these can be added to the solution to deliver the desired business outcome.

In some cases, virtualization may be sufficient to meet these requirements. In others, the engine may decide to instantiate parts of the data solution into physical tables and associated data logistics processes. Performance is just another requirement from this perspective.

Our recommendation is to frame these conversations in a way that covers how data solution virtualization can be incorporated, so that you can evolve with your technical infrastructure and requirements and let the engine provide the best mix of data solution deliverables.

Are layers still needed?

If it is feasible to fully virtualize the data solution, are all the layers that we covered in the data solution architecture chapter still relevant?

Why would one still bother with specific methodologies, such as Data Vault (or similar) at all? What value does an intermediate layer, such as the integration layer, still provide for a virtual data solution?

Is it not easier to simply define queries, views, or otherwise directly on the PSA?

The value of having layers

When the engine is in place, all data logistics components are configured as atomic processes. The design metadata provides everything the engine needs to produce these data logistics deliverables —whether virtual or physical— as well as any necessary physical data model objects.

These processes are independent and autonomous, and this allows the engine to optimize for various goals. For instance, optimization for better utilization of CPU usage, reduction of memory usage, or hard disk I/O.

The processes ultimately run on the only area where data is actually persisted – the transactional data that continually is made available in the PSA.

Any other, intermediate, layers are virtual.

This does not mean that they don't have value. The main reason for implementing intermediate layers is to *separate concerns.*

This separation of concerns provides a stable foundation for more abstract ways of (information) modeling.

The templates and conventions help to make the data solution manageable overall, and focus on logical and conceptual information modeling —which can then be translated to a physical model— including a virtual version. Using an intermediate layer for this purpose makes it easier to understand core concepts in the business, and the overall data architecture compared to directly creating queries on the PSA.

In short, it makes it possible to define data objects at a more abstract level and 'translate' this into a specific physical data model implementation using standard patterns in a way that is structured and easy to follow.

This also means that conversations on specific technical implementations become irrelevant. Are hash keys better than sequence numbers, or the 'unhashed' version of the business keys (natural business keys)? Do we even need Hub tables?

Questions such as these are less relevant, because these can be codified into the translation from the logical to the physical data model, and applied to the data logistics processes that interact with these.

Having defined layers and areas in a solution architecture assists in abstracting away complexity – keeping the solution manageable as a result.

But, the better the translation of the logical to the physical model becomes, the less visible these intermediate layers and areas will be.

Managing change and backwards compatibility

Data solution virtualization enables some truly fascinating possibilities, such as the ability to maintain version control of the data model, the metadata, the (original) data, and the relationship between the versions of them – to be able to represent the entire data solution as it was at a certain point in time. At least, in a way that is easier than creating tables and then populating these via data logistics processes.

This concept was first introduced in the data solution versioning section.

However, combining data solution versioning with data solution virtualization can take the concept of data solution versioning one step further. It is possible to 'host' two or more versions of a data solution *at the same time.*

All versions of the data solution are still related to the PSA data – at a point in time, as per the inscription timestamp. They simply represent the data solution as it was at a specific moment in time, for example as an alternative prototype that has not yet been committed or the production version of a year ago.

Virtualizing two or more versions of the data solution this way (or parts thereof) can simplify the delivery of the data to downstream consumers by managing downstream change.

Managing downstream change

A common problem that data teams face when managing data solutions, is how to manage changes in data structures without causing interruptions for consumers of the data.

Consumers rely on outgoing interfaces, and changing these interfaces may invalidate any queries, reports or services that have been built based on these interfaces.

This can cause problems, especially when code generation and automation to support the data solution is limited, because implementing and testing changes takes longer without having automation in place. Regardless, when changes are applied the data access can be interrupted until the deployment of the structural changes are complete, and the data is available again.

Consumers then need to update their logic to be compatible with the updated outgoing interfaces.

To mitigate risk of service interruptions like these, data teams often include 'decoupling views' in the ⚐ access area of the presentation layer. These views can 'soften the blow' of changes for data consumers because underlying structural changes can be implemented while simultaneously making sure the views continue to represent the status quo —wherever possible— until there is a good time to completely cut over to the new interface version.

Interface versions

Data solution virtualization offers a compelling alternative.

The involved concepts are similar to how changes in message, or API, formats in the intra-system data integration space are slowly introduced to consumers, so that they can upgrade their adapters over a period of time.

When implementing changes to an agreed format for data exchange (incoming and outgoing interfaces), you need to allow time for consumers to change their configuration from the moment when the change in the message or service format is deployed.

It is for this reason that one or more older versions of the interface continue to be supported when a new interface becomes available. The new interface is in production alongside the previous interface(s) for an agreed period of time.

This provides an extended cut-over period to allow consumers to plan the changes needed to connect to the new interface, and release these in according with their downtime requirements.

In this way, backwards compatibility is managed gracefully, over a period of time that can be agreed between the involved parties.

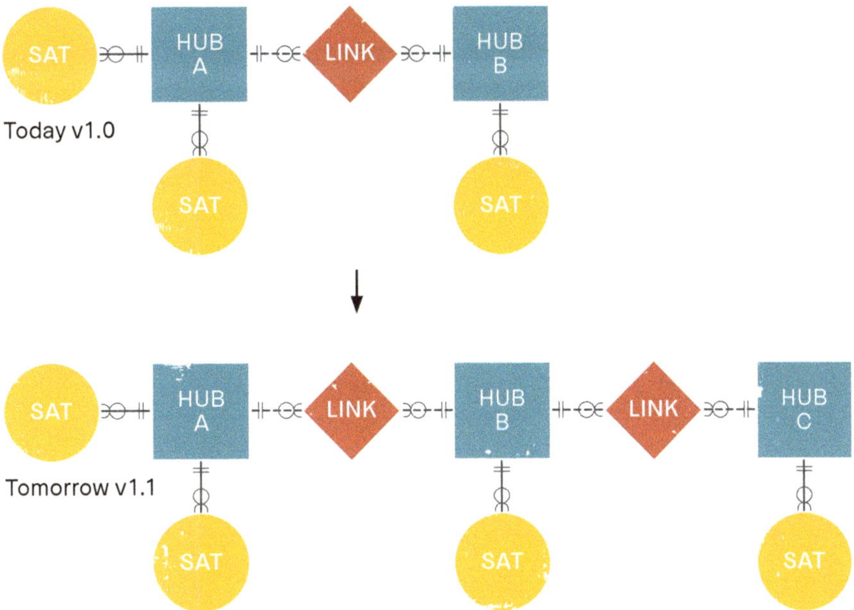

This concept can be applied to data solutions as well. Historically, this has often not been feasible due to the efforts required for the —often manual— development of the solution. But with the possibilities for automation as described in this book, and with data solution virtualization as an extreme form of this, it becomes a concept that can be considered.

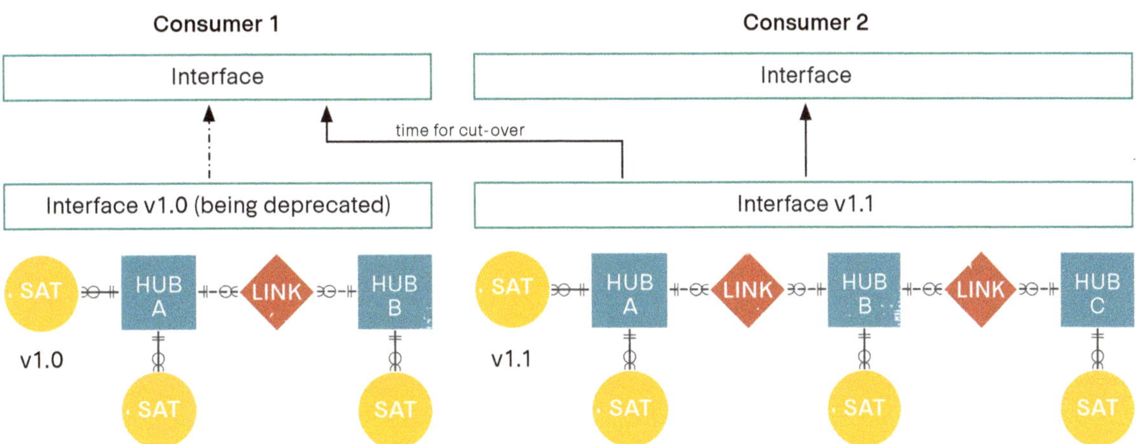

Using virtualization, a new version of the solution or interface can be deployed alongside the current production version.

For data solutions, the consumers might also include reports, data logistics processes, or services. Whatever the consumers may be, they can also take an agreed amount of time to cut over to the new version, negating the need for a 'big bang' change.

And, if at any point the data solution (and its data) require to be reverted into a representation from the past this can be supported also by applying the same principles.

Data integration technology for a virtualized solution

But wait... If all data logistics can be generated as views or compute, is specialized data logistics software still needed?

In short, yes, it is. But this is primarily to support scenarios where data needs to be loaded *onto* the data platform infrastructure, or connected to directly otherwise.

In most cases, data logistics software products are exceptional in providing connectivity to a large variety of technologies. These 'connectors' can make accessing infrastructure, services, or software that acts as data source for the data solution very straightforward.

Data logistics software can also play a role in capturing very specific business logic, for example in hosting certain transformations as a service or reusable component so this can be used by other processes. For instance to provide services that are more operationally focused, as opposed to purely analytical purposes.

Connecting to data that is hosted in technology other than the data solution has only limited support in standard query languages such as SQL. Coding environments and languages such as the .Net Framework or Python have many libraries for connecting systems, but these tend to have a higher barrier for entry whereas specialized data logistics software are often easier to use in this regards.

At the time of writing, this almost represents a full circle in the lifecycle of data logistics software: For a while, the focus on data logistics development shifted to a more visual development experience, away from —for example— coding in SQL. Now, with the widespread adoption of code generation and automation the focus is once more on scripting and code, with visual editors sometimes regarded as too cumbersome, slow, and complex to work with.

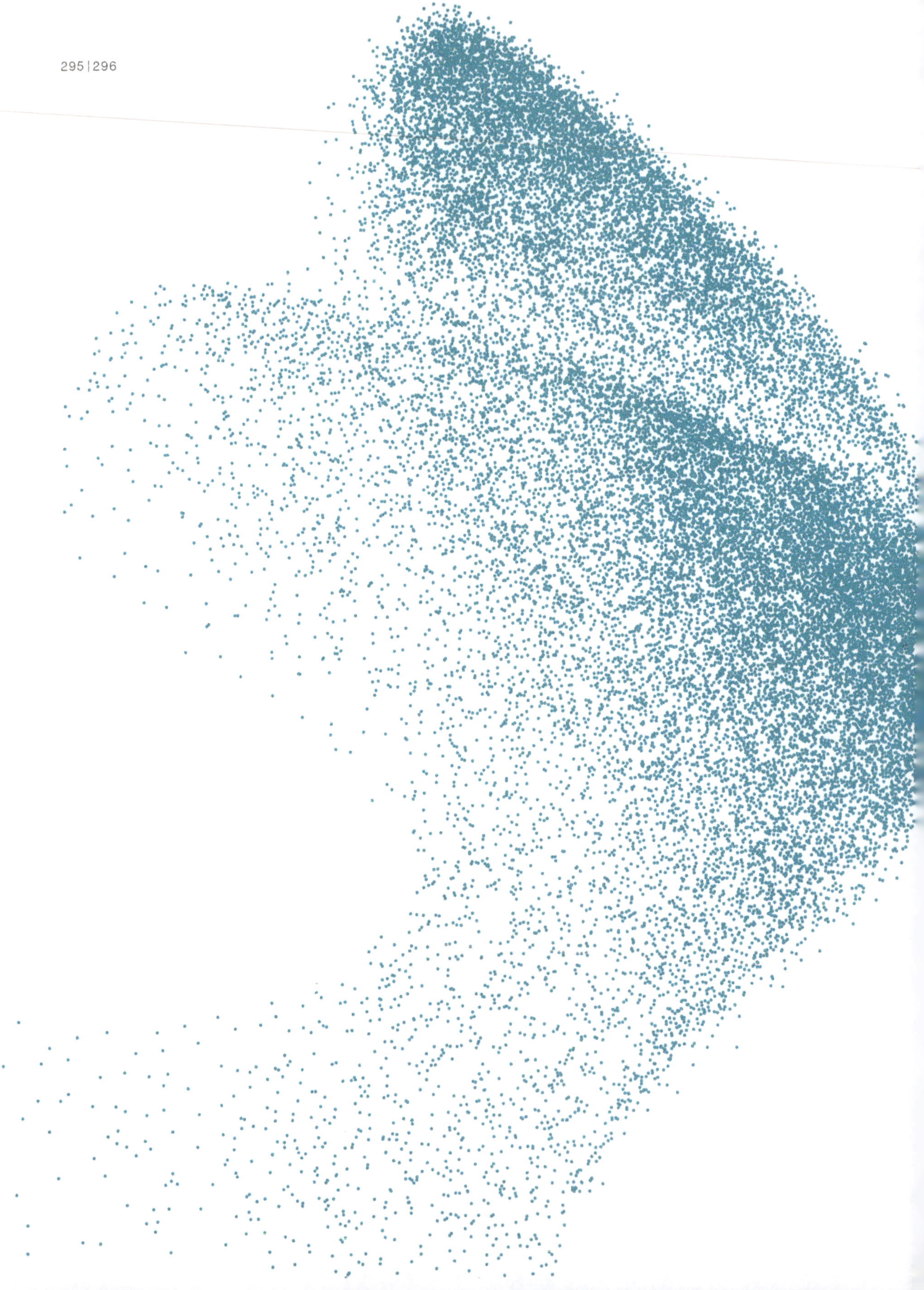

09 Getting the data in

This chapter will go into detail on what is essentially the 'back room' processes of the reference solution design, as introduced in the data solution architecture chapter.

The data solution architecture specifies what options are available, and what considerations should be made.

Now, it is time to make sure the data is loaded into the data solution.

Staging layer implementation

When it comes to getting data into the data solution, the staging layer is both one of the most complex parts of the solution to *design,* as well as one of the most straightforward ones to *develop.*

The complexity lies in the technical challenges accessing data from a wide variety of technologies. The straightforward part is that the templates themselves are relatively easy to apply.

As a brief recap from the data solution architecture chapter, the functional purpose of the staging layer is to:

- → Determine, and store, the data delta as a (transactional) series of change records
- → Log the record source
- → Set the inscription timestamp
- → Set the source timestamp
- → Log the record order (sequence)
- → Streamline the data types
- → Determine logical deletes

The staging layer consists of the landing area (LDA) and the persistent staging area (PSA). When an LDA is implemented, most of these requirements will be met by the LDA because it is the first area of the architecture that receives new data. If no LDA is implemented, the PSA will absorb the requirements otherwise addressed by the LDA.

The above requirements will be documented in either an LDA or PSA design pattern later in this chapter.

When adopting the reference architecture, the staging layer is the foundation for a flexible data solution. This layer provides a transactional view of all data changes that have been detected. Because it holds the original transactions in the PSA, it is the only layer that can *not* be virtualized.

The diagram below shows an overview of the staging layer, and the various pathways the data logistics can take depending on the solution architecture that has been defined.

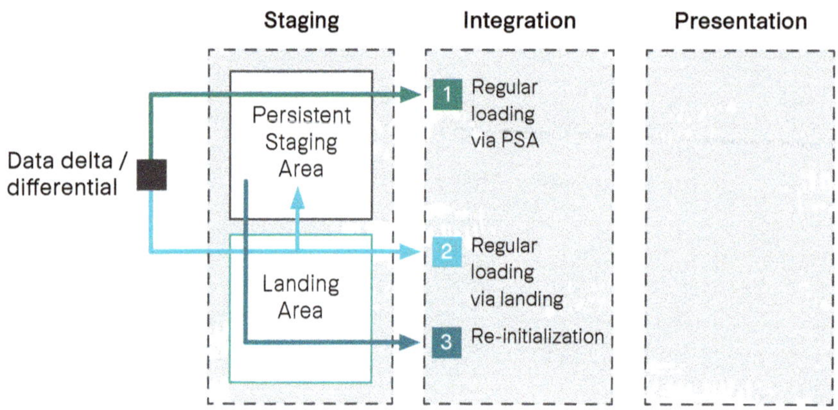

The first pathway, labeled as '1' processes the data delta into the PSA and then onwards to the integration layer. No LDA is necessary, unless required for purely technical reasons. This approach follows the reference architecture.

The second and third pathway, '2' and '3' in the diagram, adopt an LDA. This approach conforms to the 'better safe than sorry' architecture and similar designs where downstream objects can be reloaded by copying the PSA data back into the LDA – the reinitialization process.

Checksums

The staging layer marks the first time we encounter *checksums*. Checksums are widely used as a convenient way to compare the contents of multiple columns using a single value.

When comparing a record, or a part of a record, in a database table or file with another one, each column can be compared individually to determine if there are differences between the two records. A checksum provides the same functionality, but by comparing a single value that represents the record's contents.

Checksums are typically created using a hashing algorithm.

For instance, if you intend to send a bank account number without transferring the actual number, you can 'hash' the bank account details using a cryptographic hashing algorithm and send only the hashed value. The recipient can validate the contents by applying the same hash algorithm to the number they hold. If the hash values match, the sent data must contain the same value.

Similarly, a hash value is often used to ensure data integrity when sending a large amount of data, files, or binaries. By sending the data accompanied by the hash

↗ A hashing algorithm, also known as a cryptographic hash, provides a one-way encryption of its input values.

'Hashing,' the process of encrypting input data values into a hash value, is widely used to securely transfer data, assess data integrity, and authenticate. The recipient of a hash value can verify the data contents without actually having to view these.

value, the recipient can ensure that all intended data arrived correctly by comparing the hash value to their own comparison hash.

Hashing is applied in the data solution in similar ways, as a checksum to identify the contents of one, or more, columns using a single comparison value.

Using a single-value checksum, that potentially represents many columns, you can identify differences between records without having to evaluate each column individually.

Another use case for hash values is to serve as (part of the) key definition of a data object. This is called a *hash value key,* often shortened to 'hash key.'

In the staging layer, it may happen that no suitable primary key candidate is available, but is required for correct data delta detection and historization. A hash value may be used as a proxy key. This is covered in more detail in the defining a primary key section.

Later, in the integration layer, the hashed value of the business key is also one of the options to define the data object's *surrogate key.*

Checksums can also be created without using a cryptographic hashing algorithm. For instance, they can also be created by concatenating the involved data elements into a single value. However, these concatenated values tend to grow quite large and may contain characters that could impact performance in some technical environments.

A cryptographic hash value will always be the same size and structure, regardless of the number or length of its input values. For example, a hash value calculated using the SHA-1 algorithm will always return a hexadecimal value of 40 characters, even if hundreds of column values were provided as input.

Given that a hash value can often be stored as a binary type —20 bytes in the above example— it is often more efficient and convenient to opt for hash checksums over concatenated values.

Storing checksums in the data solution

Generally speaking, *anywhere* in the data solution where checksums are used for comparisons we recommend storing the resulting checksum in the target data object.

When checksums are calculated at runtime ('on the fly'), it may not always be apparent *why* certain checksum differences were encountered since the outcome of the calculation isn't stored. Small differences between the source and target of the comparison might be caused by factors that might not be immediately obvious – for example changes in incoming data types, or nullability.

Storing the checksum value when it is calculated and used removes any ambiguity around the comparison process.

At a practical level, this also prevents the checksum to be re-created, which otherwise incurs additional compute costs. Even though storage cost applies for saving the checksum, being able to select a previously computed value is often easier and more efficient.

How to create a checksum

Hashing data requires careful upfront consideration to ensure that the results of the hashing algorithm are returned as expected. The hashing approach must be defined as a pattern, and applied consistently across the data solution.

The exact result a hashing algorithm produces is dependent on many factors. Tiny differences in the technical configuration of the data platform may produce a different hash results.

This is especially important when calculating hash values across different technical environments. While it is usually possible in principle to produce the same hash value on different platforms given the same inputs and algorithm, it often requires extensive testing and trial-and-error to achieve correct comparable results.

Factors that impact the hash result include, but are not limited to:
- → Collation (e.g., casing, accent sensitivity)
- → Code page (including endianness[36])
- → String padding
- → Internal handling of NULL values

We recommended to avoid implicit conversions where possible to address these sensitivities.

To hash a value for the data solution, the following components are required in addition to the input itself:
- → An algorithm, SHA-1 is used as an example below
- → String conversion
- → NULL handling
- → Padding handling
- → String conversion
- → Sanding value

Xuefang's notes below shows an example of how a hashing calculation can be implemented using these components:

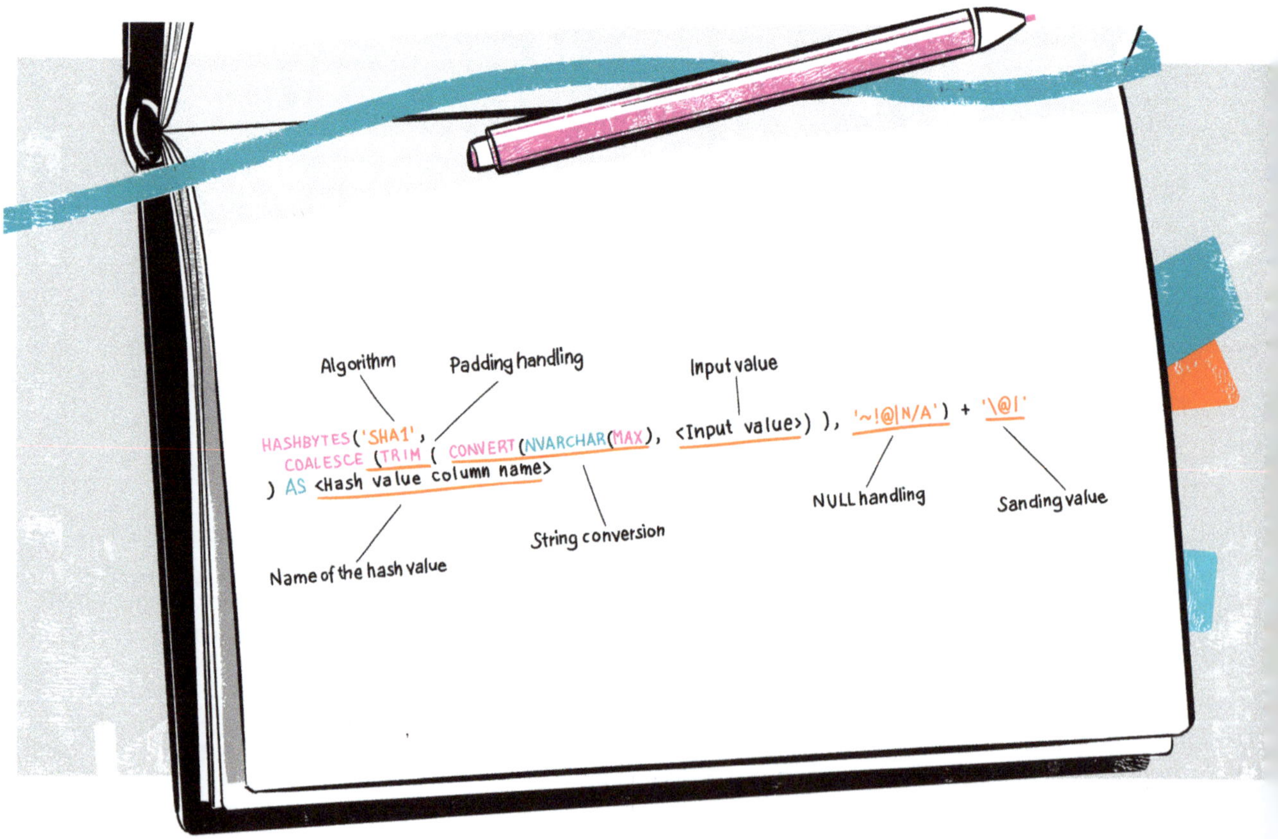

When hashing multiple values (i.e., column values of a record), each column is subject to the above approach and concatenated into a large string value before applying the hashing algorithm.

The following example applies this approach to 'hash' three column values into a single checksum:

```
HASHBYTES('SHA1',
  COALESCE (TRIM (CONVERT(NVARCHAR(MAX), [Value_1])), '~!@|N/A') + '\@|' +
  COALESCE (TRIM (CONVERT(NVARCHAR(MAX), [Value_2])), '~!@|N/A') + '\@|' +
  COALESCE (TRIM (CONVERT(NVARCHAR(MAX), [Value_3])), '~!@|N/A') + '\@|' +
) AS [Checksum]
```

The following sections go into more detail on each of the hash calculation components.

Hash algorithm

The selection of the hash algorithm determines the 'strength' of the algorithm. A stronger algorithm has a lower chance of *hash collisions,* and is safer to use for cryptographic purposes.

However, a stronger algorithm requires more computation resources and storage.

Selecting a fit-for-purpose hash algorithm requires taking the following considerations into account:

- Compute and storage costs
- Chance of hash collision, and risk-acceptance thereof
- Uniformity of value distribution
- Support by data platforms
- Security, if used for storage of sensitive data

The hashing requirements for a data solution are often not the same as its usage for true cryptographic purposes.

Encryption of data, at rest *and* in transit, is often implemented using features native to the data platform. In these cases, strong algorithms are adopted and the process is managed by the database management system.

When using hash values for checksums or hash keys, the security aspect is typically not as relevant.

Because of this, an algorithm can be considered for the data solution that is less 'secure,' also taking into account the compute, storage, and collision considerations.

Compute and storage

Stronger algorithms create hash values that are longer, they contain more characters, compared to weaker algorithms.

For example, the widely-used Message-Digest 5 (MD5) algorithm produces a 128 bit hash value, which is expressed as a 32 digit hexadecimal. This can be stored on disk as a 32 byte character field, or —preferably— as a 16 byte binary value.

Even though MD5 is not considered secure for true cryptographic purposes, it is often used in data integrity validations and checksums.

Another algorithm that is often used in data solutions is the Secure Hash Algorithm (SHA). The SHA algorithm is available in different, and increasingly stronger, versions with different compute and storage overheads:

- SHA-1 generates a 160 bit value, which can be stored as 40 byte character or 20 byte binary
- SHA-256 would generate a 256 bit value, which corresponds to 64 characters, or 32 bytes
- SHA-512 generates 512 bit values, which translates to either or 128 character positions or 64 bytes as a binary

An initial observation might be that stronger equals better, but as we covered in the previous sections, the data solution's requirements on the cryptographic 'strength' should not be confused with security of the data.

One of these considerations is the *collision rate* associated with each algorithm.

Collision

A *hash collision* ('collision') occurs when two different values return the same outcome when the hashing algorithm is applied.

Every hash algorithm contains the risk that it may generate the same outcome for more than one value, and this must be accommodated in some way.

This is a major concern in principle, because it would mean that the data solution incorrectly treats two different records as being the same. The result could be that the incoming data is not considered a change record, and dismissed accordingly.

However, it is very rare to actually encounter a collision — but not impossible.

Consider the following example:

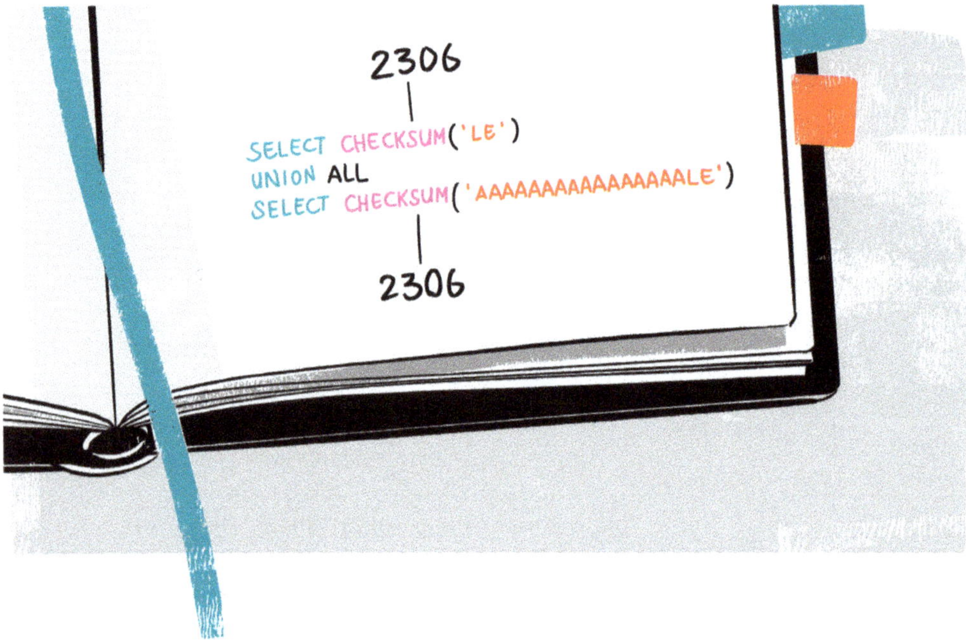

In both queries, using different input values, the outcome of the checksum algorithm is '2306.' The SQL Server checksum algorithm used in this example has a famously bad (high) collision rate, meaning that there are many combinations of values that yield the same output. It should never be used for data solutions.

However, with MD5 or SHA, or any of the stronger algorithms, this chance is lowered dramatically.

It is beyond the scope of this book to go into detail on collision probability for each of these algorithms, because many concepts and variables play a role in determining this.

Suffice it to say, the chances of a collision are really minuscule, but nonetheless exist. Various examples of hash collisions are documented as part of research projects, and so far these related to really large input values – not the type of data commonly encountered in data solutions. But, as a probability, it could be that the next collision is just around the proverbial corner.

The chance of a hash collision is so small, that most data solutions don't worry about this too much. But, it raises an interesting philosophical consideration.

Even when the risk is extremely small, does that mean the data team or architect can just accept it? Should this be something that the owners of the data get a say in? Do the benefits outweigh the risk, in case something does go wrong?

These are things to think about in the wider context of risk and data management, of which the data solution is a part of.

Is stronger also better?

Stronger algorithms have a lower collision rate, but require more storage. The 20 bytes that a SHA-1 hash value requires adds up when applying this to billions of records.

Especially when hash values are used as surrogate keys this effect is really visible – some of the intersection entities that contain multiple surrogate key references typically have the biggest I/O footprint of the entire data solution. An example of this is a Data Vault 'Link' object.

The additional compute and storage requirements that come with stronger algorithms make a real difference in cost and performance. The consideration needs to be made if a stronger algorithm is really worth this.

In our opinion, at the time of writing, opting for a relatively 'weaker' algorithm such as MD5 or SHA-1 is more than sufficient for the purposes of the data solution.

Other considerations

Other considerations regarding the hash algorithm selection are related to how well the algorithm is supported, and fit-for-purpose for, the available technical environment.

Not every data platform supports every algorithm, which is why it is often prudent to select one of the more common ones – such as MD5 or SHA.

Another consideration is how the resulting hash values are distributed. Ideally, hash output values are 'random' for all intents and purposes. They are anything but random, of course, but for the purpose of partitioning and indexing they might as well be. This behavior, in principle, supports an equal spreading across nodes in Massively Parallel Processing (MPP) environments when used as distribution keys.

But, how this works in detail is not the same across all algorithms.

A final consideration must be made when using hash algorithms for security, for example to encrypt certain sensitive data elements. This is an area where stronger algorithms should be considered.

It is beyond the scope of this book to go into a greater level of detail regarding data security, but any encryption must always be considered with other security measures because, in isolation, hash values —even stronger ones— can be compromised relatively easily. When an individual knows which approach is used, for example the pattern described in the ⚐how to create a checksum section, values can be reverse-engineered by comparing the hash values to a dictionary.

Comparing columns individually

Comparing columns individually can be considered as an alternative for using comparison checksums – especially when there is no appetite for any risk whatsoever, no matter how small. After all, staging layer data logistics processes can all be generated from design metadata, and developing logic to compare each column individually requires no additional effort.

A downside of column-to-column comparison is that the outcome of the comparison is ephemeral. After the change has been detected, there is no evidence for, or artifact of, the comparison itself.

This leads to a second alternative: it is also possible to store the concatenated string of all column values *before* the comparison is applied. Functionally, this achieves the same result as storing the output of a hashing algorithm. However, the benefit of using a hashing algorithm is that even large string values will always return a value with a predictable length – the same number of bytes.

For most tables, the concatenated values will return a string value that is quite large, and storing this might be prohibitive. Additionally, not all databases handle complex string values with many rarely used characters, as used in the NULL conversion and sanding values, with the same efficiency.

When using hash values for (surrogate) key distribution, additional options are available. These will be further covered in the core business concept section.

String conversion

The hashing algorithm is applied to a string value. If multiple column values are involved this means each value is appended (concatenated) to a large(r) string value.

Not all column values are necessarily string values, and in order to concatenate these into a single large string they require to be converted to a string type.

As a convention, we recommend to use the largest string type possible to avoid any value truncation during the conversion. This is why, in our examples, the values are always converted to NVARCHAR(MAX).

Making the conversion explicit also assists in mitigating issues related to how different databases manage implicit data type conversions. This may not be an issue if everything is running on a single database, but will help avoiding problems when different systems are involved – and are intended to use the same algorithm and its output.

NULL handling

As part of the preparation of the string value to which the hashing algorithm will be applied, NULL values should be replaced with a placeholder that is *suitably unique.*

This way, NULL values are handled explicitly following an agreed convention which further prevents implicit conversions.

'Suitably unique' in this context means that a placeholder value is used that is unlikely to appear in regular data. This is a combination of often-unused characters.

In our examples, we used '~!@|N/A' for this purpose. The 'N/A' component provides a visual cue that indicates an unknown placeholder value, and various other characters are added to improve its uniqueness – but any character string will suffice.

Padding

Padding handling refers to removing any spacing, padding, that may exist in individual string values. This is, again, intended to avoid any implicit interpretation by the database solution technology.

Different databases treat (empty) spaces differently, and treating these explicitly will ensure consistent behavior of the algorithm, especially when using the algorithm across different technical environments.

Sanding

Ensuring that a suitably unique sanding value is in place is critical to successfully implementing checksums.

Checksums algorithms are applied to a string value, and when multiple column values are involved —which is usually the case for comparison checksums— these individual column values are concatenated into a single large string value.

A sanding value is used to separate individual values so that their combinations remain unique.

For instance, if one value is 'ABC' and another one is 'DEF' then the concatenated value will become 'ABCDEF.' If another combination of values would be 'AB' and 'CDEF' then this concatenation would *also* yield 'ABCDEF.'

This has the same effect as a hash collision, incorrectly asserting that two checksums are the same when they are in fact different. This could, for example, mean that the data solution might incorrectly discard an incoming record as not being a real change record.

In our examples, we use '\@|' as the sanding value.

'ABC' and 'DEF' would then result in 'ABC\@|DEF.' 'AB' and 'CDEF' would become 'AB\@|CDEF.' Two individual combinations, by virtue of the sanding value.

Using a sanding value is essential for creating checksums, but does not fully eliminate the risk of collisions either. As with the selection of the algorithm itself, the selection of the sanding value carries a small risk that can never be entirely eliminated. However, this can be reduced to almost 0 as long as the NULL conversion uses a different value than the sanding value, and the sanding value itself uses various characters not often used in regular data.

Landing area

The landing area (LDA), when implemented, is the first area where new data is encountered from the perspective of the data solution. Because of this, a number of things need to happen here to ensure effective downstream data processing.

↗ The landing area is intended to be transient, which means that the detected data delta is only held briefly, until it has been processed downstream.

Most of the staging layer functionality will be delivered by data logistics processes that populate the LDA with data.

The LDA aims to receive —or infer— the data delta, align it to conventions and temporarily store this with the necessary audit details. This prepared data delta can then be merged into the PSA, or used for further downstream processes.

The following additional functional requirements apply specifically for the LDA:

→ Data is transient
→ Data delta is maintained until fully committed downstream

The LDA is intended to be transient, which means that the detected data delta is only held briefly, until it has been processed downstream. This is a 'truncate and insert' pattern, meaning that any new execution of these processes will overwrite the data delta that was provided the last time the process ran.'Old' data delta is removed when 'new' data delta is received by the interface.

This is specific for each individual incoming interface. Each interface will individually produce a new data delta that will replace the existing one – for that single interface.

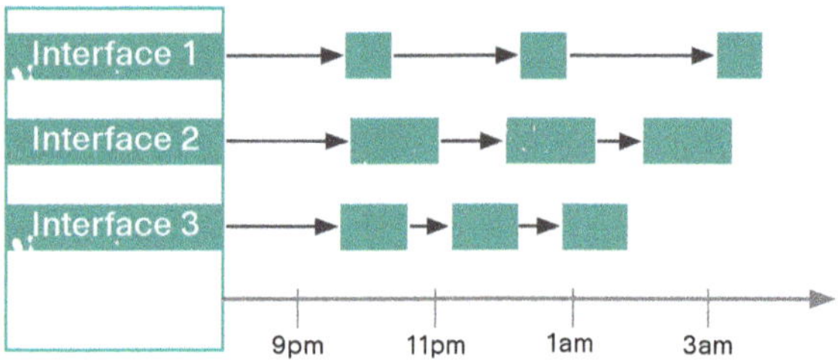

Each incoming interface manages its own wait states and data processing windows, and operates independently. This independence allows for parallel processing and reduces (processing) dependencies.

The LDA's transient nature poses a risk that data delta is lost if this data is not yet committed to the downstream areas. The staging layer orchestration therefore must protect the data delta until this has been fully committed to *all* downstream locations.

Only if all downstream areas have committed the data delta, the next LDA process can run and prepare a new data delta. This can be solved in a number of ways, which are documented in the staging layer orchestration section.

If not, the data delta may be overwritten *before* it could be processed by downstream parts of the data solution, causing a loss of data and resulting in a difference in content between the operational systems and the data solution.

This can only be repaired by performing a full compare between the data solution and the data source, resetting the delta extract timestamp in a pull interface, or restore of an earlier database backup.

If required, it is also possible to store the incoming data as-is in a separate place. An 'archive' for example, such as a file store. However, in our reference architecture the PSA performs this role so even though we would like to mention it as an option, we don't further pursue this.

Landing area data object structure

Structurally, the LDA data objects contain the same columns as the incoming data.

In addition to these, the following data solution columns are added:

- Inscription timestamp, indicating the date and time of arrival in the data solution
- Inscription record id, containing the order in which the data was received by the interface that detected and ingested the change records
- Source timestamp, capturing the moment the change took place in the operational system – as closely as possible
- Change data indicator, which tracks if a record is a change (insert or update), or detected as a logical delete
- Audit Trail Id, containing the reference to the data logistics control framework instance of the process that added the data

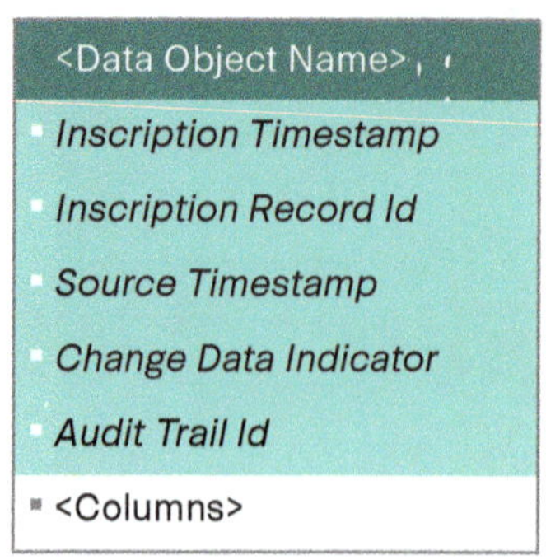

No constraints are applied in the LDA. As part of being a back-room component, as much as possible is done to prevent any technical errors – for instance ones that can be caused by violating constraints.

This means that all columns are nullable, no primary key is enforced for the data object, and no reference constraints (foreign keys) are validated.

In addition to the recommended standard columns described here, the following optional columns can be considered:

- Record source indicator
- Checksum

Inscription timestamp

The inscription timestamp is set by the staging layer processes, when the data first arrives in the data solution environment, and reused downstream.

In most architectures, this happens in the LDA.

At a high level, the inscription timestamp can be implemented in two different ways:

- As a default constraint, or
- As a metadata calculation

It is configured to capture the date and time with the highest possible detail – as a high-precision timestamp data type.

Implementing the inscription timestamp using a default constraint

If the technical environment for the data solution is a database that supports default values, the LDA data object can implement the inscription timestamp as a default constraint.

This way, no mapping is needed – the database will automatically create the value when a record is inserted. An example of this is:

```
ALTER TABLE <Data Object Name> ADD DEFAULT
(SYSUTCDATETIME()) FOR [Inscription_Timestamp]
```

Some databases, and file-based environments, do not support default constraints or similar. Or, they are supported but can't use an expression or function (only constant values). If this is the case, the inscription timestamp can also be defined in metadata.

Defining the inscription timestamp in metadata

The inscription timestamp can be defined as a calculation in metadata, at data item mapping level.

There is no source data item in this case that maps to the target inscription timestamp data item. Instead, the source data item is a data query that captures the expression that needs to be executed by the data logistics process.

For example, by using syntax as per the below:

```
{
 "sourceDataItems": [
  {
   "queryCode": "SELECT SYSUTCDATETIME()"
  }
 ],
 "targetDataItem": {
  "name": "Inscription_Timestamp"
 }
}
```

The syntax used in the example can be replaced by a DSL or similar syntax that is native to the technical environment.

Defining the inscription timestamp in metadata is often applied for file-based data solutions.

Timezones

As a centralized and standardized timestamp, we recommend recording the inscription timestamp in UTC. If needed, this UTC value can be converted to a local timezone, for instance, for auditing purposes.

Inscription record id

Similar to the inscription timestamp, the inscription record id value is also set in the staging layer and reused onwards.

The inscription record id is recorded to ensure data uniqueness in cases where the inscription timestamp alone is insufficient for this. This can be the case when multiple changes for the same key appear so fast that the precision of the timestamp is not accurate enough to distinguish this. Therefore, the inscription record id is a technical trick to uniquefy the inscription timestamp, represented as a sequential numeric field – for instance as an integer value.

The inscription record id will be part of the primary key of the corresponding PSA data object, but is not used further in the staging layer. However, it will become important in the integration layer. We will elaborate more on this in the ⚐ contextual data section.

Functionally, the inscription record id tracks the record order as the data delta is detected, processed, and committed by the interface that loads data into the staging layer.

The reason that the inscription record id needs to be recorded in the staging layer is because this is the *only* time this data can be accurately captured. This way, the order in which the data was received can always be represented correctly at any later stage.

If nothing else, the inscription record id provides some level of auditability during the loading process. The real value, however, lies in its ability to guarantee downstream deterministic processing when the inscription record id is retained in the PSA.

Similar to the inscription timestamp, the inscription record id can also be implemented as an integer using a default value, and by using a metadata expression at data item mapping level. The same limitations and possibilities apply.

A default value can be defined by most databases using a default column value. This is sometimes done by using a sequence object, or by setting an incremental value as shown here:

```
[Inscription_Record_Id] [int] IDENTITY(1,1) NOT NULL
```

Note that, in this scenario, the identity seed has to be reset each time the table is loaded as part of each data logistic process. This is important, because the inscription record id should start with the number 1 every time the data logistics process for an incoming interface is executed.

Alternatively, the inscription record id can be defined in metadata –as a data item mapping– as in the example below:

```
{
 "sourceDataItems": [
  {
   "queryCode": "SELECT NEXT VALUE FOR <my sequence"
  }
 ],
 "targetDataItem": {
  "name": "Inscription_Record_Id"
 }
}
```

When using a database sequence object, as is done in this example, this object must be created separately. Additionally, it must be reset as part of each data logistics process execution.

This can be added as a post-process SQL statement, or equivalent, in the template.

Source timestamp

The ⚐ source timestamp holds the moment the data (record) change was committed in the operational system – the system that provides the data to the data solution. It is configured as a high-precision timestamp data type, capturing date and time to the highest possible detail.

Ideally, this timestamp is evaluated separately from any columns that may be present in the source data object, for example a 'modified date' or 'last changed date.'

While these may be similar, or even the same, as the real moment of record change in the operational system, the ideal source timestamp is a system-generated value that is independent from the source data set itself — unable to be tampered with by any user.

Using an existing source data item as source timestamp exposes the data solution to integrity risks, because the data solution has no control over how data is modified in the operational system.

However, a strong candidate may not be readily available for all interface types, and in some cases using an existing column can be an acceptable risk — though not ideal.

Rationale for the source timestamp

The source timestamp exists to represent the state timeline for data delivery, *if no better suitable timestamp is available for this.* This consideration is made in the ⚐ context entity section, which contains further details on how the source timestamp is used.

The assertion of the source timestamp depends on the type of interface used to process the data into the staging layer. Not every interface is equally able to provide an accurate timestamp.

For some interfaces, there may not be a strong candidate and an approximation or proxy value must be used. Examples include the file delivery date or execution timestamp of the data logistics process that ingests the data.

For other interfaces, the source timestamp can be captured through a straight-forward data item mapping. In this scenario, the source data object already contains a suitable timestamp candidate, which can be mapped to the source timestamp directly.

In this scenario, the source data item is then *also* (redundantly) mapped to the corresponding standard data item with the same name. This makes automation easier, and reduces rework if the definition of the source timestamp is adjusted at some point in the future.

The goal is to record the best possible original moment of change, based on the available options.

We recommend to define how the source timestamp is evaluated as part of the interface agreement or definition.

In short, the evaluation of the source timestamp needs to be defined individually for each type of interface for the data solution. The selected approach then applies to all data objects that are processed using this interface.

Strategies to assert the source timestamp

This section does not contain an exhaustive list of all approaches for evaluating the source timestamp. Rather, the intent is to provide examples for common interface types as covered in the ⚐ data interface mechanisms section.

Interface type	Source timestamp evaluation strategy
Push mechanism	If the data set contains a suitable timestamp, the source timestamp can be configured as a data item mapping. This means that the providing party has included the moment of data change in the data set already. If a flat file is provided and the data does not contain a good candidate various options can be considered such as agreeing on a file-naming convention that includes the timestamp, or using file creation date details from the file properties.
Pull mechanism	If the data set does not contain a strong candidate, the data logistics execution timestamp can be considered.
Full outer join	If a suitable candidate exists in the resulting record set, then this can be mapped to the source timestamp. Otherwise, the moment of comparison determines the source timestamp. The data logistics process start timestamp can be used as an alternative, but the actual comparison timestamp is the closest proxy for the real change — even thought this may have happened much earlier in reality. This derived data must be captured by the template or data logistics process. It is not a data item that is available in the source data object.
Application Programming Interface (API)	APIs that can be used to access data from an operational system come in many shapes and forms, and do not always have a clear source timestamp column. The returned data is as per how the API is created, and usually does not represent the actual moment of change. If a suitable candidate exists in the API, then this can be mapped to the source timestamp. Otherwise the execution start timestamp of the data logistics process that ingests the data can be considered as an alternative.
Change Data Capture (CDC)	For native CDC solutions, the time of change is accessible as a data field (e.g., log sequence number or equivalent). This means the source timestamp can be defined as a regular data item mapping. This approach can apply to interfaces that rely on database triggers as well, assuming the timestamp the trigger has fired is recorded in the trigger table.
Subscription	If no strong candidate is available in the source data object, the moment the data set has been received can be used as source timestamp.
Streams and pub/sub	Streaming data almost always contains a system-generated event timestamp that identifies the message or event. This value exists in the data, and can be used to define the source timestamp.

Change data indicator

The change data indicator's purpose is to capture logical deletes. Without having a specific value to 'flag' a record, it is not possible to accurately capture the moment the record ceased to exist in the operational system – or at least when it was registered as such by the data solution.

In the reference architecture, this is covered by the ⚐determination of the data delta which includes the process of determining logical deletes.

Inserts, Updates, and Deletes

Conceptually, a record change can be due to one of the following scenarios below. The determination of which scenario applies is done using the record's primary key.

The scenarios for change data can be:

- An insert; a record that has been identified as appearing in the target data object for the first time
- An update; a record that already was there earlier, but whose values (payload) has changed
- A delete; a record that already was there earlier, but is no longer available in the providing data source

Once evaluated, the identified scenario for the record can be set in the change data indicator column.

For practical reasons, it is convenient to reduce the change data indicator values as much as possible. We recommend only using 'change' and 'delete,' not 'insert,' and using only the corresponding short codes 'C,' 'D' to reduce the storage footprint as much as possible.

This can be implemented as a fixed-length character data type so that the minimum amount of storage is used.

This way, the *first* record (for the given key) will register as 'change' ('C,' formerly know as 'insert'), and any subsequent records will be evaluated as 'change' ('C') or 'delete' ('D').

Not distinguishing between an 'insert' and 'change' simplifies the downstream templates, because otherwise additional logic will be needed in the ⚐compacting mechanisms to assert that the change from 'insert' to 'change' is actually not providing any value.

Implementing Change Data Capture

Exactly how the change data indicator is evaluated depends on the available approaches as outlined earlier in the ⚐data interface mechanisms section. In that section, we outlined the types of interfaces you may encounter when incorporating data from operational systems in the data solution.

Different technologies, platforms, organizational policies, and systems offer different options on how change data can be provided by the operational systems.

When implementing data interfaces, it is often a matter of finding the interface option that meets all, or at least most, of the requirements for the data solution – most importantly being able to:

- Determine logical deletes
- Capture all data changes

An example is the implementation of a ⚐full outer join data delta detection mechanism.

A full outer join is natively able to detect data changes, including deleted records. However, it may not be an option that is available for implementation, because this interface would require direct access to the operational system. Moreover, executing the process may significantly impact the operational systems, to the point that its users may find it unresponsive.

From a technical perspective, most database technologies would place a read lock on the table to ensure a consistent 'read' of the data for comparison – although there are various alternatives for this as well. During this time, it may be impossible for other users to access this data. For large tables, the time this takes may be prohibitive.

It is also not an approach that scales well, because the full data source is compared every time. However, it remains a good alternative for smaller data sets. One common approach is to first copy the data to the landing area, from where the data delta can be derived without further impacting the operational system's users.

Alternatives, including ⚐ pull mechanisms and ⚐ push mechanisms, provide a leaner approach where only data changes are selected or provided. This is often implemented based on a dependable, sequential value available in the data.

The challenge with interface mechanisms such as these, is that a the correct operation is dependent on this selected value *actually* being incremental. It's a column of which the data solution is not in control, so there is a reliance on an external factor —the operational system— to follow correct procedures. For example, if a user with elevated privileges updates the values used for incremental loading, this will directly impact the data solution.

Subscription and Change Data Capture (CDC) mechanisms typically apply lower-level change identification that does not rely on columns that can be manipulated by system users. These interfaces, either native or using 3rd party software, include features to interpret the database transaction log directly and through this provide a consistent flow of data changes — including deleted records.

However, there may be costs involved with solutions such as these that prevent them from being a suitable option.

Delta-based interfaces such as the push and pull mechanisms, but also including subscriptions and CDC solutions, are sometimes known to 'miss' changes for a number of reasons. If a data change has been missed, it is not possible to detect or address this without significant effort.

For all delta-based interfaces, we recommend implementing a separate full outer join supporting process that runs on a schedule that reduces impact on the operational system to acceptable levels. For example, delta-based interfaces can operate throughout the week, and the separate full outer join processes can run in the weekend. They would detect any deleted records and/or changed records that have otherwise been missed.

There is an additional benefit in being able to data changes that are essentially unexpected, by running a separate full outer join process. A full comparison from time to time may yield changes that are 'impossible' and highlight system and process defects, or even fraud.

Limitations on delta detection

It may happen that no option is available that satisfies all requirements for the data solution. This can only be resolved as a risk that must be reported and accepted by the management that is ultimately responsible for the data solution and its benefit-delivery purpose for the organization.

For example, if an operational system can provide changed data on a regular basis, but is unable to determine deleted records, this may lead to a discrepancy between the data solution and the system that provides the data.

Similarly, a system may only be able to provide an end-of-day snapshot but not provide the changes of data during the day. The data solution may miss certain data changes that can be significant.

In these examples, there may be technological or company policy limitations that prevent the data solution from using the optimal interfacing approach to determine data delta. The data solution may have to rely on what the operational system can provide.

Limitations *will* be encountered from time to time, and when these cannot be addressed it is important to ensure these are visible and any associated risks are accepted.

Audit Trail Id

The *Audit Trail Id* follows the same approach as for any entity in the data solution. This unique execution id from the data logistics process that inserts the data into the context entity will also be added to the LDA.

However, given the transient nature of the LDA, this column has limited value[37]. It will only be used for debugging purposes in case data logistics processes fail.

As a value that will be provided by the data logistics process itself, the insertion will be handled by the template. There is no need to define the Audit Trail Id in the metadata mapping.

In most cases, the Audit Trail Id is implemented as a integer value, with the option to define this as a large integer data type such as a 'bigint.' A new Audit Trail Id will be issued for every individual data logistics process execution instance, so this will add up for long-running data solutions that span many individual data logistics processes.

Descriptive columns

Any available column in the source data object is, in principle, mapped to the target LDA data object.

This is the 'payload' of the data object – the descriptive, regular, columns.

Most database technologies will add new columns to the bottom of an existing object by default. Following this convention, adding descriptive columns to the bottom of the data object is often the most convenient approach.

This usually makes it easier to physically add any new (source mapped) columns without having to reorder existing columns.

Mapping exceptions

In the LDA, all data items are mapped from the source data object to the target data object by default. In principle, there is no judgment applied to data in the back room of the solution. All data is accepted by default.

This does not mean, however, that designers are prevented from descoping any unwanted data items when there are strong reasons to do so.

An example of this is when incoming values are of a purely technical nature, and do not contain any meaningful information – as much as this can be asserted beyond a reasonable amount of doubt.

In one of the real-world examples, we connected to an operational system that would set a Yes/No value every time a user opens and closes a form in the application. When opening the form, an 'Is Used' column would be updated with 'Yes,' and this would be updated to 'No' when a users closes the form.

This mechanism was not tied to individual users, so it did not matter *which* user opened or closed the form, just that it was done by someone. Over time, this application was used by hundreds of users and each time any user opens, and closes, forms the 'Is Used' column would be update – without any way to know who actually did what.

This generated many change records with no meaningful content.

Another example is related to performance and a reduction of the amounts of data transferred from the operational system to the data solution. If a certain data object contains hundreds of columns, but only uses a small amount of these, then the redundant columns can potentially be ignored.

Ideally, and if possible, this selection is implemented in the interface that provides the data to the data solution – so that the solution does not need to make this consideration.

Or better yet, systems are continuously updated to prevent exceptions such as the boolean example from happening. At the end of the day, the best data design starts at the operational system level.

The world of data is not perfect, unfortunately, and in some cases the only remedy is to exclude columns such as these from the design.

If a data element is not mapped this will likely lead to data redundancy. But this does not need to be resolved in the LDA. This is further covered in the ⚐ redundant data section.

The PSA and integration layer are capable of managing this, and it is usually easiest to keep the LDA as straightforward as possible because the complexities involved with determining the data delta are already challenging enough.

Data type alignment

A notable feature that is implemented in the LDA is *data type alignment.*

Operational systems may span a great variety of technologies, which often leads to a range of different data types that are presented to the data solution.

To make downstream processing more resilient, these potentially different data types are mapped to a minimal set of standard data types and values in the LDA. This is in line with the intent to, as a back room process, prevent technical failures where possible.

For example, consider an operational system that provides a column with a CHAR(3) data type – a string value that can hold up to three characters.

If the corresponding LDA also uses a CHAR(3) type for the target data item, errors will occur if the operational system increases the size of this column – to a CHAR(4) for example. This would cause string truncation errors when loading this data into the LDA. Even worse: no error is raised, but characters are cut-off to satisfy the target data domain.

Having large standard data types in the data solution provides another level of protection against technical errors caused by changes in the data sources.

Data type alignment is implemented without losing detail, which means no rounding of precisions/scales or limiting string lengths (trimming).

We propose the following standard data types for our reference data solution architecture:

- → Any character data types are mapped to the longest available variable-length UTF[38] character data type (e.g., NVARCHAR(MAX))
- → All date data types that include a time component will be mapped to a high precision timestamp (e.g., DATETIME2(7))
- → All date data types without a time component are mapped to either a date data type or a high precision timestamp (e.g., DATE or DATETIME2)
- → All time data items without a date component are mapped to a time data type (e.g., TIME)
- → All decimal or numeric data types are mapped to a high precision numeric data type (e.g., NUMBER, NUMERIC(38,20))
- → All floating point data types are mapped to floating point (e.g., FLOAT)
- → All integer values –including bits and booleans– are mapped to an equivalent or larger integer data type (e.g., INT, BIGINT)
- → All blob or binary values are mapped as-is

String padding

Following this convention, a CHAR(3) data type, as used in the earlier example, would be mapped to a NVARCHAR(MAX) target data item.

The reason to use a NVARCHAR type instead of a (larger) CHAR data type is because a CHAR data type is a *fixed-length* data type, which always takes up the allocated storage, regardless of the actual contents.

Using CHAR, unused character space will be padded to the right when storing string values that are less than the fixed size, taking up unnecessary storage space. Since we advocate larger target data types, this additional storage requirement does not make it a good candidate for target data type alignment in the data solution.

Variable-length character data types (NVARCHAR, or similar) don't apply this padding. Only the actual contents are stored on disk – including an additional two bytes to record the lengths of the contents.

This means that large data types can safely be used, because only the actual content will take up storage space.

Data type conversion defaults and precision

When mapping a time data item to a high precision timestamp, depending on the technology used, the default date part may be set by the database using a default value.

For example, a time value '09:15:22.33' will be changed to '1900-01-01 09:15:22.3300000' when converted to a timestamp. This is why a time data type without a date component can only be mapped to a target time data type, and not to a timestamp.

The following example demonstrates this:

```
DECLARE @timeValue TIME = '09:15:22.33'
SELECT
  @timeValue
 ,CAST(@timeValue AS datetime2)
```

Similar behavior occurs when mapping a floating point data item to a high precision numeric data type. The value 26773e022 represents 0.0000000000000000026773.

If this value is mapped to a NUMERIC(38,20) data type, the last two digits will be rounded to 20 digits to the right of the decimal point, resulting in 0.00000000000000000268. Which is obviously not the same.

This can be reproduced using the following code:

```
DECLARE @floatNumber FLOAT = 26773e-22;
SELECT
  @floatNumber
 ,CAST(@floatNumber AS NUMERIC(38,20))
```

A floating point data type therefore must be mapped to a target floating point equivalent.

Using Unicode

The data type alignment also applies Unicode encoding (NVARCHAR) to character data types. Adopting Unicode is yet another measure to improve the data solution's resilience and flexibility. Without Unicode-encoded types, it can be difficult to integrate data from Unicode systems into a non-Unicode data solution – for example standard Oracle RDBMS installations. When the data solution is configured for Unicode, this problem does not occur.

A VARCHAR data type column is limited to an 8-bit code page, whereas Unicode encompasses many code pages, avoiding encoding conversions when reading from, and writing to, the database.

If required, it is technically always possible to validate that data is compliant to other code pages (7-bit ASCII, for example), if this is required for data delivery, while still being able to benefit from the ease of maintenance that Unicode encoding offers.

The data solution is designed to incorporate data from anywhere, and must be as welcoming for any data as possible. Even though implementing non-Unicode may be sufficient for the operational systems *currently* used in the organization, there is no guarantee that this would stay true in the future – new systems may adopt Asian characters, emojis, or similar.

Unicode provides a layer of flexibility to host data from anywhere, making the solution more future-proof.

Either UTF-8 or UTF-16 can be used. It is usually easiest to standardize on UTF-8, unless the data contains a large amount of Asian characters – in which case UTF-16 is a more storage-efficient option.

In both cases, the data can be managed without code page conversion issues.

A similar argument is also provided for collation settings, as outlined earlier in the architecture's ⚐ streamlining data types section.

Exceptions

Different operational systems may use different underlying technologies, and as a result a large variety of data types could be presented to the data solution. It may not always be immediately obvious what a suitable target data type could be.

In all cases, the purpose is to provide a layer of protection against technical failures wherever possible. When in doubt, the target data type can usually be a text data type such as NVARCHAR(MAX), in which case evaluation and conversion to a more suitable type can be implemented in the presentation layer.

Some databases may have limitations that prevent applying data type alignment to all columns. SQL Server, for example, has limitations on how many bytes a primary key index may contain. If this threshold (900 bytes for a Clustered Index, at the time of writing[39]) is exceeded, the database engine issues a warning that the index may not work correctly.

This could be encountered, for example, in the definition of a persisted staging area (PSA) object. PSA data objects typically include the original primary key in the definition of the PSA key. If the combined key exceeds system limitations, then the target data type can be scaled back to address this.

In situations such as these common sense should prevail, after all, the goal is to provide a solution that is as resilient as possible.

Some data solutions implement the convention that *all* columns are defined as a large text data type, such as NVARCHAR(MAX). The rationale for this is that it is a more straightforward data type alignment pattern to apply, and arguably one that scores well in avoiding data type conversion issues.

The downside of this approach is that a lot of information about the columns is lost in the process, and significant effort is necessary to convert the columns into formats that are appropriate for data consumption.

In addition to managing specific local interpretations ('cultures' in computer science), converting non-text values to text types has implications on sorting, calculations, and comparisons. An example is shown in section managing data type interpretation from text files.

For this reason, we prefer the data type alignment approach where the columns adopt a larger version of their original type, and address any data type conversion issues in the front room of the solution — not in the staging layer.

Optional columns

Record source indicator

A *record source indicator* column can be added in the LDA. We consider this an optional column, because the same information can also be retrieved from the control framework. The Audit Trail Id that is part of every data set, including context entities, is a reference to the data logistics process that inserted the data.

The control framework contains various administrative properties for this data logistics process, including the operational system and object from which the data was retrieved. If a specific record source label is required, it can be added here and queried if and when necessary.

One potential advantage of having the record source indicator in the data object is that this provides a visual of the data origins without having to join to the control framework.

If this information is used often, there may be performance gains associated with having the record source indicator available without requiring joins.

But conceptually, it is not required.

Checksum

Similarly, a *checksum* column can be added to the LDA design. This checksum is a single value that represents the contents of all descriptive columns.

A checksum is commonly used in data comparison mechanisms, to determine if the incoming data contains differences compared to the data that is already available in the data solution.

This is a common implementation approach for delta (change) detection, typically done by comparing the checksum value in the PSA to a checksum that based on the incoming data.

Using a checksum for comparison means that only a single value (from the incoming data set) has to be compared to another single value (as is available in the PSA) to understand if there are data changes.

An additional benefit is that the checksum column names are standard. Otherwise, all descriptive columns need to be evaluated separately to determine if there has been a data change.

The checksum value can be calculated in a number of ways, including applying a hashing algorithm, CRC[40] algorithm, or concatenating all necessary column values. Additional details on various considerations and implementation can be found in the checksums section.

Reasons to store the checksum in the LDA may be performance-related. If a checksum is used for change detection, it may be efficient to store this value in the LDA so that it can be reused to record the value in the PSA without re-calculating it during the processing from the LDA to the PSA.

For this reason, some of our examples will show the checksum as one of the LDA columns.

At the same time, if the checksum is not used in downstream processes, there is little value storing the checksum in the (transient) LDA.

In all cases, checksums can always be generated at runtime in case the decision is made to not store these in the data objects.

Landing area design pattern

This section summarizes the features of the LDA into a design pattern, supported by examples for code generation and implementation.

The full pattern, using the recommended pattern documentation *structure*, can be accessed via our website: https://dtng.link/yq0v8.

The LDA data logistics process implements the following concepts:

- → Select the in-scope columns
- → Determine the source timestamp
- → Record the inscription timestamp
- → Standardize the data types
- → Order the data set
- → Determine changes
- → Truncate and process the data into the target object

Selecting the in-scope columns

A typical, and often useful, paradigm, is to load the entire data object (table or file) when connecting to a data source for processing data into the LDA.

Or, in other words, when you only need a few data items from an object you might as well get the other data items too for essentially the same effort.

However, common sense should prevail when selecting which data items are of interest, because in some cases the data simply has no value — as we mentioned in the mapping exceptions section.

It is acceptable to limit the columns to those that matter for processing into the LDA.

Our recommendation is to process all data items when interfacing a given data object as a guideline, but allow for exceptions when some items have been identified as irrelevant beyond reasonable doubt.

Define the source timestamp, inscription timestamp, and data types

When the data set is selected, the standard data items for the source and inscription timestamp can be set as per the standards documented in the landing area data object structure section.

The data item types can be converted to their larger counterparts following the defined conventions.

Persist the data's order

Many technologies, SQL included, are non-deterministic by nature. SQL, for example, will not guarantee the same order of data retrieval and presentation if an order is not explicitly set.

To some users, this may come as a surprise. Doesn't the same result show every time the same query is run (without an ORDER BY statement), a user might ask?

This might be the case indeed, but this is often due to other factors such as caching, read patterns, and other lower-level database management operations.

The fact is, that without specifying order, results are not always guaranteed to be shown the same way.

This matters for the data solution, especially when depending on reinitialization and virtual data solution concepts. Imagine reinitializing a certain data object, only to find out the contents are wildly different.

In our reference architecture, upon arrival the order of the records is inscribed both by the timestamp of arrival (inscription timestamp) and the inscription record id. By using both the inscription timestamp and inscription record id, the data solution can guarantee deterministic downstream processing of data, because the order can always be selected in the order in which it was received.

The order of arrival is 'set in stone' in the staging layer of the reference architecture and is immutable going forward.

This does require that the data initially arrives in order, and this is why the LDA pattern strongly recommends implementing an ordering of data in the interface that processes the data into the staging layer.

Determine changes, truncate, and load

Regardless of what interface is implemented, and how the data arrives, one of the goals of the staging layer is to create a transactional view of data changes – as per the guidelines covered in the overview of the data solution design.

Once the transactional view of data changes has been prepared by the interface, the target (LDA) data object can be emptied, and the incoming data delta can be loaded into it.

This 'truncate and load' paradigm, emphasizing the transient nature of the LDA, immediately makes this pattern compliant with many of the fundamental principles for data logistics.

The pattern is modular, independent, fault-tolerant, and idempotent simply due to its transient nature.

Considerations

A few considerations apply when defining the source-to-landing data logistics processes. It is rare to have only one suitable solution for a given challenge. In most cases there are multiple correct ways to achieve the intended outcomes.

And, in some cases, this requires considerations and resulting design decisions to make things work in a certain way. We would like to share some of these considerations in this section.

Ideally, the resulting decisions made are captured in an LDA design pattern, so that the reasoning and context of the decisions can be understood by all stakeholders now, and in the future.

What columns do I really need?

This consideration is directly related to the 'selecting the in-scope columns' feature of the design pattern.

The implementation of this decision is done in design metadata, by only creating data item mappings for columns that are of interest.

We recommend to explain the reasoning in the design pattern in general, and in notes in the metadata in particular.

Moreover, any reduction of the column scope would ideally lead to a record compacting mechanism being implemented in the involved data logistics processes.

The compacting mechanic intends to remove any redundancy in data.

A decrease in column scope almost always creates some redundancy in data. This occurs when subsequent records (ordered as per the inscription timestamp) are identical save the inscription timestamp itself. The *payload* of the data is exactly the same.

This may happen because the data change in the operational system is triggered by one of the columns that are not part of the column scope.

In the introduction of this design pattern, we shared the example of an 'IsUsed' column that is continuously updated in the operational system without having any reporting value. When using native CDC (or equivalent), each change in data –including the 'IsUsed' value– will produce a change record.

When records containing only the in-scope columns are received by the data solution, there might not be a visible change between records if the change is triggered by the 'IsUsed' column (or any other column that has been taken out of scope). The other columns will still carry the same values between change records.

This only applies when a subset of columns from the source data object is processed into the data solution.

When the *full* source data object is integrated, this feature can be omitted from the design.

Not all redundant data is undesirable by definition. It is therefore important to evaluate when applying techniques to eliminate redundant data is the right thing to do.

In some (rare) situations, it may be of interested to record redundant information in case there is value in troubleshooting issues in the involved technology. Examples are malfunctions in CDC technologies, triggers, or message buffers.

There is more to cover on ⚐ data redundancy and record compacting, and the implementation details are further explained in the integration layer sections.

For now, considering data redundancy and the implementation of a record compacting feature in the PSA is recommended to be documented in the design pattern, and encoded in the templates.

Selecting the delta mechanism

An important decision to make, and document in the design pattern, is to agree on the best available and possible delta detection approach.

The 'best' interface for delta detection supports all the requirements outlined in the ⚐ staging layer implementation section, especially the ability to determine logical deletes.

The options are dependent on involved technologies, ability to potentially modify operational systems, company policies, and data volumes. Some operational systems only support certain ways of interfacing, due to the way these are managed or how warranty is supported when connecting to commercial software.

Each operational system requires individual evaluation to determine how the above-mentioned requirements can best be met, and how to manage risk if this is not the case.

A specific considerations, in addition to the above, is how an initial load can be organized. Does the interface support the ability to periodically access the full data set? Are there any windows in which the operational system should *not* be contacted for any data changes?

When using APIs, is it possible to provide parameters to manage load windows? Is the full data set always returned? Is this possible at all?

Another consideration is how logical deletes are evaluated. In some interface types, such as the Full Outer Join (FOJ) or native Change Data Capture (CDC) this is supported 'out of the box.' But in many other interface types this is not guaranteed to be supported or even possible.

If possible, aim for a technical mechanism to derive logical deletes – as opposed to relying on data points the operational system may provide, such as an 'IsDeleted' flag or indicator.

Even though we trust that operational systems are managed with the best intentions, preventing updates on their data is something that lies outside of the realm of influence of the data solution. Relying on data that is made available to the data solution might lead to missing important patterns in data that can only be tracked using a system-driven interface – one that makes it impossible (or as hard as possible) for a human operator to tamper with.

As a guideline, we assume that everything is done with the best intent and as per the best of everyone's ability. But from a system design perspective, we recommend a solution that assumes nothing.

With enough privileges, logs can be bypassed, triggers can be disabled, and changes can be made in general by covering one's tracks. All these things may lead to data changes not being visible to the data solution.

We have been involved with projects where things that 'cannot happen' invariably do. For example when commercial software states that no data is deleted, until it does happen. Or, malicious –even fraudulent– data changes where effort was made to conceal this. In other cases, the column used for the high-water mark or load window, which was considered so dependable and sequential was updated to 'insert' some records at a later stage, but the load window has already moved on.

When developing data solutions, our recommendation is to always aim for a system-driven way to determine data delta including logical deletes.

The consequence is that, for some interfaces, it may be required to also create FOJ-style interfaces in addition to the regular delta-based interface. These can run occasionally to ensure that any deleted records are identified.

The need to do so depends on various factors, which is why the considerations for this, and risk for not implementing some of these features, should be documented in the design pattern.

Restartability and recovering from failure

By its very nature, the LDA pattern is inherently deterministic and idempotent. The process can be run any time without technical failure.

However, to protect data delta that has been collected —but not yet committed downstream— care must be taken to prevent simply restarting the data logistics process. The LDA is the only place in the data solution where additional considerations on this apply, because, once a data delta has been loaded it may be lost forever if it the LDA data object is truncated too soon.

The solution for this lies in the ⚐ data logistics control framework. The batch concept in the control framework can be used to prevent accidental restarting of the LDA process until downstream processes (such as the PSA) have been completed as well.

The LDA's transient nature, and the data delta it temporarily holds, are the only exception on dependencies in the architecture. Technically, the LDA data logistics process is independent, and can be run at any time. But conceptually, this must be coupled with its downstream persisted downstream areas so that all data deltas are safely committed before the next LDA process is allowed to run.

More details on this are covered in the ⚐ staging layer orchestration section.

Timezones

Operational systems may operate in different timezones. This is often the case, of course, when systems run in different parts of the world. But it may also be the case when multiple systems run in the same single location.

Most of the challenges around this will be solved later, in the integration and presentation layers. But, it is worthwhile to capture any initial decisions around how to manage this in the LDA design pattern.

Generally speaking, we recommend to apply UTC for the standard columns of the data solution, such as the inscription and source timestamps. If and when required, these values can be translated into local time during downstream processing.

Another consideration is if it's possible to receive timezone details as part of the interface. Can the offset be provided and stored? If this is possible, then at least it's visible in data which timezone applies to the values of certain timestamp columns. If not, any details on what timestamp values represent should be documented in the design pattern and usually converted downstream.

Applying sort order

We have emphasized the role of *ordering* as part of the source-to-landing data logistics processes. The next step is to decide how to actually implement this.

The available options for this largely depend on the involved technologies, and may be limited in some cases.

Using database-to-database processes, SQL might be applied to force ordering when selecting data from the operational system. Native CDC technologies have built-in timestamps and/or transaction log sequence identifiers that can be used to persist the order of data.

FOJ mechanism, or similar, do not require ordering because only a single change per record can be detected per process run.

But a lot of interfaces don't have an ordering feature that is immediately obvious, for example when connecting to APIs. This is often a point of discussion when negotiating data interfaces between systems.

Our recommendation is to make a conscious decision on how ordering can be applied, and —where possible— add it as a requirement for integrating data into the LDA.

Whatever the outcome is, the decision should be added to the design pattern documentation.

Managing data type interpretation from text files

When data is presented to the data solution as an text file (e.g., ASCII), the data type mapping may not be immediately obvious.

If the origin of the data stems from a system that has robust controls in place manage data type constraints, these data types can potentially be adopted in the data solution. For instance, a text file may be an extract of an API or system that is well known and understood — and whose data types can safely be relied upon as well-managed.

But if this is not the case, or when risk of data ingestion issues requires to be fully mitigated, data types can be defined as character types in the data solution — at least in the back room of the solution.

This is generally the safest approach, acknowledging that the conversion to a suitable type might not always be as straightforward as it may seem.

Consider the following example:

```
DECLARE @float FLOAT = 2.6773e-22;
DECLARE @textFloatDot NVARCHAR(100) = N'2.6773e-22';
DECLARE @textFloatSemicolon NVARCHAR(100) = N'2,6773e-22';
SELECT CAST(@float AS NVARCHAR(MAX))
SELECT CAST(@textFloatDot AS FLOAT)
SELECT CAST(@textFloatSemicolon AS FLOAT)
```

In this example, a floating point is delivered in different formats. The @textFloatDot value expresses the value with a *dot* as decimal point, whereas the @textFloatSemicolon uses a *comma* to set the decimal point.

This could occur due to different systems having different configurations (cultures) for managing numeric values.

Especially when using text files as interfaces to move data between systems, this nuance could get lost, which in turns leads to conversion errors.

In the example above, assuming the data platform is configured as an English culture, the conversion from @textFloatDot would work. The conversion from the floating point value to a character also works, and the values match.

However, the conversion for @textFloatSemicolon fails because a comma is not expected for a floating point. It could be that this value was provided by a ystem that uses a German culture, and this configuration persists in the file the data was extracted to.

To work around this, it is possible to convert the data by providing the culture it should be interpreted with. A statement such as the example provided below is an option that returns the float value in the expected format.

```
SELECT TRY_PARSE
(@nvarchcharfloatWithSemicolon
AS FLOAT USING 'de-de')
```

This statement specifically converts the character value using the German culture format.

Complexities such as these tend to drive the recommendation to align columns from a text file to a character data type in the back room of the data solution, so that the front-room can be used to apply the correct conversions as part of the data delivery.

Loading data delta directly into the PSA

If you commit to having a PSA in your solution architecture, as we have done in our reference design, it may not always be necessary to implement an LDA.

An LDA is only truly necessary when you require a temporary storage ('landing') of data in the data solution environment before further processing – for example for delta detection purposes.

In some cases, data delta can be inserted directly in the PSA. Data that is already fully transactional can usually be inserted into the PSA straight away, for instance. Pub/sub events and native ('technical') CDC technologies fall into this category.

Similarly, if it is reasonable and possible to implement a FOJ comparison between a source data object and its PSA equivalent the resulting data delta can also be directly inserted in the PSA.

When following this approach, downstream processing will always take place from the PSA – locking this in the architecture. This will be covered in detail in the ⚐ staging layer orchestration section.

Without a PSA in the solution architecture, an LDA is relevant to have to capture the data delta until it has been committed to all downstream target data objects.

Avoiding data quality checks in the staging layer

In our reference solution architecture, we try to be as welcome as possible to all new data, regardless of its quality. The data solution is not there to judge, but to accurately and consistently make data available for consumption.

Many tweaks in the solution architecture, big and small, support this approach. The data type alignment and removal of constraints are examples of this in the staging layer.

Allowing 'bad quality' data to enter the data solution can sometimes feel counterintuitive, especially when the issues are obvious. Having a date of February the 30th in an incoming data set might raise some eyebrows. And, assuming the technology supports this, it will cause domain violation issues when attempting to load this into a column defined data type as a date domain – a technical error.

Even so, as we have written earlier, what is considered 'bad' data quality for some may be meaningful to others.

We recommend to accept all data, 'warts and all' into the system, so that it becomes possible to report on issues without having to implement complex data return processes and managing downstream inconsistencies related to blocked data.

A concern with rejecting data in the staging layer is this data may stay in a cycle of rejection and modification for an unknown amount of time, dependent on the business user's priorities. Adding such an additional feedback loop also adds complexity to the solution, and places greater emphasis on ensuring it is at all times visible what data has not been correctly processed yet. The concept of 'fixing' the data this way to make it fit a certain expectation also removes the fact that there an error existed in the first place, and also that it may happen again.

After all, the consumers of the data must understand the state of their data to use it correctly.

Ensuring completeness

Few technologies are perfect.

When using any delta-based interfacing approach, such as native CDC, a high-water mark, commercial middleware, trigger-driven history capture tables, and anything similar, it may happen that data changes sometimes are lost.

This is something we have experienced in every project over the years. The reasons for this are as plentiful as there are technologies and approaches for detecting data changes, but over time there is a significant chance that the reality in the operational systems slowly drifts apart from the data changes that have been received by the data solution.

And, for most interfaces, if a change has been missed it is unlikely that it is ever detected again.

The solution for this is straightforward. As a guideline, we recommend to implement a separate full comparison or reconciliation process for every delta-based interface. The quintessential example for this is a FOJ mechanism.

During regular operation, the delta-based interface can operate as usual. But, every now and then the full comparison process can 'mop up' any data changes that were missed – and detect any physical deletes to boot.

Having a full comparison process running in some quiet times for the solution, for example once per month in the weekend, can be an important safety-catch to capture missed data changes. If nothing was missed, the process will not yield any records.

But in our experience, you might be surprised what is sometimes left behind.

Automation

Only a small set of design metadata is required to generate LDA data logistics processes. This includes:

- → The relationship between the source and target data object
- → The data items, their relationships, and their data types
- → The primary key of the (source) data objects
- → The intended interface type

Using the schema for data solution automation, the relationship between the source and target data object is captured in a data object mapping. The data object mapping also contains a data item mapping that captures the source and target data items with their data types.

The data types are necessary to explicitly convert the source types into the standard LDA target types using the conventions encoded in the templates.

In many cases, the primary key details are required to support lookups and joins. Using a FOJ mechanism, for instance, the join is implemented on the primary key – which is why this must be available in the design metadata. This information is stored in the business key definition, which is a property of the data object mapping.

Lastly, we recommend recording the intended interfacing approach in the design metadata. This can be done in various ways, including using classifications or extensions.

This is especially important for LDA processes, because there are so many different possible variations. In a typical data solution, a large variety of interfaces exists to cater for the variety of technologies, systems, processes, and company policies.

In some cases, multiple different interfaces are necessary to integrate data even from a single operational system.

By recording what metadata is meant to be used by which template, the full set of data logistics processes can be automatically generated using DevOps pipelines, or similar.

Design metadata example

The following is an example LDA data object mapping.

This example assumes a physical model that has defaults defined for the inscription timestamp and inscription record id. The Audit Trail Id is also not explicitly mapped, because this will be generated by the control framework, and saved with the data.

The source timestamp is calculated by the data logistics process, for example as part of a FOJ process as described in the source timestamp section. The same FOJ process also determines the change data indicator.

These features are encoded in the template, and do not to need to be specified in design metadata.

Consider the following data object mapping:

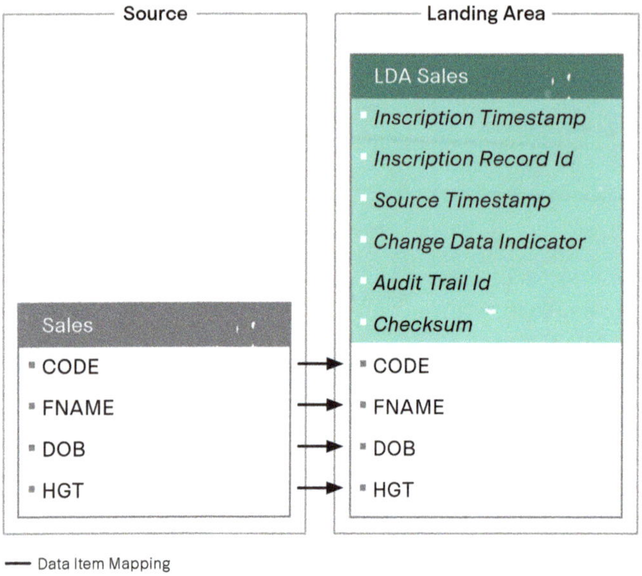

This mapping is defined in design metadata as:

```
{
 "dataObjectMappings": [
  {
   "name": "SalesMaster_to_LDA_Sales",
   "sourceDataObjects": [ { "name": "Sales" } ],
   "targetDataObject": { "name": "LDA_Sales" },
   "dataItemMappings": [
    {
     "sourceDataItems": [ { "name": "CODE" } ],
     "targetDataItem": { "name": "CODE" }
    },
    {
     "sourceDataItems": [ { "name": "FNAME" } ],
     "targetDataItem": { "name": "FNAME" }
    },
    {
     "sourceDataItems": [ { "name": "DOB" } ],
     "targetDataItem": { "name": "DOB" }
    },
    {
     "sourceDataItems": [ { "name": "HGT" } ],
     "targetDataItem": { "name": "HGT" }
    }
   ],
   "businessKeyDefinitions": [
    {
     "ordinalPosition": 1,
     "businessKeyComponents": [
      {
       "ordinalPosition": 1,
       "dataItem": { "name": "CODE" }
      }
     ]
    }
   ],
   "extensions": [
    {
     "key": "templateMapping",
     "value": "FullOuterJoin"
    }
   ]
  }
 ]
}
```

In this example, the 'CODE' column is the primary key in the operational system table 'Sales.' Data types for the data items have been omitted for brevity. There also is no need for a surrogate key in the business key definition.

This is all that is required to map a source data object to its LDA counterpart. The template that has been assigned to generate the code has been added as an extensions.

How this metadata is applied to a template is covered in the LDA solution pattern example section.

Solution pattern example

Processing data from an operational system into the data solution is, by some measures, the most difficult part of the data solution.

The possibilities for determining data delta are dependent on the systems, processes and policies that are in place for a given organization, as well as the underlying technologies and available software. Because of this there are many permutations of how data delta can be determined and loaded.

The key message is that the *best possible* incoming interface must be selected for each data set that is ingested into the data solution.

In many cases, all data objects for a given operational system are interfaced using the same pattern. But in some cases, it makes sense to specify the delta detection pattern at individual data object level.

Consider the scenario when an operational system contains a small number of very large data objects, but the majority of data objects only has a small record count. The objects with low record counts can be interfaced using a FOJ approach, whereas the large ones can be interfaced through a pull mechanism – and ideally have a separate weekly or monthly FOJ reconciliation process.

There are many implementation alternatives that achieve the same result by using different syntax. Each of these patterns may lead to specific templates for code generation. Templates are often tweaked to cater for different technical environments so that the best possible performance and efficiency can be achieved.

For this reason, various example templates are provided on our website: https://dtng.link/831oy.

A FOJ pattern is a convenient way to demonstrate many of the LDA requirements. An example LDA pattern for this is described below.

Example pattern for a LDA process

1) Truncate the data set, removing all existing records from the LDA target data object where the processed data will be stored

2) Extract the the necessary data from the source system, including key attributes and adding a checksum to assist in the comparison — excluding the change data indicator

3) Retrieve the most recent valid records from the PSA, identifying the latest available version of each record and ignoring any records marked as logically deleted

4) Compare the incoming data with the existing historical data, matching the records on their unique identifiers and comparing the checksum values:

- **a)** Mark the record as change data indicator 'C':
  - If a record is new (exists in the latest data but not in the historical data), mark it as an addition ('C')
  - If a record exists in both but has changed (based on the checksum), mark it as an update ('C')
- **b)** Mark the record as a logical delete ('D') if a record is missing (exists in the historical data but not in the new data)
- **c)** If a record is unchanged, discard it since no action is needed

5) Store only the relevant record — insert the new or updated, and deleted records into the target location

This example pattern compares a snapshot of incoming ('source') data to the 'most recent' snapshot of the data that is available in the PSA.

The most recent PSA record is evaluated as the *descending ordering* of the PSA data by the natural key, the original key as defined in the data source, the inscription timestamp, and the inscription record id.

Any 'most recent' PSA records that have the Change Data Indicator of 'D' must also be filtered out before the comparison. This information was already evaluated as not available in the source data set and identified as a logical delete, so does not need to be compared again.

The comparison itself done by means of a full outer join on the natural key.

A checksum is created for each record of the incoming data set, and compared against the checksum of the matching record from the PSA, if any. The concepts of using checksums is further detailed in the ⚐ checksums section.

If, after the comparison, the PSA key is NULL, then the record can be inserted as a new record into the landing data object, including the checksum value and the 'C' change data indicator value.

If the incoming data key is NULL, then the record is evaluated as a logical delete and inserted in the landing data object with the change data indicator as 'D.'

If both keys are present, and the checksum values are different, the record is evaluate as a change. Again, it will be inserted into the landing data object including the checksum and 'C' change data indicator value. If the checksum values are the same, the record can be discarded – there is no new data to insert.

Persistent staging area

↗ The persistent staging area represents the historical archive of all transactions that have been presented to the data solution.

In our reference architecture, the persistent staging area (PSA) it is the foundation on which the data solution is built.

The overall goal of the PSA is to provide a transactional view of all data changes. From a design and implementation perspective, this is a relatively straightforward area to develop – especially if the LDA is implemented separately and the data delta is therefore already available.

However, if no LDA is designed the PSA must also incorporate the requirements otherwise addressed by the LDA – including ensuring incoming data represents a (transactional) data delta when this is not the case already.

Persistent staging area data object structure

PSA data objects contain the same columns as LDA data objects.

There is an important structural difference, however, because the PSA will have a primary key defined on the inscription timestamp, the inscription record id, and the original primary key column(s) from the incoming data.

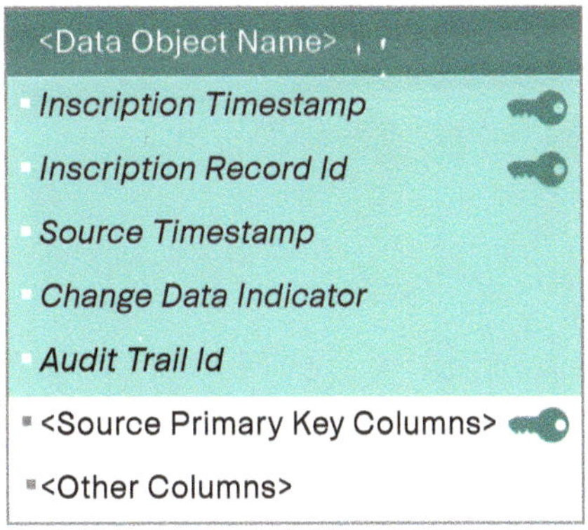

The PSA is historized, time-variant, and this is enforced by the primary key that includes the inscription timestamp. Only one version of the record may exists at a particular timestamp of arrival in the data solution.

The reason the inscription record id is *also* incorporated in the primary key is to ensure uniqueness when multiple changes for the same incoming key arrive on exactly the same time — as covered in the ⚐ inscription record id section.

As is the case for the LDA, all columns are nullable in principle, and no reference constraints (foreign keys) are enforced. An exception is made, however, for columns that are part of the primary key as most data platforms *require* these to be not nullable.

In addition to the standard columns described here, the following optional columns can be considered as well:

→ The record source indicator
→ The checksum

Inscription timestamp

The inscription timestamp for the PSA
is structurally the same as it is for the LDA.

If an LDA is available, the PSA inherits the inscription timestamp from there. In other words, when the LDA has already set the inscription timestamp, the PSA can copy its value — as opposed to setting the inscription timestamp upon insertion into the PSA.

If no LDA is implemented, the inscription timestamp
should be set by the PSA.

While it is also possible to set the inscription timestamp when inserting the record from the LDA into the PSA, there may be a delay between the data delta detection and the PSA insertion process that can become confusing for auditability.

Because of this, it is conceptually better to just copy the inscription timestamp value if it's already available, as this more accurately represents the timestamp the record became known to the data solution.

Inscription record id

Similar to the inscription timestamp approach, the inscription record id is copied from the LDA — if implemented.

When no LDA is available, and data delta is inserted into the PSA directly, the inscription record id can be evaluated there.

Modifying the inscription timestamp with the inscription record id

Since the inscription record id is part of the primary key in time-variant data objects —including the PSA— we want to address an approach commonly seen in projects but strongly advise against: modifying the inscription timestamp when loading data into the target object. This technique involves appending the inscription record id as a small additional time unit (e.g., milliseconds or microseconds).

This approach is often used to avoid adding a separate uniquification value — especially in PSA and Satellite (context) objects.

Since the inscription record id is always unique, incremental, and numerical, the inscription timestamp can be uniquefied without needing to add the inscription record id to the primary key.

Simple SQL statements can be used to implement this, for example:

```
SELECT *,
  DATEADD(microsecond,[Inscription_Record_Id],[Inscription_Timestamp]) AS [Inscription_Timestamp]
FROM <Table>
```

While this method appears simple, modifying the inscription timestamp this way introduces scalability limitations which may occur when loading large volumes of data.

When large batches of change records are processed, the inscription record id value grows into very high numbers. Using the inscription record id to modify the inscription timestamp in this case may lead to ever-larger increases of the inscription timestamp value – to the point that these modified values may 'overtake' inscription timestamp values from *later* batches.

This breaks the assertion timeline, because the actual order of arrival is lost.

Thus, while timestamp modification may seem like a simple fix, it ultimately does not scale well for enterprise-level solutions.

Therefore, for long-term scalability and consistency, we strongly recommend adding the inscription record id to the primary key rather than modifying the inscription timestamp.

Source timestamp

The source timestamp for the PSA follows the same pattern as the inscription timestamp and inscription record id, and is inherited from the LDA if available.

When an LDA is not implemented, this value is determined by the data delta detection mechanism when loading data into the PSA – as covered in the source timestamp section.

Change data indicator

Once again, the change data indicator follows the same approach as most of the standard columns for the PSA.

It is copied from the landing area, if implemented, and otherwise determined by the change data indicator evaluation when loading into the PSA.

Audit Trail Id

The Audit Trail Id for the PSA is issued for the unique execution of the PSA process.

This value is *not* copied from the LDA, as it represents the data movements from the LDA into the PSA.

This way, it is at all times possible to audit the way in which data delta was derived and ultimately processed into the PSA.

Optional columns

Record source indicator

The PSA record source indicator, if required, can be copied from the LDA or set by the PSA process directly. In all cases, the record source can be queried via the Audit Trail Id.

Checksum

A checksum is considered an optional column because similar results can be achieved through methods such as column-by-column comparison. The decision to include a checksum depends on various considerations outlined in the checksum section. Despite being optional, we include it in our examples and reference implementation as a persisted column because —in our opinion— its advantages outweigh the drawbacks.

Whenever a checksum value is used in the staging layer, we recommend to record the value in the PSA – in line with our suggestion to store any checksum used in the target data object.

Specifically for the PSA, the checksum may also be used as a natural key column when no strong key candidate exists in the incoming data. This is outlined in the defining a primary key section.

Persistent staging area design pattern

The following section summarizes the features of the PSA into a design pattern, supported by examples for code generation and implementation.

The full pattern, as always, is recommended to be captured following the *pattern documentation structure,* which can be accessed via our website: https://dtng.link/o85bw.

The ultimate goal of the PSA is to create a transactional view of all data (events) that have ever been presented to, or detected by, the data solution.

Assuming the LDA is already implemented, most of the preparation has been completed, and the data delta is available. If not, the PSA processes should also incorporate everything that has been done for the LDA.

In our reference architecture, the PSA is the centerpiece of the staging layer. The LDA exists to facilitate the preparation of the transactions, the data changes, for the PSA.

We define the PSA process as *insert-only,* where data changes are historized. This is done as per the assertion timeline, by adding the inscription timestamp and inscription record id to the primary key of the PSA object.

Simply stated, the PSA pattern can be described as *select the data delta from the landing area, and insert this into the PSA if it has not yet been processed.* Evaluating if a data delta has not yet been processed can be implemented using a lookup to the target PSA object, on the primary key.

As part of the pattern, it is recommended to implement a compacting mechanism to combat data redundancy and so that the option is available to reduce the column scope when it is appropriate to do so. The reasoning for this is the same as was already covered in the landing area design pattern.

Considerations

As with any templates, some considerations might be made, and documented in the design pattern as design decisions.

Defining a primary key

The primary key of a PSA object enforces uniqueness in transactions, ensuring that a data change can only appear once at a specific point in time – marked by the inscription timestamp and made unique by adding the inscription record id to the key.

Since the PSA is a back room process –where constraints are removed everywhere– having a primary key might seem contradictory. However, the PSA primary key is effectively fault-tolerant because it primarily relies on values controlled by the data solution itself.

The LDA prepares the delta and issues the inscription timestamp and inscription record id. If this process is configured correctly, it is simply not possible for the subsequent PSA data processing step to fail.

If the process *does* fail, there must be an issue either in the LDA pattern or with the definition of the primary key. Either way, it is preferable to receive a failure than for this issue to go unnoticed – which should, and typically does, occurs during development. Once set up and tested correctly, it is expected to never fail again.

In most cases, it is straightforward to determine what the primary key should be: it is the primary key of the original (source) data object, plus the inscription timestamp and inscription record id.

But, not in all cases.

One of the operational systems in a project we've seen had a peculiar design. In this system, the tables had primary keys defined on many columns – more columns, at least, than the unique index that was also in place for the same table.

The primary key in this case was unique, but not as unique as the unique index. This creates interesting patterns in data changes when using the primary key for change detection. Primary keys can be updated in this scenario, which triggers a two-step operation in most database systems: a delete for the previous state of the record and an insert of the new state of the record. It's a logical update. While this can happen for well-defined primary keys, it occurs much more frequently in this situation – and more importantly, not as intended!

This is just one of the many occurrences in the world of data that demonstrate the necessity of applying common sense, and not blindly trusting operational system designs.

A primary key might not be available or even NULL. There are numerous reasons this might occur, often stemming from system design, and it is not always possible to influence this from the data domain.

The solution for the PSA is that primary keys must be defined when they are missing. This can be an artificial key identified through data profiling of the operational system data. Or, in more extreme cases where no primary key can be identified at all, it is recommended to define a primary key based on the full-record checksum. This way, at least, idempotent data processing can be ensured going forward.

Reusing or recalculating checksums

As covered in the ⚐ checksum section, storing checksums in the target data object when they are used for comparison is our recommended approach.

For the PSA, the checksum is often already calculated in the LDA, so the checksum value can simply be copied.

It is not necessary to calculate the checksum again, unless the scope of columns has changed between the LDA and the PSA.

Physical storage

At the physical level, the PSA can be implemented in many ways. It could be implemented as a series of files on a storage account, or it could be a set of tables in a database.

Very large data solutions often have a PSA implemented on a scalable file storage environment, and sometimes only having the presentation layer residing in a database.

Smaller data solutions might benefit from the ease-of-use that a database PSA can provide.

In both cases, the PSA can also be stored as variant or blob object, where the entire payload is saved in JSON format (for example, or equivalent). Using this approach, the PSA data object is physically defined as the primary key and metadata columns, and a blob or variant that contains the *entire* PSA record.

All of these approaches can work, as long as the functional requirements of the staging layer, as documented in this chapter are met.

Schema drift

Schema drift occurs when data objects regularly change structure, for instance when columns are added or removed, or their position in the data set changes.

Data logistics processes tend to fail when expected columns are not present, because these processes are tied to those column names.

This is especially relevant for the PSA because of the one-to-one mapping to the data object structure in the operational system, a concept referred to as 'early binding.'

Changes to downstream processes can be handled via regular change management, but the LDA and PSA are usually impacted directly.

Defining how to manage schema drift is another consideration that influences the physical implementation of the PSA.

To a certain extent, changes in the data object structure can be automatically detected and addressed. For example, adding and removing columns is a process that can be managed automatically. But, there will always be cases when an implementation decision is required.

When new columns are added

When columns are added to a source data object, and by extent to the PSA, the implementation often is straightforward. The new data item will be mapped to the PSA, and added to the checksum.

The consequence of this decision is that usually a data change will be detected for each record in the PSA. This is because the checksum value will change, even if the new column does not hold data. The result is that the PSA will effectively double in size, because *each active record* will receive a change.

Data teams can choose to address this, if they want, by running a compacting maintenance process to eliminate full-record duplicates and ensuring the checksums are all incorporating the new column.

Because technologies keep changing, we would like to refer to our website for practical examples on how to implement this: https://dtng.link/v22oa.

When existing columns are removed

A similar dynamic takes place when a column is removed from the source data object.

The removal of the column will result in a new check-sum, which is correct given that the data payload will be significantly different. This, too, triggers a new change transaction in the PSA for each active record.

The column should not be physically removed from the PSA, as this would impact existing history and downstream usage. After all, it is a fact that the data change has existed in the past – and this must be preserved.

When columns are switching positions

Columns that 'move around' in the data object may cause issues in data logistics processes.

Most data logistics processes refer to columns by name, or use expressions to interpret patterns to match incoming fields, instead of using column positions. The order is less relevant in this case, and does not cause problems.

When relying on the ordinal position, however, a serious issue can occur when values from certain columns are inserted into incorrect columns in the staging layer.

In this case, the only real protection against this risk materializing is to ensure strong change processes across the organization, and implement test cases as outlined in the ⚐ notification and ⚐ testing sections.

When columns take on a different meaning

Arguably the most difficult scenario occurs when existing columns start to contain data that represents something entirely different. The data logistics process might not fail *technically,* but downstream impacts are likely when the –carefully modeled– data is associated with a concept it was not intended for.

As before, ensuring a robust change process in the organization, and securing this with test cases from the monitoring framework are the best options from what in reality is a limited set of alternatives.

When an existing data object ceases to exist, and appears under a different name

It may happen, that a source data object becomes end-of-life. Operational systems evolve over time, and sometimes modifications in their physical model may directly impact the PSA.

If a certain data object is no longer supported, the recommended approach is to stop the interface (via the data logistics control framework) but leave everything else as-is. The 'orphan' PSA data object will forever remain as an immutable archive of past transactions, and retain its downstream mappings to the data solution's integration layer.

Any new data objects can be treated as new interfaces, potentially being mapped to the same concepts as its previous incarnation.

Additional considerations on schema drift

Many opinions and technologies exist on the topic of schema drift, and most can be categorized as focusing on 'early binding' versus 'late binding.' This can loosely be translated at fixing the schema in the data logistics process or object definition (early binding), or accepting the inputs as-is, and interpreting these later (late binding).

A viable approach for implementing the PSA is using the afore-mentioned blob or variant data types. After all, if the PSA data is represented physically as a JSON object, the schema can change without too much *initial* impact – leaving the downstream impacts out of the consideration for now. This is a late binding approach, the schema must be interpreted upon selection from the PSA.

A similar approach is implemented in various data technologies. Schema drift support is native in certain storage account or pub/sub technologies. This is typically implemented by separating the data storage from its interpretation (schema). Both are versioned independently.

The data will always have a system-driven immutable timestamp, which fulfills the same conceptual role as the inscription timestamp in the data solution. The schema itself is version-controlled as well. This way, the *schema* at a point in time is used to interpret the *data* at a point in time.

The option is available to apply a similar concept for the data solution. By storing the PSA payload in a JSON file (or similar) the interpretation can be done downstream using a similar versioning approach.

In all cases, our recommendation is to always evaluate the data going into the PSA using test cases, so that any unexpected behavior can be detected, and acted on, automatically and rapidly.

Batching inscription timestamps

In some data solution implementations, the inscription timestamp is defined once and then applied to all records that are part of the workflow. Typically, this is the start timestamp of the data logistics process, or even sometimes the start of the top-level batch ('main batch'). All records that are part of a process run will receive this value.

This is not an incorrect approach in principle, but can sometimes be limiting for the (future) purposes of the data solution.

When using the batch, or module, timestamp for the inscription timestamp some detail, *fidelity*, is lost compared to when this is set individually for each incoming record.

The resulting limiting factor is the ability to *pinpoint* exactly when which record actually arrived in the data solution. Using the approach advocated in this book —by setting the timestamp for each individual record upon insert— this is always unequivocal.

Downstream effects of this early design decision is that 'time travel' —the approach for filtering records across the assertion timeline— later on will be more coarse because all you have is workflow-level timestamps.

Our recommendation is to *not* use the same inscription timestamp for all records that are part of a data logistics process execution.

The Audit Trail Id will always contain batch and module start and end timestamps.

Automation

To generate PSA data logistics processes, an even smaller set of metadata is required compared to the LDA.

The only components that are essential are:
- → The relationship between the source and target data object
- → The primary key of the data objects

The relationship between the source and target data object is captured in a data object mapping, which includes the data item mapping. There is no need to add the data types, because no further data type conversions are required. Everything is now driven by conventions, and there is no risk of implicit conversions.

The primary key metadata is required to ensure the data logistics process behaves in an idempotent manner. This is covered in more detail in the PSA solution pattern example.

From this point onwards, it is no longer essential to record the template type in metadata. This is still possible, of course, but the PSA process is a single, generic pattern that is applied to all data irrespective of its origins.

Design metadata example

This section outlines an example data object mapping from an LDA source data object to a PSA target data object.

Most column values can be copied directly. This can be defined in standard data item mappings, or convention-based by adding the mapping in the code generation template.

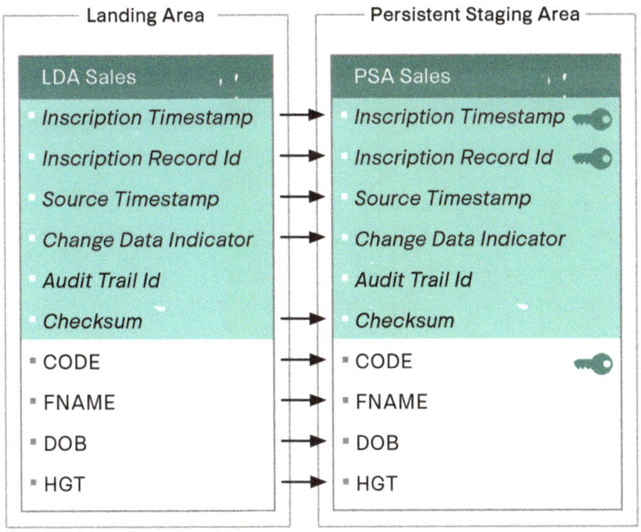

— Data Item Mapping

Note that the Audit Trail Id, as always, is not mapped. This value is provided at runtime by the data logistics control framework.

In design metadata, this is recorded as:

```
{
 "dataObjectMappings": [
  {
   "name": "LDA_Sales_to_PSA_Sales",
   "sourcedataObjects": [ { "name": "LDA_Sales" } ],
   "targetdataObject": { "name": "PSA_Sales" },
   "dataItemMappings": [
    {
     "sourcedataItems": [ { "name": "CODE" } ],
     "targetdataItem": {"name": "CODE" }
    },
    {
     "sourcedataItems": [ { "name": "FNAME" } ],
     "targetdataItem": { "name": "FNAME" }
    },
    {
     "sourcedataItems": [ { "name": "DOB" } ],
     "targetdataItem": { "name": "DOB" }
    },
    {
     "sourcedataItems": [ { "name": "HGT" } ],
     "targetdataItem": { "name": "HGT" }
    }
   ],
   "businessKeyDefinitions": [
    {
     "ordinalPosition": 1,
     "businessKeyComponents": [
      {
       "ordinalPosition": 1,
       "dataItem": {"name": "CODE" }
      }
     ]
    }
   ]
  }
 ]
}
```

For the most part, PSA data object mapping metadata is very similar to the LDA example. They are both relatively straightforward, applying direct data item mappings to target data items —which typically have the same name.

The standard framework columns, such as inscription timestamp and inscription record id are not explicitly specified in metadata. While it's possible to add these as data item mappings, the template can also operate convention-based and apply standard mappings for these columns as they are guaranteed to be available.

Bear in mind that the order of columns is significant when using checksums for comparison. The order of values in the checksum is a factor in determining the outcome, and changing the order will yield different results.

As with the LDA, the 'CODE' column, has been added to the business key definition. In the templates, this important metadata can be used to generate join/lookup conditions for a number of scenarios.

An example template that applies this metadata is covered in the PSA solution pattern example section.

Solution pattern example

Processing data into the PSA can be relatively straightforward, since —as per the reference architecture— the data delta is already available in the LDA.

In this case, loading the data can be as simple as directly copying the data delta into the PSA. This is demonstrated by the SQL statement below.

```
INSERT INTO <PSA Table (<Columns>)
SELECT <Columns>
FROM <LDA Table> LDA
```

However, this does not satisfy the *fundamental principles for data logistics*. Using the above approach, the data logistics process is not idempotent, because running it twice will cause problems. Inserting the same data for a second time will violate the primary key and unique key constraints, or insert duplicate data when this is not enforced.

For this reason, we recommend adding a 'safety catch' to check if the primary key already exists for a given point in time. If this is the case, the record can be discarded. The PSA key includes the inscription timestamp and inscription record id, and since these values are issued by the data solution they can be relied upon. Every new record in the LDA will always receive a new (later) inscription timestamp value, so if a value is presented to the PSA that already exists there it *must* mean that the record has been processed into the PSA earlier.

Having this type of safety catch is invaluable when working with time-variant data. It will prevent processing the same data delta multiple times.

Consider the updated example below:

```
SELECT <Columns>
FROM <LDA Table> LDA
LEFT OUTER JOIN <PSA Table> PSA
  ON PSA.<Key(s)> = LDA.<Key(s)>
  AND PSA.Inscription_Timestamp = LDA.Inscription_Timestamp
  AND PSA.Inscription_Record_Id = LDA.Inscription_Record_Id
WHERE PSA.<Key> IS NULL -- Prevent reprocessing
```

This approach will filter out any records that were already processed.

At a basic level, the safety catch prevents technical errors when the PSA process is accidentally run multiple times, but the underlying LDA data delta has not yet been refreshed. But this feature also facilitates *re-initialization and refactoring* when applied to the integration layer, one of the core engine components.

By virtue of the safety catch, data processing dependencies are removed. The full power of this will become visible when working with *contextual data*.

But, there is still more to add to the template to make it as flexible and robust as it can be.

Consider the example below, but also check our website for complete SQL examples and corresponding code-generation templates, as they're too large to meaningfully print in book format: https://dtng.link/gv9q3.

Example pattern for a PSA process

Extract all required columns from the LDA object

- Select the in-scope columns
- Assign a row number to each record based on its natural key(s), inscription timestamp, and inscription record id — ensuring a deterministic ordering of records

Prevent reprocessing of the data by checking if the record already exists in the PSA

- Perform a LEFT JOIN between the LDA and the PSA table. The join is based on natural key(s), inscription timestamp, and inscription record id
- If a match is found, it means the record already exists in PSA and it should be ignored to avoid duplication

```
-- Prevent reloading already processed data
LEFT OUTER JOIN <PSA Table> PSA
  ON PSA.<Key(s)> = LDA.<Key(s)>
  AND PSA.Inscription_Timestamp = LDA.Inscription_Timestamp
  AND PSA.Inscription_Record_Id = LDA.Inscription_Record_Id
```

Due to the order of operations, the filtering of the matches is defined later in the logic when using SQL:

```
WHERE PSA.<Key> IS NULL -- Prevent reprocessing
```

Retrieve the most recently received, non-deleted PSA record for each key. Multiple operations are executed to determine the latest version of each record that is not marked as deleted (change data indicator 'D'). This involves:

- Finding the most recent inscription timestamp per natural key
- Identifying the highest inscription record id within that timestamp
- Assigning a row number to establish ranking
- Filtering out logical-deleted records

```
-- Query the most recently arrived PSA record which is not logically deleted.
LEFT OUTER JOIN
(
 SELECT
  A.<Key(s)>,
  A.[Lookup_Checksum] AS [Lookup_Lookup_Checksum],
  A.[Change_Data_Indicator] AS [Lookup_Change_Data_Indicator]
 FROM <PSA Table> A
 JOIN
 (
  SELECT
   <Key(s)>,
   [Inscription_Timestamp] AS [Max_Inscription_Timestamp],
   MAX([Inscription_Record_Id]) OVER (
     PARTITION BY <Key(s)>, [Inscription_Timestamp]
     ORDER BY <Key(s)>, [Inscription_Timestamp]
   ) AS [Max_Inscription_Record_Id],
   ROW_NUMBER() OVER (
```

```
            PARTITION BY <Key(s)>
            ORDER BY <Natural Key(s), [Inscription_Timestamp] DESC
        ) AS [Max_RowNum]
      FROM <PSA Table>
    ) C
      ON A.<Key(s)> = C.<Key(s)>
  AND A.[Inscription_Timestamp] = C.[Max_Inscription_Timestamp]
     AND A.[Inscription_Record_Id] = C.[Max_Inscription_Record_Id]
     AND 1 = C.[Max_RowNum]
   WHERE A.[Lookup_Change_Data_Indicator] != 'D'
```

Compare the new record against the latest PSA record from the previous step.
Three comparisons take place:

- If the checksum differs, the record is considered changed
- If the checksum is the same but the change data indicator differs, the record is *still* considered changed
- Otherwise, the record is unchanged and ignored

Filter out records that do not require insertion

- If a record has a row number (from step 1) greater than 1, it is inserted without further checks. The LDA process, with its CDC features, already ensures any row number other than 1 is a genuine change record
- If a record has row number 1 it requires checking against the most recent PSA record.
  It is inserted only if:
  - It has a different checksum from the last recorded version
  - It has the same checksum but a different change data indicator

Insert the final data set into the PSA table

The final version of the pattern (see our website: https://dtng.link/gv9q3) is quite larger than the first example. This example also selects the data from the LDA, and implements the safety catch that comes with using time-variant data.

The template adds a new feature to the above, a check to make sure the oldest of the records in the incoming data delta (LDA) is different than the most recent record in the PSA.

Landing Area

Inscription Timestamp	Data (payload)
2023-12-02 17:59	X
2023-12-02 15:47	Y
2023-12-02 10:00	Z
2023-12-02 09:15	A

PSA

Inscription Timestamp	Data (payload)
2023-12-01 12:22	A
2023-12-01 12:10	B
2023-12-01 12:01	C
2023-12-01 11:55	A
...	...

In this approach the oldest data data record is compared against the most recent PSA record. Please note that various standard columns such as the business key(s) or inscription record id are not displayed for brevity.

If highlighted records are the same (equal checksums), the record in the data delta can be discarded because it is not really a change from the PSA's perspective. If they are different, the record can be inserted.

Any subsequent records in the data delta, after the 'oldest' one can be inserted without further consideration, because these are change records by definition.

How can this data delta and PSA records ever be different? The answer lies in potentially different column scopes for the LDA and PSA, for example when the PSA processes fewer columns than available in the LDA.

Implementing the above feature makes the template even more robust, as changes in column scopes will not break the PSA process.

No matter what happens, the PSA process can be run without failure, any time.

The ⚐record compacting section will go into more details on this process, when it happens, and why it matters. If there are strong reasons to do so, the compacting algorithm described there can also be added to the PSA pattern.

Staging layer orchestration

Even though a variety of interfacing mechanisms and technologies may be required to connect to all operational systems to the data solution, the orchestration of these processes in the staging layer is relatively straightforward.

The overall approach for integrating data, taking into account any dependencies in the order of processing, is covered in the ⚐orchestration section.

↗ The data solution ensures that any data delta that has been received or detected in the staging layer is fully committed to downstream data objects before it can be released.

However, for the staging layer a few specific guidelines apply:
- → Data delta is retained until fully committed in all downstream data objects, and
- → The data logistics processes are designed to run as often as possible

Ensuring that data delta is committed

The data solution should ensure that any data delta that has been received or detected is fully committed to downstream data objects before it can be 'released.'

This is especially important for the LDA, where data delta may be temporarily held for further processing. This data delta must not be truncated or overwritten until it has been successfully processed into its designated target data objects.

By doing so, the data solution will ensure the overall consistency of the data in the solution.

If a PSA is part of the architecture, the workflow usually stops when data is successfully committed in the PSA. Once the data is available in the PSA, it can be processed into downstream data objects independently.

If the solution architecture does *not* include a PSA, then the workflow is only completed when *all* direct downstream processes have successfully completed.

In all cases, the aim is to protect the data delta until it has been fully processed. Only then, the data delta can be truncated and the next data delta can be determined by the subsequent execution of the process.

It is the job of the data logistics control framework to ensure that this is done correctly. An implementation of the approach covered in this section often is done as per the below image:

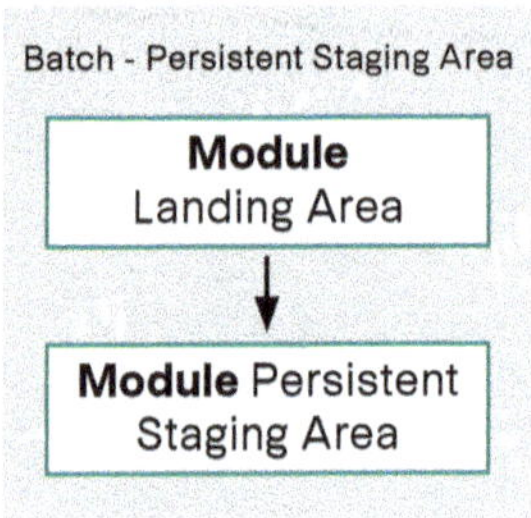

By wrapping the LDA process and PSA process —both registered as modules— in a batch, the control framework will ensure that the individual modules can not be restarted until the overall batch has been successfully completed.

Additional orchestration approaches can be feasible, and options for these rely on the specific architecture that has been selected.

Design for processing data at any frequency

Our overall recommendation is to design any data logistics process to run at any time, as an independent module.

This design pattern reduces re-engineering and increases flexibility and ease of maintenance, because the processes themselves do not require modification if the schedule may change.

However, due to the LDA's unique purpose it is an exception to this rule. An LDA module itself should *not* be run independently, because that will risk losing data delta that may not have been fully committed to downstream data objects.

Because of this, we recommend making sure the LDA is configured to be in the same batch as its downstream processes as we have outlined in the previous section.

The batch itself is still designed to run at any frequency, as is the PSA module itself.

This leads to a design where the batch with the LDA and PSA processes (the boxes in the following figure) can be run independently, processing data, and safely committing this independently of other processes.

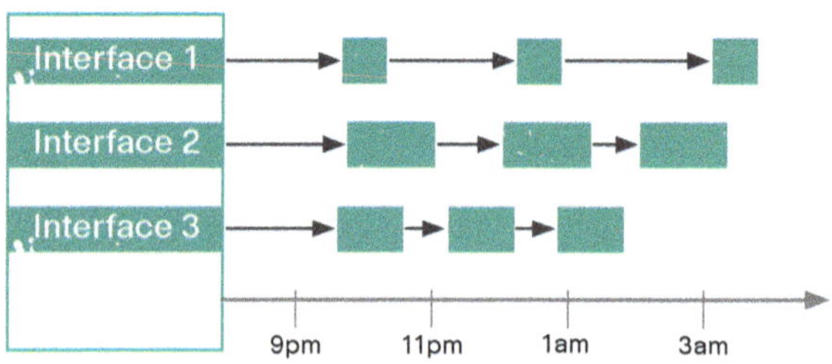

As a final note, just because the processes are designed to execute continuously, at any frequency, does not mean they have to be. The scheduling frequency, from once every period to near real-time or streaming must be meaningful for the business requirements and expectations.

It is simply one of the many ways of future-proofing the data solution.

Integration layer implementation — back room

The key purpose of the integration layer is to facilitate integration of disparate data in a flexible manner for both data ingestion and delivery.

To achieve this, we organize the data into the three main entity types that were introduced in the *overview of the data solution design.*

These are the Core Business Concepts (CBCs), the Natural Business Relationships (NBRs), and the Context entities.

↗ The key purpose of the integration layer is to facilitate integration of disparate data in a flexible manner for both data ingestion and delivery. To achieve this, we organize data into Core Business Concepts, Natural Business Relationships, and Context entities.

As we process data from the staging layer to the integration layer, the following concepts are applied:

- Design the CBCs, NBRs, and Context entities, and organize the data accordingly
- Data solution key distribution
- Historization of context and relationships

This approach is consistently implemented for both the base integration area and the derived integration area. The primary distinction between these areas is that the base integration area does not apply destructive transformations. Here, the data remains essentially 'raw,' unchanged in content from when it was received.

It is, however, *modeled* around the identified CBCs and their NBRs.

The derived integration area, on the other hand, uses the same entities but introduces a layer of business rules, transformations, and complexities that alter the data and shape it into its intended format where necessary.

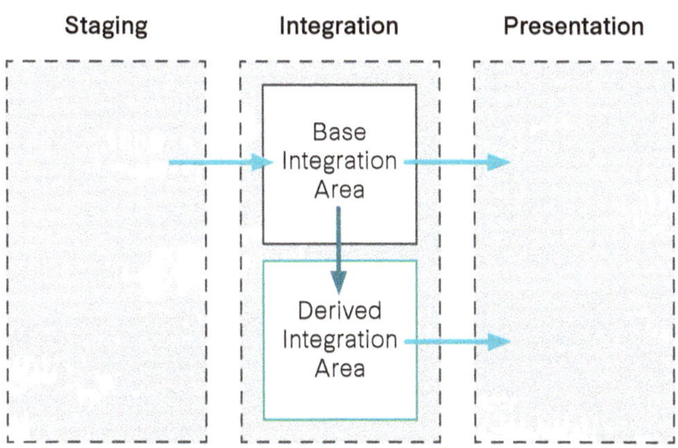

The diagram above illustrates that data arrives from the staging layer into the base integration area. From here, data that is already fit for purpose can move downstream to the presentation layer. Business rules are applied in the derived integration area only if required.

The presentation layer accepts data from both the base and derived integration areas.

A brief introduction to Data Vault

To explain the technical delivery of the integration layer, we use Data Vault methodology. While various techniques can be used to implement the integration layer, Data Vault is one of the most commonly used approaches.

Data Vault is part of a family of implementation techniques including Anchor Modeling, Focal Point, Head and Version, and various proprietary approaches, and combinations of all of these.

In this book, we maintain a clear distinction between the logical specification of the architecture and its physical implementation. The implementation can vary based on development philosophies, opinions, and technical opportunities and limitations.

We use Data Vault as our physical implementation approach and aim to use holistic naming for terms and objects whenever possible. When mapping Data Vault to the logical terms and definitions, the following applies:

- → The physical implementation of a Core Business Concept is a *Hub* table
- → Natural Business Relationships are *Link* tables in Data Vault
- → Context entities are called *Satellites*

What is Data Vault?

Data Vault concepts were first published in 2002[41] by Dan Linstedt in The Data Warehouse Newsletter (TDAN) as a series of five articles covering the fundamentals of Data Vault modeling.

Over time, the technique has evolved, and various similar dialects of Data Vault exist, maintained by different groups.

Data Vault is defined as a *detail oriented, historical tracking* and *uniquely linked set of normalized tables* that support one or more functional areas of the business:

- → Detail-oriented: storing data at the lowest available level of detail (grain)
- → Historical tracking: capturing all changes that occur
- → Uniquely linked: modeling relationships as they logically exist between business concepts
- → Normalized: separating core business concepts and their business keys (Hubs) from contextual data (Satellites)

It is a 'hybrid' data modeling approach that combines concepts from normalization (e.g., 3rd Normal Form — 3NF) and Dimensional Modeling, both traditional techniques for designing Data Warehouse platforms.

Data Vault table types

Data Vault divides the data into Hubs, Links, and Satellites.

Hubs

Hubs represent ***business entities,*** the 'things' that are meaningful to the business, part of the business processes. They are the core concepts around which the model revolves, and are used by the business to track, locate, and identify information.

Each Hub is defined by a ***business key,*** which uniquely identifies an instance of the business concept. What constitutes a business key is specific to each organization; what is critical for one may not be for another. Even when the same concepts are used across organizations, the implementation may look very different due to the variation in system landscapes.

For instance, some organizations might model different types of employees as individual Hubs, while others might only have a single 'employee' Hub. Determining the correct granularity and selecting the appropriate business key is an essential modeling task that requires a deep understanding of the business and collaboration with subject matter experts.

Links

Links represent relationships, depicting how business entities interact with each other.

The most straightforward example of a relationship is a foreign key, but relationships can, and should, also be modeled based on logical connections, regardless of their implementation in operational systems. In some Data Vault implementation approaches, transactions are modeled as relationships, while in others, they may be modeled as Hubs.

Examples of relationships include:

- An intermediary selling a policy
- Risk covered within a policy term
- Claims against a policy risk cover
- Risk cover payment transaction for a risk cover within a policy (header) made by a customer, related to a claim

Satellites

Satellites provide context, offering descriptive properties about a business entity or, depending on the Data Vault dialect, about the relationships between entities.

They contain the descriptive data that forms much of the model substance and add time variance, as they capture the data changes over time. When the context describes a CBC, it includes descriptive information about that entity and the way it changes over time. When the context pertains to a relationship (a 'Link-Satellite'), it describes the interaction between two or more CBCs and how this changes over time.

Examples of Satellite content include:

- The name and date of birth of a policyholder
- The description of a product or service
- The date and time when an incident was reported

Unified decomposition

In the introduction to the integration layer, we mentioned that one of its main goals is the reorganization of data to align with a more business-focused data model. This involves separating the original, raw data into smaller modular parts and structuring it around CBCs.

By doing so, data sets from potentially many different systems consolidate around the CBCs and its context tables, identified by the business key.

In ELM, this is called *unified decomposition*[42]. A key tenet of unified decomposition is the understanding that everything changes, and that the impact of these changes can be minimized by isolating the changing parts.

- Decomposition covers the intent to break data into smaller components to enhance flexibility, agility, and adaptability. This approach allows for capturing data that can be interpreted or modified in various ways
- Unification refers to the approach that we aim to integrate data from different systems into a common, agreed-upon standard view as well

Each data set containing the original (raw) data in the staging layer typically includes some identifiers (business keys) for CBCs, some context, and some elements that describe relationships between CBCs. The modeling effort focuses on identifying these components and mapping them to the correct entities in the target integration layer model.

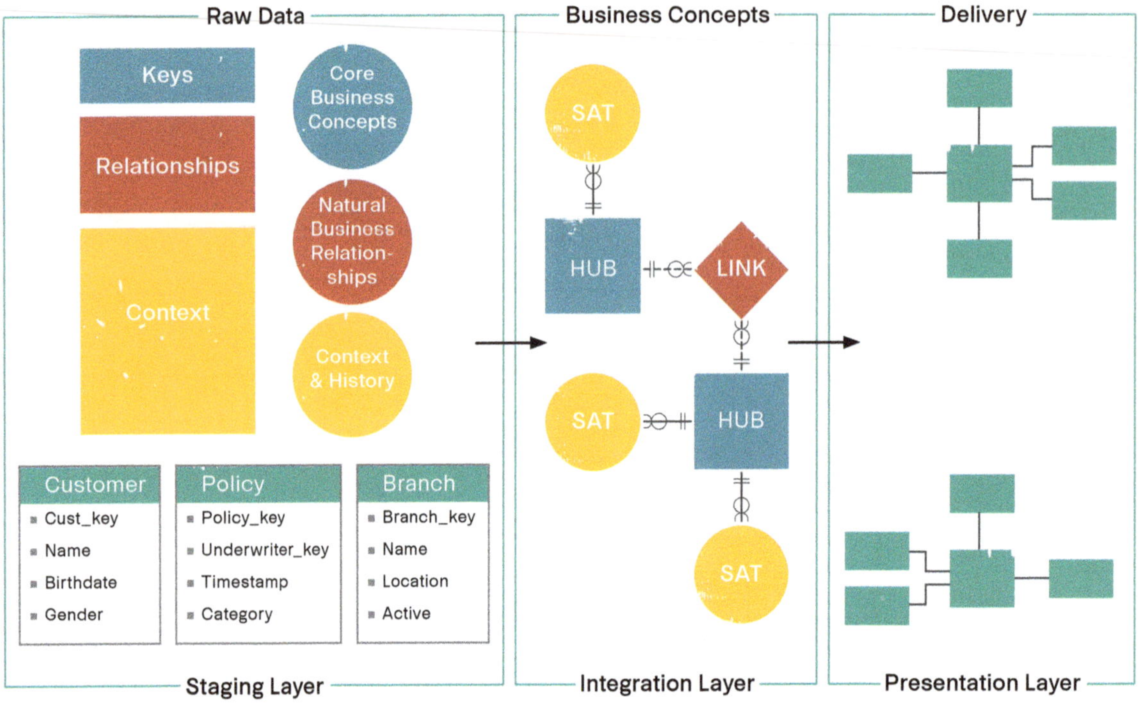

Defining whether a data element should be a CBC, NBR, or contextual property is a data modeling activity. Most projects will define an initial aspirational business or information model and begin mapping various data points to this model.

Over time, the model will evolve until it finally (and hopefully) settles into a form that is fit for purpose. For Engine Thinking, two key points are relevant:

1) The model is subject to change, and the final product is likely to differ greatly from its original concept
2) The mapping from data to the model is an interpretation that might need to be reconsidered

It's likely that a data point initially perceived as context may be *remodeled* as a CBC over the course of the data solution's lifetime.

The requirement to reconsider some of the modeling choices and refactor them in an elegant way is what data Engine Thinking is all about.

The integration layer model

The resulting model is a collection of CBCs, NBRs, and context entities:

→ CBC entities —Hub tables in Data Vault— contain the unique list of business keys that identify each instance of the CBC. Each unique instance of a CBC conforms to a single business key, which —for technical reasons— will be paired with a surrogate key in the data solution. We will cover this in detail in the ⚐ core business concept section

→ The NBRs, represented as Link tables in Data Vault, contain the unique list of relationships between business keys

→ Context entities, the Data Vault Satellites, contain historized descriptive data about the CBC (or NBR, depending on the implementation dialect)

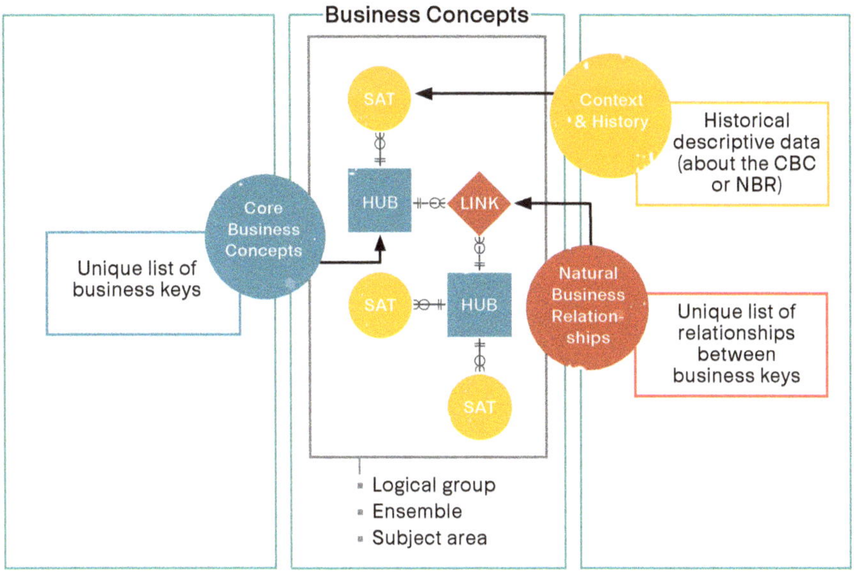

As a result, the business terms that we define (model) can be represented as an 'ensemble.' This ensemble identifies the CBC and its direct relationships and properties. When *unified*, it typically represents a meaningful business term or domain for the business consumers of the data.

Core business concepts

This section covers the details for the implementation of the Hub as the physical implementation of the CBC, as described in the corresponding architecture section.

↗ A CBC data object uniquely identifies instances of a concept, a distinct, unambiguously defined item — the *list of unique business keys*. For the physical model implementation, this is the Data Vault Hub.

Hub data object structure

Stripping it back to its essence, the Hub data object structure is as follow:

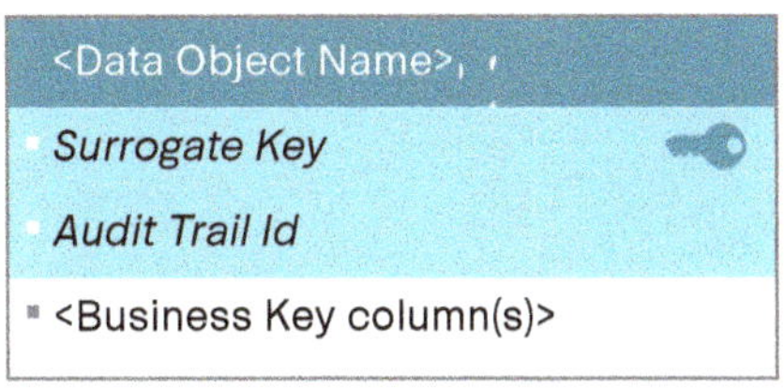

This structure includes:

- The Hub surrogate key, containing the data solution key that identifies the instance of the CBC in the data solution. In the physical model, this represents the implementation of the key distribution concept
- The Audit Trail Id, containing the reference to the control framework instance that added the data
- The column(s) which define the business key and identify the CBC instance in its original value. This may be a single column or a combination of columns, as long as this uniquely defines a single instance

Optionally, the following columns can be considered:

- The inscription timestamp, indicating the time of arrival in the data solution as inherited from the staging layer. In Data Vault, this is often called the load date timestamp (LDTS) column, but we prefer to stick to the more generic term inscription timestamp
- The record source indicator, indicating the origin of the record

Hub surrogate key

The surrogate key in the Hub is a *single column* that serves as the primary key for the physical Hub table. It can be referenced by related entities such as Satellites and Link tables, ensuring these tables inherit the same key, and ultimately satisfy referential integrity requirements.

The surrogate key is directly linked to the business key column(s), maintaining a one-to-one relationship. Conceptually, the business key could also serve as the surrogate key. However, the business key may be composed of multiple columns, transformations, or even hard-coded values.

This complexity can lead to lengthy, unpredictable, and possibly composite keys, that potentially complicates the propagation of keys across various tables that reference the Hub.

By defining a separate, single, surrogate key column it can be guaranteed that the primary key of the table is always singular. Additionally, since the surrogate key's purpose is purely technical, it can be implemented in various ways to optimize the data solution's performance.

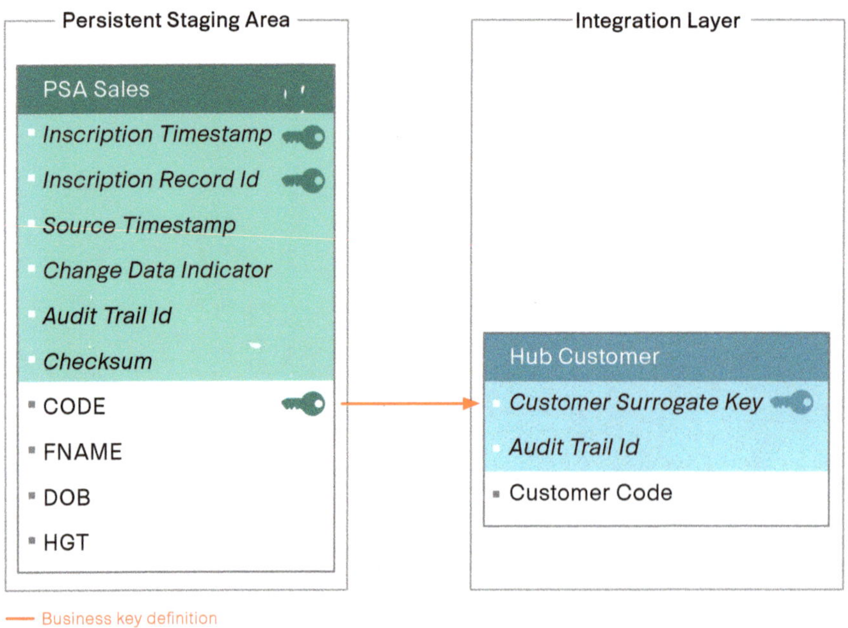

In metadata, the surrogate key is part of the business key definition metadata object.

As an example, this (also singular column 'CODE') business key definition is linked to the 'Customer_Sk' surrogate key column.

```
{
 "ordinalPosition": 1,
 "name": "Customer_Bk",
 "surrogateKey": "Customer_Sk",
 "businessKeyComponents": [
  {
   "ordinalPosition": 1,
   "dataItem": {
    "ordinalPosition": 1,
    "name": "CODE"
   }
  }
 ]
}
```

This allows the surrogate key to be generated in various ways, depending on the selected approach.

Examples include issuing numeric sequence values, creating hash value keys, or concatenating business key columns.

The exact data type for the surrogate key columns depends on the selected approach, which is covered in the surrogate key approaches section.

Business key column(s)

The values that uniquely identify a single instance of a 'thing,' the business key, can cover multiple columns, transformations, and even hard-coded values.

These values are recorded in the business key column, or columns, in the Hub table.

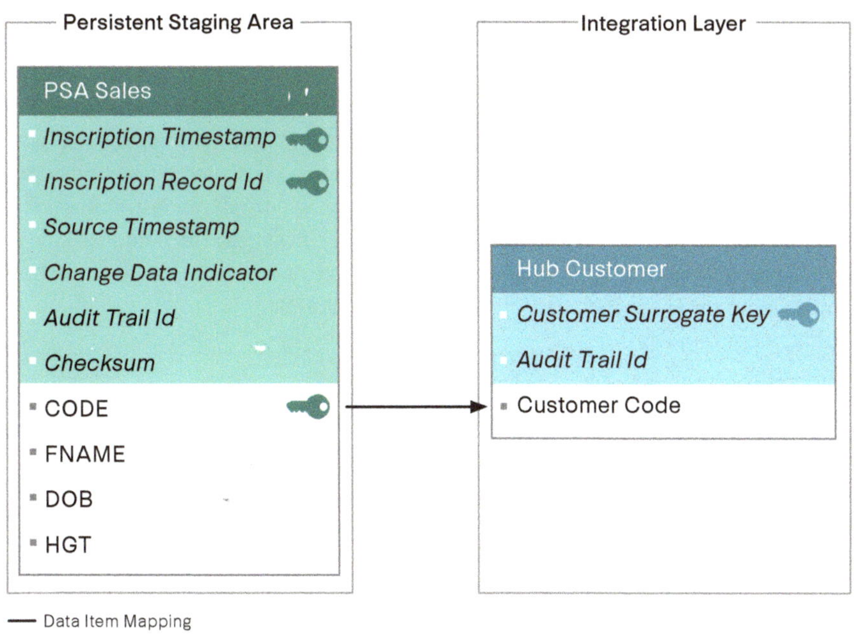

In most implementations most business keys are singular, but sometimes it is necessary to involve multiple columns to correctly define a unique instance of a CBC. In this case, all involved values are stored in the Hub as part of the business key column(s).

Implementing this using one column for each component of the business key is the most common approach, but it is not the only one. Considerations about this are available in the ⚐ complex business keys section.

Regardless of the implementation nuance, in all cases business key components are defined in metadata as a regular data item mapping.

```
{
 "dataObjectMappings": [
  {
   "dataItemMappings": [
    {
     "sourceDataItems": [ { "name": "CODE" } ],
     "targetDataItem": { "name": "Customer_Code" }
    }
   ]
  }
 ]
}
```

It is advisable to define the business key using the longest possible variable-length UTF character data type, such as NVARCHAR(1000) or NVARCHAR(MAX). This ensures that data from diverse sources can be effectively mapped to the business key columns.

Choosing an integer type for the business key can restrict interoperability with systems where business keys are stored as string values. Implementing a flexible data type for business key columns is one of the many small, yet significant, steps towards future-proofing your data solution.

Consideration should also be given to the technical infrastructure. For example, some platforms have limitations on index lengths or do not support indexing on MAX length columns.

The trick is to find the right balance for your environment, following the guideline to be as inclusive to all data as possible.

Audit Trail Id

The Audit Trail Id follows the same approach as for any table in the data solution. The unique execution id of the data logistics process that populates the data from the source data object into the Hub data object will be inserted here.

This value is *not* copied from the source data object.

Optional columns

In the introduction, we mentioned that the inscription timestamp and record source indicator can be considered as optional Hub columns.

Inscription timestamp

The inscription timestamp is inherited from the staging layer data, from the data object that maps to the Hub. The data type is therefore the same as in the staging layer – a high precision timestamp.

To deliver a data solution that is fully deterministic, the inscription timestamp should *not* be set again during the data logistics process from the staging layer to the integration layer. That would mean that a new inscription timestamp is issued every time an integration layer entity is truncated and reloaded, whereas copying the value from the staging layer will always produce the same result.

Conceptually, for a Hub, the inscription timestamp represents the first time the business key was presented to the integration layer. Or more accurately: the first data logistics process that presented the business key to the Hub. Practically, in our reference architecture it really represents the first time the business key appeared in the source data object that is mapped to, and loaded into, the Hub.

Because the sequence of data logistics processing has an impact on the exact inscription timestamp value that ultimately is stored in the Hub, its value is somewhat limited. Moreover, reloading parts of the data solution might result in different values because of the order of the data logistics processes that are run.

When building the data set for downstream processing a timestamp value can sometimes have some use. For example, when context is not yet available, it is still possible to identify when a certain key was received. This can be used to evaluate the consistency of the data and the frequency and completeness of the data logistics processes.

Additionally, this value can be used as proxy for creating initial linkages to other Hubs, for example to create a dimensional model (star schema) or equivalent. The thinking is that even though no context is yet available, it is still possible to join this business key with a starting point for its existence.

Designers must be aware, however, that this is still a technical value.

When there is genuine interest in understanding the frequency in which business key are delivered across different systems, it is possible to solve this with a dedicated Satellite.

Please refer to the ⚐ storing the business key in Satellites section for more details on this.

Record source indicator

As before, in the staging layer, the record source indicator can be seen as a redundant column, because the same information can also be retrieved from the control framework via the Audit Trail Id.

The reason we mention this as an option, is that —at the time of writing— most available Data Vault documentation considers the record source indicator a mandatory column. Conceptually, it means to record the system from which the business key originates.

However, like the inscription timestamp, the record source indicator is set only once, by whatever process first inserts the new business key. The exact value depends, again, on the sequencing of data logistics processes. If designers assume that the record source indicates the system that is the 'main' distributer of this key, the governing system, this can be misleading.

As before, we recommend to *not* include the record source indicator as a separate column in the Hub, unless there is an explicit reason to do so. If required, this can always be added later because the values will still be available in control framework.

Hub design pattern

This section summarizes the features of the Hub into a *design pattern,* supported by examples for code generation and implementation.

The full pattern, using the recommended ⚐ pattern documentation structure, can be accessed via our website: https://dtng.link/hj0ft.

The Hub data logistics process should implement the following concepts:

→ Select the distinct list of (unique) business key columns, and optionally retain the earliest inscription timestamp of each business key
→ Verify the presence of each business key in the Hub. Insert if new, discard otherwise
→ Generate the surrogate key

Operating as an insert-only process —using a lookup to determine if records should be inserted— the Hub pattern natively supports modularity, independence, fault tolerance, and idempotency. Selecting the list of unique business keys

In a Hub table, the primary content consists of unique business keys.

When mapping data from source to target objects, the business key is the sole 'source' data that will be processed. It is common that certain business keys appear multiple times within a source data object, even when only processing data deltas. For instance, if a customer orders multiple products, the customer's business key might appear in multiple records that might be processed in one pass.

It is only required to retain *one* of these appearances, because the target Hub only needs one record for each business key instance.

To achieve this, a decision must be made on which appearance of the business key to select. The preferred approach is to choose the record with the lowest (minimum) inscription timestamp among all instances of the business key.

The inscription timestamp, inherited from the staging layer, indicates when a value was first committed to the data solution. Therefore, selecting the business key with the lowest inscription timestamp signifies the first occurrence of that key in the data solution.

Applying a minimum function, or similar method, to the inscription timestamp elegantly resolves the task of selecting a single business key record from potentially many occurrences.

Assert if the business key already exists

Business keys are inserted into the Hub table only if they are not already present. A lookup is performed to verify whether the selected business keys from the previous step already exist. If they do not yet exist, they can be inserted in the Hub table. Otherwise, the records can be gracefully discarded.

Generate the surrogate key

The final step in the Hub pattern involves assigning a surrogate key to each business key before insertion.

Considerations

The following sections contain considerations that can be included in the final Hub pattern.

Complex business keys

In the business key section, we mentioned that business keys are typically singular, meaning that a single column (value) identifies the CBC.

But that is not always the case.

In most solutions, a need emerges to combine multiple data elements to achieve this identification.

There are several mechanisms to manage this, including the use of *composite keys* and *concatenated keys.*

It is also common for a single table or record to contain multiple instances of the same CBC, which can be addressed using *pivoting.*

Additionally, sometimes a business key can only be made unique by applying *transformations* or *hard-coded values.*

At the end of this section, we will also share some different ideas and concepts we have seen implemented for business keys.

Composite keys

A business key is considered composite when it is defined as a collection of columns. Each component of the business key is an individual data item mapping.

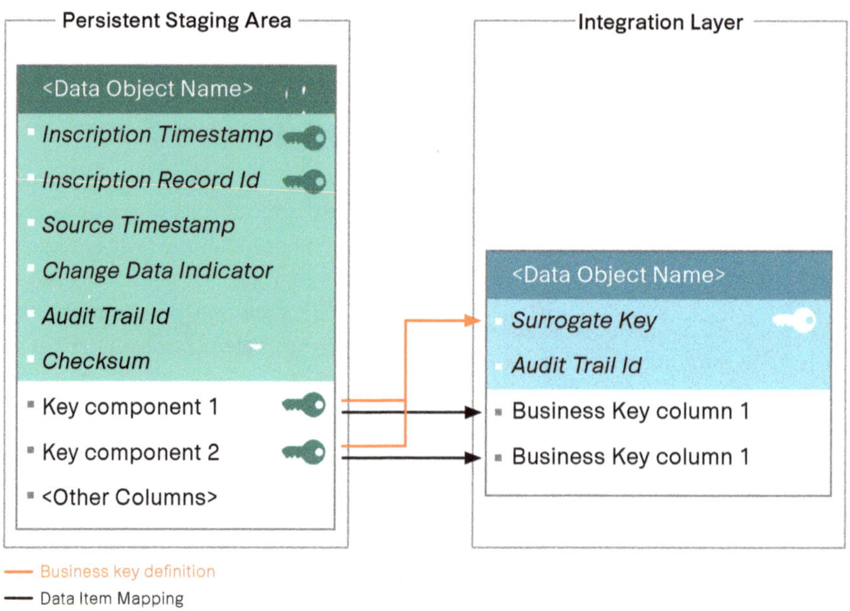

The image above illustrates that the components of the composite key are also mapped to the definition of the singular surrogate key.

Composite keys are an effective way to capture the individual original values that define the business key. When necessary, these components can be queried from the Hub table and included in downstream processing or analysis.

Composite keys are recorded in metadata as regular data item mappings. The target item where the values are stored and the role these columns play are what ultimately gives them meaning.

```
{
 "dataObjectMappings": [
  {
   "dataItemMappings": [
    {
     "sourceDataItems": [ { "name": "<key component 1>" } ],
     "targetDataItem": { "name": "<business key column 1>" }
    },
    {
     "sourceDataItems": [ { "name": "<key component 2>" } ],
     "targetDataItem": { "name": "<business key column 2>" }
    }
   ]
  }
 ]
}
```

Concatenated keys

Concatenation involves combining multiple columns (values) into a single string to form a business key, including the use of sanding delimiters to ensure uniqueness.

A concatenated key consists of multiple components, but maps to a single target business key column.

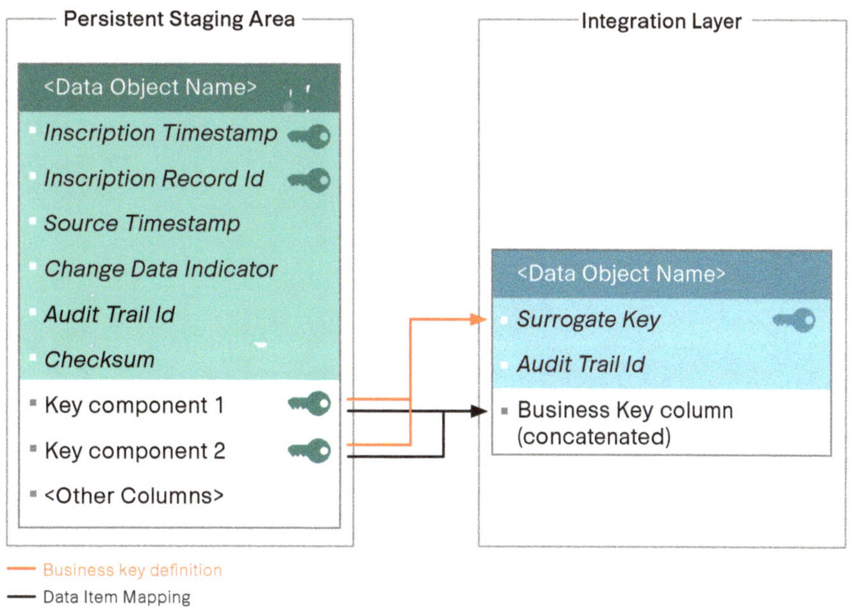

A sanding element is required whenever values are concatenated. This concept, previously covered in the sanding section of the hash algorithm, applies to concatenated keys as well.

Some automation frameworks favor concatenated keys because they ensure a consistent Hub table structure. Supporting composite keys introduces variability in the number of columns a Hub might have — which means additional coding and complexity to support this. Concatenated keys maintain a consistent column count across all Hubs.

One consideration is that a concatenated business key value often needs refinement to be fit for downstream consumption. For example, it may be necessary to remove the sanding delimiter and separate the concatenated value into its original components for reporting purposes.

For this reason, when using concatenated keys, the original business key values are often stored separately (and redundantly) in a Satellite table — the physical model counterpart of the context entity.

In metadata, concatenated keys are recorded as a data item mapping where the source data item is a data item query:

```
{
 "dataObjectMappings": [
  {
   "dataItemMappings": [
    {
     "sourceDataItems": [
      {
       "name": "concatenated key",
       "queryCode": "<key component 1> || '\\@|' || <key component 2>",
       "queryLanguage": "SQL"
      }
     ],
     "targetDataItem": { "name": "<business key column - concatenated>" }
    }
   ]
  }
 ]
}
```

Smart keys

Sometimes, identifiers in an operational system are augmented with additional attributes or metadata to facilitate the inner workings of the system and its processes.

It might not only uniquely identify a record, but could also include additional elements that have some utility for the system. These are *smart keys* —sometimes referred to as intelligent keys— and they are commonplace, sometimes so much so that they aren't really noticeable anymore.

For example, a date value like '20240630' can be considered a smart key because it consolidates year, month, and day into a single, efficient identifier.

Take the ISBN, the International Standard Book Number as another example. The ISBN is a unique identifier assigned to each edition and variation of a book. It is used as a worldwide standard for cataloging and managing books in libraries, bookstores, and online platforms.

An ISBN consists of various individual components totaling between 10 and 13 digits, each serving specific purposes. The ISBN allows publishers, retailers, and other suppliers to directly identify an individual product. As such, it has meaning as a unique identifier for a CBC — the product.

However, each component of the ISBN *also* carries its own meaning. For example, 978-3-9827180-0-2[43] contains:

- A prefix to integrate into the European Article Number system for books. ISBNs can start with either '978' or '979'
- The registration group that identifies the national, geographic, or language grouping of publishers. '3' indicates that the book is published in Germany
- The registrant. '9827180' uniquely identifies us as the specific publisher or imprint
- The publication, that identifies the edition and format of the book. '0' represents specific details about the edition and format of our book – in this case the 1st edition and print softcover
- A check digit to verify the accuracy of the ISBN, which uses a modulus to ensure the combination of values makes sense

These details illustrate how each component contributes to the unique identification of the publication. Whether these individual components hold relevance depends on the specific business context. In most cases, the combination of these components alone may suffice.

For a organizations that work with publications, such as libraries or publishing companies, the specific editions and registrations encoded in the ISBN are likely to be very relevant. For other organizations, the combined identifier, the ISBN, will probably be sufficient.

A guideline is: if the components of a smart key are used separately in the business processes then model these as individual CBCs, otherwise create a single CBC for the combination.

Should it later become evident that individual components are indeed meaningful for business operations, integrating them as separate CBCs involves relatively minor model refactoring.

Pivoting

Pivoting is a special mechanism you may sometimes need when multiple instances of the same CBC are stored across columns.

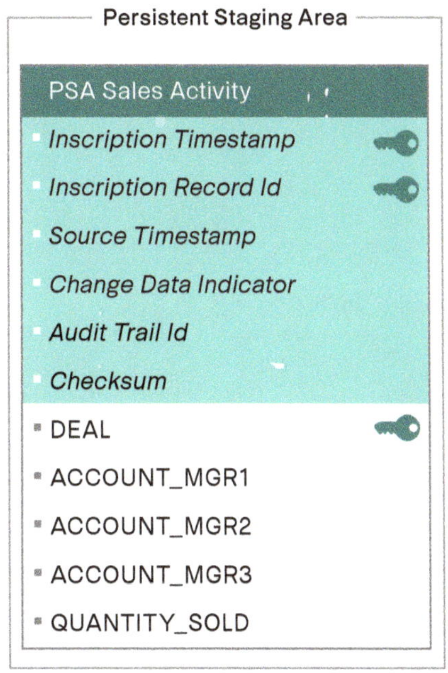

In this example, multiple 'account managers' —a core business concept in this case— can contribute to a sale. Each account manager column may represent an instance of the CBC.

There are many alternatives to implement this, and one straightforward option is to create a database view on the staging layer table.

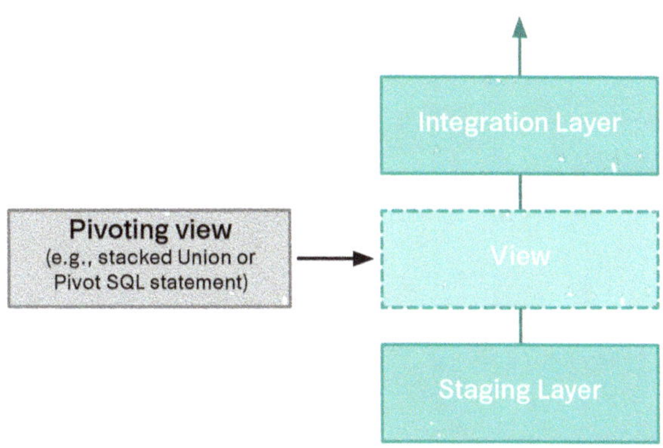

By pivoting the columns into rows, the resulting single column can be mapped to the integration layer Hub object.

An alternative is to define *multiple* separate data object mappings from the same source data object to the same target data object:

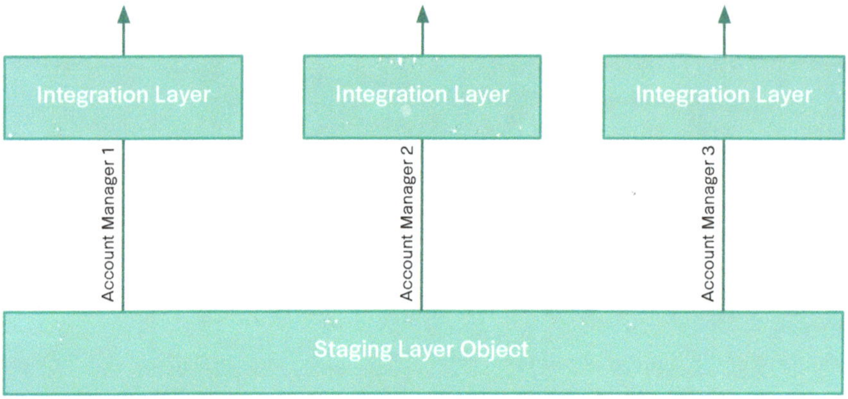

Because all mappings —three in this example— map to the same target, they will be grouped together in the same data object mapping list, as covered in the data object mapping lists section.

Transformations and hard-coded values

We have already seen transformations being used to prepare concatenated keys, but concatenation is only one of many transformations that may be required to define a business key.

Providing an overview of *all* possible transformations goes beyond the scope of this book, however, special consideration must be given to *hard-coded values.*

Hard-coded values are defined and implemented like any other transformation but require identification because they may not be used as freely in code compared to regular transformations. Classifications or extensions can be used to label these special data items.

```
{
 "dataObjectMappings": [
  {
   "dataItemMappings": [
    {
     "sourceDataItems": [
      {
       "name": "hard-coded value",
       "queryCode": "'XYZ'",
       "queryLanguage": "SQL",
       "extensions": [
        {
         "key": "isHardCodedValue",
         "value": true
        }
       ]
      }
     ],
     "targetDataItem": { "name": "<target column
      for hard-coded value" }
    }
   ]
  }
 ]
}
```

For example, when implementing *GROUP BY* statements in SQL, each component of the GROUP BY must exist in the inner query. Hard-coded values must be excluded here, and this is only possible if they can be identified in metadata – as can be done using an extension as shown in the example.

Hard-coded values are typically applicable when there is no data element available to uniquely define the business key, but it is certain (beyond reasonable doubt) that the same values actually represent different things.

How is that possible?

An example is a network of car dealerships for a particular brand of car. Many of these dealerships are franchises, and some are owned by the car manufacturer outright. As part of the agreements most dealerships use the same software for the operational systems, but how and when certain versions are deployed is mostly up to the individual dealerships.

Because of this, there are limitations to what extent IT and data governance can be applied 'top-down' from the car manufacturer headquarters to individual dealerships, which in turn results in many dealerships having their own local implementation of the operational system, as opposed to having a centralized system that all dealerships connect to.

The result of this is that each record created is uniquely identified within the scope of one system, but in a similar way to how other copies of the system do this. Each customer record, each transaction, each employee etc. is not likely to be unique when combining the data from all dealerships into a central data solution.

If there is no strong candidate to differentiate these data sets, such as a 'dealership id' for example, then the records can be *uniquefied* artificially using a hard-coded value.

This is also common for larger, multinational, companies were data points like 'country' or 'region' would uniquely identify certain data sets. But these might not always be actually available in the data.

Storing the business key in Satellites

Storing business keys in a Satellite table is another option. In this section, we're exploring various options and considerations regarding this approach –outlining how the CBC and its Hub implementation should function– and providing the directions for the engine.

As before, it is precisely these considerations that we recommend documenting in a design pattern.

In the ⚐ concatenated keys section, we mentioned that the storing the individual components in a Satellite (without the sanding element) can simplify retrieval.

This way, there's no need to parse the key into its original form when using it downstream.

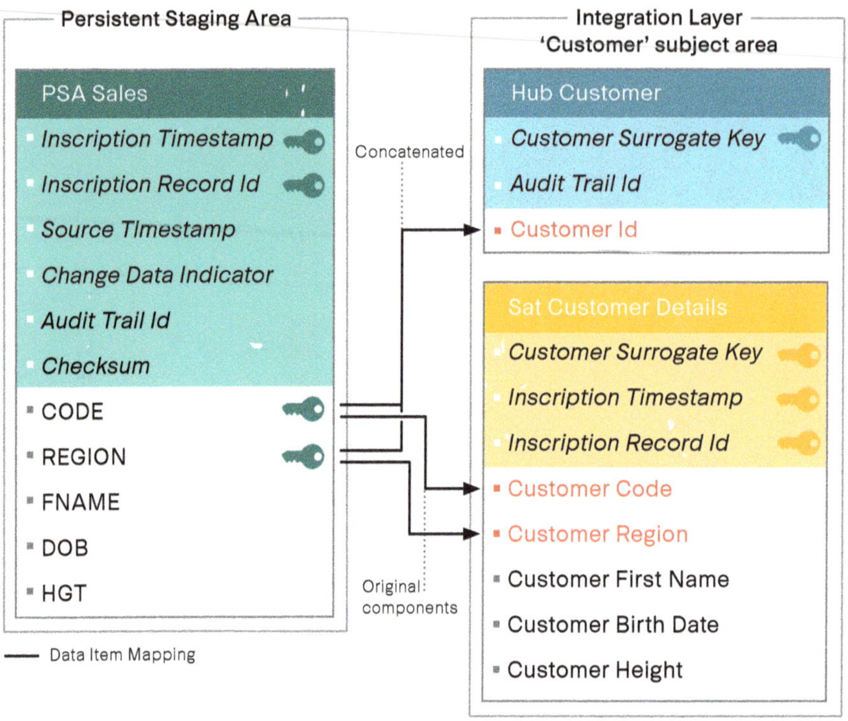

In some implementations, the business key is stored redundantly in *every* Satellite that references the Hub. This approach can arguably be justified by the ability to utilize each Satellite independently downstream, removing the need to join the Hub table altogether.

We don't necessarily recommend this, and it is not how we define our business key pattern. However, we do feel there is value in showing the many ways one can approach this subject.

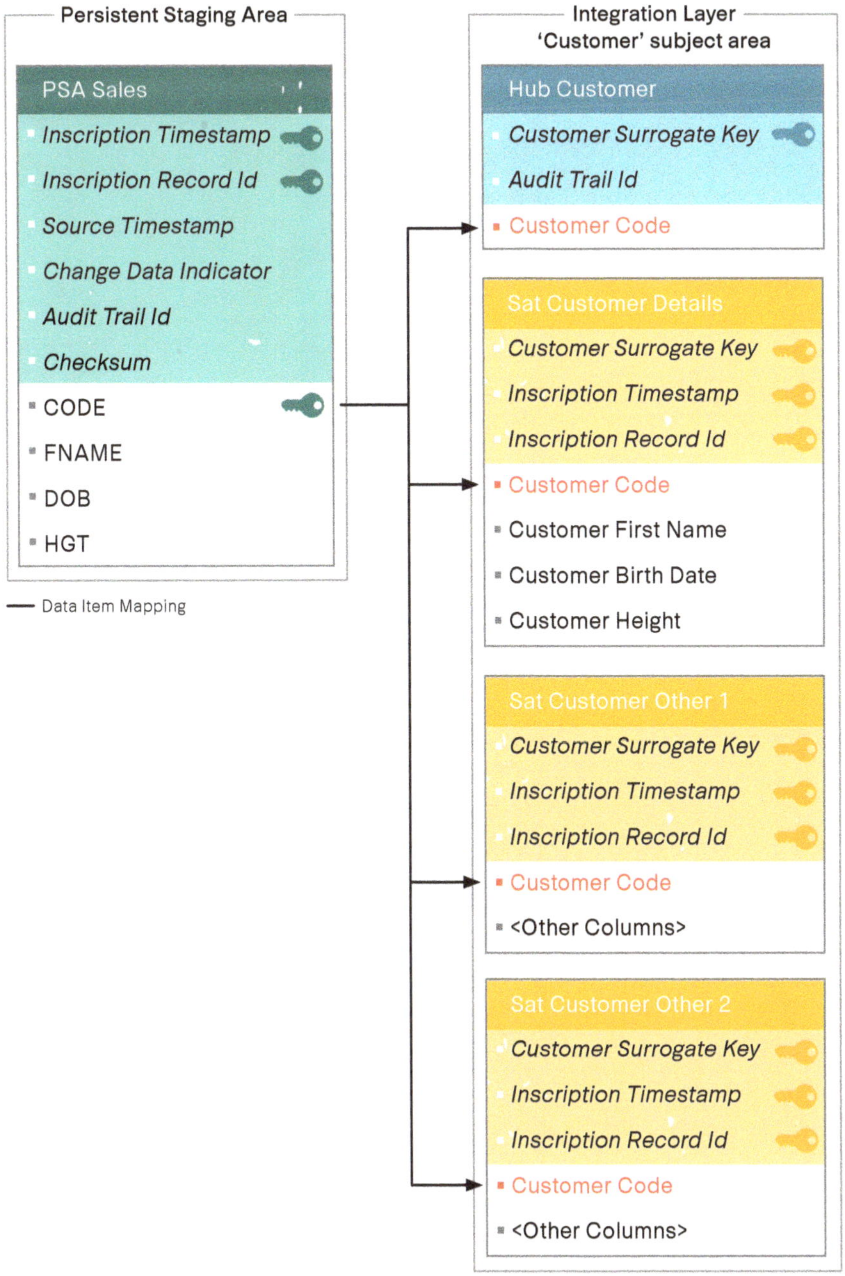
Persistent Staging Area
PSA Sales
Inscription Timestamp
Inscription Record Id
Source Timestamp
Change Data Indicator
Audit Trail Id
Checksum
CODE
FNAME
DOB
HGT
Data Item Mapping
Integration Layer
'Customer' subject area
Hub Customer
Customer Surrogate Key
Audit Trail Id
Customer Code
Sat Customer Details
Customer Surrogate Key
Inscription Timestamp
Inscription Record Id
Customer Code
Customer First Name
Customer Birth Date
Customer Height
Sat Customer Other 1
Customer Surrogate Key
Inscription Timestamp
Inscription Record Id
Customer Code
<Other Columns>
Sat Customer Other 2
Customer Surrogate Key
Inscription Timestamp
Inscription Record Id
Customer Code
<Other Columns>

A variation on this theme involves dedicating a special Satellite for the storage of the business key:

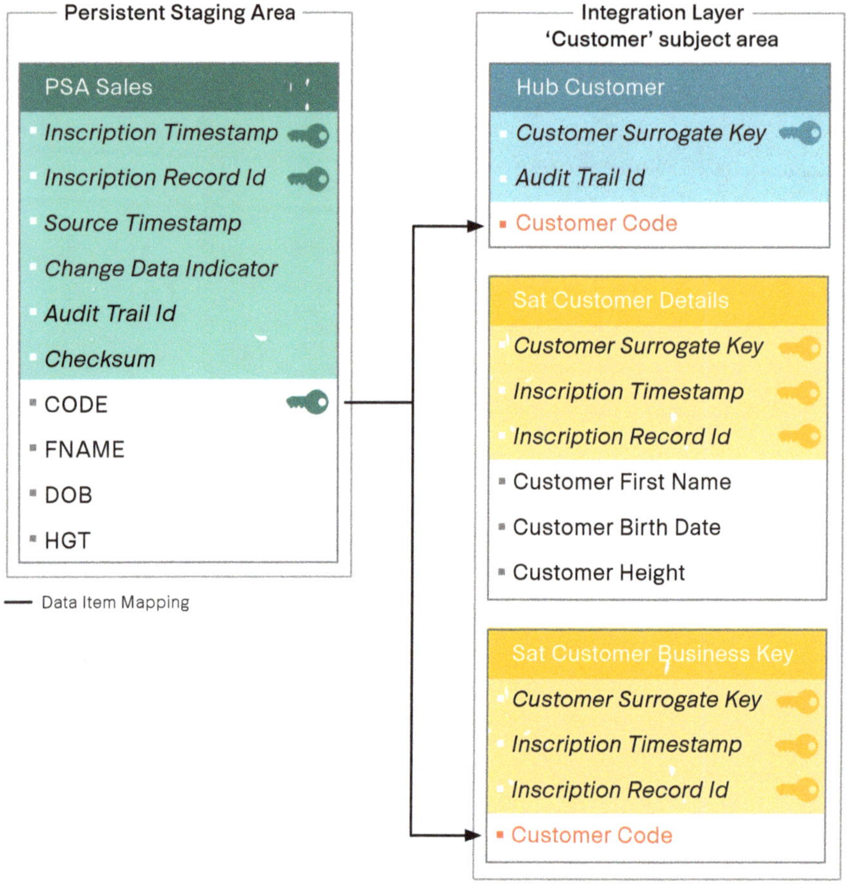

This approach offers specific benefits in complex scenarios where multiple representations of a business key exist. This typically occurs when there is no unified company-wide business key, and various unique identifiers are used across operational systems and processes. In such cases, an integrated business key may need to be established, with all candidate or alternative keys mapped to this standard.

The above example can be extended to contain all these business key candidates in one place. In ELM this is known as a 'Bag of Keys' (BOK) approach, and it can be a convenient way to manage this complexity. Introducing a BOK approach requires some special considerations for the data logistics processes however, and these are detailed in the working with alternative business keys section.

Why are we delving into these details? One reason is that these considerations should be clearly documented as part of the design pattern within the overall solution architecture. Many of these choices have trade-offs that significantly impact the final outcome.

For instance, redundantly storing each business key increases storage and I/O requirements. Is this additional footprint justified by the reduction in joins?

Another consideration is whether storing the business key in the Hub is still necessary at all.

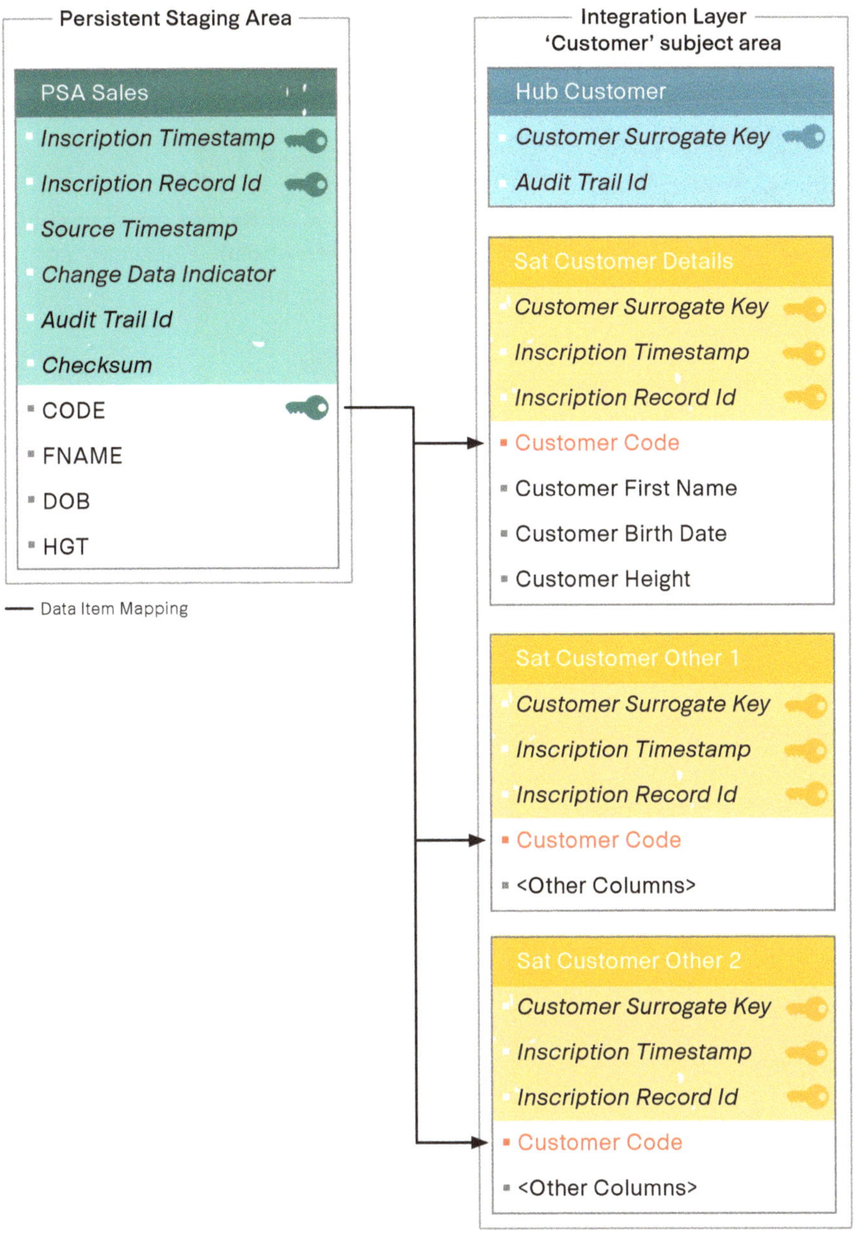

Consider the approach below. Does that alter the equation?

When business keys are redundantly stored in *all* Satellites, the necessity of *also* storing them in the Hub becomes questionable. After all, the point of doing this is for the convenience of not having to join the Hub in the first place.

Taking this line of reasoning further, if surrogate keys are consistently calculated, one might question the need for a Hub table altogether — at least in the physical model.

The engine facilitates explores such possibilities. Imagine the CBC as a logical construct only, where its business key is defined and its context described.

Based on specific circumstances, usage patterns, and optimization goals, the engine could dynamically refactor the physical model to better suit the intended purpose – possibly even eliminating the need for a Hub table. Automation ensures consistency throughout.

Is this still Data Vault? Maybe, maybe not. Does it still matter at this stage?

This thought experiment illustrates how the engine is meant to work, and that all the different considerations above are merely technical nuances that ultimately achieve the same outcome.

One of the engine's goals is to automate these optimizations tailored to the scenario at hand.

Our business key pattern

In our preferred business key design pattern, each business key component will separately be stored in the Hub. Our pattern supports composite business keys.

The Hub will, in principle, be the only place where the business key is available.

As a consequence, we acknowledge the need to join the Hub table to retrieve the business key values. Any alternative business keys will be stored in a dedicated Satellite for alternate keys.

Surrogate key approaches

Conceptually, the surrogate key provides a singular data solution key that corresponds to the Hub's business key (components) and can be referenced by other data objects.

Technically, there are many ways to implement this. In the following sections we outline the three most common approaches:

- → Hash value keys
- → Natural business keys
- → Sequence value keys

Sequence value keys

In a Data Warehouse solution, the traditional approach towards surrogate key generation is to issue a new sequence value for each new record. This is often an integer (or large integer) value managed by the database using sequence objects, or similar.

This concept has been used for a long time in dimensional modeling, and can be applied to issue surrogate keys for business keys in the Hub tables as well.

Each time a new business key is inserted into the Hub, the subsequent value from a sequence is issued and inserted with the record. This generates a sequential range of integer values that can act as surrogate key for the business key.

The example below shows how this could look with some sample data.

Surrogate Key	Audit Trail Id	Business Key	Inscription Timestamp
1	2305	CUST001	2024-10-04
2	2305	CUST002	2024-10-04
3	2305	CUST003	2024-10-04
4	2565	CUST004	2024-11-01
5	2565	CUST005	2024-11-01

A benefit of using surrogate key values is that they typically have a small storage and I/O footprint. They are efficient to use, easy to create, and predictable.

Most data platforms provide native features to generate sequential values, for instance, by using column defaults that are part of the table definition (e.g., IDENTITY) or by providing dedicated sequence objects that can be selected from. Many databases work well with integer values when joining objects, although that varies from technology to technology.

In the data solution, surrogate keys are referenced by other objects that 'inherit' the key and as such can be used to assert referential integrity. This means that the *same* sequence value that is used in the Hub *must* be used for any connecting data points, for example in Satellites and Links.

Surrogate Key	Audit Trail Id	Business Key	Inscription Timestamp
1	2305	CUST001	2024-10-04
2	2305	CUST002	2024-10-04
3	2305	CUST003	2024-10-04
4	2565	CUST004	2024-11-01
5	2565	CUST005	2024-11-01

Surrogate Key	Inscription Timestamp	Inscription Record Id	State Timestamp	Audit Trail Id	Checksum	<context>
1	2024-10-06	1	2023-01-01	2305	<>	John
1	2024-10-07	1	2023-02-01	2305	<>	Johnny
1	2024-10-09	1	2023-03-01	2305	<>	John
1	2024-11-11	1	2023-01-15	2565	<>	Jon
1	2024-12-01	1	2024-12-01	2565	<>	Jonathan

The only way to do this is by performing a *key lookup*. This is a main drawback to using sequence values, because it introduces dependencies between the data logistics processes. For a key lookup to work, the Hub object must be available first before the referencing table, the Satellite in this example, can be processed.

Dependencies between data logistics processes can have a significant impact on the overall latency in data availability, and introduce complexities in managing failures during the processing.

Hash value keys

In the ⚐ checksums section, we initially introduced the term *hash value keys,* commonly referred to as 'hash keys.' Hash keys were introduced to Data Vault methodology as an alternative to using sequence values.

A hash key is essentially the encrypted (hashed) business key, including all of its components *and* the sanding elements. This process mirrors exactly what is described in the ⚐ how to create a checksum section.

Regardless of how many components constitute a business key, its hash value will always be singular.

One of the significant advantages of adopting hash keys is their deterministic nature. Using the same business key values and hashing algorithm, the result will for intents and purposes always be the same.

When the same algorithm is applied to the same values, it consistently produces the same result — even if these values are in different data sets.

This means that a key lookup is no longer necessary.

Surrogate Key	Audit Trail Id	Business Key	Inscription Timestamp
E16FA	2305	CUST001	2024-10-04
99ABA	2305	CUST002	2024-10-04
1C10D	2305	CUST003	2024-10-04
FF98A	2565	CUST004	2024-11-01
452CA	2565	CUST005	2024-11-01

Surrogate Key	Inscription Timestamp	Inscription Record Id	State Timestamp	Audit Trail Id	Checksum	<context>
E16FA	2024-10-06	1	2023-01-01	2305	<>	John
E16FA	2024-10-07	1	2023-02-01	2305	<>	Johnny
E16FA	2024-10-09	1	2023-03-01	2305	<>	John
E16FA	2024-11-11	1	2023-01-15	2565	<>	Jon
E16FA	2024-12-01	1	2024-12-01	2565	<>	Jonathan

It is still possible to achieve the same outcome using a key lookup, and this is also one way to safeguard referential integrity in the platform. But it is no longer the *only* way.

The fact that hash keys can be generated independently opens up a number of options for the data solution. Data logistics processes that previously had a dependency on the key being available can now be *processed in parallel*. In the above example, the Hub and Satellite tables can be processed at the same time, or in any order, and the outcomes will be the same after these processes have run.

Parallel loading introduces its own complexities to the data solution. Without key lookups and enforceable constraints at runtime, referential integrity must be asserted some other way. In addition to this, checks and balances must be in place to ensure that the data selected from these objects is consistent. For instance, care must be taken to retrieve rows for which a Hub key is not yet available if the Satellite process finishes first.

These, and other, challenges will be tackled in the ⚐ orchestration section.

The deterministic nature of hash keys has another major benefit, which is that reloading a table from the PSA will *produce the exact same outcome*. Unlike sequence values —which require re-seeding and are dependent on order and volume of data— the hash value will remain the same no matter how often you truncate and load a table, given the same process and inputs.

Hash keys also enable *cross-platform linking*. In theory, the same values and algorithm should generate consistent result across different technical environments. This allows to store some data on a file system, other data in a JSON format, and the rest in a database. All three environments can be connected via hash surrogate key, which should be the same.

The wording 'in theory' and 'should' indicate that this is not always as straightforward as it might appear. In fact, ensuring that hash values indeed are the same often requires a fair amount of trial and error. This is because the outcome of the hashing algorithm is subject to all kinds of details, as covered in the how to create a checksum section.

Specifically for massively parallel processing (MPP) platforms, distributed compute etc. hash keys can be a convenient choice for the surrogate key because the generated values can make for a good distribution key for co-location and evenly-distributed data sets.

Finally, hash keys offer more versatile data logistics than sequence values. Specifically, with hash keys, the integration layer can be implemented as a set of database views or similar runtime processes, eliminating the need to persist these (save for performance considerations).

This is possible due to the deterministic behavior of hash keys. A sequence value might differ when an object is reloaded or created and run as a view, but with hash keys, the results remain consistent. Additionally, key lookups are no longer necessary which significantly simplifies the creation of these views.

The main drawbacks of using hash values in general are mostly covered in ⚐ how to create a checksum section, but when specifically using hash values as surrogate keys care must be taken when determining the indexing strategy.

Hash values are not random, of course. They are the exact opposite of random: deterministic. However, for some indexes, they might as well be. This can cause performance issues, particularly with clustered indexes in certain databases. Unlike sequence values, which are typically inserted at the end, hash keys are often inserted in the middle of the index. This can lead to fragmentation and subsequent performance issues. The extent of these issues varies by database platform, but it's important to be aware of them.

Hash keys also tend to use up a lot of storage space, which is reflected in I/O costs when working with the data. In many Data Vault solutions, the physical implementation NBRs —the Link tables— are often some of the largest tables in the overall solution even though they contain relatively few columns. This is because most columns contain hash values, which don't compress well in many database technologies.

It is beyond the scope of this book to go into too much detail on this, and how well database platform manage this varies greatly, but it is something to keep in mind.

Natural business Keys

Hash (value) keys offer new ways to think about key distribution, but the hash value itself doesn't tell you much when you look at it. You can't easily see what logic was applied to 'make things unique' — how the business key was constructed.

To do so, you need the business key component(s) themselves. After all, the hash key is nothing more than a representation of the original business key value with a hashing algorithm applied.

Natural business keys provide an alternative that addresses this. A natural business key essentially follows the hash key approach *without actually applying a hashing algorithm.* The same preparation applies, for example the null value handling and the use of a sanding delimiters. The only difference is that the 'hashing' is not done.

This way, the surrogate key still provides some value, because the involved business key components can immediately be seen. The sanding element is also clearly visible. We recommend to resist any temptations to 'clean this up' and remove the sanding element when there is only one component to the business key. It's often easier to stick with a simple, consistent approach across the board, and this is a surrogate key after all.

Surrogate Key	Audit Trail Id	Business Key	Inscription Timestamp
CUST001\@|	2305	CUST001	2024-10-04
CUST002\@|	2305	CUST002	2024-10-04
CUST003\@|	2305	CUST003	2024-10-04
CUST004\@|	2565	CUST004	2024-11-01
CUST005\@|	2565	CUST005	2024-11-01

Surrogate Key	Inscription Timestamp	Inscription Record Id	State Timestamp	Audit Trail Id	Checksum	<context>
CUST001\@|	2024-10-06	1	2023-01-01	2305	<>	John
CUST001\@|	2024-10-07	1	2023-02-01	2305	<>	Johnny
CUST001\@|	2024-10-09	1	2023-03-01	2305	<>	John
CUST001\@|	2024-11-11	1	2023-01-15	2565	<>	Jon
CUST001\@|	2024-12-01	1	2024-12-01	2565	<>	Jonathan

Natural business keys enjoy the same benefits as hash keys do. They are also deterministic, and therefore support parallel loading, independent data logistics, virtualization, deterministic reprocessing (reloading) of data, and cross-platform joins.

One of the advantages of natural business keys over hash keys is that rigorous testing of the hashing algorithm across different platforms is not required. It's easier in this regard.

An additional advantage is that natural business keys retain some of the ordering, sequential, nature of their original components. This is gentler on the indexing, mitigating some of the issues documented in the hash key section. As always, this is technology dependent, but it applies to a range of often-used database platforms.

Another advantage is that for most platforms we've seen, the natural business key is smaller *on average* compared to hash keys. A hash key always has a set size, often 16, 20 bytes or more, depending on the algorithm used. Most original business key component values are usually smaller, which shows in the natural business key size.

A smaller storage footprint yields better I/O results in most platforms.

One disadvantage of using natural business keys is that they can lead to large surrogate key values if the business key components themselves are lengthy. We stated earlier that —on average— this is not the case, but that still allows for outliers. This largely depends on the data, specifically the definition of the business key.

Another consideration is that when encryption is a requirement for the surrogate key, a hash key is the only suitable option. It may be that the surrogate key must be encrypted for genuine security reasons. In this situation, the business key components are often stored in a separate specially-secured Satellite.

A last technical note is that not all technologies handle special characters the same way. Depending on the data and the sanding element used, there are likely to be special characters in the surrogate key, which can negatively impact join performance in some database systems.

Final thoughts on surrogate key approaches

Which approach for surrogate key creation works best? To a certain extent this, as often is the case, depends on your situation. There are indications that some very large data solutions benefit from adopting hash keys, while many smaller deployments prefer the more straightforward approach of using natural business keys.

Some dialects of Data Vault advocate the use of integer keys, although we feel that the necessary introduction of processing dependencies and the inability to connect data cross-platform offset its benefits.

It is interesting to consider that, using the engine, it is possible to change the approach for surrogate key creation with a few small tweaks. Surrogate keys ultimately are only technical features. The solution can be rebuilt with another surrogate key creation approach without materially changing any data outcomes.

The engine might even generate a 'mixed' mode, where certain parts of the data solution adopt different approaches for surrogate keys. And why not? If this optimizes the system for certain directives, it might be the best overall outcome. Very large business keys, usually outliers, could be hashed while most keys would adopt a natural business key. We have seen projects getting the most out of their infrastructure using this approach.

Specific circumstances might require specific implementation decisions.

In our reference design, however, we implement natural business keys as we feel this provides the best balance between functionality, clarity, and performance. This is why the design pattern we use implements this by default.

Zero keys

Surrogate keys play a crucial role in ensuring long-term data solution consistency. By making sure surrogate keys can always 'connect' between tables, referential integrity (RI) can be maintained.

This means that any time a surrogate key (as foreign key) exists in any of the referencing (child) tables – such as Satellites or Links– there *must* be an equivalent key in the Hub. Using sequence values, this is not much of an issue, as the necessary key lookup will guarantee that RI criteria will be met.

However, using hash keys or natural business keys as the surrogate key pattern requires additional considerations. Most of these will be covered in the ⚐ orchestration section, but one piece of this puzzle is covered here: the zero key.

If, for various reasons, a Satellite (or Link) record does not contain a business key value, a zero key can be used instead. Each Hub will also have a corresponding zero record, which can then be used to satisfy RI and ultimately report on context that cannot be related to an identifiable business concept.

Without this, the data solution would not be able to process '100 % of the data, 100 % of the time,' a common Data Vault slogan.

How can this happen? There are many reasons, but in general, it means that data received at some point in time is incomplete. This can be, and often is, a data quality issue.

For instance, when a column defined as the business key is declared as an optional foreign key in the operational system. When certain conditions are met, the business key value is populated, otherwise it remains NULL. Or, the operational system may declare the column as mandatory, but this requirement is not correctly enforced, disabled, or even broken.

This would be considered an error in the operational system, but that doesn't help processing the data that already was received.

Another example: imagine a three-way relationship (Link) between the Customer, Product, and Promotion Hubs. It might be found that while 'customer' and 'product' data are consistently available, the 'promotion' data is sometimes NULL.

With the zero key in place, this data can still be loaded.

Having said this, when supporting this feature it's important to consider what it means to have unknown business keys and what it's implications really are.

In the case of the three-way Link example mentioned above, it is reasonable to review the modeling decisions made when unknown business keys occur. A redesign of parts of the model might be appropriate in such cases.

We support the use of zero keys, but treat this as a safety net rather than implicit approval for unknown business key values. If zero keys are triggered, additional investigation is required to determine why this happens. This feature makes the solution more forgiving, but is intended to prompt model improvements. Therefore, we strongly encourage placing testing framework controls on any referenced zero keys.

Because the mapping of business keys from source to target data objects is known, similar controls can be implemented on the PSA columns. This might help in early detection of the issue and facilitate modeling discussions.

Additional considerations regarding this are documented in the ⚐NULL handling for Links and ⚐NULL handling for Satellites sections.

The concept of zero keys, sometimes called 'ghost records,' 'zero records,' or 'dummy records' involves creating a default key in each Hub that represents the unknown business key. The decision to implement a zero key is a 'hard' business rule, enforced upon the creation of the Hub. In a virtual Hub, the zero key can be 'unioned' with the main data set.

The value of the zero key must be consistent with the surrogate key and business key patterns and data type, and should be the same across all Hubs.

For example a hash value of '0x00000000000000000000000000000000' with the business key value 'Unknown' can be defined as a zero key, but it's up to you how you want to handle this as long as it's consistent.

Using a natural business key, the value could simply be 'Unknown\@|.'

An interesting alternative is shown below. See how a NULL value is replaced by our standard NULL replacement string value?

```
SELECT HASHBYTES('SHA1',COALESCE(TRIM(CONVERT(NVARCHAR(MAX),
NULL)), '~!@|N/A') + '\@|')
```

Depending on various settings as covered in the checksum section, this would result in the following hash value: 0xAABA37D5A4ADE349BE93CC6DC2F72EA6D-3CA2651. The natural business key equivalent would just be '~!@|N/A\@|.'

This is our recommended solution. While the hash value is not as readily recognizable, it doesn't require checks to detect NULL values and cast them into a different value. The NULL value would automatically be interpreted as the zero key.

An added advantage of this approach is that zero keys will be automatically added wherever needed, eliminating the need for a separate record insertion process to ensure all Hubs receive a zero key.

Automation

To generate the Hub data logistics processes, we need the following metadata:

- → The mapping between the source and target data objects
- → The definition of the business key
- → The data item mapping for the business key components

The data object mapping captures the relationship between the source and target data objects, which includes the data item mapping for any of the business key components, if applicable.

There is no specific need to add data types. Everything is convention-based, and there is no risk of implicit conversions because these are standardized in the code generation template.

The business key definition captures how the business key, *as defined in the source data object,* is mapped to the surrogate key in the target data object. The specific column(s) that identify a business key, and therefore are required to calculate the surrogate key, may differ between data objects, but the result is always mapped to the same column(s) in the Hub.

Each individual business key component is a standard data item mapping. The meaning of these mappings is defined by the columns they correspond to in the target data object — the business key components.

Design metadata example

For this example, the Hub is populated from PSA data. The PSA is the source data object, and the Hub is the target data object. The Audit Trail Id, as always, is not mapped. This value is provided at runtime by the data logistics control framework.

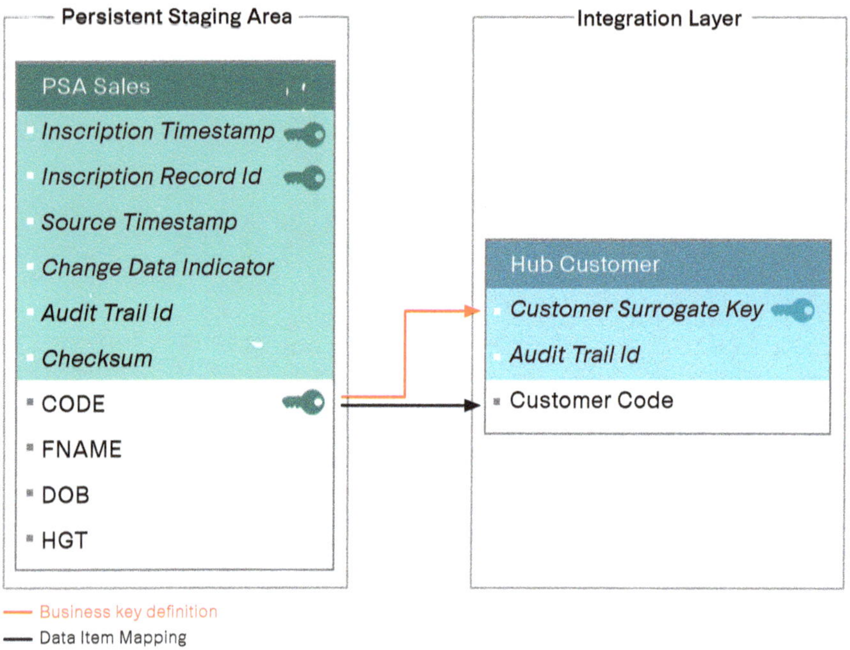

In the design metadata, this is recorded as follows:


```
{
 "dataObjectMappings": [
  {
   "name": "PSA_Sales_to_Hub_Customer",
   "sourceDataObjects": [ {"name": "PSA_Sales" } ],
   "targetDataObject": { "name": "Hub_Customer" },
   "dataItemMappings": [
    {
     "sourceDataItems": [ { "name": "CODE" } ],
     "targetDataItem": { "name": "Customer_Code" }
    }
   ],
```

```
   "businessKeyDefinitions": [
    {
      "ordinalPosition": 1,
      "surrogateKey": "Customer_Sk",
      "businessKeyComponents": [
        {
          "ordinalPosition": 1,
          "dataItem": {
            "name": "CODE"
          }
        }
      ]
    }
   ]
  }
 ]
}
```

In this example only the data items as they are known in the source data object and their order are relevant for the business definition. The mapping to the original business key components is a regular data item mapping.

In the following sections, we provide two templates as practical examples that apply this metadata.

Solution pattern example

The code generation template defines the specific approaches for surrogate key generation. The metadata itself is agnostic to the surrogate key method, allowing various technical implementations to be generated based on the provided business key definition. These implementations could include sequence values, hash keys, or natural business keys.

The solution pattern is where decisions are made on the best technical optimization. To what extent is caching implemented? Where is the majority of the compute taking place?

An example in its simplest form can look like this:

Example pattern for a Hub process

1) Select the distinct business key component(s) from the PSA data object. Exclude records where:

- **a)** The business key value is NULL
- **b)** The business key value already exists in the target object

2) Generate a surrogate key for each record where the above is true

3) Insert the new records into the target table, mapping the

- **a)** Generated surrogate key
- **b)** Audit Trail Id
- **c)** Original business key component value(s)

An example of this is shown below using SQL:

```
INSERT INTO [Hub_Customer]
(
  [Customer_Sk],
  [Audit_Trail_Id],
  [Customer_Id]
)
SELECT
  COALESCE(TRIM(CONVERT(NVARCHAR(MAX),
  [Customer_Id])), '~!@|N/A') + '\@|'
  AS [Customer_Sk], <Audit Trail Id value>
  AS [Audit_Trail_Id],
  [Customer_Id]
FROM
(
  SELECT DISTINCT [Code] AS [Customer_Id]
  FROM [Psa_Sales] psa
  WHERE
    [Code] IS NOT NULL
    AND NOT EXISTS
    (
      SELECT 1
      FROM [Hub_Customer] hub
      WHERE Psa.[Code] = hub.[Customer_Id]
  )
) sub
```

Applying a simple DISTINCT will suffice to retrieve the list of unique business keys. The NOT EXISTS check will prevent any inserts of values that already have been committed to the Hub. A LEFT OUTER JOIN can also be used instead of a NOT EXISTS to determine if the business key is already available in the Hub. It's just another variation on the same theme that can be encoded in the template.

If the inscription timestamp is part of the pattern, the earliest (lowest) inscription timestamp value is retrieved from the PSA data object. The code will be slightly more complicated. For this reason, we've added this —and corresponding code generation templates— to our website: https://dtng.link/cbp2y.

Both examples immediately satisfy the fundamental principles for data logistics. Due to the NOT EXISTS or LEFT OUTER JOIN check, the process will always prevent the re-insertion of records that have already been processed or are not required to be processed. It is natively idempotent.

Thanks to this deterministic behavior, both examples also facilitate re-initialization and refactoring.

Solution pattern example—virtual

Each data object mapping is generated as a separate executable process – a module.

These separate, independent, modules all integrate data into the Hub.

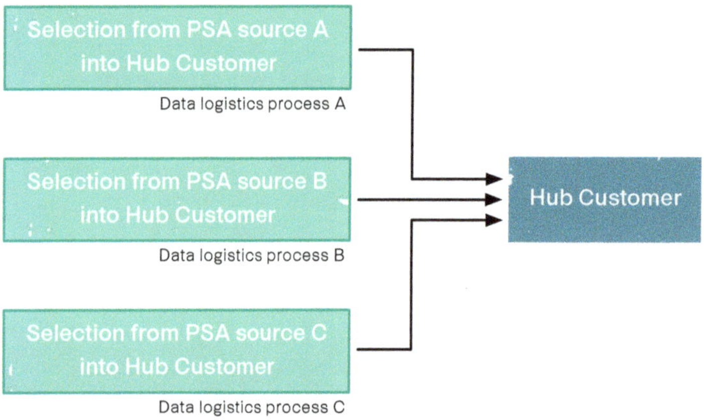

Instead of generating separate objects, the template can also be tweaked to generate individual data object mappings as SELECT components that are wrapped into a single, larger, statement – as shown below.

```
SELECT hub.*
FROM
(
 SELECT
  COALESCE(TRIM(CONVERT(NVARCHAR(MAX),[Customer_Id])), '~!@|N/A') + '\@|' AS [Customer_Sk],
  [Customer_Id]
 FROM
 (
   /* Hub Customer selection from PSA Source 'A' */
   UNION
   /* Hub Customer selection from PSA Source 'B' */
   UNION
   /* Hub Customer selection from PSA Source 'C' */
  ) all_selection
) hub
UNION
SELECT '~!@|N/A\@|' AS ZERO_KEY, 'Unknown' AS ZERO_BUSINESS_KEY
```

The same metadata can be used to generate a single database view that represents the Hub in its entirety.

Note that the zero key is 'unioned' to the view once at the bottom.

Natural business relationships

↗ An NBR data object uniquely identifies instances of relationships between CBCs, essentially forming a *list of unique relationships*. In the physical data model, this is represented by the Data Vault Link.

This section details the implementation of the Link.

Conceptually, a Link represents a connection between two or more Hubs, or sometimes a recursive relationship for a single Hub. This connection can signify an event, transaction, or any other kind of relationship.

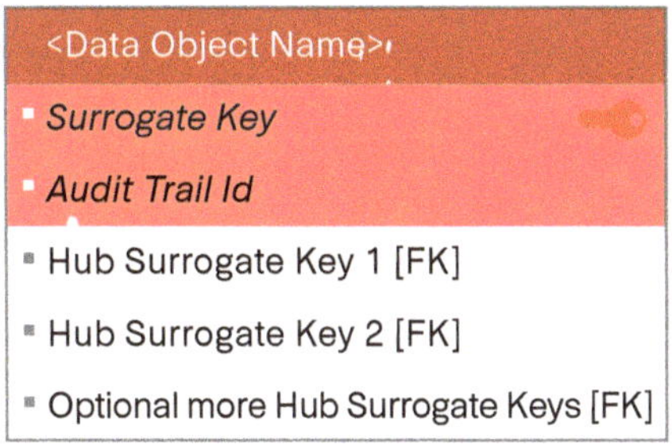

Link data object structure

A Link data object uniquely identifies instances of a relationship between two or more Hubs.

The Link data object structure includes:
- → The Link surrogate key, uniquely identifying a relationship between Hub instances
- → The Audit Trail Id, containing the reference to the control framework instance that added the relationship
- → Two or more Hub surrogate keys, listing the surrogate keys that identify the instances of the Hubs involved in this relationship

Optionally, the following column can be considered:
- → The inscription timestamp, indicating the time of arrival in the data solution as inherited from the staging layer
- → The record source indicator, indicating the origin of the record

Link surrogate key

The surrogate key in the Link is a single column that represents the primary key of the Link table. It can be referenced by related entities, specifically Link-describing Satellites, often referred to as 'Link-Satellites.' The operation of Link-Satellites is subject to various decisions and interpretations, which are covered in the ⚐ contextual data section.

The Link surrogate key is directly related to the combination of all business keys of the involved Hubs. Similar to the Hub, this combination of Hub business keys or their surrogate key equivalents could also act as the surrogate key. However, this composite-key approach would mean that the Link-Satellites inherit many columns and complexities. Using a singular surrogate key is usually easier and more efficient.

The earlier example of the SalesMaster data set has been expanded with a transaction identifier ('TRANS_ID') and product reference ('PROD_REF').

The resulting Link below represents a three-way relationship between the Customer Hub, the Sale Transaction Hub, and the Product Hub. The Link surrogate key is the unique combination of these Hubs.

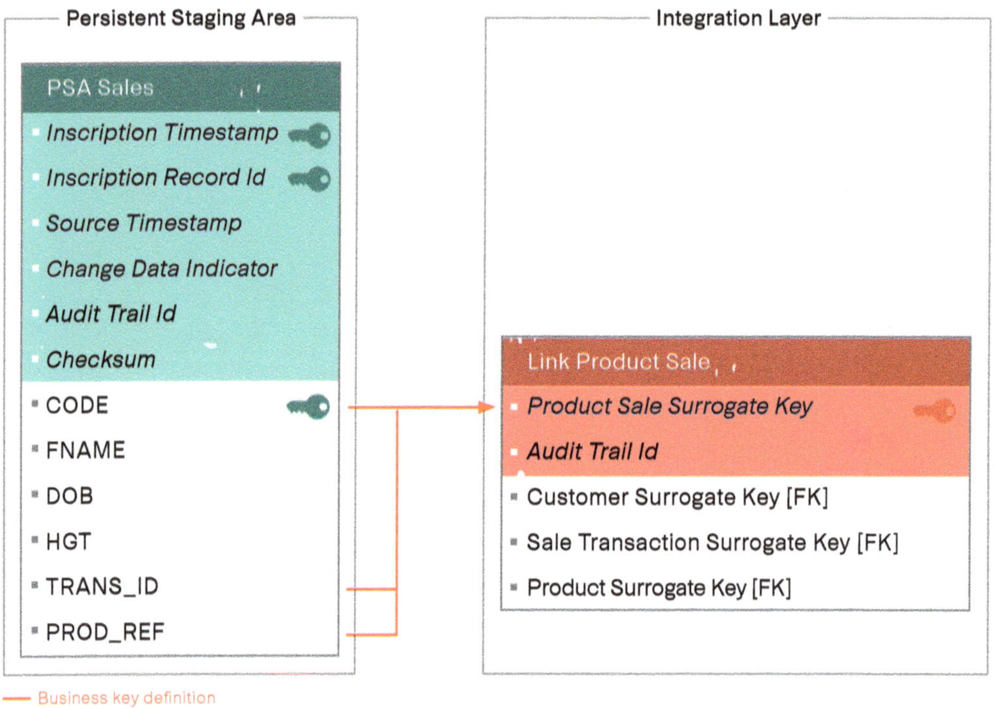

In metadata, the Link surrogate key is part of the business key definition metadata object, which also contains the individual business keys for the involved Hubs. All four business key definitions —the Link definition and the three Hub definitions— must be available in the data object mapping, but for now we only focus on the definition for the link. Hub surrogate keys for Links are covered in the next section.

```
[
 {
  "ordinalPosition": 1,
  "name": "PRODUCT_SALE_BK",
  "surrogateKey": "PRODUCT_SALE_SK",
  "businessKeyComponents": [
   {
    "ordinalPosition": 1,
    "dataItem": { "name": "CODE" }
   },
   {
    "ordinalPosition": 2,
    "dataItem": { "name": "TRANS_ID" }
   },
   {
    "ordinalPosition": 3,
    "dataItem": {"name": "PROD_REF" }
   }
  ]
 }
]
```

Hub surrogate keys

Links reference Hubs, and to ensure consistency in the data solution —particularly referential integrity— the Hub keys are part of the Link definition. Even though the reference may not always be enforced technically, they are foreign keys to the (parent) Hub.

The number of Hub surrogate key columns in a Link corresponds to the number of references in the Link.

To process the data into a Link, the individual business key definitions for each Hub must be mapped, so that the same key can be generated or retrieved.

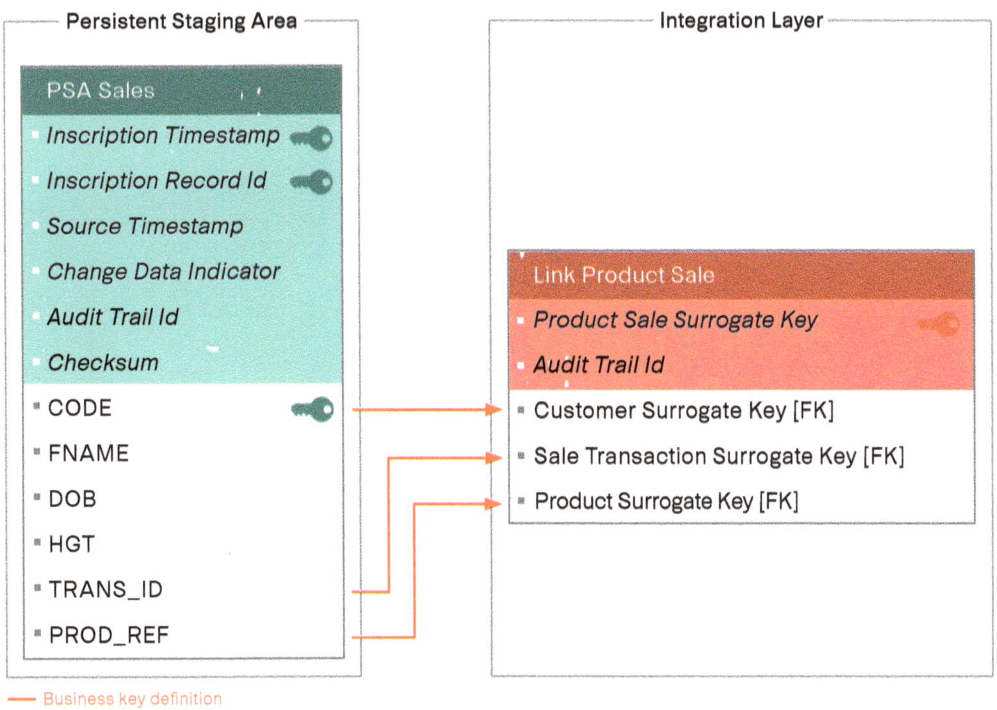

The order of business key definitions in metadata is significant. By convention, the first key in the list is the combined business key is the Link surrogate key.

Following this convention, in this example the first business key definition in this list (array) of business key definitions defines the Link surrogate key. The subsequent ones refer to each individual Hub surrogate key.

The complete example of the business key definition, combining the joint keys as well as the individual Hub keys is available below.

```
[
 {
  "ordinalPosition": 1
  /* Link business key definition from previous section */
 },
 {
  "ordinalPosition": 2,
  "name": "CUSTOMER_BK",
  "surrogateKey": "CUSTOMER_SK",
  "businessKeyComponents": [
   {
    "ordinalPosition": 1,
    "dataItem": { "name": "CODE" }
   }
  ]
 },
 {
  "ordinalPosition": 3,
  "name": "SALE_TRANSACTION_BK",
  "surrogateKey": "SALE_TRANSACTION_SK",
  "businessKeyComponents": [
   {
    "ordinalPosition": 1,
    "dataItem": { "name": "TRANS_ID" }
   }
  ]
 },
 {
  "ordinalPosition": 4,
  "name": "PRODUCT_BK",
  "surrogateKey": "PRODUCT_SK",
  "businessKeyComponents": [
   {
    "ordinalPosition": 1,
    "dataItem": { "name": "PROD_REF" }
   }
  ]
 }
]
```

Audit Trail Id

The Audit Trail Id follows the same approach as for any object in the data solution. The unique execution id of the data logistics process that populates data from the source data object into the Link data object will be inserted here.

As with the Hub, this value is *not* copied from the source data object.

Optional columns

Regarding optional columns, the Link table follows the same approach as the Hub. The inscription timestamp and record source indicator can be considered optional columns.

Inscription timestamp

To ensure deterministic processing, the inscription timestamp is inherited from the staging layer data. Essentially, the inscription timestamp represents the first time the combination of business keys was presented to the integration layer.

As with the Hub, the exact value depends somewhat on the order of data logistics processing. The same considerations as with the Hub apply here for adding this column or not and will not be repeated in this section.

Record source indicator

Similarly, the record source indicator can be retrieved from the control framework via the Audit Trail Id, making recording it here potentially redundant.

The same considerations as for the Hub apply.

Link design pattern

The below is an overview of the design pattern for the Link table, supported by examples for code generation and implementation.

As before, the full pattern, using the recommended pattern documentation structure, can be accessed via our website: https://dtng.link/g97n0.

The Link data logistics process should implement the following concepts:

- → Select the distinct combination of business key values, and optionally retain the earliest inscription timestamp for each business key combination
- → Verify the presence of each combination of business keys in the Link. Insert if new, discard otherwise
- → Generate (or retrieve) the Hub surrogate keys
- → Generate the surrogate key for the Link

As with the Hub, the Link implementation is an insert-only process that includes a lookup to determine if records should be inserted. Therefore, the Link is natively modular, independent, fault-tolerant, and idempotent.

Select the distinct combination of business key values

Link tables contain the list of unique business key combinations. To process the data into the Link, all elements (columns) of the involved business keys must be selected. As before, it may be the case that this combination of values appears multiple times in the source data object, so a form of unique selection (i.e., DISTINCT or similar) is required.

If the inscription timestamp is also incorporated into the design the same approach as applied to the Hub can be considered to ensure a unique selection while retaining the first (minimum) inscription timestamp for each combination.

Verify the presence of each combination of business keys

Business key combinations will be inserted into the Link table only if they are not already present. A lookup is performed to verify whether the combined business keys from the selection in the previous step already exist.

If they do not yet exist, they can be inserted in the Link table. Otherwise, the records can be gracefully discarded.

Generate or retrieve the Hub surrogate keys

The combination of the business keys define the Link surrogate key, uniquely identifying a relationship between Hubs. Each individual business key, representing each individual Hub, is added to the Link for reference as foreign key — though not necessarily enforced. The same surrogate key approach as outlined in the Hub section can be used here.

Generate the surrogate key for the Link

The last step in the Link pattern involves assigning a surrogate key to each business key combination before insertion.

Considerations

The following sections contain considerations that can be included in the Link design pattern.

Degenerate columns

A somewhat peculiar possible exception to the Link table structure is the concept of a *degenerate column*. This is a non-business key column that is part of the definition of the relationship, and therefore impacts the granularity.

Adding a degenerate column is a way of stating that a given value is important to guarantee uniqueness, but not important enough to warrant a Hub of its own — it's not considered a CBC.

An example of this is shown below:

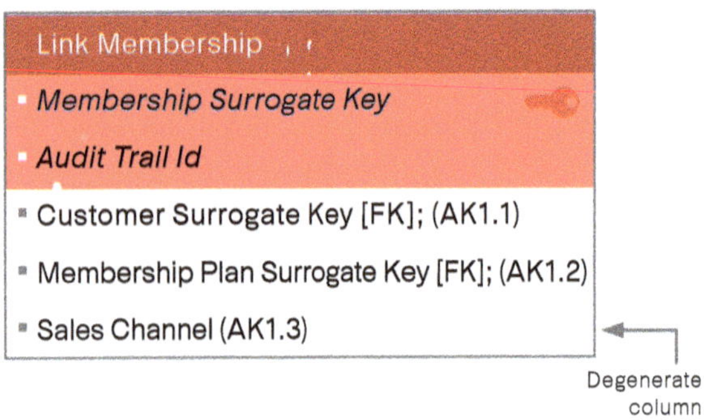

This Link table contains a reference to the Customer Hub and Membership Plan Hub. But, in this case, it's not enough to uniquely identify the relationship. To do so, a third column has been added called 'Sales Channel.'

This column *is* part of the unique constraint (regardless whether enforced or not), and is also be part of the Link surrogate key. However, it is *not* referencing other objects. There is no foreign key.

In the data object mapping metadata, a degenerate column is implemented as a standard data item mapping.

At the time of writing, there is an ongoing debate if and when implementing a degenerate column is the right thing to do. We feel it is worth mentioning the option, as it is often encountered in projects.

The obvious alternative, and our recommended approach, to using degenerate columns is to 'model these out' as Hubs. They might not be strong business concepts, and they may not have a clear definition or context yet, but that are definitive advantages from an maintenance of the physical model.

In the end, we let the engine work out the optimal physical model structure, and this is one of the options at its disposal.

Deciding how to implement transactions

Imagine a brand new coffee shop that has just opened it doors right around the corner. Everything is brand new — the machines, the tables and chairs, and, of course, its information systems. A freshly installed point-of-sale application has just been booted up when you walk in.

For this business, the following business concepts could be defined:

- A shop
- A customer
- An employee
- A product

Now, picture a transaction taking place. A customer enters the shop, and buys a cappuccino from the barista at work.

You could argue that this event represents a relationship between the following Hubs:

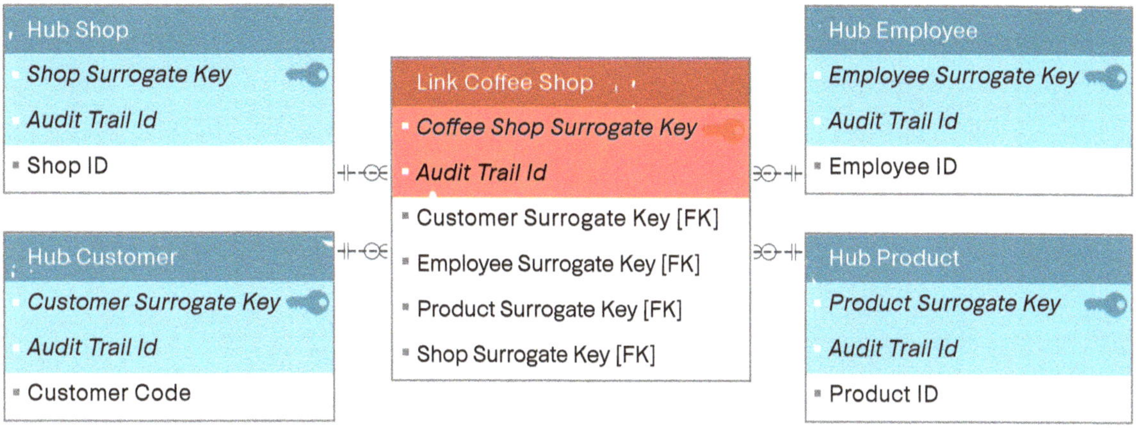

What would happen in the system during the first-ever transaction?

→ A shop record would be created in the Hub Shop
→ A customer record would be created in the Hub Customer
→ An employee record would be created in the Hub Employee
→ A product record for the cappuccino would be created in the Hub Product
→ A relationship between these would be created in the Link Coffee Shop

So far, so good. But what would happen when the same customer purchases another cappuccino from the same barista?

→ The shop record already exists, and is ignored
→ The customer record already exists, and is ignored
→ The employee record already exists, and is ignored
→ The product record already exists, and is ignored
→ The relationship record already exists, and is ignored

This is clearly not correct. This way, the second sale transaction is lost. This indicates that the model is not yet correct, as an identifier for the transaction is still missing.

Depending on your specific Data Vault implementation philosophy, the transaction identifier ('Transaction ID') could be added as a degenerate column. Let's **start with that option.**

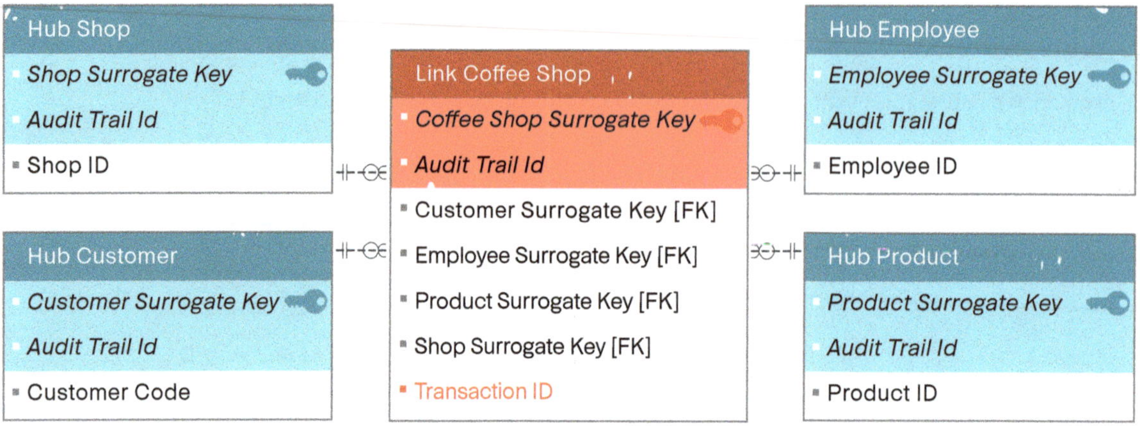

Now, each time the customer purchases a new cappuccino, a new record in the Link will be generated. But what happens if additional context about the transaction itself needs to be recorded?

Depending on your Data Vault approach this could be created as a Link-Satellite, or even added directly to the Link. This approach, sometimes called a *Transactional Link* might be sufficient and could also be beneficial for overall performance reasons.

But from a pure modeling approach there is another way: 'modeling out' the transaction as its own Hub:

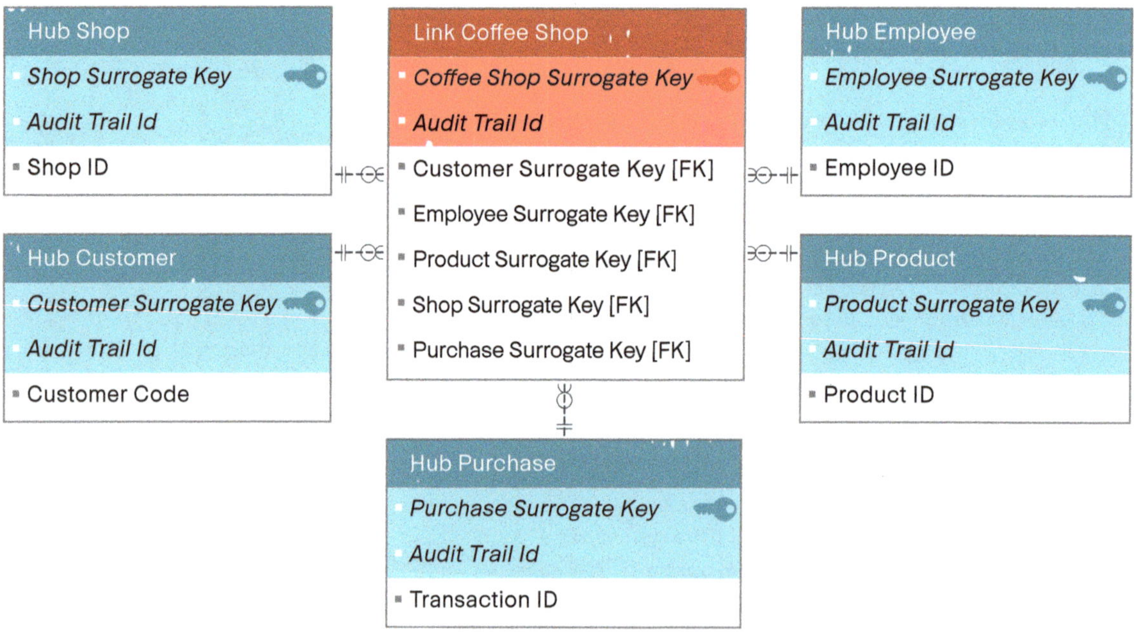

The advantage of this approach is that the new Hub Purchase, which embodies the sale transaction, serves as a potential integration point for other Links – as well as additional context describing the purchase.

Not only can any context be directly attached to the Hub, but it is also easier to connect the Hub Purchase to other business concepts that do not involve the Hubs displayed in the diagram.

This method is an effective and flexible way to expand the model. In ELM terminology, this approach is known as a *relationship describing Hub* because, in this case, the granularity of the Link is driven by the purchase.

Depending on the optimization directives, the engine would select, and implement, one of these alternatives. Except for the first example, which only serves to illustrate the requirement to model the transaction *somewhere*, the outcomes will be the same.

Using degenerate columns or separate transaction Hubs are essentially variations on the same theme, and the engine can generate both.

Same-As Links

Sometimes, different instances of the same Hub might represent the exact same thing. For example, a customer might appear in two different operational systems without a shared identifier – a true business key.

In a perfect world of data, with flawless design, governance and fully synchronized systems, this issue might never occur. However, most of us have to deal with data that is less than pristine.

Same-As Links capture this similarity relationship, and are commonly implemented when initial passive integration is not feasible. Instead, they are used as a form of data interpretation, applying logic to establish and record similarities between two keys.

In these scenarios, there isn't a relationship between different Hubs, but rather a relationship to the *same* Hub twice.

Other use cases can apply as well. We have seen this approach used to implement linkages between newer versions of a specific instance. For example, when an insurance policy, subscription, or loan renews, a new version might be automatically created with a new identifier. Tracking these linkages in a 'Link Renewal' can be a suitable use case too.

There might be a requirement to determine a 'golden customer record' because this does not (yet) exist in the organization, and it is required for integrated customer reporting. It might be essential for initiatives like Know Your Customer ('KYC'), and achieving a '360 degree view' of the customer.

A Same-As Link can to do that.

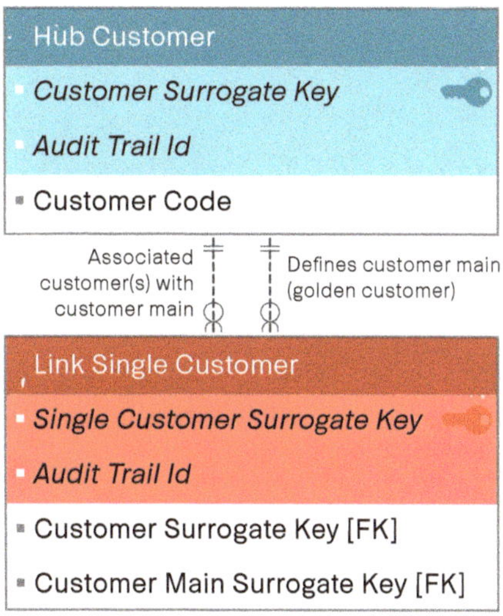

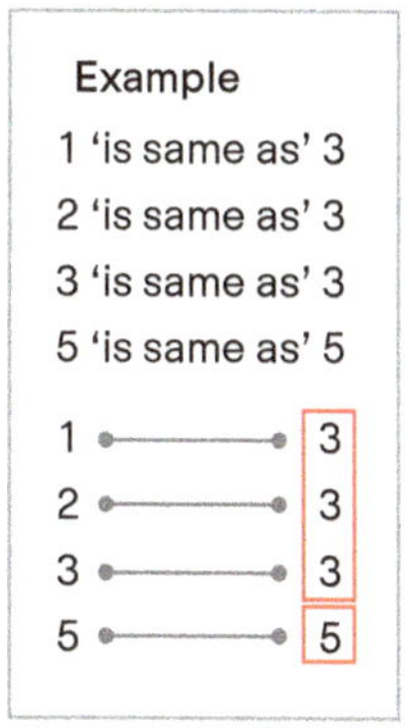

The above example is identical in structure to the hierarchical Link. However, the data it contains is very different. This is not a hierarchy, but a series of matches to assert similarity.

As with the hierarchy example, 'modeling out' is an option for Same-As Links as well:

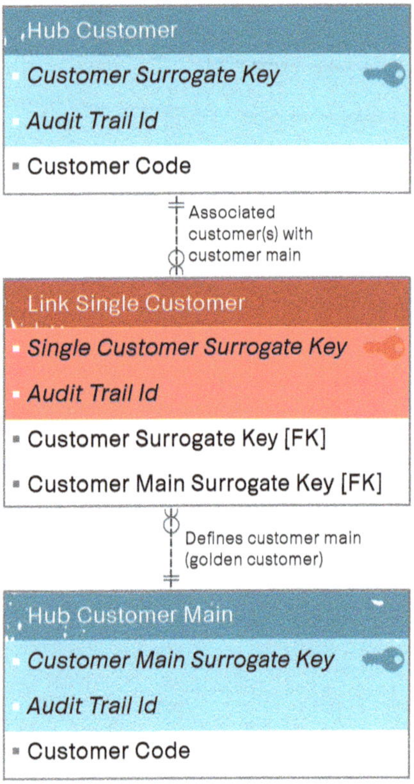

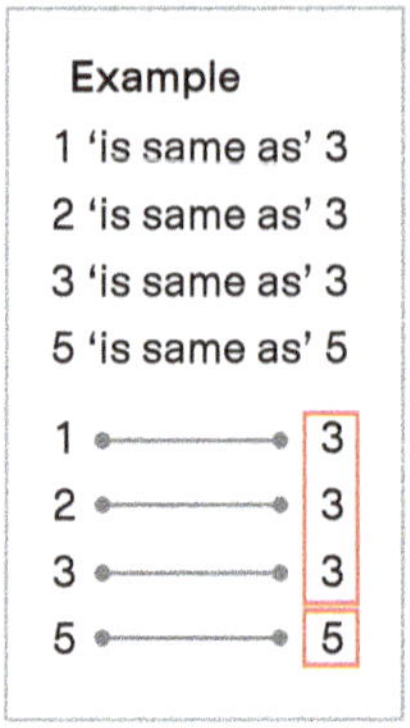

The only material difference is that a separate Hub is defined to store the integrated version, the 'golden customer key' in this case. Both approaches are tools in the engine toolbox to achieve the same outcome.

Unlike hierarchical structures, where the number of additional objects can be extensive, the number of additional objects for managing similarity will be limited in this approach. Personally, we pre-fer this second approach, and ensure our design patterns include it to manage these situations effectively.

Filtering

A common requirement when implementing Links is to apply *filtering*. This may sound counterintuitive to delivering 100 % of the data 100 % of the time, and perhaps *routing* might be a more appropriate term because that is the true goal.

Filtering (or routing) essentially involves applying a WHERE predicate or similar to select data from the staging layer, but its purpose is *not* to restrict the flow of incoming data.

Let's continue with the example from the role playing section. If we decide to model a 'Driver' Link and an 'Owner' Link we do so because these are the types of relationships between a 'Person' and a 'Vehicle' we are interested in. But the incoming data might be structured in a very different way.

In this example, the original data set contains all data including the role type. Using a qualifying criterion —in this case the 'role'— the data can be split out into different Links:

Original data

Person	Vehicle	Role	Date
John	726-ABA	Owner	2022-11-10
Peter	726-ABA	Driver	2023-04-05
Peter	726-ABA	Owner	2023-12-12

In metadata, this is supported by the *Filter Criterion* property in the Data Object Mapping.

A common scenario arises when central 'main' lists of products, customers, or other important business concepts are subdivided into more specialized subtypes. For instance, when a product is categorized as 'X,' it represents a loan, whereas if it is categorized as 'Y,' it signifies a term deposit. Most designs require some level of subtyping to create a meaningful model, and filtering is one tool in the toolbox to achieve this.

NULL handling for Links

When a business key for a Hub is NULL, there is no reason to attempt loading it. However, for a Link, the relationship can still be processed even if one of the business keys is NULL. This situation is cause for concern and indicates a need to pause, step back, and evaluate the model. A relationship with a NULL component may not be valid.

As noted in the ⚐ zero keys section, replacing NULL values with zero keys allows this data to be loaded successfully. However, this should be seen as a safeguard rather than a solution – the underlying issue should still be addressed. We recommend adding ⚐ testing framework controls to both the integration layer implementation and the staging layer objects to monitor these occurrences.

When NULL keys are detected in Links, this should trigger a model re-evaluation and potential refactoring. Additionally, a plan should be in place to handle such cases going forward. For instance, if the NULL value is due to a data quality issue or an error in the operational system that is subsequently corrected, the updated record *will* contain the business key.

What should be done with the 'old' relationship, the one that still has the NULL value? One approach is to flag these records with an ⚐ exception bitmap and exclude them from downstream selection. Another alternative is to reload parts of the impacted model with updated definitions, allowing the updated record to take precedence over the old record containing the NULL value.

Implementation

Zero keys can be implemented following the guidelines documented in the ⚐ zero key section. The surrogate key approach —whether using hash keys or natural business keys— can be automated based on how the business key is prepared. This preparation includes handling NULL values by replacing them with the default string value '~!@|N/A.'

If zero keys in the Hub are configured, using the hash value 0xAABA37D5A4ADE349BE93CC6DC2F72EA6D3CA2651 or the natural business key ~!@|N/A\@| as examples, the data automatically connects.

If a different standard value, such as 0x0000000000000000000000000000000000000000, is used in the Hub, the Link pattern can be updated with a NULL check. For example, by using the COALESCE statement or a similar method, when the business key resolves to NULL, it can be replaced by the zero key.

If *all* of the business keys for a Link are NULL, then the record can be safely discarded.

A similar approach can be implemented for sequence values as well, but there is also the option to perform a key lookup if preferred.

Depending on the specific implementation of Data Vault, Link tables may require their own zero keys as well. This only applies when using Links have their own Satellites ('Link-Satellites[44]') that contain descriptive properties, as opposed to defining Link-Satellites as objects that *only* contain validity details for the relationship.

If zero keys for Links are relevant, the same approach used for Hubs can be applied.

Automation

To generate the Link data logistics processes, we need the following metadata:
→ The mapping between the source and target data objects
→ The definition of the combined business key, and each individual business key separately
→ Any non-Hub column mappings you may need (degenerate columns) as data item mappings

The data object mapping captures the relationship between the source and target data objects.

The business key definition is always defined as an array (list) in the schema for data solution automation.

In many cases, such as the Hub, there is only one segment in this array, which is the business key definition. However, for Links this is different. The array of business key definitions contains a segment that includes all business key components across all involved business keys to define the surrogate key. Subsequent segments hold each individual Hub business key definition to facilitate the creation (or lookup) of each Hub surrogate key.

In case degenerate columns are to be supported, these can be defined as standard data item mappings.

Design metadata example

For this example, the PSA is yet again used as the source data object. This time for the Link. The Audit Trail Id, as always, is not mapped. This value is provided at runtime by the data logistics control framework.

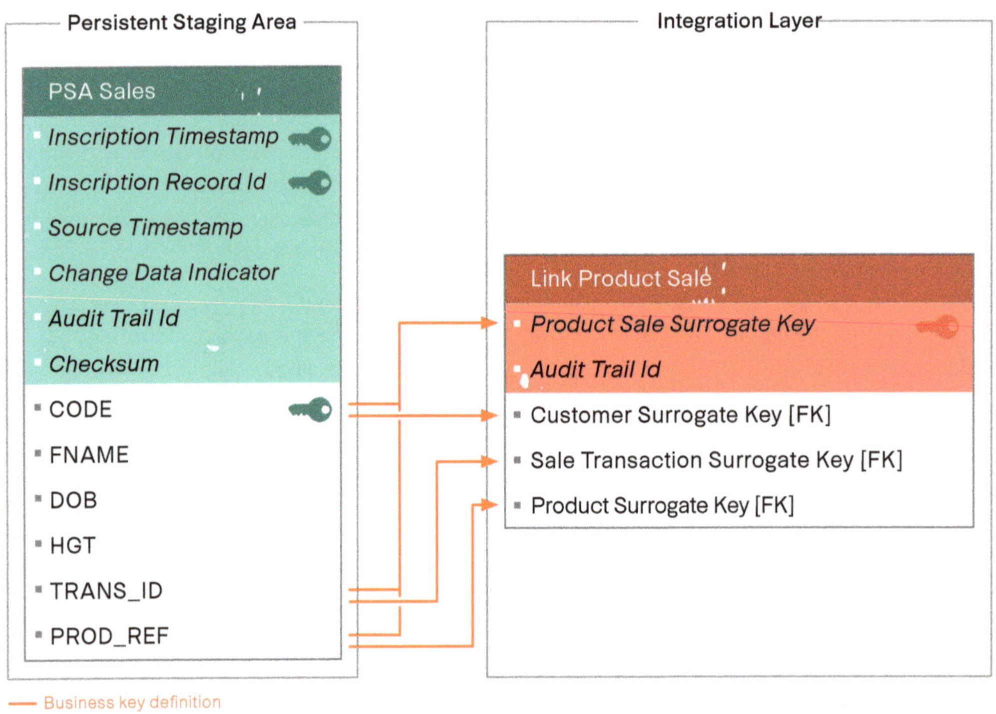

In the design metadata, this is recorded as follows:

```
{
 "dataObjectMappings": [
  {
   "name": "PSA_Sales_to_Link_Product_Sale",
   "sourceDataObjects": [ { "name": "PSA_Sales" } ],
   "targetDataObject": { "name": "Hub_Customer" },
   "businessKeyDefinitions": [
    {
     "ordinalPosition": 1,
     "name": "PRODUCT_SALE_BK",
     "surrogateKey": "PRODUCT_SALE_SK",
     "businessKeyComponents": [
      {
       "ordinalPosition": 1,
       "dataItem": { "name": "CODE" }
      },
      {
       "ordinalPosition": 2,
       "dataItem": { "name": "TRANS_ID" }
      },
      {
       "ordinalPosition": 3,
       "dataItem": { "name": "PROD_REF" }
      }
     ]
    },
    {
     "ordinalPosition": 2,
     "name": "CUSTOMER_BK",
     "surrogateKey": "CUSTOMER_SK",
     "businessKeyComponents": [
      {
       "ordinalPosition": 1,
       "dataItem": { "name": "CODE" }
      }
     ]
    },
    {
     "ordinalPosition": 3,
     "name": "SALE_TRANSACTION_BK",
     "surrogateKey": "SALE_TRANSACTION_SK",
     "businessKeyComponents": [
      {
       "ordinalPosition": 1,
       "dataItem": { "name": "TRANS_ID" }
      }
     ]
    },
    {
     "ordinalPosition": 4,
     "name": "PRODUCT_BK",
     "surrogateKey": "PRODUCT_SK",
     "businessKeyComponents": [
      {
       "ordinalPosition": 1,
       "dataItem": { "name": "PROD_REF" }
      }
     ]
    }
   ]
  }
 ]
}
```

Solution pattern example

The data logistics process for a Link is, in many ways, similar to that of a Hub. The same considerations apply, and additional background can be found in the Hub section.

Example pattern for a Link process

1) Select the distinct business keys from the PSA data object. Exclude records where:
   a) The combination of business key values is NULL
   b) The combination of business key values already exists in the target object
2) Generate a surrogate key for each record where the above is true
3) Insert the new records into the target table, mapping the
   a) Generated surrogate key for the Link
   b) Generated (or retrieved) surrogate keys for each of the Hubs

c) Audit Trail Id

d) Original business key component value(s)

Example SQL code for a Link is provided below.

```
INSERT INTO [LINK_PRODUCT_SALE]
(
 [PRODUCT_SALE_SK],
 [AUDIT_TRAIL_ID],
 [CUSTOMER_SK],
 [SALE_TRANSACTION_SK],
 [PRODUCT_SK]
)
SELECT
(
 SELECT
  HASHBYTES('SHA1',
   COALESCE(TRIM(CONVERT(NVARCHAR(MAX),[CUSTOMER_ID])), '~!@|N/A') + '\@|' +
   COALESCE(TRIM(CONVERT(NVARCHAR(MAX),[SALE_TRANSACTION_ID])), '~!@|N/A') + '\@|'
   COALESCE(TRIM(CONVERT(NVARCHAR(MAX),[PRODUCT_ID])), '~!@|N/A') + '\@|'
  ) AS [PRODUCT_SALE_SK],
  HASHBYTES('SHA1',
   COALESCE(TRIM(CONVERT(NVARCHAR(MAX),[CUSTOMER_ID])), '~!@|N/A') + '\@|'
  ) AS [CUSTOMER_SK],
```

```
HASHBYTES('SHA1',
   COALESCE(TRIM(CONVERT(NVARCHAR(MAX),[SALE_TRANSACTION_ID])), '~!@|N/A') + '\@|'
  ) AS [SALE_TRANSACTION_SK],
HASHBYTES('SHA1',
   COALESCE(TRIM(CONVERT(NVARCHAR(MAX),[PRODUCT_ID])), '~!@|N/A') + '\@|'
  ) AS [PRODUCT_SK],
  0 AS [AUDIT_TRAIL_ID]
 FROM
 (
  SELECT DISTINCT
   [CODE] AS [CUSTOMER_ID],
   [TRANS_ID] AS [SALE_TRANSACTION_ID],
   [PROD_REF] AS [PRODUCT_ID],
  FROM [PSA_SALES] psa
 ) sub
) final
WHERE NOT EXISTS
 (
  SELECT 1
  FROM [LINK_PRODUCT_SALE] link
  WHERE Final.[PRODUCT_SALE_SK] = link.[PRODUCT_SALE_SK]
 )
```

The fundamental principles for data logistics are again supported. The lookup (NOT EXIST in this example) will prevent the re-insertion of records that have already been processed, or are not required to be processed.

As always, please refer to our website for more examples and code-generation templates: https://dtng.link/q2qgp.

Contextual data

A Satellite is time-variant. It tracks historical data, changes over time, based on the assertion timeline. This means the inscription timestamp and the inscription record id is part of the primary key definition, and that data is recorded as per the order of arrival in the data solution.

The Hub or Link objects they describe are referred to as the *parent* object.

↗ Context entities contain all the columns that are describing a CBC or a NBR in detail. It is the 'what' that describes an entity. In Data Vault, the context entity is represented by the Satellite table.

Satellite data object structure

A Satellite contains data that describes a Hub or Link.

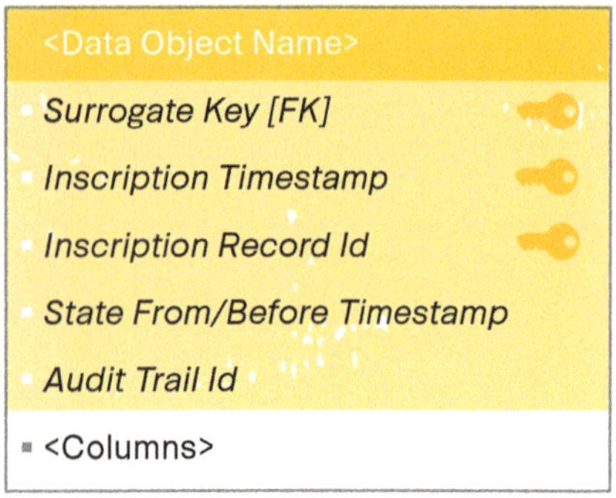

The Satellite data object structure includes:

- → The surrogate key, containing the reference to the record in the parent entity
- → The inscription timestamp, indicating the time of arrival in the data solution as inherited from the staging layer – building the assertion timeline
- → The inscription record id, containing the order in which the data was received, as inherited from the staging layer
- → The state ('from' and/or 'before') timestamp, that contains the definition of the time period for which the data should be queried in downstream processes. Either, or both, of the 'from' and 'before' should be part of the structure
- → The Audit Trail Id, containing the reference to the control framework instance that added the data
- → Any regular descriptive columns that are required to describe the parent entity

Optionally, the following columns can be considered:

- → The state ('from' and/or 'before') timestamp, to the extent that this completes the time period. For instance if the 'from' is added to the structure the 'before' can be considered optional
- → The source timestamp
- → The record source indicator
- → The change data indicator
- → The checksum

Satellites have a composite primary key. By default, the key consists of the parent entity surrogate key, the inscription timestamp, and the inscription record id. This will allow the Satellite to uniquely identify any incoming (change) record.

Additional columns may be made part of the primary key to support the multi-variant concept. This will be outlined further in the ⚐ multi-variance section.

The parent surrogate key is the same as the one in the parent entity. There is a reference between the two entities. However, this reference is usually not enforced (e.g., as a foreign key constraint) in the database or underlying storage solution.

Instead, the *referential integrity* will be safeguarded by the patterns and control framework. Test cases and monitoring will be put in place to ensure this continues to work as expected.

This approach of *lazy referential integrity* will be explained in detail in the ⚐ consistency and integrity section.

Surrogate key

The surrogate key in the Satellite references the record in its parent entity, identifying the associated Hub or Link. This surrogate key is part of the Satellite's primary key definition.

As a result, a reference exists between the Satellite and its parent, even though this is usually not enforced by database technology (if available and supported).

Thus, the keys must remain consistent between the Satellite and its parent.

Conceptually, the Satellite *inherits* the surrogate key from its parent. But in practice, this is usually generated in parallel to avoid processing dependencies.

In any case, the *business key definition* in the design metadata for the Satellite should be the same as for its parent – for the source data object from which they both are derived or loaded.

This business key definition will be used to generate the surrogate key.

The diagram below illustrates this principle. Both the Hub and the Satellite —defined in separate data object mappings— share the same business key definition. The 'CODE' column identifies the business key and surrogate key of the 'Customer' Hub and is used to generate the same surrogate key value for the Satellite.

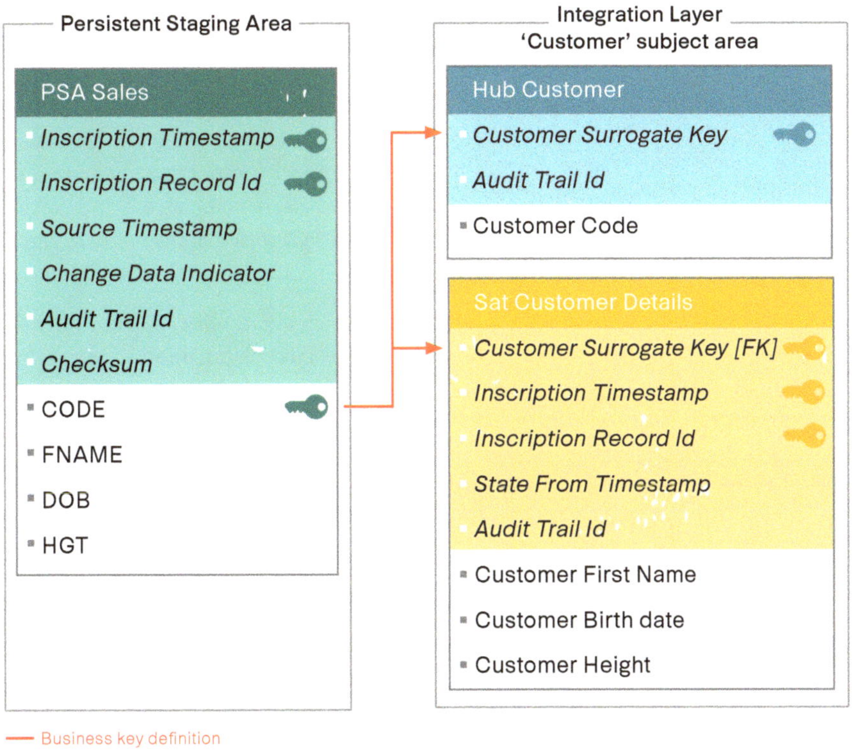

Because the process to deliver the surrogate key for the Satellite mirrors that of its parent, we refer to the surrogate key section for more details.

Inscription timestamp

The inscription timestamp is copied directly from the staging layer data object that populates the Satellite. As a result, its data type remains consistent with the staging layer — a high-precision timestamp.

To deliver a data solution that is fully deterministic, the inscription timestamp should *not* be set during the data logistics process from the staging layer to the integration layer. Resetting it would generate a new inscription timestamp every time an integration layer object is truncated and reloaded, whereas copying the value from the staging layer will always produce the same result.

Another reason for reusing the staging layer's value is that it supports a fully virtualized approach. In a virtualized Satellite, displaying a newly generated inscription timestamp with each query would lead to inconsistent outputs. Instead, copying the original value ensures stability and repeatability in query results.

From a metadata perspective, copying the inscription timestamp is simply another data item mapping.

The inscription timestamp is part of the primary key definition for the Satellite, and implements the *assertion timeline*. This is covered in more detail in the ⚐ struggling with time section.

Inscription record id

Unless the entity is *multi-variant,* the inscription record id is the third and final part of the Satellite's primary key.

Like the inscription timestamp, the inscription record id value is copied from the staging layer and is captured in metadata as a data item mapping.

It's a technical trick to *uniquefy* the inscription timestamp in cases where this value alone is not precise enough – even when it is defined as a high-precision timestamp.

The rationale for this is covered in the ⚐ logging the record order section of the architecture overview.

As described in the ⚐ PSA inscription record id section, we do not recommend merging the inscription record id with the inscription timestamp to create a unique key. Instead, we prefer adding the inscription record id directly to the Satellite's primary key.

State timestamp

The state timestamp holds the value that represents the *state timeline.* Although this column is mapped as a regular data item, it holds special significance. Conceptually, this is where the design of the state timeline occurs.

By carefully selecting the columns or calculations for the state timeline, the resulting state timestamp column will be standardized, simplifying downstream data delivery.

Having a standard column for the state timeline means that more generic templates can be applied to manage the complexities of (re)building timelines for delivery. In some cases, this might result in columns being stored redundantly in the Satellite.

The state timestamp could be a combination of different columns and, for ease of use, the original values can also be stored in the Satellite.

Assuming the source data object contains a suitable candidate, a regular data item mapping is used to map the selected source data item to the state timestamp column in metadata.

This is part of the *temporal design* of the data solution. It's often difficult at first to select the value that represents the correct moment a record value is valid, and it's something that is refined over time. It may be found that the wrong data items were mapped, which may result in a refactoring of the Satellite and corresponding reload from the PSA.

The ⚐ struggling with time section provides more detail on this topic.

Using the source timestamp as state timestamp

In exception cases, the data may not contain a suitable timestamp to build a state timeline with. In these cases the source timestamp may be used instead.

Anything is better than using the inscription timestamp to deliver data.

Due to technical exceptions, and related to certain interfacing approaches, it may happen that transactions *overtake* each other on their way into the staging layer. Since the inscription timestamp represents the time of arrival in the data solution, the later-arriving record may actually be caused by an earlier change event.

This is known to happen especially using:

→ Message-based,
→ Technical (native) Change Data Capture (CDC), or
→ Specialized middleware software for data transaction distribution

For data consumers, this means that the later-arrived record does not represent the most recent change when using this timeline for reporting, and this is likely to impact the data products that are delivered downstream.

This is the reason the source timestamp exists, and is captured as part of the staging layer data logistics. If no suitable timestamp is available to represent the state timeline, then it is our recommendation to use the source timestamp — since anything is better than using the inscription timestamp.

Audit Trail Id

The Audit Trail Id follows the same approach as for any data solution entity. The unique execution id of the data logistics process that populates the data from the source data object into the Satellite data object will be inserted here.

In a virtualized data solution, the runtime execution id from the view or procedure call is shown. In all cases, the Audit Trail Id can be referenced in the data logistics control framework for auditability.

This value is *not* copied from the source data object.

Descriptive columns

The bulk of data in the Satellite is made up of regular, descriptive, columns. They contain the true 'payload' of the data.

These columns are sometimes referred to as *non-identifying,* because the identification of the 'thing' they describe is ultimately captured in the parent entity — by its business key.

The regular columns are copied from the source data object in the staging layer. In metadata, this is recorded using standard data item mappings.

These data item mappings capture the majority of 'reshuffling' the data from the staging layer to the integration layer. Different columns in a given source data object may describe different Hubs or Links. As a result, some columns from the same source data object are mapped to different Satellites because they describe different things.

This concept of mapping data items from the same source data object to potentially different target data objects is referred to by us as *making changes in the column scope.*

We cover this in detail in the ⚐ record compacting section.

As before, the regular columns, as mapped from the source data object, are located on the bottom of the table definition by default.

Optional columns

In the introduction, we mentioned the following columns that can be considered optional for the Satellite:

These are the:

- → Source timestamp
- → Record source indicator
- → Change data indicator
- → Checksum

Source timestamp

The source timestamp is available in the staging layer, and can be mapped to the Satellite using a standard data item mapping.

However, if the source timestamp is necessary it will already be used to define (mapped to) the state timestamp which —strictly speaking— makes it redundant to record separately.

Benefits of still adding the source timestamp to the Satellite may include:

- → Visual confirmation — if the source timestamp is used for the state timestamp their values will be the same
- → The ability to deliver data against a 'source timeline' that shows how data was changed by the operational systems over time (disregarding any specific business-driven timelines)

We recommend to *not* include the source timestamp as a separate column in the Satellite, unless there is an explicit reason to do so. If required, this can always be added later because the values will still be available in the staging layer.

Record source indicator

The record source indicator can also be retrieved from the control framework. The Audit Trail Id that is part of every data set, including context entities, is a reference to the data logistics process that inserted the data.

The control framework contains various administrative properties for this data logistics process, including the operational system from which the data was retrieved. If a dedicated record source label is required, it can be added here and queried if and when necessary.

The only real advantage of having the record source indicator in the Satellite is to provide an immediate visual of its origins without having to add joins to the control framework. If this information is used often, there may be performance benefits associated with having the record source indicator available.

But conceptually, it is not required.

We recommend to *not* include the record source indicator as a separate column in the Satellite unless there is an explicit reason to do so. If required, this can always be added later because the values will still be available in control framework.

Change data indicator

The change data indicator is an optional column for Satellites. It's conceptually the same to the change data indicator column as used in the staging layer, and the purpose is also to be able to determine logical deletes.

However, in the Satellite this information must be specifically evaluated. In most cases, this can *not* be directly copied from the staging layer.

The reason for this is that, in the staging layer, the change data capture indicator represents the (status for the) full record. However, most Satellites only receive parts of this full record – and this impacts the meaning of the change data indicator.

This is the concept of column scope that is further covered in the ⚐ record compacting section.

Because the staging layer change data indicator applies to the full record, it must be separately evaluated if this (also) applies to the selected columns that are mapped to the Satellite. This may not always be necessary, and therefore we consider the change data indicator an optional —albeit important— column.

This is further outlined in the ⚐ logical CDC and ⚐ logical deletes section.

Checksum

A checksum value can simplify the detection of changes by capturing the payload of the record in a single value. This value can be used to determine if incoming data differs from existing data.

As with the PSA, whenever a checksum is used in a data logistics process, we recommend recording the value in the target data object.

For the same reasons as mentioned in the LDA and PSA sections, our examples often utilize checksums.

Satellite design pattern

An overview for the Satellite design pattern is provided below. The Satellite is one of the harder patterns to define, because of the many considerations and the time-variant aspect.

Because so many variations exist, we refer to our website for the various runnable code examples: https://dtng.link/sqyik.

The Satellite data logistics process should implement the following concepts:

→ Select the distinct data changes from the applicable columns
→ Generate (or retrieve) the relevant Hub or Link surrogate key
→ Assert that the incoming data represents a data delta (logical CDC)
→ Map the columns to the target data object

As always, the pattern must be natively modular, independent, fault-tolerant, and idempotent.

Select the distinct data changes from the applicable columns

When processing data from the staging layer into a Satellite, often only a limited set of columns (column scope) is required. The underlying object might contain hundreds of columns, but these may be mapped to various integration layer objects. It is important to select *only* the columns that apply to the target data object, and ensure that only the unique data changes are derived from this limited column set.

The implementation of this process is covered in the redundancy, compacting, and change merging section.

Generate or retrieve the relevant Hub or Link surrogate key

The Satellite's surrogate key is a foreign key reference inherited from its parent Hub or Link. It must either be retrieved or generated in same way. The surrogate key approach as is applied to the Hub or Link can be reused.

Assert that the incoming data represents a data delta

To ensure idempotent, fault-tolerant, and deterministic processing, it must be verified that the distinct data changes from the previous step represent actual changes for the target data object. This can be implemented using a lookup to the Satellite target data object to determine if the presented data represents a true change that can be added. The details of this process are covered in the logical CDC and change merging section.

Map the columns to the target data object

As a final step, the incoming data items must be mapped to the corresponding Satellite data items. For Satellites in the base integration area, no transformations are applied, but the names of the data items might differ. In the derived integration area, transformations are usually defined as part of this data item mapping.

Considerations

The following sections contain considerations that can be included in the Satellite design pattern.

Redundancy, compacting, and change merging

The concept of record compacting, or simply *compacting*, can also be referred to as record condensing or collapsing. Compacting is a mechanism for managing record redundancy, and it can be implemented throughout the data solution.

↗ Compacting removes the redundant, duplicate rows from a given data set as organized (sorted) for a given timeline.

This is important, because redundant records are likely to appear in many data solutions that retain historical, or *time-variant*, data.

Compacting removes the redundant, duplicate rows from a given data set as organized (sorted) for a given timeline. The timeline selected will depend on the area of the solution architecture to which compacting is applied.

The result is a distinct set of data changes for the data set.

In many cases, compacting reduces storage and I/O footprint, improves query performance, and generally makes it easier to interpret the data. To explain this further, we should first outline the concept of data redundancy in a data solution.

Redundant data

When developing a data solution, the incoming data set from the perspective of the target data object may be similar to this:

Surrogate Key	Inscription Timestamp	Contact Number	Email Address	Contact Preference
E92BD8	2022-10-04	0419999999	MichaelM@FastChangeCo.com	Text Message
E92BD8	2022-12-01	0410000000	MichaelM@FastChangeCo.com	Text Message
E92BD8	2022-12-05	0410000000	MichaelM@FastChangeCo.com	Text Message
E92BD8	2022-12-09	0410000000	MichaelM@FastChangeCo.com	Text Message
E92BD8	2022-12-28	0410000000	MichaelM@FastChangeCo.com	Email

Redundant

The inscription record id column is omitted to keep the examples simpler and clearer. For these examples, the inscription timestamps will be unique.

The second, third, and fourth record are completely identical except for the inscription timestamp. This means that these rows arrived at a different moment in time, one after the other in the order of arrival, but that they are otherwise the same.

The third and fourth record in this example have no intrinsic value in terms of data payload. Removing the third and fourth record will not cause loss of data, beyond losing the fact that a redundant record was ever received for this particular target data object – because the change was triggered by a column that is not relevant for this Satellite.

While this is something to consider, there are very few use cases that actually require tracking of this information.

To illustrate this, consider looking at the changes over time for this data set.

Surrogate Key	Inscription Timestamp	Contact Number	Email Address	Contact Preference
E92BD8	2022-10-04	0419999999	MichaelM@FastChangeCo.com	Text Message
E92BD8	2022-12-01	0410000000	MichaelM@FastChangeCo.com	Text Message
E92BD8	2022-12-05	0410000000	MichaelM@FastChangeCo.com	Text Message
E92BD8	2022-12-09	0410000000	MichaelM@FastChangeCo.com	Text Message
E92BD8	2022-12-28	0410000000	MichaelM@FastChangeCo.com	Email

Inscription From	Inscription Before
2022-10-04	2022-12-01
2022-12-01	2022-12-05
2022-12-05	2022-12-09
2022-12-09	2022-12-28
2022-12-28	2022-12-31

Without modifying the data, a series of inscription time periods can be derived by evaluating the inscription timestamp from the 'next' record (following the assertion timeline) as the 'before' timestamp.

This means that the data payload is valid (effective) for any point in time between the inscription from and the derived inscription before timestamp.

In this example, the data as it was valid at 2022-12-27 would be the same as if we were to query the data as of 2022-12-03.

Record compacting algorithms remove data that does not add value. The content of the data set would stay the same, but this content is provided using fewer records.

Surrogate Key	Inscription Timestamp	Contact Number	Email Address	Contact Preference	Inscription From	Inscription Before
E92BD8	2022-10-04	0419999999	MichaelM@FastChangeCo.com	Text Message	2022-10-04	2022-12-01
E92BD8	2022-12-01	0410000000	MichaelM@FastChangeCo.com	Text Message	2022-12-01	2022-12-28
~~E92BD8~~	~~2022-12-05~~	~~0410000000~~	~~MichaelM@FastChangeCo.com~~	~~Text Message~~	[illegible]	[illegible]
~~E92BD8~~	~~2022-12-09~~	~~0410000000~~	~~MichaelM@FastChangeCo.com~~	~~Text Message~~	[illegible]	[illegible]
E92BD8	2022-12-28	0410000000	MichaelM@FastChangeCo.com	Email	2022-12-28	[illegible]

When the redundant record are removed, and we were to request the data for the same time periods as before, we would get the same answers even though there are fewer records in the data set.

The effective period of the second record has been extended to the latest expiry timestamp of the removed records (2022-12-28) to cater for this.

How can this happen? It may be that, due to the changes in the *column scope,* data was provided to this target data object that didn't actually contain a change compared to the previous record. The original change that led to the record being detected and received in the staging layer may have been applied to a column that we are not interested in *for this target.* It would still be available in the PSA in its original form.

This form of data redundancy is technical in nature. It is the result of how data flows through the architecture and changes shape. From a functional, payload, perspective the data still means the same.

Column scope

Data redundancy can occur when time-variant data sets are vertically split – processed into various separate smaller target data sets (i.e., have fewer columns).

In fact, record redundancy often only becomes really noticeable when the *scope of columns* changes from one data object to another.

For example, when a single table is used to populate multiple target tables.

This is a common occurrence in the integration layer, where the data in its original staging layer structure is mapped to the target model. In many cases, data is reorganized simply by assigning data items to the right context.

A change in the scope of columns means that data is processed from a source data object that contains more columns than the target data object. To be more precise, it's the scope of columns *relative* to the target data object.

For our reference architecture, the first time column scope changes typically occur is in the integration layer – when loading data into Satellites. This is why we have chosen to introduce record compacting in this section.

Conceptually, compacting applies to any data object that contains time-variant data – which also includes the PSA. However, the need for compacting is less noticeable in the PSA, because the column scope usually does not change between the interface and the PSA.

Consider the following example:

PSA data object

Surrogate Key	Inscription Timestamp	Contact Number	Email Address	Contact Preference
E92BD8	2022-10-04	0419999999	MichaelM@FastChangeCo.com	Text Message
E92BD8	2022-12-01	0410000000	MichaelM@FastChangeCo.com	Text Message
E92BD8	2022-12-05	0410000000	MichaelM@FastChangeCo.com	Text Message
E92BD8	2022-12-09	0410000000	MichaelM@FastChangeCo.com	Text Message
E92BD8	2022-12-28	0410000000	MichaelM@FastChangeCo.com	Email

Contact Number

Surrogate Key	Inscription Timestamp	Contact Number
E92BD8	2022-10-04	0419999999
E92BD8	2022-12-01	0410000000
E92BD8	2022-12-05	0410000000
E92BD8	2022-12-09	0410000000
E92BD8	2022-12-28	0410000000

Email Adress

Surrogate Key	Inscription Timestamp	Email Address
E92BD8	2022-10-04	MichaelM@FastChangeCo.com
E92BD8	2022-12-01	MichaelM@FastChangeCo.com
E92BD8	2022-12-05	MichaelM@FastChangeCo.com
E92BD8	2022-12-09	MichaelM@FastChangeCo.com
E92BD8	2022-12-28	MichaelM@FastChangeCo.com

Here, the original data object is split into two separate target data objects. The first one is scoped to only contain the 'Contact Number' data item, whereas the second one is designed to contain only the 'Email Address' data item.

The 'contact preference' data is not used, and can be disregarded. It will always remain in the PSA in case we change our minds.

Without record compacting, the original record set will also determine the number of records in the target data objects. This creates a large amount of redundancy in the data solution.

With record compacting applied, the result is much more concise without losing any of the data payload:

PSA data object

Surrogate Key	Inscription Timestamp	Contact Number	Email Address	Contact Preference
E92BD8	2022-10-04	0419999999	MichaelM@FastChangeCo.com	Text Message
E92BD8	2022-12-01	0410000000	MichaelM@FastChangeCo.com	Text Message
E92BD8	2022-12-05	0410000000	MichaelM@FastChangeCo.com	Text Message
E92BD8	2022-12-09	0410000000	MichaelM@FastChangeCo.com	Text Message
E92BD8	2022-12-28	0410000000	MichaelM@FastChangeCo.com	Email

Contact Number

Surrogate Key	Inscription Timestamp	Contact Number
E92BD8	2022-10-04	0419999999
E92BD8	2022-12-01	0410000000

Email Adress

Surrogate Key	Inscription Timestamp	Email Address
E92BD8	2022-10-04	MichaelM@FastChangeCo.com

Reasons for applying record compacting

In our projects, we have seen redundant records make up to 70 % – 80 % of the total records in certain areas.

Sometimes, this is caused by incorrect configuration of the interfaces that provide data to the data solution. In other cases, it may be the result of loading flat files that contain the full data set each time they are provided to the data solution. This type of redundancy is the most visible in the PSA.

And because the PSA is used to provide data for downstream processing, for example into the Satellites, the effects of full data sets this redundancy can be compounding — leading to even more redundancy in the downstream data objects.

But, as we have seen in this section, redundant records will usually appear when narrowing down the column scope when moving (or interpreting) data from one object to another.

Record compacting reduces the number of rows in the data solution, which —depending on the technical environment— can have tremendous impact on performance. It is recommended to implement this as part of the data logistics processes, for reasons further outlined in the ⚐ where to apply record compacting section.

This is partly due to how record compacting reduces the Input/Output (I/O) demands on the underlying technical platforms.

Depending on the selected technical environment, and the use of available built-in data compression techniques, having more records usually mean that more storage space is required. This is known as the 'I/O footprint.'

Compression techniques at the physical storage level, such as page and columnar compression, continue to improve. However, in most cases there are still I/O benefits from applying record compacting even when advanced data compression is applied. Also, different technical environments manage physical storage and compression algorithms in different ways – so the mileage of compression may vary from system to system.

Lower I/O —due to lower record counts— means there will be fewer reads and writes to where the data is physically located on disk. Because I/O is a notorious bottleneck for overall performance, the results of compacting are often very noticeable.

There are benefits beyond immediate I/O improvements too. Query performance is improved because fewer records will have to be joined to, or merged with, other data sets during data processing. More records will mean more joins that will need to be evaluated by the infrastructure. And in the case of date joins, for example to merge timelines, the redundant records can exponentially increase the resulting data set.

The concept of merging timelines, or 'date math,' will be a main topic in the ⚐ getting the data out chapter.

During these processes, many data compression techniques will also 'decompress' data when it is retrieved from physical storage into memory, which will incur a resource cost (CPU overhead).

Record compacting is a way to keep the data solution 'in shape,' so that only data that has real value is retained, without losing any of its contents.

Lastly, when all is said and done, it is also simply easier to understand the data when every individual record is meaningful for the answers you are looking for.

Where to apply record compacting

The compacting concept is directly related to some of the *fundamental principles for data logistics.* Data logistics processes must be able to process multiple intervals (deltas) in one pass. They must also be able to be executed any time, and process whatever data is available.

For example, if the address of an employee changes multiple times during the day, and the corresponding data logistics process is run daily, then all (pending) change records should still be captured and correctly processed in a *single* execution of the data logistics process.

These requirements prevent designs that require data logistics processes to run multiple times in order to 'catch-up.' It also makes it possible to easily change processing frequencies, and supports a full reload of the integration layer from the PSA.

Last, but not least, they are fundamental principles that are required for data solution virtualization.

If you can process all available data for a given (target) data object in a single process execution, then you can use the same approach to create a view that represents the data with the same outcome.

The view would replace both the physical data object (table or file) and the data logistics process that would populate it.

It is the ultimate test to make sure the patterns work as intended, and the compacting logic is one of the core mechanisms to achieve this.

'On the fly' compacting

Compacting can be applied 'on the fly' — as part of the data logistics process *into* the target data object. This ensures that the data, or data delta, that is being processed into the target is a true delta and does not introduce any new data redundancy.

The expected outcome is that there is (still) no data redundancy after running the data logistics process to add new data to the target data object.

One of the main advantages of this approach is that the data in the solution is always as good as it can be — at least from a redundancy perspective. Another important consideration is that on the fly processing guarantees a redundancy-free target data set. Without this, the degree of redundancy becomes an unknown, a variable for further processing which may impact downstream performance in sometimes unexpected ways.

The downside is that the compacting process requires additional compute, and undeniably adds complexity to the template.

This complexity can sometimes be a barrier for implementation, especially when the project is under time pressure. With this book, we hope we can provide practical implementation guidelines to remove this barrier.

Implementing 'on the fly' compacting

Consider the following scenario: a 'Customer' within the 'PSA Sales' source data object is modeled into two separate Satellite data objects. The supporting Hub will also be modeled from the same source data object, but this has been omitted from the example for brevity.

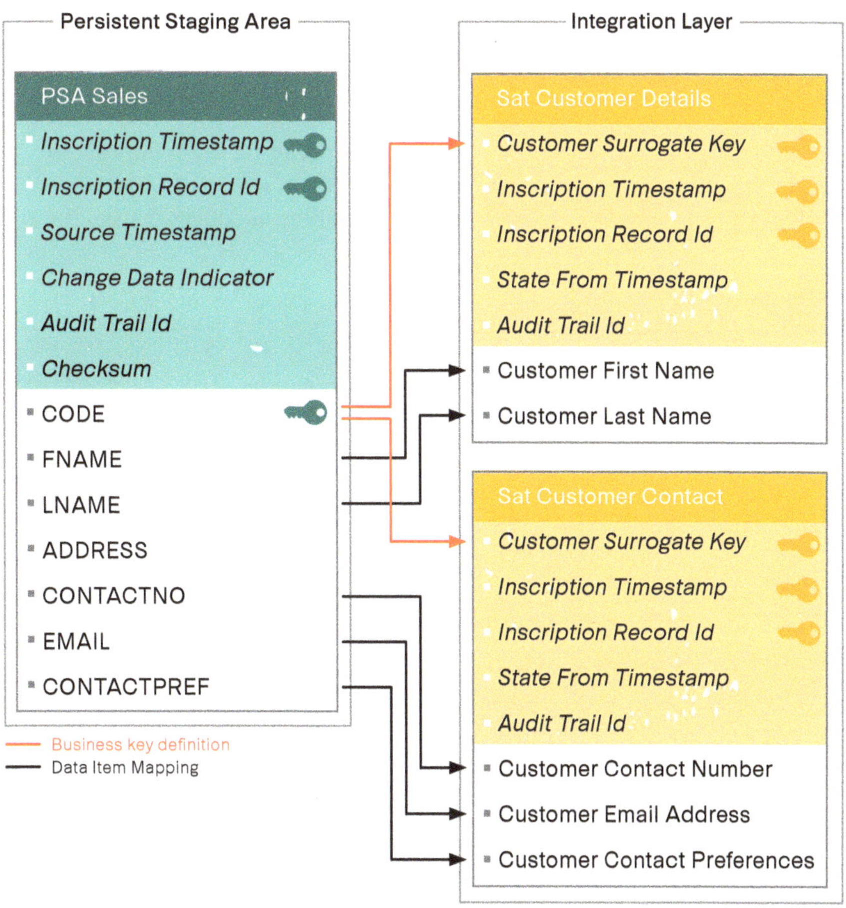

This is an example of a column scope change.

In this example, the 'CONTACTNO,' 'EMAIL,' and 'CONTACTPREF' data items are mapped to the 'Customer Contact' Satellite, while the 'FNAME' and 'LNAME' data items are mapped to the 'Customer Details' Satellite.

The 'ADDRESS' data item is not mapped. It is not required for any of the targets at this stage.

The pending data delta in staging layer data object contains a few records. If we look at this data delta, and also at how the 'Customer' data object is mapped to the targets the result is as follows:

		Mapped to the 'Customer Details' Satellite		Not mapped yet, maybe later	Mapped to the 'Customer Contact Preferences' Satellite		
CODE	Inscription Timestamp	FNAME	LNAME	ADDRESS	CONTACTNO	EMAIL	CONTACTPREF
289	2022-11-25 23:00		X				
289	2022-11-26 23:30			X			
289	2022-11-27 07:30		X				X
289	2022-11-27 09:00			X			X

In this overview, 'X' marks the column that triggered the change in the operational system. The change resulted in the data record being added to the data solution.

In the first record, the 'LNAME' changed in the operational system which is the reason the record was added. In the second change record, it was the 'ADDRESS' column that triggered the change. In all cases, the columns *other* than the column that changed will retain their values – there are no changes there.

Because different columns are mapped to different targets, not all changes are relevant. Changes are only relevant for the target when the column that has actually changed is mapped to it. Otherwise, it is just more redundant data.

The compacting algorithm aims to guarantee a redundancy-free target data set, relative for the target columns. Implementing this algorithm for on-the-fly processing involves two concepts:

→ Delta compacting: ensuring that the correct data delta is determined for in-scope columns
→ Change merging: ensuring that the resulting data set that results from the compacting step contains genuine changes relative to the target data object

Delta compacting

The delta compacting step analyzes the data delta and compacts this for its designated target(s).

Continuing with the previous example, we can examine the expected outcome when merging these changes into the 'Customer Details' Satellite, which only maps the 'FNAME' and 'LNAME' columns.

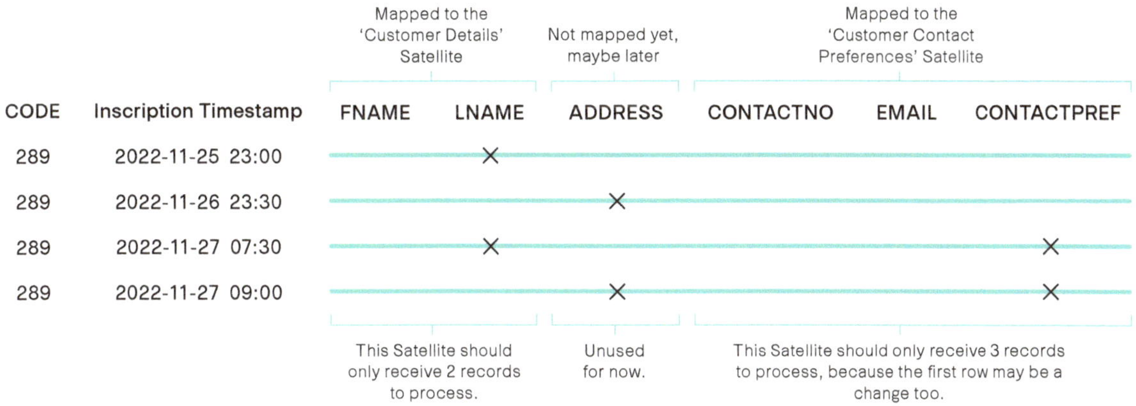

The PSA data object contains the following payload:

PSA Sales

Code	Inscription Timestamp	Change Data Indicator	FNAME	LNAME	ADDRESS	CONTACTNO	EMAIL	CONTACTPREF
289	2022-11-25 23:00	C	Michael	**Müller**	Brisbane	0410000000	MichaelM@FastChangeCo.com	Email
289	2022-11-26 23:30	C	Michael	Müller	**Sydney**	0410000000	MichaelM@FastChangeCo.com	Email
289	2022-11-27 07:30	C	Michael	**Mueller**	Sydney	0410000000	MichaelM@FastChangeCo.com	**Phone**
289	2022-11-27 09:00	C	Michael	Mueller	**Brisbane**	0410000000	MichaelM@FastChangeCo.com	**Text Message**

In this scenario, after removing redundant data within this column scope, the compacted delta merged into the 'Customer Details' Satellite should contain only *two* records. The 'LNAME' column changed twice (1st and 3rd record), but the other changes were outside this target's column scope and are not relevant.

However, the 'Customer Contact' Satellite will receive *three* change records (1st, 3rd and 4th record) after the initial delta compacting process.

This is because the first change record —the 'oldest' change based on the inscription timestamp— should *always* be considered as a change. When analyzing only the data delta, we cannot determine if the first record in a data delta is a change compared to what already exists in the target.

It is the role of the *change merging* process to assert this. During change merging, the first record in the delta is removed unless it represents an actual change compared to the most recent data (newest by inscription timestamp) in the target.

The delta compacting algorithm itself contains three steps:
1) Create a checksum for record-by-record comparison
2) Evaluate the changes over the inscription timestamp
3) Eliminate the redundant records

Creating a checksum for record-by-record comparison

The first step calculates a hash-based checksum, across all *in-scope* columns. The checksum will be used to evaluate change records in the subsequent steps.

This checksum only takes the regular columns into account, excluding the standard data solution columns and the target business key, for example:

```
SELECT
  [Inscription_Timestamp],
  [Source_Timestamp],
  [Inscription_Record_Id],
  [Change_Data_Indicator],
  -- The business key is NOT part of the change detection
  -- It is not added to the checksum
  <Business Key>,
  <Column 1>,
  <Column 2>,
  -- Calculating the checksum for in-scope columns
  -- Excluding the business key and change data indicator
  HASHBYTES('SHA1',
    COALESCE(TRIM(CONVERT(NVARCHAR(MAX), <Column 1>)), '~!@|N/A') + '\@|' +
    COALESCE(TRIM(CONVERT(NVARCHAR(MAX), <Column 2>)), '~!@|N/A') + '\@|'
  )) AS [Checksum]
FROM <table_name>
```

The process can be illustrated with the table below. The checksum column temporarily stores the hash value calculated across the in-scope columns.

Intermediate data set — Step 1: checksum

Code	Inscription Timestamp	Change Data Indicator	Checksum	CONTACTNO	EMAIL	CONTACTPREF
289	2022-11-25 23:00	C	F4A12B	0410000000	MichaelM@FastChangeCo.com	Email
289	2022-11-26 23:30	C	F4A12B	0410000000	MichaelM@FastChangeCo.com	Email
289	2022-11-27 07:30	C	A671BB	0410000000	MichaelM@FastChangeCo.com	**Phone**
289	2022-11-27 09:00	C	98CBA	0410000000	MichaelM@FastChangeCo.com	**Text Message**

Evaluating the changes over the inscription timestamp

The second step will evaluate the delta data set, including the checksum that was created in the previous step, to prepare a number of indicators for each record. These flags will be used in the next step to identify and remove redundant records.

The following evaluations are performed:

→ Checksum check – to determines if the checksum value has changed compared to the previous record (ordered by inscription timestamp and inscription record id). This detects regular changes in column values

- Change Data Capture (CDC) check – identifies if the change data indicator value changed compared to the previous record in the delta. This specifically detects logical deletes or re-inserts
- Time check – to assert if there is a difference in the inscription timestamp between consecutive records. This captures scenarios where a primary key update in the operational system results in a delete (old key) and an insert (new key) at the exact same time – a logical update at the database level

For example:

```
-- Condition 1 - make sure there are differences between the individual records
CASE
  WHEN
    LAG([Checksum],1,0x0000000000000000000000000000000000000000)
    OVER (PARTITION BY <Business Key>
    ORDER BY
      [Inscription_Timestamp] ASC,
      [Inscription_Record_Id] ASC,
      [Source_Timestamp] ASC,
      [Change_Data_Indicator] DESC
    ) = [Checksum]
  THEN 'Same'
  ELSE 'Different'
END AS [Checksum_Change_Indicator]
-- Condition 2 - make sure the change data indicator is different between rows
CASE
  WHEN
    LAG([Change_Data_Indicator],1,'')
    OVER (PARTITION BY <Business Key>
    ORDER BY
      [Inscription_Timestamp] ASC,
      [Inscription_Record_Id] ASC,
      [Source_Timestamp] ASC,
      [Change_Data_Indicator] ASC
    ) = [Change_Data_Indicator]
  THEN 'Same' ELSE 'Different'
END AS [CDC_Change_Indicator]
-- Condition 3 - make sure the inscription timestamp is ordered and evaluated)
CASE
  WHEN
    LEAD([Inscription_Timestamp],1,'9999-12-31')
    OVER (PARTITION BY <Business Key>
    ORDER BY
      [Inscription_Timestamp] ASC,
      [Inscription_Record_Id] ASC,
      [Source_Timestamp] ASC,
      [Change_Data_Indicator] ASC
    ) = [Inscription_Timestamp]
  THEN 'Same' ELSE 'Different'
END AS [Time_Change_Indicator]
```

This provides the following results for the example:

Intermediate data set — Step 2: evaluate the changes over time

Code	Inscription Timestamp	Change Data Indicator	Checksum	CONTACTNO	EMAIL	CONTACTPREF	Checksum Change Indicator	CDC Change Indicator	Time Change Indicator
289	2022-11-25 23:00	C	F4A12B	0410000000	MichaelM@FastChangeCo.com	Email	Different	Same	Different
289	2022-11-26 23:30	C	F4A12B	0410000000	MichaelM@FastChangeCo.com	Email	Same	Same	Different
289	2022-11-27 07:30	C	A671BB	0410000000	MichaelM@FastChangeCo.com	**Phone**	Different	Same	Different
289	2022-11-27 09:00	C	98CBA	0410000000	MichaelM@FastChangeCo.com	**Text Message**	Different	Same	Different

Eliminating the redundant records

Now that all necessary indicators have been established, the third and final step of the delta compacting algorithm eliminates the redundant records.

Using the change data indicator and the three additional indicators that were provided in the previous steps, a predicate is applied to only keep records that:

- Have a different checksum value and are changed records based on their change data indicator
- Have a different value in the change data indicator at different points in time, even if there are no changes in column values

This could work as follows:

```
WHERE
  -- Have a different checksum value and are change records
  ([Checksum_Change_Indicator] = 'Different' AND
   -- Inserts or changes, as per the record's change indicator value
   [Change_Data_Indicator] = 'C')
  OR
   -- Have a different value in the change data indicator at
   -- different points in time
  ([CDC_Change_Indicator] = 'Different' AND
   [Time_Change_Indicator] = 'Different')
```

Applying this logic will remove the 2nd record, as shown in the example below.

Intermediate data set — Step 3: remove redundant rows

Code	Inscription Timestamp	Change Data Indicator	Checksum	CONTACTNO	EMAIL	CONTACTPREF	Checksum Change Indicator	CDC Change Indicator	Time Change Indicator
289	2022-11-25 23:00	C	F4A12B	0410000000	MichaelM@FastChangeCo.com	Email	Different	Same	Different
~~289~~	~~2022-11-26 23:30~~	~~C~~	~~F4A12B~~	~~0410000000~~	~~MichaelM@FastChangeCo.com~~	~~Email~~	~~Same~~	~~Same~~	~~Different~~
289	2022-11-27 07:30	C	A671BB	0410000000	MichaelM@FastChangeCo.com	**Phone**	Different	Same	Different
289	2022-11-27 09:00	C	98CBA	0410000000	MichaelM@FastChangeCo.com	**Text Message**	Different	Same	Different

About using DISTINCT

When tracking changes in data over time, a SELECT DISTINCT statement cannot be used to compact the record set – even when excluding the inscription timestamp.

At first glance, applying DISTINCT may seem like a viable approach, but what would happen when the name in this examples reverts back a previous state?

Consider the following scenario:

→ On 2022-07-01, the LNAME value for key 17532 is 'Tindle'
→ On 2022-07-03, the LNAME value changes to 'Idle'
→ On 2022-07-05, the LNAME value changes back to 'Tindle'

If you apply a DISTINCT query, it would only capture two values: 'Tindle' and 'Idle.' The final change back to 'Tindle' would be ignored.

This failure to recognize an A-B-A change —where a value reverts to an earlier

Intermediate data set - A-B-A issue

Code	Inscription Timestamp	Change Data Indicator	Checksum	FNAME	LNAME	Checksum Change Indicator	CDC Change Indicator	Time Change Indicator
17532	2022-07-01 23:00	C	X72B88	Terence	**Tindle**	Different	Same	Different
17532	2022-07-26 03:30	C	Y845CF	Terence	**Idle**	Different	Same	Different
17532	2022-07-27 05:30	C	X72B88	Terence	**Tindle**	Different	Same	Different

state— makes
DISTINCT unreliable for delta tracking. Supporting this mechanism is what introduces the earlier complexity that is required to correctly evaluate changes.

For delta compacting, you always exclude the inscription timestamp —because this would be unique for each record— and also must consider logical deletes. It is the differences in the column values (checksum) that matter, and this is what DISTINCT cannot be used for.

Change merging and logical CDC

The purpose of change merging is to ensure that the data set from the compacting step contains genuine changes compared to the target data object. It is another safeguard to prevent loading redundant data.

Even after delta compacting, some resulting change records may *still* not represent actual changes when compared to the existing data in the target data object. In the architecture overview, we used the term *logical change data capture (CDC)* for this phenomenon.

In the staging layer, data changes are identified by their primary key. The whole record is considered an insert, update, or (logical) delete. However, when the column scope changes, as is often the case with Satellite tables, additional evaluation is required to determine whether an incoming record represents a true change for the intended target.

Previous sections have focused on reducing the incoming dataset to unique changes within the selected columns. The final step in the process is to verify that these changes are not already present in the target dataset.

The example below shows the original data delta, the resulting output from the delta compacting step, as well as the data that present in the target Satellite *prior* to the change merging process.

PSA Sales (Staging Layer)

Code	Inscription Timestamp	Change Data Indicator	FNAME	LNAME	ADDRESS	CONTACTNO	EMAIL	CONTACTPREF
289	2022-11-25 23:00	C	Michael	**Müller**	Brisbane	0410000000	MichaelM@FastChangeCo.com	Email
289	2022-11-26 23:30	C	Michael	Müller	**Sydney**	0410000000	MichaelM@FastChangeCo.com	Email
289	2022-11-27 07:30	C	Michael	**Mueller**	Sydney	0410000000	MichaelM@FastChangeCo.com	**Phone**
289	2022-11-27 09:00	C	Michael	Mueller	**Brisbane**	0410000000	MichaelM@FastChangeCo.com	**Text Message**

Delta compacting

Intermediate data set

Code	Inscription Timestamp	CONTACTNO	EMAIL	CONTACTPREF	Record Number
289	2022-11-25 23:00	0410000000	MichaelM@FastChangeCo.com	Email	1
289	2022-11-27 07:30	0410000000	MichaelM@FastChangeCo.com	**Phone**	**2**
289	2022-11-27 09:00	0410000000	MichaelM@FastChangeCo.com	**Text Message**	**3**

Change Merging

Sat Customer Contact (Integration Layer)

Surrogate Key	Inscription Timestamp	Contact Number	Email Address	Contact Preference
E92BD8	2020-04-04 11:00	**0419999999**	MichaelM@FastChangeCo.com	Text Message
E92BD8	2020-12-02 23:00	**0410000000**	MichaelM@FastChangeCo.com	Text Message
E92BD8	2020-12-28 23:38	0410000000	MichaelM@FastChangeCo.com	**Email**

A record number has been added to the intermediate data set — the output of the delta compacting step. This can be implemented by using a window/analytic function (or similar) to derive which of the records is the 'oldest' according to the inscription timestamp (Record Number = 1).

This record is the *only* one that needs to be evaluated against the historical data already present in the target. All other records (Record Number > 1) are considered genuine changes by definition, as the delta compacting step has already determined that they are different from the first record.

Comparing the 'oldest' record from the delta compacting output with the 'latest' record in the target, for instance with a lookup or left join, will determine if the incoming record is a true change. If the comparison shows that the incoming record is identical to what already exists, it is removed from further processing.

In this example, the record with Record Number '1' will be removed from the processing.

The final result of the delta compacting and change merging operations in the target will then be as follows:

Sat Customer Contact (Integration Layer)

Surrogate Key	Inscription Timestamp	Contact Number	Email Address	Contact Preference
E92BD8	2020-10-04 11:00	**0419999999**	MichaelM@FastChangeCo.com	Text Message
E92BD8	2020-12-02 23:00	**0410000000**	MichaelM@FastChangeCo.com	Text Message
E92BD8	2020-12-28 23:38	0410000000	MichaelM@FastChangeCo.com	**Email**
E92BD8	2022-11-27 07:30	0410000000	MichaelM@FastChangeCo.com	**Phone**
E92BD8	2022-11-27 09:00	0410000000	MichaelM@FastChangeCo.com	**Text Message**

New records

Post process compacting

Alternatively, compacting can be applied to an existing data object at any time as an independent *post process* – scheduled as part of maintenance tasks in the monitoring framework.

Using this approach, the maintenance processes periodically apply compacting to data objects to ensure any existing data redundancy is removed.

The result is that any data redundancy that exists after the regular data logistics processes have completed will be cleared out after some time, depending on the maintenance schedule.

This can be done for one, more, or all data objects at the same time depending on the scheduling of the compacting maintenance process.

The most common implementation is to configure a process that compacts a few data objects at a time over the course of a few days or so, and starts over when it reaches the end of the list of objects to process.

The benefit of this approach is that the template logic to implement compacting as post process is simpler compared to an 'on the fly' implementation.

Because of the reduced compute requirements, the process can also be slightly faster, although this does depend on the amount of redundant records (versus the speed of inserting and corresponding I/O impacts).

However, this performance gain –if any– is very likely to be omitted because of the resource-intensive removal of redundant records that were already written to disk.

The performance cost of physically removing data from disk will usually void any gains made from having a less complex insert process. The post process approach for compacting *overall* is often 'slower' than compacting on insert – on the fly.

However, if the write performance (inserts) is optimized and redundancy is not considered an issue then this can be a viable approach.

Conceptually, the 'on the fly' approach for compacting is closest to what is needed for the engine so that can be optimally tuned. Having varying levels of data redundancy introduces a variability in downstream processing that can be eliminated through on the fly processing.

And, as mentioned earlier, on the fly processing will always deliver the same outcomes when switching between virtualization and physical data storage.

Implementing post-process compacting

Implementing record compacting as a post-process is less complex compared to the on-the-fly approach. This is because the change merging step is not necessary anymore. The data is already present in the (target) data object, so any existing redundancies can be removed in one pass.

The column scope is also already known, as is the order of the data by timeline. This results in simpler logic, negating the need for the more complex evaluations required for on-the-fly compacting.

For example:

```
WITH
CompactingCTE AS
(
SELECT
  HASHBYTES('SHA1',
    COALESCE(TRIM(CONVERT(NVARCHAR(MAX), <Key>)), '~!@|N/A') + '\@|' +
     COALESCE(TRIM(CONVERT(NVARCHAR(MAX), <Column 1>)), '~!@|N/A') + '\@|' +
     COALESCE(TRIM(CONVERT(NVARCHAR(MAX), <Column 2>)), '~!@|N/A') + '\@|'
  )) AS [Checksum],
  *
FROM <table_name>
),
Subselect AS
(
SELECT
  *,
  LAG([Checksum]) OVER (PARTITION BY <Key> ORDER BY <Key>,<Timestamp>) AS [Next_Checksum],
  LAG([Change_Data_Indicator]) OVER (PARTITION BY <Key> ORDER BY <Key>,<Timestamp>) AS [Next_Change_
Data_Indicator]
FROM CondensingCTE
)
DELETE FROM Subselect
WHERE [Checksum] = [Next_Checksum]
AND [Change_Data_Indicator] = [Next_Change_Data_Indicator];
```

This code example creates a checksum that includes the key column, so that it can be used in the WHERE predicate at the end of the code. Other than that, the checksum and change data indicator are evaluated separately. This code is generic in nature, but can be modified if checksums are already available in the underlying data. Even though the logic for post-process compacting is less complex, we still prefer the on-the-fly approach.

Some of the reasons for this regarding performance versus complexity have already been covered, but there is another reason: on-the-fly processing is also conceptually better aligned to Engine Thinking.

This is the topic for the next section.

Compacting and the engine

Record compacting makes data structures malleable.

The fewer columns that are defined for the target, the *smaller* the record set will become. And conversely, the more columns are added, the *bigger* the record set will be.

Being able to apply compacting on-the-fly will immediately show the result of any changes in the physical model. This is closely aligned to Engine Thinking and data solution virtualization.

The engine will be able to simulate different structures for the best result given the parameters for optimization. A virtualized data solution will also always immediately and deterministically show the redundancy-free results – as if the object was loaded and compacting was applied.

This will allow the engine to, for example, optimize context entity structures for certain downstream query patterns. Or, it can calculate the optimal 'split' between Satellite attributes.

Record compacting significantly simplifies splitting and merging Satellites. The corresponding data set will always be adjusted for the target column scope in a deterministic way using the transactions available in the PSA.

How many context entities do we need?

As many (or few) Satellites as desired can be defined for any parent Hub or Link.

When defining an information model, having a single context entity describing a CBC or NBR is often sufficient.

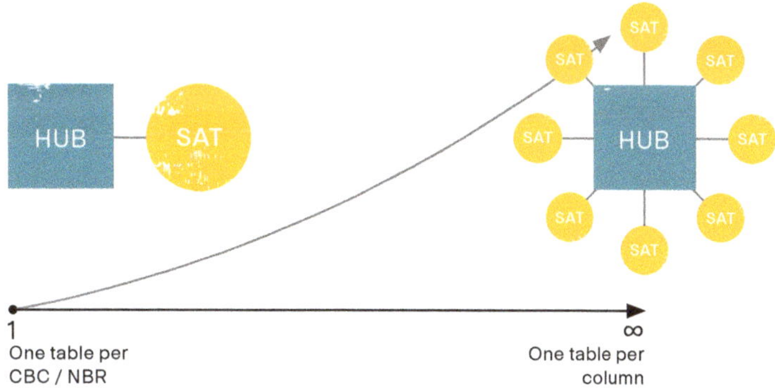

However, at the physical level, there can be as many Satellites as required. This can range from having a single table to represent the Satellite, to having a single table for each attribute – and anything in between.

Examples of how Satellites can be organized include, but are not limited to:

- → Confidential data, such as Personally Identifiable Information (PII)
- → GDPR compliance
- → Rate of change
- → Data origins
- → Data types
- → Storage types

Over time, the engine may suggest (or automatically implement) moving certain columns from one Satellite to another for performance reasons or because the definition of the data changes. For example, if certain data elements are labeled as containing PII, the columns could be automatically refactored into a more secure, designated Satellite.

This process is explained in more detail in the *Satellite splitting* section.

Satellite splitting

During Satellite splitting, columns are moved from one Satellite to another. This occurs at the physical model level, and can deliver performance gains. It can also be used to re-organize columns for functional reasons – as outlined in the *How many context entities do we need?* section.

Imagine you have a Satellite containing 1000 columns. Of this object, 999 columns change very infrequently whereas 1 column changes multiple times each day.

The resulting Satellite would contain a large amount of repeating data, because the changes in the single column that changes so often would lead to a replication of the other 999 values.

Sat Customer Contact — Fast changing column: Score

Surrogate Key	Inscription Timestamp	Contact Number	Email Address	Contact Preference	Score
E92BD8	2022-01-01 14:30	0419999999	MichaelM@FastChangeCo.com	Email	1
E92BD8	2022-01-01 14:31	0419999999	MichaelM@FastChangeCo.com	Email	0
E92BD8	2022-01-01 14:32	0419999999	MichaelM@FastChangeCo.com	Email	1
E92BD8	2022-01-01 14:33	0419999999	MichaelM@FastChangeCo.com	Email	2
E92BD8	2022-01-01 14:34	0419999999	MichaelM@FastChangeCo.com	Email	1
E92BD8	2022-01-01 14:35	0419999999	MichaelM@FastChangeCo.com	Email	0
E92BD8	2022-01-01 14:36	0419999999	MichaelM@FastChangeCo.com	Email	1
E92BD8	2022-01-01 14:37	0419999999	MichaelM@FastChangeCo.com	Email	2
E92BD8	2022-01-01 14:38	0419999999	MichaelM@FastChangeCo.com	Email	1
E92BD8	2022-01-01 14:39	0419999999	MichaelM@FastChangeCo.com	Email	0

In this scenario, the engine may create a new Satellite for the column whose data values change so often. The record compacting mechanism will then 'flatten' the original Satellite when the column has been removed.

This will result in the following two objects, refactored for better performance and storage:

Sat Customer Contact

Surrogate Key	Inscription Timestamp	Contact Number	Email Address	Contact Preference
E92BD8	2022-01-01 14:30	0419999999	MichaelM@FastChangeCo.com	Email

Sat Customer Score

Surrogate Key	Inscription Timestamp	Score
E92BD8	2022-01-01 14:30	1
E92BD8	2022-01-01 14:31	0
E92BD8	2022-01-01 14:32	1
E92BD8	2022-01-01 14:33	2
E92BD8	2022-01-01 14:34	1
E92BD8	2022-01-01 14:35	0
E92BD8	2022-01-01 14:36	1
E92BD8	2022-01-01 14:37	2
E92BD8	2022-01-01 14:38	1
E92BD8	2022-01-01 14:39	0

Compared to database technology, this is an example of *vertical partitioning*.

The mileage of this operation varies significantly depending on technical factors and the type of underlying data storage platform used. Some database management systems have very good compression algorithms that automatically manage data redundancy in a single table.

The engine compares the benefits for its optimization directives to evaluate if splitting is a good approach. This is done by creating a separate object, or set of objects, and comparing the statistics against the original.

Depending on the directives this may be on query time, I/O footprint, or other form of resource consumption.

Adding or removing columns in an existing Satellite

The engine is designed for automated refactoring, which often involves adding and removing columns from existing Satellites. Fortunately, this is a very easy process, one that is essentially covered in the ⚐ Satellite splitting section. After all, Satellite splitting really comes down to removing one or more columns from one Satellite and adding them to another.

The simplest approach to implement this is to *truncate the impacted Satellite(s) and reprocess the data from the PSA*. Thanks to deterministic processing, all involved tables will be recreated based on their new column scope.

Adding new columns when incrementally expanding the model works the same way. Once the new columns are committed to the metadata, the engine can pick them up and refactor the impacted objects.

↗ Satellite splitting, along with record compacting and deterministic patterns that follow the fundamental guidelines for data logistics, provides an exceptionally flexible and efficient way to manage structural changes in the physical model.

This is the most straightforward method for implementing such changes. However, if this approach is not feasible, the mechanisms discussed in the ⚐ corresponding PSA section apply.

Managing logically deleted records

Interpreting logical deletes, marked as the value 'D' in the change data indicator, is more complex than it first appears. From the staging layer to the integration layer, the original record set is typically divided and mapped to various target data objects in the integration layer, including multiple Satellites.

↗ The state of a given business key—active or deleted—in the integration layer is context. It's a descriptive property of a Hub or Link instance. To truly understand which column(s) the delete applies to, we first need to normalize the source data set.

In the staging layer, data changes are identified by their primary key, with the whole record considered an insert, update, or (logical) delete – technical CDC. When 'breaking up' these records and mapping parts of them to different Satellites, the meaning of a 'delete' must be reconsidered. In the integration layer, the business key may be different from the record's original primary key. There may not be a clear delete that applies to *parts* of the original record, at least not one that can be derived from technical CDC information.

We often observe the change indicator from the staging layer being propagated to *all* mapped Satellites, which is frequently incorrect. Additional logic may be required to understand the impacts of the original CDC event, especially for very denormalized source data objects.

When determining this state it is usually not sufficient to rely on technical CDC information alone. How would you determine for which columns the delete would apply and for which ones it doesn't? Restructuring occurs often in the integration layer, because data is reorganized to conform to a defined information model – irrespective of the original structure in which the data was stored.

Consider the image below, which shows the data in its original structure and as modeled in the integration layer. In this example, the CDC mechanisms are able to evaluate the change data operation for a given record, and this is recorded in the staging layer.

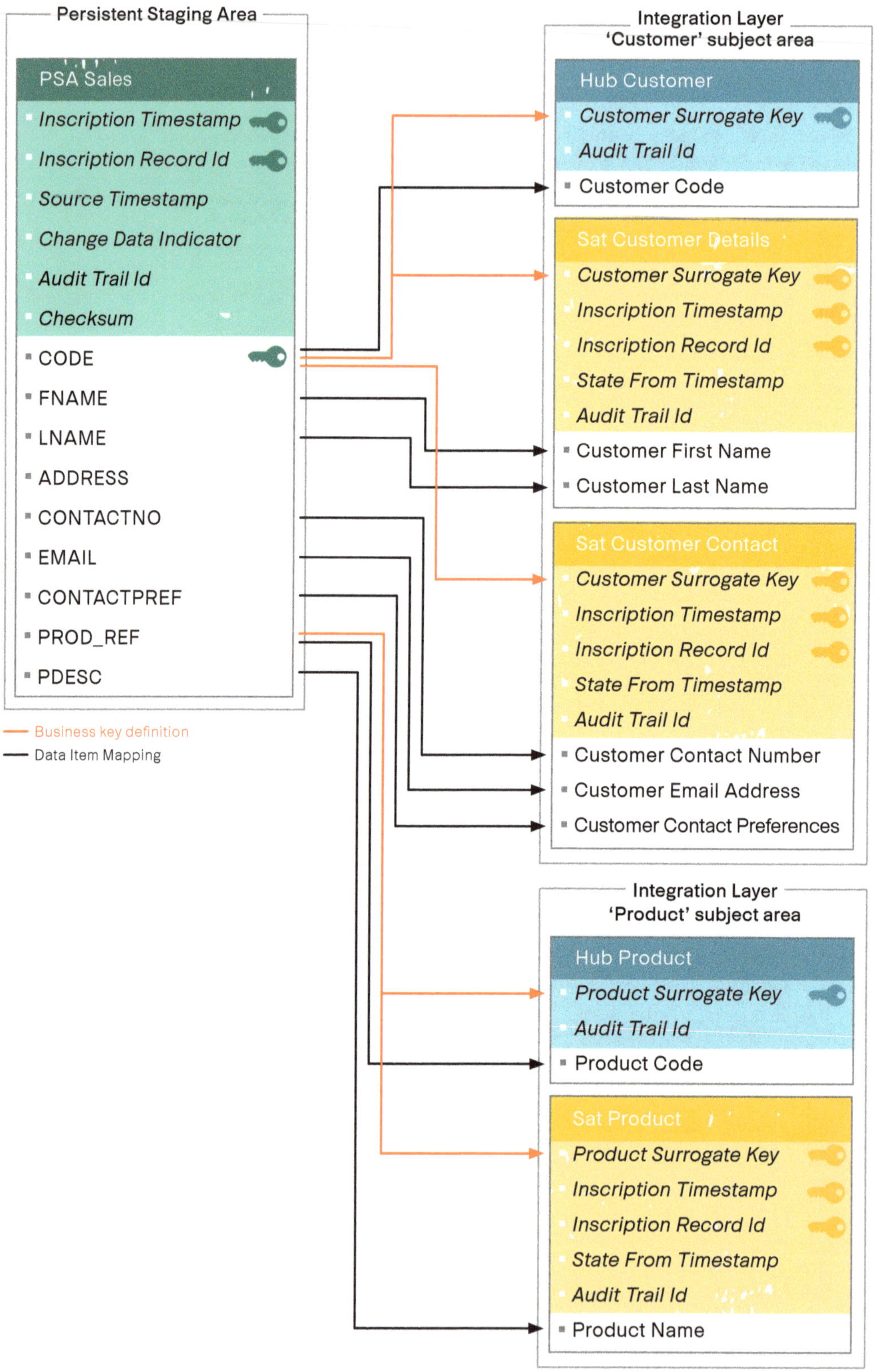
Persistent Staging Area
PSA Sales
Inscription Timestamp
Inscription Record Id
Source Timestamp
Change Data Indicator
Audit Trail Id
Checksum
CODE
FNAME
LNAME
ADDRESS
CONTACTNO
EMAIL
CONTACTPREF
PROD_REF
PDESC
Business key definition
Data Item Mapping
Integration Layer
'Customer' subject area
Hub Customer
Customer Surrogate Key
Audit Trail Id
Customer Code
Sat Customer Details
Customer Surrogate Key
Inscription Timestamp
Inscription Record Id
State From Timestamp
Audit Trail Id
Customer First Name
Customer Last Name
Sat Customer Contact
Customer Surrogate Key
Inscription Timestamp
Inscription Record Id
State From Timestamp
Audit Trail Id
Customer Contact Number
Customer Email Address
Customer Contact Preferences
Integration Layer
'Product' subject area
Hub Product
Product Surrogate Key
Audit Trail Id
Product Code
Sat Product
Product Surrogate Key
Inscription Timestamp
Inscription Record Id
State From Timestamp
Audit Trail Id
Product Name

If a record with a delete comes though (change data indicator = 'D'), what does this mean for the entities in the integration layer? Is the customer instance deleted, or could it be the product?

In this example, a denormalized data set is modeled in the integration layer. Granted, this may not be the optimal design for an operational system, but this may not be something the data solution can control.

The more denormalized the incoming data set is, the less useful the technical CDC delete information will be for deriving the state of the business keys. This is because the incoming record contains many attributes, some of which do not relate directly to the records's primary key, and these attributes are more likely to be spread out over multiple integration layer objects and possibly populate various Hubs — as is the case in this example.

However, and this is why logical CDC mechanisms are so much more elaborate than technical CDC solutions, there is more to consider than just the logical delete indication when it comes to asserting the state of a business key. Most systems have some sort of internal status or timestamp which is used to functionally determine if a business key is active or not. In these cases, this information is much more valuable.

Logical deletes do come in handy when this context is not available, and in these cases this can be stored in the integration layer as additional context for the business key. This could be done using a context entity specifically designed for status tracking, or an equivalent context entity that just contains an active or inactive flag.

Usually, the delete indication starts to diminish value quickly when you start moving data from the original record into their modeled counterparts. However, when the business key does align with the primary key in the operational system or when other context is lacking, it still has its uses.

Let's look at this example from a data perspective. The example already applies record compacting. For brevity the Hubs and Links have been omitted.

PSA Sales

Code	Inscription Timestamp	Change Data Indicator	FNAME	LNAME	ADDRESS	CONTACTNO	EMAIL	CONTACTPREF	ROD_REF	PDESC
146	2025-06-25	C	Isao	Arhosua	Tokyo	090-5678-1234	[...]	Email	250	FancyBoots
289	2025-06-25	C	Yory	Arvola	Kyoto	090-1234-5678	[...]	Email	250	FancyBoots
289	2025-06-28	C	**Yori**	Arvola	Kyoto	090-1234-5678	[...]	**Phone**	250	**FancyBoots Engine**
289	2025-09-30	**D**	Yori	Arvola	Osaka	090-1234-5678	[...]	Phone	250	FancyBoots Engine

?

Sat Customer Details

Surrogate Key	Inscription Timestamp	Change Data Indicator	First Name	Last Name
146\@|	2025-06-25	C	Isao	Arhosuo
289\@|	2025-06-25	C	Yory	Arvola
289\@|	2025-06-28	C	**Yori**	Arvola

?

Sat Product

Surrogate Key	Inscription Timestamp	Change Data Indicator	Product Name
250\@|	2025-06-25	C	FancyBoots
250\@|	2025-06-28	C	**FancyBoots Engine**

The fact that a source record is deleted should be represented in the Satellite, but which one? Should it be in any of them or both of them, or neither?

An interpretation is needed to ensure this evaluation is done correctly, and this is what we refer to as 'logical change data capture (CDC)' as opposed to the technical CDC evaluation based on the primary key.

To truly understand which column(s) the delete applies to, we first need to normalize the source data set. By understanding the inter-relationships in the data, and viewing it as a 3rd normal form model, we can make an informed decision about which data items the delete truly applies to.

In a simplified version of the incoming data set, shown below, the customer entity has a many to many relationship to a product entity.

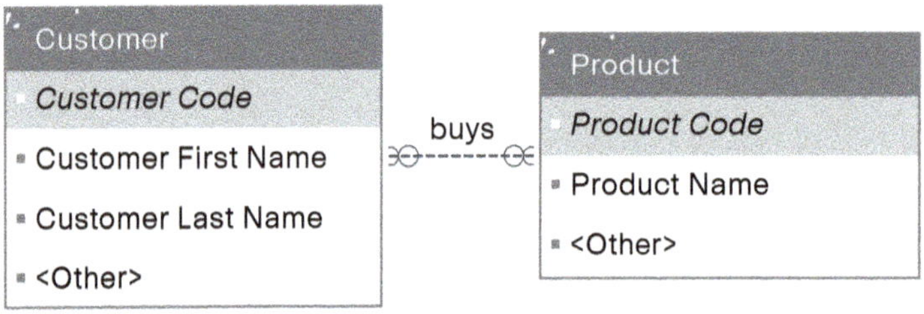

In this example, we can assert that the change data indicator really only applies to the customer code —this is the technical key which the CDC relies on— and therefore should be added to the customer Satellite and not to the product Satellite.

This would result in the following Satellite data:

PSA Sales

Code	Inscription Timestamp	Change Data Indicator	FNAME	LNAME	ADDRESS	CONTACTNO	EMAIL	CONTACTPREF	ROD_REF	PDESC
146	2025-06-25	C	Isao	Arhosua	Tokyo	090-5678-1234	[...]	Email	250	FancyBoots
289	2025-06-25	C	Yory	Arvola	Kyoto	090-1234-5678	[...]	Email	250	FancyBoots
289	2025-06-28	C	**Yori**	Arvola	Kyoto	090-1234-5678	[...]	**Phone**	250	**FancyBoots Engine**
289	2025-09-30	**D**	Yori	Arvola	Osaka	090-1234-5678	[...]	Phone	250	FancyBoots Engine

Sat Customer Details

Surrogate Key	Inscription Timestamp	Change Data Indicator	First Name	Last Name
146\@|	2025-06-25	C	Isao	Arhosuo
289\@|	2025-06-25	C	Yory	Arvola
289\@|	2025-06-28	C	**Yori**	Arvola
289\@|	2025-09-30	**D**	Yori	Arvola

Sat Product

Surrogate Key	Inscription Timestamp	Change Data Indicator	Product Name
250\@|	2025-06-25	C	FancyBoots
250\@|	2025-06-28	C	**FancyBoots Engine**

Note that the delete transaction is applied to a new record in the Satellite. This indicates that from this timestamp forward, the customer is considered to be deleted in the source data set, and these were the last known details.

The data set received in this example is flawed, of course, but we can't always control how well the received data is organized.

The more denormalized the data source is, the less likely it is that a delete indicator correctly applies to a given Satellite. The more normalized the data source, the better the chance that the delete indicator is accurate for the whole record and its contents. When in doubt, applying normalization on the data will help clarify for which columns the logical delete really applies.

Struggling with time — while getting the data in

One of the objectives of the integration layer is to *prepare the assertion and state timelines,* and the Satellite is where this is implemented. Defining, interpreting, and managing time is arguably one of the main challenges for any data solution.

↗ In the data solution, the state and assertion timelines represent an unambiguous, controlled timeline and at least one real-world timeline that the data solution does not directly control.

The concept of 'time' is broad and varied. If everything happened simultaneously, there would be no need to store historical data. We, the consumers of data, could access everything at once — in the present.

If time didn't exist, would data still be necessary? While philosophical considerations such as these are intriguing, the practical reality that time *does* exist means that data architects, data modelers and developers have to deal with it.

In the *data solution architecture,* we introduced the *state* and *assertion* timelines, and in the *staging layer implementation* we outlined the foundational building blocks to implement these.

Incorporating these two timelines in the data solution makes the data *bitemporal,* offering two default perspectives for viewing the data. This is distinguished from *unitemporal* data, which has only one defined time perspective.

This happens around us every day. As individuals, we fill out many forms for our local authorities, often filled bitemporal elements.

Tax declarations, for instance, indicate *when* money was earned and when this was submitted — capturing both the real-world events and when we reported them.

Or, after moving to a new city we might report the move (when it happened in reality) to the local authorities within three months (when we said something about it).

For businesses, we believe considerations about defining time are equally important. Decisions made earlier, with the available data back then, might be seen in a different light when looking at it from today's perspective. This is especially important if data occasionally arrives in the 'wrong' order, or when historica data is corrected.

The ability to understand the context as it was back then might be very informative to understand why things are the way the are now. We would even go as far as saying the data solution cannot be truly auditable without it.

Bitemporality in data solutions can be as complex as bending a pretzel for the first time. While well-managed time in a data solution offers powerful opportunities, it can also be overwhelming.

In these sections, we outline the various concepts at play, and how to ensure that these complex parts of the data solution are defined clearly and effectively, so that we can let the engine do the heavy lifting when it comes to using the resulting data.

Clock ticks

When introducing time into your data solution, one important concept to consider is the 'clock tick.' According to Johnston & Weis[45], "An atomic clock tick is the smallest interval (period) of time recognized by the data platform that can elapse between any two physical modifications on the platform."

↗ An atomic clock tick is the smallest time period recognized by the data platform that can elapse between any two physical modifications.

The precision of a clock tick has evolved from seconds to milliseconds, and now to nanoseconds or even smaller intervals, depending on the data platform.

These atomic clock ticks can be aggregated to clock ticks of lower granularity based on your business requirements. For example, you may want to aggregate sales revenues over months or days instead of minutes or seconds.

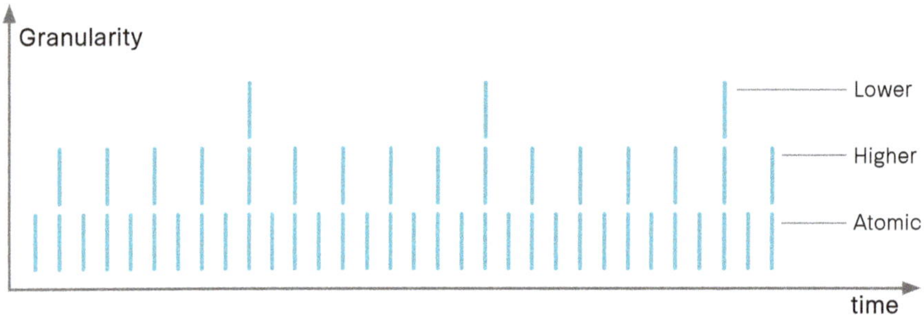

When designing a timeline for your data solution, consider the granularity of the clock tick for the data platform and each of the operational systems it integrates with. The clock tick is a hard technical limitation, so the data platform should ideally support at least the smallest clock tick across the systems involved.

However, storing data at a higher granularity than is available in the operational system means adding details to that data you can't know.

Imagine the following situation: in the first operational system, sales are stored with only a date (e.g., 15 July 2024). In the second operational system, sales are stored with a date *and* time (e.g., 16 July 2024 14:07:20).

If you want to store sales data from both systems in a *single* table, you should choose the clock tick granularity of the second operational system. However, while this allows both value to exist in the same column, this does add time information to the sales, which may result in errors in reports (e.g., some of your sales will be recorded at the time of 00:00:00). For this reason, it's often better to separate these values until the point logic can be applied to interpret these for data delivery.

To implement this, carefully evaluate which data can be safely combined and convert it to the target time data type.

The Allen Relationships

In an ideal scenario, time intervals in your data solution would follow a perfect sequence, making it easy to store and manage data. However, real-world data often presents challenges such as unexpected interval lengths and overlapping periods.

↗ The Allen Relationships identify thirteen distinct and qualitative ways how time periods may relate to each other.

To effectively manage these complexities, it's important to understand the different types of relationships between time intervals – described in the Allen Relationships[46].

The Allen Relationships identify thirteen distinct and qualitative ways how time periods may relate to each other. Below is an overview of these types and their relationships, adapted from Allen and Johnston[47].

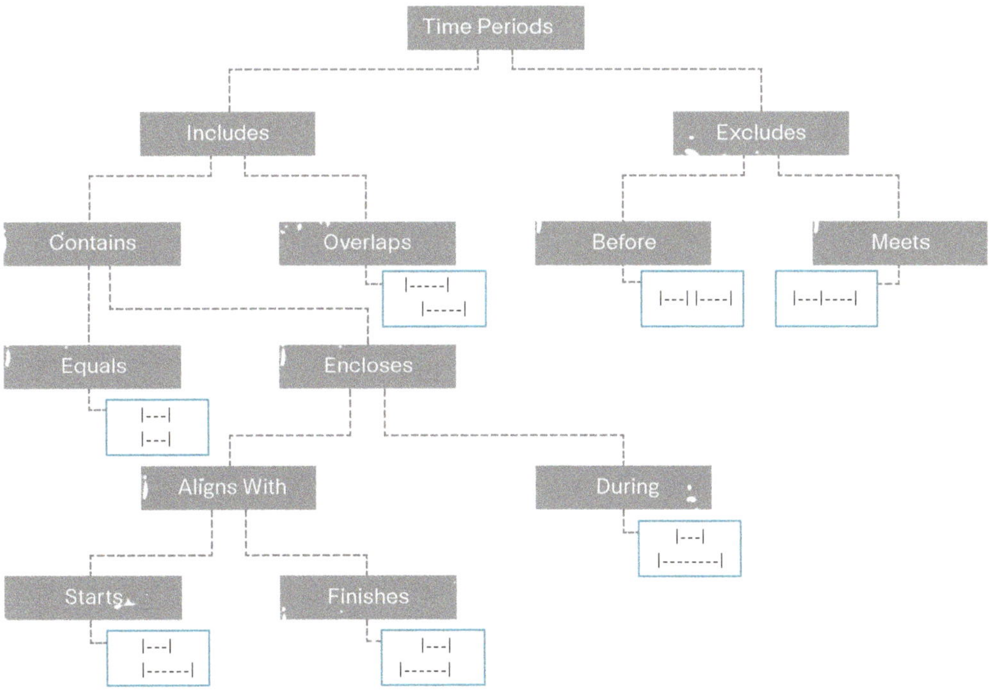

For the thirteen interactions, there are seven ways in which these interactions can manifest.

Except for the 'equals' interaction, an interaction always has an inverse counterpart.

For example the 'before' interaction between two time periods works like this:

Interaction	Interpretation
|--- X ---| |--- Y ---|	X takes place before Y
|--- Y ---| |--- X ---|	Y takes place before X (inverse)

Include interactions

Time periods that are connected in an 'include' interaction share at least one clock tick. Therefore, there is at least one clock tick for which we need to determine which data point is truly valid.

The following scenarios apply:

- Time periods with *overlaps* have the same clock ticks in common, but each period also has unique clock ticks not shared by the other
- For *equals,* both time periods have all clock ticks in common, starting and ending at the same time
- In the *starts* scenario, both time periods start at the same clock tick, but one period ends before the other
- In the *finishes* scenario, both time periods end at the same clock tick, but one period starts later than the other
- For *during,* one time period is completely contained within the other, starting later and ending earlier

Include interactions are relatively harder to implemented because of the shared clock ticks. It's essential to determine the valid data points at these shared intervals.

Exclude interactions

All time periods classified under the 'excludes' supertype have no clock ticks in common. They are much easier to handle than their 'includes' counterparts because you can store the data directly in the data platform without conflicts.

- *Before* applies when one time period occurs entirely before another period. There are no overlapping clock ticks, and there is a gap of clock ticks between the periods that are not included in either period
- *Meets* applies when an earlier time period is directly followed by the subsequent time period, without any clock ticks existing between them

Understanding the dynamics of interacting time periods helps efficient management of time in the data solution. By recognizing and properly handling these relationships, you can ensure reliable and precise data storage and reporting.

Time periods in the data solution

We will refer to these definitions in various sections that cover 'time.' For now, while importing data into the solution, it is sufficient to state that the time periods defined by the inscription timestamp always connect – they *meet.* However, the state timeline defined by the state timestamp is a different matter, which is covered in this and the getting the data out chapter.

Open or closed?

Another important consideration for managing time in the data solution is whether time periods should be *open* or *closed.* This affects how date math is implemented in practical terms, with date values being either inclusive or exclusive. This is a key decision for any data platform.

↗ The Closed-Open notation is the de facto standard. This notation ensures there are no clock ticks between time periods, regardless of the granularity of your clock ticks.

When working with temporal data, there are four ways to define how two time periods can meet. The following table shows these types using the time periods January to December 2023 and January to December 2024, based on the clock tick granularity of a month.

Closed-Closed	T1 [Jan 2023 - Dec 2023] ; T2 [Jan 2024 - Dec 2024]
Closed-Open	T1 [Jan 2023 - Jan 2024[; T2 [Jan 2024 - Jan 2025[
Open-Closed	T1]Dec 2022 - Dec 2023] ; T2]Dec 2023 - Dec 2024]
Open-Open	T1]Dec 2022 - Jan 2024[; T2]Dec 2023 - Jan 2025[

Closed-Closed

The first notation is called *Closed-Closed*. This means that the clock ticks at the borders of the time period are included. For example, the year 2023 is described by the interval from January 2023 to December 2023, with both timestamps included. Similarly, the year 2024 is defined from January 2024 to December 2024.

Closed-Open

In the *Closed-Open* notation, the starting clock tick is included in the period, but the last clock tick is excluded. This means that the last clock tick of the period is actually the first clock tick outside of the period.

In the above example it is at the same time the *first* clock tick of the second period. For example, the period for 2023 is defined as January 2023 to January 2024, excluding January 2024 itself. Here, the time period of 2024 starts with the same clock tick where 2023 'ends.'

Open-Closed

The *Open-Closed* notation includes the last clock tick of the time period, but the first clock tick represents the one *just before the first included tick*. For instance, the interval for 2023 starts right after December 2022 and includes all of 2023.

In both the Closed-Open and Open-Closed notations, you don't need to know the granularity of the clock ticks in your systems, except that there are no ticks *between* the intervals.

Open-Open

In the *Open-Open* notation, both the predecessor and successor clock ticks are excluded from the interval. The first clock tick is just before the first included tick, and the last clock tick is just after the last included tick. For example, the interval for 2023 excludes December 22 and starts from January 23, excludes January 24 and ends with December 23.

The de facto standard

In temporal literature and common relational databases, the Closed-Open notation is the de facto standard. This notation ensures there are no clock ticks between time periods, regardless of the granularity of your clock ticks. Additionally, it simplifies the use of window functions, such as lead() and lag(), in the technology of your choice.

We adopt this approach in the design patterns to implement our reference architecture. This choice influences the naming of 'timestamp' columns in the data solution. To clarify that a Closed-Open notation is implemented, we define a time period with *'from* timestamp' and *'before* timestamp.'

For reference, in a Closed-Closed notation we would use *'from* timestamp' and *'to* timestamp' in the column naming.

As a result, when defining time periods for commonly-used temporal columns, such as the inscription timestamp and state timestamp, we use the following naming conventions:

- 'Inscription from timestamp' up to (but not including) 'inscription before timestamp'
- 'State from timestamp' up to (but not including) 'state before timestamp'

Consider this in the context of the earlier date math introduction:

'Zero record'

Person Key	Colour	Change Timestamp	Expiry Timestamp
25	Unknown	1900-01-01	2022-06-05
25	Red	2022-06-05	2022-07-23
25	Blue	2022-07-23	2023-03-16
25	Green	2023-03-16	9999-12-31

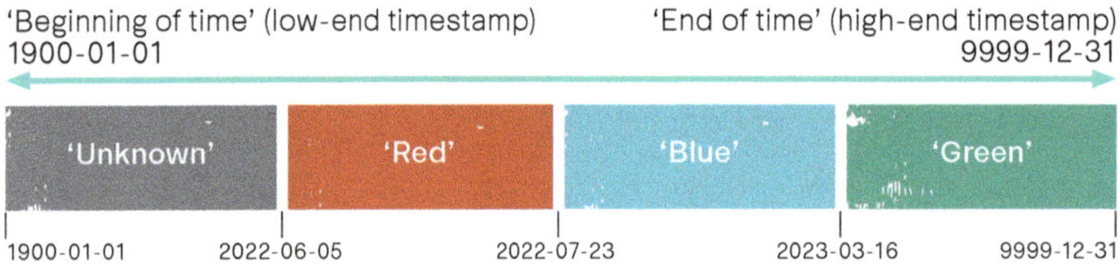

A time period, sometimes referred to as an 'effective period' or 'validity period,' can be evaluated by retrieving the corresponding timestamp from the subsequent record for the key.

In our design pattern, we implement this as 'from timestamp' and 'before timestamp' to emphasize the Closed-Open approach. The 'end date' or 'expiry date' is the before timestamp, indicating the time period just before the new record begins.

In practical terms, this means retrieving the value in a certain time period is done by selecting the value that is greater or equal (>=) than the from timestamp you're looking for, and smaller than (<) the before timestamp.

Mapping the state timestamp

Defining the state timeline involves mapping the selected column from the source data object (PSA) to the state (from/before) timestamp column. In metadata, this is a standard data item mapping, but it carries special significance.

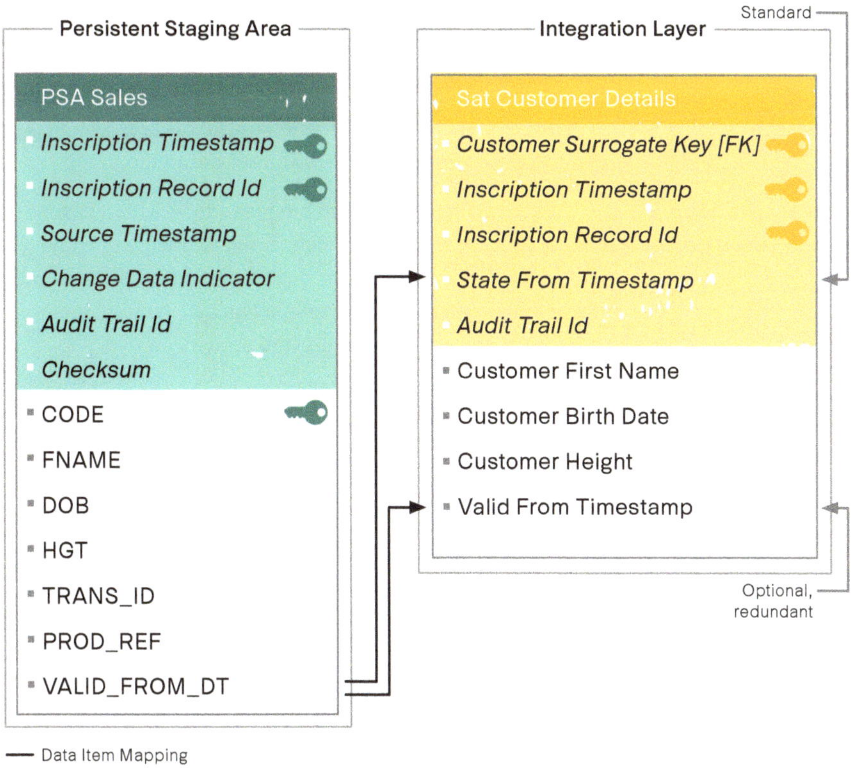

In this example, the 'VALID_FROM_DT' column in the staging layer is mapped to the state from timestamp standard column. While a suitable candidate for the state timeline is available in this case, this is not always guaranteed.

If necessary, the same data item can *also* be included in the Satellite in its original form ('Valid From Timestamp') — marked as 'redundant' for clarity.

As mentioned in the ⚐ state timestamp section, if no adequate alternative is available we recommend mapping the state from timestamp from the source timestamp in the staging layer.

This is always preferable to using the inscription timestamp.

At this stage, it's important to note that the *end* of the time period initiated by the state timestamp can also be represented using a standard column. In this book, this concept is referred to as the 'state before timestamp,' which will be covered in detail in the section on ⚐ end-dating.

Receiving and integrating data from multiple time zones

Timestamp data can be presented to the data solution in different time zones. This variation may occur because systems are physically located in different geographical areas than the data solution, or they might be configured to operate in specific time zones regardless of their physical location.

As a general guideline, when receiving timestamp data it's important to determine the time zone in which the data is delivered and convert it to a standard time zone in the integration layer.

The de facto standard for this conversion is Coordinated Universal Time (UTC). An alternative approach is capture the UTC offset for each timestamp, allowing it to be converted later.

For some data types, the UTC offset can be stored *with* the timestamp (e.g., datetimeoffset). In other cases, the time zone information might be provided separately from the timestamp, for example as a separate UTC offset value or an identifier for the timezone.

Both approaches —converting to UTC and storing the UTC offset and retaining the original timestamp format— are viable, but the first option is generally simpler. In either scenario, timestamp values can be represented in both UTC and local time.

However, converting to UTC alone is not the complete solution. Time zones can change throughout the year, and specific rules —such as daylight saving time adjustments— may apply to certain time zones. The UTC offset is not always fixed.

These shifts can lead to scenarios where transactions appear to occur 'twice' in history or seem to overtake each other in time, even if they happened sequentially. This situation is expected and correct when daylight saving time adjustments are considered.

For instance, if you need to combine data with time-critical elements, such as reporting on SLAs, it's crucial to ensure the reported times reflect the actual time in the relevant time zone, including any time zone shifts (e.g., daylight savings). To accurately interpret this information, queries must account for time zone shifts, specifying whether the reported time was before or after the adjustment.

Various platforms address this issue differently. For example, SQL Server offers the 'AT TIME ZONE' function, which can handle challenges like daylight saving time shifts, though there are some exceptions to this feature.

Implementing time zones

In our reference solution, timestamp data may require a conversion to UTC going from the staging layer into the integration layer. In metadata, this conversion is recorded as part of the standard data item mapping.

We consider this a hard business rule, which is why this is managed from the staging to integration layer. But for solutions that move the temporal design downstream, this conversion can also be implemented in the derived integration area.

In our experience, properly implementing the temporal design in the integration layer significantly simplifies the presentation layer, preventing the need for disparate solutions for the struggle with time.

Any specific timezone conversions required for consumption can be managed in the presentation layer, converting from the standard format to the required delivery format.

However, it is important to note that this information is not always available, or easy to determine. In some cases, the timezone may not be known initially. Understanding which time zones apply to specific data points can become clearer over time through data usage and analysis.

A good practice is to revisit the design when new insights emerge, update the metadata with the relevant timezone information, and allow the engine to refactor the affected parts of the solution.

Insert only, or not?

One way to classify data logistics processes, and even the data solution overall, is by determining whether they follow an *insert-only paradigm*. In an insert-only data solution, data logistics processes only insert records into data objects, and never update existing records.

The PSA is often implemented using an insert-only approach. Incoming data changes, already prepared to be transactional in nature, are simply stored (inserted) in the order they are received.

Hubs and Links also follow an insert-only approach; if a qualifying record does not exist, it is inserted. There is never a need to update it.

For Satellites, the same principle largely applies. Updating data received from operational systems —especially in the back room of the solution— goes against the core principles of the data solution.

However, exceptions exist when the concept of end-dating is involved. End-dating, explained in detail in the next section, may require updating an existing record when a newer version becomes available. The time period is 'closed' by setting the end timestamp, which technically constitutes an update transaction on an existing record. The process is therefore no longer strictly insert-only.

There is much to say in favor of the insert-only approach. This paradigm enforces a transactional view of data logistics, making it easier to refactor and is inherently dynamic, as derived values are calculated at runtime. This approach eliminates the need to consistently update values to maintain accurate time periods, thereby avoiding associated risks such as delays, failures, and rollbacks – issues that do not affect runtime evaluations.

From a technical standpoint, it simplifies management, as there is no need for concurrency control mechanisms such as locks to prevent read/write conflicts at the storage level. And in some technologies, an in-place update is not even supported.

Additionally, incorporating the necessary code into data logistics processes is often straightforward, and the performance cost of calculating changes is typically lower than the I/O penalties associated with physically storing (and retrieving) updates.

Implementing a complete insert-only approach for the entire data solution is both possible and viable, whether using Data Vault or other methodologies.

We recommend to apply insert-only wherever possible.

Implementing an insert-only approach, while initially straightforward, can become more complex when downstream preparing and merging time-variant data. This complexity often leads to a practical decision to persist some end-dating columns to simplify handling.

End-dating

Although the engine is capable of managing this process, it's essential for us to understand and work with it effectively as well.

↗ End-dating is defined as evaluating a *before timestamp* for a given *from timestamp*.

Defining a time period requires both a start and end timestamp.

Sometimes both of these values are already provided in the data. In other cases, you may need to calculate the record's time period.

This involves determining when a record is no longer valid, which occurs when its payload changes to a different value, or set of values.

This concept is often referred to as *end-dating* or *expiry-dating.* However, based on the terminology used in previous sections, referring to it as 'before dating' might be more precise as it aligns with the 'timestamp before' concept in a Closed-Open approach.

Nonetheless, we continue using 'end-dating' since this term is more widely recognized and understood in the industry.

End-dating is defined as evaluating a 'before timestamp' for a given 'from timestamp.' Unless it is already available, this is typically derived by using the from timestamp of the next record, sorted by the key and from timestamp.

Setting the before timestamp creates a visible per-record 'timeline,' 'time slice,' or 'date range.' We refer to this as *time periods.* For an example of this, please refer to the ⚐ open or closed section.

Apply or derive?

How, and to what extend, end-dating requires implementation depends largely on the data that is received. There are two possibilities.

1) In a perfect world, the operational systems may provide a full state time period, and we can map this to the state from timestamp and state before timestamp
2) When this is not reliable —or simply not available— the state or inscription before timestamp can be derived using the already available from timestamps

In all cases we prefer to address temporal challenges early in the integration layer.

These two approaches are covered in the subsequent sections.

Adding before timestamp columns to the physical model

In this book, we have chosen to persist the before timestamp for the state timeline, the *state before timestamp.*

We haven't included it as a standard column in the Satellite definition because its evaluation depends on various factors, which are covered in these sections. In some cases, it needs to be derived entirely, which can be done at runtime.

In rare instances, the situation might be reversed. The state before timestamp could be a standard column, while the state from timestamp is optional. This occurs when the operating system *only* provides the end timestamp for a time period. This is the primary reason for the ambiguity in the ⚐ Satellite data object structure section.

However, in our examples, we often add the 'missing' state timestamp, mostly the state before timestamp, as we believe its visibility assists in understanding the various concepts.

We do not recommend to persist the before timestamp for the assertion timeline (i.e. an 'inscription before timestamp') unless there is a strong reason to do so. The reason for this is that we, too often, encounter solutions that use the assertion timeline for date range queries and combining data for downstream consumption. While there may be use cases for this, they are rare. If one of these use cases apply, an 'inscription before timestamp' can always be added.

In most scenarios, it's safest to use the inscription timestamp *for filtering only* and rely on the state timeline for any date math and combination of data sets. Not having the 'inscription timestamp before' in the solution reinforces this practice.

Mapping end-dating

If the operational system already provides complete time periods, these values can be selected directly and mapped as standard data items.

If this is the case, the state before timestamp can be added to the solution architecture as a standard Satellite column. The solution will still be able to support an insert-only approach – including a full state timeline.

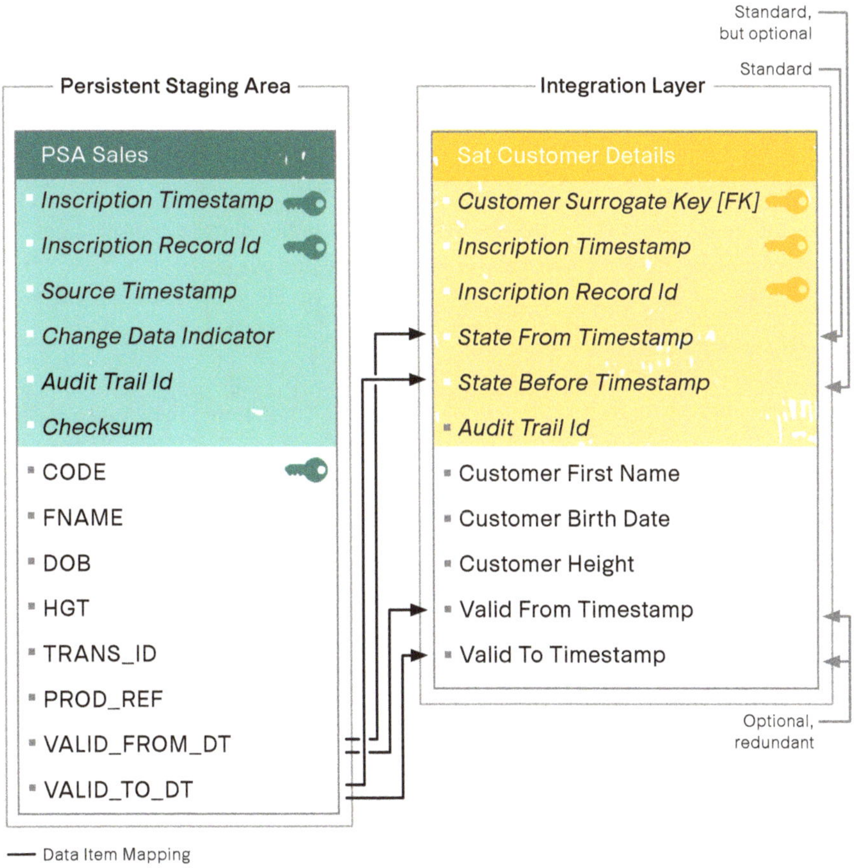

In this example, the 'VALID_TO_DT' column in the staging layer is mapped to the state before timestamp column as the operating system provides a Closed-Open time period.

Determining whether this approach is viable is part of the temporal design process. For this to work effectively, the before timestamp ('VALID_TO_DT') must be tightly controlled by the operational system, ensuring there are no overlaps or gaps.

This is a risk for the data solution that must be managed, and testing framework controls are recommended to be in place to ensure ongoing consistency of the time periods.

If significant (temporal) data quality issues need to be addressed the original values can be retained as separate data item mappings, and fixes on the state timeline can be applied to ensure the availability of correct time periods.

It is often beneficial for all parties to recognize these issues early so they can (ideally) be addressed in the operational system or at the incoming interface between the operational system and the data solution.

These and other considerations are further covered in the section covering ⚐ bitemporal implementations.

Deriving end-dating

Before timestamps can always be derived using the from timestamps. Since they can be derived at runtime, they do not necessarily need to be stored alongside the data.

For a given from timestamp, such as the inscription or state timestamp, the before timestamp can be derived using code like this:

```
LEAD(<timestamp>,1,'9999-12-31')
OVER (PARTITION BY <key>
   ORDER BY <timestamp>)
```

This code selects the corresponding timestamp from the next row in order of the key and timestamp. When no next record is available, the high-end timestamp '9999-12-31' value is used as default.

When working with time periods, it is highly recommended to have a standard default high-end value indicating the absence of a before timestamp. This value can be any date far in the future, as long as it is applied consistently. We use 9999-12-31, as it is unlikely we will receive records dated this far ahead.

'On the fly' evaluation of the before timestamp supports an insert-only approach for data ingestion. The advantage is that the above code can be easily added to queries whenever a before timestamp is needed. This ensures the derived before timestamps are always correct based on the input data and logic, unlike previously stored before dates that might become inaccurate if they haven't been properly updated.

However, calculating the before timestamp each time a query runs incurs a performance cost due to the relatively expensive window function operation. Additionally, it adds complexity to the integration layer, requiring familiarity with SQL code like the example above and additional knowledge to interpret the data for point-in-time selections.

One key point to remember is that a time period applies to the entire record, encompassing *all* its columns and values.

As seen in the ⚐ redundancy, compacting, and change merging section, the column scope can change due to various factors, including the definition and evolution of the data model, as well as reasons like Satellite splitting. This dynamic will occur again when selecting specific columns from potentially many Satellites to deliver the presentation layer.

Each time the column scope changes, the time periods needs to be recalculated, which is easier when done at runtime and when required.

Persisting before timestamps

Persisting the before timestamp to disk has pros and cons too. When the before timestamp is stored as a physical column in the Satellite, it incurs an I/O cost.

Additionally, the process is no longer insert-only. Updating the before timestamp, such as changing '9999-12-31' to a new value when changes are detected, requires an update operation. There are also concerns about consistently updating these values to ensure they always provide the correct time periods – an issue that runtime evaluations do not face.

An example SQL statement for closing any time periods that require this can be found on our website: https://dtng.link/57mbg.

We have encountered various data solutions where the insert part of the Satellite data logistics process runs separately from the before-dating updates. If the insert process succeeds but the update process fails, the time periods can become inconsistent, leading to overlaps and downstream problems. Therefore, if before timestamps *are* persisted, we recommend ensuring that the before-dating logic is part of the same module. This way, Satellite inserts and updates can be committed or rolled back as a single functional unit — a single module.

There are cases where persisting the before timestamp is beneficial, even though it moves away from a full insert-only approach. For example, when data platforms charge more for compute resources but less for storage, it may be more cost-effective to persist the 'before timestamps.'

A special edge case in favor of persisting columns arises when the data solution supports driving keys. This will be covered in the ⚐ corresponding section.

The engine can switch between runtime and persisted before timestamps, where they are not directly mapped, based on directives for cost or performance optimization.

Modeling time in Satellites

In the reference solution architecture, we standardize Satellites with an assertion timeline and a state timeline. The assertion timeline is created automatically, and the state timeline is mapped to the best available option.

These Satellites are always structurally configured to support bitemporality.

However, for completeness, we would like to provide a brief overview of other options, such as nontemporal and unitemporal approaches, before delving into bitemporality.

Nontemporal

In a nontemporal environment, data simply 'is,' without any reference to time. For example, a customer record's personal details will always represent the current state until updated. When updated, the previous state is gone forever. For instance, if a customer changes their phone number, it will no longer be possible to retrieve the previous one, nor will there be any record of when, or how often, this change occurred.

↗ Nontemporal data simply is, without any reference to time.

Even today, systems can be nontemporal. In fact, one use case for implementing data solutions is to ensure that any previous states *can* be reproduced, even if the operational system cannot do so.

A specific example of nontemporal environment are events, as generated by a streaming technology. Measuring a temperature via a sensor, for example. In these cases, it is highly unlikely, improbable, or even technically impossible, to receive updates. In this specific scenario, the only information received is the temperature 'now.' There is no time component in this case, and no historization.

Unless there are compelling reasons to do otherwise, we still recommend to implement this as a uni- or bitemporal Satellite. This approach avoids the complexity of defining separate patterns and templates, thereby simplifying the overall solution. However, it's important to note that —strictly speaking— this is not bitemporal data, as the values will never change over time.

Unitemporal

↗ Unitemporal data defines a single timeline, which by default is the assertion timeline.

A unitemporal Satellite represents the traditional way Satellites are documented in most Data Vault methodology. This Satellite type defines a single timeline, which by default is the assertion timeline.

For instance, to track how often and why a customer's address changes, a timeline is added to the data. By recording a timestamp each time an address change occurs, we can capture past and present addresses, as well as how frequently the changes happen.

This way, the Satellite is unitemporal – adopting an assertion timeline represented by the inscription timestamp. Data changes are recorded in the order they arrive.

A unitemporal Satellite is defined with a primary key that consists of the following columns:

→ The surrogate key
→ The inscription timestamp
→ The inscription record id

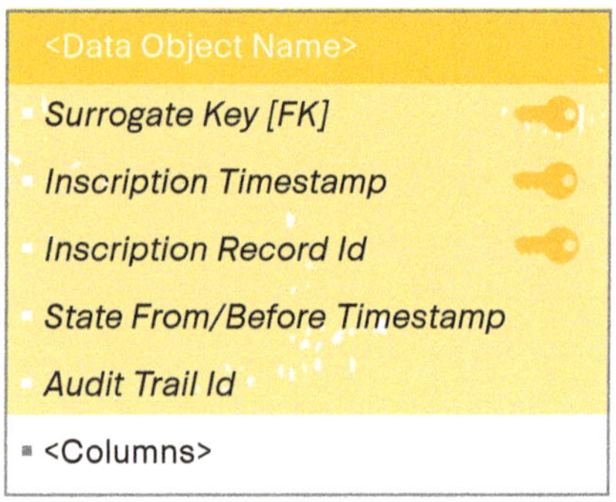

However, this approach often faces a common challenge: the recorded history may not align with the reality business users expect.

An address change that was received today might actually reflect a change that happened some time ago. This could be a correction, or the addition of an older address that wasn't yet recorded in the system. In such cases, the order of data arrival doesn't match when the customer actually changed addresses – and might result in showing the 'wrong' (older) address as the most current one.

If the goal is to understand when certain addresses were valid regardless of when the change was received, a different perspective on time is needed: the state timeline – represented by the state timestamp.

This approach moves towards defining a bitemporal Satellite. A fully bitemporal Satellite enables queries about the past, present, and even future state of a customer's address, independent of when the changes were made, and reflects the historical understanding at a given point in time.

We'll explore bitemporal concepts in the next sections, but for now, a Satellite that tracks changes solely on the assertion timeline (inscription timestamp) remains unitemporal, even if the state timestamp *is* mapped. The state timestamp in this case is not necessarily a timeline yet, and it is not part of the primary key. In reality, it's still just another descriptive attribute.

Compared to bitemporal implementations, any issues related to the (completeness of the) state timeline are not yet resolved in an unitemporal Satellite.

A Satellite can also be unitemporal if it uses *only* the state timeline, effectively replacing the inscription timeline. However, this introduces a risk due to the tight coupling between operational systems and the data solution. If state timestamps are modified or added retrospectively, the data solution will be directly impacted. For this reason, we don't recommend this approach.

Before diving further into bitemporal concepts, we will illustrate how to visualize unitemporal data, and combine unitemporal Satellites for data delivery. In this pattern, bitemporal challenges are addressed as the data leaves the integration layer.

This serves as a useful introduction to how a fully bitemporal approach resolves these issues upfront.

Visualizing (uni)temporal data

At this stage, we would like to introduce a technique for visualizing data changes over time. We can use both the assertion timeline ('ATL,' when data was received) and the state timeline ('STL,' when data applies) to display changes over time on a Cartesian plane. The y-axis represents the ATL, and the x-axis represents the STL.

We will use this visual to cover different scenarios involving both unitemporal and bitemporal challenges. For now, since we're still covering unitemporal data, we *only need to consider the ATL*—the y-axis.

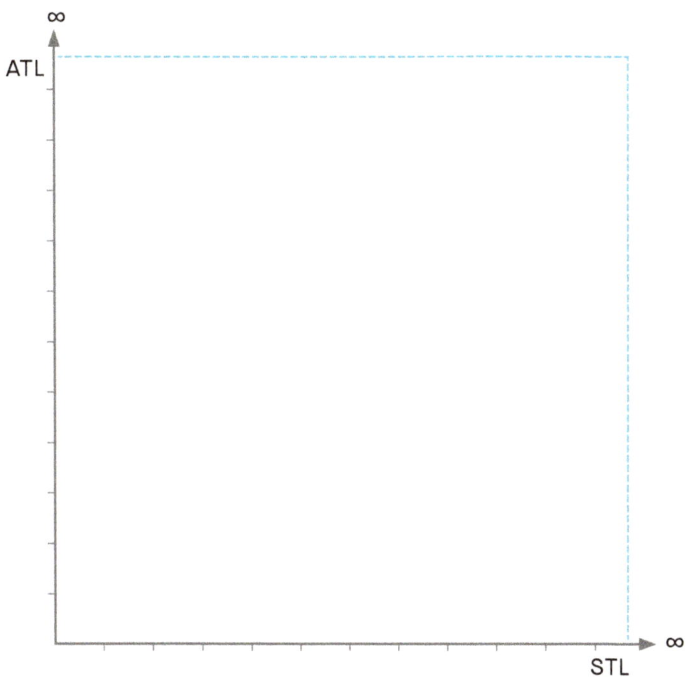

A simple unitemporal example —disregarding the STL for now— could be as follows. In this example, the inscription timestamps are unique, and the inscription record id has been omitted for brevity.

Sat Customer Address

Surrogate Key	Inscription Timestamp	Address
CUST_34	2015-06-01	Utrecht
CUST_34	2019-01-01	Frankfurt
CUST_34	2022-01-01	Brisbane
CUST_34	2025-06-01	Temptation City

In this example, omitting various columns, the changes over time for a customer's address are shown in the order in which they were detected and received by the data solution. In reality, these changes trickle into the data solution with large intervals and we're observing the changes back in time from today's perspective. When building the visualization, we're replaying these transactions one at a time.

The first appearance of the customer record is in 2015-06-01, apparently the customer is reported to be living in 'Utrecht' at that time. At least, we know at that time we received data indicating this.

On the Cartesian plane, a 'block' is added to visualize this:

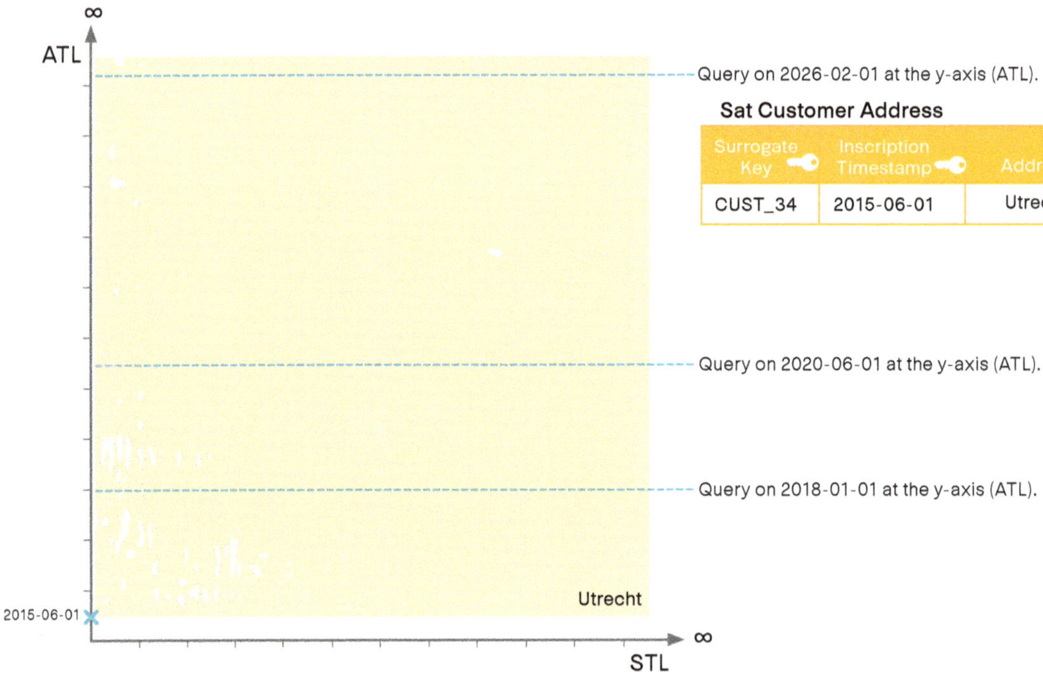

Sat Customer Address

Surrogate Key	Inscription Timestamp	Address
CUST_34	2015-06-01	Utrecht

When the first record arrives, all we know is that from 2015-06-01 onwards the customer's address is 'Utrecht.' Before that, we don't know, and we haven't received any other data to indicate otherwise later. So, for all intents and purposes, at any time we query the data solution for data later than 2015-06-01, the address is always 'Utrecht.'

The dotted lines in the diagram illustrate this. These are the points in time we retrieve (query) the data from according to the ATL — horizontal lines crossing the y-axis.

An update on the customer's address details is received on 2019-01-01, resulting in a new block (record) on the Cartesian plane. This new record state begins at 2019-01-01, which also means that the before inscription timestamp of the previous record becomes known.

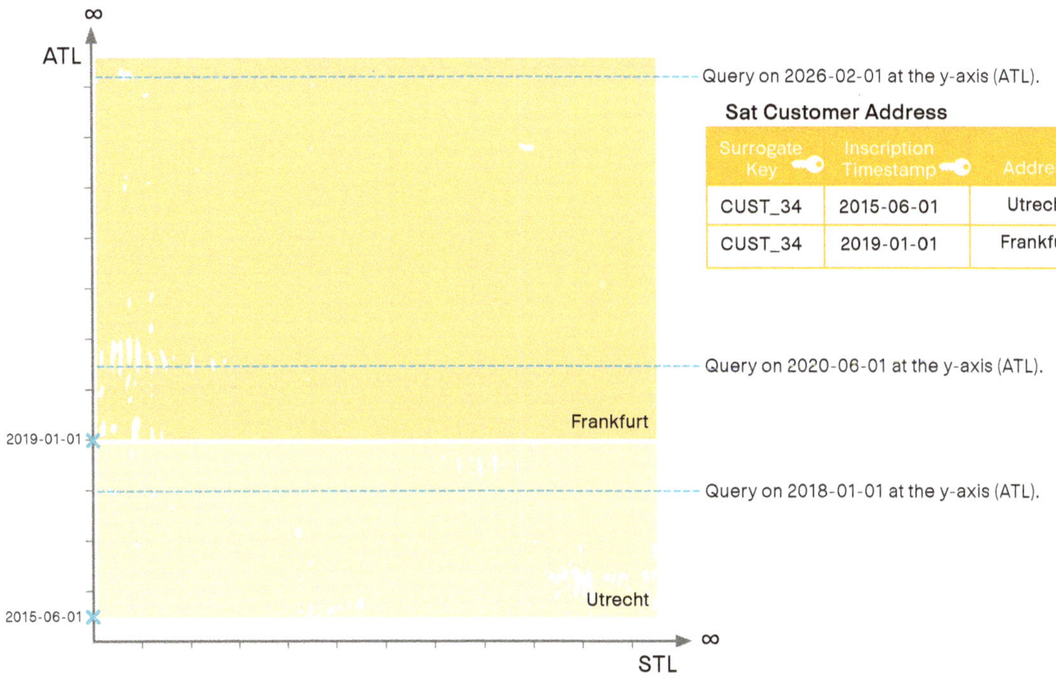

Sat Customer Address

Surrogate Key	Inscription Timestamp	Address
CUST_34	2015-06-01	Utrecht
CUST_34	2019-01-01	Frankfurt

Querying the data at the different ATL points-in-time will return the corresponding different values. The first query (2018-01-01) will return 'Utrecht,' but any query after 2019-01-01 will now return 'Frankfurt.'

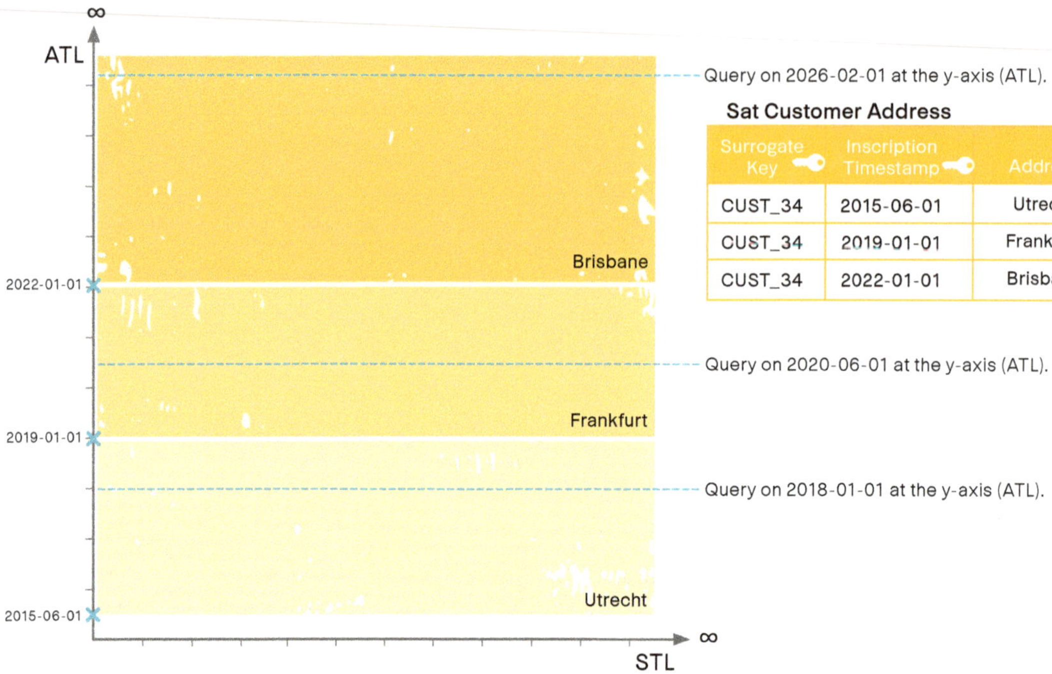

Sat Customer Address

Surrogate Key	Inscription Timestamp	Address
CUST_34	2015-06-01	Utrecht
CUST_34	2019-01-01	Frankfurt
CUST_34	2022-01-01	Brisbane

Subsequently, new address changes are received, indicating the address change to ‘Brisbane’ at 2022-01-01 and ‘Temptation City’ at 2025-06-01.

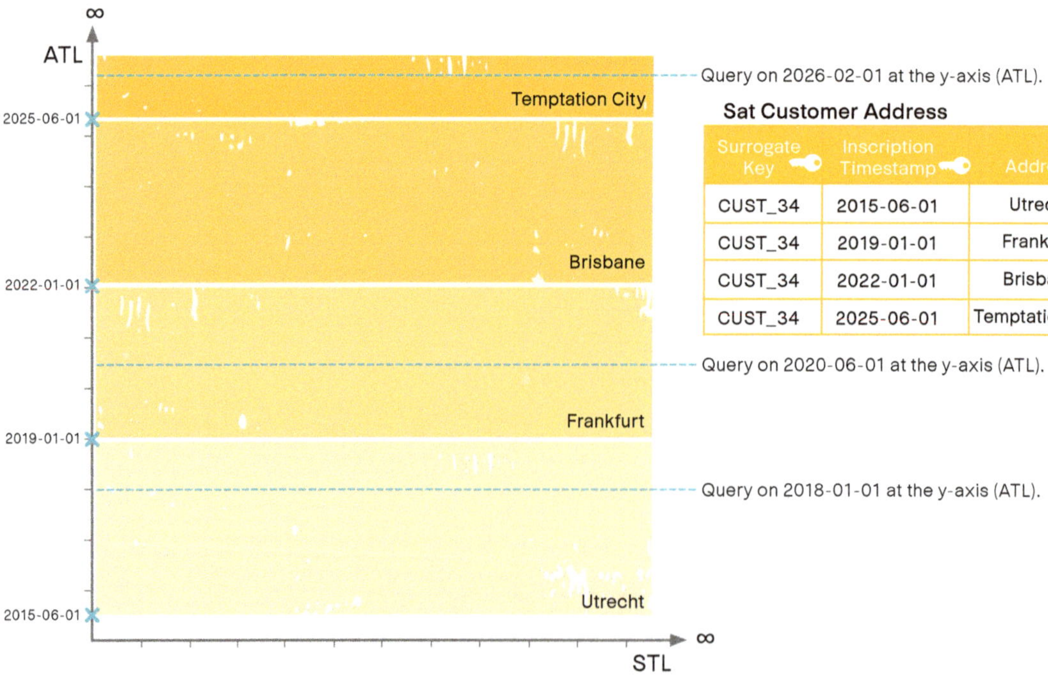

Sat Customer Address

Surrogate Key	Inscription Timestamp	Address
CUST_34	2015-06-01	Utrecht
CUST_34	2019-01-01	Frankfurt
CUST_34	2022-01-01	Brisbane
CUST_34	2025-06-01	Temptation City

This unitemporal data example shows how data can be queried at various points in time. The third change —'Brisbane'— will not be returned by the example's query points but of course any query when the timestamp is greater than or equal to 2022-01-01 and lower than 2025-06-01 will do so.

Late-arriving transactions

Imagine you are tasked with providing the January end-of-month sales report. Eager to impress, you stay up until just past midnight to send the results as soon as they're available. Once midnight hits, you check that all the data has been correctly loaded into the data platform. Satisfied, you generate the report and it shows 100 units sold – a good result.

A few days later, your manager calls. She has just run the same report, but her results show 80 units sold.

What's going on? To understand the discrepancy, we need to examine the data using both the assertion and state timestamps.

For example, on January 4th, 4 units are sold which brings the balance to 4. On January 7th, another 16 units are sold, raising the balance to 20. Then on January 22nd, 60 more units are reported, bringing the balance to 80.

Inscription Timestamp	Transaction Unit	Period	Balance Unit
2023-01-25	+20	January	100
2023-01-22	+60	January	80
2023-01-07	+16	January	20
2023-01-04	+4	January	4

Finally, on January 25th, another 20 units are sold, ending the month with a total of 100 units sold.

But on February 3rd, a correction comes in that applies to the January reporting period. It turns out that the sales figures from January 4th and 7th were incorrect and needed adjusting. The sales representative (correctly) created an adjustment of -20 units dated January 10th but committed this transaction *after* the closing of the month. It wasn't added to the system until February 3rd, which is also when it was received by the data solution – but it still applies to the January reporting period.

Inscription Timestamp	Transaction Unit	Period	Balance Unit
2023-02-03	-20	January	80
2023-01-25	+20	January	100
2023-01-22	+60	January	80
2023-01-07	+16	January	20
2023-01-04	+4	January	4

This kind of late-arriving, or back-dated, record can appear in many forms depending on the system and interface involved. In this example, the operational system logged the correction as a separate transaction (-20 units), but it could just as easily have been an update to the original record. In that case, the values for the January 4th and January 7th records would have been updated to 0 but detected as a regular change record.

In this scenario, the operational system might not even retain the original values and may only be able to show the current state of the data. However, if the staging layer is properly designed, the interface to the data solution would detect this as a data change, capturing the updated values. The data solution could then still show the old and updated values as though they were received as a correction.

Regardless of how the data is received, if the records had been processed at the 'right' time, the overview would have appeared like this:

Inscription Timestamp	Transaction Unit	Period	Balance Unit
2023-01-25	+20	January	80
2023-01-22	+60	January	60
2023-01-10	-20	January	0
2023-01-07	+16	January	20
2023-01-04	+4	January	4

If the adjustment had been received on January 10th —as intended— the reported balance for January would have been different. So, when you ran the report at month-end, 100 units was the correct result based on the data available at that time. After the correction, the correct result became 80 units.

Both perspectives are valid based on the data at the time of reporting, but how can this be managed?

Applying the visualization

If we map the first transaction to the plane it results in the below visual. Keep in mind that the focus is still on unitemporal data, and therefore the ATL, the y-axis, is the main focus. However, we will start adding STL values to illustrate the different variations between pure unitemporal data and full bitemporal perspectives.

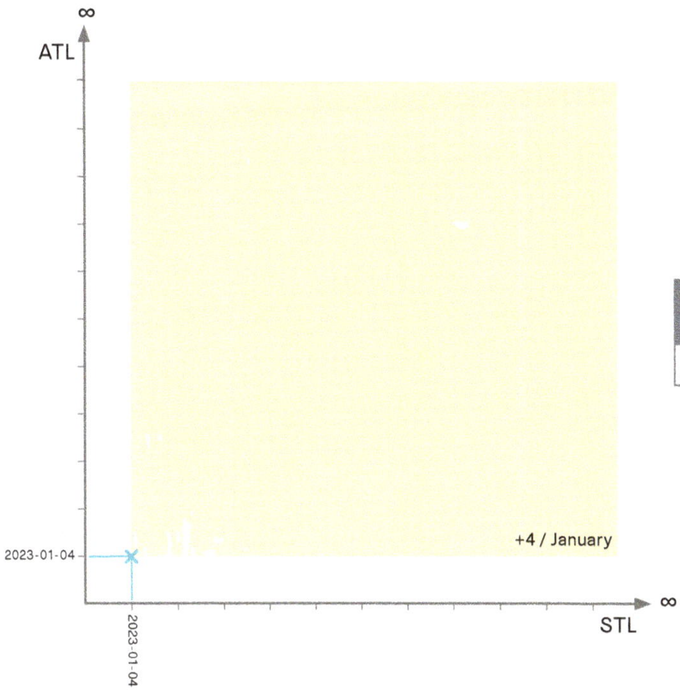

Inscription Timestamp	State Timestamp	Transaction Unit	Period	Balance Unit
2023-01-04	2023-01-04	+4	January	4

The inscription timestamp and the state timestamp are to be understood as a coordinate point on the Cartesian plane. This is how the lower left corner (the point) of the new rectangle is determined. Like coordinates on a map.

The transaction value and balance are added next to each point to demonstrate the impact of the data change.

The record arrived on January 4th – the inscription timestamp. This marks the lower edge of the blue square that represents the validity of the record. Below that edge, before January 4th, there is nothing. The record did not exist yet.

The same applies for the state timestamp, which is also January 4th. This is represented by the left side of the square. To the left of this edge, there is nothing which indicates there was no valid state prior to this timestamp. The top and right side of the square represent the high-value timestamp, the 31st of December 9999 for instance, that represents the end of the validity period.

When we map the subsequent transactions to the plane, a pattern of data changes emerges. The transactions that were received in January are now visible, and the transaction received on the 3rd of February has not happened yet.

The horizontal dotted line that intersects with the ATL y-axis represents the point in time the report was run, just after midnight on the 1st of February. It sums up the four transactions for the 'January' period received *before* February 3rd –the dotted line– which results in a balance of 100.

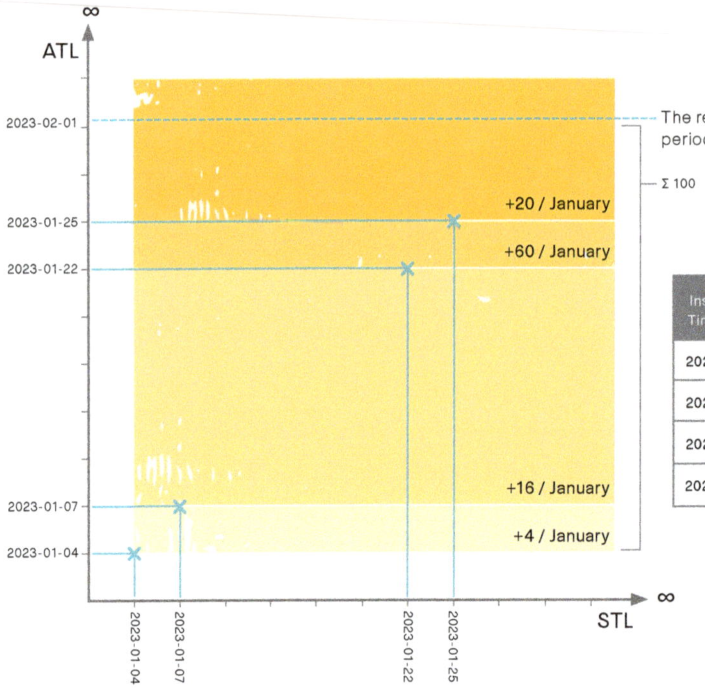

Inscription Timestamp	State Timestamp	Transaction Unit	Period	Balance Unit
2023-01-25	2023-01-25	+20	January	100
2023-01-22	2023-01-22	+60	January	80
2023-01-07	2023-01-07	+16	January	20
2023-01-04	2023-01-04	+4	January	4

When the February 3rd adjustment is introduced, it highlights that the correction applies to a previous point in the state timeline, but was received later on the assertion timeline. This transaction arrived after the earlier ones, so it appears higher up along the assertion timeline axis. However, because the correction applies to an earlier point in time, it shifts slightly to the left on the state timeline axis.

The dotted line in the diagram represents the moment the report was run for the second time, a few days later. Now the balance for the January reporting period reflect 80 units.

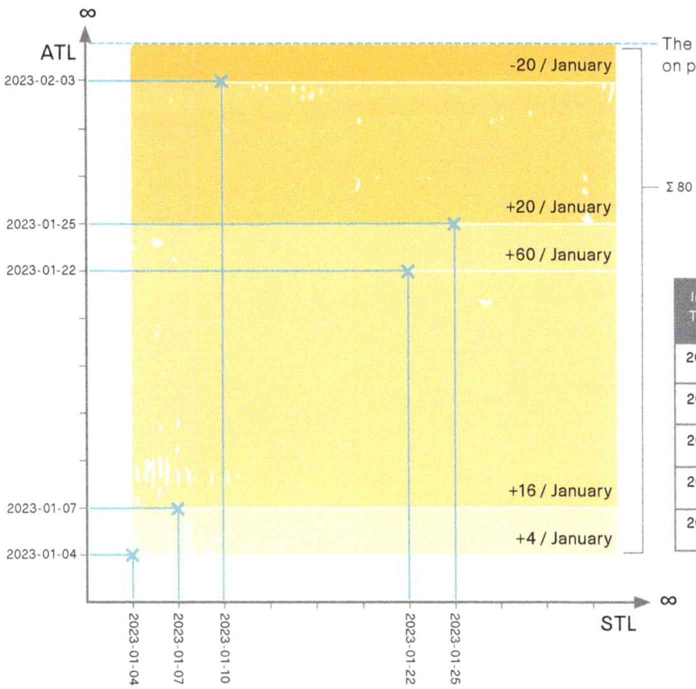

Inscription Timestamp	State Timestamp	Transaction Unit	Period	Balance Unit
2023-02-03	2023-01-10	-20	January	80
2023-01-25	2023-01-25	+20	January	100
2023-01-22	2023-01-22	+60	January	80
2023-01-07	2023-01-07	+16	January	20
2023-01-04	2023-01-04	+4	January	4

All transactions are now visible on the Cartesian plane, and we can now traverse the y-axis to go back-and-forth in time following the asserting timeline.

In the data solution, this point-in-time perspective of the balance can always be replicated by navigating back along the assertion timeline. Technically, this involves filtering out records with an inscription timestamp later than the point in time being viewed, excluding any records with an inscription timestamp greater than this point in time.

This technique of 'as-of' data retrieval, by applying filters on the inscription timestamp, allows the data solution to reproduce the exact state of the data at any given moment. This capability becomes invaluable as the the organization's data maturity increases.

We will dive deeper into this in the ⚐ getting the data out chapter.

Merging unitemporal Satellites into a bitemporal data set

In this section, we'll cover how to combine two unitemporal Satellites (additionally including the state timestamps) into a single data set for delivery. This section also serves as an introduction to bitemporal complexities, simplified to focus on key concepts.

We want to make clear that, in a bitemporal approach, the issues encountered here are resolved when processing the data *into* the Satellite. They —the problems— occur only due to the fact that the Satellite are unitemporal, even if they appear to be bitemporal. The state timelines are not fully completed — as we will see. Completing these will become the focus of the bitemporal approach.

In this example, we combine the unitemporal 'Customer' Satellite with the unitemporal 'Customer Contact' Satellite. Both describe the Customer Hub, but each has its own cadence of data changes.

Each Satellite includes a business time period (state before/after timestamps), which can be used to join the data at the correct business-representative point in time in the data object 'Customer Overview.'

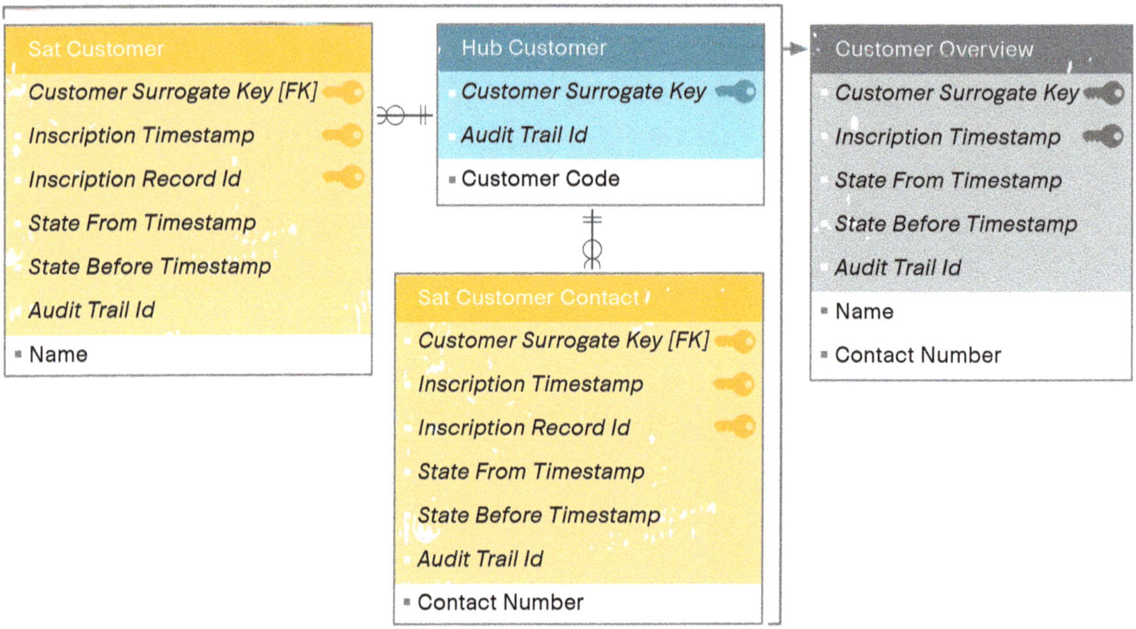

The data in this example is shown below. The Hub contents are omitted for brevity.

Sat Customer

Surrogate Key	Inscription Timestamp	State From Timestamp	State Before Timestamp	Customer Name
CUST_4	2015-04-01	2015-02-01	9999-12-31	Jonathan
CUST_4	2017-02-02	2017-01-01	9999-12-31	John
CUST_4	2018-01-01	2018-01-01	9999-12-31	Jon

Sat Customer Contact

Surrogate Key	Inscription Timestamp	State From Timestamp	State Before Timestamp	Contact Number
CUST_4	2016-01-01	2016-01-01	9999-12-31	123
CUST_4	2019-01-01	2019-01-01	9999-12-31	999
CUST_4	2019-02-01	2016-06-01	2019-01-01	345
CUST_4	2023-01-01	2025-01-01	9999-12-31	111

Correction of the past.

The 'Customer' Satellite contains data in a correct order. The 'Customer Name' changed in a chronologically correct order — for both the inscription timestamp and state from timestamp.

In the 'Customer Contact' Satellite, the 'Contact Number' incurs a backdated adjustment (record 3). The contact number 123 is replaced by 345 for the time period 2016-12-01 to 2019-01-01.

When interpreting time-variant data, we should base our analysis on the real-world history of events, irrespective of their arrival — the state timestamps.

We can reorder these data changes to align to this perspective using the state from timestamp. With the benefit of hindsight, we're reviewing (business) history from today's perspective after all. The typical result of combining the unitemporal Satellites is shown below:

Sat Customer

Surrogate Key	Inscription Timestamp	State From Timestamp	Customer Name
CUST_4	2015-04-01	2015-02-01	Jonathan
CUST_4	2017-02-02	2017-01-01	John
CUST_4	2018-01-01	2018-01-01	Jon

Sat Customer Contact

Surrogate Key	Inscription Timestamp	State From Timestamp	Contact Number
CUST_4	2016-01-01	2016-01-01	123
CUST_4	2019-01-01	2019-01-01	999
CUST_4	2019-02-01	2016-06-01	345
CUST_4	2025-01-01	2025-01-01	111

Combined data set (by State From Timestamp)

Surrogate Key	Inscription Timestamp	State From Timestamp	Customer Name	Contact Number
CUST_4	2015-04-01	2015-02-01	Jonathan	Null
CUST_4	2016-01-01	2016-01-01	Jonathan	123
CUST_4	2019-02-01	2016-06-01	Jonathan	345
CUST_4	2017-02-02	2017-01-01	John	345
CUST_4	2018-01-01	2018-01-01	Jon	345
CUST_4	2019-01-01	2019-01-01	Jon	999
CUST_4	2025-01-01	2025-01-01	Jon	111

The state before timestamp is omitted for brevity. Simply reviewing the data changes over the state time, the outcome might seem logical at first glance.

Even if the data is merged correct, from a unitemporal perspective, the result *is incorrect from business point of view.*

The underlying reasons for this are what can make dealing with time in data solutions so challenging.

Replaying history

To explain why this result is not truly correct, we must replay the sequence of changes as they occurred —following the assertion timeline, but keeping the state timeline in mind— and evaluate the impact of each new change as it was received.

We should evaluate each record with only the data available at that point in time, excluding any 'future' records that had not yet been received (at that time). We can do this by filtering out records with an inscription timestamp later than the point in time than the data change that is evaluated.

So, instead of looking backwards in history from today's perspective,
we simulate building up the history over time by filtering out later transactions.

To illustrate this, we use the Cartesian plane from the previous sections.

Let's start with the first Satellite and see how its data changes can be represented on the plane. The inscription timestamp and the state timestamp are used as coordinate points (the green crosses).

The first change carves out a section in the plane that represents the record's validity based on both the assertion and state timelines.

- → The record arrived on 2015-04-01, marked by the bottom edge of the square, representing the inscription timestamp. Before this date, no record existed
- → The state timestamp is 2015-02-01, meaning the record is considered valid starting two months before it was received. This is shown by the left edge of the square. To the left of this edge, there is nothing which indicates there was no valid state prior to this timestamp

The top and right sides of the square represent the high-end value dates (e.g., 9999-12-31), which indicate the end of the validity period.

To be precise, this is the bitemporal representation of the unitemporal data. This is necessary to show the correct merging of the two satellites on their state (business) timelines.

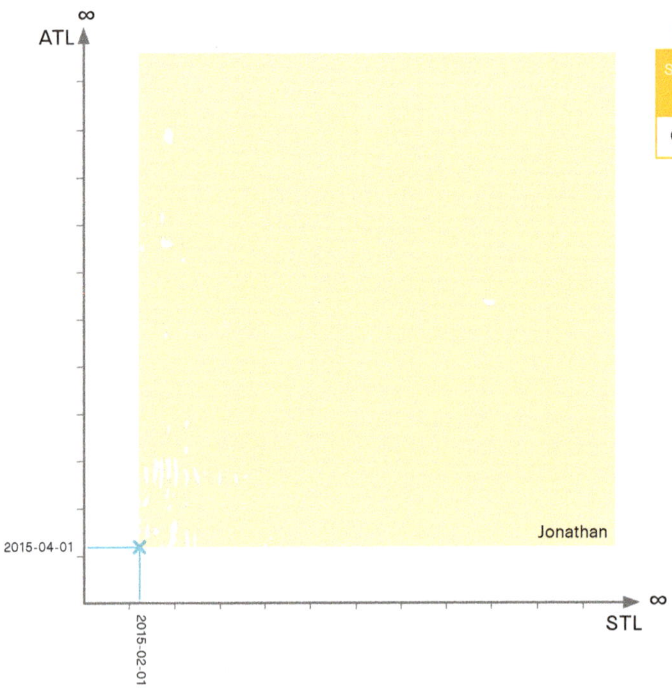

Sat Customer

Surrogate Key	Inscription Timestamp	State From Timestamp	State Before Timestamp	Customer Name
CUST_4	2015-04-01	2015-02-01	9999-12-31	Jonathan

Now let's add other two changes to the plane:

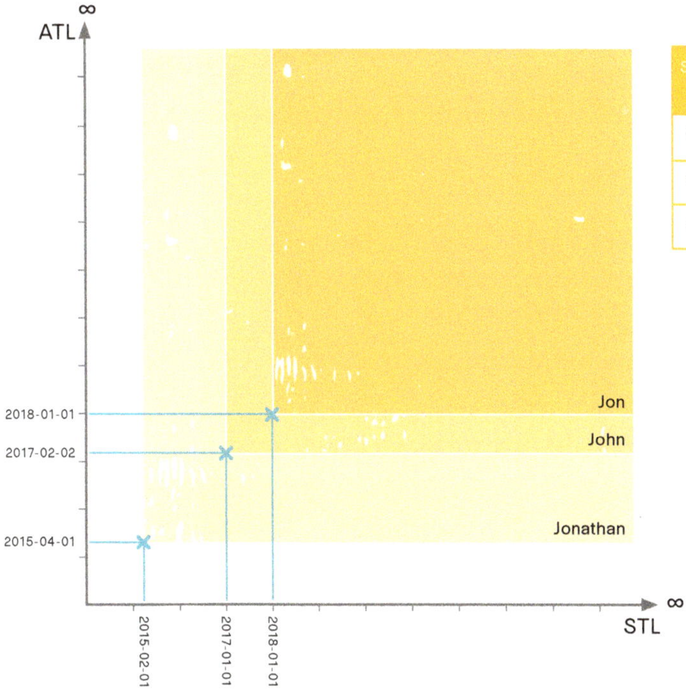

Sat Customer

Surrogate Key	Inscription Timestamp	State From Timestamp	State Before Timestamp	Customer Name
CUST_4	2015-04-01	2015-02-01	9999-12-31	Jonathan
CUST_4	2017-02-02	2017-01-01	9999-12-31	John
CUST_4	2018-01-01	2018-01-01	9999-12-31	Jon

These changes are sequential for both timelines. Each record continues to carve out smaller sections in the plane. The creation of a new section serves as a visual indication when the earlier record is considered end-dated.

We can do the same for the second Satellite. The diagram below sees all four data changes mapped to the plane:

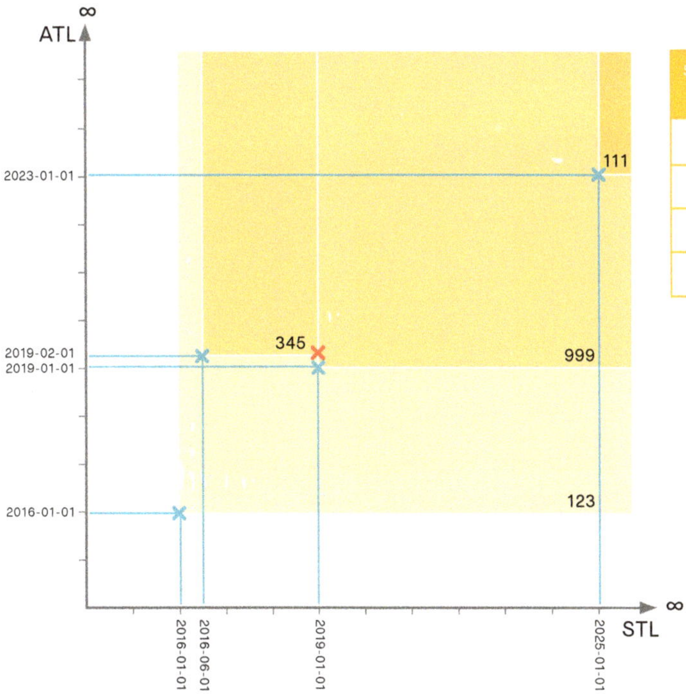

Sat Customer Contact

Surrogate Key	Inscription Timestamp	State From Timestamp	State Before Timestamp	Contact Number
CUST_4	2016-01-01	2016-01-01	9999-12-31	123
CUST_4	2019-01-01	2019-01-01	9999-12-31	999
CUST_4	2019-02-01	2016-06-01	2019-01-01	345
CUST_4	2023-01-01	2025-01-01	9999-12-31	111

As always, each block on the plane represents a record. The third record from the top —with number '345'— is as mentioned before a backdated adjustment . This is a correction that was received later. Because of this, it moves slightly to the left to indicate the earlier state timestamp. The red cross represents the coordinate of the inscription timestamp and the state before timestamp for this record. Without this end timestamp coordinate, this data set would have overwritten all data younger than ATL = 2019-02-01 and STL = 2016-06-01.

Combining the data

When combining the two data sets, we need to perform a point-in-time join using the state timestamps. The detailed implementation of this process will be covered in later sections, but we can preview the expected result set by *overlaying* the two diagrams.

The outcome is a merged view of the data sets, as illustrated in the diagram below.

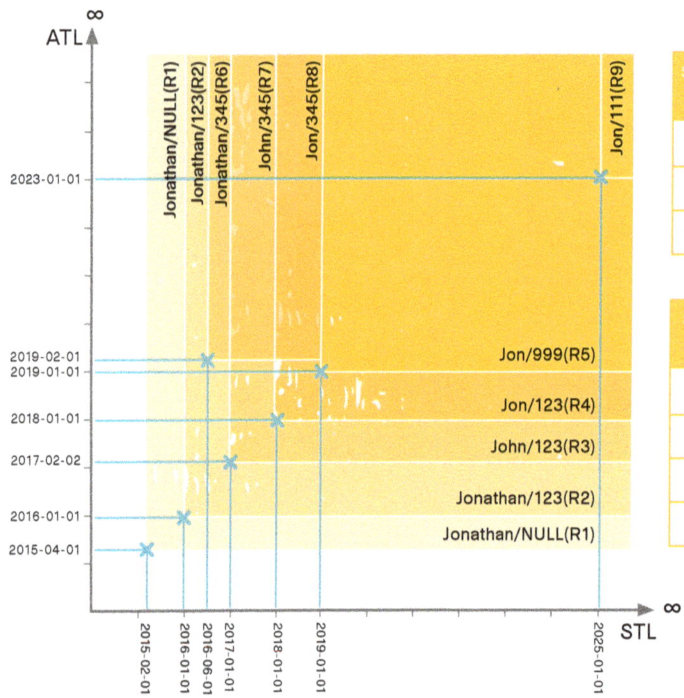

Sat Customer

Surrogate Key	Inscription Timestamp	State From Timestamp	State Before Timestamp	Customer Name
CUST_4	2015-04-01	2015-02-01	9999-12-31	Jonathan
CUST_4	2017-02-02	2017-01-01	9999-12-31	John
CUST_4	2018-01-01	2018-01-01	9999-12-31	Jon

Sat Customer Contact

Surrogate Key	Inscription Timestamp	State From Timestamp	State Before Timestamp	Contact Number
CUST_4	2016-01-01	2016-01-01	9999-12-31	123
CUST_4	2019-01-01	2019-01-01	9999-12-31	999
CUST_4	2019-02-01	2016-06-01	2019-01-01	345
CUST_4	2023-01-01	2025-01-01	9999-12-31	111

In the diagram, we can now see that the combined data set reflects the most current data according to the STL – the top 7 vertical blocks. This corresponds to the combined set used in the introduction, looking back at history from today's perspective.

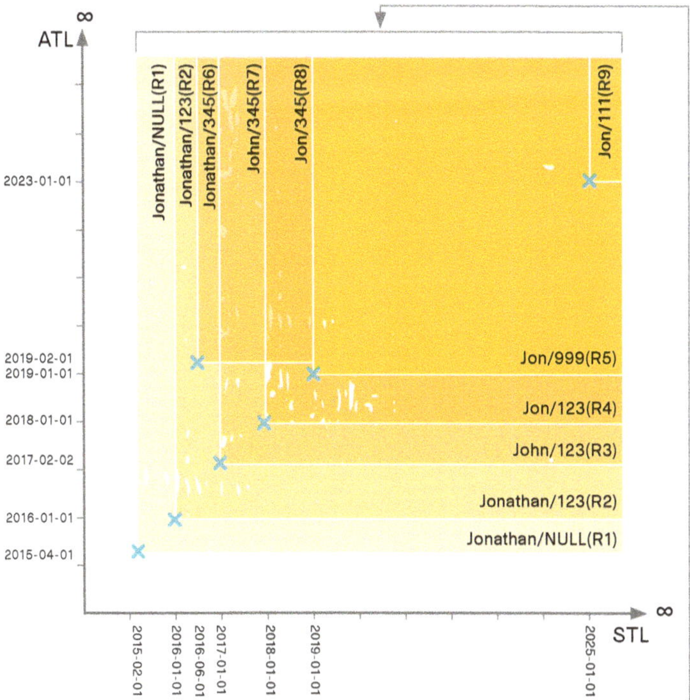

Combined data set (by State From Timestamp)

Surrogate Key	Inscription Timestamp	State From Timestamp	State Before Timestamp	Customer Name	Contact Number	Square Number
CUST_4	2015-04-01	2015-02-01	9999-12-31	Jonathan	NULL	R1
CUST_4	2016-01-01	2016-01-01	9999-12-31	Jonathan	123	R2
CUST_4	2019-02-01	2016-06-01	2017-01-01	Jonathan	345	R6
CUST_4	2017-02-02	2017-01-01	2018-01-01	John	345	R7
CUST_4	2018-01-01	2018-01-01	2019-01-01	Jon	345	R8
CUST_4	2019-01-01	2019-01-01	9999-12-31	Jon	999	R5
CUST_4	2025-01-01	2025-01-01	9999-12-31	Jon	111	R9

This is where something interesting happens. Instead of the original 7 blocks, after overlaying both planes we now have a total 9 blocks. The intersections between the two diagrams have created data combinations which were not visible in the initial combined data set based on the state timeline.

These are highlighted in red writing in the diagram below:

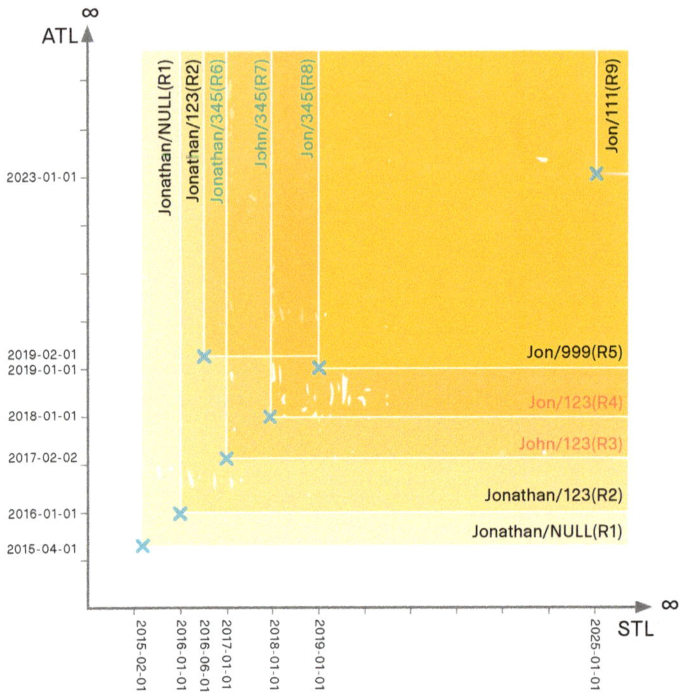

On the other hand, the three green highlighted blocks represent the changes that *would have occurred* if the backdated record had arrived at the intended time. They hold an alternative view of the history based on when data was availabl – a different perspective aligned to the STL.

The following diagram is now a true bitemporal data set, visible here because there are three different records that share the same primary key. In this case, records 6–8 have the *same* inscription timestamp.

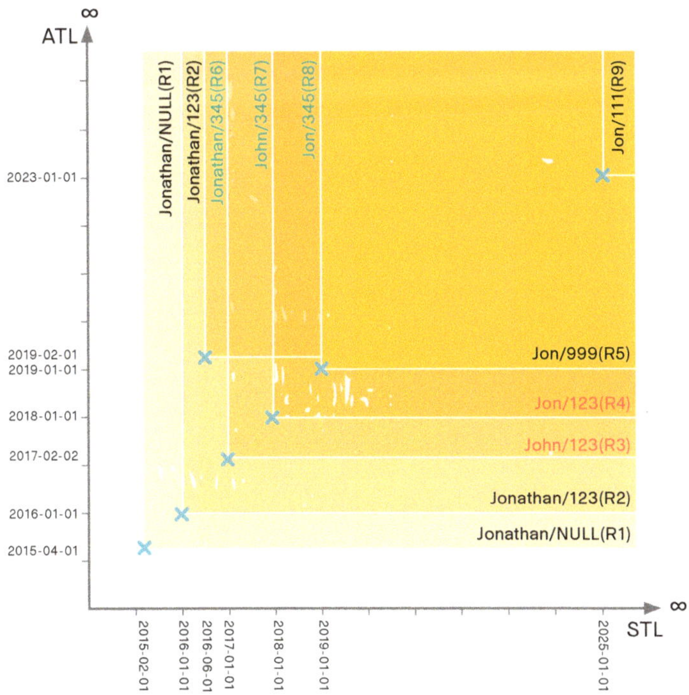

Combined data set

Surrogate Key	Inscription Timestamp	State From Timestamp	State Before Timestamp	Customer Name	Contact Number	Square Number
CUST_4	2015-04-01	2015-02-01	9999-12-31	Jonathan	NULL	R1
CUST_4	2016-01-01	2016-01-01	9999-12-31	Jonathan	123	R2
CUST_4	2017-02-02	2017-02-02	9999-12-31	John	123	R3
CUST_4	2018-01-01	2018-01-01	9999-12-31	Jon	123	R4
CUST_4	2019-01-01	2019-01-01	9999-12-31	Jon	999	R5
CUST_4	2019-02-01	2016-06-01	2017-01-01	Jonathan	345	R6
CUST_4	2019-02-01	2017-01-01	2018-01-01	John	345	R7
CUST_4	2019-02-01	2018-01-01	2019-01-01	Jon	345	R8
CUST_4	2025-01-01	2025-01-01	9999-12-31	Jon	111	R9

In a bitemporal data set, including bitemporal Satellites, the state from timestamp is added to the primary key for this exact reason.

Looking in detail

In a bitemporal environment, backdated adjustments create a 'ripple' effect with changes that continue until the next regular change – the two records in the previous section. To understand why this happens, let's break down the process step by step, as the data arrives.

The first five records, in the order of arrival across both data sets, are straightforward. Both the inscription and state timestamps are incremental for each record, and no backdated adjustments have occurred yet.

Sat Customer

Surrogate Key	Inscription Timestamp	State From Timestamp	State Before Timestamp	Customer Name	Order STL	Order ATL
CUST_4	2015-04-01	2015-02-01	9999-12-31	Jonathan	1	1
CUST_4	2017-02-02	2017-01-01	9999-12-31	John	3	3
CUST_4	2018-01-01	2018-01-01	9999-12-31	Jon	4	4

Sat Customer Contact

Surrogate Key	Inscription Timestamp	State From Timestamp	State Before Timestamp	Contact Number	Order STL	Order ATL
CUST_4	2016-01-01	2016-01-01	9999-12-31	123	2	2
CUST_4	2019-01-01	2019-01-01	9999-12-31	999	5	5

Combined data set (by State From Timestamp)

Surrogate Key	Inscription Timestamp	State From Timestamp	State Before Timestamp	Customer Name	Contact Number	Square Number
CUST_4	2015-04-01	2015-02-01	9999-12-31	Jonathan	NULL	R1
CUST_4	2016-01-01	2016-01-01	9999-12-31	Jonathan	123	R2
CUST_4	2017-02-02	2017-01-01	9999-12-31	John	123	R3
CUST_4	2018-01-01	2018-01-01	9999-12-31	Jon	123	R4
CUST_4	2019-01-01	2019-01-01	9999-12-31	Jon	999	R5

Now, consider what happens when a backdated record arrives.

Sat Customer

Surrogate Key 🔑	Inscription Timestamp 🔑	State From Timestamp	State Before Timestamp	Customer Name	Order BTL	Order ATL
CUST_4	2015-04-01	2015-02-01	9999-12-31	Jonathan	1	1
CUST_4	2017-02-02	2017-01-01	9999-12-31	John	3 -> 4	3
CUST_4	2018-01-01	2018-01-01	9999-12-31	Jon	4 -> 5	4

Sat Customer Contact

Surrogate Key 🔑	Inscription Timestamp 🔑	State From Timestamp	State Before Timestamp	Contact Number	Order BTL	Order ATL
CUST_4	2016-01-01	2016-01-01	9999-12-31	123	1	2
CUST_4	2019-01-01	2019-01-01	9999-12-31	999	5 -> 6	5
CUST_4	2019-02-01	2016-06-01	2019-01-01	345	3	6

Correction of the past.

Combined data set (by State From Timestamp)

Surrogate Key 🔑	Inscription Timestamp 🔑	State From Timestamp	State Before Timestamp	Customer Name	Contact Number	Square Number
CUST_4	2015-04-01	2015-02-01	9999-12-31	Jonathan	NULL	R1
CUST_4	2016-01-01	2016-01-01	9999-12-31	Jonathan	123	R2
CUST_4	2017-02-02	2017-01-01	9999-12-31	John	123	R3
CUST_4	2018-01-01	2018-01-01	9999-12-31	Jon	123	R4
CUST_4	2019-01-01	2019-01-01	9999-12-31	Jon	999	R5
CUST_4	2019-02-01	2016-06-01	2019-01-01	Jonathan	345	R6

This new record in the 'Customer Contact' Satellite with value '345' arrives later than the records received so far, but applies to an earlier point in time. Because we always use state timestamps for joining, the 'Customer Name' in the other Satellite that matches the number '345' as of 2016-06-01 is 'Jonathan'– the value recorded on 2015-02-01 in the 'Customer' Satellite.

With the benefit of hindsight, we know that name will change again to 'John' on 2017-01-01, but that change *hasn't occurred* yet by 2016-06-01.

For all intents and purposes, this is a regular record being added to the result set. But this is not all, additional records will need to be added that spawn from the same change.

These are the two new blocks from the Cartesian plane.

Sat Customer

Surrogate Key	Inscription Timestamp	State From Timestamp	State Before Timestamp	Customer Name	Order STL	Order ATL
CUST_4	2015-04-01	2015-02-01	9999-12-31	Jonathan	1	1
CUST_4	2017-02-02	2017-01-01	9999-12-31	John	3 -> 4	3
CUST_4	2018-01-01	2018-01-01	9999-12-31	Jon	4 -> 5	4

Allen Relationship — Correction applies like:
- Overlaps
- During
- Finishes

Sat Customer Contact

Surrogate Key	Inscription Timestamp	State From Timestamp	State Before Timestamp	Contact Number	Order STL	Order ATL
CUST_4	2016-01-01	2016-01-01	9999-12-31	123	1	2
CUST_4	2019-01-01	2019-01-01	9999-12-31	999	5 -> 6	5
CUST_4	2019-02-01	2016-06-01	2019-01-01	345	3	6

Correction of the past.

Combined data set (by State From Timestamp, order by ATL)

Surrogate Key	Inscription Timestamp	State From Timestamp	State Before Timestamp	Customer Name	Contact Number	Square Number
CUST_4	2015-04-01	2015-02-01	9999-12-31	Jonathan	NULL	R1
CUST_4	2016-01-01	2016-01-01	9999-12-31	Jonathan	123	R2
CUST_4	2017-02-02	2017-01-01	9999-12-31	John	123	R3
CUST_4	2018-01-01	2018-01-01	9999-12-31	Jon	123	R4
CUST_4	2019-01-01	2019-01-01	9999-12-31	Jon	999	R5
CUST_4	2019-02-01	2016-06-01	2017-01-01	Jonathan	345	R6
CUST_4	2019-02-01	2017-01-01	2018-01-01	John	345	R7
CUST_4	2019-02-01	2018-01-01	2019-01-01	Jon	345	R8

These two new records are created because, from the perspective of the backdated adjustment (2016-06-01), there are known future changes that must be accounted for, specifically on 2017-01-01 and 2018-01-01. This 'ripple effect' continues until the next regular change, occurring on 2019-01-01.

The Allen relationships explain this in more detail:

- The R2 record of the combined data is applied as 'Overlaps,' and results in the creation of record R6 and its the new state from timestamp
- R3 is a 'During' containing the adjustment record, and creates R7
- Record R4 is a 'Finishes' relationship

Prior to this moment, there was no way to predict the arrival of this backdated change (received on inscription timestamp 2019-02-01). Therefore, two different versions of history now exist, each depending on the assertion timeline.

So, the two additional rows are the ones that *would have been created* if this change would have been at the intended moment. If we would have received this row at 2016-06-01, instead of 2019-02-01 as we have now, the normal change detection would have led to the creation of these two rows in the future.

We would not have known this back then, but we do know this was going to happen with the information we have received up to and including the present.

The final record is a regular change, completing the merge of the two Satellites.

Sat Customer

Surrogate Key	Inscription Timestamp	State From Timestamp	State Before Timestamp	Customer Name	Order STL	Order ATL
CUST_4	2015-04-01	2015-02-01	9999-12-31	Jonathan	1	1
CUST_4	2017-02-02	2017-01-01	9999-12-31	John	3 > 4	3
CUST_4	2018-01-01	2018-01-01	9999-12-31	Jon	4 > 5	4

Sat Customer Contact

Surrogate Key	Inscription Timestamp	State From Timestamp	State Before Timestamp	Contact Number	Order STL	Order ATL
CUST_4	2016-01-01	2016-01-01	9999-12-31	123	2	2
CUST_4	2019-01-01	2019-01-01	9999-12-31	999	5 > 6	5
CUST_4	2019-02-01	2016-06-01	2019-01-01	345	3	6
CUST_4	2023-01-01	2025-01-01	9999-12-31	111	7	7

Correction of the past.

Combined data set (by State From Timestamp, order by ATL)

Surrogate Key	Inscription Timestamp	State From Timestamp	State Before Timestamp	Customer Name	Contact Number	Square Number
CUST_4	2015-04-01	2015-02-01	9999-12-31	Jonathan	NULL	R1
CUST_4	2016-01-01	2016-01-01	9999-12-31	Jonathan	123	R2
CUST_4	2017-02-02	2017-01-01	9999-12-31	John	123	R3
CUST_4	2018-01-01	2018-01-01	9999-12-31	Jon	123	R4
CUST_4	2019-01-01	2019-01-01	9999-12-31	Jon	999	R5
CUST_4	2019-02-01	2016-06-01	2017-01-01	Jonathan	345	R6
CUST_4	2019-02-01	2017-01-01	2018-01-01	John	345	R7
CUST_4	2019-02-01	2018-01-01	2019-01-01	Jon	345	R8
CUST_4	2025-01-01	2025-01-01	9999-12-31	Jon	111	R9

Time travel

Now the combined data set is complete let's revisit the additional records again, because these make the out-come bitemporal. A consequence of bitemporality is that multiple record (for the same key) may share the same point in time — as we've experienced with the ripple effect caused by the backdated adjustment.

It can be helpful to consider this from another perspective — where the ATL and STL are viewed next to each other.

The example from the previous section prior to the occurrence of the backdated adjustment can be visualized as a timeline that depicts the ATL on top, and the STL on the bottom:

Combined data set (by State From Timestamp, prior backdated adjustments)

Surrogate Key	Inscription Timestamp	State From Timestamp	State Before Timestamp	Customer Name	Contact Number	Square Number
CUST_4	2015-04-01	2015-02-01	9999-12-31	Jonathan	NULL	R1
CUST_4	2016-01-01	2016-01-01	9999-12-31	Jonathan	123	R2
CUST_4	2017-02-02	2017-01-01	9999-12-31	John	123	R3
CUST_4	2018-01-01	2018-01-01	9999-12-31	Jon	123	R4
CUST_4	2019-01-01	2019-01-01	9999-12-31	Jon	999	R5

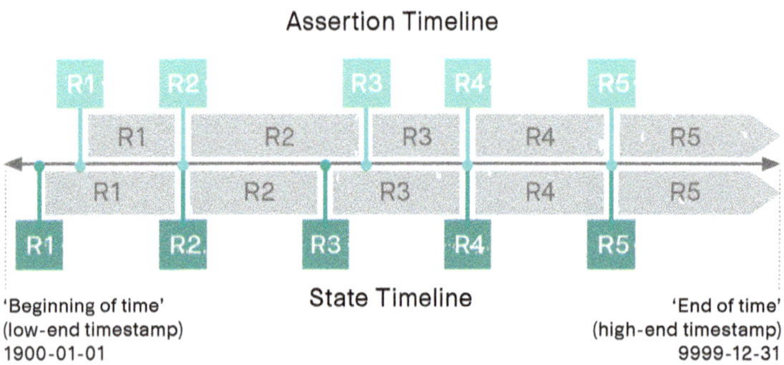

So far, the timelines increase in sync, but this will change when the additional records caused by the backdated adjustment appear.

The diagram below, including all backdated changes, shows the impact of these records. Record R3 and R7, for example, have different context for the *same* state from timestamp (2017-01-01). The same applies to record R4 and R8. Depending on your assertion timeline perspective (selection), you would retrieve either of these values.

If you 'travel back in time' and query the data set from a point in time before the 2019-02-01 inscription timestamp, you would see the values as they were known then. Querying from the inscription timestamp 2019-02-01 onward gives you the context that includes the backdated changes.

Combined data set (by State From Timestamp, order by ATL)

Surrogate Key	Inscription Timestamp	State From Timestamp	State Before Timestamp	Customer Name	Contact Number	Square Number
CUST_4	2015-04-01	2015-02-01	9999-12-31	Jonathan	NULL	R1
CUST_4	2016-01-01	2016-01-01	9999-12-31	Jonathan	123	R2
CUST_4	2017-02-02	2017-01-01	9999-12-31	John	123	R3
CUST_4	2018-01-01	2018-01-01	9999-12-31	Jon	123	R4
CUST_4	2019-01-01	2019-01-01	9999-12-31	Jon	999	R5
CUST_4	2019-02-01	2016-06-01	2017-01-01	Jonathan	345	R6
CUST_4	2019-02-01	2017-01-01	2018-01-01	John	345	R7
CUST_4	2019-02-01	2018-01-01	2019-01-01	Jon	345	R8
CUST_4	2025-01-01	2025-01-01	9999-12-31	Jon	111	R9

Data set including backdated changes

Data set before 2019-01-02

Travel back to 2019-01-01

Plotting these changes on the timeline, as shown in the diagram below, provides a different visual to highlight this behavior:

- Records R6, R7, and R8 arrive at the same point in time but apply to earlier state timestamp values
- The state timestamps for record pairs R3, R7, and R4, R8, are in the same positions
- R2 is split into R2.1 and R2.2, and R6 replaces R2.2
- R7 replaces R3 and R8 replaces R4 from the today's perspective

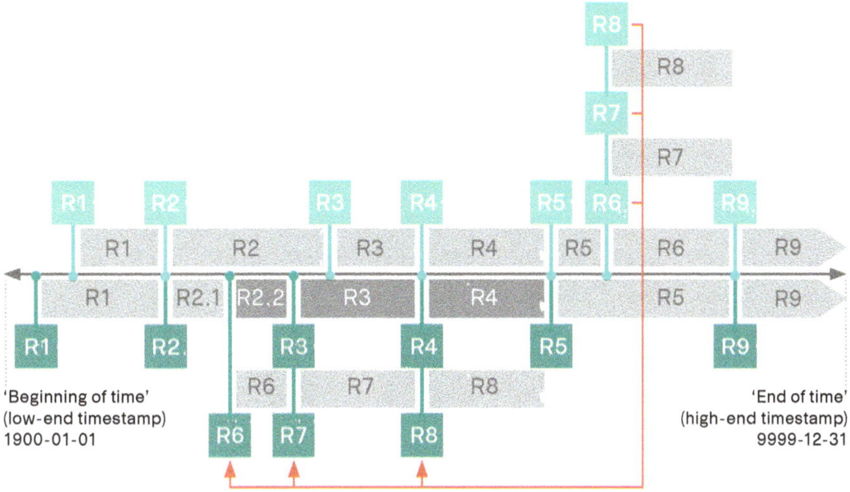

State Timeline

In a bitemporal data set, the query results depend on the assertion timeline you specify. This could be the most recent perspective (the highest inscription timestamp), or any point in the past.

Tackling bitemporal complexities upfront

This section addresses some of the challenges of working with bitemporal data, and is intended as an introduction to the considerations involved in defining bitemporal Satellites.

The pattern discussed in this section can also apply to the process of 'getting the data out,' as it ultimately involves combining two unitemporal Satellites for (bitemporal) delivery. However, the same challenges can also be tackled upfront by designing the Satellite as bitemporal from the start.

This presents a key decision in the solution architecture: when designing Satellites as unitemporal, the approach outlined in this section, along with the subsequent sections, must be implemented when handling data in the front room of the solution. When Satellites are designed as bitemporal, these concepts must be applied when the data is ingested into the object.

There are different possible approaches for this, and these are further covered in the where to implement temporal design section.

Additionally, data quality and uniqueness have not yet been addressed. When combining unitemporal Satellites, as described in this section, it is often necessary to apply some form of *uniquification* to ensure that the state timestamps are unique for joining purposes, preventing duplicates in the result set. These duplicates could otherwise arise from timeline overlaps introduced by combining multiple data sets. This topic will be further explored in the ⚐ getting the data out chapter.

Bitemporal approaches, as we will see in the next section, inherently resolve this issue upfront.

Viewing late-arriving transaction as bitemporal

Now that we've explored bitemporality and backdated adjustments, let's revisit the example of late-arriving transactions. To analyze this from a bitemporal perspective —correctly visualizing both the ATL and STL— we can make the following observations:

→ The summary of the balance is once again 100 when running the report if only the ATL is considered
→ But, if the STL is considered as well —selecting data with state timestamps up to and including January 31st— the balance is 80

If the STL is used to aggregate the values for the 'January period' where the state timestamps fall in January, the balance is correct each time the report is run after the backdated transaction has been received.

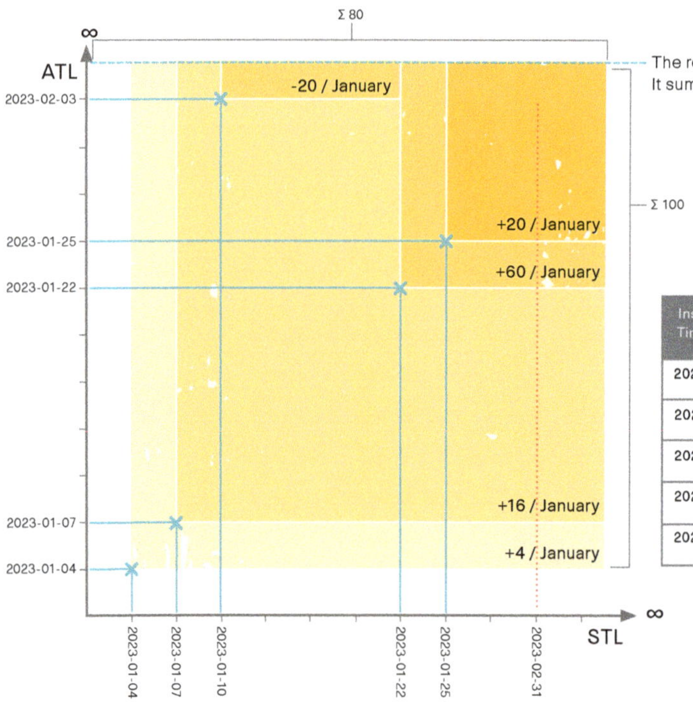

Inscription Timestamp	State Timestamp	Transaction Unit	Period	Balance Unit
2023-02-03	2023-01-10	-20	January	80
2023-01-25	2023-01-25	+20	January	100
2023-01-22	2023-01-22	+60	January	80
2023-01-07	2023-01-07	+16	January	20
2023-01-04	2023-01-04	+4	January	4

Bitemporal

↗ Bitemporal data defines two timelines, to separate the reception of an event from when it applies in reality — represented by the assertion and state timelines.

There may be a requirement to know when an event was recorded in the data solution, and when it is true in reality.

For example, what data went into last year's profit and loss calculation, and what adjustments were made this year? Which future price did the business plan for blue jeans last year? When did the business define the discount period for the blue jeans?

Changes can be made to data that apply to the past, present, and future. For instance, the fact that a customer has moved can be recorded once the customer informs us of the new address. We were, however, unaware of the move until the notification. A customer could also let us know today that a move is planned two months in the future.

To separate the reception of an event from when it applies in reality, two perspectives of time are required that work together: a bitemporal approach – enabled by the assertion and state timelines.

In the reference architecture, bitemporality is implemented using three timestamp columns:
→ Inscription timestamp; representing the assertion timeline – used for filtering only
→ State from timestamp; the state timestamp, representing the start of a state time period
→ State before timestamp; the end of a state time period using an Closed-Open approach

The challenge is to ensure that any possible form of the Allen Relationships can be mapped onto this structure. For example, a data logistics process could add a new record with a 'During' Allen Relationship which disrupts the existing state timeline.

These, and many more, situations require handling as part of the data logistics processes for bitemporal Satellites.

A bitemporal Satellite is defined with a primary key that consists of the following columns:
→ The surrogate key
→ The inscription timestamp
→ The inscription record id
→ The state from (or state before) timestamp

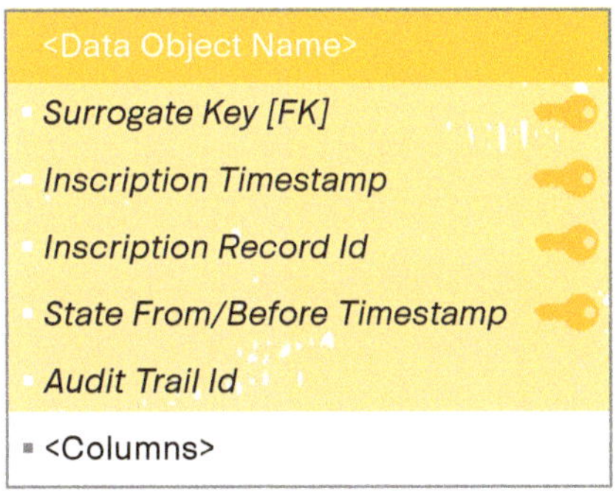

Receiving a complete time period

A record containing a complete time period is one that includes both a start and an end indicator, specifying the range during which the values are valid.

In an ideal world, the operational system provides a full history of changes, with each record having a state from and state before timestamp.

When the data is supplied with a complete time period for each record *and* no corrections are ever applied, the timeline is already well-defined, and can be processed to the integration layer without any issues.

For example, consider the following 'Product Price' data set. This sample contains a complete timeline where the price for jeans changes over time. These records all arrive at the same moment — 2025-06-01.

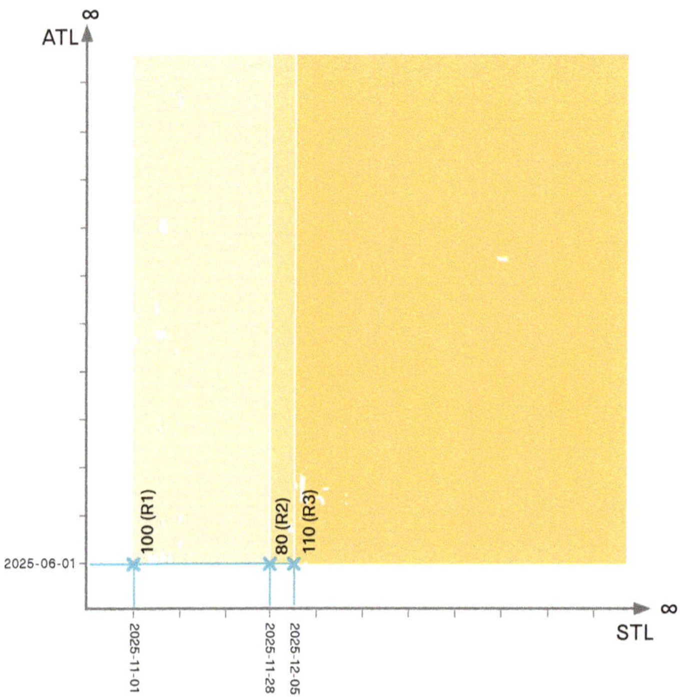

PSA data object — Product Price

Product	Inscription Timestamp	Valid From	Valid To	Price	Square Number
Jeans	2025-06-01	2025-11-01	2025-11-28	100	R1
Jeans	2025-06-01	2025-11-28	2025-12-05	80	R2
Jeans	2025-06-01	2025-12-05	9999-12-31	110	R3

Initial data set

Initially, the seller plans to sell the jeans for $100 until 2025-11-28, when the price drops to $80 as part of the Black Friday promotion. After the promotion, the price increases to $110 and remains like this until further notice.

This information is received ahead of time on 2025-06-01 during the first module execution.

However, when corrections are received, the construction of a complete and consistent state timeline becomes more complicated even when both state from and state before timestamps are available. This can occur, for example, when values in the operational system are updated directly and detected as data changes. Or, when pricing teams plan future prices or correct past prices.

Consider the example below. The 'square number' is synonymous to a record number. The squares will later be visualized on the Cartesian Plane.

PSA data object — Product Price

	Product	Inscription Timestamp	Valid From	Valid To	Price	Square Number
Initial data set	Jeans	2025-06-01	2025-11-01	2025-11-28	100	R1
	Jeans	2025-06-01	2025-11-28	2025-12-05	80	R2
	Jeans	2025-06-01	2025-12-05	9999-12-31	110	R3
Delta data set 1	Jeans	2025-06-11	2025-11-01	2025-11-28	95	R4
	Jeans	2025-06-11	2025-11-28	2025-12-15	82	R5
Delta data set 2	Jeans	2025-06-12	2025-11-01	2025-11-15	100	R6

In a subsequent module execution (delta data set 1), records are received that contain corrections on some of the prices within spe-cific periods. Presumably, these changes were updated in the operational system and arrived at the data solution as change records.

As part of a second delta data set (delta data set 2), another correction is applied. The accumulated history in the PSA now clearly shows the different prices that would apply for the different periods, depending on when the data became available.

The PSA table is an accurate representation of the data changes received over time, but the state timeline is no longer consistent.

For example, if we query the price of jeans from today's (ATL) perspective with STL 2026-01-01 there would be no record to match. With today's ATL perspective, we would only receive R6.

The record for this point in time —STL 2026-01-01— was provided with the initial data set as R3, but is no longer visible from today's (ATL) perspective. The STL is incomplete, and to restore this timeline, so values can be retrieved for any point in time, further adjustments are needed.

Understanding the time relationships

To understand what needs to be done, it helps to consider the Allen Relationships. In this example, the records received at 2025-06-11 —delta data set 1— are involved with three relationship interactions:

PSA data object — Product Price

Product	Inscription Timestamp	Valid From	Valid To	Price	Square Number
Jeans	2025-06-01	2025-11-01	2025-11-28	100	R1
Jeans	2025-06-01	2025-11-28	2025-12-05	80	R2
Jeans	2025-06-01	2025-12-05	9999-12-31	110	R3
Jeans	2025-06-11	2025-11-01	2025-11-28	95	R4
Jeans	2025-06-11	2025-11-28	2025-12-15	82	R5

Equals (R1, R4): |---| |---|

Overlaps (R3, R5): |-----| |-----|

Starts (R2, R5): |---| |------|

For delta set 1, the following can be asserted:

- R4 equals R1, and therefore 'replaces' R1 entirely
- R5 starts at the same clock tick as R2, and shares some of that time period. However, R2 ends earlier than R5
- This leads to an overlap with R3, where both time periods (records) have clock ticks in common, but each record also has unique clock ticks

PSA data object — Product Price

Product	Inscription Timestamp	Valid From	Valid To	Price	Square Number
Jeans	2025-06-01	2025-11-01	2025-11-28	100	R1
Jeans	2025-06-01	2025-11-28	2025-12-05	80	R2
Jeans	2025-06-01	2025-12-05	9999-12-31	110	R3
Jeans	2025-06-11	2025-11-01	2025-11-28	95	R4
Jeans	2025-06-11	2025-11-28	2025-12-15	82	R5
Jeans	2025-06-12	2025-11-01	2025-11-15	100	R6

Starts (R4, R6): |---| |------|

For data delta set 2, R6 starts at the same clock tick as R4 but ends earlier.

The consequences of these interactions depend on the specific Allen Relationships involved. You may need to insert as little as one new record (for relationships like meets, before, or equals) or as many as three (for during) to preserve a complete and accurate history, ensuring the data's validity is correctly configured.

If the time period is not yet in a Closed-Open notation, it needs to be changed into it.
We elaborate on this further in the interpreting Closed-Closed time periods section.

Repairing the timeline

To 'repair' the state timeline, additional records must be added to address these issues. Once these are in place, it will once again be straightforward to time-travel.

The first delta data set will —due to the overlap of R5 and R3— create one additional record: R7 is added to preserve the unaltered portion of R3.

- → R1, R2, and R3 are end-dated to 2025-06-11 (ATL - inscription before timestamp)
- → R7 preserves the context of R3 where it is not overlapped by R5
- → R7 is a copy of R3 with an updated state from timestamp. It shares the same inscription timestamp as R5

PSA data object — Product Price

Product	Inscription Timestamp	Valid From	Valid To	Price	Square Number
Jeans	2025-06-01	2025-11-01	2025-11-28	100	R1
Jeans	2025-06-01	2025-11-28	2025-12-05	80	R2
Jeans	2025-06-01	2025-12-05	9999-12-31	110	R3
Jeans	2025-06-11	2025-11-01	2025-11-28	95	R4
Jeans	2025-06-11	2025-11-28	2025-12-15	82	R5

Delta data set 1

Sat Product Price

Surrogate Key	Inscription Timestamp	State From Timestamp	State Before Timestamp	Price	Inscription Before Timestamp	Square Number
Jeans	2025-06-01	2025-11-01	2025-11-28	100	2025-06-11	R1
Jeans	2025-06-01	2025-11-28	2025-12-05	80	2025-06-11	R2
Jeans	2025-06-01	2025-12-05	9999-12-31	110	2025-06-11	R3
Jeans	2025-06-11	2025-11-01	2025-11-28	95	9999-12-31	R4
Jeans	2025-06-11	2025-11-28	2025-12-15	82	9999-12-31	R5
Jeans	2025-06-11	2025-12-15	9999-12-31	110	9999-12-31	R7

Additional record

The second delta data adds R8 to preserve the unaltered portion of R4:

- → R4 is end-dated as of 2025-06-12, preserving the context of R4 where it is not overlapped by R6
- → R8 is a copy of R4 with an updated state from timestamp. It shares the same inscription timestamp as R6

PSA data object — Product Price

Product	Inscription Timestamp	Valid From	Valid To	Price	Square Number
Jeans	2025-06-01	2025-11-01	2025-11-28	100	R1
Jeans	2025-06-01	2025-11-28	2025-12-05	80	R2
Jeans	2025-06-01	2025-12-05	9999-12-31	110	R3
Jeans	2025-06-11	2025-11-01	2025-11-28	95	R4
Jeans	2025-06-11	2025-11-28	2025-12-15	82	R5
Jeans	2025-06-12	2025-11-01	2025-11-15	100	R6

Delta data set 2 (last row)

Sat Product Price

Surrogate Key	Inscription Timestamp	State From Timestamp	State Before Timestamp	Price	Inscription Before Timestamp	Square Number
Jeans	2025-06-01	2025-11-01	2025-11-28	100	2025-06-11	R1
Jeans	2025-06-01	2025-11-28	2025-12-05	80	2025-06-11	R2
Jeans	2025-06-01	2025-12-05	9999-12-31	110	2025-06-11	R3
Jeans	2025-06-11	2025-11-01	2025-11-28	95	2025-06-12	R4
Jeans	2025-06-11	2025-11-28	2025-12-15	82	9999-12-31	R5
Jeans	2025-06-11	2025-12-15	9999-12-31	110	9999-12-31	R7
Jeans	2025-06-12	2025-11-01	2025-11-15	100	9999-12-31	R6
Jeans	2025-06-12	2025-11-15	2025-11-28	95	9999-12-31	R8

Additional record (last row)

Visualizing the results

The Cartesian Plane visualization of the ATL and STL confirms this: records R7 and R8 were created to restore timeline consistency.

For convenience, the ATL can be used to visualize which records represent the most recently received records and their corresponding STL. But sorting the values by the primary key is equally effective.

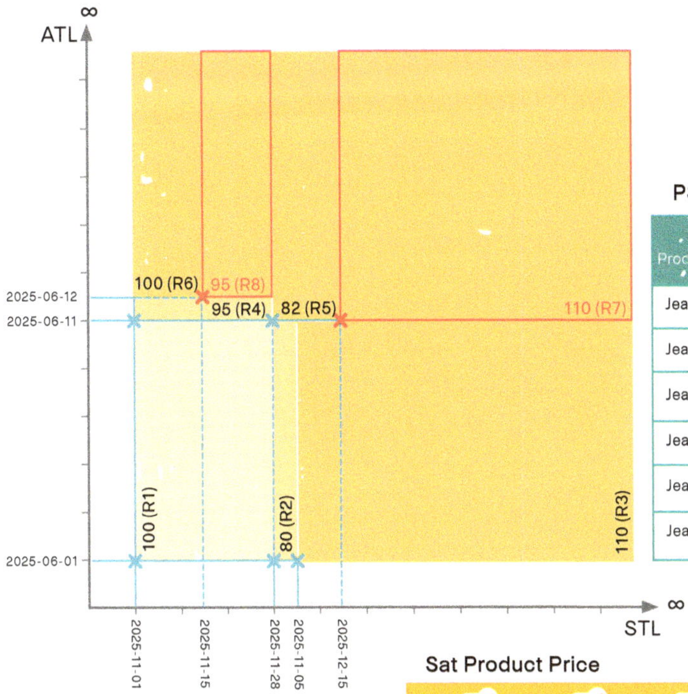

PSA data object — Product Price

Product	Inscription Timestamp	Valid From	Valid To	Price	Square Number
Jeans	2025-06-01	2025-11-01	2025-11-28	100	R1
Jeans	2025-06-01	2025-11-28	2025-12-05	80	R2
Jeans	2025-06-01	2025-12-05	9999-12-31	110	R3
Jeans	2025-06-11	2025-11-01	2025-11-28	95	R4
Jeans	2025-06-11	2025-11-28	2025-12-15	82	R5
Jeans	2025-06-12	2025-11-01	2025-11-15	100	R6

Sat Product Price

Surrogate Key	Inscription Timestamp	State From Timestamp	State Before Timestamp	Price	Inscription Before Timestamp	Square Number
Jeans	2025-06-01	2025-11-01	2025-11-28	100	2025-06-11	R1
Jeans	2025-06-01	2025-11-28	2025-12-05	80	2025-06-11	R2
Jeans	2025-06-01	2025-12-05	9999-12-31	110	2025-06-11	R3
Jeans	2025-06-11	2025-11-01	2025-11-28	95	2025-06-12	R4
Jeans	2025-06-11	2025-11-28	2025-12-15	82	9999-12-31	R5
Jeans	2025-06-11	2025-12-15	9999-12-31	110	9999-12-31	R7
Jeans	2025-06-12	2025-11-01	2025-11-15	100	9999-12-31	R6
Jeans	2025-06-12	2025-11-15	2025-11-28	95	9999-12-31	R8

With these adjustments, a complete timeline is maintained for each 'phase' of the assertion timeline:

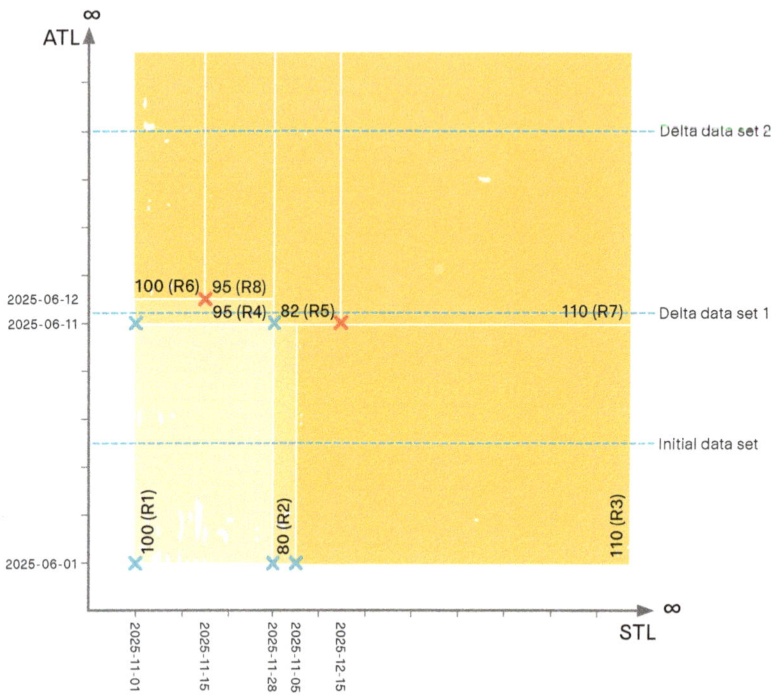

The dotted line (delta data set 2) representing the query from today's (ATL) perspective. This represents what is expected by the business, since this is what is currently available in the operational system. These are four prices, valid for four distinct time periods. **The previously missed STL 2026-01-01 is now included:**

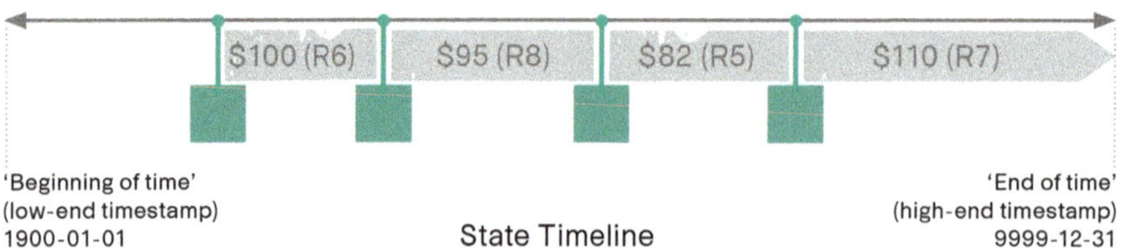

This section has demonstrated how to manage complete time periods with corrections. For implementation details, refer to the solution pattern section for Satellites.

While we have covered the essential bitemporal challenges, many additional scenarios exist depending on the specific use case. For more details, visit our website: https://dtng.link/30s91.

Receiving an incomplete time period

When a time period is incomplete, the data can only be described using either the 'from' timestamp *or* the 'before' timestamp — but one of them is missing. In this scenario, decisions must be made how to interpret the data. Since we *only* define 'from' and 'before' timestamps for the state timeline, we refer to the state timeline everywhere in this section when mentioning 'from' or 'before.'

The most common situation is that a 'before' timestamp is not received. But it should be, because not receiving this data might cause problems, or at least requires decisions to be made. In such cases, the de facto standard is to assume the data is valid indefinitely. After all, we don't have any information indicating otherwise. In practice, we apply the high-end timestamp to the before timestamp.

We can argue, that this is a *finishes* or *meets* Allen Relationship. Since the 'before' timestamp is unknown, it could also represent the first clock tick of a yet-to-be-received time period.

Consider the following example of exchange rates between the Australian Dollar (AUD) and the Euro (EUR), where the rates change over time but without specifying how long each rate remains valid.

PSA data object — Exchange Rate

Base Currency	Target Currency	Inscription Timestamp	Valid From	Exchange Rate
AUD	EUR	2024-07-25	2024-07-23	1.35
AUD	EUR	2024-07-25	2024-07-24	1.278
AUD	EUR	2024-07-25	2024-07-25	1.3

Intermediate data set — Add missing timestamp

Base Currency	Target Currency	Inscription Timestamp	Exchange Rate	State From Timestamp	State Before Timestamp
AUD	EUR	2024-07-25	1.35	2024-07-23	2024-07-24
AUD	EUR	2024-07-25	1.278	2024-07-24	2024-07-25
AUD	EUR	2024-07-25	1.3	2024-07-25	9999-12-31

In this case, we can derive the missing before timestamp from the next available record in the sequence. If no successor record exists, the high-end timestamp is applied.

If late-arriving data is received —for instance on 2024-07-26— there may be different interpretations of how to handle the missing before timestamp.

The following diagram shows two possible interpretations:

PSA data object — Exchange Rate

Base Currency	Target Currency	Inscription Timestamp	Valid From	Exchange Rate
AUD	EUR	2024-07-25	2024-07-23	1.35
AUD	EUR	2024-07-25	2024-07-24	1.278
AUD	EUR	2024-07-25	2024-07-25	1.3
AUD	EUR	2024-07-26	2024-07-22	1.3

Interpretation 2

Interpretation 1

Intermediate data set 1 — Backdated missing record 'overwrites'

Base Currency	Target Currency	Inscription Timestamp	Exchange Rate	State From Timestamp	State Before Timestamp
AUD	EUR	2024-07-25	1.35	2024-07-23	2024-07-24
AUD	EUR	2024-07-25	1.278	2024-07-24	2024-07-25
AUD	EUR	2024-07-25	1.3	2024-07-25	9999-12-31
AUD	EUR	2024-07-26	1.3	2024-07-22	9999-12-31

Intermediate data set 2 — Backdated missing record 'inherits'

Base Currency	Target Currency	Inscription Timestamp	Exchange Rate	State From Timestamp	State Before Timestamp
AUD	EUR	2024-07-26	1.3	2024-07-22	2024-07-23
AUD	EUR	2024-07-25	1.35	2024-07-23	2024-07-24
AUD	EUR	2024-07-25	1.278	2024-07-24	2024-07-25
AUD	EUR	2024-07-25	1.3	2024-07-25	9999-12-31

Interpretation 1 'overwrites' data that is still considered valid. The newly received record 'replaces' the rates valid from 2024-07-23 onwards. These records were previously assumed to be valid indefinitely but are now 'lost.' This highlights that assuming indefinite validity without a before timestamp can be problematic.

Interpretation 2 'inherits' the before timestamp from its successor. In the updated data set above, the rates from 2024-07-23 are still valid. Without a PSA this interpretation is very difficult to achieve.

The appropriate interpretation depends on the business process that generates the data. Ideally, temporal data quality issues —such as missing records and incomplete time periods— should be addressed at the interface level, if possible.

Interpreting Closed-Closed time periods

When operational systems deliver time periods in a Closed-Closed notation, there is even more to investigate. Specifically, we need to determine the granularity of the time periods: are the intervals (clock ticks) measured in days, hours, seconds, or something else?

This should be carefully documented in the interface. To interpret the data correctly, the data solution must translate the time periods into the default Closed-Open notation, otherwise there is a risk of unintended overlaps or gaps.

Changing the granularity from minute (higher) to month (lower) and keeping the Closed-Closed notation —as shown in the diagram below— would create an overlap of the time periods. January 2024 would then be part of *both* time periods, and consequently a select on January 2024 would return both records.

PSA data object — clock tick granularity: minute — type: Closed-Closed

Surrogate Key	First Name	Last Name	Department	State From Timestamp	State To Timestamp
A01	Terence	Tindle	Controlling	2015-06-05 10:31	2024-01-05 16:59
A01	Terence	Tindle	DMCE	2024-01-05 17:00	2024-12-21 17:18

↓

Target data object — clock tick granularity: month — type: Closed-Closed

Surrogate Key	First Name	Last Name	Department	Inscription From Timestamp	State From Timestamp	State To Timestamp
A01	Terence	Tindle	Controlling	2024-01-05 16:45	June 2015	January 2024
A01	Terence	Tindle	DMCE	2024-01-05 16:45	January 2024	December 2024

In a Closed-Open notation, there is no overlap caused by the change in granularity.

However, there is another risk of losing data due to gaps in the timeline if clock ticks are changing from a lower (day) to a higher (minute) granularity when using a Closed-Closed notation:

PSA data object — clock tick granularity: day — type: Closed-Closed

Surrogate Key	First Name	Last Name	Department	State From Timestamp	State To Timestamp
A01	Terence	Tindle	Controlling	2015-06-05	2024-01-05
A01	Terence	Tindle	DMCE	2024-01-06	2024-12-21

↓

Target data object — clock tick granularity: minute — type: Closed-Closed

Surrogate Key	First Name	Last Name	Department	Inscription From Timestamp	State From Timestamp	State To Timestamp
A01	Terence	Tindle	Controlling	2024-01-05 16:45	2015-06-05 00:00	2024-01-05 00:00
A01	Terence	Tindle	DMCE	2024-01-05 16:45	2024-01-06 00:00	2024-12-21 00:00

In the above example, there is no valid data for the time period from '2024-01-05 00:01' to '2024-01-05 23:59' — essentially losing almost an entire day. The system adds the time component 00:00 to the date since there is no information about the time in the source data object. Gaps such as these may cause serious problems downstream in the data solution.

For instance, if a salary is paid to the employee at '2024-01-05 15:53' an empty result will be returned when joining the employee details to this transaction because there is no corresponding entry in the employee data set. The transaction falls right in the timeline gap.

Switching from Closed-Closed to Closed-Open

To change a Closed-Closed to a Closed-Open notation the 'state *to* timestamp' of the predecessor needs to inherit the 'state *from* timestamp' of the successor record. This becomes then the new 'state before timestamp.'

This can be done in an intermediate step as shown in the diagram below:

PSA data object — clock tick granularity: day — type: Closed-Closed

Surrogate Key	First Name	Last Name	Department	State From Timestamp	State To Timestamp
A01	Terence	Tindle	Controlling	2015-06-05	2024-01-05
A01	Terence	Tindle	DMCE	2024-01-06	2024-12-21

Intermediate data set — Change notation : day — type: Closed-Closed -> Closed-Open

Surrogate Key	First Name	Last Name	Department	State From Timestamp	State To Timestamp
A01	Terence	Tindle	Controlling	2015-06-05	~~2024-01-05~~ 2024-01-06
A01	Terence	Tindle	DMCE	2024-01-06	2024-12-21

Target data object — clock tick granularity: minute — type: Closed-Open

Surrogate Key	First Name	Last Name	Department	Inscription From Timestamp	State From Timestamp	State To Timestamp
A01	Terence	Tindle	Controlling	2024-01-05 16:45	2015-06-05 00:00	2024-01-06 00:00
A01	Terence	Tindle	DMCE	2024-01-05 16:45	2024-01-06 00:00	2024-12-21 00:00

The resulting timeline is now Closed-Open with the granularity of minutes, and without gaps.

This approach solves the issues when changing the granularity, from higher to lower as well as vice versa.

Where to implement temporal design?

At the time of writing, there is no standard for implementing (bi)temporality in Data Vault.

In our reference design, we address these complexities in the integration layer, specifically in the base integration area. This approach, part of what we call 'temporal design,' is based on the belief that a correct definition of time is crucial for a valid model and must be addressed upfront. By handling temporality here, we not only ensure the integrity of the data model but also introduce efficiencies: the complexity only needs to be managed once for a given data set, instead of being repeatedly tackled for potentially different downstream data deliveries.

In contrast, some Data Vault implementations manage bitemporality further downstream. In this approach, the creation of a state timeline may be seen as a business requirement and therefore solved 'on the way out' of the data solution – in the front room. Typically implemented in the derived integration area or the presentation layer.

This approach prioritizes data processing speed and simplicity, but it also tends to make the model more technical and sacrifices some clarity and accuracy from a business perspective.

The previous sections are ultimately about evaluating the incoming data for consistency in the timelines. Adding additional records, transforming to a Closed-Open notation all contribute to what has been referred to as a consistent timeline, without gaps, overlaps etc.

An overarching concept when working with time-variant data and building timelines is *uniquification*. The goal is to ensure that each value in a timeline is unique, so you always get a (unique, single) return value when querying the data at any point in time.

Either you solve this on the way into the integration layer, or on the way out – but it *has* to be solved. This concept will be revisited in the getting the data out chapter, where it becomes especially relevant for unitemporal Satellites, as the bitemporal approach discussed in previous sections already addresses this issue.

Another thing to consider is that temporal inconsistencies are a common cause of poor data quality in data solutions, and given the importance of representing data correctly in time we believe that addressing temporal issues as close as possible to the incoming interface is generally preferable.

Ideally, these issues would be addressed in the interface or operating system.

For these reasons, we standardize on a bitemporal implementation to manage this complexity upfront in our reference architecture – into the integration layer. This delivers a data solution that is easier to manage and can meet future data delivery requirements without needing architectural changes.

Both the 'back room' and 'front room' approaches for solving temporal challenges can be successful, but each approach requires different design and solution patterns, so it is a fundamental decision to make in the overall data solution architecture. This consideration drives decisions about 'do we need bitemporal Satellites, or not?' It's often a matter of deciding *where* these concepts are implemented in the solution.

From an automation perspective, this involves carefully assigning each data object to the appropriate template – for example, determining which Satellites should be unitemporal and which should be bitemporal, or applying a pattern to merge unitemporal data sets into a bitemporal result set downstream. And, of course, These decisions may evolve over time and be refactored using the PSA.

In all cases, these concepts are critical to delivering the 'right' data, and as a guideline we believe that solving these issues earlier ensures greater consistency and clarity in the overall model.

Current record indicators

Data solutions sometimes add 'current record indicators' to their time-variant tables. These indicators represent the most recent record for a selected timeline, which is often, and by default, the assertion timeline (inscription timestamp) – something that we do not recommend.

A current record indicator can be derived similarly to the before timestamp value. For example:

```
LEAD('N',1,'Y')
OVER (PARTITION BY <Key>
   ORDER BY <Date>)
```

As with before timestamps, the current record indicator can be stored in the table as a column or evaluated on the fly.

We mention this because it is a common practice, but we don't recommend using it unless there is a clear use case.

One reason is that current record indicators disrupt an 'insert-only' approach to data processing, as they require updating when newer records appear. While some data platforms offer solutions like computed or virtual columns to manage this, these are not always feasible due to cost, complexity, or performance issues.

Additionally, current record values are conceptually redundant. For instance, the high-end timestamp (e.g., 9999-12-31) always signifies the current record for a given timeline.

More importantly, the current record indicator value represents only a *specific* timeline, often the assertion timeline, which can be misleading. The most recent state of the assertion timeline has limited application.

Ultimately, a current record indicator is a redundant data point. If implemented at all, it is most beneficial to only apply it to the state timeline.

Multi-variance

We have defined Satellites as data objects that describe the context of business keys in a Hub. However, an exception exists for Satellites that are *multi-variant,* sometimes referred to as 'multi-active,' or 'multi-valued.'

↗ Multi-variance occurs when a Satellite describes not only its parent but includes an additional primary key column or columns.

Multi-variance occurs when a Satellite describes not only its parent Hub (or Link, depending on the implementation) based on the inscription timestamp and inscription record id, but *also* includes an additional primary key column (or columns).

To be more precise, multi-variance occurs when a Satellite contains multiple valid records for a given business key, made unique by adding another —degenerate— column.

Or, you might say it simply violates 3rd normal form. It can be said that the use of a multi-variance satellite is always an indication, a symptom, that the information model and the underlying assumptions should be reviewed. With a few exceptions, the multi-variance satellite will then disappear.

The existence of multi-variance is a concession to reality. It exists because there is a need to handle situations where the data just doesn't quite fit the ideal of the target model. You want to associate a Satellite to a Hub, but it just doesn't match the grain.

In these cases, you may want to associate the Satellite to the Hub *per something else*, another column that shifts the granularity to the desired level while still referring to the intended Hub.

Multi-variant Satellites are always separated from other Satellites with the same parent because they have a different primary key definition. As a result, they cannot be combined with Satellites that follow the regular (Hub) key definition, as they do not share the same grain.

The classic implementation of a multi-variant Satellite involves adding this 'other' column to the primary key of the Satellite:

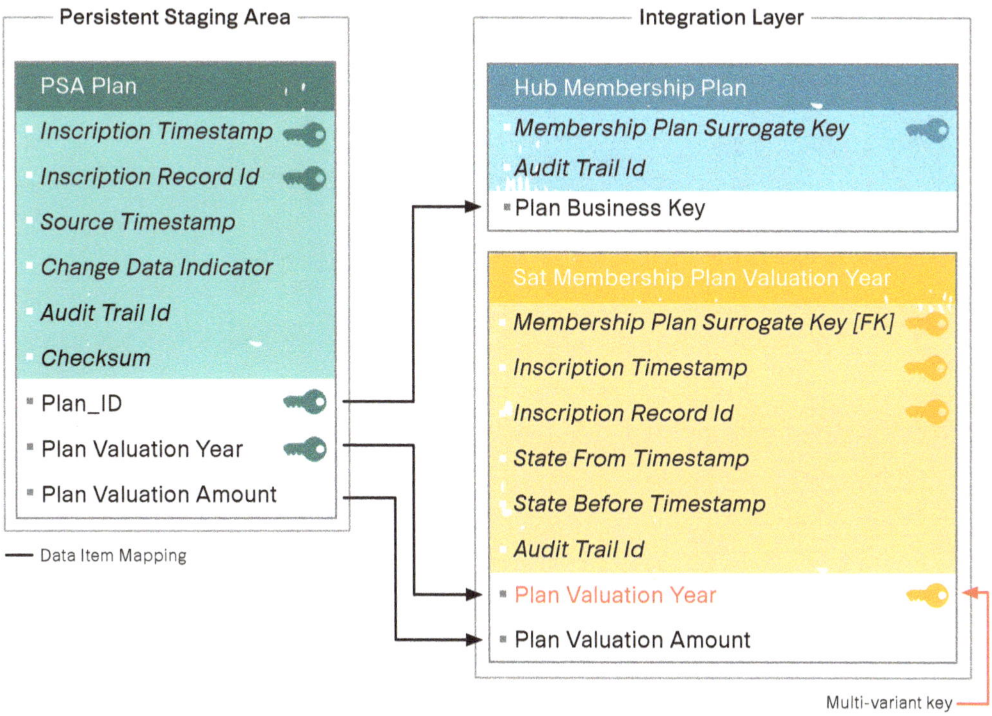

In this example, consider a Membership Plan Hub, which includes a yearly valuation of associated funds. These funds, referred to as the 'plan valuation amount,' do not directly describe the plan itself but rather provide details about the plan for a given year.

A more precise explanation is that if there are multiple active plan values for a specific plan at a specific point in time, the 'plan valuation year' acts as a multi-variant key. As a result, the Satellite containing this data is considered multi-variant.

You could argue that multi-variance breaks the Satellite pattern. After all, the Satellite is not describing the Hub anymore, at least not *directly.*

Implementing multi-variance presents several challenges. It requires special considerations in data logistics patterns and code generation templates, and requires a deep understanding of the physical model to correctly integrate different data sets.

A major drawback is that multi-variant keys assume immutability; any change in the value of a multi-variant key itself creates issues, such as leaving an old time period open when a new one is initiated.

There are various ways to implement multi-variance, as well as alternatives that bypass the concept entirely. While none of these approaches are inherently right or wrong, we believe some are more effective than others. Ultimately, we recommend avoiding multi-variance in the physical model whenever possible. With a conceptual representation of the information model, the physical implementation can remain flexible.

The engine can use directives to manage these considerations in various ways, as discussed in the following sections.

Adding a multi-variant key to a Satellite

The classic implementation of multi-variance is adding a column to the primary key to the Satellite.

Sat Membership Plan Valuation Year

<table>
<tr><th>Membership Plan Surrogate Key</th><th>Inscription Timestamp</th><th>Plan Valuation Year</th><th>Plan Valuation Amount</th></tr>
<tr><td>PLANA\@|</td><td>2022-07-02</td><td>2022</td><td>110000</td></tr>
<tr><td>PLANA\@|</td><td>2023-12-31</td><td>2023</td><td>50000</td></tr>
<tr><td>PLANA\@|</td><td>2022-02-06</td><td>2025</td><td>1250</td></tr>
</table>

Various columns, including the inscription record id, have been omitted for brevity in various examples.

One advantage of this approach is that it limits the number of data objects in the physical model, and allows for the flexible incorporation of new instances – such as new valuation years. When a new valuation year is introduced, the model can handle it naturally.

However, this method also has several disadvantages. It requires additional considerations in data patterns and code generation templates. For instance, the system must detect and account for the multi-active column as part of the key, especially when performing operations like row condensing, identifying the 'most recent row,' and handling end-dating and joins.

Moreover, this approach complicates both the development and interpretation of the data solution. The context is stored at a different level, requiring in-depth understanding to retrieve accurately. Issues often arise when the chosen multi-variant key is not as immutable as initially assumed, leading to complexity in data retrieval.

Even simple queries can cause problems. A common query pattern is to select the 'most recent' or 'current' value from a Satellite, typically based on the surrogate key. However, with multi-variance, the additional key column must be considered. Failing to do so can result in multiple 'current' records for the same key, which can be confusing for users or worst case reporting wrong results without recognizing it.

Adding a separate object for each multi-variant instance

Multi-variance can also be 'modeled out' into separate data objects. This simplifies the data logistics pattern, code generation and data retrieval, but is not always feasible.

In this example, a separate data object is created for each 'Plan Valuation Year.'

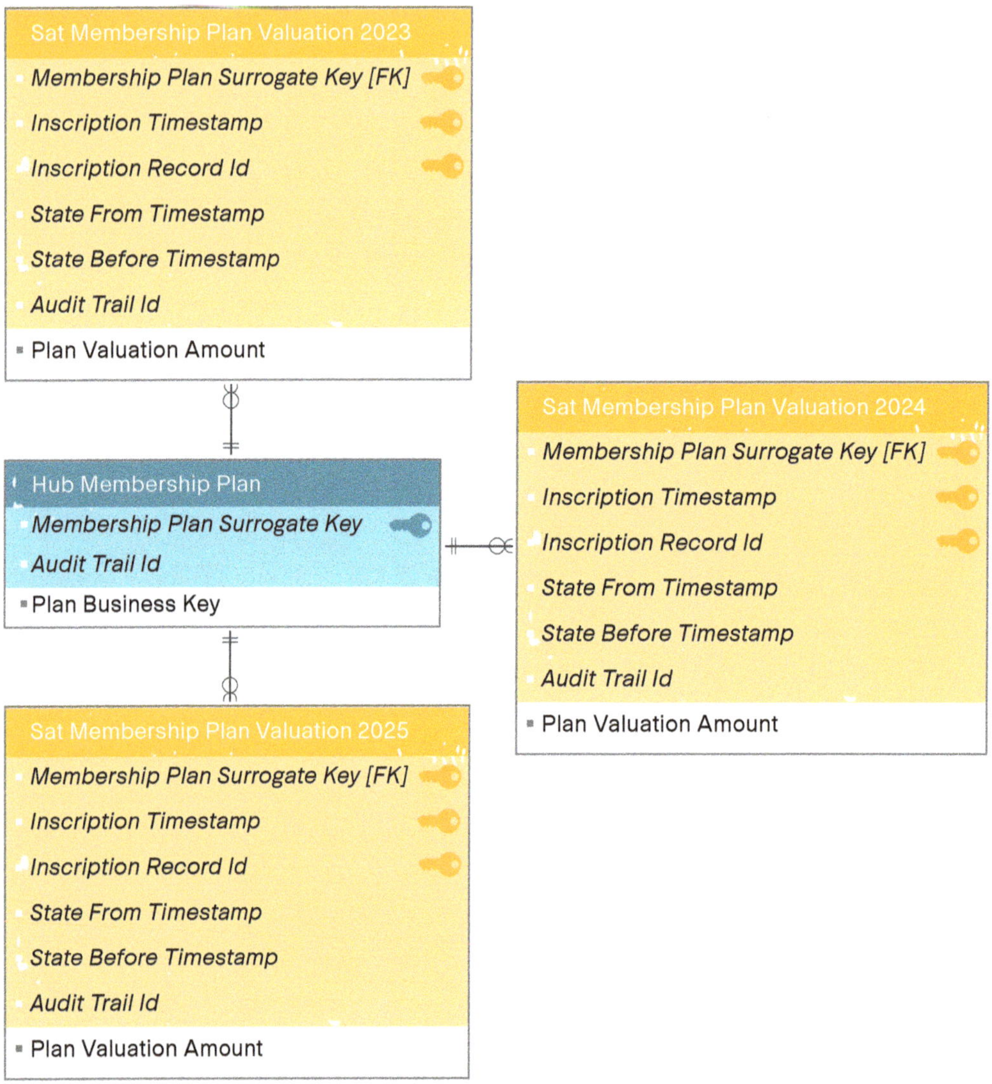

The advantage of this approach is that it allows for the reuse of the regular Satellite pattern. It's like having a normal Satellite, only more of them. Implementation-wise, this involves defining a filter criterion in the data object mapping to ensure that data is routed to the appropriate objects.

This approach works well when a limited number of fixed options are available, for example a distinct set of subtypes for a given concept.

However, this approach has a notable limitation: it does not scale well. If there are many multi-variant keys, a corresponding number of data objects will be required. Additionally, when a new multi-variant key emerges, a new table must be created and connected using a new data object mapping with the appropriate filter condition.

This step can sometimes be overlooked, leading to delays in data availability since the new object must first be defined and implemented.

Creating a dependent Hub

As an alternative to implementing a multi-variant Satellite, one can also create a dedicated Hub at the granularity that would otherwise correspond to the multi-variant key.

This 'dependent' Hub can then be connected to the main Hub using a Link. A dependent Hub is sometimes referred to as a 'weak' Hub because it may not represent an agreed-upon business concept, and is more technical in nature.

This example defines a 'Hub Plan Valuation Year' as a dependent Hub:

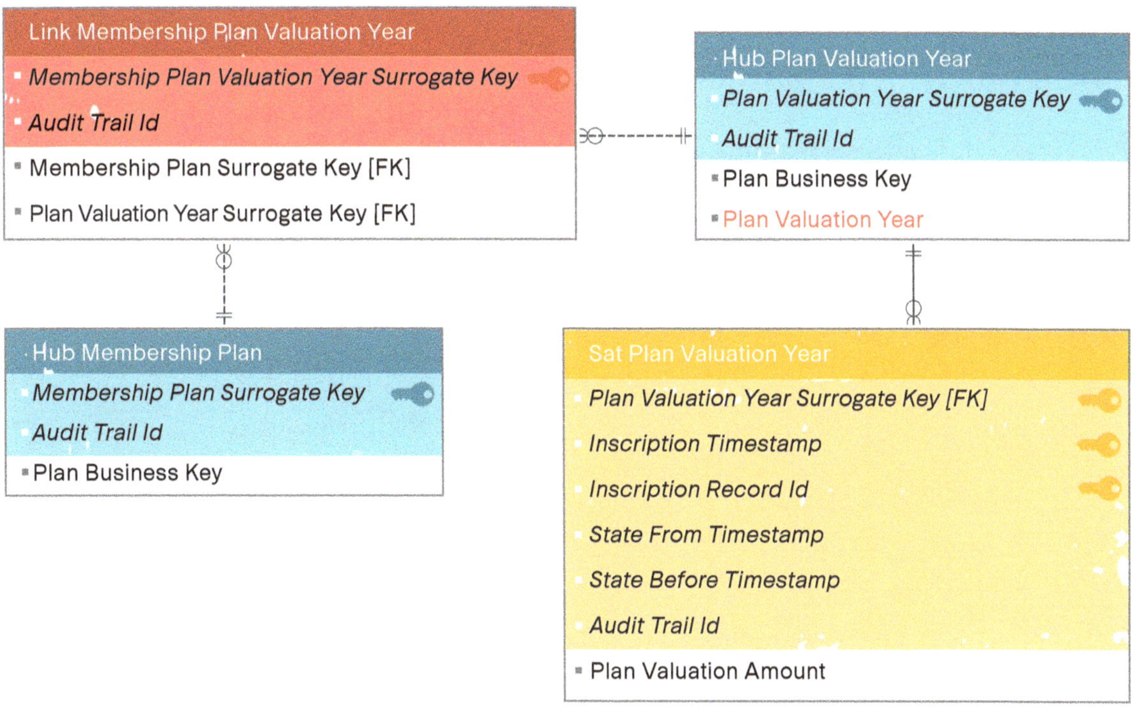

The advantage of this approach is that it achieves the same outcomes as a classic multi-variant Satellite *without* requiring a dedicated pattern to support the additional primary key component. This can simplify the design and implementation process.

However, the disadvantage is that it 'sacrifices' part of the model to be more technical rather than aligned with business concepts. This is not inherently problematic, but it does raise considerations about the purpose of each component within the physical model. This decision applies more to the physical model than the logical model, reflecting a trade-off between technical and business-oriented modeling.

In this sense, the term 'weak' is somewhat of a misnomer. It is just more technical in nature, but works and acts the same as any other Hub in the model, which is why prefer the term dependent Hub instead.

Conceptually, this is no longer multi-variant because the primary key no longer includes any degenerate columns. As we mentioned in the introduction, some approaches allow the implementation to bypass multi-variance entirely, and this is one such method.

Introducing a peg-legged Link

The previous alternatives can also be combined into a hybrid approach: implementing a so-called 'peg-legged Link' and attaching a Satellite to it.

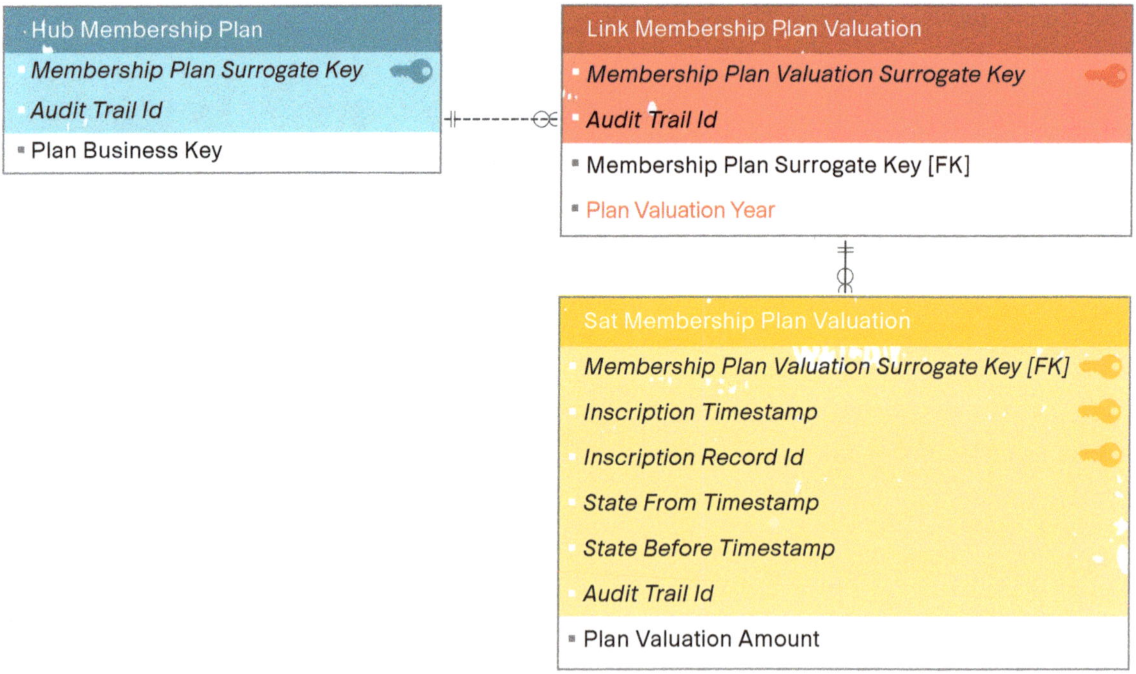

This approach combines various concepts covered earlier into a new implementation. The multi-variant key is used as a degenerate column in the Link. While we don't recommend this method, we include it to illustrate the many ways this challenge can been addressed.

At this point, it's time to disembark the wild ride of our imagination, and find some solid ground to make implementation decisions.

What to look out for when designing multi-variance

Excluding dependent Hubs, which are no longer multi-variant, the single most important thing to understand when adopting a multi-variant approach is the *immutable* property of the multi-variant column. This means that there should be little or no (business) reason to change its value once it has been set.

Various methods can ensure immutability, including governance policies and technical techniques like using deterministic or consistent sequences.

However, it's important to recognize that implementing multi-variance involves relying on the data being received. This reliance introduces a risk that the data team must be aware of and willing to accept. To some extent, you are at the mercy of the data you receive.

This closely relates to the interpretation and detection of deltas, including logical deletes. If a multi-variance column value changes —indicating that it was actually mutable— the records associated with the old key value for that time period need to be end-dated. This is because the new value will initiate a new time period in the Satellite for the new key.

This is where issues are likely to arise. From a data solution perspective, operational systems can't always be trusted, and some columns may not be as immutable as intended. We've encountered problems when values used as multi-variant columns were later updated, sometimes directly at the database level by support teams, bypassing the application.

How to select a solution approach

The choice of approach largely depends on personal preferences and philosophical views regarding the role of the (physical) model in representing data. All methods can ultimately be made to work.

However, when considering higher-level modeling abstractions, by using the engine's graph model abstraction and concepts like collapsing and expanding, the specifics of the physical model become less critical. In these cases, the physical model often serves as a runtime execution layer that may not be frequently examined.

The classic multi-variant concept presents certain challenges that can complicate its use.

For these reasons, and those discussed in earlier sections, we prefer the dependent Hub approach to address multi-variant challenges.

Exception bitmap

↗ An exception bitmap can track multiple errors in a single value, enables tailoring of downstream data quality requirements, and negates the need for reject processes.

Error handling in the back room of the data solution is a contradiction in terms. After all, the back room does not judge data, and is focused on getting the data into the integration layer while eliminating any potential cause of failure. Various architectural tweaks, such as deterministic and atomic data logistics, larger data types, and the removal of constraints, are implemented to prevent errors from occurring in the first place.

Where then, does error handling fit in?

The key difference in approach is that errors can still be *detected,* but records are not *rejected* because of them. We believe the most elegant solution is to implement this using an *exception bitmap.*

When running data logistics processes, many details in the data might not meet expectations. A single records might contain multiple errors. The challenge lies in capturing *all* these issues in a single execution and capture them at the individual record level, and in a way that is flexible to easily add, remove, or change checks without changing the physical structure of the data object.

A bitmap is a great solution for this.

Imagine there is a centralized list of exception checks, each numbered uniquely is given a bit value which is a proxy of its position in a bitmap.

Exception bitmap

Scenario	Description	Bit position
1	Invalid date in text field	1
2	No customer for transaction	2
3	No transaction date	4
4	Invalid email address	8
5	Invalid phone number	16
6	Existing customer but no data found	32
7	New customer but data exists	64
8	Placeholder for future check	128

When errors are detected, the corresponding bit values will be selected, and the resulting error code is the sum of these bit values.

For example, if errors 2 and 6 are detected, their corresponding bit values (2 and 32, respectively) are added together, resulting in an error code of 34 (2 + 32). This integer value can then be stored with the record, providing a concise way to track and identify possibly multiple errors in a single value.

Exception bitmap

Scenario	Description	Bit position
1	Invalid date in text field	1
2	No customer for transaction	2
3	No transaction date	4
4	Invalid email address	8
5	Invalid phone number	16
6	Existing customer but no data found	32
7	New customer but data exists	64
8	Placeholder for future check	128

The integer value of 34 can be represented in its binary (bitwise) form, hence the term 'bitmap': 00100010. In this bitmap, the 'ones' indicate which checks have failed (errors detected), while the 'zeros' indicate checks that were successful (no errors detected).

This example can be described using binary positional notation:

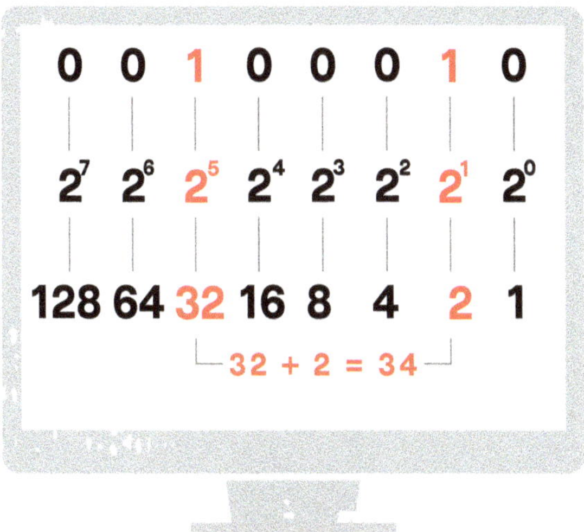

Each bit in the binary value corresponds to a specific error check, with the position of the bit indicating the check's unique number. For instance, in the binary representation 00100010, the 1 in the second and sixth positions —reading from right to left— indicates that errors 2 and 6 were detected.

Evaluating exceptions and implementing checks often involves business logic, but it is not limited to it. Any meaningful code can be incorporated into the exception bitmap logic to assess each test case.

For instance, to validate scenario 2 ('no customer for transaction'), the implementation might include logic such as:

```
CASE Error_Bit_2
 WHEN (Transaction_ID IS NOT NULL
    AND Customer_ID IS NULL)
 THEN 1
 ELSE 0
END
```

Assuming other checks follow similar logic or are defaulted to 0, the full bitmap can be calculated and stored as an integer value:

```
COALESCE(Error_Bit_1,0) * 1 +
COALESCE(Error_Bit_2,0) * 2 +
COALESCE(Error_Bit_3,0) * 4 +
COALESCE(Error_Bit_4,0) * 8 +
COALESCE(Error_Bit_5,0) * 16 +
COALESCE(Error_Bit_6,0) * 32 +
COALESCE(Error_Bit_7,0) * 64 +
COALESCE(Error_Bit_8,0) * 128
```

To conveniently retrieve all error results for a given record by interpreting its integer bitmap representation, data platforms often support a 'bitwise join' feature. This feature can automatically decode the bitmap to identify which checks have triggered errors.

For example:

```
SELECT
 reject.*,
 error_table.description
FROM
<reject_tablename> reject,
ERROR_CODE_REFERENCE error_table
WHERE BITAND
(
 reject.error_code,error_table.bit_mask_value
) = error_table.bit_mask_value
```

This concept is applicable throughout the data solution, but it often is most relevant in Satellite tables and later in the presentation layer. Exception checks, such as those using a bitmap, are usually independent processes that can be applied to any data object.

These checks can either be integrated into regular data logistics processes or run as standalone tasks. We would recommend to run this as a separate process to separate the standard data logistics from these kinds of additional controls.

This way, the data logistics processes remain modular.

No rejects

It might seem obvious, but it's important to note: implementing an exception bitmap offers an alternative to the traditional practice of using reject tables. In the reject table approach, records identified as erroneous are separated, reviewed, and potentially sent back to their origins for correction or updating.

However, following the principles and guidelines discussed in this book, we believe that rejecting errors can be subjective. What is considered an error in one area of the business might not be seen as such in another. An exception bitmap addresses this by providing a detailed and identifiable collection of errors. This allows each consuming party to select the level of data quality they deem acceptable, enabling a more nuanced and flexible approach to error handling.

By using an exception bitmap, data quality requirements can be tailored to specific needs without the need for outright rejection of records, facilitating more inclusive and adaptable provisioning of data for consumption.

Measuring results over time

One often overlooked benefit of using exception bitmaps is their utility in tracking improvements in data quality over time. The bitmap value can be stored with each Satellite record and treated as any other value that may change over time. When issues are detected, they can be reported to relevant parties responsible for enhancing the fitness-for-purpose of data within the organization – such as data stewards, data management teams, or business owners of operational systems.

Assuming these teams are informed about data concerns, they can address root causes in the underlying systems and processes. The data solution itself records what happens without making judgments or corrections. Instead, the responsibility for fixing data issues lies with the operational systems and business processes within the organization.

As improvements are implemented, the data quality should improve, allowing records to pass checks that previously failed. This results in a better (typically lower) bitmap value over time, reflecting enhanced data quality and providing a clear, quantifiable measure of progress.

Satellites for Links

Relationships are often time-variant, and can have unique properties.

Consider a relationship between a car and a driver. Some data might not describe either of these business concepts but applies to their relationship, for example the familiarity a driver has with a particular car.

A person might be very familiar with a large SUV but less familiar with the manual car owned by their grandparents. This 'familiarity' property is specific to the relationship between the driver and the car, not to either entity individually. And, of course, familiarity may change over time, the more the driver gains experience with the car.

Traditionally, in Data Vault, there has been the idea that that all descriptive attributes of a relationship can be placed in a Satellite that describes this relationship, a *Link-Satellite,* as shown in the image below.

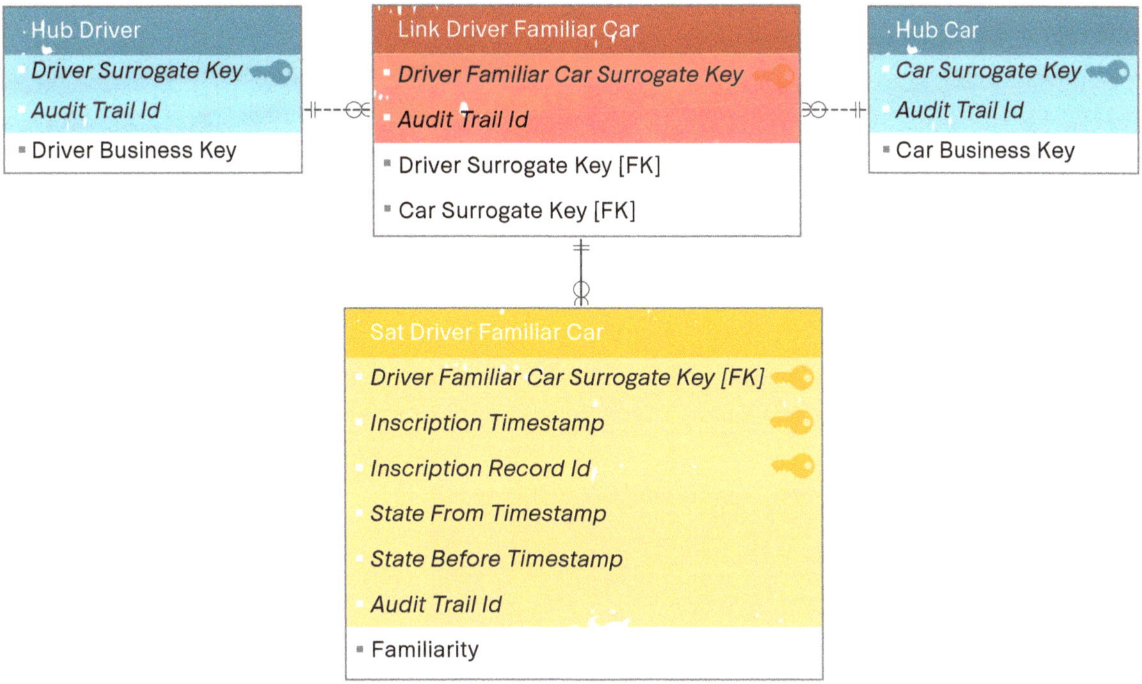

While this might seem logical at first, it introduces drawbacks and complexities, which we will discuss in the Link-Satellites, when, and how? section.

We mention this classic form because it is still commonly seen in projects, though we do not recommend using it — as detailed in the upcoming sections.

Regardless, in most cases, Link-Satellites are necessary to manage the end-dating process (validity) for relationships. Although the example above does not include a time element, as soon as time-variance is introduced, it must be managed appropriately.

The section Driving keys and relationship end-dating will explain how this can be implemented.

Link-Satellites, when, and how?

When considering whether and how to add Link-Satellites in a Data Vault model, a useful guideline is to take a step back and consider the information model. How should the data and its relationships be defined?

For example, consider an *employee* that *works* in a *department*. A department can have many employees. Both the employee and department have their own descriptive attributes.

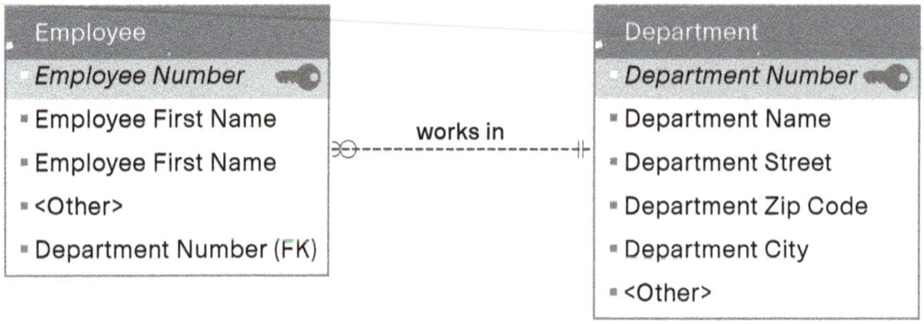

In a Data Vault physical model, each entity is typically created as a Hub and Satellite combination, while the relationship between them becomes a Link without a Link-Satellite.

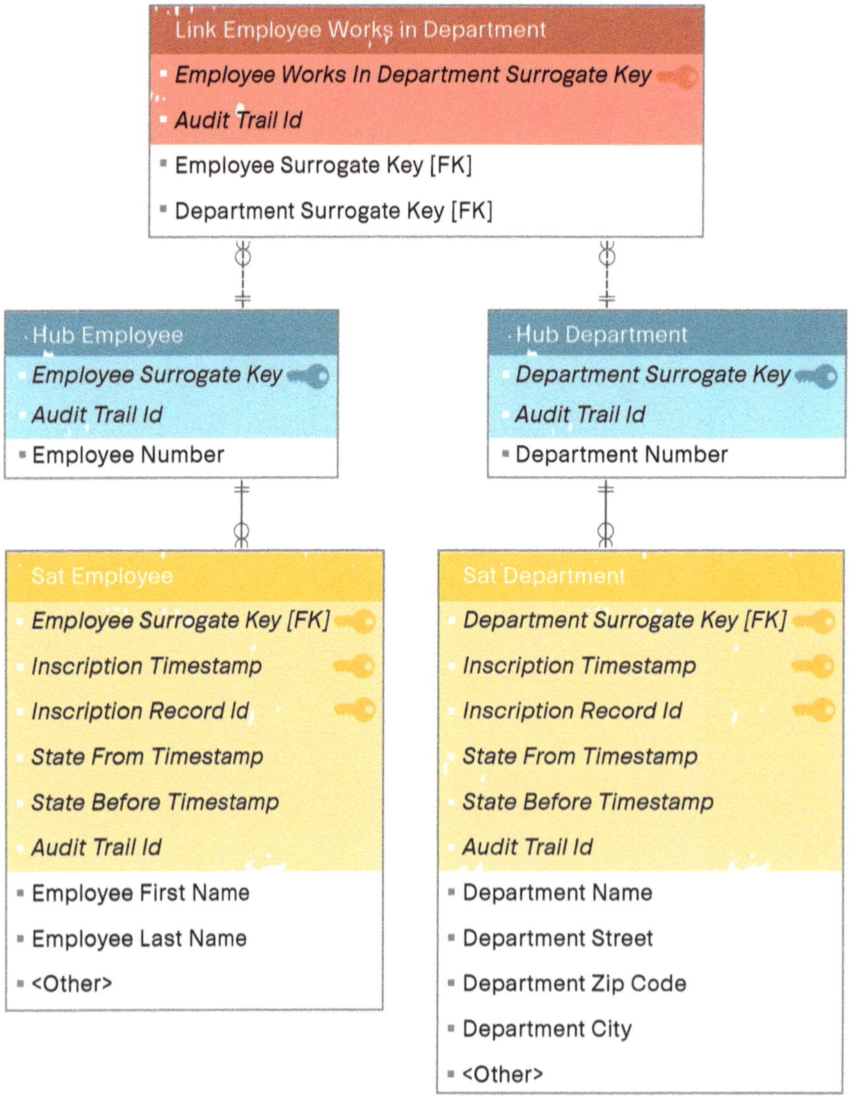

This is based on the notion that:
1) The attribute that identifies the entity becomes the business key
2) Any descriptive attributes are placed in a Satellite
3) The relationship itself is represented by a Link

If we follow this line of thinking, a Link-Satellite is not created because the information model doesn't actually specify a relationship with descriptive attributes. For example, if an employee switches departments, the change is reflected in the *employee* entity — where the department they work in is updated.

If a relationship *would* need descriptive properties, the data modeler would define an associative entity. This associative entity would contain any attributes that describe the relationship.

And here's the thing: following the rules above, the associative entity would be treated *as another Hub-and-Satellite* combination, rather than as a Link-Satellite.

But what would happen when an employee changes departments?

The information model in this example doesn't cater for any historization. However, the physical model, the Data Vault, natively supports technical historization in the Satellites by virtue of the inscription timestamp and inscription record id.

To capture changes in the relationship, a Link-Satellite can be added. This is only used for the technical historization of changes in the Link, by applying the driving key mechanism. It does not contain any descriptive attributes for the relationship — because there aren't any. The only purpose of this Link-Satellite is to manage the time periods, which is why we refer to it as an *end-dating Link-Satellite.*

As a result, if an employee changes departments, there will be *two* relationship records for that employee. One record will be end-dated when the new relationship takes effect.

Now let's assume the information model *does* contain descriptive attributes for the relationship. As per our earlier comment, these would appear as an associative entity in the information model:

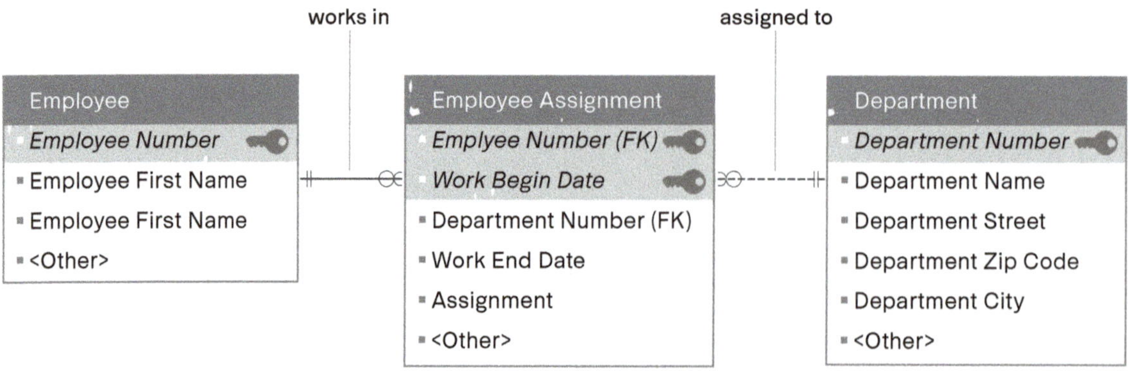

In this example, an employee can have a start date in a new department ('Work Begin Date'), an assignment, and an end date for that assignment ('Work End Date'). This model can also specify past or future assignments.

For instance, an employee might take on the role of a data modeler ('Assignment') starting on 2025-01-01 ('Work Begin Date') and ending on 2025-03-31 ('Work End Date').

Following the above rules, the associative entity is created as a Hub-and-Satellite combination.

However, the two relationships should *not* be represented as two separate Links without Satellites.

The reason for this is that having two separate relationships would not conform to the information model. The associative entity represents a *single* relationship between the employee and the department, and the physical model should reflect this as well.

Therefore, in the Data Vault model, the associative entity is implemented as *one* Link, *one* Hub, and *one* Satellite.

The purpose of the 'Hub Employee Assignment' and its Satellite is to accurately represent the original (many-to-many) relationship along with its descriptive attributes. In ELM, this approach is sometimes called a 'keyed instance' or a 'relationship describing Hub,' and we highly recommend this practice.

This is a form of a ⚐ dependent Hub. It may not have come up as part of the data modeling workshop when discussing business terms, and may not initially be perceived as a business concept the same way as would be the case for 'employee' or 'department,' but it is a natural result from interpreting the information model.

Additionally, with this approach, there is no longer a need for an end-dating Satellite on the Link, as this is now managed within the 'Sat Employee Assignment.'

The updated modeling guidelines, now including this final point are:

1) The attribute that identifies the entity becomes the business key
2) Any descriptive attributes are placed in the Satellite
3) The relationship itself is represented by a Link
4) An associative entity in the information model is implemented as a Hub, Satellite, and Link combination

This approach not only aligns more closely with the information model —and accurately reflects how the business operates— but it is also simpler from an implementation standpoint. In contrast, using a traditional Link-Satellite, as introduced earlier, requires a separate pattern and code generation template. Although very similar to a regular Satellite, the Link-Satellite approach still differs because it requires access to all business keys that define the relationships in the metadata.

The engine can deliver both forms, because these are ultimately variations on the same theme, but as a directive to the engine, we let this approach take precedence when the physical model is generated.

Driving keys and relationship end-dating

In the previous section, we introduced the concept of an *end-dating Link-Satellite.*

Unlike a regular Satellite, this type of Link-Satellite typically contains no descriptive columns. It is sometimes referred to as an 'effectivity' Link-Satellite.

The primary purpose of the end-dating Link-Satellite is to determine the validity of a relationship over time. This design allows for the implementation of different relationship cardinalities (such as many-to-many, many-to-one, or one-to-one) without altering the structure of the Link itself.

By using an end-dating Link-Satellite, a data modeler can manage the temporal aspect of relationships between two or more Hubs, enabling flexible design of relationship cardinalities in the physical model.

For the most part, this is *only* required when there only is a technical historization of the data, such as is the case in this example:

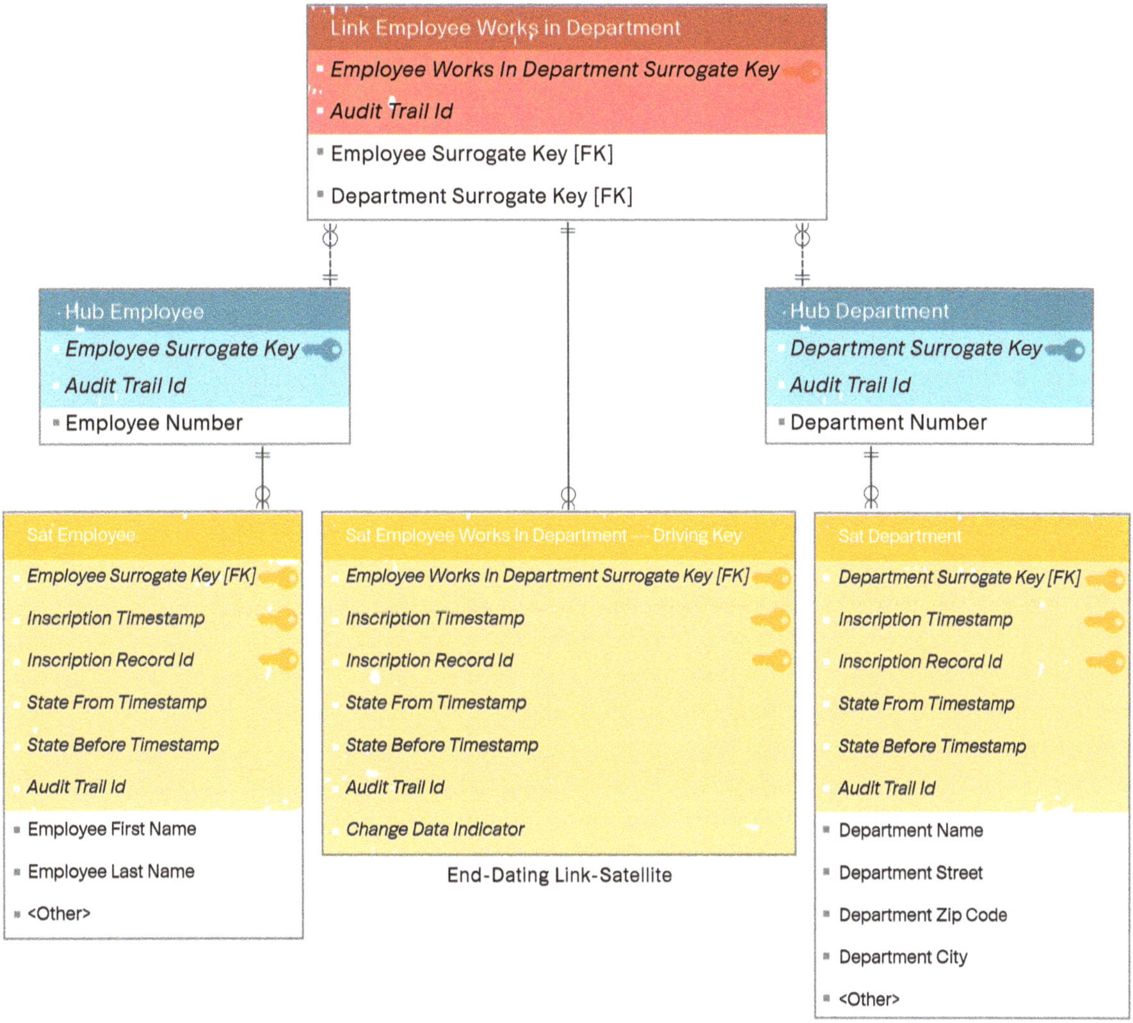

End-Dating Link-Satellite

In this scenario, when an employee moves to another department a new record in the Link will be created.

Staging Layer

Employee	Department	Inscription Timestamp
John	Human Resources	2025-01-02
John	Marketing	2025-03-05

Link

Employee	Department
John	Human Resources
John	Marketing

At this stage a decision needs to be made. The Link is not time-variant, so which of these two records is valid, and when?

In this case, a rule can be implemented to state that an employee can only be part of one department, at a point in time. In effect, the relationship is now defined as one-to-many with the department being the 'one'.

The employee is now the *driving key*, when this person moves to another department, it drives the mechanism to end-date its previous relationship to the (other, previous) department.

That is what is happening in the example below:

Staging Layer

Employee	Department	Inscription Timestamp
John	Human Resources	2025-01-02
John	Marketing	2025-03-05

Link

Employee	Department
John	Human Resources
John	Marketing

End-Dating Link-Satellite

Employee	Department	Inscription Timestamp	State From Timestamp	State Before Timestamp
John	Human Resources	2025-01-02	2025-01-02	2025-03-05
John	Marketing	2025-03-05	2025-03-05	9999-12-31

In this example, the employee acts as the driving key. When John moves from Human Resources to Marketing, this triggers the end-dating of the state time period during which John worked in Human Resources.

We previously mentioned that this approach concerns technical historization only. There simply is no better alternative, so the best we can do is identify that a relationship has changed when a newer version exists that uses the same driving key.

However, because this is the best available option, we still map these values to the state timeline columns, and adhere to the end-dating approach for regular Satellites.

Appointing a driving key is an interpretation —a business rule— and it might not always be correct. If it turns out to be incorrect, the metadata can be updated, and the solution can be refactored to reflect the new interpretation. In our experience, this situation occurs frequently and is another reason to consider implementing a PSA.

Before we go into pattern and implementation details, consider what happens when John switches back to Human Resources.

Staging Layer

Employee	Department	Inscription Timestamp
John	Human Resources	2025-01-02
John	Marketing	2025-03-05
John	Human Resources	2025-09-01

Link

Employee	Department
John	Human Resources
John	Marketing

End-Dating Link-Satellite

Employee	Department	Inscription Timestamp	State From Timestamp	State Before Timestamp
John	Human Resources	2025-01-02	2025-01-02	2025-03-05
John	Marketing	2025-03-05	2025-03-05	2025-09-01
John	Human Resources	2025-09-01	2025-09-01	9999-12-31

Even though a change is detected in the data delta, there is *no* new relationship created in the Link, because the unique relationship between John and Human Resources already existed. However, this change *is* reflected in the Link-Satellite.

This situation illustrates a pattern known as the A-B-A pattern, where data reverts to an earlier state after a change. In such cases, evaluating an end-dating Link-Satellite *must* rely on data from the staging layer, not directly on the Link. This approach avoids common pitfalls associated with trying to evaluate changes directly from the Link data, which will not accurately reflect the temporal dynamics of the relationships.

Driving keys and insert-only

Driving keys present an interesting complication for end-dating, especially when adopting an insert-only approach. Standard window functions for end-dating cannot be immediately applied to determine the before timestamp.

To accurately calculate the before timestamp, the driving key column itself is required as additional information:

```
SELECT
  <timestamp> AS FROM_TIMESTAMP
  ,LEAD(<timestamp>,1,'9999-12-31')
   OVER (PARTITION BY <driving key
   in Link)>
     ORDER BY <timestamp>)
   AS BEFORE_TIMESTAMP
FROM <Link> link
JOIN <(Link)Satellite> sat
ON link.<Link key> = sat.<Link key>
```

Let's have a look at an updated version of the employee and department example:

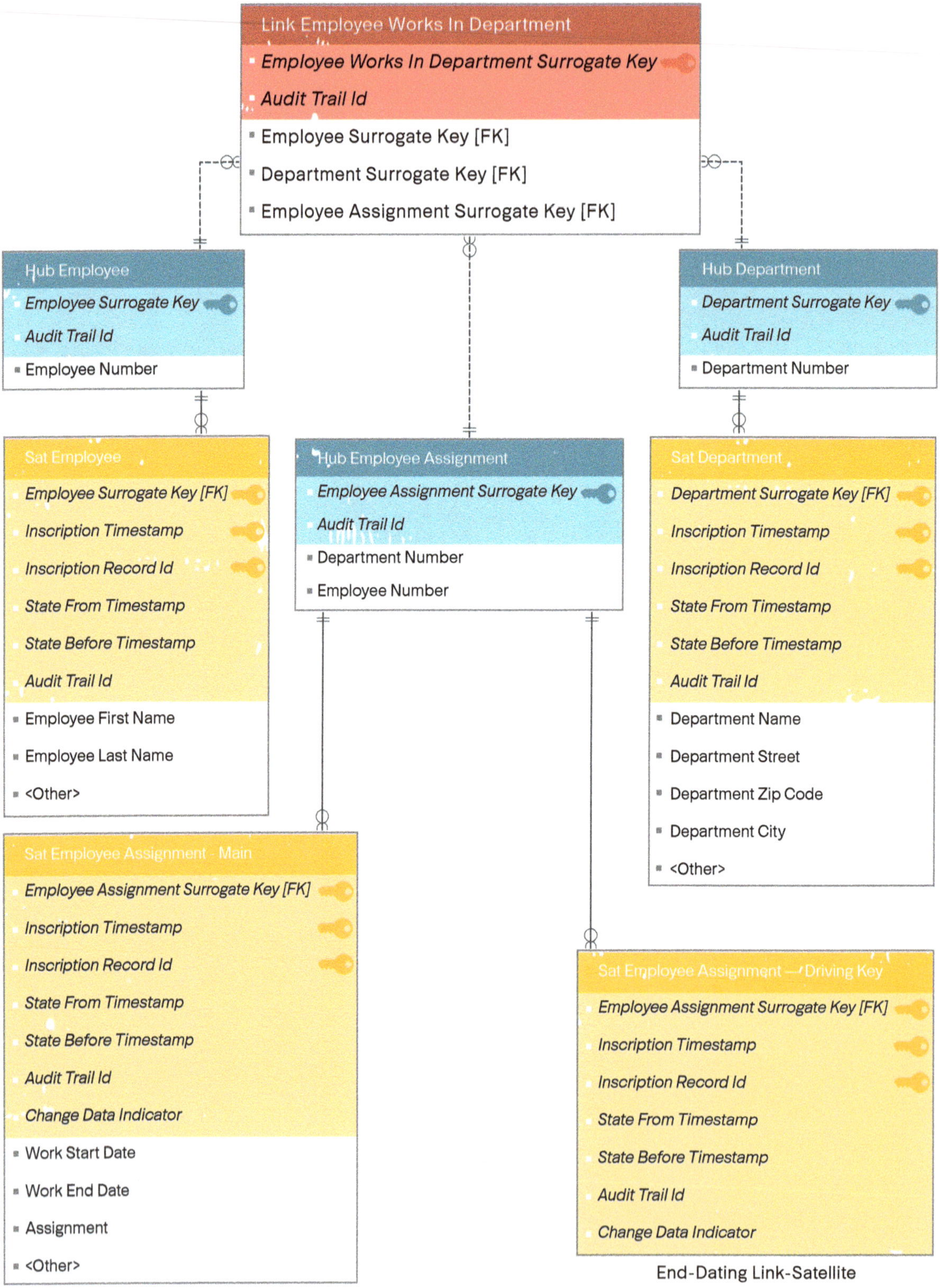

End-Dating Link-Satellite

In this example, regular history for the relationship is associated to a dependent Hub called 'Hub Employee Assignment.'

However, the relationship's validity period might also need to be evaluated separately using the driving key mechanism. This is managed in the 'Sat Employee Assignment – Driving Key' object.

Implementing and retrieving the validity time period data requires knowing which column is the driving key, which can be encoded in the design metadata.

An example of this is:

```
LEAD([State_From_Timestamp],1,'9999-12-31')
OVER (PARTITION BY [Employee Number]
   ORDER BY [State_From_Timestamp])
AS [State_Before_Timestamp]
```

In this example, the driving key is the 'Employee Number,' one of the business key columns in the parent Hub. Alternatively, the Employee Surrogate Key from the Link could also be used – they both represent the same CBC. Either way, these columns are not readily available, and require the parent Hub or Link to be joined, as well as the selection of the driving key column.

With an insert-only approach, this may not always be apparent in the physical model, leading to mistakes when deriving the before timestamp for the driving key-based Satellite at runtime. These mistakes occur if the Satellite is treated the same as a regular Satellite, where the window function is applied to the surrogate key. In this case, the driving key should be included.

This issue does *not* arise if the insert-only approach is not followed and the values are persisted.

For comparison, and to highlight the difference between two Satellites for the same Hub, deriving the before timestamp a regular Satellite 'Sat Employee Assignment – Main' would look like this:

```
LEAD([State_From_Timestamp],1,'9999-12-31')
OVER (PARTITION BY [Employee Assignment Surrogate Key]
   ORDER BY [State_From_Timestamp])
AS [State_Before_Timestamp]
```

In other words, this directly applies the Hub surrogate key. This assumes the before timestamp is not mapped already – please refer to the mapping end-dating section for background on this.

Modifying the approach for insert-only

However, it is still possible to use an insert-only approach in a way that bypasses the need to understand when and where to implement driving key-specific logic.

For this purpose, an alternative method is available:

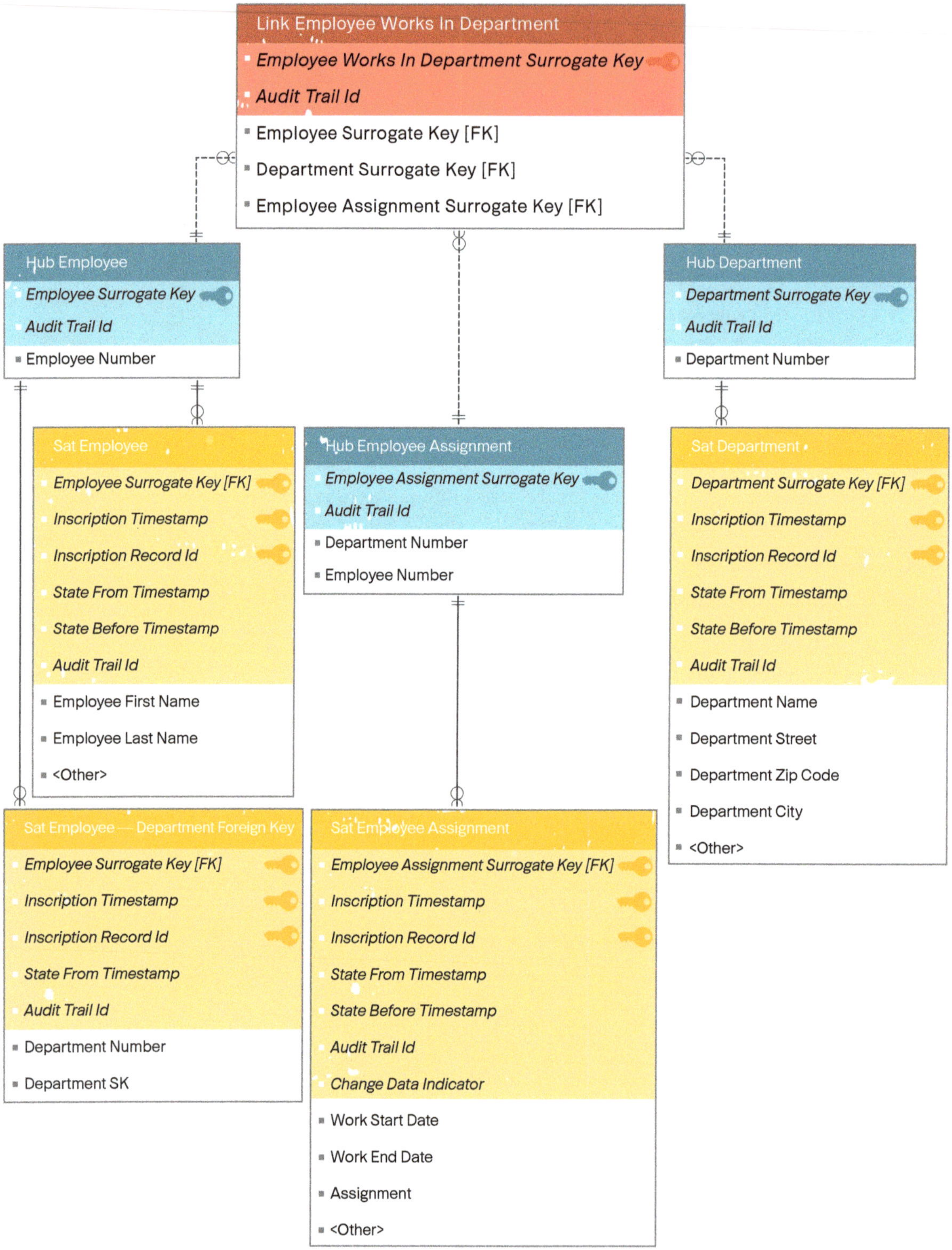

Link Employee Works In Department
Employee Works In Department Surrogate Key
Audit Trail Id
Employee Surrogate Key [FK]
Department Surrogate Key [FK]
Employee Assignment Surrogate Key [FK]
Hub Employee
Employee Surrogate Key
Audit Trail Id
Employee Number
Hub Department
Department Surrogate Key
Audit Trail Id
Department Number
Sat Employee
Employee Surrogate Key [FK]
Inscription Timestamp
Inscription Record Id
State From Timestamp
State Before Timestamp
Audit Trail Id
Employee First Name
Employee Last Name
<Other>
Hub Employee Assignment
Employee Assignment Surrogate Key
Audit Trail Id
Department Number
Employee Number
Sat Department
Department Surrogate Key [FK]
Inscription Timestamp
Inscription Record Id
State From Timestamp
State Before Timestamp
Audit Trail Id
Department Name
Department Street
Department Zip Code
Department City
<Other>
Sat Employee — Department Foreign Key
Employee Surrogate Key [FK]
Inscription Timestamp
Inscription Record Id
State From Timestamp
Audit Trail Id
Department Number
Department SK
Sat Employee Assignment
Employee Assignment Surrogate Key [FK]
Inscription Timestamp
Inscription Record Id
State From Timestamp
State Before Timestamp
Audit Trail Id
Change Data Indicator
Work Start Date
Work End Date
Assignment
<Other>

This example still implements a dependent Hub for the relationship, tracking the regular relationship context. However, the driving key mechanism is moved to the employee Hub, making it explicit in the model that the department is the foreign key of the one-to-many relationship.

This adjustment reflects reality more accurately, as it involves tracking changes of the foreign keys for the department over time.

This also simplifies the deriving of the before timestamp, because the regular pattern can now be used for the driving key, which is now located in 'Sat Employee – Department Foreign Key':

```
LEAD([State_From_Timestamp],1,'9999-12-31')
OVER (PARTITION BY [Employee Surrogate Key]
   ORDER BY [State_From_Timestamp])
AS [State_Before_Timestamp]
```

Consumers no longer 'need to know' which key to partition by for creating the intended time periods. Additionally, the regular Satellite pattern can be used, meaning there is only one Satellite pattern required for all contextual data. This provides a reliable way to support an insert-only paradigm while avoiding driving key complexities.

Note that both the business key as well as the surrogate key can be used in the driving key Satellite, it doesn't matter. We've displayed both to illustrate this option.

These examples highlight the options available at the physical implementation level to simplify some of these complexities.

NULL handling for Satellites

When a business key for a Hub is missing (NULL), there is no reason to try to load it. For a Satellite, it can be considered to still load the record when the business key is missing.

To implement the handling of missing business keys for Satellites, the unknown business key can be connected to the Hub zero key, either by performing a lookup or by replacing the empty value with the standard zero key value as defined in the ⚐ zero keys in the Hub section.

However, the value of doing so is limited. Loading a Satellite record without the business key is somewhat contradictory. After all, how can one attach something to a thing that doesn't exist?

If this happens, the only thing we really know is that business keys are missing. While we can infer something about the context of this missing key, we can't connect it to anything meaningful. At the very least, this data behavior indicates a potential data quality issue and could signify possible improvements in the model. Is there perhaps another business key that would work better?

Having said that, we do recommend allowing this to occur and therefore adding this feature to the design pattern. The reason for this is that we want to be aware of this situation so that we can still process the data, run data platform checks on it using the ⚐ testing framework, and be alerted to this through the ⚐ monitoring framework so that changes to rectify this phenomenon can be implemented.

When notified of this issue, changes in the model or operational system can be considered to address it, and the engine can refactor the implementation accordingly.

As with the Link NULL handling, decisions must be made what to do when the business key becomes known for the record. Using additional logic, these situations can be identified and flagged, for example by using an ⚐ exception bitmap, and excluded from downstream processing.

Combining multiple data sources in a Satellite

In the base integration area, Satellites that describe the same Hub are typically separated by their origins. For example, a 'customer' Satellite from one operational system is likely to be distinct from the 'customer' Satellite from another.

This is the de facto approach for adding Satellites in the base integration area. It's not the only approach, of course, but it's the one that is most commonly used. There are a few reasons for this, primarily because it's by far the easiest to implement.

Since we're still in the back room of the data solution, we keep the transformation logic in the data solution to an absolute minimum, only implementing it where we can fully control the outcome to avoid errors.

Consider the example below:

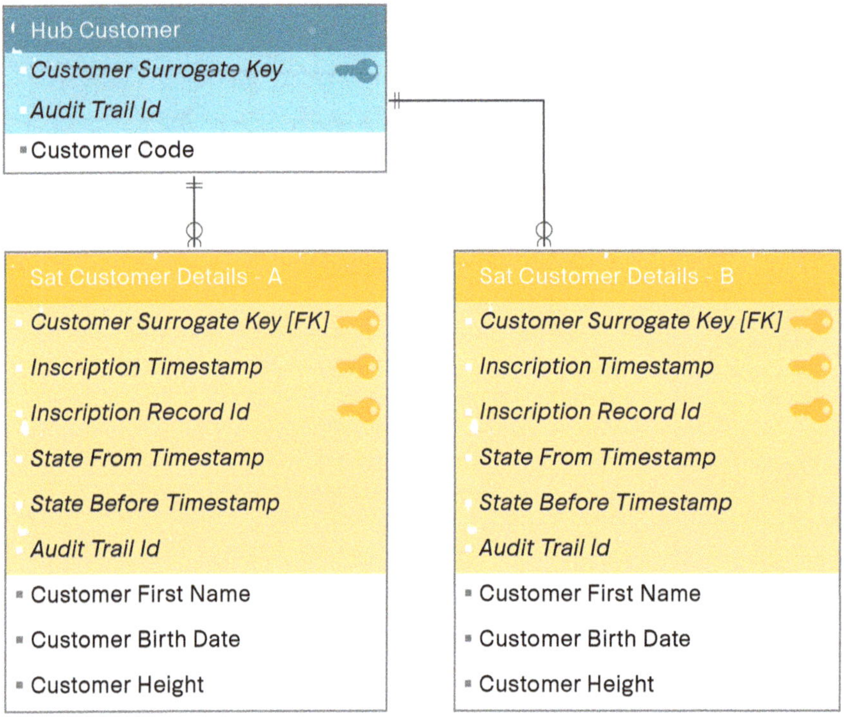

Two operational systems, A and B, both deliver context that describes the customer. At first sight, it might seem convenient to create a single Satellite that is populated by both systems. But in practice, this can only be done in very specific and rare cases.

To understand why, we have to examine the data and its structure more closely. For example, the customer height might be recorded in centimeters in system A, and in inches in system B.

PSA customer - System A

Customer Code	Inscription Timestamp	Customer First Name	Customer Birth Date	Customer Height
C415	2025-11-01 23:00	John	1990-02-04	200
C415	2025-11-11 10:00	John	1990-02-04	199

PSA customer - System B

Customer Code	Inscription Timestamp	Customer First Name	Customer Birth Date	Customer Height
C415	2025-11-05 17:30	John	NULL	78
C415	2025-11-19 08:00	John	1990-02-04	78

When combining this into a single Satellite the result would introduce an odd 'flip-flopping' effect, in both the height and date of birth columns — the red highlighted cells. A false impression is created that the customer continues to grow and shrink over time.

Sat Customer Details

Surrogate Key	Inscription Timestamp	Customer First Name	Customer Birth Date	Customer Height
C415\@|	2025-11-01 23:00	John	1990-02-04	200
C415\@|	2025-11-05 17:30	John	NULL	78
C415\@|	2025-11-11 10:00	John	1990-02-04	200
C415\@|	2025-11-19 08:00	John	1990-02-04	78

This hypothetical example intends to illustrate what kind of problems may occur when merging data in the base integration area. Encountering a situation like this where multiple data sets have the exact same structure is rare. It is much more common for designers to 'bundle' similar columns in Satellites, but this results in the exact same issues.

For example, creating a single Satellite containing only the customer height, and taking only the height columns from both source data objects results in the same incorrect outcome.

'Merging' data from various source data objects in a single Satellite can only be done when:

- → The column structures match, and
- → The data sets are completely separate, with no overlap in business keys, and
- → The data sets are identical in meaning

This is extremely rare. In most cases, combining data is a task for the derived integration area.

Automation

To generate the Satellite data logistics processes, we need the following metadata:

- → The mapping between the source and target data objects
- → The definition of the business key
- → The mapping between the source and target data items

The data object mapping captures the relationship between the source and target data objects.

The business key definition, as with the Hub and Link, captures how the business key is defined in the source data object. For a Satellite, this must be the exact same definition as is used for the parent Hub or Link in their mapping from the respective source data object.

Each individual data item mapping, including any renames and transformations are captured in a list of standard data item mappings.

Design metadata example

As with earlier examples on the specification of the design metadata, the 'PSA Sales' once again acts as the source data object for the Satellite mapping. The metadata is agnostic of its unitemporal or bitemporal implementation, this is determined by which code generation template is applied.

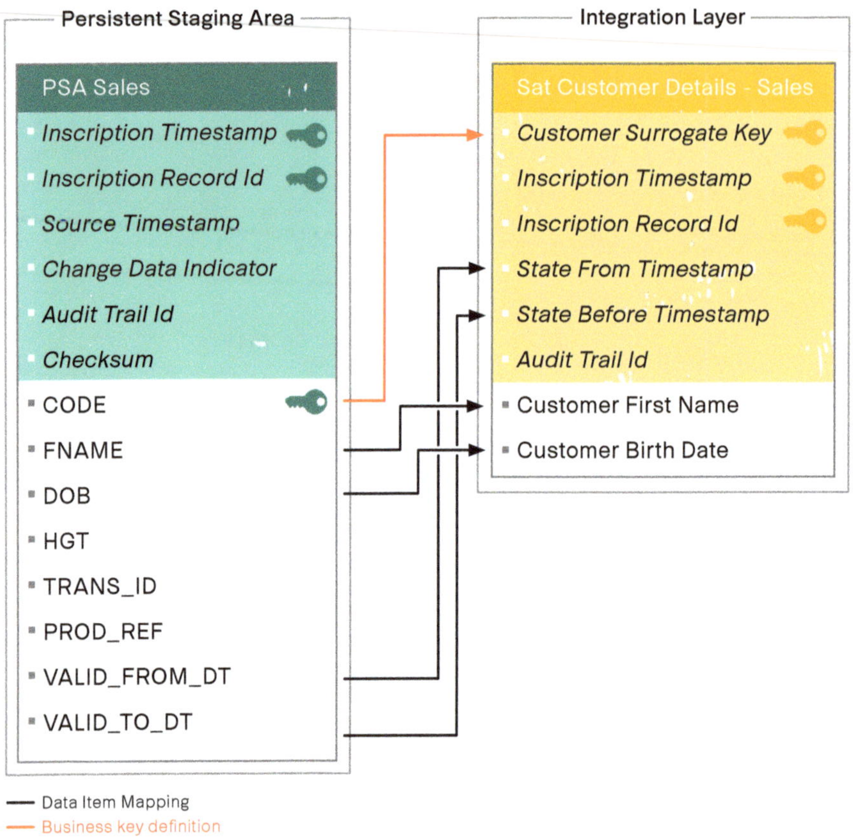

In this example, the following columns are mapped as regular data item mappings:

- → 'FNAME,' which is mapped to 'Customer First Name'
- → 'DOB,' which is mapped to 'Customer Birth Date'
- → 'VALID_FROM_DT' has been selected as the state from timestamp candidate
- → 'VALID_TO_DT' has been selected as the state before timestamp candidate

The business key definition remains the same as used for the (parent) 'Customer' Hub.

In this example, the data contains a suitable state before timestamp (VALID_TO_DT). If this is not available, however, the state before timestamp must be derived and would initially be set to the high-end value of 9999-12-31. In this scenario, it would not be mapped because there is no matching source data item.

In addition, for an intended bitemporal implementation the state before timestamp column must be part of the primary key in the target data object – as described in the ⚐ bitemporal section.

This Satellite has a 'Sales' suffix in the name, indicating it is a dedicated Satellite for the 'Sales' data set. There might be more Satellite tables that contain customer details but are populated by other source data objects.

In the design metadata, this can be recorded as follows:


```
{
 "dataObjectMappings": [
  {
   "name": "PSA_Sales to Satellite Customer Details - Sales",
   "sourceDataObjects": [ { "name": "PSA_Sales" } ],
   "targetDataObject": { "name": "Satellite Customer Details - Sales" },
   "businessKeyDefinitions": [
    [
     {
      "ordinalPosition": 1,
      "name": "CUSTOMER_BK",
      "surrogateKey": "CUSTOMER_SK",
      "businessKeyComponents": [
       {
        "ordinalPosition": 1,
        "dataItem": { "name": "CODE" }
       }
      ]
     }
    ]
   ],
   "dataItemMappings": [
    {
     "sourceDataItems": [ { "name": "FNAME" } ],
     "targetDataItem": { "name": "CUSTOMER_FIRST_NAME" }
    },
    {
     "sourceDataItems": [ { "name": "DOB" } ],
     "targetDataItem": { "name": "CUSTOMER_DATE_OF_BIRTH" }
    },
    {
     "sourceDataItems": [ { "name": "VALID_FROM_DT" } ],
     "targetDataItem": { "name": "STATE_FROM_TIMESTAMP" }
    },
    {
     "sourceDataItems": [ { "name": "VALID_TO_DT" } ],
     "targetDataItem": { "name": "STATE_BEFORE_TIMESTAMP" }
    }
   ]
  }
 ]
}
```


As before, the Audit Trail Id is not mapped because this will be added by the data logistics process. Additionally, as with the PSA example, the remaining standard framework columns are not explicitly mapped in metadata, as these are added by the code generation template.

Solution pattern example

The data logistics process for a Satellite is among the more complex patterns in data architecture. It can be implemented using either a ⚐ uni-temporal or ⚐ bitemporal approach, depending on the requirements. Conceptually, it resembles the PSA pattern but in-cludes additional features based on specific design considerations.

See our website for a full solution pattern example: https://dtng.link/d8bgw.

In the following sections, we will explore how to implement both approaches in detail.

Preparing the Satellite

The preparation process is the same for both unitemporal and bitemporal Satellites.

Since the complete code is lengthy, we'll focus on the separate components in the following sections while referring to code we've covered in earlier sections, like the record compacting.

See our website for a full SQL example for preparing Satellites: https://dtng.link/en9go.

The overall process

The high-level Satellite preparing process can be expressed as pseudo code below, highlighting the important steps in order of operation:

```
SELECT
  <Compacting selection>
FROM
(
  SELECT
    <Compacting preparation>
  FROM
  (
    SELECT
      <Inner selection>
    FROM
  ) compacting_preparation
) compacting_selection
WHERE <compacting filter>
```

Inner selection

The first step in the order of operation is the 'inner selection,' which fetches the data from the PSA.

In this step of the process, the data item mappings are applied, which results in columns being aliased to their intended target name. This also includes the mapping to the state timestamp(s).

```
SELECT
  [Inscription_Timestamp],
  [Source_Timestamp],
  [Inscription_Record_Id],
  [Change_Data_Indicator],
  [CODE],
  [VALID_FROM_DT] AS [State_From_Timestamp],
  [VALID_TO_DT] AS [State_Before_Timestamp],
  [FNAME] AS [CUSTOMER_FIRST_NAME],
  [DOB] AS [CUSTOMER_DATE_OF_BIRTH],
  HASHBYTES('SHA1',
    COALESCE(TRIM(CONVERT(NVARCHAR(MAX),
    [VALID_FROM_DT])), '~!@|N/A') + '\@|' +
    COALESCE(TRIM(CONVERT(NVARCHAR(MAX),
    [VALID_TO_DT])), '~!@|N/A') + '\@|' +
    COALESCE(TRIM(CONVERT(NVARCHAR(MAX),
    [FNAME])), '~!@|N/A') + '\@|' +
   COALESCE(TRIM(CONVERT(NVARCHAR(MAX),
   [DOB])), '~!@|N/A') + '\@|'
  ) AS [Checksum]
FROM [Psa_Sales] inner_selection
```

The checksum is created using the SHA1 algorithm in this step. This will be used later in the compacting process and for comparison against the target data object.

The business key column is selected as-is. This will be used to determine the surrogate key in subsequent steps.

Filters, including load windows, can be added here if required, for example:

```
WHERE [Inscription_Timestamp] > <LoadWindowAfter>
 AND [Inscription_Timestamp] <= <LoadWindowTo>
```

Compacting preparation

In the next selection, the data from the inner selection is enhanced with the necessary evaluations for the compacting mechanism. These are the columns described in the delta compacting section. To reduce the amount of code in each example, we'll refer to these section for the technical implementation details.

```
SELECT
  [Inscription_Timestamp],
  [Source_Timestamp],
  [Inscription_Record_Id],
  [Change_Data_Indicator],
  [Checksum],
  [CODE],
  [State_From_Timestamp],
  [State_Before_Timestamp],
  [CUSTOMER_FIRST_NAME],
  [CUSTOMER_DATE_OF_BIRTH],
```

```
  -- Condition 1
  <Delta compacting condition 1>
  [Checksum_Change_Indicator]
  -- Condition 2
  <Delta compacting condition 2>
  [CDC_Change_Indicator]
  -- Condition 3
  <Delta compacting condition 3>
 [Time_Change_Indicator]
FROM
(
  <Inner selection>
) compacting_preparation
```

Compacting selection

In the third step, the data is compacted by filtering out the redundant data from the result set so far.

Additionally, this is the step where the surrogate key is created.

```
SELECT
  COALESCE(TRIM(CONVERT(NVARCHAR(MAX),
  [CODE])), '~!@|N/A') + '\@|' AS [CUSTOMER_SK],
  <variable> AS [Audit_Trail_Id],
  [Inscription_Timestamp],
  [Inscription_Record_Id],
  [Change_Data_Indicator],
  [Checksum],
  [State_From_Timestamp],
  [State_Before_Timestamp],
  [CUSTOMER_FIRST_NAME],
  [CUSTOMER_DATE_OF_BIRTH]
FROM
(
 <Compacting preparation>

) compacting_selection
WHERE
  ([Checksum_Change_Indicator] = 'Different' AND
   [Change_Data_Indicator] = 'C')
  OR
  ([CDC_Change_Indicator] = 'Different' AND
   [Time_Change_Indicator] = 'Different')
```

The compacting implementation for a bitemporal approach differs slightly from the unitemporal solution shown here. While both approaches are similar, the bitemporal method also considers the state timeline during compacting. For examples of how compacting varies based on intended outcomes, visit: https://dtng.link/en9go.

At this stage, the logic represents a virtual unitemporal Satellite – when executed against the PSA as is the case for this example.

It's also a great option to introduce the Audit Trail Id, though this can be added in various places. As with other similar examples, the fetching of the audit trail id is not added to keep the focus on the Satellite logic. In a typical implementation this would be provided as a parameter (or similar) provided by the control framework.

Loading an unitemporal Satellite

A unitemporal Satellite represents the traditional way Satellites are documented in Data Vault methodology.

See our website for a full example of SQL code for an unitemporal Satellite: https://dtng.link/apn5c.

To process data to a unitemporal Satellite, the compacted subset —the outcomes of the compacting selection step in the previous section— is compared against the target data object. When loading data into a physical Satellite object, the mechanisms for ⚐ preventing reprocessing and ⚐ change merging are applied to ensure that records are not duplicated or redundantly processed.

```
INSERT INTO [Sat Customer]
(
  [CUSTOMER_SK],
  [Inscription_Timestamp],
  [Inscription_Record_Id],
  [State_From_Timestamp],
  [State_Before_Timestamp],
  [Change_Data_Indicator],
  [Checksum],
  [Audit_Trail_Id],
  [CUSTOMER_FIRST_NAME],
  [CUSTOMER_DATE_OF_BIRTH]
)
SELECT
  [...]
FROM
(
  SELECT
  compacting_selection.[CUSTOMER_SK],
  compacting_selection.[Inscription_Timestamp],
  compacting_selection.[Inscription_Record_Id],
  compacting_selection.[State_From_Timestamp],
  compacting_selection.[State_Before_Timestamp],
  compacting_selection.[Change_Data_Indicator],
  compacting_selection.[Checksum],
  Compacting_selection.[Audit_Trail_Id],
  compacting_selection.[CUSTOMER_FIRST_NAME],
  compacting_selection.[CUSTOMER_DATE_OF_BIRTH],
  CAST(ROW_NUMBER() OVER (
    PARTITION BY compacting_selection.[CUSTOMER_SK]
    ORDER BY compacting_selection.[CUSTOMER_SK],
          compacting_selection.[Inscription_Timestamp],
          compacting_selection.[Inscription_Record_Id]
  ) AS INT) AS KEY_ROW_NUMBER,
```

```
  target_object.[Checksum] AS [Lookup_Checksum],
  target_object.[Change_Data_Indicator] AS [Lookup_Change_Data_Indicator]
  FROM
  (
    <Compacting selection>
  ) compacting_selection
  -- Prevent reprocessing
  LEFT OUTER JOIN [Sat Customer] target_object
    ON compacting_selection.[CUSTOMER_SK] = target_object.[CUSTOMER_SK]
    AND compacting_selection.[Inscription_Timestamp] = target_object.[Inscription_Timestamp]
    AND compacting_selection.[Inscription_Record_Id] = target_object.[Inscription_Record_Id]
  WHERE satellite.[CUSTOMER_SK] IS NULL
 ) final
-- Change merging
WHERE
(
  KEY_ROW_NUMBER = 1
  AND (( [Checksum] != [Lookup_Checksum] )
    -- The checksums are different
    OR ( [Checksum] = [Lookup_Checksum]
     AND [Change_Data_Indicator] != [Lookup_Change_Data_Indicator])
    -- The checksums are the same but the CDC is different
    )
)
OR
(
  -- It's not the most recent change in the set, so the record can be inserted as-is
  KEY_ROW_NUMBER != 1
)
```

The fundamental principles for data logistics are again supported. The prevent reprocessing step, implemented using a LEFT OUTER JOIN, ensures that already-processed records are not reinserted while the change merging removes any data redundancy compared to the target. Both mechanisms are the same as applied in the PSA pattern.

Loading a bitemporal Satellite

The data logistics process for a bitemporal Satellite is implemented on the same preparing data process —the compacted subset— as the unitemporal Satellite. In addition, the compacted subset must also provide the state before timestamp column.

Compared to an unitemporal Satellite, the bitemporal process 'fixes' the timelines where required and therefore includes more steps.

See our website for a full SQL example of a bitemporal Satellite process: https://dtng.link/zc4ld.

Example pattern for a bitemporal Satellite process

1) Compare all records from the compacted subset against the target data object. Select only records, which have yet not been processed—the 'prevent reprocessing' mechanism

2) Compare the new records to the existing records in the target data object to determine if time periods are overlapping. We refer to 'right' and 'left' in this context, referring to representing a timeline for a record from left (earlier) to right (later) in time. If overlapping time periods exists, create new records to preserve the overlapping portions, for:

   a) The 'left' part of the existing record ('existing left')

   b) The 'right' part of the existing record ('existing right')

3) Insert all records —the new, preserved 'existing right,' and preserved 'existing left'— into the target object, mapping the surrogate key for the Satellite, Audit Trail Id, and all contextual column(s).

The process can be expressed as pseudo SQL code below, highlighting the important steps in order of operation:

```
WITH
NewRecords AS
(
  SELECT [...]
  (
    <Compacting selection>
  )
  LEFT JOIN
    <Prevent reprocessing>
)
, ExistingRight AS
(
  -- All new records, and all most recent records from the
  -- target object with overlapping time periods
  SELECT [...] FROM <NewRecords>
  UNION
  SELECT [...] FROM <target data object with overlaps>
)
, PreserveRightPartOfExistingRecords AS
(
  -- Duplicate the existing record, preserving the right portion
  SELECT
     NewRecords.[CUSTOMER_SK]
    -- Use the new inscription timestamp and record id
    ,NewRecords.[Inscription_Time-stamp]
    ,NewRecords.[Inscription_Record_Id]
```

```
    -- Replace the existing state from timestamp with new state before timestamp
    ,COALESCE(NewRecords.State_Before_Timestamp,'9999-12-31') AS [State_From_Timestamp]
    -- Keep the existing state before timestamp
    ,ExistingRight.[State_Before_Time-stamp]
    -- Map the available existing data
    ,ExistingRight.<available columns>
    -- Order the records — Only the most recent record is of interest
    ,ROW_NUMBER()
      OVER (PARTITION BY ExistingRight.[CODE]
                ,NewRecords.[State_Before_Timestamp] -- New State From Timestamp
      ORDER BY ExistingRight.[Inscription_Timestamp] DESC
            ,ExistingRight.[Inscription_Record_Id] DESC)
      AS rownum
  FROM <NewRecords>
  JOIN <ExistingRight>
    ON NewRecords.[CUSTOMER_SK] = ExistingRight.[CUSTOMER_SK]
  WHERE
    -- Compare only with previous records
    NewRecords.[Inscription_Timestamp] > ExistingRight.[Inscription_Timestamp]
   -- Find Allen Relationship (right)
  AND COALESCE(NewRecords.State_Before_Timestamp,'9999-12-31') > ExistingRight.[State_From_Timestamp]
  AND COALESCE(NewRecords.State_Before_Timestamp,'9999-12-31') < ExistingRight.[State_Before_Timestamp]
)
, ExistingLeft AS
(
  -- All preserved right part records and
  -- all new records, and all most recent records from the
  -- target object with overlapping time periods
  SELECT [...] FROM <PreserveRightPartOfExistingRecords>
  UNION
  SELECT [...] FROM <NewRecords>
  UNION
  SELECT [...] FROM <target data object with overlaps>
)
, PreserveLeftPartOfExistingRecords AS
(
  -- Duplicate the existing record, preserving the left portion
  SELECT
     NewRecords.[CUSTOMER_SK]
    -- Use new inscription timestamp and record id
    ,NewRecords.[Inscription_Timestamp]
    ,NewRecords.[Inscription_Record_Id]
    -- Keep the existing state before timestamp
    ,ExistingLeft.[State_From_Timestamp] AS [State_From_Timestamp]
    -- Replace the existing state before timestamp with new state from timestamp
    ,NewRecords.[State_From_Timestamp] AS [State_Before_Timestamp]
```

```
    -- Map the available existing data
    ,ExistingLeft.<available columns>
    ,[...]
    -- Order the records - Only the most recent record is of interest
    ,ROW_NUMBER()
      OVER (PARTITION BY ExistingLeft.[CODE]
                ,NewRecords.State_From_Timestamp    -- New State Before Timestamp
      ORDER BY ExistingLeft.[Inscription_Timestamp] DESC
           ,ExistingLeft.[Inscription_Record_Id] DESC)
      AS rownum
  FROM <NewRecords>
  JOIN <ExistingLeft>
    ON NewRecords.[CUSTOMER_SK] = ExistingLeft.[CUSTOMER_SK]
  WHERE
  -- Compare only with previous records
    NewRecords.Inscription_Timestamp > ExistingLeft.Inscription_Timestamp
  -- Find Allen Relationship (left)
  AND NewRecords.State_From_Timestamp > ExistingLeft.State_From_Timestamp
  AND NewRecords.State_From_Timestamp < ExistingLeft.State_Before_Timestamp
)
INSERT INTO [Sat Customer]
(
  [CUSTOMER_SK],
  [Inscription_Timestamp],
  [Inscription_Record_Id],
  [State_From_Timestamp],
  [State_Before_Timestamp],
  [Change_Data_Indicator],
  [Checksum],
  [Audit_Trail_Id],
  [CUSTOMER_FIRST_NAME],
  [CUSTOMER_DATE_OF_BIRTH]
)
SELECT <PreserveLeftPartOfExistingRecords>
WHERE rownum = 1
UNION
SELECT <PreserveRightPartOfExistingRecords>
WHERE rownum = 1
UNION
SELECT <NewRecords>
```

NewRecords selection

In the initial selection of records, the 'prevent reprocessing' step is applied to ensure that the fundamental principles for data logistics are supported. **The lookup (LEFT OUTER JOIN in this example) will prevent the re-insertion of records that already have been processed:**

```
-- Select only records which have yet not been processed (prevent reprocessing)
LEFT OUTER JOIN [Sat Customer] target_object
  ON compacting_selection.[CUSTOMER_SK] = target_object.[CUSTOMER_SK]
  -- ATL check
  AND compacting_selection.[Inscription_Timestamp] = target_object.[Inscription_Timestamp]
  AND compacting_selection.[Inscription_Record_Id] = target_object.[Inscription_Record_Id]
  -- STL check
  AND compacting_selection.[State_From_Timestamp] = target_object.[State_From_Timestamp]
WHERE target_object.[CUSTOMER_SK] IS NULL
```

Compared to earlier (unitemporal) examples, the addition of the STL check is important because the state from timestamp is now part of the Satellite's primary key.

ExistingRight selection

This step compares new records with the most recent existing records in the target data object. From the ATL perspective, only currently valid records are considered; records that have already been end-dated are excluded.

To determine the current 'existing records' to preserve for the right part, the records that overlap with the data from 'NewRecords' must be selected from the current target data object.

Additionally, the records from NewRecords must be incorporated using a UNION. This ensures that, in the case of a full load from the PSA, for instance when refactoring, earlier overlaps are also recognized — represented as 'ExistingRight.'

```
ExistingRight AS
(
  -- All new records and all records from the target objects with overlapping time periods
  SELECT *
  FROM <NewRecords>
  UNION
  SELECT target_object_as_is.<same columns as NewRecords>
  -- Select the most recent records from the target object
  FROM [Sat Customer As Is] target_object_as_is
  INNER JOIN NewRecords
  ON NewRecords.[CUSTOMER_SK] = target_object_as_is.[CUSTOMER_SK]
  -- Find Allen Relationship (right)
   AND NewRecords.[State_Before_Timestamp] > target_object_as_is.[State_From_Timestamp]
   AND NewRecords.[State_Before_Timestamp] < target_object_as_is.[State_Before_Timestamp]
)
```

PreserveRightPartOfExistingRecords selection

When joining the 'NewRecords' and the 'ExistingRight' records, a new record must be created to preserve the right part of the existing record's time period when overlapping time periods are found.

```
FROM <NewRecords>
INNER JOIN <ExistingRight>
  ON NewRecords.[CUSTOMER_SK] = ExistingRight.[CUSTOMER_SK]
WHERE
-- Compare only with previous records
  NewRecords.[Inscription_Timestamp] > ExistingRight.[Inscription_Timestamp]
-- Find Allen Relationship (right)
AND COALESCE(NewRecords.State_Before_Timestamp,'9999-12-31')
> ExistingRight.[State_From_Timestamp]
AND COALESCE(NewRecords.State_Before_Timestamp,'9999-12-31')
< ExistingRight.[State_Before_Timestamp]
```

This returns a copy of the existing record from the 'ExistingRight' data set, replacing the existing state from timestamp with the new state before timestamp. The new inscription timestamp and inscription record id are also added, while all context columns preserve the existing data.

```
-- Use the new inscription timestamp and record id
,NewRecords.[Inscription_Timestamp]
,NewRecords.[Inscription_Record_Id]
-- Replace the existing state from timestamp with new state before timestamp
,COALESCE(NewRecords.State_Before_Timestamp,'9999-12-31') AS [State_From_Timestamp]
-- Keep the existing state before timestamp
,ExistingRight.[State_Before_Timestamp]
-- Map the available existing data
,ExistingRight.<available columns>
```

The resulting data set needs to be grouped by the business key and the new state from timestamp, ordered by the inscription timestamp and inscription record id. Only the most recent record is of interest.

```
-- Order the records: only the most recent record is of interest
,ROW_NUMBER()
  OVER (PARTITION BY ExistingRight.[PRODUCT_NAME]
           ,NewRecords.[State_Before_Timestamp] -- New state from timestamp
  ORDER BY ExistingRight.[Inscription_Timestamp] DESC
      ,ExistingRight.[Inscription_Record_Id] DESC)
AS rownum
```

ExistingLeft selection

Similar to the SQL in the 'ExistingRight' step, existing records that overlap with data from 'NewRecords' must be considered.

This selection involves three key steps:

1) Incorporate previously generated preserved right existing records ('PreserveRightPartOfExistingRecords')
2) Incorporate all records from 'NewRecords'
3) Select the overlapping most recent records from the current target data object to preserve the left part

These records will be combined using UNION.

```
ExistingLeft AS
(
  SELECT *
  FROM <PreserveRightPartOfExistingRecords>
  -- Only the most recent record is of interest
  WHERE rownum = 1
  UNION
  SELECT *
  FROM <NewRecords>
  UNION
  SELECT target_object_as_is.<same columns as NewRecords>
  -- Select only the most recent records from target object
  FROM [Sat Customer As Is] target_object_as_is
  INNER JOIN <NewRecords>
     NewRecords.[CUSTOMER_SK] = target_object_as_is.[CUSTOMER_SK]
  -- Find Allen Relationship (left)
   AND NewRecords.[State_From_Timestamp] > target_object_as_is.[State_From_Timestamp]
   AND NewRecords.[State_From_Timestamp] < target_object_as_is.[State_Before_Timestamp]
)
```

PreserveLeftPartOfExistingRecords selection

This step is very similar to the 'PreseveRightPartOfExistingRecords' one. The new records are again compared with the existing records, and a record is created for overlapping periods.

However, this part focuses on the *left* portion of the record.

```
  FROM <NewRecords>
  INNER JOIN <ExistingLeft>
    ON NewRecords.[CUSTOMER_SK] = ExistingLeft.[CUSTOMER_SK]
  WHERE
  -- Compare only with previous records
    NewRecords.Inscription_Timestamp > ExistingLeft.Inscription_Timestamp
  -- Find Allen Relationship (left)
  AND NewRecords.State_From_Timestamp > ExistingLeft.State_From_Timestamp
  AND NewRecords.State_From_Timestamp < ExistingLeft.State_Before_Timestamp
```

As before, this returns a copy of the existing record. The existing state before timestamp is replaced with the new state from timestamp, the new inscription timestamp and inscription record id are added, and the regular context is preserved.

```
-- Use the new inscription timestamp and record id
,NewRecords.[Inscription_Timestamp]
,NewRecords.[Inscription_Record_Id]
-- Keep the existing state before timestamp
,ExistingLeft.[State_From_Timestamp] AS [State_From_Timestamp]
-- Replace the existing state before timestamp with new state from timestamp
,NewRecords.[State_From_Timestamp] AS [State_Before_Timestamp]
-- Map the available existing data
,ExistingLeft.<available columns>
-- Order the records: only the most recent record is of interest
,ROW_NUMBER()
   OVER (PARTITION BY ExistingLeft.[PRODUCT_NAME]
              ,NewRecords.State_From_Timestamp -- New state before timestamp
   ORDER BY ExistingLeft.[Inscription_Timestamp] DESC
        ,ExistingLeft.[Inscription_Record_Id] DESC)
AS rownum
```

Union and insert

The final step is to UNION all of the records —the new ones, the preserved ones on the right, and the preserved ones on the left— and load these into the target data object.

Other integration layer considerations

The following sections contain the remaining general considerations that can be included when designing the integration layer.

Managing reference data

In some cases, certain codes, pointers, or similar standardized data elements may appear frequently across the data landscape. Each of these codes or pointers may have its own contextual data, such as a description or a set of standard values, providing further explanation for the code in question.

In many other cases, the codes themselves carry implicit meanings that people within the same area understand without needing additional descriptions. In some instances, these descriptions may not even be available in the data, as can be the case when using some industry-standard notations.

Examples of reference data include specific codes of operational systems, industry standard codes like country or language, and conversion rates (e.g., currency, weight, temperature). These are just a few examples, as the range of what can be considered reference data is wide and varied.

This type of data can be defined as reference data. In many operational systems, reference data is stored in often large 'code' tables, which contain a centralized list of all descriptions, labels, and other supporting information.

Adding reference data

As mentioned in the introduction of reference data, it might not even physically exist as data in the organization. If it does, it's simply a matter of applying the same data logistics patterns we've used so far. However, if it does *not* exist, it may need to be added. There are a few options for this.

One alternative is using managed landing area tables – special types of landing area tables. They are identical to landing area tables in terms of structure, but they are not truncated, and the tables and content are managed by the data solution team. Changes made are automatically versioned by the PSA, for example, via a FOJ delta detection mechanism.

Managed landing area tables are versatile and can be applied in various situations where data is not available in regular operational systems. We'll also see managed landing area tables again in the front room of the solution, as an alternative to complex transformation logic.

In terms of implementation, the managed landing area tables are populated through a one-off upload or manual data entry. For downstream processing they are treated as any other landing table.

Other options include defining a proxy operational system to hold the reference data, which can be updated in place and interfaced following standard staging layer practices.

Unconnected Hubs

↗ With an unconnected Hub it is possible to directly join reference data through a trusted relationship. A trusted relationship in this case is not a reference that can or should necessarily be defined and enforced through referential integrity.

Additional decisions are necessary when modeling reference data in the integration layer.

If certain frequently-used codes appear in many Satellites, providing descriptions for these codes in each table can add complexity to data logistics processes due to joins or lookups, and result in significant data redundancy by storing the same text multiple times.

To address this, reference data is often modeled as a Hub-and-Satellite combination, even if it might not be considered a true CBC. In this approach, the code serves as the business key, and the description is part of the Satellite's context.

However, it might not be meaningful to create a Link between the reference data Hub and the numerous Hub-and-Satellite combinations containing the code. In a typical solution, the sheer number of Links required could defeat the purpose of modeling reference data as a Hub-and-Satellite combination in the first place, which is to reduce complexity and data redundancy in Satellites.

In many cases, it might be more practical to directly join reference data as a *trusted relationship* to the corresponding codes in the Satellite, meaning without having to go through a Link. A trusted relationship in this case is not a reference that can or should necessarily be defined and enforced through referential integrity, but we trust it anyway.

This can be done either in the integration layer or in the presentation layer.

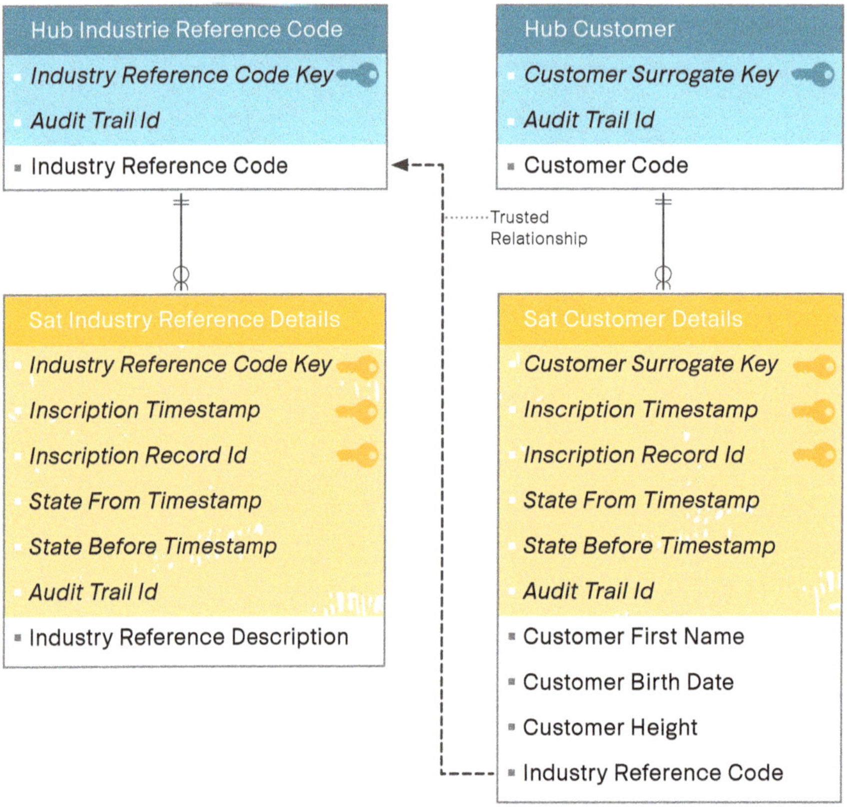

In all cases, however, the temporal aspects of the trusted relationship need to be taken into account. This is further covered in the ⚐ struggling with time – while getting the data out section.

CBC, or not?

Reference data often is an interesting topic to discuss. Like most modeling decisions, labeling some data as 'reference data' can imply a certain interpretation, influencing the overall model. What one considers a reference value, another might see as a CBC — depending on the situation and use case.

Take a currency code, for example. In many cases, this might lead to the creation of a reference data entity that includes descriptive information for the currency code (e.g., the country the code belongs to). The code itself may exist in many context entities.

However, in other areas —possibly within the same organization— a currency code is a CBC, serving as an integration point for various transactions and other relationships, such as in stock-trading or foreign-exchange contexts. In such instances, if the currency code is modeled as a reference table, it cannot be used as an integration point without breaking patterns or requiring refactoring.

On a positive note, following the Engine Thinking approach, this change in the model can be detected, and the solution automatically refactored accordingly. An ambition to strive for.

Orchestration

Orchestration refers to the management and coordination of data logistics processes, ensuring that tasks are performed in the correct sequence and according to defined schedules and dependencies.

How this works exactly is encoded in the data logistics control framework, either by convention or registration of the involved modules and batches.

The modular design of each individual data logistics process provides various options for defining orchestration. Do all tasks run as part of a large batch workflow, a hierarchy of batches, or completely independently? This modular design supports any of these options.

Whether a module runs on a set frequency as part of a broader batch or as often as possible as a stand-alone process, the design of the process itself does not change.

This feature allows for incredible flexibility in orchestration. The degree of data freshness and the latency between changes occurring in operational systems and their availability in the data solution can be considered a business requirement, which may change over time. Being able to adjust the frequency of data processing and prioritize certain data sets is invaluable in the long run.

Ideally, we aim to:
- → Process data as soon as it is available and dependencies are met
- → Achieve near real-time processing
- → Reduce individual data deltas
- → Distribute the impacts of data processing

Large workflows that run infrequently tend to process large amounts of data when they do run. Additionally, many modules need to process this data around the same time, usually before a certain deadline tied to service level agreements. If delays occur, they can become choke points for resources needed for subsequent steps, causing further delays.

As a guideline, 'staggering' the data logistics processes helps distribute the impacts and resource consumption to stay within acceptable thresholds. This is the intention behind the bullet points mentioned above.

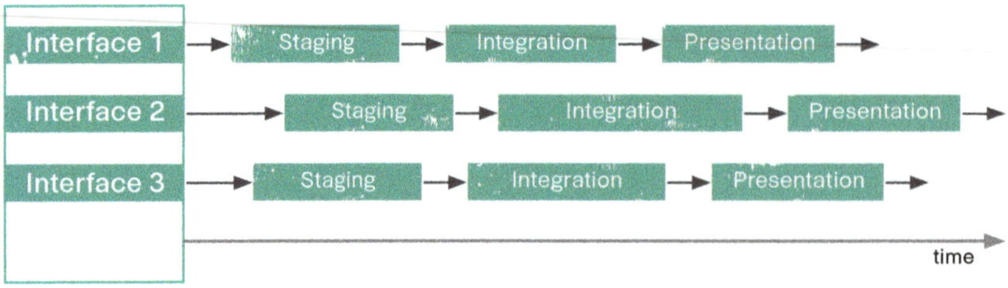

In the subsequent chapters, we will cover various considerations for orchestration, culminating in a mechanism that allows for fully independent and parallel processing applicable to every process in the architecture.

Integrity processing, for a reason

To meet the goals outlined in the introduction to integration layer orchestration, all data logistics processes should be designed without (processing) dependencies.

This approach results in an increased number of data logistics processes but offers significant flexibility and ease of maintenance. Although many of these processes may *seem* redundant, they are critical for the overall flexibility of the data solution, including orchestration and partial refactoring when the model is updated.

The key concept here is that for referencing ('child') objects, such as Satellites or Links, there *must be* a corresponding integrity mapping from the same source to the referenced ('parent') object:

- For a Satellite process, there should be a corresponding Hub (or Link, if traditional Link-Satellites are supported) integrity process for the same source data object.
- For a Link process, there should be corresponding integrity processes for all connected Hubs for the same source data object.

The intent is that referencing objects are not reliant on a 'central' list of business keys that needs to be processed prior to loading these Satellites or Links.

Some systems may contain a central 'customer' or 'product' data set that *should* include all necessary keys for these CBCs. It is theoretically possible to create a batch where the customer and product Hubs are loaded first, and subsequently process the related Satellites and/or Links, potentially from other source data objects that also have this key along with additional context.

Relying on such a central customer or product data set assumes that the system will ensure these keys are correctly propagated throughout the system. However, this assumption often proves to be incorrect. Additionally, when business keys are expected to be distributed across multiple operational systems, the timing may not align with data processing.

In both scenarios, referential integrity may not be satisfied; a Satellite might not be able to connect to its parent Hub, rendering the data unusable. Another issue with relying on central data sets is the introduction of dependencies that make refactoring more difficult. When reloading certain parts of the system, the main data sets must be processed first.

It is much easier to implement the seemingly redundant integrity processes mentioned in the introduction to this section.

Let's look at an example.

An example of seemingly redundant processing

An imaginary source data object, 'A,' contains transactions for customer placing orders.

This source data object is mapped to, and populates, the following target data objects:

→ Hub Order
→ Hub Customer
→ Link Customer Order
→ Satellite Order

A second source data object, 'B,' contains details describing the customers. It can be considered a central 'customer' table containing the main details.

This is mapped to the following target data objects:

→ Hub Customer
→ Satellite Customer

The mappings for these would like this:

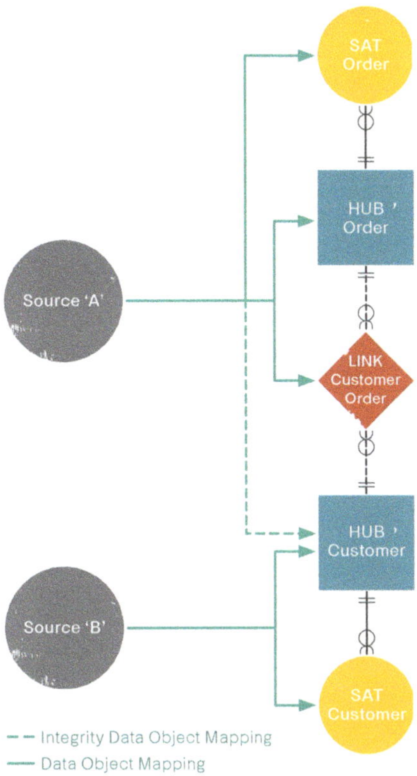

What would happen if source 'A' runs first? And what if source 'B' runs first? Let's examine each scenario.

Scenario 1: source 'A' runs first

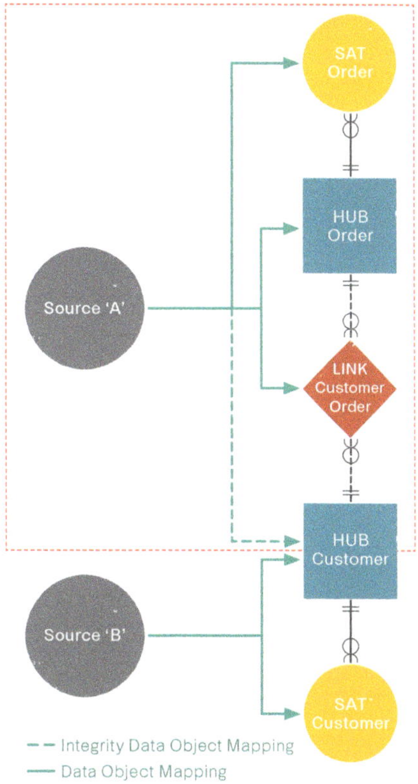

The data flowing from source 'A' into the target data objects is done via four separate mappings. If the source data object contains a data delta, these four mappings would constitute a data logistics unit of work. All four processes must finish before the data delta can be released – a concept first mentioned in the ⚐ staging layer orchestration section, which will further be covered in the ⚐ batch design section.

In this scenario, a record in the Hub Customer object is created if the customer placing an order does not yet exist. Since this record is created now, it can be connected to the order via the Link Customer Order. At this stage, nothing is known about the customer except for the business key.

When source 'B' runs, additional details for the customer might be added to the Satellite, but no new record in the Hub Customer is created because the customer entry was already created by source 'A.'

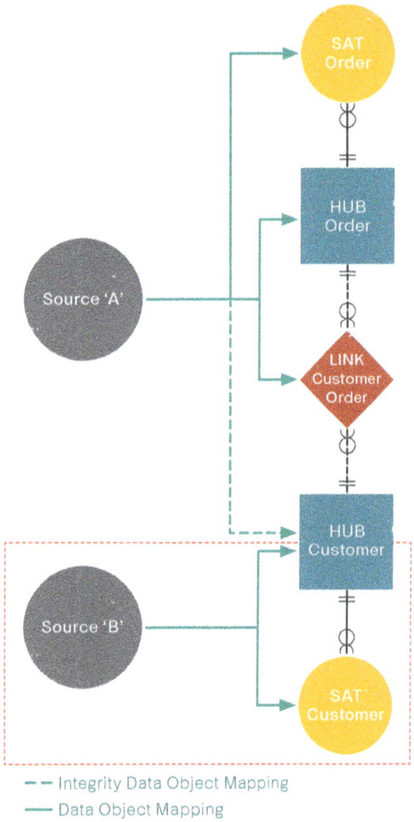

Scenario 2: source 'B' runs first

In this scenario, a customer record is created along with its descriptive properties. We know who the customer is, but not any orders this person might have placed.

That will become known when source 'A' runs. At this stage, the customer already exists as an instance in the Hub Customer. The other target data objects are updated as usual.

In both scenarios, the end result is the same. Sources 'A' and 'B' can be run in any order without causing issues. This is made possible by the seemingly redundant integrity mapping to Hub Customer for source 'A,' created by following the rule that a Satellite process should have a corresponding Hub process for the same source data object.

Processing without redundancy

Without this redundancy, the assumption would be that source 'B,' considered the main customer table, would have to be loaded first, creating a dependency between both sources.

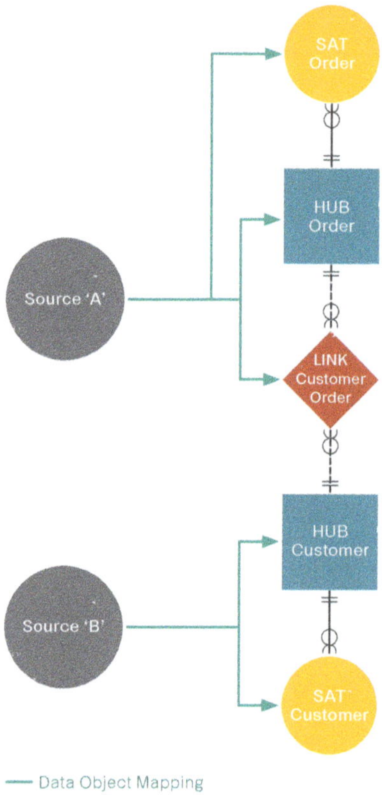

As mentioned in the introduction, assumptions such as these carry risks and generally rely on how well the operational systems manage their data internally.

For example, if there are integrity issues in the system and some orders are attributed to customers not present in the main customer table (source 'B'), data can be lost —or at least delayed— because the customer business keys are missing. The same can occur when there are delays in the deliver of certain data sets which should contain a central list of business keys.

Integrity processing ensures all data can be managed in any of these scenarios.

Batch design, dependencies, and integrity

The seemingly redundant integrity processing introduced in the previous section marks a significant step forward in reducing data logistics dependencies. However, some dependencies remain to be managed.

Building on the previous examples, a classic batch pattern that processes data directly downstream may look like this:

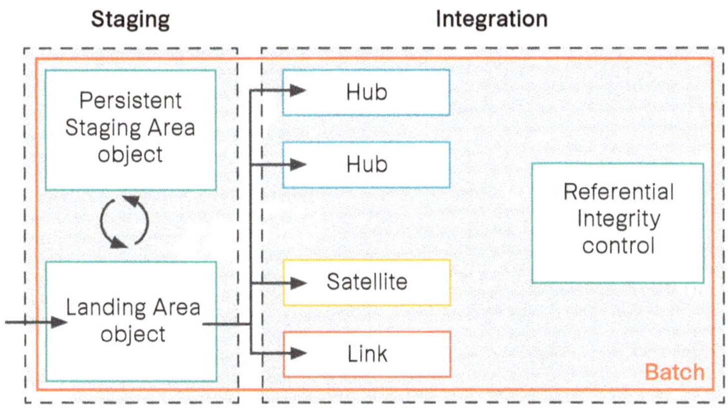

This batch pattern aligns more closely with a traditional or better safe than sorry solution architecture, where the PSA is not the source data object for the integration layer.

However, it's a convenient way to introduce lower-level dependencies and serves as an introduction to parallel processing. We will build on these concepts when we align the PSA with our reference architecture.

If a given LDA data set is mapped to two Hubs, a Satellite, and a Link, all these processes must finish before the batch can be restarted. This is safeguarded by the data logistics process control using the concepts covered in the idempotence and data logistics process transaction control section.

An optional control can be added in the from of a referential integrity check to ensure that all data is accounted for.

For example, by using logic such as:

```
SELECT
  COUNT(*) AS REFERENTIAL_INTEGRITY_ISSUES,
  'SAT_CUSTOMER'
FROM SAT_CUSTOMER sat
JOIN
(
  SELECT
    COALESCE (TRIM (CONVERT(NVARCHAR(MAX),
    CUSTOMERID)), '~!@|N/A') + '\@|' AS
    CUSTOMER_SK
  FROM [LANDING_CUSTOMER]
) Ind
  ON sat.CUSTOMER_SK = Ind..CUSTOMER_SK
LEFT JOIN HUB_CUSTOMER hub
  ON sat.CUSTOMER_SK = hub.CUSTOMER_SK
WHERE HUB.CUSTOMER_SK IS NULL
```

This control limits the referential integrity (RI) validation to the delta currently held in the landing area object. However, by removing this restriction, the control can be applied to the entire Satellite for instance as a final check after the end-to-end process.

This batch-level transaction control is one way to manage data consistency in the solution, and it applies to certain solution architecture types including the aforementioned ones. In this pattern, RI cannot be enforced by the data platform itself, but the separate RI control module will assert if RI can be satisfied after the fact — 'lazy RI.'

Using key lookups

This kind of consistency can also be safeguarded at the module level by applying key lookups. For the hash and natural business key approach, this is optional and not recommended; for an integer value, it is required.

Consider the example below. There is no separate RI control because dependencies and consistency are managed at the module level.

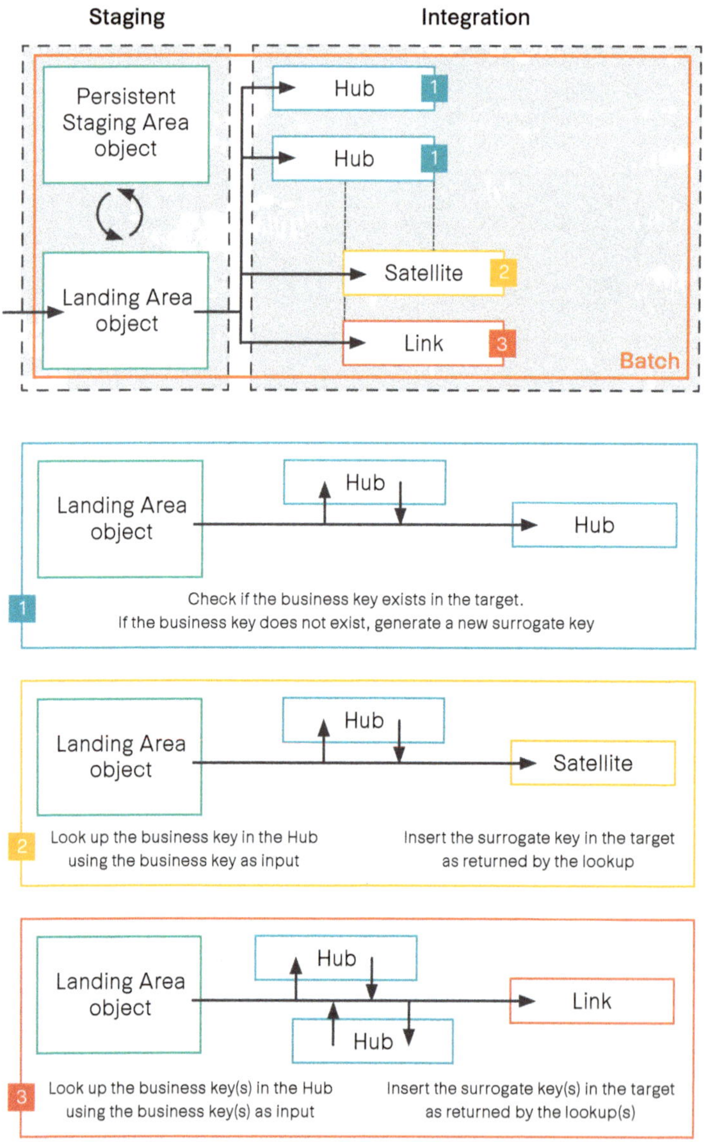

Each module performs a key lookup to retrieve the surrogate key. If this key cannot be found, it results in a technical error, causing the module to be flagged as 'failed.' Consequently, the batch process will also report a failure, ensuring that the data delta is not overwritten.

For this to work, dependencies must be defined between the modules that are part of the batch. In this example, the Hub tables need to be processed first (step '1'). Once the Hub that the Satellite relies on is completed, the Satellite module can start (step '2'). After both Hub modules are completed, the Link module can start (step '3').

As you can imagine, the need for key lookups and corresponding dependencies within the batch extends the overall loading process compared to the first example. This is one reason to consider natural business keys over integer values.

In both examples, the self-contained nature of the batch allows it to be run at any time. This design simplifies the process of changing refresh frequencies, as the scheduling can be adjusted without modifying the batch or the individual data logistics processes — the modules. This also means that each module and/or batch can run as often as possible, continuous and independent.

In the next section, we will explore what it means to remove all dependencies by aligning with our reference architecture and positioning the PSA as the source for the integration layer modules.

Continuous parallel processing

Loading all data, all the time. How does that work in practice?

This section expands on the application of RI and consistency checks covered in the ⚐ batch design, dependencies and integrity section.

The concepts outlined in this section explain how to ensure consistency and integrity in a fully independent parallel loading environment where processes run as often as possible.

State machine

To implement a fully continuous and parallel data processing approach, a mechanism is needed to that starts data logistics modules and/or batches whenever appropriate. After all, there is no set schedule when certain processes will start. Instead, each process can run again as soon as possible after it has finished, depending on various directives and the available capacity.

↗ A state machine is a service that manages a limited number of processing slots and determines which process to run based on specific directives.

A great way to manage this is a *state machine.*

A state machine is a service or daemon that manages a limited number of processing 'slots' and determines which process to run based on specific triggers or inputs. The state machine retrieves the next process to run from a queue, a list of eligible modules and/or batches that have been prioritized for certain directives.

State machine

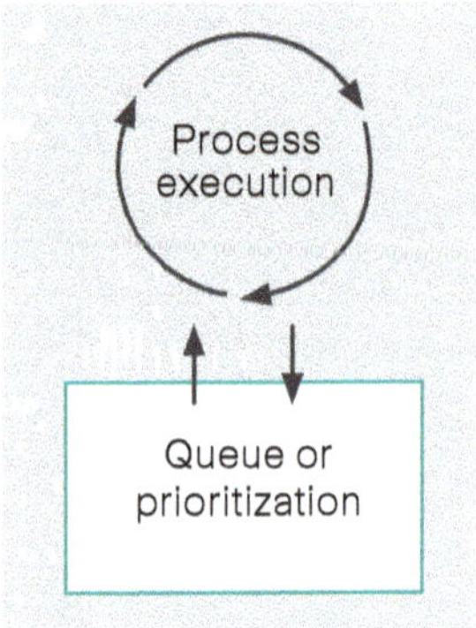

These directives are specific to each organization and technical environment. For instance, the goal can be to optimize cost, memory pressure or the delivery of data sets that are considered more important. Based on these directives, the state machine can efficiently utilize the available resources.

In this implementation, the state machine is a process that runs continuously and checks if there is an available spot free every iteration. When this is the case, the module or batch that is on the top of the prioritized queue will be run.

An example of a state machine implemented using SQL can be found on our website: https://dtng.link/995kq.

A data solution can add multiple state machines, for modules and/or batches depending on the process organization. A typical implementation has dedicated state machines for each of the main solution architecture layers; staging, integration and presentation.

Positioning the PSA

To align to the reference architecture, we position the PSA as the source for processing data into the base integration area:

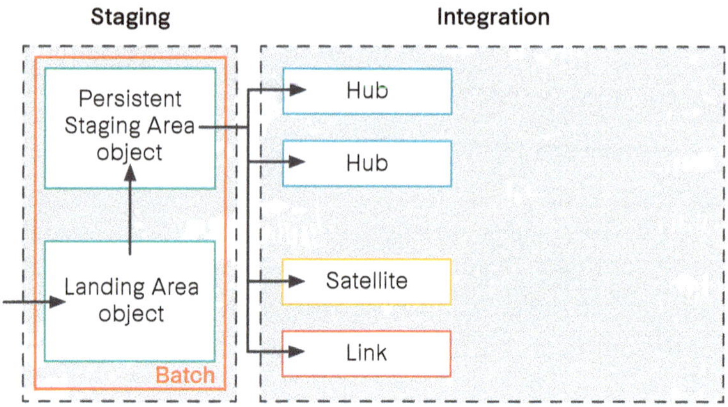

If an LDA is required (e.g., for delta detection), it should be combined in a batch process together with the PSA, as detailed in the ⚐ staging layer orchestration section. Once this batch is complete, all downstream modules can be loaded at any time, and in any order.

In this design, the staging layer batch can be configured to run frequently, even continuously, *alongside* the downstream integration layer modules.

The underlying concept is to apply *load windows,* to avoid (re)loading the entire PSA for each downstream process. A load window defines the range (time period) of data that can be selected by a given data logistics process using timestamps that mark the time period, the start and end, of the load window.

This time period is following an Open-Closed notation. For this reason, we prefer using the 'after' convention for the beginning of the time period, which is exclusive, and the inclusive 'to' convention for the end of the time period. The to timestamp of the load window sets a 'high-water mark' indicating up to which point data has been loaded.

The goal is to select all data that can be processed (including the to timestamp) while avoiding re-processing data that has already been handled (excluding the after timestamp).

When the process runs again, the 'to' from the previous load window becomes the 'after' for the new load window, and a new timestamp is determined based on the available data.

A load window set on the PSA for a particular target data object is conceptually similar to processing a data delta in a LDA object.

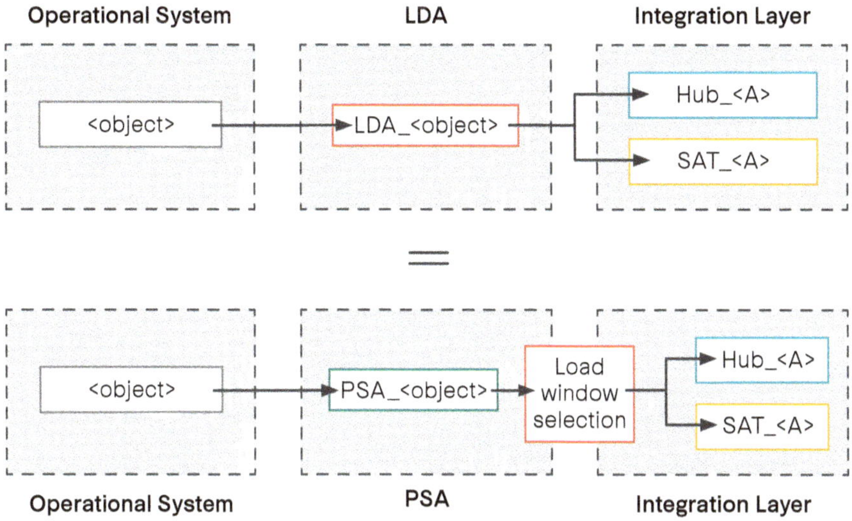

By utilizing load windows managed by individual data logistics processes, each process can operate independently and continuously. As a result, each data object mapping —such as Hubs, Links, and Satellites— manages its own load window for each source data object.

In other words, each data object mapping manages its personal load window.

Batch-based PSA design

When adopting a PSA, the batch pattern introduced in the ⚐ batch design, dependencies and integrity section can still be used. However, this updated pattern aligns more closely with our reference solution architecture while continuing to support the earlier approach — and more.

Using this pattern, the options to either perform lazy RI or key lookups remain available, depending on the selected surrogate key approach. **In line with the previous sections, this can be orchestrated as follows:**

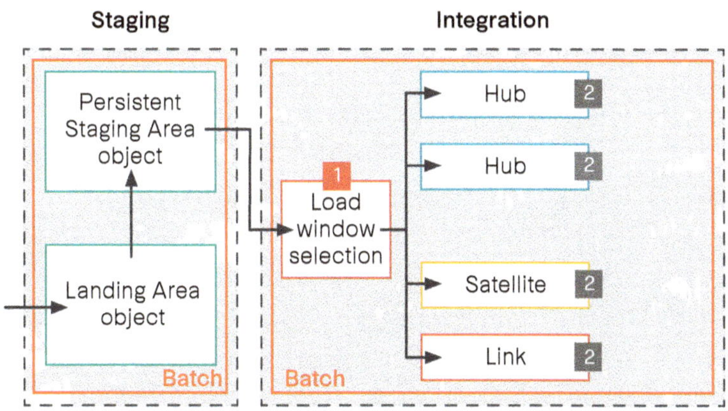

In this example, the load window conceptually replaces the landing area object. Once defined, all downstream processes must complete this data delta before the batch can be restarted.

Alternatively, RI can be asserted within the batch, sacrificing some flexibility and extending the length of the overall workflow.

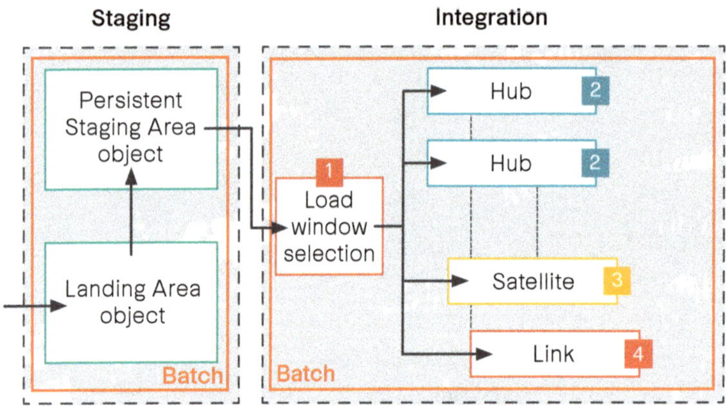

In this situation, after the load windows are established, the Hub modules must finish before their dependent objects. Once all processes are completed, the batch can be restarted.

The PSA introduces new options, as the data delta is always accessible in the PSA. As a result, the integration layer modules no longer need to be batched.

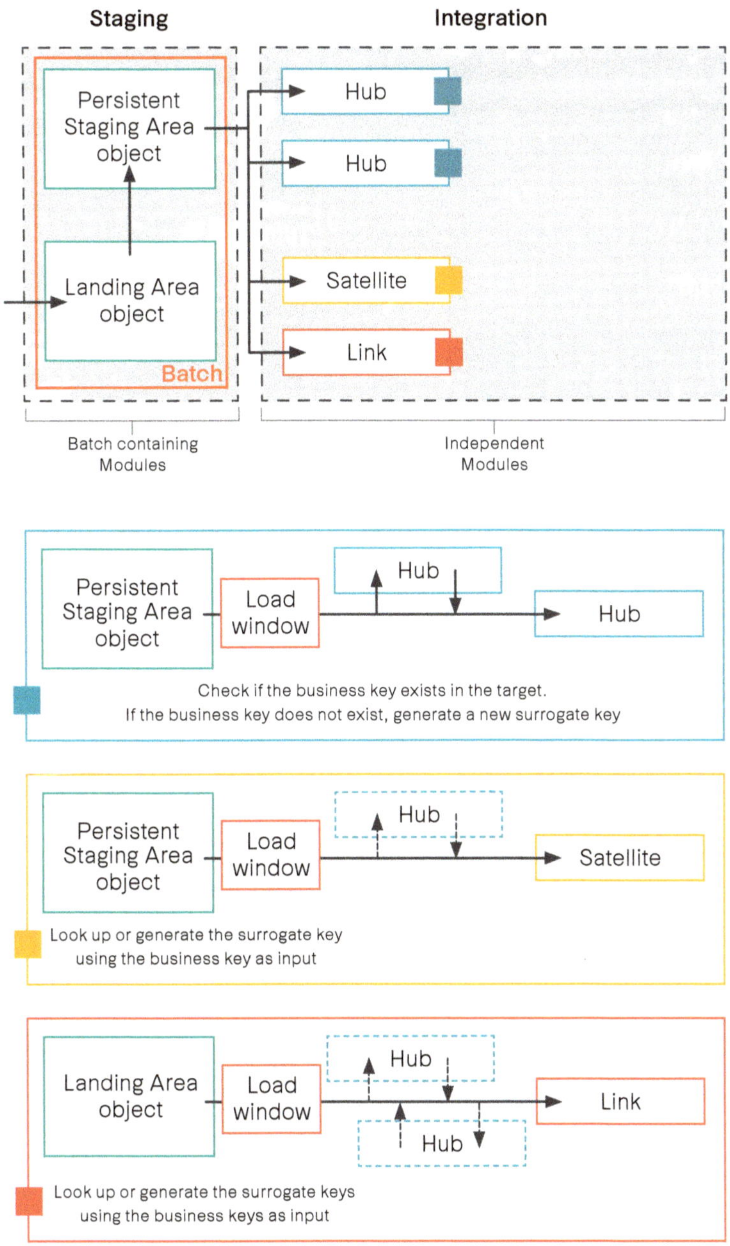

In this approach, the load window is created as part of each module, allowing them to run independently.

Creating load windows

Load windows are managed in the data logistics control framework. At the beginning of an integration layer or presentation data logistics process, a load window can be evaluated and committed to the process control object.

This central view allows the history of data selections for each individual module to be reviewed:

Load Window

Module Id	Audit Trail Id	Inscription Timestamp	Load Window After	Load Window To
7500	100	2025-01-02	1900-01-01	2025-01-02
7501	101	2025-01-03	1900-01-01	2025-01-03
7502	102	2025-01-05	1900-01-01	2025-01-05
7500	103	2025-01-06	2025-01-02	2025-01-06

Selection for module 7500

Module Id	Load Window After	Load Window To
7500	1900-01-01	2025-01-02
7500	2025-01-02	2025-01-06

The inscription timestamp values available in the PSA data objects can be used to define the load window.

Since these timestamps are issued by the data solution, they provide a reliable and sequential method to ensure there are no gaps in the selection process. It's also important to note that a default low-end value of 1900-01-01 is applied the first time a load window is created for a specific data object mapping.

Each module can then use its own most-recent load window to select the correct range from the PSA, using code such as:

```
WHERE [Inscription_Timestamp] > <LoadWindowAfter>
  AND [Inscription_Timestamp] <= <LoadWindowTo>
```

Recording the creation timestamp of a load window is often useful for additional auditability, for consistency this is also referred to as an inscription timestamp. Load windows can be created later, or even be predefined, to cover a historical range and reload certain parts of the data solution — a topic of the completing the engine chapter.

Since staging layer and integration processes can run in parallel, defining the load window requires careful consideration. Data may be written to the PSA data object while one or more downstream processes are reading from it. The control framework manages this transaction isolation, a concept referred to as application-level ACID, detailed in the idempotence and data logistics process transaction control section.

The principle is to only select records from the PSA that have been successfully committed: the load window is based solely on the inscription timestamps of records where the Audit Trail Id corresponds to a module instance with a successfully completed execution status ('Succeeded').

Records associated with a failed execution status ('Failed') should be omitted, as the framework must first address any issues.

Similarly, records associated with an executing status ('Executing') must also be ignored, as these may still fail, and loading them would constitute a 'dirty read.' Once issues are resolved, or the process has completed successfully, the records associated with these Audit Trail Ids will be incorporated into the load window next time the module runs.

The following example illustrates how the control framework guarantees this transaction control:

Module Instance

Audit Trail Id	Module Id	Start Timestamp	Execution Status
1	7500	2025-01-02	Succeeded
2	7500	2025-01-03	Succeeded
3	7500	2025-01-05	Failed
4	7500	2025-01-06	Executing

Load Window

Audit Trail Id	Module Id	Inscription Timestamp	Load Window After	Load Window To
5	7599	2025-01-05	1900-01-01 00:00	2025-01-03 00:02
6	7599	2025-01-06	2025-01-03 00:02	2025-01-03 00:02

PSA data object

Audit Trail Id	Inscription Timestamp	Payload columns
1	2025-01-02 00:00	<>
1	2025-01-02 00:02	<>
2	2025-01-03 00:01	<>
2	2025-01-03 00:02	<>
3	2025-01-05 00:01	<>
4	2025-01-06 00:01	<>

This diagram shows a PSA data object that has been gradually be populated over multiple module executions. When records are inserted, the inscription timestamp is set as usual.

After examining the control framework, we know that the executions associated with Audit Trail Id 1 and 2 have been successful. However, Audit Trail Id 3 reports an error. Some, or perhaps all, records have already been written to the PSA object.

The module with Audit Trail Id 4 is still executing. This module instance recovers the failure of instance with Audit Trail Id 3, and completes the process when it finishes.

When downstream processes create their load window, they can use this information to determine up to what inscription timestamp data is safe to process from this particular PSA object. In this example, a sample downstream process run twice – with Audit Trail Ids 5 and 6.

The first time the downstream module runs (Audit Trail Id 5), a new load window is created up to the point of the last successfully completed PSA module instance, selecting the maximum inscription timestamp associated with this Audit Trail Id 2.

The second time (Audit Trail Id 6), the underlying PSA process is still running, so there is no new data to process yet. The load window is created with a 'after' and 'to' timestamp that is the same, indicating that the process has run, but that there was no data ready to be selected.

How many records are part of the load window depends on the execution frequency of the downstream processes. The more they run, the smaller the load windows are and the fewer records are processed each time. If they don't run for a while, they will catch up by selecting more records using a broader load window.

This allow for incredible flexibility in the scheduling of data logistics processes, fully optimizing resources for various directives.

Interpreting load windows

Over time, a history of load windows is built up that can be queried from the control framework.

For example, let's assume a PSA data object is mapped to three downstream integration layer objects:

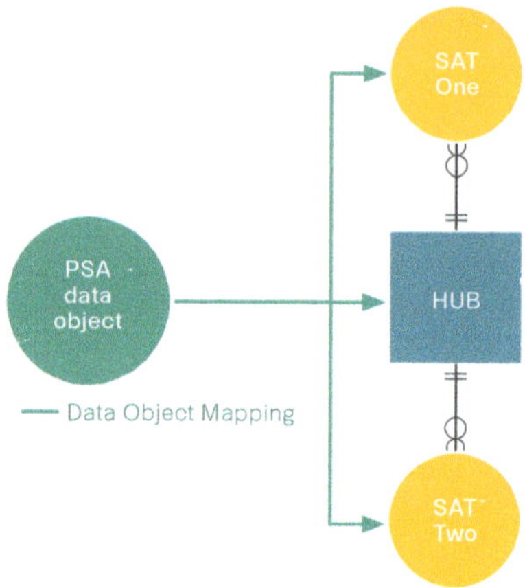

In this scenario, all four involved objects are populated by processes that run independently. Because of this, there is no set schedule for when they run, and some might run more than others.

When reviewing the history of load windows, the result might look like this:

Load Window

Audit Trail Id	Module	Inscription Timestamp	Load Window After	Load Window To
10101	Hub	2025-01-01 12:00	1900-01-01 00:00	2025-01-01 11:10
10202	Satellite 1	2025-02-01 16:00	1900-01-01 00:00	2025-02-01 15:05
10303	Satellite 2	2025-03-01 15:05	1900-01-01 00:00	2025-03-01 15:01
10404	Hub	2025-02-01 19:00	2025-01-01 11:10	2025-02-01 18:05
10505	Satellite 1	2025-03-01 15:15	2025-02-01 15:05	2025-03-01 15:09
10606	Hub	2025-03-01 15:15	2025-02-01 18:05	2025-03-01 15:09
10707	Satellite 2	2025-03-01 18:00	2025-03-01 15:01	2025-03-01 17:45
10808	Satellite 1	2025-05-01 12:00	2025-03-01 15:09	2025-05-01 10:02
10909	Hub	2025-05-01 13:00	2025-03-01 15:09	2025-05-01 10:02
101010	Satellite 2	2025-05-01 13:30	2025-03-01 17:45	2025-05-03 10:02

PSA data object

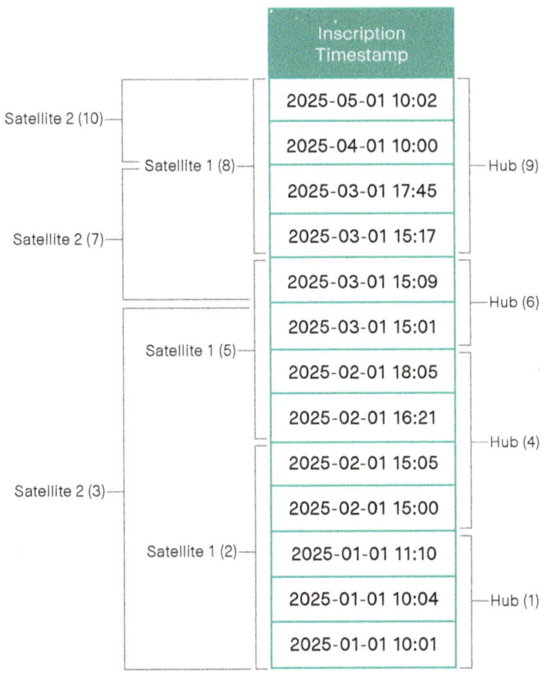

The regular PSA columns have been omitted for brevity, as only the inscription timestamp is relevant for this example since it's used to determine the load window. For the sake of this example, all data logistics process executions have been successful.

The diagram on the left illustrates the selections from the perspective of the PSA, while the table on the right displays the load windows as queried from the control framework.

Running modules without dependencies like this requires careful attention to ensure that referential integrity can be maintained at specific points in time. In the example above, some records processed by the Satellite 1 module (Audit Trail Id 10202) may not yet be available in the parent Hub. Once the Hub module (Audit Trail Id 10404) processes, referential integrity can be re-established for all records that were processed by the Satellite 1 module (Audit Trail Id 10202).

How this can be managed is the topic of the eventual consistency section.

Eventual consistency

In the previous sections, we discussed how there are moments when RI cannot be enforced for certain objects. In a fully continuous and parallel environment, these kinds of 'leap-frogging' effects are common.

The further the module executions are in the past, the greater the chance that RI is in order. However, the closer to the present we get, the likelihood of inconsistencies increases. Despite this, we can be confident that, over time, the data will again become consistent.

Therefore, caution should be exercised when querying the integration layer data in a continuous parallel data processing approach so that only consistent data is selected.

A straightforward algorithm can be used to determine the *consistency timestamp,* the point in time when it is certain that the data from the various involved objects can be safely combined. This timestamp is closely tied to the frequency of data processing. The more often processes run, the closer the consistency timestamp is to the present. Conversely, if processes run less often, there will be a larger gap between the consistency timestamp and the present.

This gap between the time data can be safely consumed, the consistency timestamp, and the present is the *latency.* It is an indicator for data freshness and processing uptime, and can be a powerful metric for data consumers.

In practical terms, the consistency timestamp is used as a filter criterion for downstream data selection, ensuring that incomplete data is not exposed.

Let's explore how this works in the next section.

Deriving the consistency timestamp

In a large and complex data solution that supports parallel continuous processing, many processes are likely to run multiple times, often in parallel, and in no particular order.

In practice, this means that —for instance— a Satellite process may execute several times before the corresponding Hub data is processed. RI will only be satisfied once the Hub data catches up.

However, the situation is more nuanced. In the previous example, the Hub might have a load window that extends *further* than the most recent load windows of the multiple Satellite runs. Therefore, we must consider these load windows together to accurately determine when RI can be asserted.

To illustrate, consider the example below, which involves one Hub and two Satellites required for a specific data delivery. For clarity, the timestamps and processing are represented as days instead of timestamps.

Load Window

Audit Trail Id	Module	Inscription Timestamp	Load Window After	Load Window To
10101	Hub	2025-01-02	1900-01-01	2025-01-02
10202	Satellite 1	2025-01-03	1900-01-01	2025-01-03
10303	Satellite 2	2025-01-05	1900-01-01	2025-01-05
10404	Hub	2025-01-06	2025-01-02	2025-01-06
10505	Satellite 1	2025-01-07	2025-01-03	2025-01-07
10606	Hub	2025-01-10	2025-01-06	2025-01-10
10707	Satellite 2	2025-01-11	2025-01-05	2025-01-11
10808	Satellite 1	2025-01-14	2025-01-07	2025-01-14
10909	Hub	2025-01-14	2025-01-10	2025-01-14
101010	Satellite 2	2025-01-14	2025-01-11	2025-01-14

Looking at this data, we review this history of events from today's perspective.

As of 2025-01-14, all processes are caught up, and all available data in the PSA has been processed into the Hub and Satellites. However, during the processing of each individual load window, only the data that was ready in the PSA at that time would have been considered.

The load windows, which represent the available data delta, are based on the inscription timestamps in the PSA. For process 1 (the process numbers corresponds with the 'Audit Trail Id' in the load window table), this means that on 2025-01-02, the Hub process ingested all available data up to that date.

When the first Satellite runs a day later, on 2025-01-03 as process 2, additional data is available in the PSA, so data up to 2025-01-03 is loaded for the Satellite. When the second Satellite runs, as process 3, it processes this and additional data that has since become available in the PSA — up to 2025-01-05.

At this point, RI cannot be satisfied for Satellite records with an inscription timestamp later than 2025-01-02.

This scenario can be visualized in a way that better illustrates these gaps and overlaps:

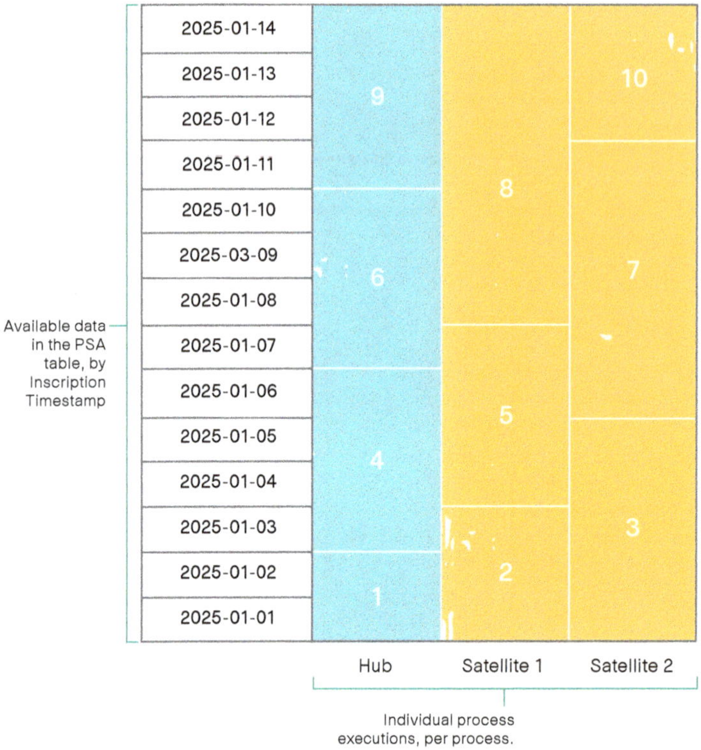

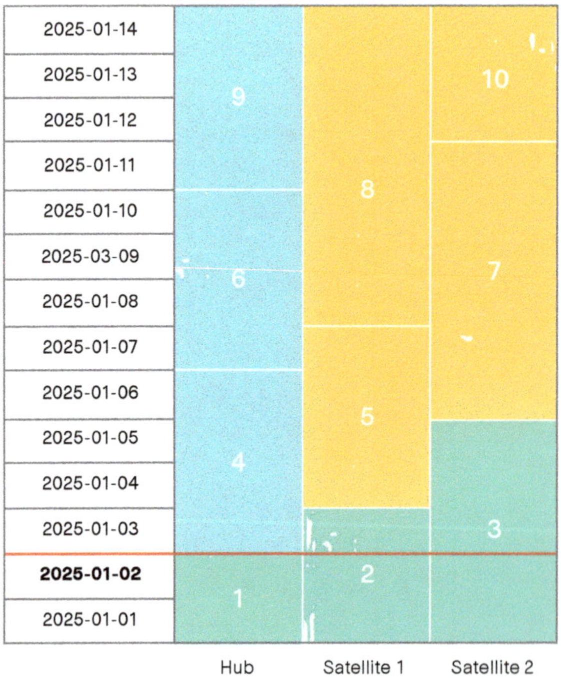

This visual helps identify the point up to which RI can be asserted. When processes 1, 2, and 3 have successfully completed, the data is consistent up to the inscription timestamp of 2025-01-02. Beyond this point, there are no corresponding values in the Hub yet, because it has run only once so far.

Since the inscription timestamp values from the PSA are propagated to the integration layer objects, we can use these to filter out any records with timestamps later than 2025-01-02 when joining these tables.

Remember, we're viewing this history from today's perspective. At the point in time when process 3 completed, the subsequent processes *had not yet run,* so we must exclude them from our evaluation.

Now, let's say we want to calculate the consistency timestamp for a specific date, such as 2025-01-09. At this point, processes 6, 8, and 7 are still running and therefore cannot be used to assert RI. This is because data can only be considered valid when it has been fully committed by the control framework. Only data associated with a successfully completed process, as indicated by the Audit Trail Id, can be safely selected. Additionally, processes 9 and 10 haven't run as of yet, while processes 1 to 5 have been completed.

To find the answer, we need to identify which processes have been successfully completed and the data deltas associated with these processes – the load windows. By understanding these load windows, we can determine the most recent point in time when there was overlap, indicating potential consistency.

We're not interested in processes that had earlier successful runs relative to the measurement date (2025-01-09); instead, we focus on the most recent ones. This means we can exclude execution instances 1 and 2, as they were superseded by more recent completions, processes 4 and 5, respectively.

To determine the most recent point of overlap, we need to understand the latest successful executions for the involved objects. The most recent overlap point is determined by the *end* of the load window from the process that completed *first,* as the other load windows might capture more data, simply because they have started later and there might be new data in the PSA to process.

This is illustrated in the following diagram:

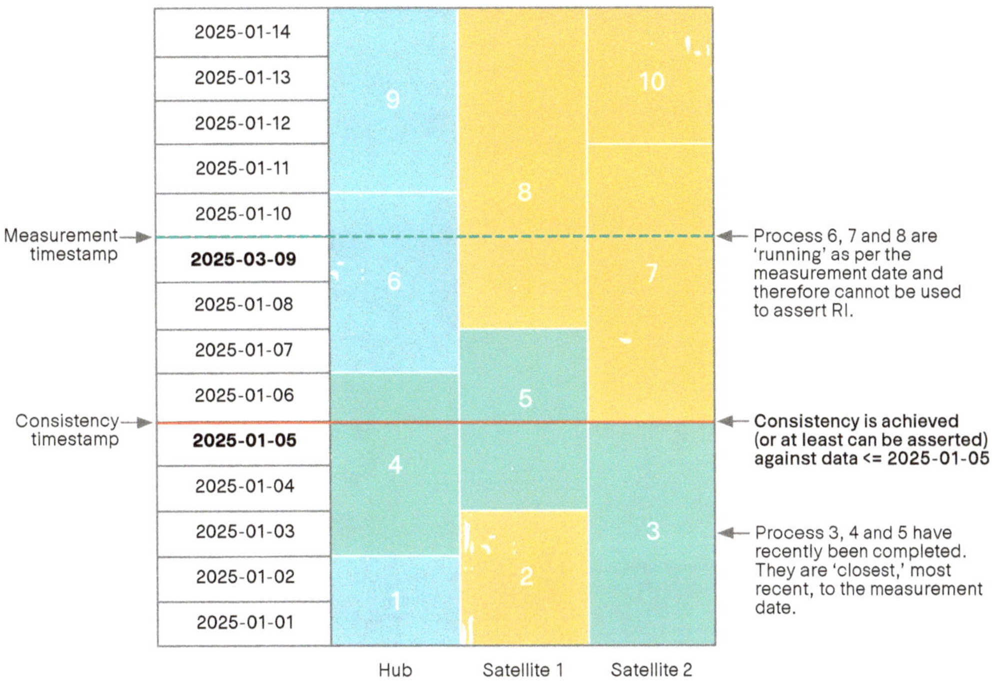

The diagram shows that if we measure at 2025-01-09, the most recent successful executions are processes 3, 4, and 5, with the minimum load window before this timestamp being 2025-01-05. We should only select data from the involved objects with timestamps smaller than or equal to this date, as any later data is not yet consistent.

To summarize, the following steps can be used to determine the point in time when RI can be assessed:

1) Using a measurement timestamp as input, retrieve the most recent successfully completed processes relative to this timestamp
2) Select the minimum (lowest) load window to timestamp from the result of the previous step. This value is the consistency timestamp

In other words, for a given point in time data will be consistent up to the lowest load window before timestamp of the most recently successfully completed process instance involved with the target data objects.

Using the consistency timestamp, we can filter out any data that does not yet satisfy RI before providing it to downstream consumers. Over time, the environment will eventually become consistent, and the consistency timestamp (an inscription timestamp) can act as a load window for downstream processes.

For practical examples of how this can be implemented, please refer to our website: https://dtng.link/995kq.

In practice, the measurement timestamp is typically 'now' as data is often pushed to downstream targets as soon as it is received. However, this logic applies equally well to both current and historical timestamps.

Returning to the example, the same visual can illustrate the lagging effect of the consistency timestamp, or latency, over time:

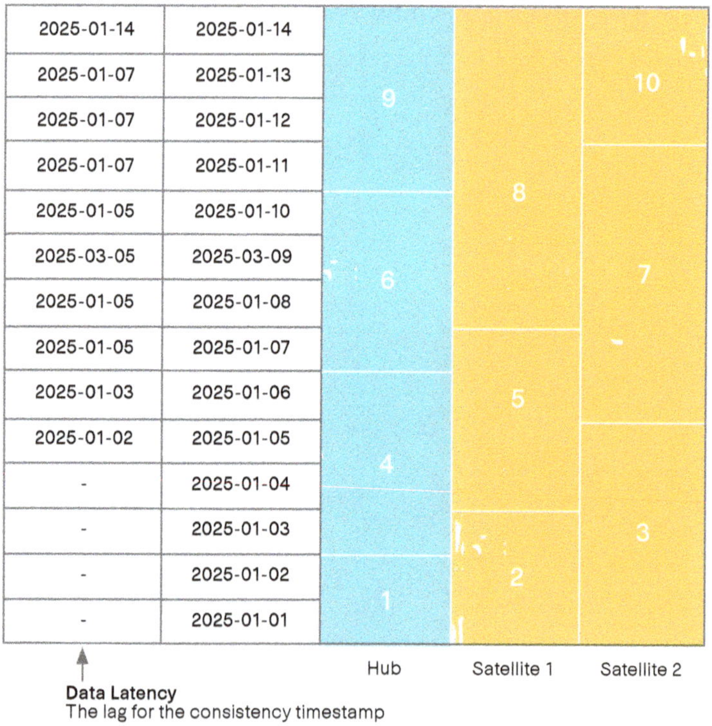

The latency, derived from the consistency timestamp, determines up to what point in time data can be selected. The acceptable size of this latency —whether a day or a minute— is essentially a business requirement. Adopting parallel and continuous processing allows the data platform to be flexible in delivering data, but determining whether a specific latency is acceptable depends on a discussion between requirements and available resources. This is the topic of the next section.

Moving closer to the Engine

The consistency timestamp is influenced by the scope of objects involved in a data delivery. Fewer objects lead to smaller latency, while adding more objects increases latency. This mechanism can be a powerful tool for prioritizing data processing, helping to manage competing priorities within an organization.

For instance, if a particular data mart is deemed more important, the data logistics processes supporting it can be prioritized by the state machine, running more frequently. This prioritization reduces latency for that specific data delivery, though likely at the expense of others. Due to the limited capacity of the state machine, other processes may run less frequently as a result.

In some ways, this mimics the complexities of managing scarce resources that exist almost everywhere. The team responsible for operating the data solution must continually optimize limited resources, whether processing capacity, memory, space, or cost. Decisions about resource utilization must be made effectively, as they are always constrained.

Having a mechanism like the consistency timestamp aids in these discussions. Ultimately, the data solution serves the business and aligns with its vision and strategy. Deciding which data set should take priority can be made a business decision based on priorities, rather than a purely technical one made by the data team.

This ability to prioritize is one of the main benefits of a parallel and continuous orchestration approach. Achieving the same level of flexibility with a large 'main' or 'daily' workflow is much more challenging.

There are many other benefits, including (but not limited to):

- → Data can be processed soon after it is made available, keeping the data deltas small and reducing processing time
- → Data can be provided near real-time or at any desired frequency by adjusting prioritization or the speed at which the state machine cycles through the processes, simplifying orchestration management
- → Resources can be used more effectively by spreading out processing, avoiding peaks in resource consumption.
- → The absence of dependencies in processing significantly simplifies the overall management of the data solution.
- → The priority of individual processes, or groups of processes required for certain deliveries, can be adjusted on the fly. For example, if a single process is dragging down latency, it can be configured to run more frequently.

In the full implementation, all layers of the data solution run continuously, in parallel:

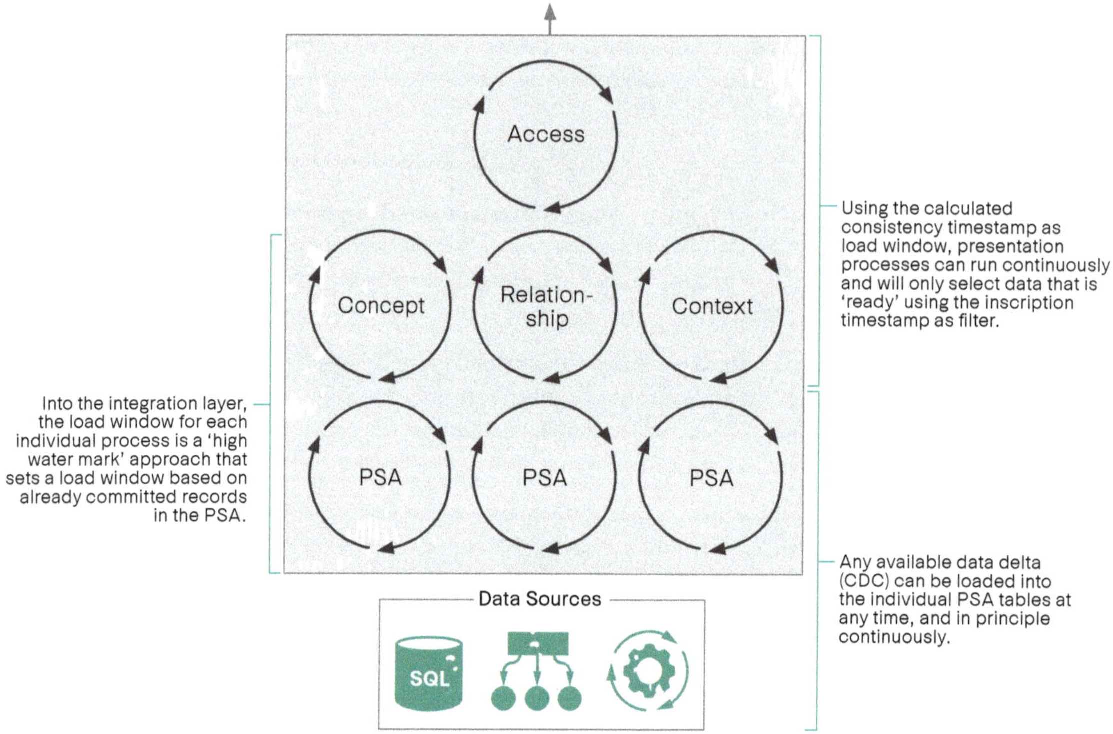

For Engine Thinking, this approach is a powerful. Instead of waiting for all downstream processes to complete before maintaining data deltas, each process can execute in any order as directed by the state machine. Additionally, when parts of the solution are refactored, they are immediately rebuilt in their new form as soon as the state machine picks them up.

Prioritization can be based on any set of parameters or system metrics, moving the solution closer to a self-optimizing configuration.

Race conditions

↗ A race conditions occurs when at least two processes, or threads, attempt to access the same resource at the same time.

A *race condition* is a term that is most commonly associated with computer science and coding. A race conditions occurs when at least two processes, or threads, attempt to access the same resource at the same time – causing problems in the system. Race conditions are a common issue for multi-threaded applications.

The data solution, as per our reference architecture, is a form of a multi-threaded application, and race conditions can occur here too.

By far the most occurrences of race conditions relate to Hub and Link processes. These are the integration points of the data solution, and often many data logistics processes write to some of the Hubs and Links.

For instance, if two processes start around the same time targeting the same Hub —one from a source data object and the other from a different one— they may both simultaneously check for the existence of a business key in the Hub. If both processes find that the business key does not yet exist, they might both attempt to insert it. This can lead to primary key violation issues (if enforced) or duplicate records (if not enforced).

These kinds of issues can be puzzling at first. After all, if the impacted process restarts chances are that it *will* run successfully. This time, the lookup will detect the business key so the process will not attempt to insert it, and complete successfully.

Having a restart or retry feature in the control framework or scheduling might 'fix' this, but a better approach is to prevent this issue from happening at all.

There are various solutions for this, including:
1) Implement data logistics dependencies
2) Combining data logistics processes for the same target
3) Detect and avoid potential conflicts
4) Semaphores

Implementing dependencies

Race conditions can be easily predicted. Whenever one or more data logistics processes involve the same target data object, there is a risk of race conditions unless these processes are configured to never run simultaneously. A straightforward way to avoid these issues is to ensure that processes targeting the same data object are never executed at the same time.

In many data solutions, a 'batch' style orchestration loads multiple, or even all, Hubs and Links in sequence. In such cases, race conditions do not occur. However, the obvious downside is that the overall refresh of the data solution is limited. Completing a cycle takes longer when some or all processes run sequentially.

While this is a tried-and-tested approach, we believe it is not the best one.

Combining data logistics

Another alternative is to change the technical delivery of the data logistics processes. Instead of running separate modules for each source data object targeting the same target data object, the process code can be generated as a single process where all source data objects are combined.

This means that instead of having many modules targeting a Hub or Link, there will be one module that contains all mapped source data objects. Technically, this can be implemented using a UNION statement or similar approach.

The downside of this approach is some inflexibility and delays in scheduling. To load a single data delta for one of the source data objects, all of them must be processed.

However, in certain technical environments, this can be beneficial, especially if extensive caching is involved to support the key lookups.

Another consideration is deployment. When source data objects are processed in separate modules, adding, changing, or removing a data logistics process does not impact other modules. However, if a single combined module is used, any modification will affect the entire module, potentially requiring additional testing overhead to proceed through the deployment process.

Detect and avoid

Another alternative for managing race conditions is to detect the potential occurrence of two data logistics processes targeting the same data object simultaneously. This particularly applies to the ⚐ state machine orchestration paradigm, where no dependencies are applied. In this case, each process can run in any order, depending on priority and available resources.

The order of processing can account for this by de-prioritizing modules with the same target data object automatically when there is a risk of them running simultaneously.

For example, using code such as:

```
ROW_NUMBER() OVER
  (PARTITION BY MODULE.DATA_OBJECT_TARGET
  ORDER BY CASE COALESCE(EXECUTION_STATUS_CODE,'S')
      WHEN 'E' THEN 1
      ELSE 2 END, END_DATETIME) AS BY_DATA_STORE
WHERE BY_DATA_STORE = 1
```

This is an elegant way to prevent race conditions in an environment that is fully parallel-loaded.

Semaphore

A final, but certainly not the least, alternative for managing race conditions is to implement a semaphore. This approach can apply to any orchestration approach, but like the 'detect and avoid' approach is applied best in situations where there are little or no dependencies.

In this implementation, each module writes a semaphore for its target data object in a dedicated semaphore object. Other modules check this semaphore object to see if their target data object is currently in use by any module. If it is, the control framework will postpone the module until the semaphore is released. Once the semaphore is released, the module execution begins immediately.

Joining objects in the PSA

While the integration layer is typically the preferred place for complex joins, there are scenarios where performing them upstream, in the staging layer, may be a practical solution.

In an ideal world, we would recommend against joining tables in the staging layer because this involves bringing forward complexities and considerations that are usually best addressed in the integration layer.

However, in certain situations, staging layer joins can simplify downstream processes, making them a valid approach worth considering. We should not entirely discard this pattern either.

A common use case arises when specific data items must be linked to a downstream object, but the necessary identifier (business key) is not directly available. The business key may exist in another object that can be accessed via foreign key references.

In simple terms, the business key and required context are scattered across several tables connected by foreign key relationships.

When joining data in the staging layer, it should *always* be done using PSA data objects, as they provide the full historical context needed to ensure correct joins. The landing area, being transient, is unsuitable for this purpose, as its tables may be empty at any given time.

In all cases, it's recommended to avoid introducing business logic or transformations that alter the nature of the data. The goal of the staging layer is to accurately ingest and historize raw data, leaving any interpretation or transformation for the integration and presentation layers.

Customer, Category, Category Group

To illustrate how the pattern for joining PSA objects works, consider the following scenario:

→ A customer must be assigned to a category, and
→ A category may contain many customers
→ Every category must belong to a category group, a category group may cover many categories

In this example, you might want to define the category and category group names as direct descriptive properties of a 'Customer' CBC. The category and category group could be a classification of the customer, and it may not be required to define these as separate CBCs and corresponding relationships.

In this case we can consider joining the PSA tables to produce a single result set for easier downstream processing.

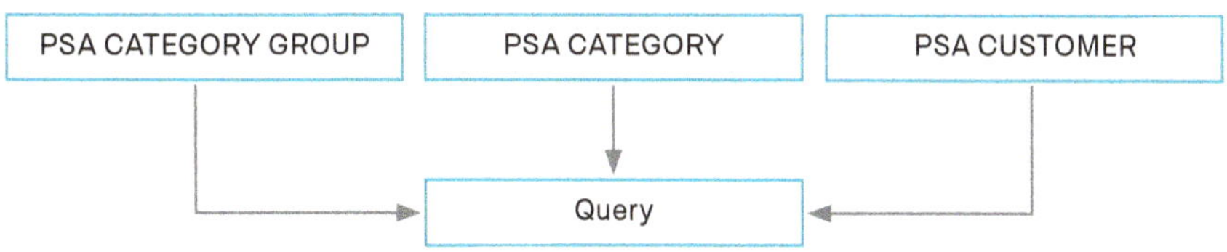

The key to this pattern is acknowledging that all three tables may experience data changes at different times and rates. For example, the category group name might be updated, but this change doesn't directly affect the category or customer tables. The update only applies to the category group table, as foreign key values in the referenced tables remain unchanged.

However, this change does impact the result when all three tables are joined together.

Each table may receive updates at different intervals, so the join query must account for these combined changes across all involved tables. In this example, though, we are primarily interested in changes from the customer's perspective.

We don't need to include categories or category groups that aren't referenced by any customer since the goal is to add customer context to the Customer CBC.

This consideration drives the approach for joining the tables, as shown in the diagram below.

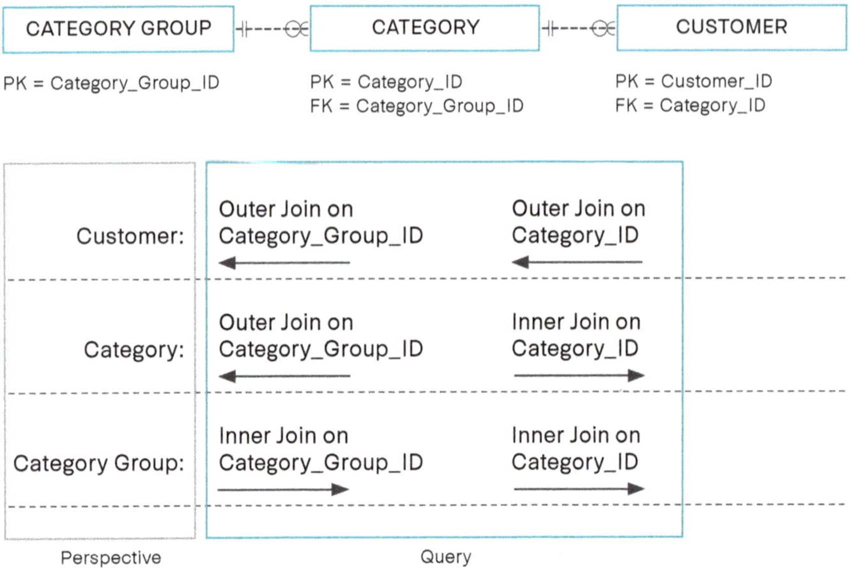

To capture the combined changes across all tables, we start from each table and join the others. In this scenario, three separate queries are required, each starting from a different table's perspective.

Using the customer table as starting point, the category can be outer-joined directly from the customer table. After this, the category group can be outer-joined via the category table. Both joins are outer joins because we don't want to 'lose' customer records because the category or category group is not (yet) available. This should not be possible according to the original Entity-Relationship diagram, but we also have to consider the data logistic intervals. Some data may not yet be loaded.

When starting from the perspective of the category table, the customer table can be inner-joined. This is because we are only interested in categories that are associated to customers. The join to the category group is an outer join again, since we don't want to miss out on customer/category records that do not happen to have a category group yet.

Lastly, the category group starting point inner-joins to the other table. Only categories and customers that are referenced are of interest.

Each of these queries provides a subset of relevant changes. Hence, the combined result set (union) of these three queries will provide the final result.

How to join in the PSA

When joining time-variant (historized) tables, such as those in the PSA, it's essential to account for the 'time' element. Each PSA record represents a version of the data as it existed at a specific point in time, ordered by the inscription timestamp. However, the inscription timestamp is a technical value used to track when the data became available to the solution for auditing purposes. As such, it is not the best candidate for joining data.

Instead, the key to accurate joins is aligning data based on the moment it was valid, which is often more relevant than when it was ingested. Many data sets include their own validity periods, which are the values expected by data consumers – the state timeline.

This introduces challenges when joining tables in the PSA, as you must join them using the appropriate timeline, effectively bringing forward complexities typically addressed in the integration layer, as we've covered in the ⚐ struggling with time section.

Not only is the state timeline not fully prepared yet, it potentially exposes the solution to data quality issues (e.g., overlaps, gaps, duplications) caused by inconsistent timestamp values.

These challenges are not insurmountable, but must be adequately considered and investigated.

Let's look at an example involving two of the three tables from the previous scenario. The inputs for the join are the customer and category tables. For both objects the 'from' and 'before' values for the state timestamp are provided, following the Open-Closed notation.

PSA Customer

Inscription Timestamp	State From Timestamp	State Before Tmestamp	Customer ID	Favorite Color	Category ID
2023-01-24	2023-01-22	2025-03-29	100	Yellow	A
2023-03-30	2023-03-29	2023-06-22	100	Orange	A
2023-06-22	2023-06-22	9999-12-31	100	Purple	A

PSA Category

Inscription Timestamp	State From Timestamp	State Before Tmestamp	Category ID	Category Name
2018-01-01	2018-01-01	2020-01-01	A	First Category Name
2020-01-01	2020-01-01	2023-02-01	A	Second Category Name
2023-02-01	2023-02-01	2024-01-01	A	Third Category Name
2024-01-01	2024-01-01	9999-12-31	A	Fourth Category Name

To correctly join the tables at their shared points in time, we use the date range provided by the state timeline for the correct point-in-time join.

Following this pattern, each table is queried separately. The final result is the union of these queries, capturing relevant changes from both the customer and category perspectives.

An example of this pattern is provided below:

```
-- Customer perspective
SELECT
 Customer.InscriptionTimestamp
,Customer.StateFromTimestamp
,Customer.CustomerId
,Customer.FavouriteColour
,Category.CategoryId
,Category.CategoryName
FROM Customer
LEFT JOIN
(
 SELECT
   StateFromTimestamp
  ,StateBeforeTimestamp
  ,*
 FROM Category
) Category
 ON Customer.CategoryId = Category.CategoryId
AND Customer.StateFromTimestamp >= Category.StateFromTimestamp
AND Customer.StateFromTimestamp < Category.StateBeforeTimestamp

UNION ALL

-- Category perspective
SELECT
 Category.InscriptionTimestamp
,Category.StateFromTimestamp
,Customer.CustomerId
,Customer.FavouriteColour
,Category.CategoryId
,Category.CategoryName
FROM Category
INNER JOIN
(
 SELECT
   StateFromTimestamp
  ,StateBeforeTimestamp
  ,*
 FROM Customer
) Customer
ON Category.CategoryId = Customer.CategoryId
AND Category.StateFromTimestamp >= Customer.StateFromTimestamp
AND Category.StateFromTimestamp < Customer.StateBeforeTimestamp
```

Applying this, or similar patterns, results in this data set:

Combined Data Set

Inscription Timestamp	State From Timestamp	State Before Tmestamp	Favorite Color	Category ID	Category Name
2023-01-22	2023-01-22	2023-02-01	Yellow	A	Second Category Name
2023-02-01	2023-02-01	2023-03-29	Yellow	A	Third Category Name
2023-03-29	2023-03-29	2023-06-22	Orange	A	Third Category Name
2023-06-22	2023-06-22	2024-01-01	Purple	A	Third Category Name
2024-01-01	2024-01-01	9999-12-31	Purple	A	Fourth Category Name

Records driven by changes in 'Customer'

Records driven by changes in 'Category'

The evaluation of the state before timestamp in the resulting data set is not included in the query example for brevity, but can be derived using the various approaches covered in the ⚐ struggling with time section.

What would happen when adding the customer group to the SQL code? This would require a third query to be *unioned* with the others, this time from the category group perspective, and so on.

For additional practical examples of how this pattern can be implemented, please refer to our website: https://dtng.link/8cfug.

Alternative solutions

There are always multiple ways to implement a workable solution. This particular use case —the absence of the desired business key in the necessary table— can also be addressed in the integration layer using *alternative approaches,* such as the ELM 'Bag of Keys' or Data Vault 'Key Satellite' concepts.

Each approach, as is often the case, comes with its own advantages and trade-offs. Solving this in the integration layer using one of the aforementioned methods introduces additional complexity related to key lookups, automation challenges, and data loading dependencies. On the other hand, generating PSA join queries is relatively straightforward using simple metadata — but only once the appropriate timeline for joining has been established.

Working with alternate business keys

In the previous section, we discussed using joins in the staging layer to retrieve data items from different objects. This approach is often used to obtain a business key that is missing from one of the data sets, but is necessary to link to a Hub.

An alternative to performing joins in the staging layer is using an ELM 'Bag of Keys' (BOK), also known as a Data Vault 'Key Satellite'. We will use the more generic ELM term BOK to describe these concepts.

In this approach, a dedicated Satellite is defined to store all the business key candidates, as covered in the section on ⚐ storing the business key in Satellites.

A typical implementation is illustrated in the diagram below:

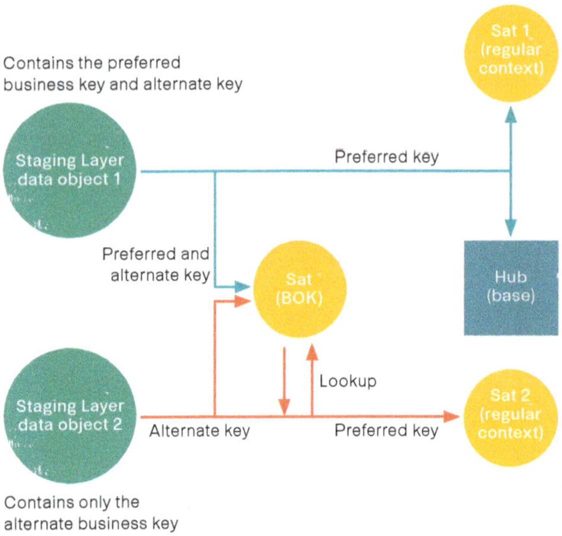

In this example, the first staging layer object contains both the preferred business key values and a different, alternate, version of the key, which could be a system-specific internal sequence value. This alternate key can be related back to the preferred business key through a foreign key reference. The second staging layer object only contains this alternate business key.

Only the preferred business key values are processed into the Hub, and the Satellite mapped to the first staging layer object can be processed directly. However, because the second staging layer object does not contain the preferred key, it cannot directly connect the Satellite to the Hub. To resolve this, the first object provides both key alternatives to a dedicated BOK Satellite. The second object then uses the BOK Satellite as a lookup to retrieve the preferred business key, using the alternate key as input.

Because of this dependency, there is no need to map the second staging layer object to the Hub – the possible values are restricted by the data provided by the first object.

A downside of this approach is that it introduces data processing dependencies. The BOK Satellite must be refreshed and available before processing the context Satellite, due to the key lookup. To ensure consistent processing, it is recommended to combine all involved modules into a batch.

Applying the BOK in the derived integration area

Another variation of this approach is to load all business keys into the Hub initially, then define the preferred business key later in the derived integration area using a BOK. Compared to the previous example, this method simplifies the back room loading process by removing the two-step lookup dependency, though it may require additional objects.

The diagram below illustrates how two staging layer objects are integrated in this way. The first object contains both the preferred and alternate business key values, while the second contains only the alternate key.

Both objects can process data independently into the Hub and their respective Satellites. In this scenario, the Hub contains a mix of business key values, including both the preferred and alternate versions. Even though both staging layer objects are mapped to the same Hub, the data remains logically separated.

This approach can also benefit from a Same-As Link (or similar) to connect the base and derived Hubs, though this has been omitted from the diagram for simplicity.

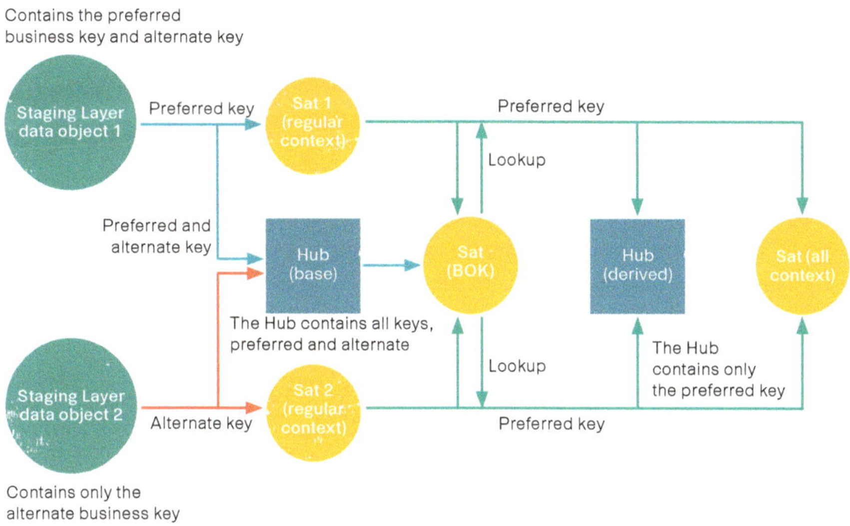

There are several variations of this approach. In one version, illustrated below, a single Hub is used for all four Satellites, with each Satellite referring to a subset of keys in the Hub.

The integrated Satellite, which contains columns from both Satellites, refers to the preferred business key and relies on the BOK for any columns provided by the second staging layer object.

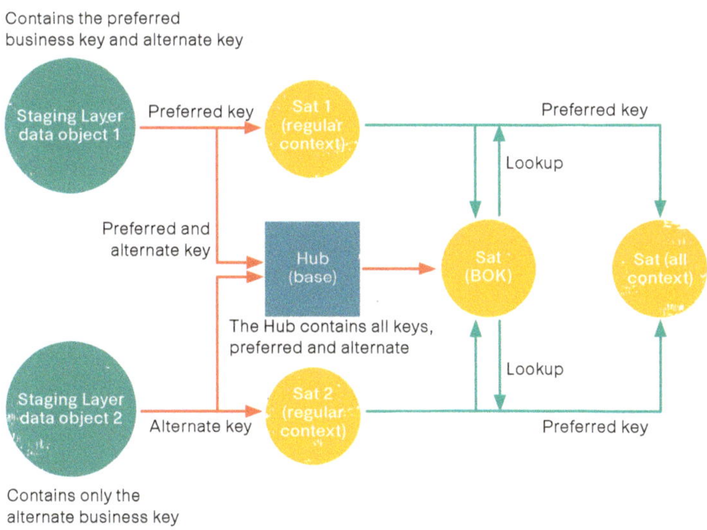

While we acknowledge these are available options to consider, whenever possible we recommend ⚐ joining the data objects in the PSA and replacing the alternative key with the preferred key upstream. Nevertheless, the alternate key can also be loaded into the BOK using one of the alternatives outlined in this section.

Testing

In the development lifecycle, the integration layer is often the first meaningful opportunity to integrate the ⚐ testing framework. After all, even though business rules and transformations that materially alter the data have not yet been applied, the data structure has undergone a dramatic change compared to the original data in the PSA.

At this point, we can introduce tests to ensure these new data structures meet expectations. By adding tests to the testing framework, we embed the knowledge gained during design and implementation into a shared repository. This repository can later support data platform controls, such as monitoring and regression testing.

Even though we're introducing the testing framework in more detail as part of the integration layer, controls can also be placed on the staging layer objects. However, this is typically considered later in the lifecycle of the data solution as part of data quality monitoring.

For more examples of testing framework checks, please visit our website: https://dtng.link/7lgql.

Essential integration layer controls

The essential controls outlined in this section are designed to ensure that design and development practices have been correctly followed. If the data platform is properly configured, these controls should never fail. As such, they are more technical in nature.

Examples of such controls include:
→ Detecting violation of uniqueness constraints and expectations
→ Validating the completeness of timelines
→ Checking if referential integrity has been satisfied

The following sections will provide detail on defining and automating each of these controls.

Uniqueness

Uniqueness controls ensure that no values violate primary key or unique key constraints. These are only required when the data platform does not enforce these constraints natively.

For an example of a uniqueness check on a Hub business key, please visit our website: https://dtng.link/yhlr3.

This test returns a failure if the business key appears more than once — which should never happen. While extremely rare, this could even uncover a hash collision when hash keys are being used as surrogate keys. More commonly, however, this test identifies issues with incorrect development practices, such as suboptimal patterns or templates.

Similar uniqueness checks can be applied to all surrogate keys, Links (where the combination of Hub surrogate keys must be unique) and Satellites (where the combination of the surrogate key, inscription timestamp, and inscription record id must be unique).

These checks can be automatically generated for each Hub, Link, and Satellite using a code generation template like this:

```
{{#each dataObjectMappings}}
{{#if @first}}

BEGIN
 DECLARE @TestResult VARCHAR(10) = 'Fail';
 DECLARE @TestOutput VARCHAR(MAX);
 DECLARE @Issues INT = 0;
 BEGIN TRY
  SELECT @Issues = COUNT(*)
  FROM [{{targetDataObject.name}}] sat
  WHERE NOT EXISTS
  (
  {{#each relationships}}
   SELECT 1 FROM [{{dataObject.name}}] hub
  WHERE 1=1
  {{#each businessKeyDefinitions}} AND sat.{{surrogateKey}} = hub.{{surrogateKey}}{{/each}}
 {{/each}}
  )

  SET @TestOutput = CONVERT(VARCHAR(10),@Issues)+' issue(s) were found.';

  IF @Issues = 0
   BEGIN
    SET @TestResult = 'Pass'
   END
 END TRY
 BEGIN CATCH
  SET @TestOutput = ERROR_MESSAGE();
  SET @TestResult = 'Fail'
 END CATCH

 SELECT @TestOutput AS [OUTPUT], @TestResult AS [RESULT];
END
```

Both the {{dataObject}} and {{dataObjectMappings}} (data object mapping list) can be applied to deliver these outcomes, but this example is created for the data object mapping list. The first occurrence of each mapping in {{dataObjectMappings}} is selected, because for the purposes of this check only the target data object is necessary, and this is the same for all mappings in the list.

Completeness in temporality

A common integration layer control is to assert completeness of timelines. When there are gaps or overlaps in timelines, it may result in missing or duplicate records respectively in downstream usage.

This type of control is only required when the 'before' timestamps of the given timeline are available, which depends on the approach used as outlined in the ⚐ struggling with time section.

Assuming a 'from' and 'before' timestamp are available, logic can be applied as a test. For an example of completeness in temporality check, please visit our website: https://dtng.link/qgxzk.

Even thought inscription timeline is evaluated in this example, similar logic can be applied to any timeline that has a physical 'from' and 'before' column. Typically, this applies to the state timeline but the inscription timeline can be asserted as well. The above example code checks the entire table for timeline consistency, but this can be applied to smaller record sets as well, for example when using load windows to process data delta downstream.

As with the uniqueness controls, both the {{dataObject}} and {{dataObjectMappings}} can be used for test code generation and, as before, this example is created for the data object mapping list.

```
{{#each dataObjectMappings}}
{{#if @first}}

BEGIN
 DECLARE @TestResult VARCHAR(10) = 'Fail';
 DECLARE @TestOutput VARCHAR(MAX);
 DECLARE @Issues INT = 0;
 BEGIN TRY
  WITH OrderedRanges AS
  (
   SELECT
    {{#each businessKeyDefinitions}}{{surrogateKey}},{{/each}}
    {{inscriptionTimeStampColumn}},
    {{inscriptionTimeStampBeforeColumn}},
    LAG({{inscriptionTimeStampBeforeColumn}}) OVER (
     PARTITION BY {{#each businessKeyDefinitions}}{{surrogateKey}}{{/each}}
     ORDER BY {{#each businessKeyDefinitions}}{{surrogateKey}}, {{/each}}
     {{inscriptionTimeStampColumn}})
     AS PREVIOUS_{{inscriptionTimeStampBeforeColumn}}
   FROM [{{targetDataObject.name}}] sat
  )
  ,Evaluation AS
  (
```

```
  SELECT
   {{#each businessKeyDefinitions}}{{surrogateKey}},{{/each}}
   {{inscriptionTimeStampColumn}},
   {{inscriptionTimeStampBeforeColumn}},
   PREVIOUS_{{inscriptionTimeStampBeforeColumn}},
   CASE
    WHEN PREVIOUS_{{inscriptionTimeStampBeforeColumn}} IS NOT NULL
     AND {{inscriptionTimeStampColumn}} >
        PREVIOUS_{{inscriptionTimeStampBeforeColumn}} THEN 'Gap'
    WHEN PREVIOUS_{{inscriptionTimeStampBeforeColumn}} IS NOT NULL
     AND {{inscriptionTimeStampColumn}} <
        PREVIOUS_{{inscriptionTimeStampBeforeColumn}} THEN 'Overlap'
    ELSE 'No Issue'
   END AS TEMPORAL_INCONSISTENCY_ISSUE
  FROM OrderedRanges
  WHERE
   (PREVIOUS_{{inscriptionTimeStampBeforeColumn}} IS NOT NULL
    AND {{inscriptionTimeStampColumn}} >
       PREVIOUS_{{inscriptionTimeStampBeforeColumn}} )
   OR
   (PREVIOUS_{{inscriptionTimeStampBeforeColumn}} IS NOT NULL
    AND {{inscriptionTimeStampColumn}} <
       PREVIOUS_{{inscriptionTimeStampBeforeColumn}} )
 )
 SELECT @Issues = COUNT(*)
 FROM Evaluation

 SET @TestOutput = CONVERT(VARCHAR(10),@Issues)+' issue(s) were found.';

 IF @Issues = 0
  BEGIN
   SET @TestResult = 'Pass'
  END
 END TRY
 BEGIN CATCH
  SET @TestOutput = ERROR_MESSAGE();
  SET @TestResult = 'Fail'
 END CATCH

 SELECT @TestOutput AS [OUTPUT], @TestResult AS [RESULT];
END
```

Referential integrity

The purpose of RI tests is to ensure that a 'child' object correctly references its parent object.

For example, ensuring that a Satellite correctly references its parent Hub.

The form of these tests may vary depending on the orchestration approach and only applies when the data platform does not already enforce RI.

RI checks as outlined in this section are an example *lazy RI,* a validation that is applied *after* the data has been inserted, not as a prevention of data being inserted incorrectly.

A typical approach to implementing RI checks is through a left-outer join or exists statement.

For an example of a RI control check, please visit our website: https://dtng.link/ftndm.

The code can be adjusted for specific scenarios. For instance, in a batch processing approach, you could validate RI only on the data delta processed from a landing area. In a continuous parallel loading paradigm, the consistency timestamp can also be incorporated.

Generating RI tests is straightforward since the necessary design metadata is already available: this test reuses the same metadata used to generate the data logistics processes.

Starting from the Satellite, the {{targetDataObject}} and {{relationships}} properties can be used to generate the above code, or similar, using a (simplified) template such as this:

```
{{#each dataObjectMappings}}
{{#if @first}}

BEGIN
 DECLARE @TestResult VARCHAR(10) = 'Fail';
 DECLARE @TestOutput VARCHAR(MAX);
 DECLARE @Issues INT = 0;
 BEGIN TRY
  SELECT @Issues = COUNT(*)
  FROM [{{targetDataObject.name}}] sat
  WHERE NOT EXISTS
  (
  {{#each relationships}}
   SELECT 1 FROM [{{dataObject.name}}] hub
  WHERE 1=1
  {{#each businessKeyDefinitions}} AND sat.{{surrogateKey}} = hub.{{surrogateKey}}{{/each}}
 {{/each}}
  )

  SET @TestOutput = CONVERT(VARCHAR(10),@Issues)+' issue(s) were found.';

  IF @Issues = 0
   BEGIN
    SET @TestResult = 'Pass'
   END
 END TRY
 BEGIN CATCH
  SET @TestOutput = ERROR_MESSAGE();
  SET @TestResult = 'Fail'
 END CATCH

 SELECT @TestOutput AS [OUTPUT], @TestResult AS [RESULT];
END
```

Notification

The controls covered in the previous sections focus on adherence to the solution architecture. During design and implementation, they assist to ensure development stays on the right track.

After production deployment, the testing framework can continue to track if these expectations continue to be met. And, when expectations are not met, we want to be notified.

To achieve this, tests should be run regularly, typically on a schedule independent of the data platform's data logistics processes.

As recommended in the testing framework, tests are ideally implemented as modules in the control framework, so that they can be grouped (batched) and scheduled at a suitable frequency.

This approach informs the data platform team and provides time-series data on issues such as:

- Regression of known issues; are certain issues reappearing regularly?
- System and process health; do all objects continue to conform to conventions?
- Risk management; are there any issues appearing that are likely to affect consumers and require immediate mitigation?

When a test fails, alerts can be sent via available channels, such as email, portal notifications, or internal communication platforms.

Tests and notifications for the control framework

So far, tests have been created as part of the development process and typically apply to data objects. In a production context, however, various tests can also be applied to the control framework, which holds critical information about how the data platform operates.

These tests directly target the control framework repository and are invaluable for maintaining the health of the platform, alerting the team to exceptions that may arise during data logistics process execution.

Examples of such tests include:

- Data loading expectations; is data arriving, complete, and being processed correctly on the expected schedule?
- Framework hygiene; is the administration of processes (batches and modules) and runtime monitoring in sync with the design?
- Latency; does the delay between receiving data and providing this to consumers exceed acceptable thresholds?

A common test is ensuring no failures occur in the module and batch executions. Are there any modules or batches that do not have a most-recent execution status that indicates 'success?' Additionally, tests can identify processes that are running longer than expected or those not running at all, which may indicate incorrect administration of data logistics processes in the control framework. Keeping the framework up to date helps differentiate between processes that should be running but aren't and those mistakenly registered that can be removed.

When using workflows, such as a 'daily run' that execute a hierarchy of batches, a check can be considered to ensure no batch lacks a parent, except the top-level batch in the hierarchy.

These tests are generic in nature and do not necessarily require generation from metadata.

For more examples of control framework checks, please visit our website: https://dtng.link/qeyrb.

Back room and front room

Getting data *into* the data solution corresponds to the back room of the data solution.

In these sections, we've covered the essential physical model components, how to work with them, what considerations to make, and ultimately how to implement them in a flexible way.

As part of this, we've made various key decisions, such as:

- Determining business concepts, and defining business keys
- Defined where the various data elements need to be housed
- Ensure the temporal challenges are addressed

These steps have advanced the data towards a state of usefulness, clearly modeled, while minimizing issues through careful orchestration, data logistics patterns, and architecture configuration. At this stage, we have a data solution that can be refactored dynamically and deterministically, is resilient, and includes a full audit trail and data lineage.

In other words, it provides a robust foundation to build data products for the final consumers. This will often require business rules and transformation logic, which will be handled in the front room of the data solution, the topic of the ⚐ getting the data out chapter. Here, we will cover the second part of the integration layer and the final piece of the solution architecture: the presentation layer.

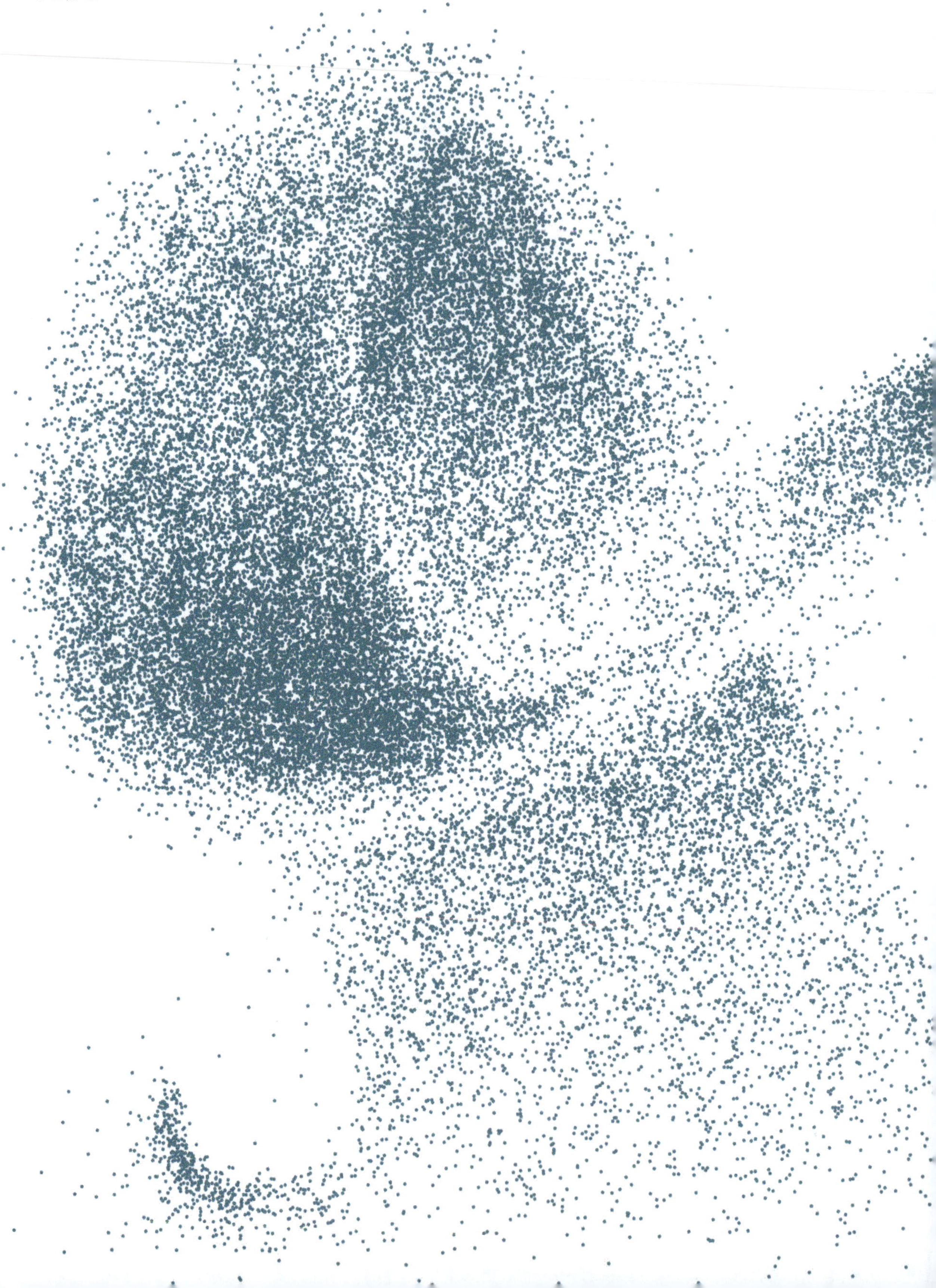

10 FastChangeCo – getting the data in

The team has gathered a large amount of content to define an approach for loading the data into the staging and integration layers, one that can be automated as well.

To discuss their results, and to celebrate the official launch of the DMCE department, Sylvia organizes a two-day offsite. It's held nearby, though far enough to feel like a refreshing break from daily routines.

Over the course of the two days, the 'Solutions & Brews,' as it's quickly dubbed, turns out to be a great success. The team draws on the vision and strategy, the decision register, and the first training modules from the DMCE Academy to fully understand all the decisions and goals established so far.

By the end of the offsite, everyone agrees that the developed concepts and procedures align well with the overarching vision and strategy.

Michael is especially pleased to see some of his narratives woven into the concept descriptions, including one of his favorite stories about car dealers which illustrates the complexities of business keys.

He's glad to see the growing number of examples incorporated throughout the concepts, as they clarify the reasoning behind each decision. This addition, he notes, reduces the need for follow-up discussions within the team.

MVP — Increasing time to value

Michael and the team start the new week with fresh motivation after the DMCE offsite. He's particularly pleased that they've defined the MVP and established a clear methodology. Now, they can officially begin working on the MVP and start loading the initial data.

Michael anticipates a steep learning curve for the team in the coming weeks as they apply the agreed-upon concepts. Yet, he has full confidence in their abilities. He expects that, especially in the beginning, some parts of the MVP may not be implemented perfectly. However, as the team gains experience, becomes familiar with the data, and refines the models, each subsequent 'restart' of the data solution from the PSA will be an improvement – incorporating all the rework and corrections.

From experience, Michael knows challenges lie ahead. That's why keeping everyone motivated and sustaining the momentum from Solutions & Brews is crucial.

His top priority is to drastically reduce development times, which have historically frustrated data solution users at FastChangeCo. In his early conversations at the company, he learned that the prolonged time required to develop even a single feature had eroded user confidence and trust in the existing data solutions.

This must change. Maintaining user confidence is essential – not only to secure continued financial support but also to ensure that the team experiences the satisfaction of delivering new features quickly.

The road to automation

To tackle the challenges of lengthy development cycles, Michael wants to explore ways to incorporate automation, albeit sparingly, within the MVP. His focus remains on delivering the MVP itself – automation itself is not the end goal. He shares this vision with the team, emphasizing that any initial automation should only support, not overshadow, the core objectives.

Xuefang, Amal, Yerodin, and the rest of the team agree with Michael's perspective. They're eager to see how the concepts will take shape and excited about the potential for innovation.

The team spends the rest of the meeting defining the scope for basic automation, which includes:
→ Creating design metadata
→ Developing templates for code generation
→ Implementing essential logging with the Audit Trail Id

For now, other supporting frameworks will be excluded from the MVP.

Amal raises a point: "Shouldn't we also generate the DDL[48] for the data objects using design metadata?" Xuefang makes a note and agrees, "Yes, that would certainly help speed up rolling out these features."

Sensing the team's enthusiasm, Michael holds back on commenting, curious to hear other perspectives. Yerodin shares his thoughts: "I like the idea, but there's a risk we might lose focus on the MVP's core objectives and end up building something that doesn't provide immediate value to our users. Could that make us seem slow again?"

Michael is pleased to see Yerodin keeping the team focused on the MVP's primary goals despite all these good ideas. Recognizing the value in both points of view, Xuefang and Amal add their suggestion to the backlog for future consideration.

Finally, the team updates the decision register, documenting their intention to keep automation for the MVP at a minimum. Any further automation ideas will serve as future criteria for tool selection.

Minimizing environments

Yerodin continues the conversation. "In my view, FastChangeCo projects set up way too many environments – multiple ones for development, testing, integration, and production. Reducing the number of environments could really help speed up delivery."

"What do you mean?" asks Zalika, back from her days at university.

"Well," Yerodin explains, "in some projects, there were so many environments we didn't even know where we were supposed to test. And they often weren't consistent. For example, we'd find the 'test' environment being used to develop patches, while one of the development environments was used for acceptance testing. Just figuring out *where* to test took ages, not to mention waiting for deployments between environments. So much time was lost just getting the environment in a usable state."

"Got it, that does sound confusing," Zalika replies.

Yerodin continues, "I propose we cut down to the bare minimum of environments, as Amal, Xuefang, and Diego suggested in the metadata, automation and code generation concept. We need a clear definition of each environment's purpose."

Michael sees an opening to share a story. "In one project I worked on, we had twelve different databases for testing alone. Even with all those environments, the feature rolled out to production often didn't perform. One reason was that each environment had different database configurations, which led to optimization assumptions that didn't hold in production. Plus, we kept creating new environments whenever a new 'need' came up."

Amal jumps in, picking up the discussion's momentum. "I think we're all on the same page. Let's agree on a central integration environment, a dedicated production environment, and individual development environments for each developer. The development environments must be easy to create and remove, for instance a production copy that can be quickly provisioned. At the latest when we go into production with The Resurrection."

Though Michael is a little disappointed to cut his story short, he's pleased the discussion is moving in the right direction. The team agrees on a simpler, clearer environment structure that will streamline their development process.

Deployment on time

"Delivering added value at the shortest possible intervals – that's what we committed to in our 'Vision and Strategy,'" Michael says, standing up. "Are the steps we've discussed enough to build the MVP in line with that guiding principle?"

"I think we're on the right track," Amal replies, joining him by the window. Together, they gaze at the bright blue sky over the nearby mountains. "By focusing on only the essential automation and reducing the number of environments, we should be able to deliver new features quickly for the MVP."

Michael nods, "I've seen projects where features were rolled out to production twice a day – morning and afternoon. Except Fridays. We only released in the morning then to avoid Friday afternoon issues. Nobody wants an early Saturday wake-up for troubleshooting."

The team's goal is clear: as soon as a feature is ready, it should be rolled out. Ideally, they aim for twice a week, but once at the very least. Their success will depend on maintaining focus and and ensuring a steady flow of work in Kanban.

Data modeling for the MVP

Zalika has rejoined the team, officially this time, fresh from graduating and eager to be part of the group. Having completed her Master's thesis and passed her exams with flying colors, she proudly presents her work to the team.

Based on her research into various Fact-Oriented Modeling (FOM) approaches, Zalika recommends adopting Fully Communication-Oriented Information Modeling (FCO-IM) as the method for developing information models within DMCE.

She explains her reasoning: FCO-IM focuses solely on modeling information that is explicitly communicated. This results in a simpler and more uniform information model, reducing complexity during implementation.

Additionally, FCO-IM's structured methodology, supported by tools, streamlines the analysis process and prevents redundancy by automatically matching previously analyzed facts.

These features make it an efficient and practical choice, particularly for large-scale projects like those at FastChangeCo.

After reviewing her thesis and understanding her reasoning, the team's data modelers agree with her recommendation.

The decision to adopt FCO-IM is promptly recorded in the decision register. At the same time, the team realizes that while they had previously decided to use Data Vault for physical modeling, this decision hasn't yet been formally documented. They make a note to revisit and confirm it in the decision register.

Information model

Zalika enthusiastically begins creating the FCO-IM data model for the MVP. She reaches out to Philomena Pavlovic, an experienced application developer and business analyst, whom she hasn't officially met before.

As a subject matter expert, Philomena is the main point of contact for the business aspects of important objects for ReCol such as 'customer,' 'product,' 'order,' 'returns,' and 'supplier.'

Zalika introduces Philomena to the philosophy behind FastChangeCo's new data solution. "All 'marbles' (data) in the information hub must correspond to fundamental business objects," she explains. "There should be no marbles in the raw data or information hub without business significance."

"In the PSA, however, we can have 'unknown' marbles, which represents data that needs further examination from a business perspective. Over time, we'll analyze, define, and assign them to specific business requirements. This unknown data will also be available for future research and innovation, because it may hold value we're not aware of at this stage."

"Our task now," she continues, "is to analyze these marbles with the help of the information model – giving them meaning, defining them, and placing them in FastChangeCo's business context."

Philomena nods. "I'm curious to see exactly how we'll do that. Can we use our existing data models?"

The DMCE team had already considered this. Unfortunately, most existing data models were outdated, incomplete, or otherwise in poor condition. Many business object definitions were either missing, unclear, or tautological. Defining that 'the customer is a customer of FastChangeCo' is not very helpful!

Recognizing this, the team committed to improving the general understanding of business objects by defining them more precisely.

For example:
A FastChangeCo customer is a natural person of legal age who has made at least one purchase from FastChangeCo. It does not matter whether it is an active or inactive customer.

"Verbalization with FCO-IM has been incredibly helpful," Zalika explains. "A clear definition of core business objects simplifies the physical implementation of the data solution, reducing ambiguity. It leaves as little room for interpretation as possible."

The two of them go into more detail about modeling with FCO-IM and Philomena listens intently to Zalika's explanations.

She is drawn to this approach of verbalizing sample data to create information models, and appreciates how it allows her to model using clear, precise sentences. She is keen to see the outcomes of this method.

Together, she and Zalika draft the sentences for the MVP model, and Philomena is relieved that she does not have to deal with unfamiliar data modeling tools. Instead, she and Zalika can work through the business relationships in a simple text file using concrete examples such as:

[Product Name]
"The name of the product 10023 is FancyBoots"
"The name of the product 12045 is MegaBoots"
[Product Price]
"The price of product 10023 is 149.99"
"The price of product 12045 is 199.99"
[Order Line Item]
"In order 128736, order line item 1 is the product 10023"
"In order 128736, order line item 2 is the product 12045"
[Order Date]
"Order 128736 was placed on 2025-05-05"
"Order 129774 was placed on 2025-06-02"

From these, and many more, sentences, Zalika derives[49] the FCO-IM information model:

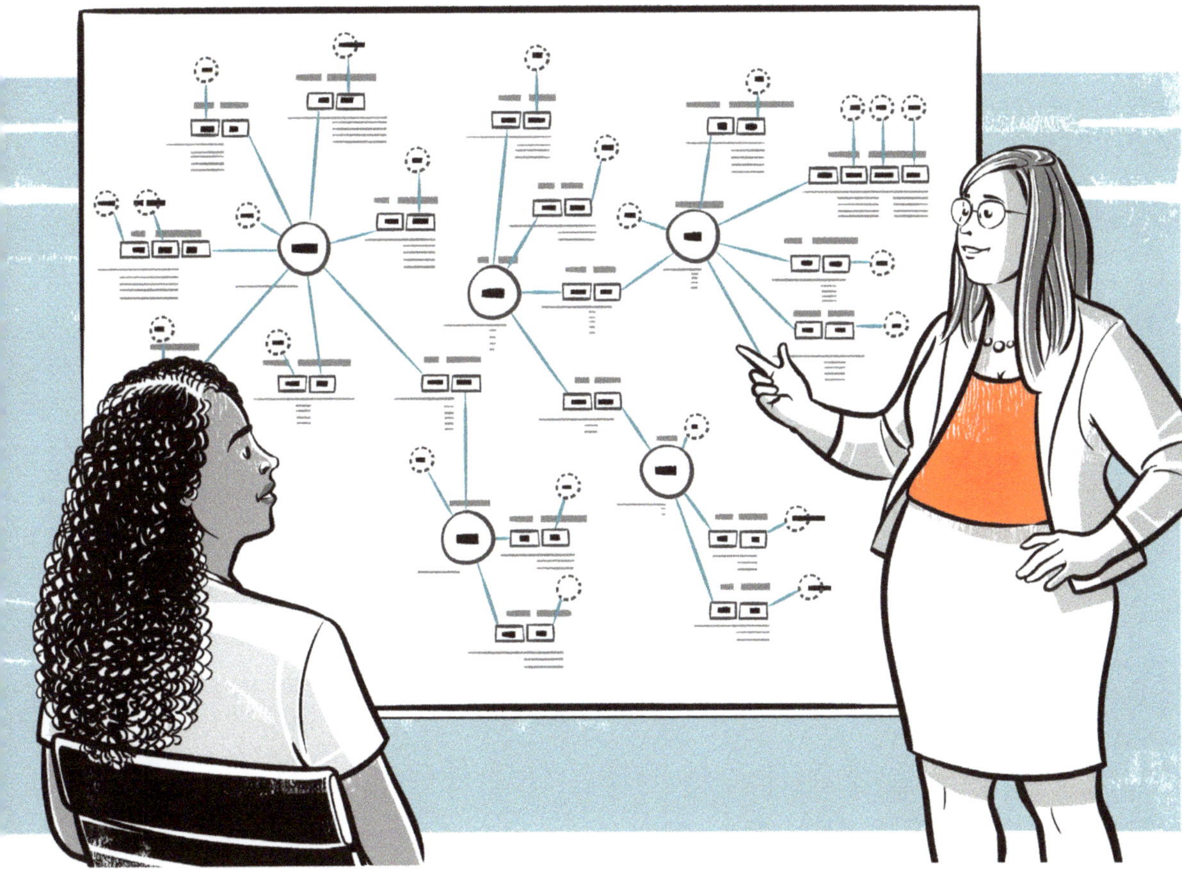

After completing the model, Philomena turns to Zalika and admits, "I was skeptical at first, having never heard of FCO-IM, but now I can say this is the first data model I can accept as 100 % correct, based on what I know today."

As the workshop continues, they complete the MVP's first feature by modeling the 'product' and 'order' business objects.

Not only does this approach make sense to Philomena, but it also enables her to validate product master data and analyze turnover for individual products – tasks she typically performs in isolation using outdated reports.

For the first time, she feels confident that the data model truly aligns with the business reality.

Data Vault data model

The next afternoon, the team gathers to review the Zalika's information model. As they examine it, they quickly notice how different it looks from any model they've created before.

After giving a broad overview, Zalika pauses and scans the room, waiting for questions. At first, there's silence – no one seems ready to speak up. She resists the urge to fill the gap, knowing from experience that sometimes all it takes is a moment.

Finally, Amal breaks the quiet. "How do we create a Data Vault model from this? Do we need a different tool?"

Relieved that the discussion has begun, Zalika shakes her head. "No, we can derive the Data Vault structures directly from the information model. I've written a few algorithms for this."

As she speaks, she opens her laptop and begins running scripts. "But we still need to verify the results carefully. It would be premature to assume this process works flawlessly just yet."

Zalika demonstrates to everyone how easy it is to prepare the FCO-IM data model for a Data Vault data model, then derive the DDL from it.

"Nice," Amal says, clearly intrigued. "So we can use these scripts to start building our integration layer right away?"

Zalika nods, pleased that her explanation has resonated.

Michael glances at the time. "Let's take a 10-minute break before we continue – I have another question I want to go over afterward."

Managing metadata

After the break, everyone returns refreshed, chatting about Zalika's modeling approach.

Michael waits for the room to settle before speaking. "We agreed to start the MVP with minimal automation. The engine needs design metadata for that, right? But where does it come from? Can we generate it from the information model, like the Data Vault DDLs?"

"Yes, we can derive some of it from the information model," Zalika replies. "However, certain parts –especially those needed for mapping– will have to be provided manually. That said, we should start setting up a Git repository to store everything: design metadata, fact sentences, all of it."

"Agreed," Amal adds. "From now on, all artifacts must go into Git. After the MVP, the engine will be able to generate DDLs from that metadata – that's where we want to get. Maybe we'll have tool support for this down the line, but that's a discussion for another time."

Michael nods. "That's enough of an answer for me. Sounds like we're moving in the right direction. I'm curious to see how it all develops."

He glances out the window. "Let's call it a day. Hope everyone enjoys the great weather this evening."

Gathering his teapot and cup, Michael leaves the room, chatting cheerfully with Zalika.

Building the staging layer

It's happening — the data machine is starting!

With the first building blocks of the MVP in place, the team is eager to begin development. The vision for the data solution is steadily coming to life.

Michael is thrilled with the progress so far, and for Sylvia, this milestone carries significant weight. Both recognize its importance from their own perspectives.

To kick off MVP development, Sylvia and Michael have decided to organize a hackathon — the first one for 'The Resurrection.' Sylvia has secured FastChangeCo's conference area for four days, giving the team dedicated time to collaborate intensively. By working together on the initial deliverables, they can quickly address any questions or challenges that arise.

The primary objective: ensure that at least the 'product' and 'order' business objects are implemented in the PSA and integration layer — loaded with data[50].

Landing area

Shortly after the hackathon begins, the first questions arise.

The team had expected the LDA and the PSA to come together quickly — a straightforward one-to-one data copy into the LDA, some CDC logic to populate the PSA, and everything would fall into place.

In an ideal world, this might have been the case. But FastChangeCo's data reality is more complicated.

The team quickly realizes that the interfaces they intended to reuse only provide technical identifiers from the source systems, perform full extracts each time, and lack the business keys they actually need.

This is not how they expected to integrate the 'product' and 'order' business objects. While the information model flags this as a data quality issue, the team decides to store the data as-is in the PSA.

Yerodin recalls how previous projects required countless workarounds to address this issue. "We built an extra layer to load all the data and then —by joining multiple tables— replaced technical identifiers with business keys. That approach created a massive maintenance overhead and constant synchronization problems."

He stands up, pacing nervously. "This is a challenge for the MVP. We should put in the work now rather than push the problem down the road. Ignoring it would go against our vision of delivering real business value."

Michael had anticipated these kinds of obstacles. That's why he, Sylvia, and Jeff agreed to have a few IT professionals on standby during the first HackMatrix — a name that emerged after just a few hours of collaboration.

Amal suggests addressing the data quality issues as early as possible, ideally at the source.

"You're absolutely right, Amal," Yerodin says. "I was a bit stuck in old ways, and didn't realize that was an option too. That makes a lot of sense."

Through discussions with the IT team, the DMCE team ensures that business keys are added to each incoming interface. Instead of replacing the existing technical identifiers with the business key, they modify the interfaces to avoid breaking dependent processes. These interfaces are also used by others, after all.

"Another advantage of having both business keys and technical IDs," Amal adds, "is that we might need both in cases where an interface can't be updated quickly. "We can use a BOK satellite in such cases, as we described in ⚐working with alternate business keys."

Fortunately, the IT team is able to implement the interface update quickly, minimizing delays. Michael hopes that IT collaboration will become the norm rather than an exception when interface issues arise in the future. With the correct business key in place, defining logical CDC mechanisms for the PSA becomes much easier. The team can now move forward with integration — though that's not yet the focus of the HackMatrix.

If this were the only problem, Michael thinks, that would be fortunate. But his experience tells him otherwise.

Analyzing the source data objects

This early encounter with data quality issues prompts the team to check in with Diego.

"Always profile the data thoroughly if possible, even for an MVP," he advises. "You might not always be able to do this directly in operational systems, but if you can, you should. Otherwise, load an extract into the LDA or PSA for closer inspection. This will save you from a lot of refactoring later."

Agreeing with his advice, the DMCE team takes a step back to analyze the data in the LDA related to the two business objects.

While reviewing the order data, they notice something unusual – a date that doesn't seem valid. The aging mainframe system is returning February 30 as a date.

"Classic issue," Diego remarks.

Apparently, the mainframe consistently outputs this invalid date, which obviously doesn't conform to the LDA's date data type. According to their ⚐data type alignment standards, any date without a time component is mapped to a date type – but clearly, something has gone wrong.

A brief discussion follows: should they fix this issue while loading the LDA?

Yerodin hesitates. "In a previous project, we struggled with this. Our order reports didn't match the mainframe's reports – especially around February and March. Later, we discovered the mainframe had its own 'complex' rules for handling invalid dates. In leap years, February 30 was assigned to February 29. In other years, it was pushed to March 1."

"That's exactly why we avoid data quality checks in the staging layer," Amal adds.

They decide to store the problematic values as-is by converting the column to an NVARCHAR() type. Later, they will implement a business rule in the integration layer to translate the invalid dates correctly.

"This is a great example of how to apply the ⚐exception bitmap concept," Amal notes. "Let's add it to the backlog."

Analyzing columns

While analyzing the product data, Zalika doesn't find any errors in the date columns.

However, she notices that some columns contain only spaces or empty strings. Curious, she brings it up with the team, but even Yerodin doesn't have an explanation.

Adding to the mystery, other columns contain timestamps and flags that don't seem to have an obvious purpose.

Michael has a hunch but suggests Zalika discuss the findings with Philomena. "A subject matter expert can help determine whether this data is meaningful or just operational noise."

When Zalika and Philomena review the data together, they uncover the issue: the empty strings and spaces actually represent NULL values – unknown or undefined data.

Some columns that contain values that are unclear are added to the PSA. The columns that contain technical information relevant only to the operational system hold no business value, and Philomena agrees they are irrelevant to both the data solution and the MVP.

Unlike previous FastChangeCo projects, the team decides to focus solely on data relevant to the MVP. Any non-essential columns from product and order will be ignored in the integration layer, but will still be retained in the PSA for full transparency.

Persistent staging area

The first minor hurdles of the MVP have been successfully overcome. With the final analysis of the source data complete and ignoring the identified unnecessary columns, the team has loaded the first data into the LDA.

Now, they shift their focus to building the PSA. Following the design, they include a change data indicator and checksum column in each PSA table. This will make it easier to identify new, changed, or deleted records when comparing the full data extract using a FOJ.

Pre-calculation of business keys hash values

As Xuefang and Amal take a break, Xuefang brings up an interesting thought.

"I heard somewhere that surrogate keys and checksums for Data Vault Satellites should be generated on the way *into* the data solution," she says.

"As far as I remember, the idea was that surrogate key values only need to be calculated once this way. Well, when using hash values or natural business keys as the surrogate key approach I mean. Should we bring this up with the team?"

Amal agrees, and after the break, Xuefang presents the question to the group.

The team listens to Xuefang's comment, and considers whether the surrogate key values should be generated on the way to the LDA, when moving data from the LDA to the PSA, or even later when processing data from the PSA to the integration layer.

The discussion that follows is inconclusive.

"Maybe this is something to check with Diego?" Michael suggests.

Shortly afterward, the team shares their debate with Diego, keen to get his perspective.

"As you've recognized, one advantage of generating surrogate keys early —using hash values or natural business keys— is that they only need to be calculated once and can be reused downstream," Diego begins.

But," he continues, "the downside is that this approach couples the integration layer tightly to the staging layer. The layers are no longer independent."

Zalika frowns. "What do you mean by that?"

"Well, imagine you're modifying the Data Vault model – maybe adding a new Hub based on an existing PSA table. That means you would also have to modify the PSA table to add this new Hub surrogate key column."

"Got it ..." Zalika nods.

Diego continues, "Ideally, you want to keep the staging and integration layers independent. That way, changes in the integration layer don't force refactoring in the PSA."

"I see, that does seem to go against what I consider good software design," Zalika remarks. "If every change forces a cascade of updates, refactoring becomes a nightmare."

Diego agrees with her point, but also says that this approach can make sense for some projects. For example, it could work in a streaming environment where data might be inserted directly in the integration layer in a Kappa architecture where no staging layer exists.

"Let me also give you an example of when pre-calculating hashes didn't work out," he says.

Michael, who loves hearing about real-world experiences, listens intently.

"For one project, we decided to generate hash-based surrogate keys and checksums while loading data into the staging layer, so pre-calculating the hash values. It was actually pretty easy to load the data from the staging layer into the integration layer with this approach."

"But there's a catch, right?" Zalika asks.

Diego smiles. "In a way, yes. It turned out that generating hash values early was actually counterproductive given the amount of data involved. We had a dataset with over one billion records, but some of the included business keys had only 3,000 or so distinct values. Instead of computing the hashes just 3,000 times, we recalculated them a billion times while loading into the LDA. And since we were dealing with a full extract every time, this became a performance and cost concern."

He pauses for a quick sip of his drink, allowing the team some time to process what was just said.

"The result? It was a huge computational overhead to calculate these hashes and store them in the staging layer – just for a one-time usage. The system slowed down so much that the loading windows became unmanageable. We decided to move the hash calculation to the data logistic processes that were loading the integration layer, and calculate it only for unique values."

"How much faster was it after that?" Zalika asks, thinking back to her university lessons on optimization.

"The cycle time dropped to about one-twentieth of what it had been. Of course, the difference wasn't as noticeable for smaller tables, but at scale, it was a game-changer."

Michael nods. "That makes sense. But the bigger issue here is still layer dependencies. Our entire engine concept is designed for decoupling – right down to independent modules."

Amal agrees. "If we tie surrogate key generation to the PSA, any change in the integration layer forces us to refactor the PSA and its data logistics. That's unnecessary complexity. A stable PSA and a flexible integration layer are key to agility and time-to-market."

Diego looks at Amal and Michael. "I'd like to add," he says, "that perhaps in the future, the engine could decide when to calculate hash values. After all, it would be capable of managing this refactoring internally."

Michael laughs. "That's an exciting vision!"

After further discussion, Michael calls for a decision. The hackathon won't last forever, and they need to move forward.

They recognize the benefits of creating the PSA without needing to know every Hub, Link, or Satellite that will be built in the integration layer. And so, the team decides that surrogate keys should be calculated as natural business keys during processing from the PSA into the integration layer.

The decision is logged, and they proceed to build the PSA.

Duplicate data records

The next day at the HackMatrix, the team discovers duplicate records in the orders data they've just loaded into the brand new PSA table.

"How do we deal with this? Can we just delete these redundant records?" Xuefang, who found the issue turns to Amal.

Amal shakes her head. "Not so fast. There are several reasons why duplicates might exist, and we shouldn't delete them without understanding the cause."

She continues, "True duplicate records, in the sense of actual redundant data, can occur when columns that trigger a change aren't included in the interface – presumably because they aren't relevant to the data solution. For example, if the system logs each time a user clicks a button in the same table as personal details, we might only care about the personal details, not every button click. If that button-click column isn't included in the interface, from our perspective the operational system logs changes for no reason. As a result, we receive the updated records but can't see why they changed, making them appear redundant."

"There could also be errors in the interface itself," she adds. "For example, an incorrect join in the data selection could cause technical redundancy – records that aren't truly duplicates but appear to be due to a flawed extraction process."

Michael chimes in, "And then there are the *supposed* duplicates."

In these cases, the records aren't actually redundant, even though they appear to be. You might encounter an A-B-A problem, where a value (A) is updated to something else (B) and then reverted back to its original value (A). If the sequence of these changes isn't accounted for during data delivery or in the PSA, it can look like record A is duplicated, even though record B should exist between them."

"Right, so first we need to figure out why these duplicates exist," Zalika concludes.

"Exactly," Amal agrees. "Only when we understand the cause we can decide how to handle them."

After consulting the operational system experts, the team rules out technical redundancy with near certainty.

"Can you help us understand this from a business perspective Yerodin?" Michael asks.

Yerodin, pleased to have his own story to tell, unravels the mystery. He recognizes the issue from an earlier project.

"What happens in stock when we're packing products can be interesting," he begins. "Products are stored in compartments, and the operational system tracks how many are available at each one. Now, imagine someone orders two identical pairs of shoes — say, 'FancyBoots, size 44.' However, there's only one pair left in one location, while more are available elsewhere."

He gestures as he explains. "The system generates packing instructions, so workers know where to pick from. In this case, the order line 'FancyBoots, size 44 – quantity: 2' gets split into two:

→ 'FancyBoots, size 44 – quantity: 1 – compartment 3487'
→ 'FancyBoots, size 44 – quantity: 1 – compartment 9037'

Since there's only one pair left in compartment 3487, the packers know exactly where to pick the other from."

"But for the data solution," he continues, "we receive two records from stock inventory logistics but without the compartment numbers. That info wasn't in the interface. This makes them look like duplicate transactions, but they're not. The total quantity is still two, just as in the original order. If we delete one, we'd be altering the order incorrectly."

"The records are 'duplicated' by the stock inventory logistic processes. The duplicates only exist from *our* perspective," Yerodin concludes, taking a sip of water.

"That's really interesting," says Michael, sipping his green tea. "I've never come across this before." The others smile, realizing that Michael for once doesn't have his own story to share.

Amal nods. "This is why we never delete records from the PSA. Even if they look like duplicates, they're still unique within that layer."

"Duplicates can also occur when column scope is reduced while loading data into the integration layer, such as to a Satellite," she adds. "If the column that triggered a change isn't included, the record will appear duplicated."

"This is why we've documented ⚐record compacting in detail in our concept," she continues. "The key is understanding *why* the duplicates exist – only then can we decide if and how compacting should be applied when moving data into the integration layer."

"And if it's technical redundancy," Yerodin adds, "that should be fixed at the source, in the incoming interface."

Building the integration layer

More than half of the HackMatrix is now over, and it's high time to work on the integration layer. Michael and his team are well aware of this.

Despite the remaining tasks, Michael takes a moment to appreciate how much the team has already accomplished in such a short time.

All data-related questions have been answered and the key concepts have firmly taken root in the team's collective knowledge. And, of course, the order and product data is now available in the PSA.

Meanwhile, the team has laid the foundation for the data logistic control framework, ensuring that an Audit Trail Id and basic process logging are in place. This is more than Michael had expected at this stage.

Feeling satisfied with the team's progress, he continues to monitor the MVP's development throughout the remainder of the HackMatrix. So far, he and Sylvia seem to have made the right decisions.

He notices Amal already leveraging the control framework data to develop the load window mechanism, which will be essential for moving data from the PSA into the integration layer.

As he prepares a green tea, Michael reflects, "The load window elegantly identifies which records should be processed in the integration layer. Without it, the process would be far more cumbersome."

Even at a HackMatrix, there's always time for tea.

At the same time, Xuefang and Yerodin are creating the necessary Data Vault objects for the MVP. They're deriving these objects from the information model and validating them against their modeling guidelines:

- → The attribute that identifies the business concept becomes the business key: 'order' and 'product'
- → Descriptive attributes are placed in the Satellite: some Satellites for 'order' and 'product'
- → Associative entities in the information model are implemented as Hub, Satellite, and Link combinations – in this case the relationship between 'product' and 'order,' representing the products ordered

As Michael observes the team in action, he feels optimistic. At the very least, they should be able to load the raw data into the integration layer before the hackathon ends. And with any luck, they'll also resolve the remaining open issues – bringing the MVP one step closer to production.

Data logistics processes

Though not yet supported by code generation templates, the team continues developing the first data logistics processes based on design metadata. They register these as modules in the control framework and use them to load Data Vault objects in the integration layer with data from the PSA. Due to time constraints, they agreed that code generation template development wasn't essential for the MVP.

With this and other pragmatic decisions aimed at ensuring the MVP's timely completion and value delivery the team is making significant progress.

In the past 24 hours, things have gone almost too smoothly, Michael thinks. With just a few hours left, he plans to wrap up the event with a summary of achievements and a list of remaining tasks to get the MVP into production. Maybe there's even time to share a story or two.

But as the hackathon draws to a close, new, critical questions emerge – enough for Michael to pause further MVP development to address them properly. "I can skip one of my stories," he muses.

Xuefang, Amal, and Yerodin raise concerns about how to document business logic and rules in a way that's transparent and easily understood by everyone. Too often, these rules remain only in developers' minds, and over time, the reasoning behind them is lost.

"At uni, I learned that business logic often extends beyond a single use case," Xuefang says. "So we need to document it in a way that's both flexible and extendable – not just capturing the rules clearly but also linking back to where they've been implemented."

The team agrees they need a permanent, sustainable, solution. However, they decide to add this to the backlog for two reasons

1) There's not enough time left in the hackathon to solve it properly.
2) Business rules belong to the 'front room' of the data solution – which isn't the focus of this event.

Deciding for a timeline

The team is committed to continuing the development of the data logistics processes. With the processes for business keys (Hubs) and relationships (Links) already running smoothly, the team now turns their focus to developing context entities – the Satellites.

"The inscription timestamp and the inscription record id are always transferred as-is," Amal summarizes.

"From this, the assertion timeline is formed, which is used to filter the data."

Zalika adds, "The state timeline is a bit more complicated. We need to determine the business timestamp for each data object. Ideally, the data already contains a business timeline with complete and chronologically correct time periods."

"But if that's not the case," Amal continues, "we use the best available timestamp. We've already assigned the best available timestamp to the source timestamp column."

"Oops!" Xuefang exclaims. "I think we forgot to define the source timestamp in the staging layer. We should definitely address that; it must have slipped through with all the other tasks."

Amal nods. "Absolutely. It's only one column to add – on both the LDA and PSA data objects. We should be able to fix that quickly."

"But which source timestamp do we use for 'product?' And which one for 'order?'" Zalika asks.

Xuefang considers this. "That's a good question."

Zalika offers a solution. "I'm meeting with Philomena later to discuss the business timelines for the context entities, I'll also clarify which values are suitable as source timestamps. I can use the list of approaches we discussed for evaluating source timestamps."

Michael agrees. "It's unfortunate that we missed the column, but that's the nature of working on an MVP. Luckily, we should be able to fix it quickly. Let's follow Zalika's suggestion. And to make sure we stay fresh, let's take a longer lunch break today. There's room for that in a hackathon!"

Meeting with Philomena

After the break, the team continues developing the data logistics processes for the Satellites, while Zalika heads to meet Philomena.

Together, Zalika and Philomena work on determining which state timeline and source timestamp is right for this data. This decision is crucial for historization when loading the Satellites.

For the 'product' entity, the two of them quickly agree on the state timeline. Philomena explains that the 'VALID_FROM' and 'VALID_TO' columns for 'product' describe the validity period. This can be the validity of a price, a specific variant of the product that is only available for a certain period of time, or product data that is already recorded for the future – and is only valid in the future.

'VALID_FROM' is mapped to the state from timestamp, and 'VALID_TO' to the state before timestamp. Thankfully, it isn't necessary to adjust the time period as it is already delivered as Open-Closed.

"But what about the 'order'?" Zalika asks. "I assume the 'ORDER_DATE' is the correct timestamp for the state from timestamp. That's when the order was placed in the operational system, right?"

Philomena thinks for a moment. "Actually, an order doesn't have a true business history. It's simply a fixed point in time. Our system doesn't allow retroactive changes to orders."

"However, the 'ORDER_DATE' is only exact to the day, and contains no time fraction. So, 'ORDER_DATE' isn't the best candidate for the state timestamp. The 'SCST' column —Shopping Cart Send Timestamp— would be better. It captures when the order was sent by the customer and logged into the system. It is a true timestamp."

Zalika nods. "It's more complex than I initially thought."

Philomena agrees. "It's not always easy for the business side, either. Sometimes processes deviate from our original business definitions, or they're interpreted differently."

"For example, the 'ORDER_DATE' is a legacy column. It's important, but was implemented based on the system limitations at the time. That's why it can have issues, like a February 30th date. We need to handle that, but it's not ideal for analysis."

Zalika recalls what Amal had mentioned earlier about the ⚐ 'World of Data.' "We work on the assumption that operational systems are inherently imperfect, and without historical context, we can't fully understand the data. This is a great example for that."

Philomena smiles. "I think that's a very good way to look at it."

After a short break, during which Philomena grabs an ice-cold Repsi Cherry and Zalika prepares a fresh maté, Zalika picks up the thread again.

"OK, so we'll use the 'SCST' column as the state from timestamp for the order and map this to the Satellite's state timeline."

Finding the source timestamps

Zalika ponders for a moment and continues: "We have already defined the state timeline for the 'product.' But which timestamp do we use as source timestamp? We haven't discussed that yet."

Philomena thinks for a moment. "I believe there's a timestamp for changes made by users. Look for a 'Modified Date' column, or something similar. In the GUI, we can see both a Creation Date and a Last Modified Date for products. The latter should work for our needs."

Zalika checks the staging layer for the 'product' entity and finds the 'CHNG_DT' column, which contains both the date and time of the last change. Using the GUI, Philomena and Zalika check individual samples to ensure that the displayed timestamp matches the data.

But it doesn't feel right to Zalika. She pauses for a moment and considers how the source timestamp is actually defined. She remembers that the source timestamp determines the point in time at which the change was detected in the system.

The 'CHNG_DT' is indeed a timestamp that documents a change, but is controlled by the operational system. What they need is something that is as close as possible to the moment the actual change occurred in the operational system, without relying on administrative values — something system-generated, which cannot be changed manually. Looking further, they discover that the process that triggers the full extract from the operational system provides a 'start timestamp' at the beginning of the data extraction.

This seems like a good choice for the source timestamp, so they decide to go with that.

Based on their understanding of the source timestamp, the two decide that this 'start timestamp' should also be used for the 'orders.'

With their analysis complete, Zalika is ready to present their decision to the rest of the team. They move forward with implementing the staging layer, marking the first major refactoring in the project, and begin creating the corresponding mappings.

Reject tables

While the team remains focused on developing processes and metadata, Michael prepares another one of his teas. The previous evening, he attended a Japanese tea tasting at *T-Time,* where he was particularly impressed by Yabukita White Tea – an exquisite and rare white tea from Japan.

As he watches the team work with concentration, his thoughts drift back to the days when the Data Warehouse still relied on reject tables.

How far we've come, he reflects. The team has not only moved past this rigid approach but has fundamentally shifted its mindset. By eliminating RI constraints and optimizing data type flexibility, they've removed the main reasons for rejecting records in the first place. But more importantly, they've embraced a new philosophy: all data is welcome – warts and all. The thought brings a smile to his face.

Noticing this, Xuefang asks, "Michael, what's so funny? Want to share?"

Michael chuckles. "I was just thinking about one of my earlier projects. We used reject tables back then. The fact that we no longer do that –not even for records containing February 30– made me smile. We don't discard those 'warts' anymore; we load them."

The rest of the team grins.

"Was that the project you mentioned when we talked about RI?" Amal asks.

"Not quite," Michael replies. "That project had reject tables because RI prevented loading due to missing parent records. But there was a similar case – records were rejected because they failed 'data quality rules.' Just like our February 30 issue.

"At the time, instead of finding a way to load the data, we simply parked those records. The idea was that subject matter experts would review and correct them. Or at least, they should have. But in reality, it was a tedious, thankless task that no one wanted to do. Over time, millions of Euros were literally piled up in the data records in rejection tables – they were completely absent from the reports."

Yerodin shakes his head. "That's crazy. Didn't the controlling department notice?"

"We wondered the same thing. Apparently not. And honestly, during the project, we didn't realize how much data was accumulating either. We didn't monitor it, and only caught it by chance."

Michael pauses, then says, "Looking back, we should've kept a closer eye on the reject tables. But to be fair to our team, the responsibility lay with the subject matter experts. Long story short, the situation got out of hand. That's why I'm glad we've moved on." He takes a sip of his tea, enjoying the moment.

Amal turns to the team and grins. "OK, then let's make sure Michael never has a story like that to tell about us. Let's use the rest of the HackMatrix to finish loading the integration layer."

Bringing the MVP to production

At the end of the HackMatrix, the team presents the results to Sylvia. They walk her through how stable the loading of the PSA already is, and how the the data is subsequently loaded into the budding integration layer.

With his modest Python skills, Yerodin has put together a simple module visualization using the logging data from the control framework.

Michael turns to Sylvia with a grin. "The decisions we've made so far are really paying off. Basically, the team is following the agreed methods for loading data into the staging and the integration layers. Of course, given the MVP's constraints, not everything is in place yet."

Sylvia looks around at the team with a satisfied nod. "It's clear how much you've all grown together over the last few weeks. I'm hearing far fewer debates about the concepts you've developed, and everything seems to be in line with the agreed vision and strategy of *The Resurrection*. Great progress!"

As the MVP presentation continues, the team explains their plan to run fully in parallel. Sylvia raises an eyebrow, and Amal clarifies, "That just means, in principle, all modules *could* run in parallel."

Sylvia glances at her watch – she has a board meeting coming up. She turns back to the team. "As I said, I'm really impressed with what you've accomplished in the MVP. I'm looking forward to seeing the first report or dashboard."

She pauses before adding, "But, as I've learned from the DQM, there's still a long way to go before this is production-ready." With that, she heads off to her board meeting.

Michael picks up the thread. "We should start defining a process for getting the MVP into production. We've already described the fundamentals and rules of the data quadrant model, and this MVP would be fully absorbed into DQ-I. That means all artifacts need to fully align with the design patterns. But let's not go too deep into that now – first, let's outline the high-level to-dos."

Zalika suddenly groans. "We didn't even get to show Sylvia our Git process! I made some great illustrations for that."

Michael waves it off. "That's fine. It would've been too much detail anyway. And your illustrations weren't for nothing – they're part of our Git process documentation now. They really help explain how it works."

Zalika shrugs, satisfied.

The team moves on to brainstorming the open points from the hackathon. They also go over what's actually needed to take the MVP in production.

Amal summarizes the remaining high-level tasks:

- *Second phase of the MVP (front room):*
  - *Implement business and data quality rules*
  - *Add reference data to support business rules and data quality improvements*
  - *Correctly providing timelines, also when merging data sets*
  - *Configuring outbound interfaces*
  - *Include helper objects to improve performance*
- *Production-readiness – after phase 2:*
  - *Implement the testing framework and exception bitmap to conform to DQ-I and DQ-II*
  - *Establish orchestration for dependencies in the integration layer (e.g., business rules that must be executed in a specific order). No immediate need for this within the MVP, but it's something to consider*
  - *Deploy to production*
- *Post production support:*
  - *Stabilize deployment*
- *Out of scope:*
  - *Sandboxes*
  - *Turning off legacy reporting. This can only happen once all required features are supported – which is outside of the MVP scope. We'll log a technical debt ticket in the backlog*

The list is certainly not complete, but that wasn't the aim of the brainstorming session. The team agrees to log the outstanding work in the backlog and work through this later.

'The Resurrection' has to keep moving forward. It's time to investigate how the data can be accessed and made available for reports and dashboards.

With that, the team heads to their quiet research and development space, focusing on the steps of the second phase of the MVP.

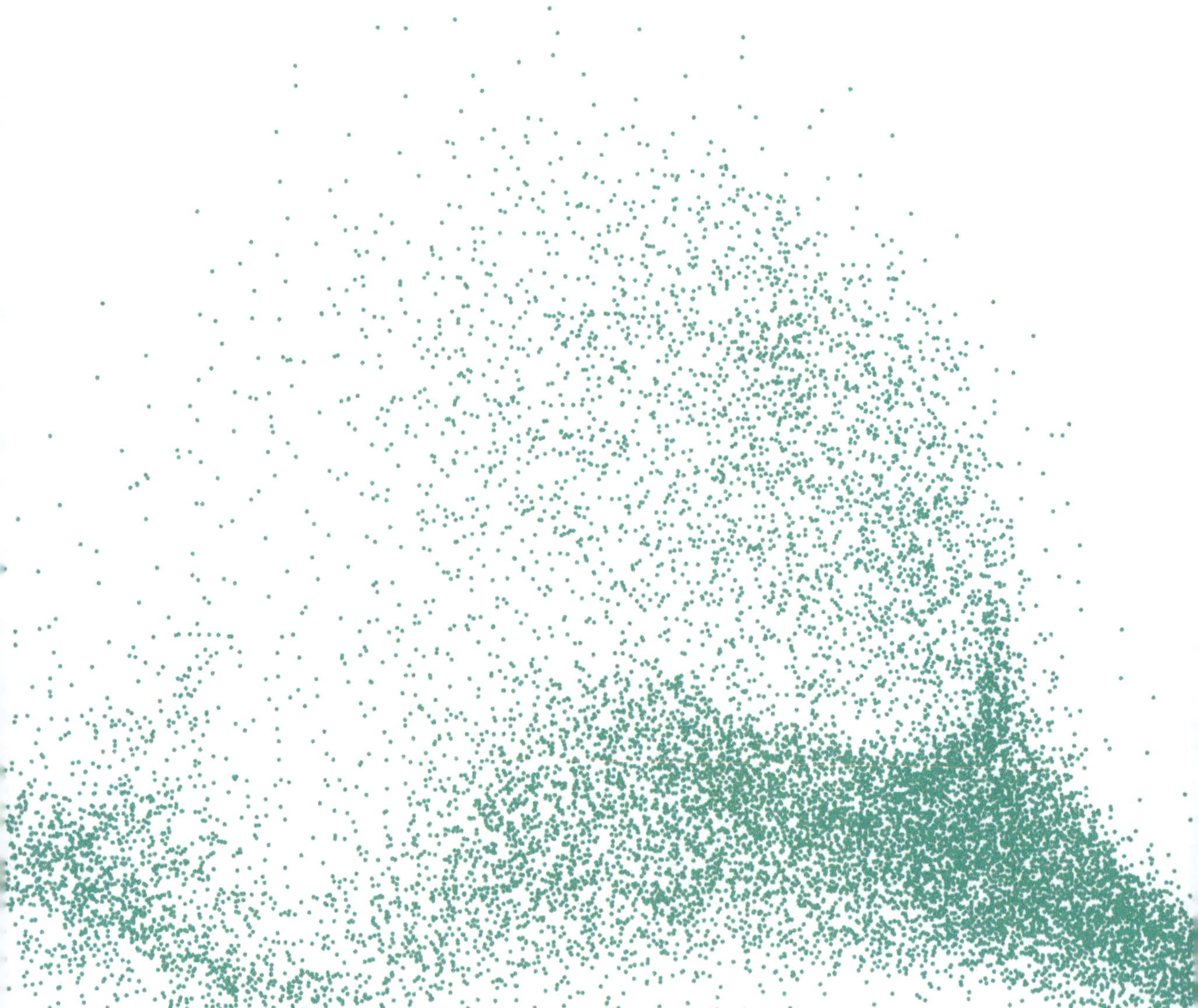

11
Getting the data out

The development 'heavy lifting' is now done: the data is integrated into the data solution. A lot has happened: operational systems have been connected, historization is in place, the information model is taking shape, the essential frameworks are in place, and timelines have been repaired where required.

But we're not there just yet. Two major areas of focus remain:

→ How interpretations —'business logic'— are added to complete the alignment of the data to the information model
→ How the data can be prepared for delivery and consumption

This chapter will go into detail on the 'front room' of the architecture. Let's prepare the data for delivery.

Integration layer implementation — front room

At first glance, the front room of the integration layer —the derived integration area— looks and feels a lot like the base integration area. The derived integration area is, in a sense, 'more of the same': the same objects, patterns, and templates apply. The notable difference is the application of business logic —transformations that alter the meaning of the data— are applied here.

In these sections, we'll use the terms 'transformations,' 'business logic,' and 'business rules,' or simply 'rules' interchangeably.

The derived integration layer focuses on:

→ Application of rules
→ Exception handling

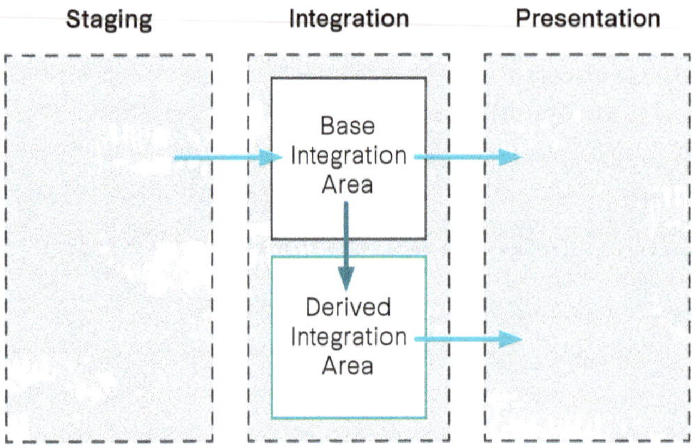

At the end of the day, this is an architecture decision on how to interpret certain methodologies. How you 'do' things, and to what extent 'rules' are followed.

Even though the engine supports full refactoring we prefer to specifically define the derived integration area for business logic implementation.

It's a form of separation of concerns, and we feel it's a useful convention to highlight where business logic resides in the architecture.

When using Data Vault as the physical modeling technique, the derived integration area adds additional Hubs, Links, and Satellites to the model. At least, to the extent that this is necessary to conform data to the information model, by applying business rules. Together, these two areas are the physical implementation of the information model.

This also explains why this area is optional. When no transformations or additional objects are necessary to map the data to the model, there is no need for derived integration area objects.

Why have a derived area when you have a PSA?

Before starting discussing the front room in earnest, there is a philosophical topic worth discussing: when it's possible to deterministically reprocess the entire data solution in the spirit of the virtual data solution, then what's the benefit of having a separate area for business logic implementation?

After all, the base integration area is *also* an interpretation, albeit one without fundamentally altering the data. And interpretations change or can be outright wrong — a core tenet of Engine Thinking.

Moreover, due to the ability to reprocess the integration layer in its entirety, one could argue it's permitted to implement transformation that modify the meaning of the data —destructive transformations— on the way *into* the base integration area.

When these transformations are modified, parts of the system can be rebuilt, the same way as done when refactoring (parts of) the model.

Some projects don't define a derived integration area for this reason — they have a PSA to fall back on.

Where to apply business logic

Unfortunately, in the real world, data doesn't always fit the intended model. Transformations are necessary to reshape the data into a form and meaning that provides actionable information to consumers.

In earlier chapters, we have emphasized the importance of addressing this complexity at the system level as part of broader data management efforts. However, due to various constraints, some degree of business logic implementation is unavoidable — so that the burden of adding this complexity does not fall on data consumers.

Generally speaking, and having taken the decision to include the derived integration area in the architecture, the implementation of these transformations can be done in two key locations:

- → On the way to the presentation layer
- → Within the derived integration area

The choice between these options depends on the scope of the business logic — to what extent the business logic is *enterprise-wide.* This concept was first introduced in the architecture's derived integration area section, and essentially means if transformations are used more than once.

If the transformation is specific to a single data delivery, implementing it in the presentation layer may be the simplest approach. However, if the same logic is required across multiple deliveries, it is more efficient to implement it once in the derived integration area, allowing for reuse and reducing redundant coding.

Raw Vault, Business Vault

In the physical implementation using Data Vault methodology, the base integration area and derived integration area align to 'raw' and 'business' Data Vault objects.

The term 'business' can be a bit of a misnomer in this context, as both the 'raw' and 'business' Data Vault objects should be business-focused. After all, the objects represent the physical implementation of the organization's information model.

Business logic is implemented as data logistic processes to load new Hubs, Links, and Satellites that complement the existing (raw) model.

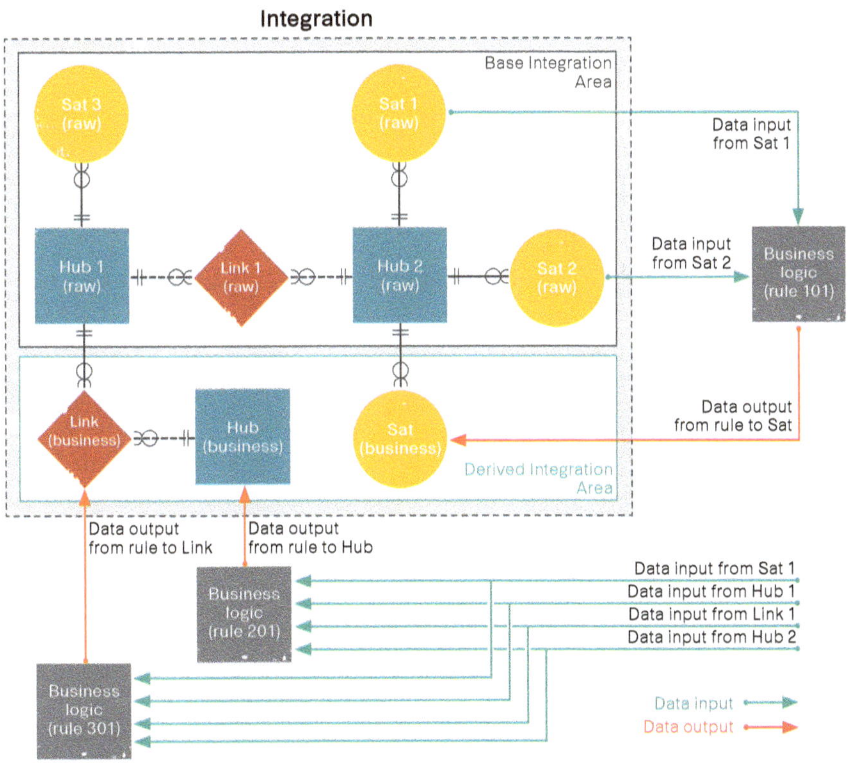

Raw and business Data Vault don't represent separate layers, and there is no need to pass through a 'Business Data Vault' to be able to deliver data. Objects should only be added if and when necessary.

Translating intent to code

Now, let's focus on the actual transformations – the business rules themselves.

At a high level, we define a separation between the functional intent and the technical implementation.

A *business rule* in this context is the technology independent explanation of the transformation that should be applied. An *implementation rule* –technology-dependent– specifies how these data transformations are applied in practice.

Implementation rules must be linked to a business rule, and each business rule can be referred to by one or more implementation rules.

Business rules capture the logic required by business experts without considering technical implementation. Because of this, business rules can be expressed in a language that best supports the subject matter experts – much like the information model.

The business rule bitmap

A *business rule bitmap* provides a structured way to list rules, assign unique identifiers, and link applied rules to affected data. It follows the same principle as an ⚐ exception bitmap, but while an exception bitmap tracks exception scenarios in data, a business rule bitmap records business logic transformations.

The mechanism is straightforward:
→ Each business rule is assigned a unique bit position (a binary identifier)
→ When a rule is applied, its corresponding bit position is activated
→ The final recorded value is the sum of all active bit positions

This idea is illustrated with an example below:

Business rule bitmap

Rule	Description	Bit position
1	Add GST	1
2	Define Order Of Dependents	2
3	Calculate Earned	4
4	Calculate Written	8
5	Invalid phone number	16
6	Determine Owner of Cover	32
7	Standardize Address	64
8	Remove GST	128

In this example, rule 2 and rule 6 are applied:
- → Rule 2 has a bit position of 2
- → Rule 6 has a bit position of 32
- → The recorded value is 34 (2 + 32)

In binary, 34 is represented as 001000010 (read from right to left).
Each 1 indicates an active rule at that bit position.

This approach efficiently tracks and links multiple rules to a single record within the data platform, providing a compact and structured way to manage transformations. When annotating code, the individual rules can be reference directly. When using Git, or similar, a URL can be added to directly refer to the rule's details.

Documentation of business rules

Business rules change over time as improvements and refinements are made. These updates can be implemented deterministically, raising an important question for the data solution's architect:
- → Should the latest version of a rule be applied retroactively to all historical data?
- → Should rule changes only affect data from the moment the rule is updated?
- → Can both approaches be supported?

To manage this, we consider it a best practice to structurally record business rules in a repository for transparency and auditability, and so that version control is applied to understand changes to these rules over time.

We recommend to:
- → Assign a unique identifier to each business rule
- → Refer to rule identifiers in both code and data for traceability
- → Extend the business rule bitmap with a validity period and additional details that benefit the explanation (technology-independent)

The goal is to maintain a managed, version-controlled list of business rules that are directly linked back from their implementation — both from the code where they are applied and from the data they affect.

Let's expand on rule 2 (Define Order of Dependents) and rule 6 (Determine Owner of Cover):

Business rule bitmap

Rule	Effective From Timestamp	Effective Before Timestamp	Audit Timestamp	Reasoning	Implementation Pseudo Code
2	1900-01-01	2025-01-19	2025-01-10	Select the order of creating defines the order as this information is not captured.	Rank Customers on Policy by [MODIFIED DATE].
2	2025-01-19	9999-12-31	NULL	For the Travel policies the order of creating defines the order as this information is not captured. For Roadside assistance this is captured however and can be used directly.	If the [Plan_Code] is 'Travel' then rank Customers on Policy by [MODIFIED DATE]. If the [Plan_Code] is 'Roadside' then select the [DEPENDENT_NR] value.
6	1900-01-01	9999-12-31	2025-01-15	If the order of the customer on the policy is the first, then this is the owner of cover.	Rank the order of customers on a policy using [Define Order of Dependents] and select the Rank = 1.

The rule identifiers refer to the business rule bitmap's unique identifiers, but additional details have now been added.

An effective from and effective before timestamp are introduced, indicating the range of data the rule is, or should be, applied against based on the data's inscription timestamp.

By applying the validity period to the inscription timestamps, the data delivery can be scoped to the full range of data or re-applied deterministically when refactoring.

An audit timestamp can be added as well. Business rules are discussed from time to time, and it can be helpful to create a record of when it was last reviewed (and optionally by whom).

An alternative approach is to introduce a new rule for each updated version instead of relying on a validity period. This works as long as it remains clear when an old rule is no longer valid and which data it applies to.

Documentation of implementation rules

Implementation rules don't require separate documentation in the same way business rules do. The code itself —linked to business rule identifiers— serves as the documentation.

Clear coding standards, inline comments and annotations, along with consistent structures and conventions, all contribute to making the code 'readable.' In this way, the intent behind the code is documented through the business rules, and the implementation can be reviewed directly within the codebase.

Implementation

The implementation of business rules in data solutions is a deep and complex topic, with many approaches and differing opinions on the best method.

Options range from:
- → Code-based solutions (using 3rd- or 4th-generation languages)
- → Business rule engines or similar declarative tools
- → Domain Specific Languages (DSLs)
- → Dedicated data integration software in various forms

The underlying distinction is to what extent the business rule implementation lies in a more 'technical' or a more 'business' domain.

How much technical background should a 'business person' have to correctly implement transformation rules on data?

Many data integration tools are seen as too technical, while abstract business-rule engines may be too limited – or too cumbersome when exposed via APIs. Over time, opinions shift back-and-forth between code-based and GUI-driven approaches.

Code provides structure, but can become too complex for non-technical users. On the other hand, GUI-based rule definitions can be slow to developers, difficult to debug at scale, and are often tied to vendor capabilities and limitations.

Ultimately, what matters in all scenarios for Engine Thinking is the ability to capture the rules in metadata. The business rule bitmap (or equivalent) is a key component, providing the unique numbering of rules and the ability to ensure these can be referenced in code and data.

In the ⚐ schema for data solution automation, we introduced the data query concept to house business logic. Any content can be added here, provided it is be understood by the platform (e.g., compiler, interpreter).

Many of the techniques and concepts mentioned in this section allow business logic to be captured in design metadata this way. This is often done using a form of DSL – a specialized, purpose-built language that allows standardized documentation of logic.

SQL, itself a DSL, is a common choice, but other DSLs —including open-source initiatives— can also be used to support the automation. One of the benefits of using a broadly-supported language like SQL is that it's easier to switch technologies. Using third-party DSLs and software-specific syntax may result in vendor lock-in.

As long as business logic is structured and standardized, it can define transformations at both the entity and attribute levels as part of source-to-target mappings.

The engine can then read these definitions and compile them into executable code as part of the code generation process.

Considerations

The following sections contain considerations for implementing the derived integration area.

Implementing a business rule as a view

One implementation approach for business rules that we frequently see in projects is the use of views.

This is related to the implementation approach, and the way business rules are captured in metadata. Instead of applying logic at the item level via a data query, it can also be applied at the object level using mechanisms like database views, functions, stored procedures, or equivalent solutions.

Rather than having a detailed set of instructions applied to data —often on a row-by-row basis— a common solution is to implement business logic in views using DSLs (including SQL) or code such as Python, Scala, and similar languages.

The considerations of the implementation sections still apply: to what extent is the implementation 'too technical' for subject matter experts to review? Can this be addressed with clear documentation based on the business rule bitmap, and peer reviews on the implementation side?

Either way, using a view (or equivalent) can be a convenient way to encapsulate all transformation in a single object, which can then be added as a source data object in the data object mapping.

Parallel processing

Derived integration area objects are typically sourced from base integration objects. This creates a dependency: base integration data must be available before the derived integration area can complete.

However, this dependency exists only at the *data* level. It is still possible to implement parallel processing —up to the level of continuous operation— by following the same patterns used in the base integration area.

Load windows can be applied to base integration area objects when processing data into the derived integration area, just as they are used when loading data from the PSA into the base layer.

When applying load windows to non-time-variant objects —such as Hubs or Links— we recommend ensuring that their contents (typically business keys and relationships) are always described using their corresponding context objects.

This is important because the context's inscription timestamp can then be used as a temporal reference for filtering. On their own, business keys and relationships carry little meaning – they require context to determine their status (e.g., whether they are active or relevant at a given point in time).

What timestamps to pick when creating new data?

Derived integration area objects follow the same conventions as base integration area objects, meaning they share the same standard columns – including the inscription timestamp and state timestamp(s).

A key question arises for newly created records: what values should be assigned to data that has been transformed by business rules?

For the inscription timestamp, the moment the new record was created can be used. The inscription record id follows the order in the dataset, sorted by inscription timestamp.

The assignment of state timestamps depends on the specific business context. In most cases, the new state timeline values should align with the approach used in the base integration area.

In short, derived integration area objects should follow the same temporal approach as their base integration counterparts to maintain consistency the implementation of timelines – so that data can easily be delivered in the presentation layer.

User managed landing objects

In some data solutions, complex logic is implemented to replicate calculations that are not formally available in operational systems but are manually performed by subject matter experts on a regular basis. These calculations tend to be detailed and fast-changing. For instance, the kind of complexity often found in spreadsheets used by actuaries, accountants, and sales teams.

In many cases, only the outcome of these calculations —such as an indexing figure or a correction factor— needs to be applied to the data. However, to determine this outcome, the entire calculation process must be replicated within the data solution.

While formalizing these processes within the data solution may be the right approach —especially if the goal is to phase out spreadsheets or bespoke applications— there is an alternative when moving complexity into the system is neither desirable nor realistic: User Managed Landing Objects (UMLOs).

The role of UMLOs

UMLOs can be used to store ⚐ reference data, including the results of complex calculations that are impractical or undesirable to reproduce within the data solution itself.

These objects follow the same conventions as other LDA objects, but unlike standard LDA objects, UMLOs:

- → Do not originate from a formal operational system 'source'
- → Are *not* truncated
- → Have basic logging applied

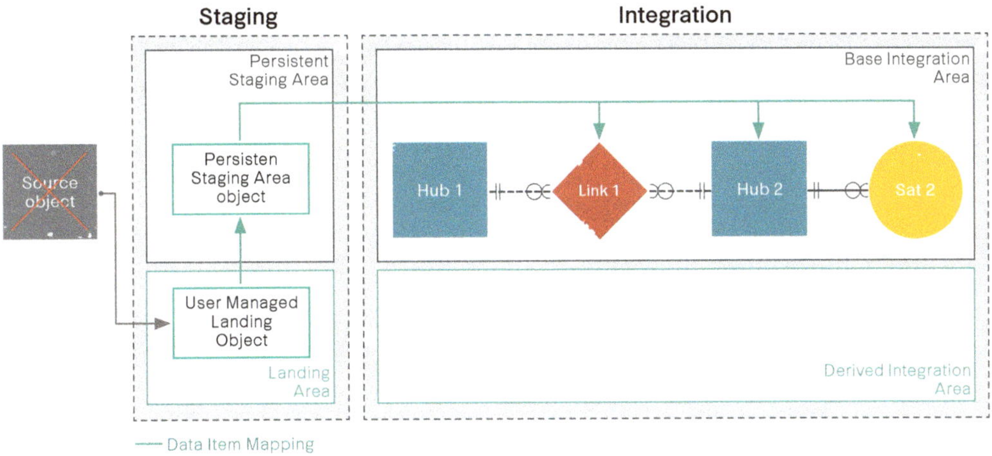

With UMLOs, only the final calculated values are recorded, while the underlying logic remains outside the data solution. It's a form of business logic that can be directly controlled by subject matter experts without actually having this logic implemented. Calculations can be changed without requiring engineering support to modify the data solution. The subject matter expert can simply update the values in the UMLO as needed.

UMLOs are processed downstream in the same way as other LDA objects – into the PSA and beyond when following the reference architecture. This automatically provides auditability and versioning.

Logging

To enhance transparency, we recommend including simple standardized logging when using UMLOs. This logging can be as straightforward as adding columns to automatically capture:

- When a record is changed
- Who made the change

The moment of change –when the subject matter expert commits a new record, or updates and existing one– conceptually is the source timestamp for UMLOs. But it can also be used to record the moment of reception of the data change by the data solution: the inscription timestamp.

Depending on the platform's technical features, logging can often be automated. For example, by implementing triggers or auto-update fields. Additionally, graphical user interfaces (GUIs) or front-end applications can be developed to facilitate data entry while ensuring logs are maintained.

Logging is an important safety net for the data solution. Values managed by subject matter experts often play a critical role in reporting. Especially when the data solution is integrated in operational processes, or automations are built on top off the solution it's essential to have a way to show why data is delivered the way it is.

For example, if an subject matter expert incorrectly enters an indexing value that is applied to delivered data, it could disrupt operational processes. By adding logging columns, the PSA automatically provides a full audit trail, so that it is always clear why data behaves the way it does.

Example — reference data

The following example illustrates how a UMLO is used to capture a mapping between an 'account' and a 'district.' In this scenario, this mapping data –including the district– is not available in operational systems but is maintained by subject matter experts based on conventions or agreements.

The mapping could also stem from a calculation, a business rule, or a simple manual assignment. This is a common use case for adding reference data to the data solution.

For brevity, the PSA is omitted from the example. However, when following the reference architecture it would be included in the flow of data.

User Managed Landing Object – District Mapping

Account	District Code	Modified By	Inscription Timestamp
Active	North	Yerodin	2025-02-04 15:37 10:00
Inactive	West	Yerodin	2025-02-04 15:53 10:00
High-Value	West	Yerodin	2025-02-04 16:02 10:00
Overdue	South	Yerodin	2025-06-04 09:12 49:00

Hub Account

Account Surrogate Key	Audit Trail Id	Account
Active\@|	2389	Active
Inactive\@|	2389	Inactive
High-Value\@|	2389	High-Value
Overdue\@|	2389	Overdue

Hub District

District Surrogate Key	Audit Trail Id	District Code
North\@|	2305	North
West\@|	2305	West
South\@|	2305	South

Link Account maps to District

Account to District Surrogate Key	Audit Trail Id	Account Surrogate Key	District Surrogate Key
Active\@|North\@|	2346	Active\@|	North\@|
Inactive\@|West\@|	2346	Inactive\@|	West\@|
High-Value\@|West\@|	2346	High-Value\@|	West\@|
Overdue\@|South\@|	2346	Overdue\@|	South\@|

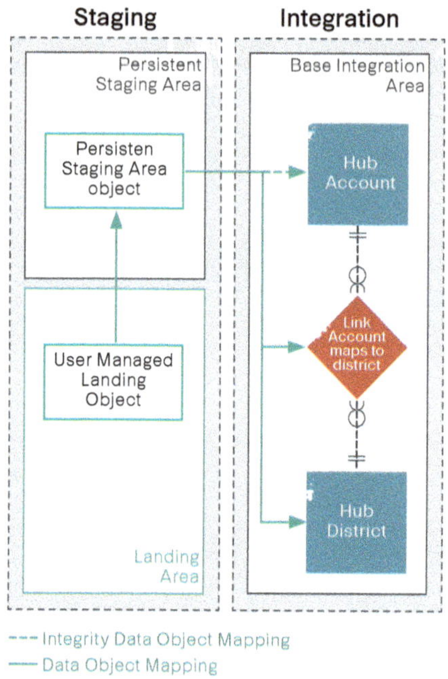

The UMLO containing 'district mappings' is modeled as any other object, and defined in metadata using data object mappings. It functions the same as any other incoming data set.

In this example, while the account Hub may already exist, the district is required for reporting purposes. Subject matter experts can directly influence reporting by updating the values in the UMLO.

Example — indexing

The example below is similar to the previous one. However, this example is less obviously reference data. Here, the 'Increase %' is the result of complex calculations which are performed by subject matter experts outside of the data solution. The resulting index, which increases the costs of renewal plans, becomes context of the renewal, and can be used in downstream reporting to modify figures from other data points.

In this example, both the 'plan' and the 'renewal' plans represent the Plan CBC. In this example, however, the context for the relationship between plans —the renewal— is implemented using a relationship-describing Hub to avoid using Link-Satellites: the renewal Hub.

Another way to implement this is to use ⚐ same-as Links and not explicitly model the renewal Hub.

User Managed Landing Object – Auto Subscriptions

Plan Code	Renewal Plan Code	Increase %	Modified By	Inscription Timestamp
FamilyPlus	Comprehensive	2	Yerodin	2025-02-04
GroupIdeal	Comprehensive	2	Yerodin	2025-02-04
LargerLife	Comprehensive	2	Yerodin	2025-02-04
Overdue	Standard	3	Yerodin	2025-06-04

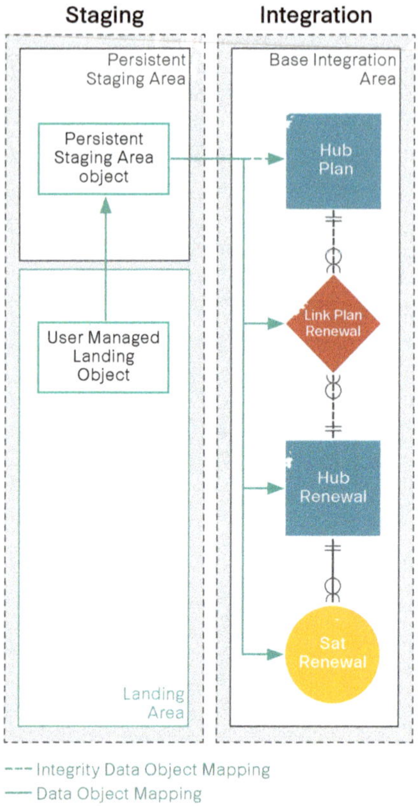

Hub Renewal

Renewal Surrogate Key	Existing Plan Code	New Plan code
FamilyPlus\@|Comprehensive\@|	FamilyPlus	Comprehensive
GroupIdeal\@|Comprehensive\@|	GroupIdeal	Comprehensive
LargerLife\@|Comprehensive\@|	LargerLife	Comprehensive
Fit4One\@|Standard\@|	Fit4One	Standard

Hub Plan

Account Surrogate Key	Plan Code
FamilyPlus\@|	FamilyPlus
GroupIdeal\@|	GroupIdeal
LargerLife\@|	LargerLife
Fit4One\@|	Fit4One
Comprehensive\@|	Comprehensive
Standard\@|	Standard

Sat Renewal

Renewal Surrogate Key	Inscription Timestamp	State Before Timestamp	Increase %
FamilyPlus\@|Comprehensive\@|	2025-02-04	9999-12-31	2
GroupIdeal\@|Comprehensive\@|	2025-02-04	9999-12-31	2
LargerLife\@|Comprehensive\@|	2025-02-04	9999-12-31	2
Fit4One\@|Standard\@|	2025-06-04	9999-12-31	3

Link Plan Renewal

Plan Renewal Surrogate Key	Audit Trail Id	Existing Plan Surrogate Key	Renewal Surrogate Key
FamilyPlus\@|FamilyPlus\@|Comprehensive\@|	45790	FamilyPlus\@|	FamilyPlus\@|Comprehensive\@|
GroupIdeal\@|GroupIdeal\@|Comprehensive\@|	45790	GroupIdeal\@|	GroupIdeal\@|Comprehensive\@|
LargerLife\@|LargerLife\@|Comprehensive\@|	45790	LargerLife\@|	LargerLife\@|Comprehensive\@|
OFit4One\@|Fit4One\@|Standard\@|	45797	Fit4One\@|	Fit4One\@|Standard\@|

This, and the previous example, show how UMLOs can be used to provide necessary data points without implementing complexity in the data solution — and shifting control and accountability to subject matter experts.

Presentation layer implementation

The final layer in the data solution architecture is the presentation layer. Much of the work done in previous layers and areas is done to simplify the process of getting the data out — and enable to do this pattern-based.

Following the data solution architecture, the presentation layer focuses on:
- → Formatting data for final delivery (outgoing interface)
- → Establishing the right level of detail for data delivery (granularity)
- → Implementing business rules not yet covered by earlier layers
- → Selection of timelines and 'date math'
- → Displaying data changes over time

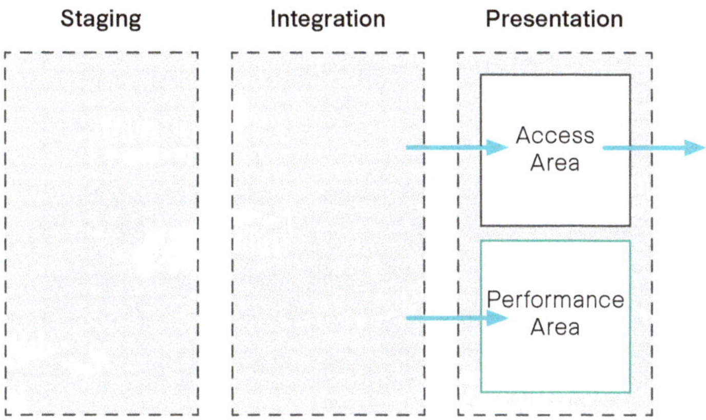

The presentation layer can retrieve data from both the base and derived integration areas.

If the data is already fit for purpose, the final preparation for delivery is relatively straightforward. If not, additional business rules and performance optimizations can be applied to the extent the derived integration area has not already catered for this.

Struggling with time — while getting the data out

The struggle with time to get the data 'out' is much easier with all the preparation done on timelines in the integration layer — when getting the data 'in.'

However, there are still a few important concepts to tackle.

The integration layer already delivers complete timelines following the Open-Closed notation. If this is not the case, then this must be implemented or derived as part of this step — which means the complexity covered in the earlier ⚐ struggling with time section must be managed here.

Timelines and snapshots

↗ Timelines display the changes over time, using a validity period. Snapshots create a record for each point-in-time view of the data.

Generally speaking, data can be delivered in two primary ways: as timeline or as snapshot.

Timelines capture changes over time, with each row explicitly marked by its validity time period using Open-Closed notation (from timestamp —inclusive, before timestamp— exclusive). This is the same structure used in Satellites.

Snapshots offer a point-in-time view of the data. They're generated by querying the timeline data to extract what was valid at a specific moment — such as daily, end-of-month, or hourly.

These two representations are two sides of the same coin. They both describe temporal truth and can —conceptually— be transformed into one another. For example, you can derive a snapshot from a timeline by filtering for specific timestamps, or build a timeline by chaining a sequence of snapshots together and deriving a before timestamp, the time periods, again.

Timelines have less, or no, data redundancy and are more versatile. They are, however, more complex to develop. Snapshots are relatively easy to implement but require much more processing and storage, typically contain data redundancy, and are less scalable overall.

They're not fundamentally different in concept — only in representation and intent. That said, they are not technically the same. Their structure, performance implications, and best-use scenarios differ depending on the delivery needs and situation.

Various use-cases can be implemented for both. Some outgoing interfaces require snapshots. In other cases, snapshots are delivered because of time pressure since timelines are more complex to develop and test.

Timelines

Timelines are the default structure for delivering data in the presentation layer.

A classic example is a Slowly Changing Dimension – Type 2 ('SCD 2'), which captures historical changes using validity ranges.

When applying the patterns for combining multiple time-variant objects —outlined in the following sections— the resulting output will follow a timeline format by design.

Please refer to our website for examples: https://dtng.link/4pgg7.

Joining two time-variant objects

When joining two datasets that contain changes over time —time-variant objects— a standard pattern can be used:
The greatest of the two from timestamps is smaller than the smallest of the two before timestamps.

Everything else we do is a variation of this theme.

Consider the following example, which joins a Hub with two Satellites:

```
SELECT
 Hub.<Key>, -- Hub Key
 (CASE
   WHEN Sat1.<From Timestamp> > Sat2.<From Timestamp>
   THEN Sat1.<From Timestamp>
   ELSE Sat2.<From Timestamp>
 END) AS <From Timestamp>, -- Greatest of the two from timestamps
 (CASE
   WHEN Sat1.<Before Timestamp> < Sat2.<Before Timestamp>
   THEN Sat1.<Before Timestamp>
   ELSE Sat2.<Before Timestamp>
 END) AS <Before Timestamp>, -- Smallest of the two before timestamps
 * -- Any other columns as required
FROM <Hub> Hub
JOIN <Satellite 1> Sat1
  ON Hub.<Key> = Sat1.<Key>
JOIN <Satellite 2> Sat2
  ON Hub.<Key> = Sat2.<Key>
WHERE
 (CASE
  WHEN Sat1.<From Timestamp> > Sat2.<From Timestamp>
  THEN Sat1.<From Timestamp>
  ELSE Sat2.<From Timestamp>
 END) -- Greatest of the two from timestamps
<
 (CASE
  WHEN Sat1.<Before Timestamp> < Sat2.<Before Timestamp>
  THEN Sat1.<Before Timestamp>
  ELSE Sat2.<Before Timestamp>
 END) -- Smallest of the two before timestamps
```

This sample SQL query returns only the overlapping intervals in the selected timeline, following the concepts introduced in the ⚐ 'date math' section. The timeline itself is kept intentionally generic. This technique works for any timeline, assuming it is complete. In practice, the state timeline should be used as the basis for joining time-variant data.

SQLs of this example can be found on our website: https://dtng.link/52lr0.

While this example uses explicit CASE statements, most SQL dialects support built-in GREATEST() and LEAST() functions, which can simplify the syntax significantly.

To better understand what's happening, consider the simplified example below:

Sat Wind Condition

City Surrogate Key	Inscription Timestamp	State From Timestamp	State Before Timestamp	Wind Condition
Lo Stagnone\@l	2025-04-10	2025-04-10	2025-04-11	Not good
Lo Stagnone\@l	2025-04-11	2025-04-11	2025-04-14	Great
Lo Stagnone\@l	2025-04-14	2025-04-14	9999-12-31	Extreme

Sat Weather

City Surrogate Key	Inscription Timestamp	State From Timestamp	State Before Timestamp	Weather
Lo Stagnone\@l	2025-04-10	2025-04-10	2025-04-12	Sunny
Lo Stagnone\@l	2025-04-12	2025-04-12	2025-04-13	Partly cloudy
Lo Stagnone\@l	2025-04-13	2025-04-13	2025-04-14	Cloudy
Lo Stagnone\@l	2025-04-14	2025-04-14	9999-12-31	Rain

Combined data set (for kite surfing)

City Surrogate Key	Inscription Timestamp	State From Timestamp	Weather	Wind condition
Lo Stagnone\@l	2025-04-10	2025-04-11	Sunny	Not good
Lo Stagnone\@l	2025-04-11	2025-04-12	Sunny	Great
Lo Stagnone\@l	2025-04-12	2025-04-13	Partly cloudy	Great
Lo Stagnone\@l	2025-04-13	2025-04-14	Cloudy	Great
Lo Stagnone\@l	2025-04-14	9999-12-31	Rain	Extreme

The 'greatest of the two from timestamps is smaller than the smallest of the two before timestamps' approach compares the overlaps.

This can be shown in the combined data set (for kite surfing) including all the 'overlaps' that are presented here:

Wind condition	Wind From	Wind Before	Weather	Weather From	Weather Before	Greatest From Timestamp	Smallest Before Timestamp	Valid Indicator
Not good	2025-04-10	2025-04-11	Sunny	2025-04-10	2025-04-12	2025-04-10	2025-04-11	Valid
Not good	2025-04-10	2025-04-11	Partly cloudy	2025-04-12	2025-04-13	2025-04-12	2025-04-11	Invalid
Not good	2025-04-10	2025-04-11	Cloudy	2025-04-13	2025-04-14	2025-04-13	2025-04-11	Invalid
Not good	2025-04-10	2025-04-11	Rain	2025-04-14	9999-12-31	2025-04-14	2025-04-11	Invalid
Great	2025-04-11	2025-04-14	Sunny	2025-04-10	2025-04-12	2025-04-11	2025-04-12	Valid
Great	2025-04-11	2025-04-14	Partly cloudy	2025-04-12	2025-04-13	2025-04-12	2025-04-13	Valid
Great	2025-04-11	2025-04-14	Cloudy	2025-04-13	2025-04-14	2025-04-13	2025-04-14	Valid
Great	2025-04-11	2025-04-14	Rain	2025-04-14	9999-12-31	2025-04-14	2025-04-14	Invalid
Extreme	2025-04-14	9999-12-31	Sunny	2025-04-10	2025-04-12	2025-04-14	2025-04-12	Invalid
Extreme	2025-04-14	9999-12-31	Partly cloudy	2025-04-12	2025-04-13	2025-04-14	2025-04-13	Invalid
Extreme	2025-04-14	9999-12-31	Cloudy	2025-04-13	2025-04-14	2025-04-14	2025-04-14	Invalid
Extreme	2025-04-14	9999-12-31	Rain	2025-04-14	9999-12-31	2025-04-14	9999-12-31	Valid

The WHERE predicate in the SQL ensures that only records with a valid overlap are returned.

However, this approach only works well when *exactly* two time-variant objects are involved. Extending it to more than two requires significantly more complex logic. While it's possible to iteratively join a third, fourth, or more time-variant tables —using CTEs, for example— this becomes cumbersome and harder to maintain.

A more scalable approach builds upon the core concepts of this section and allows for combining any number of time-variant objects in a single statement. That more advanced method is the topic of the next section

Combining multiple time-variant objects

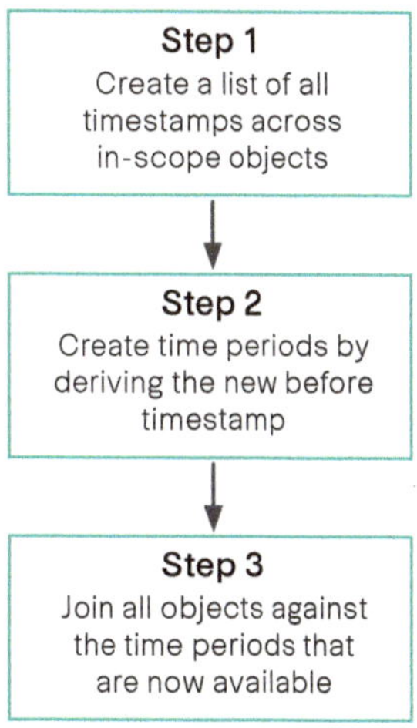

When working with multiple time-variant tables, a different approach is needed to combine them in one go. The key idea is to create a shared timestamp range across all involved objects, and then join each object against this unified timeline.

Please refer to our website for various examples on how this pattern can be applied, as the code can become quite verbose: https://dtng.link/erjut.

Combine all from timestamp values

Start by creating a combined set of all available from timestamp values across the relevant time-variant tables. This is done using a UNION, which effectively compiles a list of all change timestamps.

The result is a list of all changes across all in-scope objects.

This is also an ideal place to add a zero record. This ensures a complete timeline from the earliest possible timestamp (low-end timestamp value):

```
-- Creation of a zero key for the timeline
SELECT Hub.<Key>, CONVERT(DATETIME2(7), '1900-01-01') AS [From_Timestamp] FROM <Hub> Hub
UNION
-- Combined set of all available from timestamp values
SELECT Sat1.<Key>, Sat1.<From Timestamp> AS [From_Timestamp] FROM <Satellite 1> Sat1
UNION
SELECT Sat2.<Key>, Sat2.<From Timestamp> AS [From_Timestamp] FROM <Satellite 2> Sat2
```

As before, the timeline is intentionally kept generic. In practice, the state timeline applies here. This is the ideal place to add filters, including the required additional selections for bitemporal data sources.

Derive time periods

Next, use a window function to derive the before timestamp value, the end of each time period, from the from timestamp values:

```
-- Creation of time periods
SELECT
 <Key>,
 [From_Timestamp],
 LEAD(FROM_TIMESTAMP,1,'9999-12-31')
 OVER (PARTITION BY <Key>
     ORDER BY [From_Timestamp] ASC)
 AS [Before_Timestamp]
FROM
(
 <results from step 1>
) Timestamps
```

This creates a continuous, unified, timeline that can be joined against.

Join each time-variant object

Now, join the time-variant objects (and optionally, non-time-variant objects like Hubs) against the unified timeline based on the from and before timestamps.

Any required columns from the involved objects that are necessary for delivery can be added here.

```
SELECT
 Hub.<Key>,
 -- Data Item Mappings for the Hub
 Hub.<Business Key>,
 -- Data Item Mappings for Satellite 1
 Sat1.<Column 1>,
 Sat1.<Column 2>,
 Sat1.<Column 3>,
```

```
 -- Data Item Mappings for Satellite 2
 Sat2.<Column 1>,
 Sat2.<Column 2>,
 -- New timeline
 TimePeriods.[From_Timestamp]
 TimePeriods.[Before_Timestamp]
FROM
(
 <results from step 2>
) TimePeriods
-- Joining the Hub, for the business key
INNER JOIN <Hub> Hub
  ON TimePeriods.<Key> = Hub.<Key>
-- Joining the context for Satellite 1
LEFT OUTER JOIN <Satellite 1> Sat1
  ON TimePeriods.<surrogate key> = Sat1.<surrogate key>
 AND Sat1.<From Timestamp> <= TimePeriods.[From_Timestamp]
 AND Sat1.<Before Timestamp> > TimePeriods.[Before_Timestamp]
-- Joining the context for Satellite 2
LEFT OUTER JOIN <Satellite 2> Sat2
  ON TimePeriods.<surrogate key> = Sat2.<surrogate key>
 AND Sat2.<From Timestamp> <= TimePeriods.[From_Timestamp]
 AND Sat2.<Before Timestamp> > TimePeriods.[Before_Timestamp]
```

Since each object is joined against the unified timeline, the scope of objects can easily be extended. However, each additional object will impact the granularity: the more change records are added in step 1, the more records will be returned.

The result may resemble a dimension, a point-in-time (PIT) table, or a full historical snapshot.

Next steps

The resulting time periods represent the most granular level of history available, based on all changes across all joined tables. The attributes you select may not be directly linked to each timestamp in the range – some may appear redundant. This is expected behavior and mirrors what you see in Satellite tables when column scope changes.

Depending on which attributes you expose this may lead to redundancy in the result, but these can easily be handled by adding compacting to the code, similar to the one used in the Satellites.

By applying compacting on top of this query, it becomes easy to:

- → Present a historized (i.e., SCD 2) dimension
- → Generate a true PIT snapshot or timeline
- → Or simply visualize all changes over time

In the next section, we'll explore compacting strategies and alternative approaches to handle this efficiently.

Compacting in the presentation layer

When combining multiple time-variant data objects into a unified timeline, the result often includes more records than needed – especially when you're only selecting a subset of attributes. In these cases, compacting helps reduce redundancy by removing records where nothing has actually changed in the selected output.

This technique is essential when preparing data for delivery, for instance when building certain types of PIT tables or historical dimensions.

The core idea is simple: compare each record with the previous one. If no column values have changed, the current record can be safely discarded. This works because, while a change in a Satellite may have triggered a new time period, that change may not affect any of the attributes selected in the final output.

To implement this, we calculate a checksum across the selected columns, compare adjacent rows, grouped by business key and ordered by the timeline, and filter out records where the checksums are the same.

Generating a checksum

The first step is to use a hashing function to create a single value that represents the contents of each record – excluding the business key, from timestamp, and before timestamp.

For example:

```
HASHBYTES('SHA1',
 COALESCE(TRIM(CONVERT(NVARCHAR(MAX),Sat1.<Column 1>)), '~!@|N/A') + '\@|' +
 COALESCE(TRIM(CONVERT(NVARCHAR(MAX),Sat1.<Column 2>)), '~!@|N/A') + '\@|' +
 COALESCE(TRIM(CONVERT(NVARCHAR(MAX),Sat1.<Column 1>)), '~!@|N/A') + '\@|' +
 COALESCE(TRIM(CONVERT(NVARCHAR(MAX),Sat2.<Column 1>)), '~!@|N/A') + '\@|' +
 COALESCE(TRIM(CONVERT(NVARCHAR(MAX),Sat2.<Column 2>)), '~!@|N/A') + '\@|' +
) AS [Checksum]
```

Compare the current record to the previous one

When the checksum is available, a windows function (LAG) can be applied to access the checksum of the previous record:

```
LAG([Checksum], 1, 0x0000000000000000000000000000000000000000)
OVER(PARTITION BY Hub.<Key>
    ORDER BY [From_Timestamp] ASC)
AS [Previous_Checksum]
```

Filter out unchanged records

Now, filter to include only records where the checksum has changed:

```
WHERE [Checksum] <> [Previous_Checksum]
```

This removes any redundant records – those representing a new timestamp but no meaningful change in the selected column values.

Overview

This compacting logic wraps neatly around the output from the previous section:

```
SELECT
 Final.*,
 [From_Timestamp],
 LEAD([From_Timestamp],1,'9999-12-31')
 OVER(PARTITION BY Hub.<Key>
    ORDER BY [From_Timestamp] ASC)
 AS [Before_Timestamp]
FROM
(
 SELECT
  Calculate_Checksum.*,
  LAG([Checksum], 1, 0x0000000000000000000000000000000000000000)
  OVER(PARTITION BY Hub.<Key>
     ORDER BY [From_Timestamp] ASC)
  AS [Previous_Checksum]
 FROM
 (
```

```
    SELECT
      *,
      HASHBYTES('SHA1',
       COALESCE(TRIM(CONVERT(NVARCHAR(MAX),Sat1.<Column 1>)), '~!@|N/A') + '\@|' +
       COALESCE(TRIM(CONVERT(NVARCHAR(MAX),Sat1.<Column 2>)), '~!@|N/A') + '\@|' +
       COALESCE(TRIM(CONVERT(NVARCHAR(MAX),Sat1.<Column 3>)), '~!@|N/A') + '\@|' +
       COALESCE(TRIM(CONVERT(NVARCHAR(MAX),Sat2.<Column 1>)), '~!@|N/A') + '\@|' +
       COALESCE(TRIM(CONVERT(NVARCHAR(MAX),Sat2.<Column 2>)), '~!@|N/A') + '\@|'
      ) AS [Checksum]
    FROM
  (
    <results from previous section - combining multiple time-variant objects>
    ) Timeline
   ) Calculate_Checksum
) Final
WHERE Final.[Checksum] <> Final.[Previous_Checksum]
```

Note that as a last action, a new before timestamp is calculated. Once redundant records have been filtered out, the timeline may again be incomplete. Recalculating the before timestamp using a final LEAD() function ensures the resulting time ranges are again correct and continuous.

Please refer to our website for an example: https://dtng.link/a8j0r.

Combining data with different granularity

The pattern for combining time-variant objects so far has focused on a single Hub key — for example, integrating a customer Hub and its associated Satellites to create a complete view of customer details over time.

This might be sufficient for many scenarios, but what happens when you need to include additional Hubs (and their Satellites) in the timeline?

Adding Hubs can shift the grain of the timeline. It's helpful to think of this in terms of hierarchy levels: What is the lowest-level Hub — the one with the highest granularity? And which Hubs are 'higher up' in the hierarchy? These higher-level Hubs become attributes or contextual properties of the lowest level, similar to what happens in dimensional modeling. Changes in these higher levels trigger new change records in the timeline.

We'll touch on this further in the final section of this chapter.

A practical approach is to begin with the lowest-level Hub, build its timeline (including its Satellites), and then incrementally add higher-level Hubs and their contextual data.

This is done by traversing the model via Links, connecting Hubs and their context:

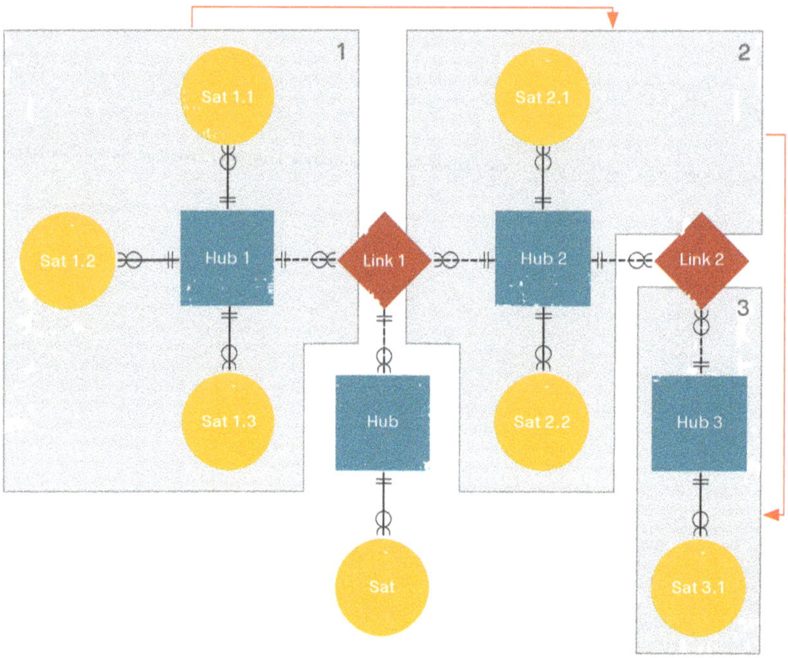

Implementation

The strategy builds on the concepts introduced earlier in this section. Here, you create and join timelines one Hub at a time —or all data which is at the same granularity to be precise— following the standard approach for ⚐ combining multiple time-variant objects. The result is a unified timeline capturing changes across all relevant Hubs and Satellites.

At each step, include the necessary key(s) to point to the next Hub in the chain. This way, the final timeline is constructed in stages – in this example:

→ Combine Hub 1 with its three Satellites
→ Add Hub 2 and its two Satellites
→ Add Hub 3 and its associated Satellite

Link pointers

The joins between timelines are performed via shared keys, which serve as pointers between the timelines. In a Data Vault physical model, these are found in Links.

These Link keys must be present at each step, so they can be used to join to the next timeline:

```
SELECT
 Link1.<Hub2 Key>,
 ...
FROM
(
 -- Timeline 1 definition
) TimePeriods
LEFT OUTER JOIN <Link1>
 ON TimePeriods.<Hub1 Key> = Link1.<Hub1 Key>
```

Now, the timeline from step 1 contains the pointer needed to join the timeline from Hub 2.

However, the time-variance of the Link must also be considered – for instance when implemented as an end-dating Link-Satellite. If the relationship's time-variance is handled by a dedicated Satellite, no extra action is needed. But if not, you'll need to account for the validity of the relationship in the timeline definition.

This can be done in the initial unified timeline step, where all from-timestamps are combined, by adding another UNION block:

```
-- Original part for combining all timestamp values
SELECT Hub.<Key>, CONVERT(DATETIME2(7), '1900-01-01') AS [From_Timestamp] FROM <Hub> Hub
UNION
SELECT Sat1.<Key>, Sat1.<From Timestamp> AS [From_Timestamp] FROM <Satellite 1> Sat1
UNION
SELECT Sat2.<Key>, Sat2.<From Timestamp> AS [From_Timestamp] FROM <Satellite 2> Sat2

-- Added Link-Satellite
UNION
SELECT Hub.<Key>, <From Timestamp> AS [From_Timestamp]
FROM
(
 SELECT
  Link.Hub.<Key>,
  Lsat.<From Timestamp>
 FROM <Link> Link
 INNER JOIN <Link Satellite> Lsat
 ON Link.<key> = Lsat.<key>
) sub
```

Joining the timelines

Timelines are joined using the overlap condition introduced earlier: *the greatest of the two from timestamps is smaller than the smallest of the two before timestamps:*

```
-- Combine timeline 1 and timeline 2 using standard overlap logic
SELECT
 CASE
  WHEN T1.[From_Timestamp] > T2.[From_Timestamp] THEN T1.[From_Timestamp]
```

```
    ELSE T2.[From_Timestamp]
  END AS [From_Timestamp],
  CASE
    WHEN T1.[Before_Timestamp] < T2.[Before_Timestamp] THEN T1.[Before_Timestamp]
    ELSE T2.[Before_Timestamp]
  END AS [Before_Timestamp],
  T1.*,
  T2.*
FROM Timeline1 T1
LEFT OUTER JOIN Timeline2 T2
  ON T1.<Hub2 Key> = T2.<Hub2 Key>
WHERE
  (CASE
    WHEN T1.[From_Timestamp] > T2.[From_Timestamp] THEN T1.[From_Timestamp]
    ELSE T2.[From_Timestamp]
  END)
<
  (CASE
    WHEN T1.[Before_Timestamp] < T2.[Before_Timestamp] THEN T1.[Before_Timestamp]
    ELSE T2.[Before_Timestamp]
  END)
```

The LEFT JOIN in this pattern is significant, because there may not be a relationship to the higher level.

Where to apply compacting?

Compacting can be done at various points in this process:

- After each join step: reduces data volume early and improves performance, but adds complexity (though standardized/pattern-based)
- At the end of the process: simpler to implement (only once) but may involve handling larger result sets

Filtering

One of the golden rules in data integration is: filter as early as possible – and this applies to timelines as well. If filters are needed, the best place to apply them is during the initial selection phase, where from timestamp values are collected across all time-variant objects (as described in the combine all timestamps section).

Filtering at this stage ensures that only relevant records are carried forward into the timeline construction and subsequent joins. It also prevents unnecessary redundant rows from appearing later on – especially once compacting logic is applied.

What filtering is applied exactly is subject to requirements. However, in the next sections we would like to share some examples on how to get creative using filtering for time periods, including how to apply filtering on bitemporal objects.

Frequency compacting

When merging timelines, even minute differences in change timestamps can lead to a large number of output records – each unique timestamp (or time period) results in a separate entry.

In cases where only periodic values are needed (e.g., hourly, daily, or monthly), you can reduce noise by applying frequency-based compacting. This technique groups changes by a predefined time period and retains only the most relevant record per group.

The level of frequency depends entirely on your use case:
→ For financial transactions, every change may be relevant
→ To track customers changing address details, once a day might suffice

Consider a case where two Satellites and a Hub are joined, resulting in changes spread across different timestamps.

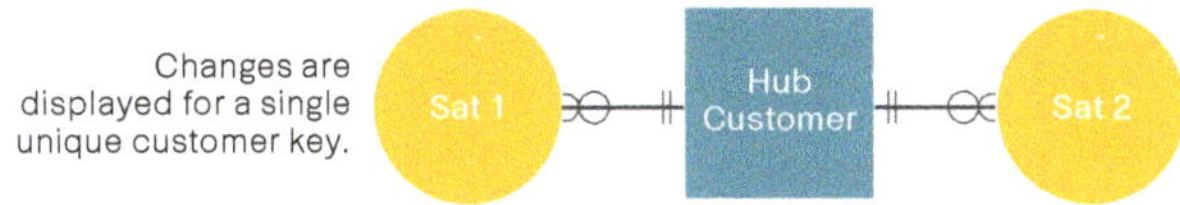

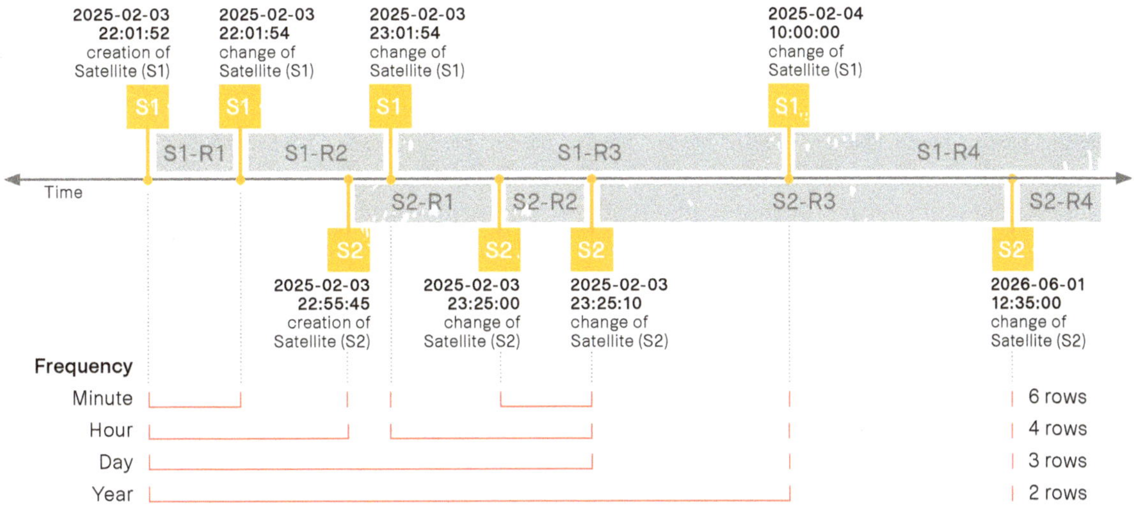

The frequency displayed in this diagram shows the grouping in which the changes fall. Without grouping, the changes would create 8 records.

A grouping for all the changes that fall in the granularity of a minute yields 6 records, whereas the grouping of records at year granularity returns 2.

This is the essence of frequency compacting.

Implementation

To create a 'frequency compacter,' the following pattern can be followed:
→ Group values by your chosen frequency (e.g., minute, hour)
→ Order changes by timeline – from timestamp, descending
→ Use FIRST_VALUE() or equivalent to select the latest value within each group
→ Filter to retain only those latest records

For example:

```
-- Organize the values within the selected frequency
-- Order the dates in descending order, and select the first value
<Selection>,
[From_Timestamp],
FIRST_VALUE([From_Timestamp])
  OVER (PARTITION BY <Key>,
            <Date Part of ([From_Timestamp])>
     ORDER BY [From_Timestamp] DESC)
  AS [Time_Compacter]
-- Keep only the latest record within the selected frequency
WHERE [From_Timestamp] = [Time_Compacter]
```

Continuing the earlier example, let's group changes by hour and retain the most recent record in that timeframe:

```
<Selection>,
[From_Timestamp],
FIRST_VALUE([From_Timestamp])
  OVER (PARTITION BY <Key>,
     DATEPART(YEAR,[From_Timestamp]),
     DATEPART(MONTH,[From_Timestamp]),
     DATEPART(DAY,[From_Timestamp]),
     DATEPART(HOUR,[From_Timestamp])
     ORDER BY [From_Timestamp] DESC)
  AS [Time_Compacter]
```

Applying this code to the sample data yields the following result:

Group	Surrogate Key	From Timestamp	Time Compacter
Group 1	FastChangeCo\@I	2025-02-03 22:01:52	2025-02-03 22:55:45
Group 1	FastChangeCo\@I	2025-02-03 22:01:54	2025-02-03 22:55:45
Group 1	FastChangeCo\@I	2025-02-03 22:55:45	2025-02-03 22:55:45
Group 2	FastChangeCo\@I	2025-02-03 23:01:54	2025-02-03 23:25:10
Group 2	FastChangeCo\@I	2025-02-03 23:25:00	2025-02-03 23:25:10
Group 2	FastChangeCo\@I	2025-02-03 23:25:10	2025-02-03 23:25:10
Group 3	FastChangeCo\@I	2025-02-04 10:00:00	2025-02-04 10:00:00
Group 4	FastChangeCo\@I	2026-06-01 12:35:00	2026-06-01 12:35:00

In this case, only four highlighted re-cords are retained — each representing the latest snapshot for a given hour. Frequency-based condensing is a hard split: values just seconds apart may fall into separate groups. For instance 22:59:59 and 23:00:01 will be two separate rows when condensing at minute level even though the gap is only 2 seconds.

For example, try out this query:

```
SELECT DATEDIFF(MINUTE,
'2025-01-01 16:59',
'2025-01-01 17:01')
```

This returns 2. Even this two-second gap across the minute boundary creates separate rows.

Continuous gap compacting

Continuous gap compacting groups records not by fixed time periods (like hour or day), but based on their proximity in time — assessing whether changes occur within a meaningful frequency threshold.

Let's look again at the example from the previous section:

This time, however, we group records based on how close together the changes are in time, or how long a record was valid (e.g, the time periods in minutes). Each time period which has less minutes than the threshold will be skipped from the result set.

Implementation

The following pattern can be applied:

→ Order the changes by timestamp within each business key
→ Measure the time gap between each change and the next one
→ Retain the record only if the gap exceeds a defined threshold (or if it's the last record)

For example:

```
-- Organize the values within the selected frequency
-- Calculate the time difference with the next row (lead ascending)
DATEDIFF (MINUTE,
  [From_Timestamp],
  LEAD([From_Timestamp])
  OVER (PARTITION BY <Key>
     ORDER BY [From_Timestamp])
) AS [Gap_Minutes]
[...]
-- Keep only the latest record within the selected frequency
WHERE [Gap_Minutes] >= <threshold>
  OR [Gap_Minutes] IS NULL
```

Continuing the same sample data, this example groups changes by proximity within 30 minutes and retains only the latest change in each cluster:

```
DATEDIFF (MINUTE,
  [From_Timestamp],
  LEAD([From_Timestamp])
  OVER (PARTITION BY <Key>
      ORDER BY [From_Timestamp])
) AS [Gap_Minutes]
[...]
WHERE [Gap_Minutes] >= 30
  OR [Gap_Minutes] IS NULL
```

Applying this code to the sample data retains the latest record which exceeds each 30-minute threshold:

	Surrogate Key	From Timestamp	Gap to Successor (in min)
Group 1	FastChangeCo\@l	2025-02-03 22:01:52	0
	FastChangeCo\@l	2025-02-03 22:01:54	54
Group 2	FastChangeCo\@l	2025-02-03 22:55:45	6
	FastChangeCo\@l	2025-02-03 23:01:54	24
	FastChangeCo\@l	2025-02-03 23:25:00	0
	FastChangeCo\@l	2025-02-03 23:25:10	635
Group 3	FastChangeCo\@l	2025-02-04 10:00:00	694.235
Group 4	FastChangeCo\@l	2026-06-01 12:35:00	NULL

This approach condenses the data by ignoring micro-changes that occur too frequently to be meaningful, and instead surfaces the last known value in each group.

This is useful when your goal is to reduce 'change noise' and focus on material changes spaced meaningfully apart. For instance using sensor data that sends intermittent bursts of data, or when certain changes are always 'batched up' in operational systems.

Temporal data selection

When combining data objects, the selection of from timestamp values —used to define the time periods— must also be constrained by the assertion timeline.

Do you want to view history as it was received today, or as it appeared at the end of last month?

To answer that, a filter must be applied to limit records based on the inscription timestamp.

This is typically done by adding a predicate during the timestamp collection phase — that is, when combining all from timestamp values from involved objects.

How this is implemented depends whether the solution uses unitemporal or bitemporal objects.

Bitemporal

For bitemporal objects, filtering must account for both the inscription from timestamp and the inscription before timestamp.

This is because backdated adjustments — changes that arrive later but apply to earlier time periods — can cause ripples in the state timeline — a concept extensively covered when getting the data in.

Without explicitly specifying the validity of the assertion timeline, multiple records may be returned due to overlaps in the state timeline at different points in the assertion timeline.

```
DECLARE @Assertion_Filter_Timestamp DATETIME2(7) = SYSUTCDATETIME();

[...]
WHERE
-- Assertion timeline
    [Inscription_From_Timestamp]  <= @Assertion_Filter_Timestamp
  AND [Inscription_Before_Timestamp] > @Assertion_Filter_Timestamp
```

Where do the inscription from and before timestamps come from?

Standard bitemporal objects typically store only the inscription timestamp.

In this approach, the inscription from timestamp is simply the inscription timestamp itself, while the corresponding before timestamp is derived using a window function.

We didn't add these from and before timestamps earlier —so we can follow an insert-only processing approach— but this means that the inscription before timestamp must be evaluated at runtime.

Alternatively, it's possible to store the before timestamp directly in the Satellite, but doing so would require updates to maintain the assertion timeline.

Unitemporal

For unitemporal objects, the approach is simpler, because the assertion timeline only needs to be constrained based on the inscription timestamp:

```
DECLARE @Assertion_Filter_Timestamp DATETIME2(7) = SYSUTCDATETIME();

[...]
WHERE
-- Assertion timeline
    [Inscription_From_Timestamp]  <= @Assertion_Filter_Timestamp
```

This predicate ensures that only records below a given assertion timeline boundary are returned.

The remaining records can then be merged along the state timeline.

The inscription timestamp will never contain future timestamps as it is added to each record upon insert. That's why the <= filter is sufficient here.

Snapshots

A snapshot is a straightforward way to retrieve point-in-time information from the integration layer. The idea is simple: for each record or key, return the value that was valid at a specific moment in time — based on the available time period data.

To create a snapshot, filter the data using the following condition:

- Snapshot timestamp >= from timestamp
- Snapshot timestamp < before timestamp

For example, to return the data valid at 2025-04-08 16:00:07.320, you can use the following SQL:

```
SELECT *
FROM <data object>
WHERE '2025-04-08 16:00:07.320' >= [From_Timestamp]
 AND '2025-04-08 16:00:07.320'  < [Before_Timestamp]
```

We use >= and < because the time ranges in the integration layer follow the Open-Closed notation. Thanks to the preparation done earlier, there's no gap between the before timestamp of one record and the from timestamp of the next — they are identical.

Using <= instead of < would result in duplicate rows.

Please refer to our website for examples: https://dtng.link/8kk8t.

In the next sections, we'll explore the advantages and trade-offs of using snapshots as a delivery mechanism.

Combining data

In the pattern for creating a timeline from multiple time-variant objects, we explored how additional data —spanning multiple Hubs, Links, and Satellites— can be joined to build a unified timeline. While powerful, this timeline-based approach is relatively complex (though highly standardized).

For snapshot-based approaches, the process is much simpler.

Although the model is still traversed the same way —navigating via Links to reach other Hubs— each time-variant object joined along the way applies the same snapshot selection logic.

This consistent filtering simplifies the retrieval of point-in-time values across the entire model.

Granularity and redundancy

The following example demonstrates how a dataset with time periods can be converted into a series of monthly snapshots, using a timestamp field to 'pick' a snapshot date. In this case, the snapshot is taken at end-of-month (EOM) granularity, one for each month in 2025.

The example contains five sample records and a recursive statement to generate 12 snapshot timestamps. For each one, the corresponding valid record is selected.

You can find the query and example output on our website: https://dtng.link/b0zlj.

```
WITH [Sample] AS
(
 SELECT '100\@|' AS [Surrogate_Key],
    NULL AS [Column_Value],
    CONVERT(DATETIME2(7),'1900-01-01') AS
[From_Timestamp],
    CONVERT(DATETIME2(7),'2025-02-01') AS
[Before_Timestamp]
 UNION
 SELECT '100\@|' AS [Surrogate_Key],
    'A' AS [Column_Value],
    CONVERT(DATETIME2(7),'2025-02-01') AS
[From_Timestamp],
```

```
    CONVERT(DATETIME2(7),'2025-02-15') AS [Before_Timestamp]
UNION
SELECT'100\@|' AS [Surrogate_Key],
    'B' AS [Column_Value],
    CONVERT(DATETIME2(7),'2025-02-15') AS [From_Timestamp],
    CONVERT(DATETIME2(7),'2025-03-20') AS [Before_Timestamp]
UNION
SELECT '100\@|' AS [Surrogate_Key],
    'C' AS [Column_Value],
    CONVERT(DATETIME2(7),'2025-03-20') AS [From_Timestamp],
    CONVERT(DATETIME2(7),'2025-09-20')AS [Before_Timestamp]
UNION
SELECT '100\@|' AS [Surrogate_Key],
    'D' AS [Column_Value],
    CONVERT(DATETIME2(7),'2025-09-20') AS [From_Timestamp],
    CONVERT(DATETIME2(7),'9999-12-31') AS [Before_Timestamp]
)
,[Dates] AS
(
  -- Create a list of 12 months (end-of-month timestamps)
  SELECT [Snapshot Timestamp] = EOMONTH(CONVERT(DATETIME2(7),'2025-01-31'))
  UNION ALL
  SELECT [Snapshot Timestamp] = EOMONTH(DATEADD(MONTH, 1, [Snapshot Timestamp]))
  FROM DATES
  WHERE [Snapshot Timestamp] < CONVERT(DATETIME2(7),'2025-12-31')
)
SELECT *
FROM [Sample]
JOIN [Dates]
 ON [Snapshot Timestamp] >= [From_Timestamp]
 AND [Snapshot Timestamp] <  [Before_Timestamp]
```

The ‘Sample’ CTE component contains time-period data with clearly defined validity ranges using Open-Closed notation:

Surrogate Key	Value	From Timestamp	Before Timestamp
100\@|	NULL	1900-01-01	2025-02-01
100\@|	A	2025-02-01	2025-02-15
100\@|	B	2025-02-15	2025-03-20
100\@|	C	2025-03-20	2025-09-20
100\@|	D	2025-09-20	9999-12-31

The ‘Dates’ CTE component generates 12 snapshot points —one per month— using the EOMONTH() function to define each end-of-month timestamp in 2025.

When creating snapshots for each of these months, the result is as follows:

Surrogate Key	Value	From Timestamp	Before Timestamp	Snapshot Timestamp
100\@|	NULL	1900-01-01	2025-02-01	2025-01-31
100\@|	B	2025-02-15	2025-03-20	2025-02-28
100\@|	C	2025-03-20	2025-09-20	2025-03-31
100\@|	C	2025-03-20	2025-09-20	2025-04-30
100\@|	C	2025-03-20	2025-09-20	2025-05-31
100\@|	C	2025-03-20	2025-09-20	2025-06-30
100\@|	C	2025-02-20	2025-09-20	2025-07-31
100\@|	C	2025-03-20	2025-09-20	2025-08-31
100\@|	D	2025-09-20	9999-12-31	2025-09-30
100\@|	D	2025-09-20	9999-12-31	2025-10-31
100\@|	D	2025-09-20	9999-12-31	2025-11-30
100\@|	D	2025-09-20	9999-12-31	2025-12-31

The resulting dataset shows one record per snapshot timestamp, representing the value that was valid at that point in time.

The output clearly shows the redundancy that is created as a result. Some values (e.g., ‘C’ and ‘D’) appear in multiple records because they were valid across many months. This is expected behavior – snapshots duplicate values across time points when the underlying values remain unchanged.

Notice that value ‘A’ disappears completely. It was valid only from 2025-02-01 and before 2025-02-15, but no snapshot timestamp falls within that time period. This shows how snapshot granularity (e.g., monthly) can impact fidelity – the topic of the next section.

While you technically could apply compacting to reduce redundancy in the result set, doing so would defeat the purpose of snapshots. Consumers would no longer be able to directly retrieve specific snapshots (e.g., month-end) with confidence. Compacting would effectively convert the snapshot output back into a time-period format.

Fidelity

While snapshots are easier to create and consume, they come with a trade-off: loss of fidelity. For example, once you generate a daily snapshot, it’s no longer possible to meaningfully convert it into hourly resolution – because the finer-grained detail is no longer available.

Unless you regenerate snapshots from the integration layer (which retains full historized context), that data is lost.

Let’s continue the example from the previous section by compacting the snapshot data back into a timeline format.

This version of SQL reuses the ‘Dates’ CTE from earlier, but instead of treating each timestamp as a separate snapshot, it compacts consecutive records with the same values into broader time periods.

```
...<sample and dates CTE components
from previous section>
,[Snapshots] AS
(
 SELECT * FROM [Sample]
 JOIN [Dates]
  ON [Snapshot Timestamp] >= [From_Timestamp]
  AND [Snapshot Timestamp] < [Before_Timestamp]
)
,[Checksum_CTE] AS
(
 -- Create a checksum for record comparison
 SELECT
  HASHBYTES('SHA1',
   COALESCE(TRIM(CONVERT(NVARCHAR(MAX),
   [Column_Value])), '~!@|N/A') + '\@|'
  ) AS [Checksum],
  *
 FROM Snapshots
)
,[PreviousChecksum] AS
(
```

```
  -- Query the previous checksum using LAG()
  SELECT
   [Surrogate_Key],
   [Column_Value],
   [From_Timestamp],
   [Checksum],
   LAG([Checksum])
   OVER (PARTITION BY [Surrogate_Key]
       ORDER BY [From_Timestamp])
   AS [Previous_Checksum]
  FROM [Checksum_CTE]
),
Compacting AS
(
  -- Remove redundant records
  SELECT
   [Surrogate_Key],
   [Column_Value],
   [From_Timestamp],
   [Checksum],
   [Previous_Checksum]
  FROM PreviousChecksum
  WHERE [Previous_Checksum] IS NULL OR [Checksum]
  != [Previous_Checksum]
)
-- Display the final results
SELECT
   [Surrogate_Key],
   [Column_Value],
   [From_Timestamp],
   LEAD([From_Timestamp],1,'9999-12-31')
   OVER (PARTITION BY [Surrogate_Key]
       ORDER BY [From_Timestamp] ASC)
   AS [Before_Timestamp]
FROM Compacting
```

This returns the following record set:

Surrogate Key	Value	From Timestamp	Before Timestamp
100\@I	NULL	1900-01-01	2025-02-15
100\@I	B	2025-02-15	2025-03-20
100\@I	C	2025-03-20	2025-09-20
100\@I	D	2025-09-20	9999-12-31

This query compacts consecutive records with the same column values into a single record with a valid time period including a from timestamp and a before timestamp.

However, you'll notice that the value 'A' is still not available in the result. This is because its time period did not overlap with any of the snapshot timestamps — and once the data is reduced to snapshots, that level of detail is no longer recoverable.

When you reduce granularity (e.g., from time periods to monthly snapshots), data loss is inevitable unless you re-query the integration layer.

It's always best to generate snapshots directly from the integration layer, which retains the most detailed view in time-period format. If downstream consumers need to pivot often between different levels of granularity, a ⚐ timeline approach for data delivery might suit better.

As always, you can find the full query and example output on our website: https://dtng.link/7m3f2.

Filtering

Filtering for snapshots ensures that only records relevant at the snapshot's specific point in time are selected, typically following the state timeline. In contrast, timeline filtering primarily focuses on limiting records along the assertion timeline.

As with timeline filtering, additional filters can be applied to meet specific requirements.

Temporal data selection

In our reference architecture, time-variant objects are bitemporal by default. This means that both the state timeline and assertion timeline must be considered in queries.

To retrieve a valid snapshot from bitemporal data sources, you must apply filters on both timelines:

```
DECLARE @Assertion_Snapshot_Timestamp DATETIME2(7) = SYSUTCDATETIME();
DECLARE @State_Snapshot_Timestamp DATETIME2(7) = CAST('2025-02-25'
AS DATETIME2(7));

SELECT *
FROM <data object>
WHERE
-- Assertion timeline
    Inscription_From_Timestamp  <= @Assertion_Snapshot_Timestamp
  AND Inscription_Before_Timestamp > @Assertion_Snapshot_Timestamp
-- State timeline
  AND State_From_Timestamp  <= @State_Snapshot_Timestamp
  AND State_Before_Timestamp > @State_Snapshot_Timestamp
```

This query delivers a point-in-time snapshot for the state timeline as of 2025-02-25, using the most recently asserted data (up to the current UTC timestamp on the assertion timeline).

When querying the state timeline, be aware that it may already include future-dated values – for instance, planned price changes or upcoming contracts. If your snapshot is intended to reflect current reality, make sure your timestamp doesn't accidentally pull in future-effective records.

Similarly, for unitemporal selections a limitation on the inscription timestamp is sufficient. This approach is the same as applied to the ⚐ timeline sections on filtering:

```
DECLARE @Assertion_Snapshot_Timestamp DATETIME2(7) = SYSUTCDATETIME();

[...]
WHERE
-- Assertion timeline
  [Inscription_From_Timestamp] <= @Assertion_Snapshot_Timestamp
```

Performance area

↗ The performance area is an optional area, focusing on performance and efficiency in data delivery.

The performance area contains supporting objects, such as point-in-time (PIT) objects, aggregates, and similar helper constructs.

Objects in the performance area

The exact structure of performance area objects is less critical than the efficiency they deliver. Consequently, these objects are often less standardized.

To maintain practicality, this section will demonstrate the implementation of various forms of PIT objects, as they are commonly employed in projects. Many of these forms are variations on similar concepts, and all forms can be delivered as timelines or snapshots and can be created with the corresponding patterns.

In all cases, the intent is to reduce the 'heavy lift' when querying the integration layer by creating an intermediate object that combines values from several underlying objects:

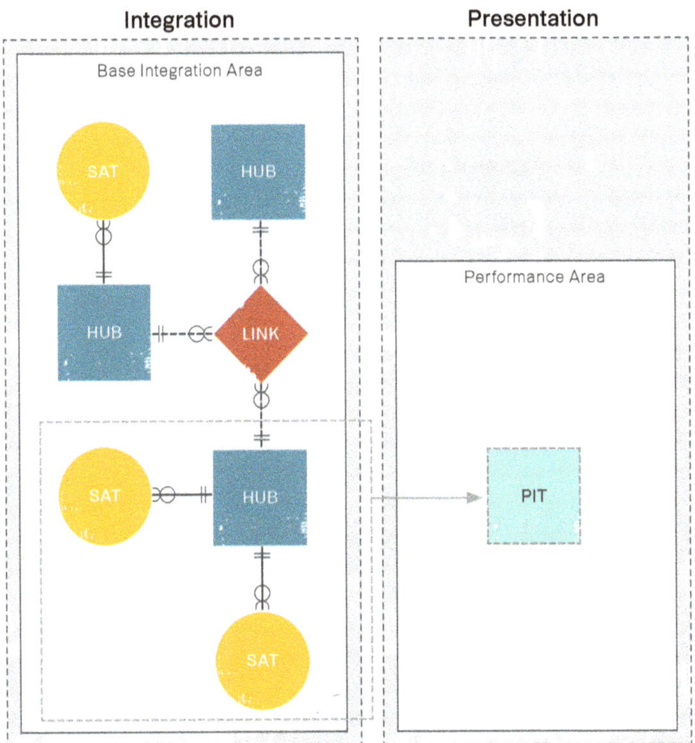

The key consideration for the performance area is to adhere to ⚐ fundamental principles of data logistics, most notably deterministic and independent behavior. This approach allows performance-oriented objects to be neatly integrated into the architecture, avoiding bottlenecks and supporting parallel processing.

Performance area data object structure

When designing performance area objects, the physical structure varies depending on whether a timeline-based or snapshot-based approach is selected.

This decision influences the object's structure, its data logistics pattern, and the method by which data is ultimately retrieved.

Both patterns are sufficiently generic to support a wide range of object variations, including traditional Data Vault PIT tables as well as fact and dimension tables within a dimensional modeling context.

In this section, we'll focus on PIT tables as a representative use case.

Traditional PIT tables, whether snapshot-based or timeline-based, typically do not contain descriptive (contextual) attributes. Instead, they store keys that facilitate performance improvements by enabling efficient joins during data delivery in the access area.

While it's possible to include descriptive columns in PIT tables, doing so aligns them more closely with dimension or fact tables—a concept briefly discussed in the ⚐ virtualization section. For our purposes, we'll mostly concentrate on the technical implementation of PIT tables as collections of keys intended for downstream joining. It does illustrate, however, how similar these patterns are, and we will briefly touch on this in the ⚐ optional columns section.

Snapshot-based

Snapshot-based PIT objects capture the state of data at specific points in time, such as end-of-day snapshots. For this purpose they contain a snapshot timestamp.

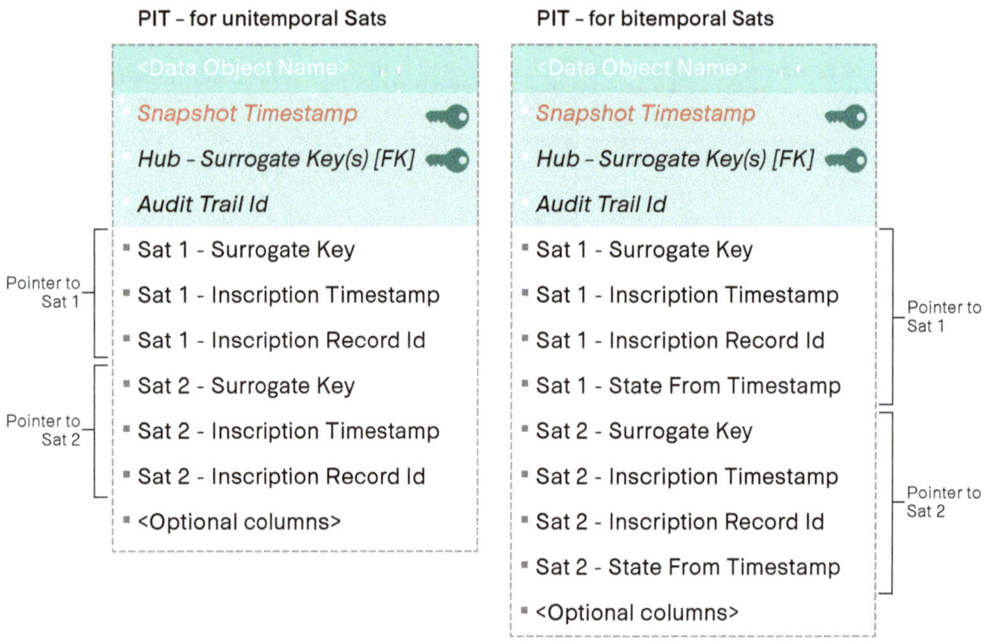

This example shows the pointers (join keys) for two Satellites, but additional ones can be added as needed. The key principle is to include enough information to join the relevant Satellites and return a single record per time period. In this example, both Satellites are linked to the same Hub. However, if they relate to different Hubs —or if more Hubs are involved— their corresponding Hub keys should also be included and become part of the primary key.

As with Satellites, the indication of 'time' impacts the structure. Bitemporal approaches include the state timestamp.

Snapshot-based objects include:

→ A snapshot timestamp indicating the point in time the key combinations are valid for
→ Any Hub Surrogate Keys related to the involved Satellites
→ The Audit Trail Id, containing the reference to the control framework instance
→ The primary key components from each involved Satellite as these are required for joining (the pointer):
  → Surrogate key
  → Inscription timestamp
  → Inscription record id
  → State from/before timestamp of each bitemporal Satellite

Optionally, the following columns can be considered:

→ A PIT-specific key can be added, which can be helpful to deliver downstream objects including dimension and fact tables. This can act as alternate key, be a sequence, or something different – as long as it uniquely identifies the record
→ Any descriptive columns

Timeline-based

Timeline based PIT tables represent data changes over time. They are essentially dimensions without descriptive columns.

Structurally they are very similar —though not exactly the same— as their snapshot-based counterparts. The real difference lies in the contents: the storage of data as a timeline.

Instead of a snapshot timestamp, they use an state from timestamp as part of the primary key, indicating when the key combinations became valid.

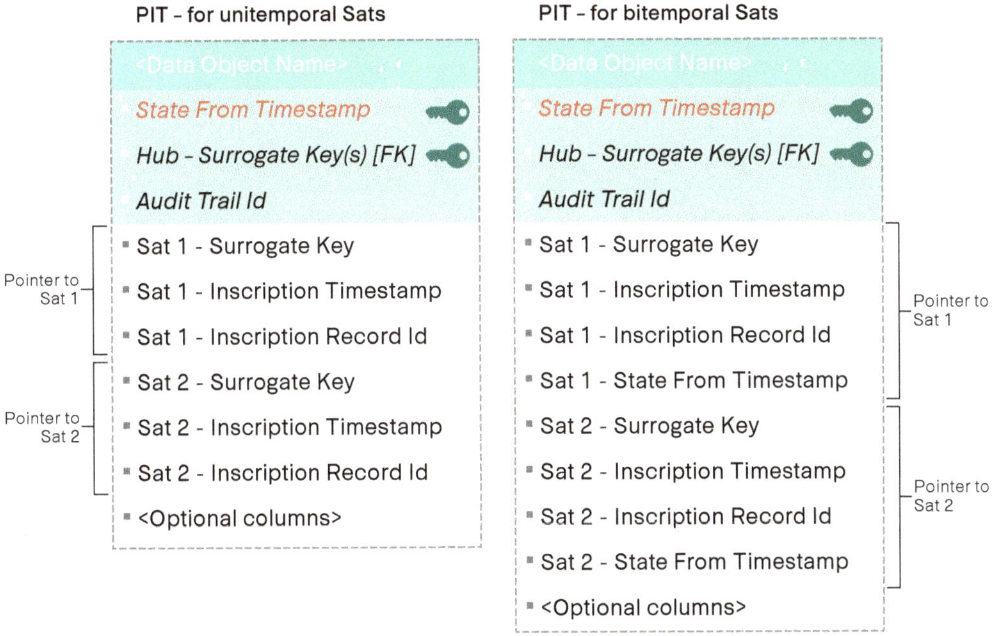

Timestamp

The 'timestamp column' refers either to the snapshot timestamp or the state from timestamp, depending on whether the object follows a snapshot-based or timeline-based approach. Both are high-precision timestamp fields, differing only in name — though the distinction reflects the fundamental difference in how the data is stored.

The value of this column is derived from the applied data logistics template and is not explicitly defined in metadata.

In a ⚐ timeline-based approach, the value from the unified timeline is assigned to the state from timestamp. In a ⚐ snapshot-based approach, the snapshot's point-in-time values are mapped to the snapshot timestamp.

Hub surrogate key(s)

The surrogate keys from the involved Hubs define the grain of the PIT object and form part of its primary key.

The number of Hub keys included depends on how many Hubs participate in the PIT.

If needed, business key components can be added for convenience — either as regular data item mappings in metadata or later in the access area by joining the relevant Hubs to the PIT object.

In metadata, Hubs are mapped to a performance area object using data object mappings. This mapping itself contains all necessary information for the code generation processes to add the Hub's surrogate key, as it is a property of the data object.

Audit Trail Id

As always, the Audit Trail Id follows the same approach as followed so far: this is the unique execution id of the data logistics process that populates the data.

Satellite pointer(s)

The purpose of a PIT is to support joins with Satellites —allowing descriptive columns to be added for data delivery— such that each join returns exactly one record per time period or snapshot timestamp.

To achieve this, the PIT object must include all necessary pointers to uniquely identify the corresponding records.

**This includes the following columns f
or each of the involved Satellites:**

- → Surrogate key – referencing the Hub or Link
- → Inscription timestamp – indicating the position on the assertion timeline
- → Inscription record id – the sequence value assigned in the Satellite to ensure uniqueness for the inscription timestamp
- → State from/before timestamp – required for bitemporal data delivery; represents the state timeline's validity period for the record

Thanks to the preparation work done in the integration layer —and to some extent even in the staging layer— joining on the columns listed above reliably returns a single valid record per time period. In these earlier steps, the state timeline has been aligned and corrected (where needed), the inscription timestamp has been consistently applied, and uniquefied using the inscription record id.

This significantly simplifies data delivery from the integration layer.

Satellites are also mapped to performance area objects using data object mappings. Since the pointer values listed above follow a highly standardized structure, they can be handled through convention-based logic in the code generation process.

Optional columns

The following columns can be considered optional for performance area objects, particularly PIT objects, as discussed in these sections:

- → Key
- → Descriptive columns

However, as noted in the introduction, the structure is less important than the results these objects provide. Therefore, flexibility and common sense should guide their design.

Key

PIT objects provide a convenient location to create keys for downstream use – for instance, as dimension keys (and consequently fact keys). These keys are not intended to serve as the primary key of the PIT object, although they *can* be implemented that way, turning the standard primary key structure into a unique constraint.

Their primary purpose is to simplify key distribution in the access area, particularly for dimensional models. For this reason, PIT keys are often implemented as integers, though any deterministic approach is valid.

Deterministic PIT keys

When refactoring the data solution or delivering data virtually, both performance and access area structures —including time-variant objects like PITs and dimensions— may be truncated and reloaded (or generated as views). In these cases, it's essential that any generated keys remain the same: they must be deterministic.

This is especially important in dimensional modeling. If dimension keys are generated non-deterministically, a dimension reload would also require a reload of all referencing fact tables – otherwise, foreign key relationships may break. The same applies indirectly to PIT objects as the source for dimensional model objects. To support full automation, the PIT and dimension structures must be reloadable without affecting downstream objects.

This also enables these objects to be represented via database views (or similar).

To meet this requirement, the PIT implementation must generate keys in a deterministic manner. This key is functionally equivalent to combining the primary key columns of the PIT and can be generated using a simple algorithm: using a window function (e.g., ROW_NUMBER) to sort by the inscription timestamp (and inscription record id), the state timestamp, and then the involved Hub key(s).

```
ROW_NUMBER() OVER
( ORDER BY
  [Inscription_Timestamp],
  [Inscription_Record_Id],
  [State_From_Timestamp],
  <Hub Surrogate Key(s)>
) AS [PIT_Key]
```

This ordering ensures determinism because:

- The inscription timestamp and inscription record id are strictly sequential and guaranteed by the data solution
- The state from timestamp is also incremental in concept, though it may be impacted by backdated or late-arriving records – but in those cases, the inscription timestamp will still reflect a later processing time
- The Hub surrogate key(s) anchor the PIT record to a specific CBC instance. This adds an additional layer of security that the key will be unique, even though in all likelihood the first three columns already guarantee uniqueness

Any structural change –such as compacting or altering the record set– can influence key generation. Therefore, the engine must be able to detect such changes and trigger the rebuild of referencing objects when necessary.

Also, with timeline-based approaches, this algorithm should be applied before a compacting algorithm is applied as the compacting itself might influence the outcomes: when time periods are removed to address data redundancy the ordering will change.

Alternative approaches also exist, such as adding sequence values in Hubs or Satellites (not as primary keys, but as contextual identifiers). These, too, can serve as building blocks for PIT or dimension keys. However, such methods come with trade-offs beyond the scope of this book.

In most cases, the approach outlined above –using a window function for key generation– is simple, reliable, and easily implemented in the presentation layer. For that reason, we recommend it as the default pattern.

Descriptive columns

As mentioned in the introduction to this section, we primarily focus on PIT objects that do not contain descriptive columns – although the pattern does support this. Still, it's important to acknowledge that this option exists. Some solutions make extensive use of it by creating large, wide PIT objects that include all necessary columns for delivery – in some cases even embedding business logic. The more descriptive columns are added, the more the PIT table resembles a dimension, especially when a dedicated key is added and defined as 'primary key.'

In this approach, a significant portion –or even the entirety– of the delivery model in the access area can be derived from a single PIT. This is a valid design choice, effectively keeping the access area 'light' by focusing solely on structure, while shifting the complexity into the PIT process.

Any additional columns are defined in metadata as regular data item mappings, part of the data object mapping from the Satellite to the PIT.

Performance area design pattern

The performance area is an optional area in the architecture, focusing on performance and efficiency in data delivery processes. As always, the pattern must be modular, independent, fault-tolerant, and idempotent.

In this step —if utilized— the following concepts are applied:

- Choose an approach for data preparation:
  - Snapshot approach: capture data at specific points in time
  - Timeline approach: maintain a continuous record of data changes over time
- Combine the relevant objects and data from the integration layer
- Select in-scope columns, compact if required
- Issue deterministic keys

f the performance area is omitted, the responsibilities outlined above must be managed within the access area, which may impact performance and maintainability.

Choose an approach for data preparation

The decision to implement either a snapshot-based or timeline-based approach is a foundational one that influences all subsequent steps.

Will the solution introduce a bit more complexity —albeit in a standardized way— in order to gain greater fidelity and flexibility? Or will it opt for a snapshot-based approach that is simpler to implement but may require more ongoing maintenance? To some degree, combinations are also possible (dependent on requirements), for instance delivering the performance area as a timeline but the final outgoing interface in the access area as a series of snapshots.

Based on this choice, the appropriate code generation template can be selected:

- A timeline-based approach merges available time-variant data into a continuous, aligned series of time periods.
- A snapshot-based approach captures the state of data at predefined intervals.

Combine the relevant objects and data from the integration layer

Based on the selected approach (timeline or snapshot), the required integration layer objects are joined together – either through a time-variant join or by selecting values valid at a specific point in time.

This is also the stage where filtering is applied as needed.

Issue deterministic keys

With the data joined and ready, a deterministic key can be assigned – if this is part of the design.

Select in-scope columns, compact if required

This step is relevant when descriptive columns are included and a timeline-based approach is used – snapshot-based outputs often contain redundancy by design. If descriptive data is present, any redundant records can be identified and resolved using the compacting techniques described in the presentation layer ⚐ compacting section.

Considerations

The following sections can be considered for the performance area design pattern.

Compacting, again?

When applying the PIT pattern as described in this section, the PIT data object records only the key combinations from the associated Satellites. Subsequently, when joining these Satellites to the PIT table to retrieve descriptive columns —such as during the loading of access area objects— there's a potential for data redundancy.

This redundancy arises because the descriptive columns become known only *after* the join operation. Any duplication can be identified and addressed only at that stage.

To mitigate this, an additional layer of compacting may be necessary post-join to eliminate redundant records. This is consideration to make when deciding whether to create access area structures directly from the integration layer, or to implement interim performance area objects.

Snapshot maintenance

Snapshot-based methods are generally straightforward to implement; however, they can introduce long-term overhead. This is especially true for high-frequency snapshots, such as hourly captures, or when dealing with large data volumes, as these snapshots often contain significant data redundancy.

To maintain efficiency, it's advisable to implement a regular maintenance routine that includes the removal of outdated snapshots.

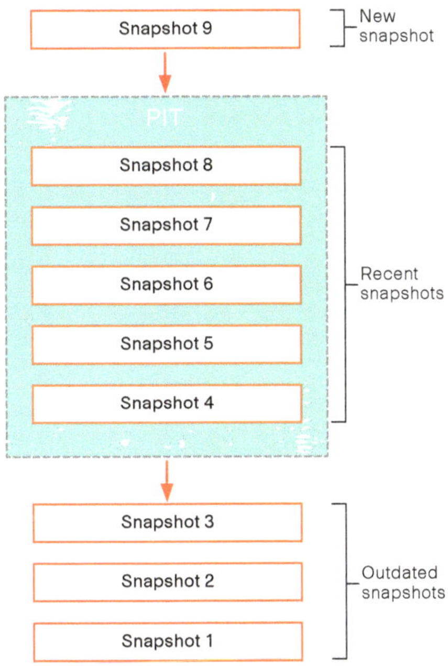

The definition of 'outdated' is a business requirement, and should align with your organization's data retention policies and compliance requirements. Removing outdated snapshots can be a maintenance task that runs periodically across the data solution.

When unchecked, snapshot objects can grow substantially in size, potentially impacting storage resources, system performance and cost.

Establishing a maintenance process contributes to the overall manageability of the data solution. When required, snapshots can always be re-created from integration layer data.

Bridges

As part of our overview of performance area objects, we would like to briefly discuss bridge tables, which are sometimes referenced in the context of the Data Vault physical model. Bridge tables are akin to PIT tables, but specifically combine, or 'bridge,' various Hubs and Links.

The selection of involved Hubs and Links defines the grain.

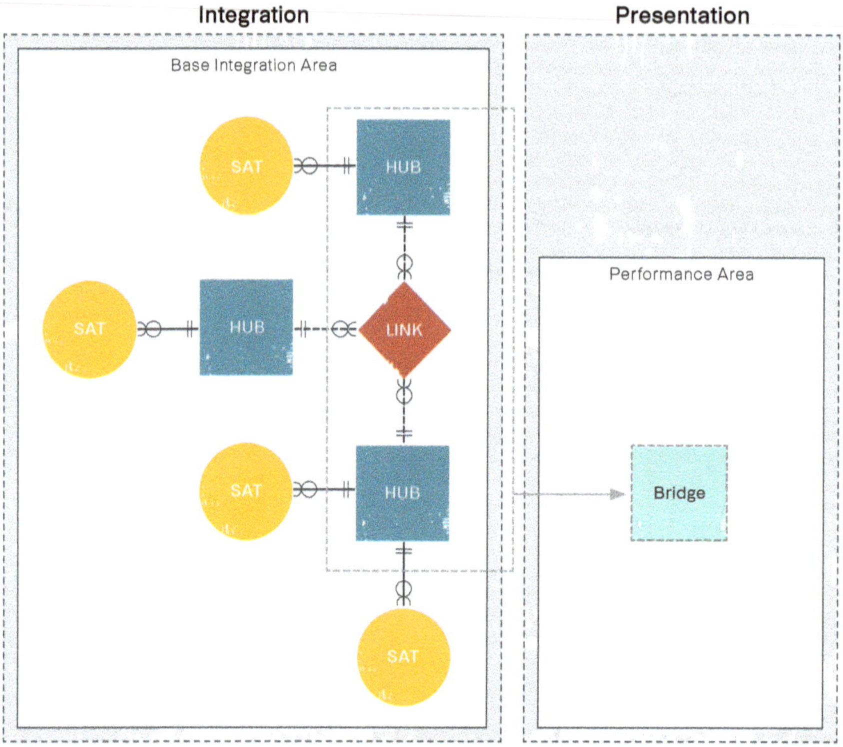

Fundamentally, bridge objects contain only Hub and Link keys, without storing contextual information. Due to this structure, bridge tables are typically created as snapshots. The primary rationale behind bridge tables is to pre-join certain underlying components, allowing the join operation to be performed once and reused multiple times downstream.

Bridge tables are closely related to PIT tables, and in some projects, contextual information is also stored within bridge objects, further aligning them with snapshot-based PIT structures.

Due to their similarity and overlap with PIT objects, we won't cover bridge objects as a separate solution pattern. However, the logic is straightforward: at the selected snapshot timestamp, store the combination of keys. The involved Hub keys define the bridge primary key.

Do we need both Hub and Satellite keys?

The essential PIT structure includes references to both the Hub surrogate key and the Satellite surrogate keys. At first glance, this might seem redundant – after all, if the Hub key is present, wouldn't that also apply to the Satellites?

However, there are good reasons for including both.

First, when multiple Hubs are involved, having the Satellite surrogate keys explicitly in the PIT removes ambiguity. It ensures that Satellites can always be joined reliably, without having to second-guess which Hub key to use.

The second reason relates to the join strategy. Consider what happens when a Satellite has no record for a particular time period. In that case —following the reference architecture— the PIT will contain a NULL pointer for that Satellite.

This can occur, for example, when creating a snapshot for a moment in time where no corresponding Satellite record is valid. If NULL pointers are present, caution is needed when joining the Satellites for their descriptive columns: an INNER JOIN would incorrectly filter out these PIT records due to the missing Satellite references.

There are two ways to handle this:
→ Add a zero key to each Satellite to facilitate INNER JOINs
→ Use a LEFT OUTER JOIN when joining Satellites

In all cases, including the Hub key separately ensures that the business key instance is always present even when some Satellite context is missing.

Zero keys in Satellites
Adding zero keys to Satellite allows NULL pointers in the PIT to be replaced with a default value (the zero key) during processing. With these in place, Satellites can be reliably inner-joined.

There are a few ways to implement this, including (but not limited to):
→ Adding a zero record *per business key*. This approach is sometimes seen in projects, but it is not advisable. It significantly increases the Satellite size with very little benefit. After all, we don't need a full timeline per business key in Satellites because this is further managed when merging time-variant data sets
→ Adding a *single* zero key to each Satellite representing NULL values. This record connects to the Hub zero key and serves as a default for NULL pointers. If using zero keys in Satellites, this is the preferable approach

Using a LEFT OUTER JOIN
This is our recommended approach, as it avoids the need for zero records altogether.

Either way, zero key records or LEFT JOINs will result in NULL or unknown values — but these can easily be handled later in the presentation layer.

Automation

Generating PIT objects —and similar presentation layer structures such as dimensions and even fact tables— requires relatively little design metadata. Most of the implementation is driven by conventions.

Only a few essential components are needed:
→ The relationships between the source and target data objects, including all involved Hubs and Satellites
→ Any data item mappings for descriptive columns

Each individual relationship between a source data object and the target performance area object is captured as a separate data object mapping. These mappings also include the corresponding data item mappings for any descriptive columns provided by that source. All of these are then grouped into a data object mapping list, since they share the same target data object.

In the presentation layer, it's again recommended to include the template type in metadata — this determines whether the snapshot or timeline-based code generation template should be applied.

Design metadata example

In this example, a PIT object is created from a Hub and two bitemporal Satellites:

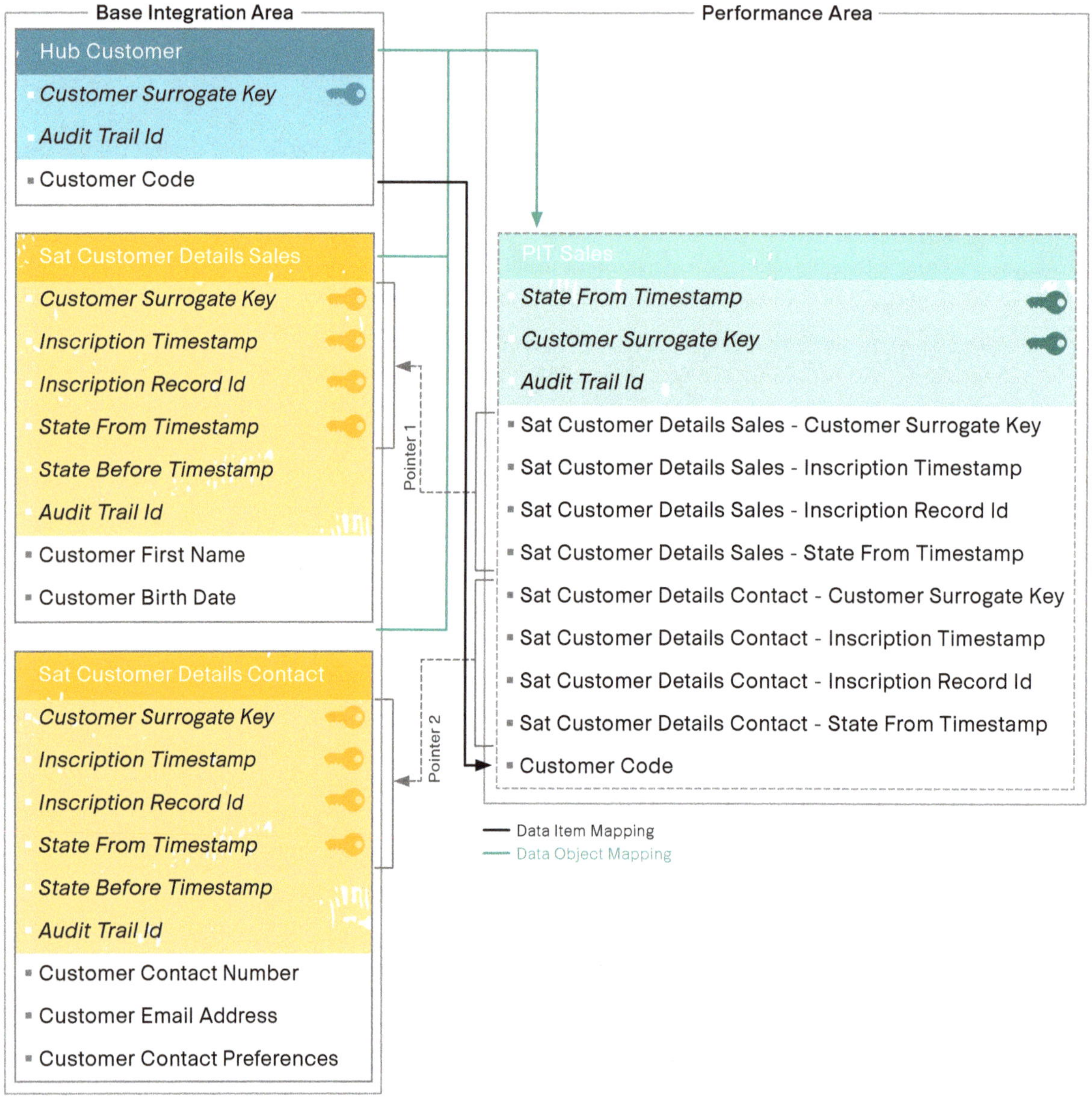

For illustration purposes, the Customer Code column is added as a data item mapping to show that additional columns can be included if needed. Other than that, the implementation is fully driven by conventions, based on the available data object mapping – which are explicitly shown in this example for this reason.

For instance, the 'Customer Surrogate Key' column can automatically be added if a data object mapping is available. Likewise, the Satellite pointers (e.g., surrogate key, inscription timestamp, inscription record id) and state timestamp columns are standardized and can also be added automatically.

The design metadata to define this PIT structure is encoded as follows:

```
{
 "dataObjectMappings": [
  {
   "name": "Hub_Customer_to_PIT_Sales",
   "sourceDataObjects": [
    {
     "name": "Hub_Customer"
    }
   ],
   "targetDataObject": {
    "name": "PIT_Sales"
   },
   "dataItemMappings": [
    {
     "sourcedataItems": [
      {
       "name": "Customer_Code"
      }
     ],
     "targetdataItem": {
      "name": "Customer_Code"
     }
    }
   ]
  },
  {
   "name": "Sat_Customer_Details_Sales_to_PIT_Sales",
   "sourceDataObjects": [
    {
     "name": "Sat_Customer_Details_Sales"
    }
   ],
   "targetDataObject": {
    "name": "PIT_Sales"
   }
  },
  {
   "name": "Sat_Customer_Details_Contact_to_PIT_Sales",
   "sourceDataObjects": [
    {
     "name": "Sat_Customer_Details_Contact"
    }
   ],
   "targetDataObject": {
    "name": "PIT_Sales"
   }
  }
 ]
}
```

A notable difference compared to earlier examples is that multiple data object mappings are defined and combined in the data object mapping list. While this isn't the only way to implement this pattern, it's a clear and structured approach that makes it easy to track which data item mappings originate from which source objects.

Any additional descriptive columns from the Satellites can be added to the mapping when needed.

When objects such as this are created from many underlying objects, it is often helpful to include the *relationships* between objects in metadata. This way, more complex joins can be automated as well. To support this, information can be added via the relationship object.

For a Satellite, this could be:

```
"relationships": [
  {
    "type": "Foreign Key",
    "relatedDataObject": {
      "name": "Hub_Customer",
      "businessKeyDefinitions": [
        {
          "ordinalPosition": 1,
          "surrogateKey": "Customer_Surrogate_Key",
          "businessKeyComponents": [
            {
              "ordinalPosition": 1,
              "dataItem": {
                "name": "Customer_Code"
              }
            }
          ]
        }
      ]
    }
  }
]
```

Alternatively, a simpler version to provide only the pointer if the business key definition is not required (e.g., for creating hash values etc.).

```
"relationships": [
  {
    "type": "Inner Join",
    "relatedDataObject": { "name": "Hub_Customer" },
    "dataItemMappings": [
      {
        "sourcedataItems": [ { "name": "Customer_Surrogate_Key" } ],
        "targetdataItem": { "name": "Customer_Surrogate_Key" }
      }
    ]
  }
]
```

Combining unitemporal Satellites

In our reference solution architecture, we've standardized on bitemporal Satellites, as this provides the most flexibility for data delivery and resolves time-related issues early in the process.

However, unitemporal Satellites are commonly seen in projects as well. We would like to briefly illustrate how small the differences are at this stage, and what adjustments are needed to adapt the approach for a unitemporal input.

For the metadata definition itself, there is no difference.
The main distinction lies in how the underlying structures are defined:

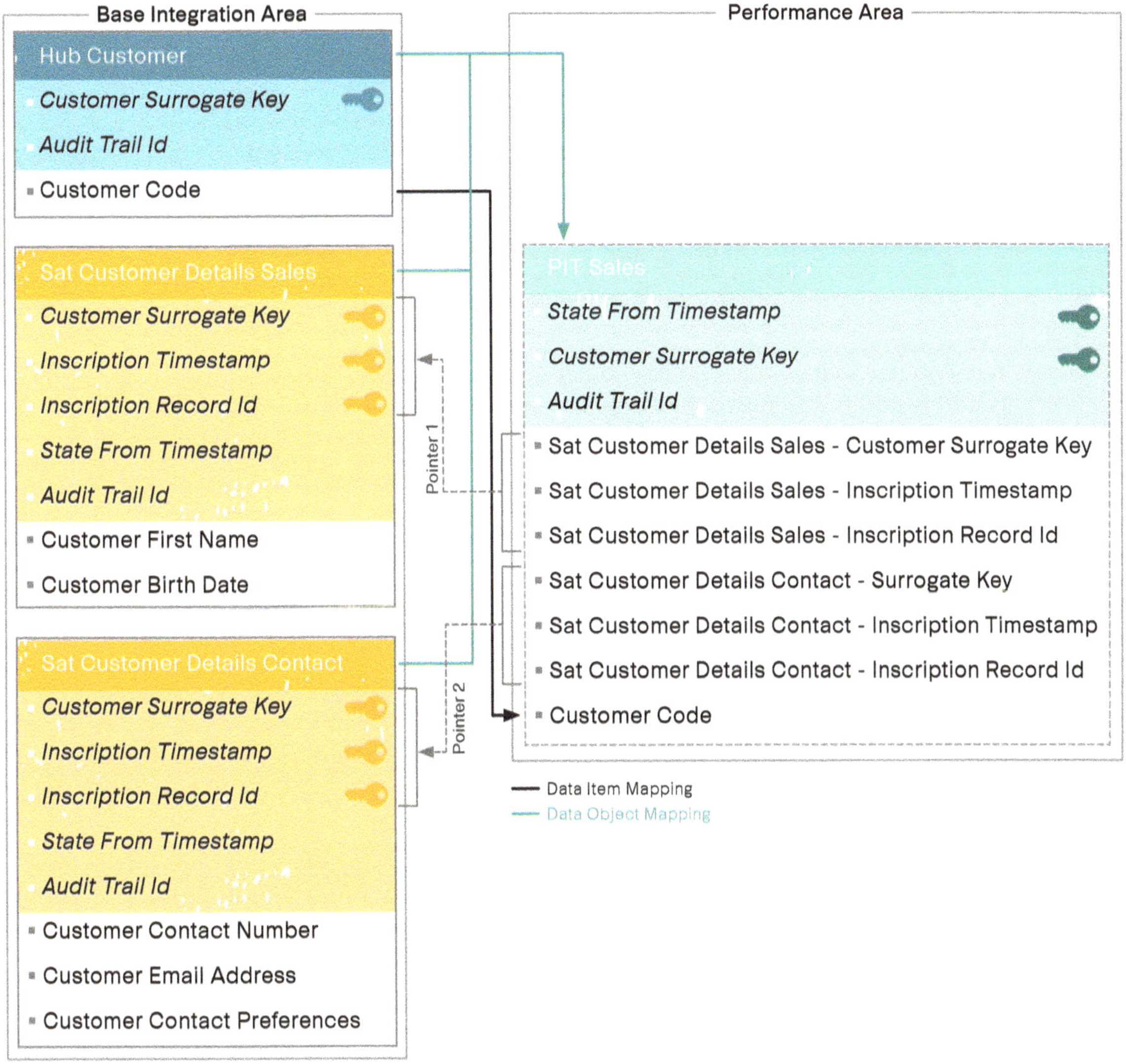

In a unitemporal design, the state from timestamp is no longer part of the Satellite definition and therefore does not need to be included in the pointer.

From a design and implementation perspective, however, that's really the only change.
The timeline in the PIT object can still be constructed based on (unitemporal) state from timestamps

Solution pattern example

Taking the PIT as an example performance area solution pattern, the implementation depends on whether a timeline-based or snapshot-based approach is selected. Both can be implemented using the same design metadata.

At this stage, the pattern is a summary of concepts already covered — but for completeness, a brief example of each approach is provided below.

As always, you can find a full example of the solution pattern on our website: https://dtng.link/xtpkt.

Timeline-based

The timeline-based approach follows the steps described earlier in the timelines sections. Since those have already been explained in detail, we won't repeat the approach here. However, it may be helpful to review the full query, as applied to the example design metadata below.

Note that filtering on the assertion timeline is applied on the inner-most section, where the timestamps are combined. The inscription from timestamp and inscription before timestamps assumed to be part of the Satellite structure in this example, but can otherwise be derived at runtime using a window function.

```
DECLARE @Assertion_Filter_Timestamp DATETIME2(7) = SYSUTCDATETIME();

SELECT
 -- New timeline
 TimePeriods.[From_Timestamp],
 TimePeriods.[Before_Timestamp],
 -- Hub surrogate key(s)
 Hub.[Customer_Surrogate_Key] AS [Hub_Customer_Customer_Surrogate_Key],
 -- Pointer Satellite 1
 Sat1.[Customer_Surrogate_Key] AS [Sat_Customer_Details_Sales_Customer_Surrogate_Key],
 Sat1.[Inscription_Timestamp] AS [Sat_Customer_Details_Sales_Inscription_Timestamp],
 Sat1.[Inscription_Record_Id] AS [Sat_Customer_Details_Sales_Inscription_Record_Id],
 Sat1.[State_From_Timestamp] AS [Sat_Customer_Details_Sales_State_From_Timestamp],
 -- Pointer Satellite 2
 Sat2.[Customer_Surrogate_Key] AS [Sat_Customer_Details_Contact_Customer_Surrogate_Key],
 Sat2.[Inscription_Timestamp] AS [Sat_Customer_Details_Contact_Inscription_Timestamp],
 Sat2.[Inscription_Record_Id] AS [Sat_Customer_Details_Contact_Inscription_Record_Id],
 Sat2.[State_From_Timestamp] AS [Sat_Customer_Details_Contact_State_From_Timestamp],
 -- Additional columns
 Hub.[Customer_Code]
FROM
(
 -- Creation of time periods
 SELECT
  [Customer_Surrogate_Key],
  [From_Timestamp],
  LEAD([From_Timestamp],1,'9999-12-31')
    OVER (PARTITION BY [Customer_Surrogate_Key]
```

```
    ORDER BY [From_Timestamp] ASC)
   AS [Before_Timestamp]
 FROM
 (
  -- Creation of a low-end timestamp for the timeline
  SELECT
   Hub.[Customer_Surrogate_Key],
   CONVERT(DATETIME2(7),'1900-01-01') AS [From_Timestamp]
  FROM [Hub_Customer] Hub
  UNION
  -- Combined set of all available from timestamp values
  SELECT Sat1.[Customer_Surrogate_Key], Sat1.[State_From_Timestamp] AS [From_Timestamp]
  FROM [Sat_Customer_Details_Sales] Sat1
  WHERE Sat1.[Inscription_From_Timestamp] <= @Assertion_Filter_Timestamp
   AND Sat1.[Inscription_Before_Timestamp] > @ Assertion_Filter_Timestamp
  UNION
  SELECT Sat2.[Customer_Surrogate_Key], Sat2.[State_From_Timestamp] AS [From_Timestamp]
  FROM [Sat_Customer_Details_Contact] Sat2
  WHERE Sat2.[Inscription_From_Timestamp] <= @Assertion_Filter_Timestamp
   AND Sat2.[Inscription_Before_Timestamp] > @ Assertion_Filter_Timestamp
 ) Timestamps
) TimePeriods
-- Joining the Hub
INNER JOIN [Hub_Customer] Hub
 ON TimePeriods.[Customer_Surrogate_Key] =  Hub.[Customer_Surrogate_Key]
-- Joining Satellite 1
LEFT JOIN [Sat_Customer_Details_Sales] Sat1
 ON TimePeriods.[Customer_Surrogate_Key] = Sat1.[Customer_Surrogate_Key]
 AND Sat1.[State_From_Timestamp] <= TimePeriods.[From_Timestamp]
 AND Sat1.[State_Before_Timestamp] > TimePeriods.[Before_Timestamp]
-- Joining Satellite 2
LEFT JOIN [Sat_Customer_Details_Contact] Sat2
 ON TimePeriods.[Customer_Surrogate_Key] = Sat2.[Customer_Surrogate_Key]
 AND Sat2.[State_From_Timestamp] <= TimePeriods.[From_Timestamp]
 AND Sat2.[State_Before_Timestamp] > TimePeriods.[Before_Timestamp]
```

This logic creates a PIT object, which can then be wrapped in an INSERT statement that only inserts if the object's primary key doesn't already exist. Use NOT EXISTS or LEFT JOIN as needed.

This PIT object is essentially a dimension without descriptive columns or a dimension key. These can easily be added – which is why the same pattern works for dimensions as well.

What is the benefit from creating a PIT like this, instead of directly creating the dimension? After all, the 'heavy lift' of joining the time-variant data into a unified timeline is done anyway. Does it really help to separate the process, by creating a PIT and joining the descriptive column later in the access area?

The answer, unfortunately, is very situation-dependent. In many projects, skipping the PIT and going straight to the dimension is viable.

However, a PIT can be a solid architectural choice when:

→ Multiple marts can use the PIT
→ The PIT is created as a very wide object that can support parts, or the full, dimensional model it can make sense
→ You seek a clean separation of concerns between date-math logic and presentation in the access area

As a final note, a distinctive feature of the access area is the ability to define historization behavior at the column level.

Timeline-based PIT objects already represent historization – similar to a Slowly Changing Dimension (SCD) Type 2. When building access area structures, any historization method can be derived from these PITs, allowing you to shape the output precisely to the needs of each consuming system.

Snapshot-based

Snapshot-based PITs are simpler to implement, but require external input to determine the snapshot timestamp(s). In this example, we use a variable – but it could also come from a date list, snapshot table, or batch process as used in the ⚐ earlier snapshot examples.

The snapshot logic, using a fixed selection timestamp and bitemporal inputs, looks like this:

```
DECLARE @Assertion_Snapshot_Timestamp DATETIME2(7) = SYSUTCDATETIME();
DECLARE @State_Snapshot_Timestamp DATETIME2(7) = CAST('2025-02-25' AS DATETIME2(7));

SELECT
  -- New snapshot timestamp
  @StateSnapshotTimestamp AS [Snapshot_Timestamp],
  -- Hub surrogate key(s)
  Hub.[Customer_Surrogate_Key]  AS [Hub_Customer_Customer_Surrogate_Key],
  -- Pointer Satellite 1
  Sat1.[Customer_Surrogate_Key] AS [Sat_Customer_Details_Sales_Customer_Surrogate_Key],
  Sat1.[Inscription_Timestamp]  AS [Sat_Customer_Details_Sales_Inscription_Timestamp],
  Sat1.[Inscription_Record_Id]  AS [Sat_Customer_Details_Sales_Inscription_Record_Id],
  Sat1.[State_From_Timestamp]   AS [Sat_Customer_Details_Sales_State_From_Timestamp],
  -- Pointer Satellite 2
  Sat2.[Customer_Surrogate_Key] AS [Sat_Customer_Details_Contact_Customer_Surrogate_Key],
  Sat2.[Inscription_Timestamp]  AS [Sat_Customer_Details_Contact_Inscription_Timestamp],
  Sat2.[Inscription_Record_Id]  AS [Sat_Customer_Details_Contact_Inscription_Record_Id],
  Sat2.[State_From_Timestamp]   AS [Sat_Customer_Details_Contact_State_From_Timestamp],
  -- Optional columns
  Hub.[Customer_Code]
FROM [Hub_Customer] Hub
```

```
-- Sat Customer Details Sales (in subquery to derive inscription before timestamp)
LEFT JOIN
(
 SELECT
   *,
   [Inscription_Timestamp] AS [Inscription_From_Timestamp],
   LEAD([Inscription_Timestamp],1,'9999-12-31')
   OVER (
     PARTITION BY [Customer_Surrogate_Key]
       ORDER BY [Inscription_Timestamp] ASC
   ) AS [Inscription_Before_Timestamp],
 FROM [Sat_Customer_Details_Sales]
) sat1
ON
 -- Assertion timeline
    sat1.[Inscription_From_Timestamp] <= @Assertion_Snapshot_Timestamp
 AND sat1.[Inscription_Before_Timestamp] > @Assertion_Snapshot_Timestamp
 -- State timeline
 AND sat1.[State_From_Timestamp]  <= @State_Snapshot_Timestamp
 AND sat1.[State_Before_Timestamp] > @State_Snapshot_Timestamp
-- Sat Customer Details Contact (in subquery to derive inscription before timestamp)
LEFT JOIN
(
 SELECT
   *,
   [Inscription_Timestamp] AS [Inscription_From_Timestamp],
   LEAD([Inscription_Timestamp],1,'9999-12-31')
   OVER (
     PARTITION BY [Customer_Surrogate_Key]
       ORDER BY [Inscription_Timestamp] ASC
   ) AS [Inscription_Before_Timestamp],
 FROM [Sat_Customer_Details_Contact]
) sat2
ON
 -- Assertion timeline
    sat2.[Inscription_From_Timestamp] <= @Assertion_Snapshot_Timestamp
 AND sat2.[Inscription_Before_Timestamp] > @Assertion_Snapshot_Timestamp
 -- State timeline
 AND sat2.[State_From_Timestamp]  <= @State_Snapshot_Timestamp
 AND sat2.[State_Before_Timestamp] > @State_Snapshot_Timestamp
```

This is an example of a snapshot from bitemporal sources, creating a snapshot from historical data (state timeline) from today's perspective (assertion timeline). The inscription before timestamp is derived in this example, following the explanation in the filtering sections.

As with the timeline approach, you can materialize this snapshot using an INSERT wrapped in a check to prevent duplicates or constraint violations — ensuring idempotence. A LEFT JOIN or NOT EXISTS ensures the snapshot for the given timestamp doesn't already exist.

Access area

↗ The access area is the final area in the architecture. It makes data available to consumers through outgoing interfaces.

By the time data reaches the access area, most preparation work has already been completed – especially if a performance area is in place. If not, the responsibilities typically handled in the performance area must be addressed here instead.

Assuming the performance area exists, the primary focus of the access area is to:
- → Transform data to the required delivery format, defined by the outgoing interface
- → Define the historization behavior at column-level
- → Set the appropriate granularity; establishing the right level of detail for data delivery
- → Apply remaining business logic; logic that hasn't been addressed in previous layers

In essence, the access area is where data is finalized for consumption. It ensures the right structure, scope, and business meaning are applied before delivery to downstream applications or users.

Access area data object structure

When defining access area structures, there are virtually no limitations – anything goes. However, in practice, this area is often implemented as one or more *data marts.*

A typical data mart is structured around facts and dimensions:
- → Facts represent measurable events or transactions, aligned to a defined grain. These records can typically be aggregated
- → Dimensions provide descriptive context for the facts. Each column in a dimension is configured based on its historization behavior

We'll keep the following sections relatively short, as there is already extensive documentation available on the design and implementation of dimensional models, covering a wide variety of approaches including –but not limited to– snowflake models, mini-dimensions, historized facts, junk dimensions, dimensional bridges, the list goes on.

The basic structure for these objects is as follows:

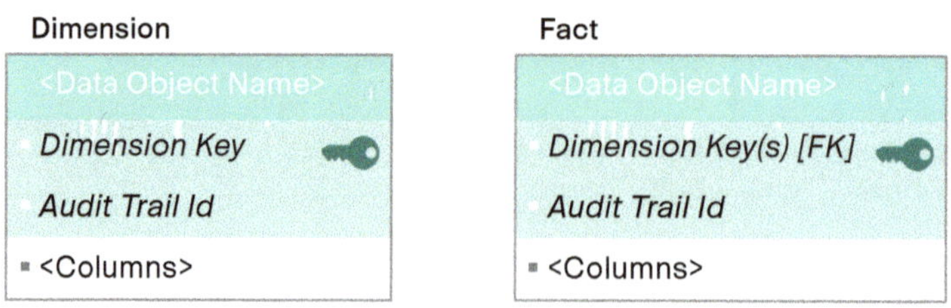

Dimension objects

A dimension includes:
- → A dimension key that uniquely identifies the record
- → An Audit Trail Id
- → One or more descriptive columns

Optionally, the following columns can be considered:
- → From/Before Timestamps
- → Checksums

Fact objects

A fact table typically includes:
- → A combination of dimension keys, representing the grain
- → An Audit Trail Id
- → Descriptive columns —in fact tables— these often consist of metrics or aggregatable values, such as quantities, amounts, or durations

Dimension key(s)

A dimension key is a surrogate key that uniquely identifies each record in a dimension object. It is typically a stable, system-generated value —often an integer— that simplifies joins between fact and dimension objects. This ensures consistent linkage and efficient query performance, especially in historized dimensions (e.g., SCD 2), where multiple records may describe the same business key over time.

In the reference architecture described in this book, dimension keys are generated deterministically — either within the PIT object or directly in the dimension when skipping the PIT. The key requirement is that the dimension can be truncated and reproduced exactly as it was, including the same dimension keys. That way, everything stays aligned across your data model during refactoring without potentially rebuilding large parts of the model. And, of course, this enables a virtualization approach.

Dimension keys serve as the primary key of the dimension and act as foreign keys in fact tables. The grain of a fact table is determined by the dimensions linked to it, and the combination of dimension keys stored in the fact table forms its composite primary key.

Dim Product

Product Key	From Timestamp	Before Timestamp	Audit Trail Id	Product Identifier	Cost Price
9001	2025-01-10	2025-06-04	285100	Shoe IXA	25
9002	2025-06-04	9999-12-31	285301	Shoe IXA	35

Fact Sales

Customer Key	Product Key	Transaction Date Key	Audit Trail Id	Quantity Sold
18515	9001	20250101	19011	1
18516	9001	20250102	19012	2
18517	9001	20250103	19011	2

Dim Date

Date Key	Audit Trail Id	Day	Month	Year
20250101	104	1	January	2025
20250102	104	2	January	2025
20250103	104	2	January	2025

Dim Customer

Customer Key	From Timestamp	Before Timestamp	Audit Trail Id	Customer Identifier	Customer First Name	<columns>	Customer Contact Preference
18515	2025-12-01	2025-12-23	285124	100	Michael	<...>	Phone
18516	2025-12-23	9999-12-31	285125	100	Michael	<...>	Email
18517	2025-12-02	9999-12-31	285124	200	Amal	<...>	Text

In this example, a sales fact table is described by the customer, product, and date dimensions. The dimension keys reflect changes over time – for instance, in the customer or product details – and those changes are visible in the fact data. Date, time, or timestamp values can be connected to a date dimension that supports aggregation to higher levels – day, month, and year in this example. This allows the measures (descriptive columns in the fact) to be reported against these levels.

Granularity also plays a role here. In reality, sales don't always occur exactly at midnight – they happen throughout the day. However, if the fact table stores (aggregates) data at day-level granularity, this becomes the lowest level of time-based aggregation supported by the current model. If more detailed analysis is needed –say, by hour– the fact table can be refactored accordingly and connected to a more granular time dimension.

Audit Trail Id

The Audit Trail Id continues to serve its purpose in the access area. Capturing the unique execution identifier of the data logistics process that processed the data. However, access area objects introduce a slight twist. In specific scenarios, it may be useful –or even necessary– to include a *second* Audit Trail Id to track updates applied to the data.

In the reference architecture, we promote an insert-only approach for processing data. But with certain historization types, this pattern no longer holds up. For example, SCD 1 implementations (particularly SCD 1A, where changes are overwritten across the entire history) separate the insert from the update. Since updates modify existing records, the insert-only principle doesn't apply here.

In these cases, having a second Audit Trail Id can be helpful: one to log the original insert, and another to track the most recent update. This allows you to distinguish between the initial data load and subsequent changes made to the record (the most recent update in this case).

That said, if you're using a virtualization approach, this distinction becomes irrelevant. Since there's no physical update being applied, a single Audit Trail Id is sufficient to track the execution context.

Descriptive columns

The descriptive columns are what it's all about in the access area – they're the values that truly matter to data consumers. In dimensions, these columns describe the context for fact records. In fact tables, they represent the measures – values meant to be counted, aggregated, or reported at different levels of detail.

This is an interesting point to pause on. Descriptive columns –whether from dimensions or facts– originate in the integration layer, where they're simply *columns.* It's only when we model them in the access area that they take on their specific role – whether descriptive or quantitative. In other words, their meaning is driven by the model, not by the source.

Viewed this way, any column from the integration layer can act as either a descriptive value or a measure – or even both. For example, a column like 'number of sales,' which clearly looks like a measure, could also be used descriptively to classify products into categories such as low-volume or high-volume.

The possibilities are nearly endless – a creative playground for experimenting with different access area models.

And thanks to virtualization and automated refactoring, it's easy to explore and evolve these models over time.

Optional columns

Given the breadth of options for designing outgoing interfaces –particularly dimensional models– the following list of optional columns should be considered a starting point. Many additional columns can be invented or applied depending on the specific implementation flavor or concept.

As such, the list below is not exhaustive, but a foundation to build on:

→ Checksums
→ From and Before Timestamps

Checksums

Checksums, though optional, are especially useful in (materialized) dimensions to detect changes – just as they are in the staging and integration layers. The way checksums are used depends on the historization approach.

We'll go into more detail in the ⚐ types of history section, but in short: historization is defined at the column level, and it can be helpful to group columns with the same historization type into a dedicated checksum. For example, all SCD 1 columns might be represented by a single checksum. If this checksum differs from the previous record for the same business key, the affected columns can be updated. Similarly, if a checksum representing SCD 2 columns changes, a new record is inserted.

As with other uses of checksums, this approach is optional and can be replaced by comparing individual columns directly if preferred.

From and before timestamps

Time periods can be added to access area objects when tracking changes over time is needed. This is considered optional, as not every object requires historization. For example, in SCD 0 and certain SCD 1 implementations (and their variations), time-based tracking is unnecessary.

However, when historization is required, it's standard practice to include from and before timestamp columns to represent the validity period of each record.

Access area design pattern

This section provides a high-level overview of an access area design pattern. Because there are so many possible permutations for delivering data, it's not feasible to define a single pattern that fits every scenario. However, most data deliveries follow variations on a common theme. Describing delivery in terms of a dimensional model often serves as a helpful foundation — even when alternative structures are used.

A typical process for delivering a dimension includes the following steps:

- → Select the data from the underlying performance or integration layer objects; apply compacting if required
- → Calculate SCD 1 and SCD 2 checksums to support the desired historization behavior
- → Lookup the target record in the dimension table and compare it using the checksums
  - → Insert a new record if the record does not exist, or if the SCD 2 checksum indicates a historized change, else discard the row
  - → Update the existing record if only the SCD 1 checksum differs. If no differences are found, discard the row

This approach builds on the data preparation patterns introduced in the performance area. As noted earlier, the pattern itself is highly generic and supports a wide range of presentation layer objects. The real nuance lies in where —and how— specific parts of the process are applied.

Considerations

As always, each area has specific considerations unique to its context, which should be incorporated into the final design pattern.

Types of history

When defining an outgoing interface —such as a classic Kimball dimension— it's essential to define the method of historization, which determines how changes in values are tracked over time.

Historization is specified at the attribute (column) level and is considered a property of the information model. It is encoded in metadata, which can then be used to generate the physical model and drive the corresponding data logistics. This ensures that historical data is presented in line with the model, and the corresponding business expectations.

Each column is assigned a history classification, and depending on the type, changes may affect just the column in question or the entire record.

While we won't go in extensive detail here —since high-quality documentation on this topic[51] is readily available— we'll provide a brief summary of commonly used types of historization. These are typically referred to as 'slowly changing dimensions' — using the abbreviation 'SCD.'

SCD 0 — retain original (no change)

A passive approach where values are assumed not to change. Common examples include date of birth, the original creation date of a record, or calendar properties. No history is tracked, as these values are expected to remain constant and only the initial state has to be preserved.

SCD 1A — overwrite history across all records

When a value changes, the new value overwrites the old one across *all* records. No history is retained.

This approach is suitable when tracking history is unnecessary.

SCD 1B — overwrite only the current record

A slight variation of SCD 1A. Instead of updating all records, only the current (most recent) record is updated. This is often used for corrections, such as spelling errors, where the latest version is sufficient and historical changes are not meaningful.

SCD 2 — create new record for change

History is tracked by inserting a new record and closing the most recent corresponding record whenever a change occurs in a column tagged as SCD 2. This is the most common approach to tracking detailed attribute changes over time.

SCD 3 — store history in separate column

The previous value of a changing attribute is stored in a separate column (e.g., previous_name). Typically, only the most recent previous state is retained, but as many columns can be added as previous states that need to be captured.

SCD 4 — separate table for historical values

Volatile attributes are moved into a separate mini-dimension table. One table holds the current record; another stores some, or all, historical changes.

SCD 5 — snapshots

The SCD 5 (1+4) method of implements versions of tables for every period in time. Also known as 'snap-shotting.'

This method uses full table snapshots to represent different time periods. It allows access to both current and historical values without requiring a join through a fact table.

SCD 6 — current and historical column pair

A combination of SCD 1A, 2, and 3 — also known as 'twin time stamping' or the 'hybrid approach.' Each change inserts a new record (SCD 2), while current and previous values are stored in dedicated columns (SCD 3), and the current record is updated (SCD 1A). This allows for querying both current and historical states directly.

SCD 7 — dual foreign keys in fact table

The fact table contains two foreign keys: one referencing the current (SCD 1) dimension record and another referencing the historical dimension record (SCD 2).

Conditional updates

As a small but important side note: when working with SCD 1 approaches, remember that updates are *conditional.* This stems from the separation of assertion and state timelines within the data solution.

Traditionally, SCD 1 methods dictate that column values are updated when a newer version is presented.

However, in a bitemporal framework, 'newer' must be seen from the state timeline's perspective. Even if new data is introduced to the access area, it might contain backdated or future-dated values.

To ensure updates are only applied when the incoming data's state timestamp is more recent than the existing value, a conditional predicate can be added:

```
WHERE <incoming>.[State_From_Timestamp] >=
<existing>.[State_From_Timestamp]
```

This obviously requires the from timestamp to be added to the object, but ensures that only data with a more recent state timestamp 'updates' the existing records. Additionally, this predicate can be extended to exclude certain future-dated values, depending on specific requirements.

Applying remaining business logic updates

In the reference solution architecture, most business logic is already applied in the derived integration area — particularly if the transformation is considered sufficiently generic or enterprise-wide. Even transformations used only once can be added there to fully isolate the implementation of business logic.

However, if a transformation is specific to a particular data delivery —such as a single data mart— it can also be implemented later in the presentation layer. At that point, it may be added either in the performance area or directly in the access area. Both approaches are valid, as long as they are applied consistently.

That said, when applying logic in the presentation layer, we recommend placing it in the access area for clarity and separation of concerns. Doing so keeps the performance area focused on technical preparation, and the access area dedicated to any final transformations needed for consumption.

As in previous layers, business logic can be implemented using standard patterns and defined in metadata through a data query object.

Automation

Presentation layer structures —including dimensions and fact objects— are generally straightforward to define in metadata. At a minimum, the following elements are required:

→ The data object mapping between the source and target data objects
→ Any data item mappings for descriptive columns

As in the performance area, each individual mapping between a source data object and a target access area object is captured as a separate data object mapping. These mappings include the corresponding data item mappings for any descriptive columns provided by that source. All such mappings are grouped into a data object mapping list, as they share the same target data object.

As with all presentation layer mappings, it's recommended to include the template type in metadata, since this largely determines the final implementation.

Design metadata examples

To illustrate the use of design metadata in the access area, we'll walk through examples both with and without a performance area object. For clarity, each scenario will be covered in a separate section.

Defining a dimension from a PIT

In the first example, a dimension is created based on a traditional PIT object. The descriptive columns are sourced from their respective Satellites.

Note that this example includes a from and a before timestamp, indicating that at least some columns follow SCD 2 historization. This isn't explicitly defined in metadata, as the convention is to use the state timeline to manage this behavior.

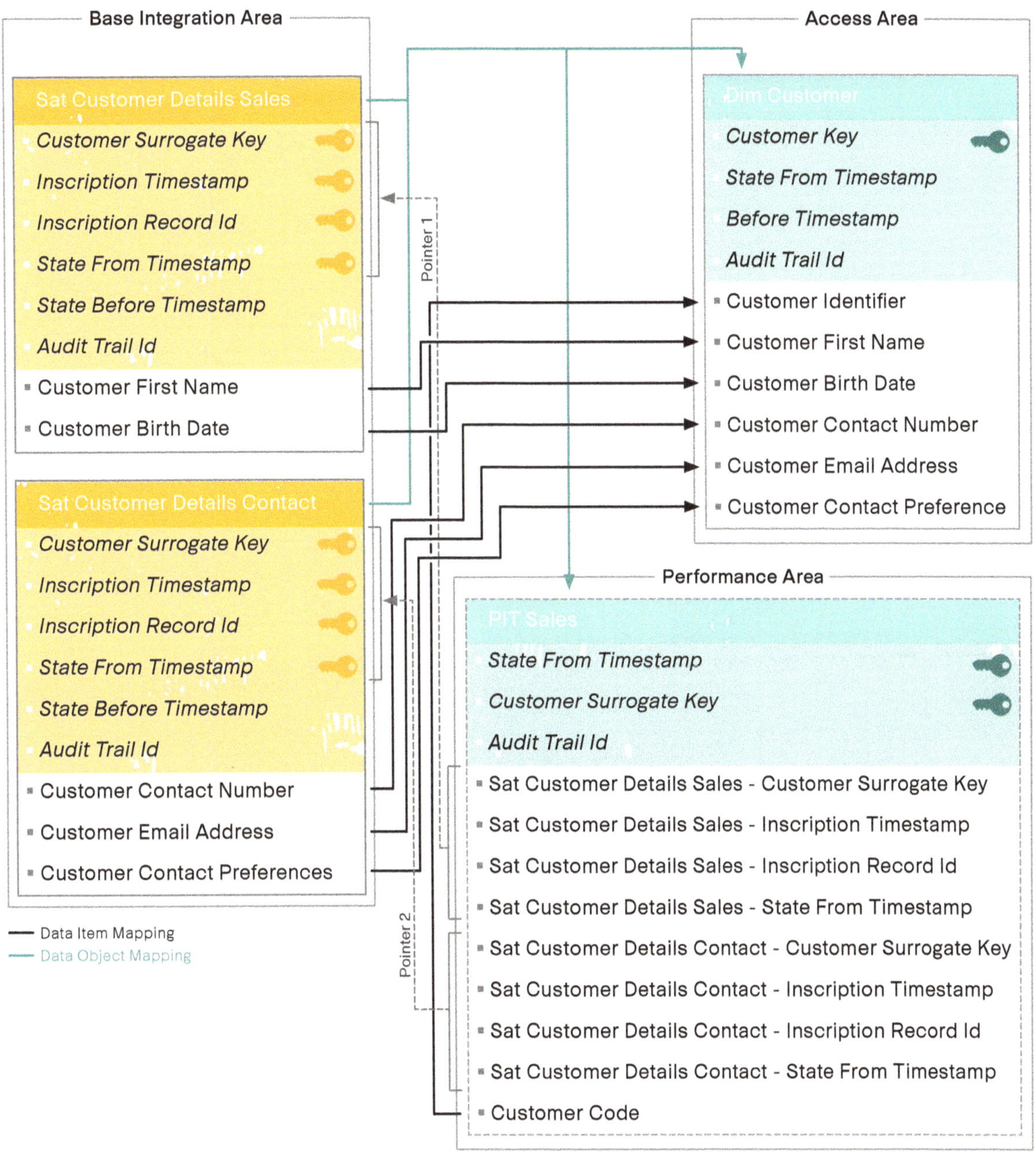

The business key for the customer CBC —the 'Customer Code'— is already available in the PIT, so the Hub does not need to be explicitly added to the metadata.

The design metadata to support this is shown below. To keep things readable, some repeating segments have been removed and replaced with placeholder notes:

```
{
 "dataObjectMappings": [
  {
   "name": "PIT_Sales_to_Dim_Customer",
   "sourceDataObjects": [ { "name": "PIT_Sales" } ],
   "targetDataObject": { "name": "Dim_Customer" },
   "dataItemMappings": [
    {
     "sourcedataItems": [ { "name": "Customer_Code" } ],
     "targetdataItem": { "name": "Identifier" }
    }
   ],
   "relationships": [
    {
     "type": "Left Join",
     "relatedDataObject": { "name": "Sat_Customer_Details_Sales" },
     "dataItemMappings": [
      {
       "sourcedataItems": [ { "name": "Customer_Surrogate_Key" } ],
       "targetdataItem": { "name": "Sat_Customer_Details_Sales_Customer_Surrogate_Key" }
      },
      {
       "sourcedataItems": [ { "name": "Inscription_Timestamp" } ],
       "targetdataItem": { "name": "Sat_Customer_Details_Sales_Inscription_Timestamp" }
      },
      {
       "sourcedataItems": [ { "name": "Inscription_Record_Id" } ],
       "targetdataItem": { "name": "Sat_Customer_Details_Sales_Inscription_Record_Id" }
      },
      {
       "sourcedataItems": [ { "name": "State_From_Timestamp" } ],
       "targetdataItem": { "name": "Sat_Customer_Details_Sales_State_From_Timestamp" }
      }
     ]
    },
    { same as above for Sat_Customer_Details_Contact }
   ]
  },
  {
   "name": "Sat_Customer_Details_Sales_to_Dim_Customer",
   "sourceDataObjects": [ { "name": "Sat_Customer_Details_Sales" } ],
   "targetDataObject": { "name": "Dim_Customer" },
   "dataItemMappings": [
```

```
      {
        "sourcedataItems": [ { "name": "Customer_First_Name" } ],
        "targetdataItem": {
          "name": "First_Name",
          "extensions": [
            {
              "key": "Historization",
              "value": "SCD2"
            }
          ]
        }
      },
      {
        "sourcedataItems": [ { "name": "Customer_Birth_Date" } ],
        "targetdataItem": {
          "name": "Birth_Date",
          "extensions": [
            {
              "key": "Historization",
              "value": "SCD1"
            }
          ]
        }
      }
    ]
  },
  { ... same as above for Sat_Customer_Details_Contact }
 ]
}
```

This dataObjectMappingList contains three distinct data object mappings:

→ The PIT to the dimension
→ The Satellite Customer Details Sales to the dimension
→ The Satellite Customer Details Contact to the dimension

In the first mapping, the PIT is connected to the target dimension. Only one data item mapping is defined —'Customer Code'— as it's the only descriptive column present in the PIT. The more interesting part here is the relationships section, which defines how the Satellites should be joined using their pointer values. For this example, a more generic approach is chosen to demonstrate the usage of the relationships object.

While it's also possible to define these joins within the Satellite mappings themselves, this approach provides a clear and centralized overview using the PIT as starting point generating the code.

The second and third mappings connect the respective Satellites to the dimension and define the data item mappings that supply the descriptive columns. Some data item mappings include an extension to indicate the historization type. If it's missing, the column is treated as not requiring historization.

The code generation template will then do the rest.

Defining a dimension from integration layer objects

To illustrate how closely aligned presentation layer patterns are, this section shows how to create a dimension directly from Satellites – without first generating a PIT object. In this alternative approach, no intermediate performance objects are involved.

While similar to the earlier example with a PIT, in this case, the target data object is a dimension.

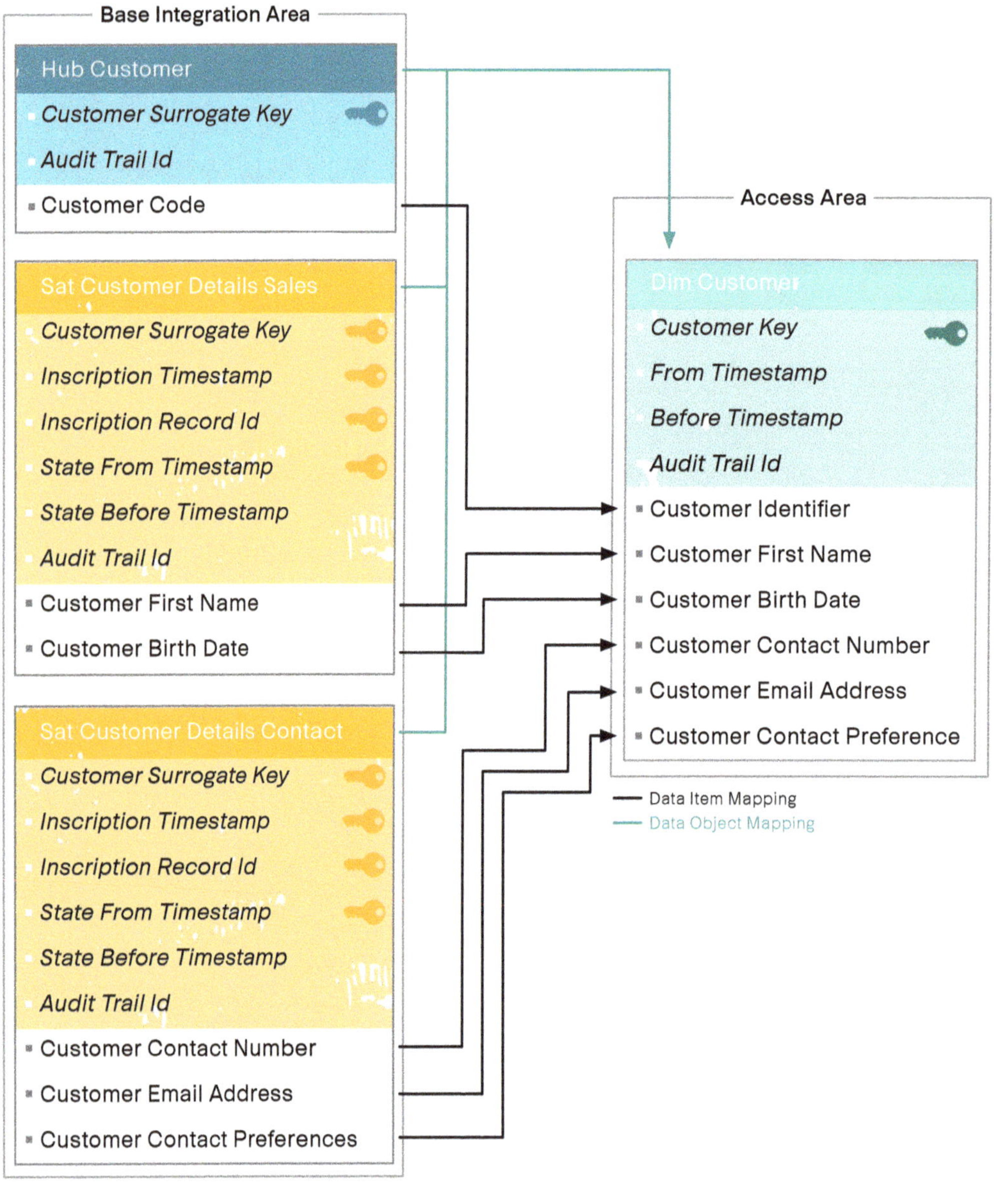

Compare to the PIT-based example, the metadata to directly combine the integration layer objects is largely similar:

```
{
 "dataObjectMappings": [
  {
   "name": "Hub_Customer_to_Dim_Customer",
   "sourceDataObjects": [
    {
     "name": "Hub_Customer"
    }
   ],
   "targetDataObject": {
    "name": "Dim_Customer"
   },
   "dataItemMappings": [
    {
     "sourcedataItems": [ { "name": "Customer_Code" } ],
     "targetdataItem": { "name": "Identifier" }
    }
   ],
   "relationships": [
    {
     "type": "Left Join",
     "relatedDataObject": { "name": "Sat_Customer_Details_Sales" },
     "dataItemMappings": [
      {
       "sourcedataItems": [ { "name": "Customer_Surrogate_Key" } ],
       "targetdataItem": { "name": "Sat_Customer_Details_Sales_Customer_Surrogate_Key" }
      }
     ]
    },
    { same as above for Sat_Customer_Details_Contact }
   ]
  },
  {
   "name": "Sat_Customer_Details_Sales_to_Dim_Customer",
   "sourceDataObjects": [
    {
     "name": "Sat_Customer_Details_Sales"
    }
   ],
   "targetDataObject": {
    "name": "Dim_Customer"
   },
```

```
"dataItemMappings": [
 {
  "sourcedataItems": [
   {
    "name": "Customer_First_Name"
   }
  ],
  "targetdataItem": {
   "name": "First_Name",
   "extensions": [
    {
     "key": "Historization",
     "value": "SCD2"
    }
   ]
  }
 },
 {
  "sourcedataItems": [
   {
    "name": "Customer_Birth_Date"
   }
  ],
  "targetdataItem": {
   "name": "Birth_Date",
   "extensions": [
    {
     "key": "Historization",
     "value": "SCD1"
    }
   ]
  }
 }
]
},
{ same as above for Sat_Customer_Details_Contact }
]
}
```

The only material difference is that instead of the PIT, the Hub object is added and provides the Customer Code data item mapping.

Defining a fact object

The definition of a fact object follows the same general approach as a PIT or dimension, but selects a different kind of descriptive column – specifically, metrics that can be aggregated across the connected dimensions.

In this example, additional Satellites are introduced and joined through a PIT, following the PIT construction method discussed earlier. While the PIT structure and its join pointers are shown in the diagram for clarity, they are not directly part of the fact object's metadata – except for the Product Sale Transaction Satellite, which must be joined to retrieve the required descriptive columns.

The fact object sources primarily from the PIT, which combines multiple Satellites. However, the metric –the actual measure to be aggregated– is added separately as contextual information.

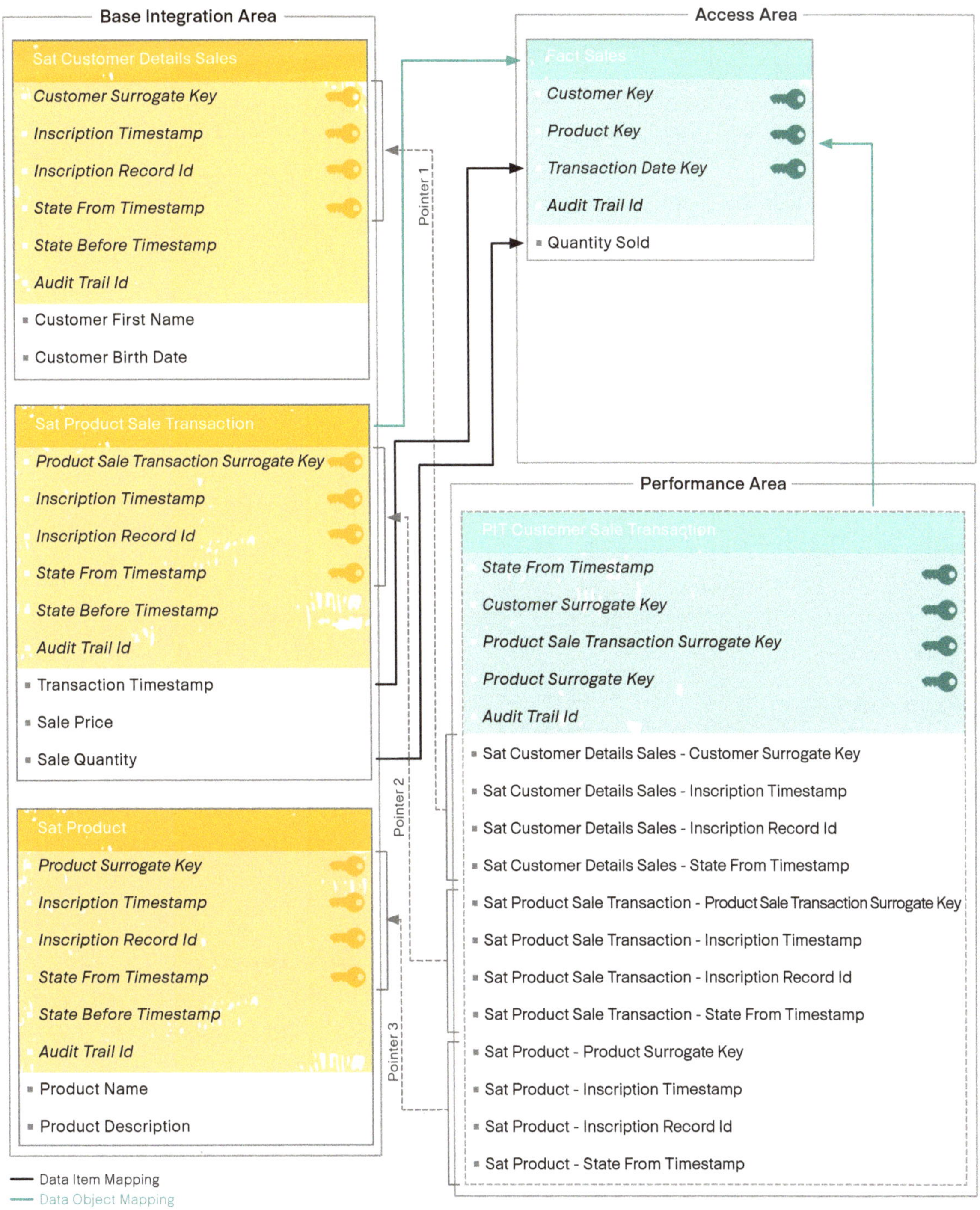
Base Integration Area
Sat Customer Details Sales
Customer Surrogate Key
Inscription Timestamp
Inscription Record Id
State From Timestamp
State Before Timestamp
Audit Trail Id
Customer First Name
Customer Birth Date
Sat Product Sale Transaction
Product Sale Transaction Surrogate Key
Inscription Timestamp
Inscription Record Id
State From Timestamp
State Before Timestamp
Audit Trail Id
Transaction Timestamp
Sale Price
Sale Quantity
Sat Product
Product Surrogate Key
Inscription Timestamp
Inscription Record Id
State From Timestamp
State Before Timestamp
Audit Trail Id
Product Name
Product Description
Pointer 1
Pointer 2
Pointer 3
Access Area
Fact Sales
Customer Key
Product Key
Transaction Date Key
Audit Trail Id
Quantity Sold
Performance Area
PIT Customer Sale Transaction
State From Timestamp
Customer Surrogate Key
Product Sale Transaction Surrogate Key
Product Surrogate Key
Audit Trail Id
Sat Customer Details Sales - Customer Surrogate Key
Sat Customer Details Sales - Inscription Timestamp
Sat Customer Details Sales - Inscription Record Id
Sat Customer Details Sales - State From Timestamp
Sat Product Sale Transaction - Product Sale Transaction Surrogate Key
Sat Product Sale Transaction - Inscription Timestamp
Sat Product Sale Transaction - Inscription Record Id
Sat Product Sale Transaction - State From Timestamp
Sat Product - Product Surrogate Key
Sat Product - Inscription Timestamp
Sat Product - Inscription Record Id
Sat Product - State From Timestamp
Data Item Mapping
Data Object Mapping

In this overview, note that the PIT itself is only referenced as part of a data object mapping. No data item mappings are defined for the PIT in this case, although it could also be valid to include the metric within the PIT. To maintain consistency with the examples shown so far —and to highlight the flexibility of this approach— the metric is mapped directly from the original Satellite.

Additionally, a data item mapping is defined for the transaction timestamp, as this value is used to derive the foreign key for the date dimension – a special case. Other dimension keys are generated at runtime.

The corresponding metadata is structured as follows:

```
{
 "dataObjectMappings": [
  {
   "name": "PIT_Customer_Sale_Transactions_to_Fact_Sales",
   "sourceDataObjects": [ { "name": "PIT_Customer_Sale_Transactions" } ],
   "targetDataObject": { "name": "Fact_Sales" },
   "relationships": [
    {
     "type": "Left Join",
     "relatedDataObject": { "name": "Sat_Product_Sale_Transaction" },
     "dataItemMappings": [
      {
       "sourcedataItems": [ { "name": "Customer_Surrogate_Key" } ],
       "targetdataItem": { "name": "Sat_Product_Sale_Transaction_Surrogate_Key" }
      },
      {
       "sourcedataItems": [ { "name": "Inscription_Timestamp" } ],
       "targetdataItem": { "name": "Sat_Product_Sale_Transaction_Inscription_Timestamp" }
      },
      {
       "sourcedataItems": [ { "name": "Inscription_Record_Id" } ],
       "targetdataItem": { "name": "Sat_Product_Sale_Transaction_Inscription_Record_Id" }
      },
      {
       "sourcedataItems": [ { "name": "State_From_Timestamp" } ],
       "targetdataItem": { "name": "Sat_Product_Sale_Transaction_State_From_Timestamp" }
      }
     ]
    }
   ]
  },
```

```
  {
    "name": "Sat_Product_Sale_Transaction_to_Fact_Sales",
    "sourceDataObjects": [ { "name": "Sat_Product_Sale_Transaction" } ],
    "targetDataObject": { "name": "Fact_Sales" },
    "dataItemMappings": [
     {
      "sourcedataItems": [
       { "dataQueryCode": "SELECT CAST(CONVERT(CHAR(8), [Transaction_Timestamp], 112) AS INT)"
}
      ],
      "targetdataItem": { "name": "Transaction_Date_Key" }
     },
     {
      "sourcedataItems": [ { "dataQueryCode": "COUNT([Sale_Quantity]" } ],
      "targetdataItem": { "name": "Quantity_Sold" }
     }
    ],
    "extensions": [
     {
      "key": "Aggregation",
      "value": "GROUP BY ALL"
     }
    ]
  }
 ]
}
```

The calculations are defined using a dataQuery, which guides the code generation template to apply the necessary aggregations. The 'GROUP BY ALL' flag in the extensions section signals that the result should be grouped across all dimension keys defined for the fact object.

Solution pattern examples

The access area implementation uses the same fundamental approach as the performance area and can follow either a snapshot-based or timeline-based pattern. Since both approaches have already been covered in detail, we won't repeat that content here.

Instead, we'll focus on timeline-based examples, as they align most closely with the structure and behavior of a traditional SCD 2 dimension.

In the next sections, we'll cover the creation of access area objects with and without using performance area objects based on the corresponding design metadata examples.

See our website for solution pattern examples: https://dtng.link/qa5xf.

Creating a dimension from a PIT

With a PIT available, constructing a dimension becomes relatively straightforward. The heavy lifting has already been done in previous layers, so this implementation only needs to join in the descriptive columns from the Satellites. **The result is concise and efficient code:**

```
SELECT
 -- Customer dimension key
 ROW_NUMBER() OVER
 (ORDER BY
  [PIT_Sales].[Sat_Customer_Details_Sales_Inscription_Timestamp],
  [PIT_Sales].[Sat_Customer_Details_Sales_Inscription_Record_Id],
  [PIT_Sales].[Sat_Customer_Details_Sales_State_From_Timestamp],
  [PIT_Sales].[Customer_Code]
 ) AS [Customer_Key],

 -- Time periods
 [PIT_Sales].[State_From_Timestamp] AS [From_Timestamp],
 LEAD([PIT_Sales].[State_From_Timestamp],1,'9999-12-31')
  OVER (
    PARTITION BY [PIT_Sales].[Customer_Surrogate_Key]
      ORDER BY [PIT_Sales].[State_From_Timestamp] ASC
  ) AS [Before_Timestamp],

 -- Descriptive columns
 [PIT_Sales].[Customer_Code]               AS [Identifier],
 [sat1].[Customer_First_Name]              AS [First_Name],
 [sat1].[Customer_Birth_Date]              AS [Birth_Date],
 [sat2].[Customer_Contact_Number]          AS [Contact_Number],
 [sat2].[Customer_Email_Address]           AS [Email_Address],
 [sat2].[Customer_Contact_Preferences]     AS [Contact_Preference]
FROM PIT_Sales

-- Join Satellite 1: Customer Details Sales
LEFT JOIN [Sat_Customer_Details_Sales] sat1
ON
    PIT_Sales.[Sat_Customer_Details_Sales_Customer_Surrogate_Key]    = sat1.[Customer_Surrogate_Key]
  AND PIT_Sales.[Sat_Customer_Details_Sales_Inscription_Timestamp]   = sat1.[Inscription_Timestamp]
  AND PIT_Sales.[Sat_Customer_Details_Sales_Inscription_Record_Id]   = sat1.[Inscription_Record_Id]
  AND PIT_Sales.[Sat_Customer_Details_Sales_State_From_Timestamp]    = sat1.[State_From_Timestamp]

-- Join Satellite 2: Customer Details Contact
LEFT JOIN [Sat_Customer_Details_Contact] sat2
ON
    PIT_Sales.[Sat_Customer_Details_Contact_Customer_Surrogate_Key]    = sat1.[Customer_Surrogate_Key]
  AND PIT_Sales.[Sat_Customer_Details_Contact_Inscription_Timestamp]   = sat1.[Inscription_Timestamp]
  AND PIT_Sales.[Sat_Customer_Details_Contact_Inscription_Record_Id]   = sat1.[Inscription_Record_Id]
  AND PIT_Sales.[Sat_Customer_Details_Contact_State_From_Timestamp]    = sat1.[State_From_Timestamp]
```

The only derived values here are the dimension key and the before timestamp, both calculated using standard window functions. Optionally, these can be pre-generated in the PIT to simplify this logic even further.

Adding a materialization wrapper

To persist the dimension as a physical object —rather than exposing it purely as a view— wrap the final selection in an INSERT INTO statement.

This allows you to insert only new or changed records, supports incremental loading, and aligns with data logistics principles:

```
INSERT INTO [Dim_Customer]
(
 [Customer_Key],
 [From_Timestamp],
 [Before_Timestamp],
 [Identifier],
 [First_Name],
 [Birth_Date],
 [Contact_Number],
 [Email_Address],
 [Contact_Preference]
)
SELECT *
FROM
(
 <Selection query>
) AS ChangeRecords
WHERE NOT EXISTS
(
 SELECT NULL
 FROM [Dim_Customer] Existing
 WHERE Existing.[Customer_Key] = NewRecords.[Customer_Key]
)
```

Overlaying historization

So far, all columns have been treated as SCD 2 by default. If specific historization approaches are defined in metadata (e.g., mix of SCD 1 and SCD 2 columns), you can calculate dedicated checksums for each group.

These checksums are then used to detect updates or insertions in the target object, or be used to represent history in different ways as the final step of the query or view.

The below logic can be added to the original selection to prepare the checksums based on the design metadata:

```
-- Type 1 Checksum (e.g., descriptive non-historized changes)
HASHBYTES('SHA1',
  COALESCE(TRIM(CONVERT(NVARCHAR(MAX), [Customer_Birth_Date])), '~!@|N/A') + '\@|' +
) AS [Checksum_SCD1],

-- Type 2 Checksum (e.g., historized changes)
HASHBYTES('SHA1',
  COALESCE(TRIM(CONVERT(NVARCHAR(MAX), [Customer_First_Name])), '~!@|N/A') + '\@|' +
  COALESCE(TRIM(CONVERT(NVARCHAR(MAX), [Customer_Contact_Number])), '~!@|N/A') + '\@|' +
  COALESCE(TRIM(CONVERT(NVARCHAR(MAX), [Customer_Email_Address])), '~!@|N/A')
  COALESCE(TRIM(CONVERT(NVARCHAR(MAX), [Customer_Contact_Preferences])), '~!@|N/A')
) AS [Checksum_SCD2]
```

With these details available, the dimension can be queried (LEFT JOIN) to compare checksums, separating inserts and updates (or use a merge statement).

The insert part manages the SCD 2 columns:

```
INSERT INTO Dim_Customer
(
 [Customer_Key],
 [From_Timestamp],
 [Before_Timestamp],
 [Identifier],
 [First_Name],
 [Birth_Date],
 [Contact_Number],
 [Email_Address],
 [Contact_Preference],
 [Checksum_Type1],
 [Checksum_Type2]
)
SELECT
 Selection.[Customer_Key],
 Selection.[From_Timestamp],
 Selection.[Before_Timestamp],
 Selection.[Identifier],
 Selection.[First_Name],
 Selection.[Birth_Date],
 Selection.[Contact_Number],
 Selection.[Email_Address],
 Selection.[Contact_Preference],
 Selection.[Checksum_Type1],
 Selection.[Checksum_Type2]
FROM <Selection query> Selection
LEFT JOIN Dim_Customer Dim
 ON Selection.[Customer_Key] = Dim.[Customer_Key]
```

```
WHERE Dim.[Customer_Key IS NULL
  OR Selection.[Checksum_SCD2] <> Dim.[Checksum_SCD2]
```

And, the update component looks after the SCD 1 columns:

```
UPDATE Dim
SET
 Dim.[Customer_Birth_Date] = Selection.[Customer_Birth_Date]
FROM Dim_Customer Dim
FROM <Selection query> Selection
 ON Dim.[Customer_Key] = Selection.[Customer_Key]
WHERE Selection.[Checksum_SCD1] <> Dim.[Checksum_SCD1]
```

Representing historization in a virtual dimension

If you're preparing a virtual object (e.g., a view, function, query, or similar) to represent a historized dimension there's no physical update – so you simulate the update logic by presenting the latest value for SCD 1 attributes alongside historized (SCD 2) records.

This is a common approach in virtualization and ensures the query result reflects the expected current and historized state.

To implement this, you represent the latest SCD 1 columns by:

- → Partitioning the data by business key or surrogate key
- → Ordering by the timeline column (e.g., From Timestamp) descending
- → Using FIRST_VALUE() or LAST_VALUE() window functions to retrieve the most recent SCD 1 values
- → Keeping the original SCD 2 values so that these show changes over time

This can be implemented as a (variation of) the following code:

```
WITH HistorizedDimension AS
(
 SELECT
  Dim.[Customer_Key],
  Dim.[From_Timestamp],
  Dim.[Before_Timestamp],
  Dim.[Identifier],
  Dim.[First_Name],               -- SCD 2
  Dim.[Contact_Number],           -- SCD 2
  Dim.[Email_Address],            -- SCD 2
  Dim.[Contact_Preference],       -- SCD 2
  -- Type 1: latest birth date per customer
  FIRST_VALUE(Dim.[Customer_Birth_Date]) OVER
  (
   PARTITION BY Dim.[Customer_Surrogate_Key]
   ORDER BY Dim.[From_Timestamp] DESC
  ) AS [Customer_Birth_Date]      -- SCD 1
 FROM Dim_Customer Dim
)
SELECT *
FROM HistorizedDimension;
```

See our website for a full SQL example for creating a dimension from a PIT: https://dtng.link/2cw2s.

Creating a dimension from integration layer objects

The overall pattern for creating a dimension from integration layer objects large-ly mirrors the original PIT process, with just a few minor adjustments. To keep things readable, we'll break it into smaller steps and briefly explain each.

The overall process

The high-level process can be expressed as pseudo code below, highlighting the important steps in order of operation:

```
DECLARE @Assertion_Filter_Timestamp
DATETIME2(7) = SYSUTCDATETIME();

SELECT
 <Final column formatting and aliasing>
FROM
(
 SELECT
  <Checksum comparison>
 FROM
 (
  SELECT
   <Checksum preparation>
  FROM
  (
   SELECT
    <Integration layer column selection>
   FROM
   (
    SELECT
     <Derive time periods>
    FROM
```

```
      (
       <Combine all from timestamp values>
      ) Timestamps
     ) Timeperiods
     JOIN <Integration layer objects>
    ) Timelines
   ) Calculate_Checksum
  ) Final
WHERE <Checksum comparison filter>
```

Combine all from timestamp values

This inner selection follows the same approach as the PIT and gathers all relevant timestamp values that represent changes across the involved objects.

```
-- Creation of a low-end timestamp for the timeline
SELECT
 Hub.[Customer_Surrogate_Key],
 CONVERT(DATETIME2(7), '1900-01-01') AS [From_Timestamp]
FROM [Hub_Customer] Hub
UNION
-- Combined set of all available from timestamp values
SELECT
 Sat1.[Customer_Surrogate_Key],
 Sat1.[State_From_Timestamp] AS [From_Timestamp]
FROM [Sat_Customer_Details_Sales] Sat1
-- The from and before inscription timestamps are either available, or derived at runtime
WHERE sat1.[Inscription_From_Timestamp]  <= @Assertion_Filter_Timestamp
 AND sat1.[Inscription_Before_Timestamp] > @Assertion_Filter_Timestamp
UNION
SELECT
 Sat2.[Customer_Surrogate_Key],
 Sat2.[State_From_Timestamp] AS [From_Timestamp]
FROM [Sat_Customer_Details_Contact] Sat2
-- The from and before inscription timestamps are either available, or derived at runtime
WHERE sat2.[Inscription_From_Timestamp]  <= @Assertion_Filter_Timestamp
 AND sat2.[Inscription_Before_Timestamp] > @Assertion_Filter_Timestamp
```

The inscription before timestamp may not be available, as covered in the temporal filtering sections. This can be derived at runtime, as shown in the PIT example. For brevity, this code is not repeated but the same window function can be applied.

Derive time periods

This step, too, follows the PIT pattern closely generating the before timestamp using a standard window function:

```
-- Creation of time periods
SELECT
 [Customer_Surrogate_Key],
 [From_Timestamp],
 LEAD(From_Timestamp,1,'9999-12-31')
  OVER (PARTITION BY [Customer_Surrogate_Key]
   ORDER BY [From_Timestamp] ASC)
  AS [Before_Timestamp]
FROM
(
 <Combine all from timestamp values>
) Timestamps
```

Join integration layer objects

This step differs slightly from the PIT example: selecting descriptive columns instead of pointer columns.

```
SELECT
 Hub.[Customer_Surrogate_Key],
 -- Data Item Mappings for the Hub
 Hub.[Customer_Code],
 -- Data Item Mappings for Satellite 1
 Sat1.[Customer_First_Name],
 Sat1.[Customer_Birth_Date],
 -- Data Item Mappings for Satellite 2
 Sat2.[Customer_Contact_Number],
 Sat2.[Customer_Email_Address],
 Sat2.[Customer_Contact_Preferences],
 -- New timeline
 TimePeriods.[From_Timestamp],
 TimePeriods.[Before_Timestamp]
FROM
(
 <Derive time periods>
) TimePeriods
-- Joining the Hub, for the business key
 INNER JOIN [Hub_Customer] Hub
  ON TimePeriods.[Customer_Surrogate_Key] = Hub.[Customer_Surrogate_Key]
-- Joining the context for Satellite 1
 LEFT JOIN [Sat_Customer_Details_Sales] Sat1
  ON TimePeriods.[Customer_Surrogate_Key] = Sat1.[Customer_Surrogate_Key]
  AND Sat1.[State_From_Timestamp] <= TimePeriods.[From_Timestamp]
  AND Sat1.[State_Before_Timestamp] > TimePeriods.[Before_Timestamp]
```

```
-- Joining the context for Satellite 2
LEFT JOIN [Sat_Customer_Details_Contact] Sat2
  ON TimePeriods.[Customer_Surrogate_Key] = Sat2.[Customer_Surrogate_Key]
 AND Sat2.[State_From_Timestamp] <= TimePeriods.[From_Timestamp]
 AND Sat2.[State_Before_Timestamp] > TimePeriods.[Before_Timestamp]
```

Creating the checksum and dimension key

Now that we have descriptive columns, we can calculate a checksum to prepare the ⚐ compacting mechanism. In this step —still before compacting is applied— the ⚐ surrogate dimension key is also created using a window function.

```
SELECT
 *,
 ROW_NUMBER() OVER (ORDER BY
  [Inscription_Timestamp],
  [Inscription_Record],
  [From_Timestamp],
  [Customer_Code]
 ) AS [Dimension_Key],
 HASHBYTES('SHA1',
  COALESCE(TRIM(CONVERT(NVARCHAR(MAX),[Customer_First_Name])), '~!@|N/A') + '\@|' +
  COALESCE(TRIM(CONVERT(NVARCHAR(MAX),[Customer_Birth_Date])), '~!@|N/A') + '\@|' +
  COALESCE(TRIM(CONVERT(NVARCHAR(MAX),[Customer_Contact_Number])), '~!@|N/A') + '\@|' +
  COALESCE(TRIM(CONVERT(NVARCHAR(MAX),[Customer_Email_Address])), '~!@|N/A') + '\@|' +
  COALESCE(TRIM(CONVERT(NVARCHAR(MAX),[Customer_Contact_Preferences)), '~!@|N/A') + '\@|'
 ) AS [Checksum]
FROM
(
 <Join integration layer objects>
) Timelines
```

Preparing checksum comparison

To support compacting, the previous checksum value is retrieved. This will be used to filter out duplicate records in the final step – implementing the compacting.

```
SELECT
 Calculate_Checksum.*,
 LAG([Checksum], 1, 0x0000000000000000000000000000000000000000) OVER(
 PARTITION BY [Customer_Surrogate_Key]
 ORDER BY [From_Timestamp] ASC) AS [Previous_Checksum]
FROM
(
 <Creating the checksum>
) Calculate_Checksum
```

Finalizing the query

The final step of the dimension preparation selects the required columns, including the dimension identifier and time periods. In this step, the column names are also aliased to match the design metadata specification.

At the end of the query, the filter implements compacting by only retaining records where the current checksum differs from the previous checksum.

```
SELECT
 [Dimension_Key] AS [Customer_Key],
 From_Timestamp,
 LEAD(From_Timestamp,1,'9999-12-31')
   OVER (
     PARTITION BY [Customer_Surrogate_Key]
       ORDER BY From_Timestamp ASC
   ) AS [Before_Timestamp],
 [Customer_Code] AS [Identifier],
 [Customer_First_Name] AS [First_Name],
 [Customer_Birth_Date] AS [Birth_Date],
 [Customer_Contact_Number] AS [Contact_Number],
 [Customer_Email_Address] AS [Email_Address],
 [Customer_Contact_Preferences] AS [Contact_Preference]
FROM
(
 <Preparing checksum comparison>
) Final
WHERE Final.[Checksum] <> Final.[Previous_Checksum]
```

Adding materialization and historization wrappers

To persist the dimension as a physical object and apply historization approaches, the same approach can be used as with the PIT-based dimension creation.

See our website for a full SQL example for creating a dimension from integration layer objects: https://dtng.link/hwbgz.

Creating a fact object

As with dimensions, the implementation of a fact table follows the same overall approach outlined so far. The key difference is that only the descriptive columns intended to serve as measures are selected, alongside the dimension keys for all referenced dimensions.

If any aggregation is required to align the measures to the defined grain of the fact table, it should be performed at this stage.

Based on the metadata configuration provided earlier, the following SQL logic can be generated to populate the 'Fact Sales' object. This logic follows the same pattern established in the performance and access areas and assumes the use of a PIT to facilitate joins across Satellites.

The metadata indicates that the metric ('Quantity Sold') is sourced from a Satellite and should be aggregated. Additionally, the transaction timestamp is used to derive a 'Transaction Date Key' that references the date dimension.

The SQL below reflects the aggregation and mappings defined in metadata:

```
SELECT
  -- Runtime-generated dimension keys (if not persisted in PIT)
  -- Customer Dimension Key
  ROW_NUMBER() OVER (
  ORDER BY
    PIT.[Sat_Customer_Details_Sales_Inscription_Timestamp],
    PIT.[Sat_Customer_Details_Sales_Inscription_Record_Id],
    PIT.[Sat_Customer_Details_Sales_State_From_Timestamp],
    PIT.[Sat_Customer_Details_Sales_Customer_Surrogate_Key]
  ) AS [Customer_Key],
  -- Product Dimension Key
  ROW_NUMBER() OVER (
  ORDER BY
    PIT.[Sat_Product_Inscription_Timestamp],
    PIT.[Sat_Product_Inscription_Record_Id],
    PIT.[Sat_Product_State_From_Timestamp],
    PIT.[Sat_Product_Product_Surrogate_Key]
  ) AS [Product_Key],

  -- Transaction Date Dimension Key
  CAST(CONVERT(CHAR(8), sat.[Transaction_Timestamp], 112) AS INT) AS [Transaction_Date_Key],
  -- Aggregated metric
  COUNT(sat.[Sale_Quantity]) AS [Quantity_Sold],

FROM PIT_Customer_Sale_Transactions PIT

-- Join to the Satellite providing the metric and timestamp
LEFT JOIN Sat_Product_Sale_Transaction sat
  ON PIT.[Sat_Product_Sale_Transaction_Surrogate_Key]                = sat.[Customer_Surrogate_Key]
 AND PIT.[Sat_Product_Sale_Transaction_Inscription_Timestamp]        = sat.[Inscription_Timestamp]
 AND PIT.[Sat_Product_Sale_Transaction_Inscription_Record_Id]        = sat.[Inscription_Record_Id]
 AND PIT.[Sat_Product_Sale_Transaction_State_From_Timestamp]         = sat.[State_From_Timestamp]

GROUP BY
 PIT.[Customer_Surrogate_Key],
 PIT.[Product_Surrogate_Key],
 CAST(CONVERT(CHAR(8), sat.[Transaction_Timestamp], 112) AS INT)
```

Adding materialization wrappers

Fact tables can be persisted using the same approach as used for dimensions – for example, by applying a LEFT JOIN or EXISTS clause to insert only new records.

See our website for a full SQL example for creating a fact: https://dtng.link/nt6ex.

Considering performance area objects to support the access area

As these sections illustrate, there is often little real difference between certain forms of PIT objects and more traditional objects in the access layer.

The approaches, concepts, and implementations are closely related: remove descriptive attributes from the pattern but keep surrogate keys and timestamps, and you get a classic Data Vault PIT object. Add a few attributes, assign a surrogate key, and introduce a timeline, and you have a fully-fledged SCD 2 dimension.

This flexibility underscores the importance of carefully considering when and how to implement performance-focused objects. Persisting data always introduces overhead – keeping persisted data synchronized requires effort. Some projects implement a dedicated layer of PIT objects as a consistent pattern across the board. Others opt not to use PITs at all, delivering facts and dimensions directly from the integration layer using the same underlying pattern.

While individual access area objects and PIT objects are often quite similar, there can be value in creating a very wide performance area object – one that includes pointers, descriptive columns, or both. Such a wide object can serve as a shared foundation for one or more data marts, including prepared deterministic surrogate keys:

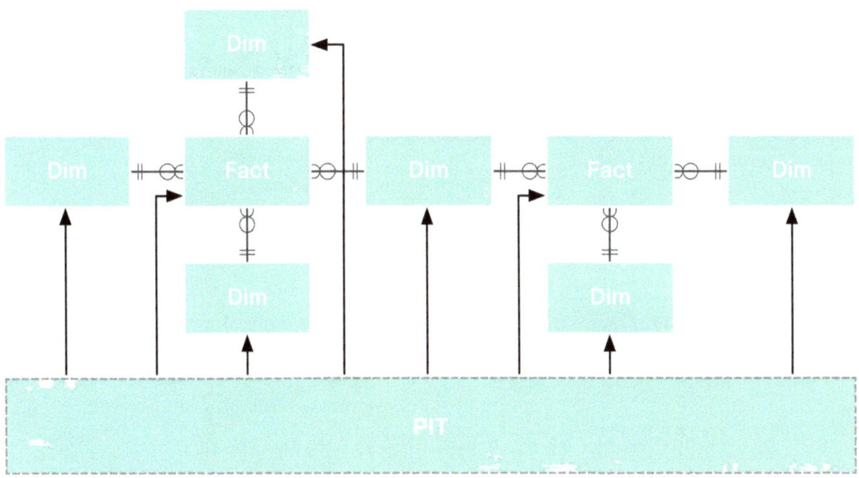

Using this approach may require additional aggregation when processing dimensions and facts. However, it's worth considering in scenarios where performance benefits can be gained in the access area. This highlights yet another advantage of the performance area: its flexibility to consolidate all required data into a single object that supports streamlined delivery to the access layer.

Performance objects in virtual solutions

In virtualized data solutions, performance objects may not be necessary at all. A dimensional model can be delivered directly from the integration layer – for instance as a layer of views. However, if performance doesn't meet expectations, the engine can still generate and maintain a physical layer of performance objects even when the integration layer remains fully virtual.

Our recommendation: be mindful of these dynamics and make deliberate decisions about where and how to implement performance area objects. Often, the simplest path –with less overhead and fewer moving parts– is to deliver data directly from the integration layer.

Still, the architecture should allow for both approaches as needed. Flexibility is key and, as always, these options and considerations should be documented in your solution architecture.

Bringing it all together

At this stage, it's beneficial to revisit how data flows through the solution from ingestion to delivery.

Ingesting data delta into the PSA

Consider three interfaces that process data into the PSA.

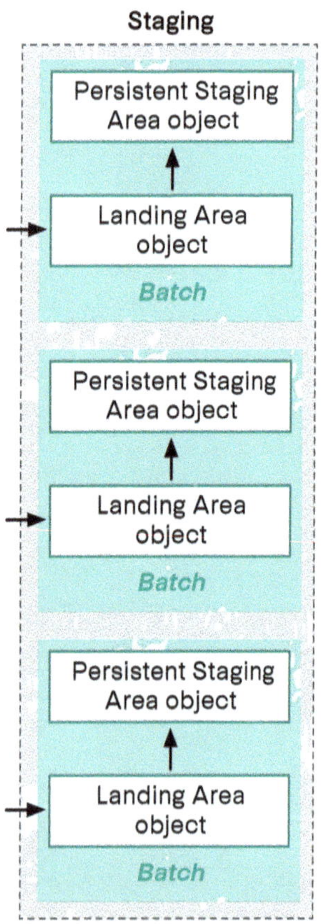

These interfaces are processed as batches, because the LDA data must be committed to the PSA before the delta detection can restart.

Mapping data to the information model

Once the data is available in the PSA, it can be processed into the integration layer. Here, it's mapped to physical model objects derived from the information model.

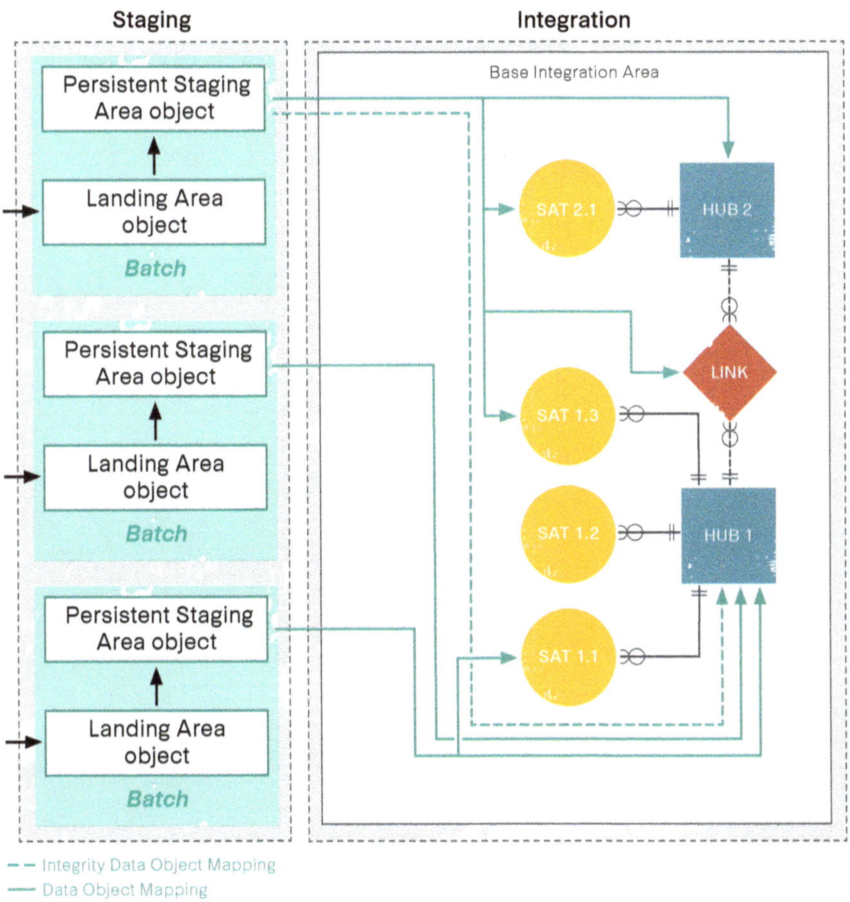

In this example, the three PSA objects are mapped to a Link, two Hubs, and four Satellites. These objects constitute the base integration area.

Adhering to continuous parallel processing principles, these individual modules can run independently and as frequently as needed. Beyond the PSA, all processes operate individually and autonomously, eliminating the need for further orchestration. They can, of course, also be run batch-based.

Adding business logic

If necessary, derived objects can be added to the solution. For instance, the model can be enhanced with an additional Satellite in the derived integration area.

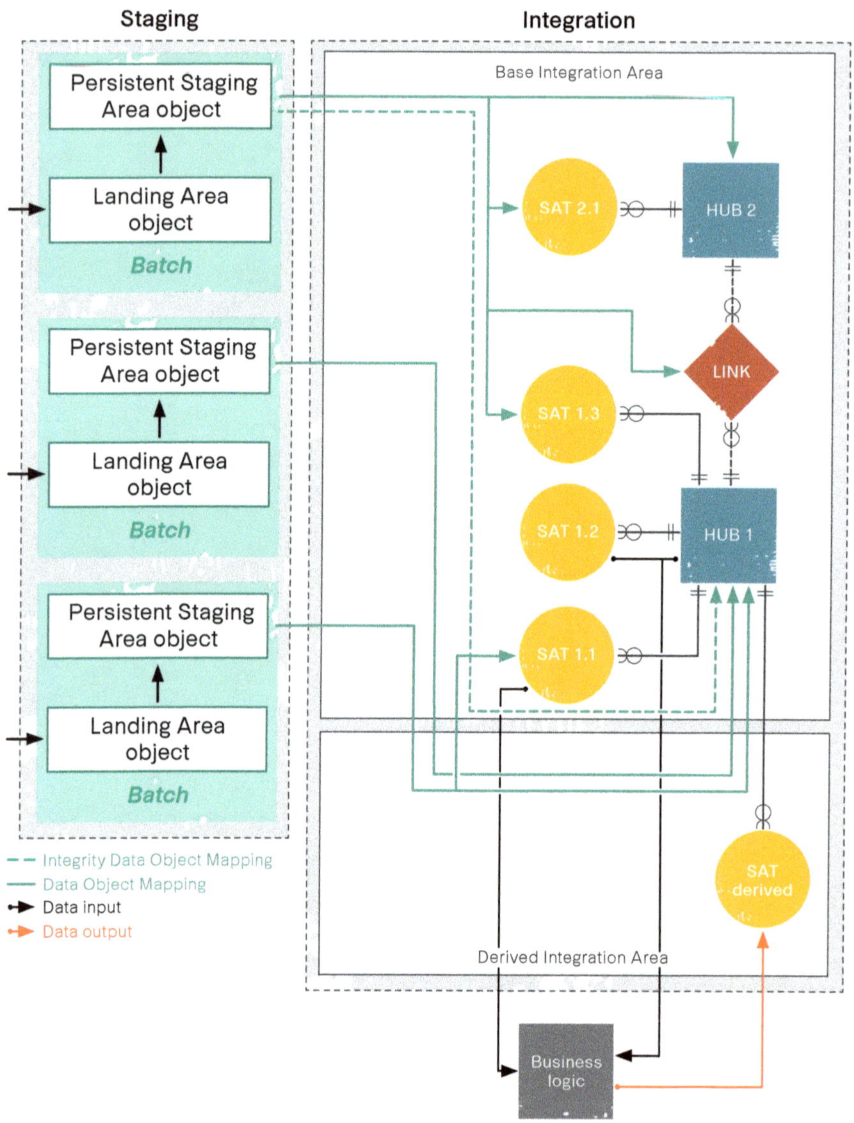

Considering performance

The next step involves adding performance area objects, such as bridge and PIT objects.

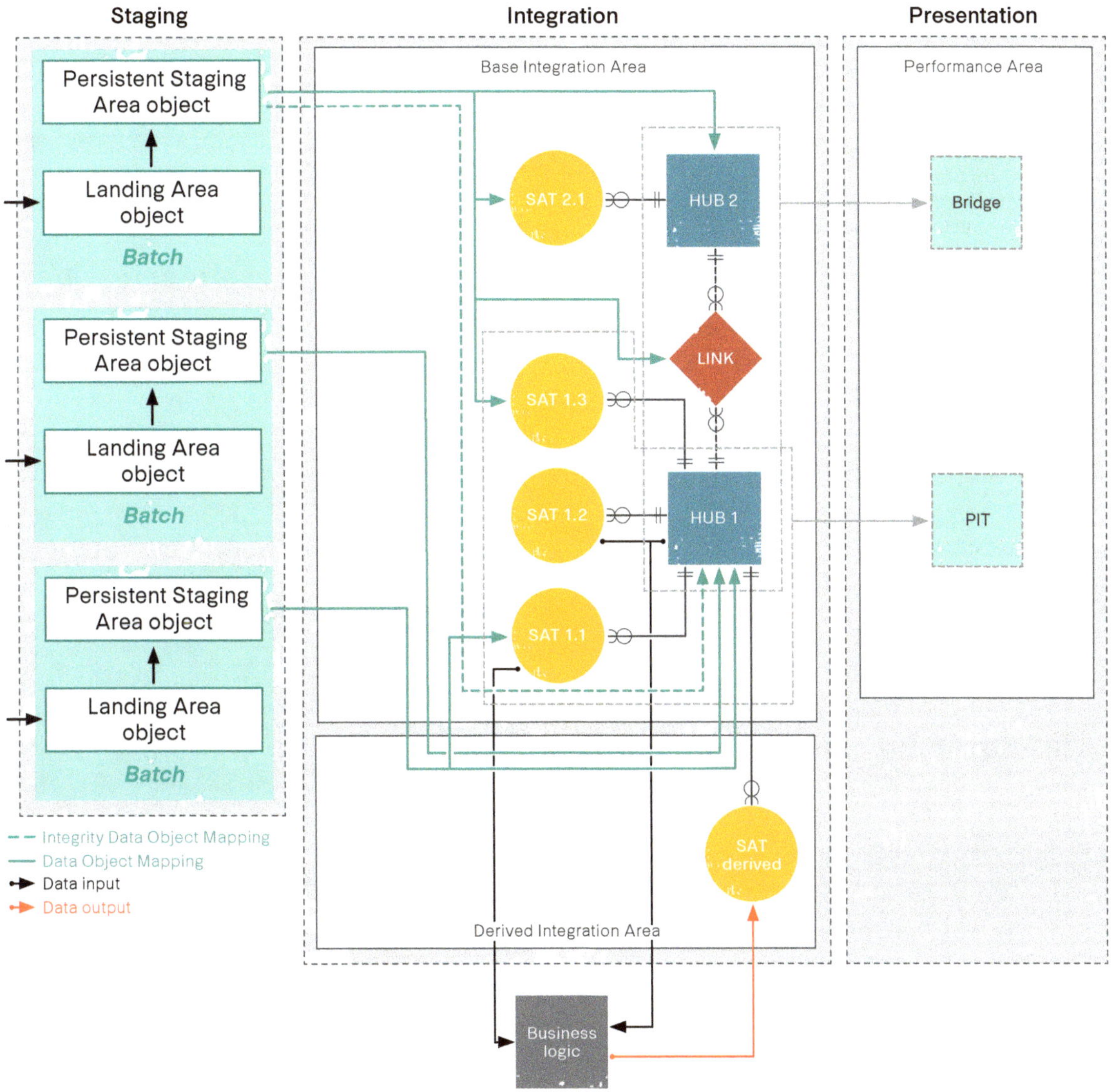

The PIT table is created from the three base Satellites describing the Hub and includes the derived Satellite. The bridge combines two Hubs and a Link.

Constructing the dimension

Finally, the dimension can be constructed from the available objects. In this example, it is fundamentally built using two Hubs, their associated Satellites, and a Link. These may belong to the same CBC or Ensemble – though this isn't necessarily the case.

This pattern allows data from any CBC to be combined; however, not every combination will have business relevance. For instance, Hub 1 and Hub 2 might represent a 'customer' and a 'sales region,' forming a meaningful classification or hierarchy. Alternatively, they could represent a 'product' and a 'warehouse.' Other combinations —such as 'customer' and 'product'— may be technically possible but lack meaningful business interpretation.

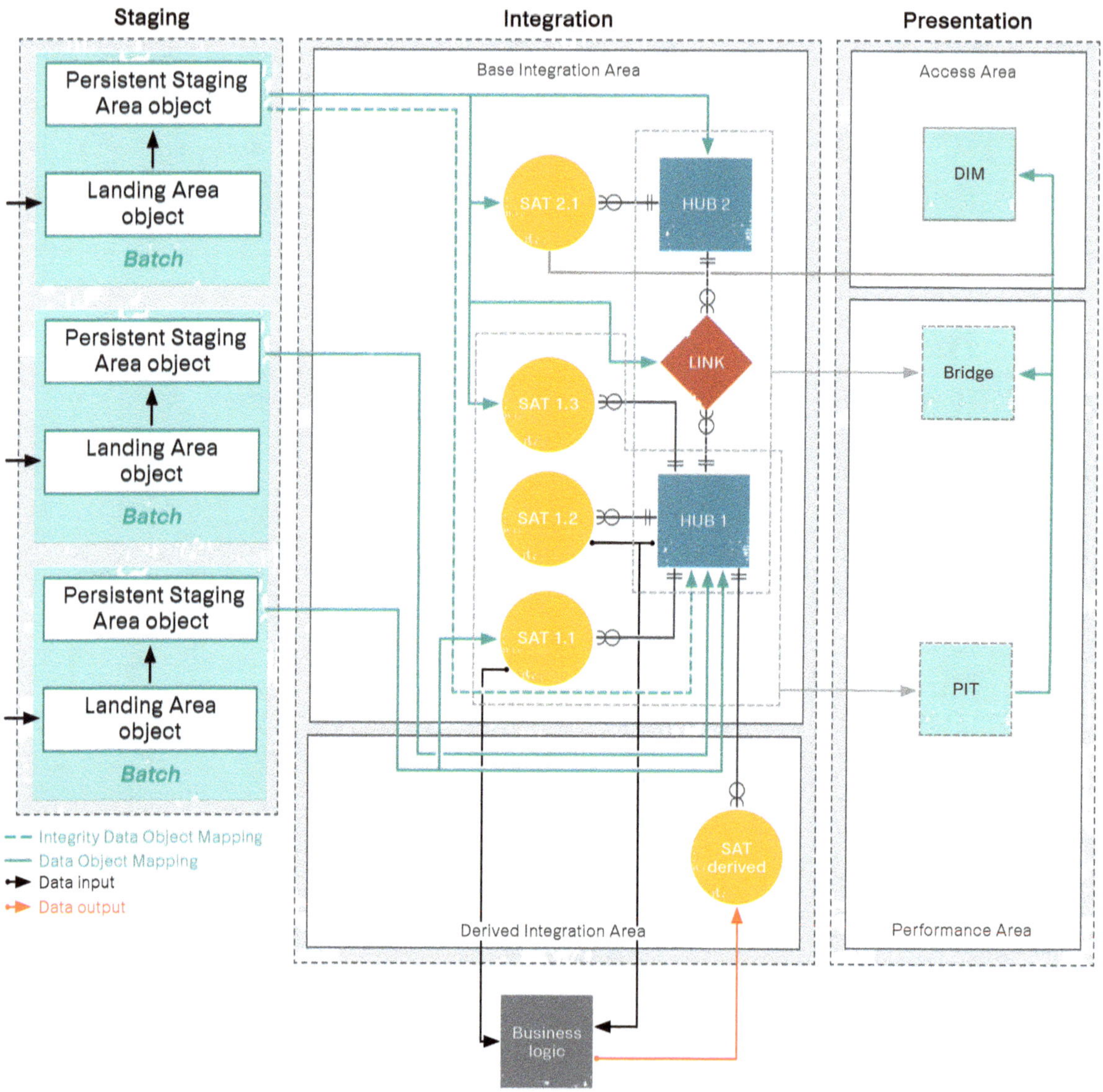

The dimension accesses data through the PIT and combines it with the other Satellite (which isn't included in the PIT). However, using the patterns described in this chapter, it could also utilize the original Satellites. The PIT serves as an interim object, assuming that other presentation layers benefit from it as well. The dimension might select some columns from the PIT and others from the underlying Satellites. Nonetheless, if a PIT exists, it's often more convenient to incorporate the necessary columns there first.

All involved components can run independently, either using load windows or by managing snapshots (inserting a new snapshot only if one doesn't already exist). While there are no technical loading dependencies, functional dependencies do exist. As discussed in the integration layer orchestration sections, no data is 'lost' if a process runs before its dependent processes have completed; the data is simply picked up in the next process run.

The following diagram illustrates this concept, and shows that while dependencies on data exists, this does not impact its processing.

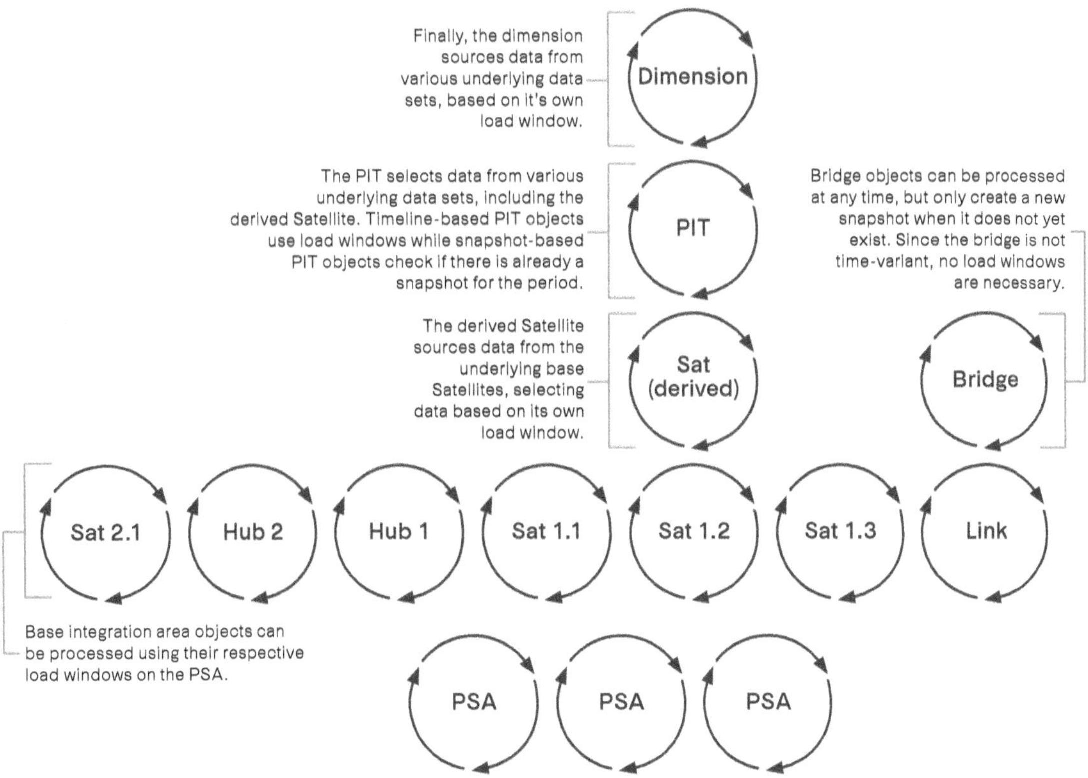

12 FastChangeCo — Getting the data out

The Resurrection is making great strides!

After an intensive phase of research and development, the team has gathered a wealth of knowledge.

To review their progress, Sylvia once again turns to the team's proven format: an offsite. This time, she adds a unique twist — the meeting takes place in the conference area of a theme park. A clever move, she thinks. After demanding work sessions, the team can unwind on rollercoasters in the late afternoon and evening.

Dubbed 'Rollercoasters & Pretzels,' the offsite proves to be another success. The team methodically reviews their achievements. Has the vision and strategy been adhered to?

This type of evaluation has become second nature; they move through decisions with precision, discussing each point thoroughly. By the end, there is consensus — the developed concepts align seamlessly with their overarching vision.

The next step quickly emerged: a hackathon to kick off the second phase of the MVP — the 'front room.' Recalling their previous hackathon's rapid success boosts the team's excitement.

The focus is clear: implementing business and data quality rules, and building a data mart to support the RelCol report. It's a challenge the team is excited to take on.

Michael is immediately on board. Planning for the second HackMatrix begins — setting the stage for the next leap forward in The Resurrection.

The MVP's dimensional model

At the start of the HackMatrix, Zalika focuses on modeling the outgoing interface for the MVP: the dimensional data model.

During the first hackathon, Zalika and Philomena had already created the information model using FCO-IM. The data model is based on *verbalization* — sentences with specific examples stored in text files.

Zalika is considering a fact table for 'orders' and a dimension for 'products.' This aligns with the scope agreed on with Philomena.

However, as she models the product dimension, Zalika realizes she's uncertain in which temporal form Philomena expects the data. Should she only deliver the current state of the data —from today's perspective— or also the changes over time?

They had discussed the report's required attributes but never explicitly addressed the temporal aspect — perhaps assuming everyone was on the same page?

But assumptions are a weak foundation for design decisions, let alone implementation. Zalika knows she can't decide this alone; Philomena needs to weigh in.

Fortunately, their prior work on handling time in the data solution means they have options. Zalika reflects that they can basically provide all temporal variants in the data mart.

Spontaneously, she calls Philomena.

"Philomena, I need to clarify something about the data for the report. Can we talk?"

They agree to meet after lunch.

In the meantime, Zalika annotates the FCO-IM model by defining which objects are part of a fact or a dimension, so that she can generate the appropriate metadata.

Meeting with Philomena

In the company café, Zalika lays out her question about the temporal aspect of the product dimension.

Philomena takes a sip of her Roka Rola – her usual Repsi was, regrettably, sold out.

Since I want to use this report to validate product master data and analyze orders, I need to see how prices change over time," she muses aloud. "Just having today's price won't work. An essential analysis is comparing the actual order price to the planned product price at that time."

Zalika nods, sipping her maté.

"Got it. So, we'll structure the product dimension to retain historical values – what we call a slowly changing dimension, Type 2. That way, changes over time remain traceable."

With the decision made, they chat casually until Philomena finishes her Roka.

Back at her laptop, Zalika updates the FCO-IM model, incorporating the new historical tracking requirements. Later, in the HackMatrix, she and Amal will translate this into physical tables or views.

Building the access layer

Meanwhile, the rest of the team is working on setting up the access layer. As outlined in their design, the front room is responsible for interpreting raw data from the back room, integrating it as needed, and enriching it with additional information.

The team wants to combine different data sources and make it analyzable together as soon as the MVP is ready. However, given the current limited scope, this is only partially feasible. Once the RelCol report is fully implemented, the full range of concepts will likely come into play.

At this point, everyone agrees that the data must be validated and that business rules must then be used to respond to the results. That shared understanding sets the stage for the launch of the third HackMatrix.

Data validation

The energy in the conference room is palpable as the team gathers around the large table. On the wall, the Kanban board titled 'MVP – RelCol' tracks their progress. Now, it's finally time to implement the second phase.

Michael flips through his notes. "We should start with the most critical data validation tests," he says. "Let's prioritize our test scenarios."

Amal nods, opening her laptop. "I suggest starting with validating data against domain values." She turns the screen so everyone can see the data profiling results from the staging layer.

"We noticed an issue in the 'ORDER_DATE' column," she explains. "February 30 isn't a valid date – it doesn't fit the date domain. To ensure all data loads, we converted the column to NVARCHAR() in staging."

Xuefang frowns. "A classic problem, as Diego pointed out. We can load the data, but we need a solution for further processing – like a business rule."

"Let's pull this issue from the backlog and implement it using the exception bitmap," Amal suggests. "It's the perfect test case."

Yerodin, always an advocate for data quality, raises his hand, eyes shining. "I have more ideas for validation," he says, listing them on his tablet.

"We could add plausibility checks to catch unusual values," he explains. "Or consistency checks across tables – something we often needed in controlling."

While Yerodin is talking, Michael is taking notes. "Thanks Yerodin, these are really valuable inputs."

He checks his watch. "We'll capture all of Yerodin's ideas, but for this hackathon, let's focus on a few key validations. Time is limited."

The team nods. Amal steps up to the whiteboard, drawing a fourquadrant diagram. "Remember our DQM framework? We're moving from DQ-III to DQ-I, improving data quality through testing and validation against the information model."

"The solution," she continues, "is to flag data that fails certain tests. This way, we handle data both in the incoming layers (DQ-I, back-room) and the delivery layers (DQ-II, front-room) – without filtering or removing anything."

Xuefang nods. "Exactly. We never delete data – we just mark it. That way, everything stays in the system, but we know what's problematic."

Amal pulls up a presentation. "I've prepared an example of how we can implement the exception bitmap," she says, projecting a diagram onto the wall.

For the next few hours, they focus on the first test cases – validating date formats and detecting invalid values like February 30.

By the afternoon, they have a working exception bitmap. Michael looks around, satisfied. "This is a big step. With this methodology, we can continuously monitor and improve data quality."

The foundation for robust data quality monitoring has been laid. Now, the next challenge: responding to flagged data with business rules – and improving it where necessary.

As evening falls, Michael decides to wrap up. "Let's pick this up tomorrow – fresh and ready to go."

Documenting business rules

Michael invited Philomena to today's Hackmatrix, assuming that as a subject matter expert, she would play a key role in defining business rules. Fortunately, she was able to join on short notice. When she arrives at the conference room, the team is already continuing their discussion from the previous day.

Xuefang, Amal, and Yerodin raise concerns about documenting business logic and rules in a way that is transparent and easily understood. Too often, these rules exist only in developers' minds, and over time, their reasoning is lost.

"At university, I learned that business logic often extends beyond a single use case, so our documentation needs to be both flexible and extensible," Xuefang notes. "That means not only capturing the rules clearly but also linking back to their implementation."

The team agrees that a sustainable, long-term solution is necessary. Xuefang glances at Michael, wondering if he has a relevant story to share – he does, much to his quiet amusement.

"I remember when Diego and I first tackled a similar problem," Michael begins. "We clicked right away – not just personally, but in how we approached problem-solving. But I'm already digressing," he adds with a smile, prompting Xuefang to turn away briefly to suppress her amusement. Everyone is familiar with Michael's tendency to go off on tangents.

"Anyway, back then, Diego and I needed to document business rules in a way that was both transparent and comprehensible. The key concept we developed was separating 'business rules' from 'implementation rules.'"

Michael pauses, looking for his tea. Yerodin, smiling, points towards the sideboard. After retrieving his tea, Michael continues, "Business rules capture the logic required by business experts without considering technical implementation. They should be described independently of any technology."

Taking a sip of green tea, he adds, "Developers then derive implementation rules from these business rules. Each business rule is linked to one or more implementation rules that specify how the necessary data transformations are applied. We used a numbering system to uniquely identify both types of rules, making them traceable across documentation, code, and data models."

Michael sketches an example on the whiteboard, illustrating the separation between business and implementation rules. "This approach ensures clarity and traceability."

Michael places the pens back on the whiteboard.

Turning to Philomena, he shifts the discussion. "Yerodin highlighted a data quality issue with the 'ORDER_DATE' column in the order table. Some records contain invalid dates."

Philomena nods. "Yes, some records have impossible dates like February 29, 30, or 31. These errors make it difficult to analyze the data accurately, so we need to address them."

Michael continues, "Yerodin suggested that the correction for dates like February 30 depends on whether it's a leap year. In leap years, this date should be mapped to February 29; otherwise, it should be adjusted to March 1."

Philomena looks thoughtfully out the window, recalling similar data quality challenges during reporting cycles. After a brief pause, she turns back to Michael and Yerodin. "We deal with these kinds of issues regularly. We should establish a clear business rule to standardize how we handle them."

Michael nods. "Exactly. Could you draft an initial version outlining the approach?"

"I can certainly try," Philomena responds. "It would still be a draft, but it would provide a starting point."

"Let's take a short break," Yerodin suggests. "In the meantime, I'd like to help Philomena outline the rule. I have some ideas based on previous data-cleansing projects."

The team agrees, stretching their legs before tackling the issue with fresh energy after the break.

During the break, Philomena and Yerodin draft the following business rule:

Business Rule Number: BR-2025-1000345

- *Short Description: Cleansing date columns in 'Order'*
- *Related Implementation Rules:*
  → *IR-2025-3000754*
- *Creation Date: 2025-09-08*
- *Version: 1.0.0*
- *Effective From Date: 2025-09-08*
- *Effective Before Date: 9999-12-31*
- *Audit Date: 2025-09-08*
- *Responsible subject matter expert: Philomena Pavlovic*
- *Responsible engineer: Yerodin van Dusseldorp*
- *Data Set: Order*
- *Columns:*
  → *order date (ORDER_DATE)*
  → *order expected payment date (ORDER_EXPA_DATE)*
  → *order shipment schedule date (ORDER_SHSH_DATE)*
- *Rule:*

Is leap year?	*Wrong date:*	*New, corrected date:*	*Exception bit set?*
1	*20xx-02-30*	*20xx-02-29*	*Yes*
1	*20xx-02-31*	*20xx-03-01*	*Yes*
0	*20xx-02-29*	*20xx-02-28*	*Yes*
0	*20xx-02-30*	*20xx-03-01*	*Yes*
0	*20xx-02-31*	*20xx-03-01*	*Yes*

→ *All other dates do not need to be corrected.*
→ *The all dates, including corrected values, should be saved in a column with the date data type.*
→ *All of these an exception bitmap must be set*

After the break, Philomena and Yerodin present their draft business rule to the team.

Amal reviews it carefully. "I like it – it's clear and concise. But why assign an implementation rule number if it doesn't exist in our documentation system yet?"

"Good question," Yerodin replies. "The number is currently a placeholder for technical documentation. Philomena and I are considering creating a structured document format for implementation rules as well."

Philomena runs a hand through her hair. "This could significantly improve our data quality over time. Having a consistent approach for documenting these issues would save us countless hours of troubleshooting."

Curious about past methods, Yerodin asks Michael, "What documentation system did your previous project use? Michael furrows his brow. "I think it was just a wiki, accessible through a browser. The key thing was having a central location for all rules."

With no further questions from the team, Michael nods approvingly. "I like this approach. Let's document both business and implementation rules and refine the process as needed."

Xuefang, who has been quiet, raises her hand. "I'd suggest documenting implementation rules directly in the code, referencing the business rule number. That way, they stay close to where they're applied."

Michael considers this. "That makes sense. In Diego's and my project, we needed clear documentation to provide instructions to our outsourcing partner. Linking rules directly in the code would have made things much easier."

The team exchanges glances, recognizing the potential of merging their ideas. By aligning business and technical documentation, they can create a more efficient and sustainable system that benefits both developers and business users.

The team adds the approach for business rule documentation to the decision register, including that implementation rules don't require separate documentation: the code itself serves as the documentation.

Designing the RelCol data mart

After a short break, Amal and Zalika are back at the whiteboard, designing the physical data mart structures: a fact table for the order data and a historized dimension for the product data.

"The fact table will combine data from the sales Hub and its Satellite." Amal says. "For the product dimension, we'll collect the data from the product Hub and its Satellites."

"And we're building the dimension in the traditional Kimball style – as a Slowly Changing Dimension Type 2," she continues, tracing the structure and mappings from the integration layer on the whiteboard. "The fact table will be transactional."

Zalika nods. "And we link the order facts to the product dimension using a dimension identifier, an integer? There are quite a few approaches discussed in the literature."

"Using a dimension key," Amal confirms. "We'll use a surrogate key –a positive integer– not a natural business key or a hash value."

"For performance reasons?" Zalika asks, making a few notes.

"Yes. We've seen in past projects that non-integer join keys can significantly impact performance," Amal replies, leaning back in her chair. "Especially with the reporting tool Philomena uses."

"With other tools it might be different," she adds. "That's why it's important to talk to the experts for each tool and find the best way to deliver the data."

"Including the structures, like the schema of the outgoing interface?" Zalika asks.

"Exactly. We need to determine the ideal data type for the columns the tool uses to join data, and the schema is part of that," Amal says. "For the RelCol report, a dimensional model –a star schema– is ideal. But for other tools, it could be a JSON file or a key-value pair table."

They discuss this for a while until Amal suddenly stops. "We don't have a calendar dimension yet," she says, frowning. "We probably need that too."

She turns to Zalika. "Could you call Philomena and check? Also, ask whether a standard calendar is sufficient or if we need to include FastChangeCo's shifted fiscal year."

Zalika opens the video conferencing app and sends a message. Within seconds, Philomena starts a video call.

After a brief conversation, Zalika ends the call and turns to Amal. "Yes, we'll need both – the regular calendar and the fiscal year."

She takes a sip of her maté. "How exactly does the fiscal year work at FastChangeCo?"

"Our fiscal year starts four months after the calendar year," Amal explains. "Not sure why. But it means we'll need extra columns for fiscal months, quarters, and so on."

Zalika nods slowly. "And how have we handled that up to now?"

"As far as I know," Amal says, propping her chin on her hand, "people just added it manually in reports – over and over again." She shakes her head. "We should handle this once, properly, in the data solution.

Zalika's eyes light up. "We could treat the calendar data as reference data – a User Managed Landing Object, like we defined in our concept." She taps her pan against the table. "Maybe Diego has something ready that could save us time during the hackathon."

"Good thinking," Amal says, smiling. "That way, Philomena can update the fiscal calendar herself, and we don't need everything to be perfect right away."

Sure enough, Diego has a structured calendar dataset ready – complete with fiscal year columns. Amal and Zalika gratefully use it as the foundation for their calendar dimension.

The whole team works intently on their respective tasks. Pleased with the momentum, Michael decides not to interrupt and instead orders pizza and drinks for everyone.

When the food arrives, the smell of fresh pizza fills the room. Everyone looks up, smiling – ready for a well-deserved break.

Dimension identifiers

After lunch, Xuefang and Yerodin rejoin the group.

"We've created the derived data objects," Yerodin says, taking a seat at the conference table. "These store corrected dates whenever data validation detects an issue and the business rule determines a valid replacement."

Xuefang slides her notebook to the center of the table so everyone can see. "We built a data quality Satellite for this: 'Sat Order Data Quality.' As Yerodin mentioned, we only store corrected values there. If data exists in the satellite, it takes precedence over the original."

"That's cool!" Zalika says, leaning over to look at the notebook. "We can use a simple COALESCE in SQL to pull the corrected value into the fact table."

"And perfect timing," Amal adds. "We were just about to start on the product dimension. Want to help us with the fact logic?"

Yerodin and Xuefang jump in without hesitation.

"OK Zalika, let's start building the product dimension as a view," Amal says. "We've already got the calendar dimension in place." They turn to the screen and begin working side by side.

But it doesn't take long before they hit a snag. A one-to-one dimension key per business key isn't enough – they also need a unique id for each version of the context data. Amal runs her fingers thoughtfully through her hair.

"This complicates things," Zalika murmurs. "How can we create an id that is deterministic?"

Zalika takes a sip of her maté. "May we need to implement a PIT table. We can use it to add dimension keys to both the fact and dimension views. It would also be beneficial for performance, because we only have to implement these more complex joins once. I think doing this in the view would make it too slow."

They recall a concept they discussed earlier: first, perform a time-accurate join of the required data, then store the generated dimension key in a PIT table created specifically for this purpose.

Across the table, Xuefang looks up from the fact table view. "That would let us store the temporal join result together with the corresponding historized dimension key — and link directly to the right records in the Satellites."

"Good idea," Amal says, standing up. She grabs a marker and begins sketching the source objects, data flows, and PIT table on the whiteboard.

The others watch as her sketch grows into a mostly complete data model — data mappings, join logic, and all. It ends up looking strikingly similar to their earlier diagrams from the *getting the data out* concept.

"Let's prove our concept of a PIT. If performance is sufficient, we should integrate the logic directly in a view instead of using a PIT. The pattern is very similar anyway," Amal says, putting her pens back on the whiteboard. "We should always aim to virtualize the access layer."

Zalika takes detailed notes while Yerodin and Xuefang begin planning the next implementation steps.

Performance optimization

Yerodin pauses for a moment, thinking. "Looking at this now... shouldn't we add foreign keys to improve access? I worked on a project where some SELECT queries were painfully slow because there were no foreign keys. The database ended up generating poor execution plans."

Just then, Michael, passing by and overhearing the discussion, stops and joins the group. He sets his teacup down on the table and leans casually against the doorframe.

"Yerodin, we've already had a thorough discussion about foreign keys," Michael says in a friendly but firm tone. "We documented the decision —along with its pros and cons— in the decision register. Sure, we'll run into performance issues at times — but that's exactly why we defined helper objects in our concept: PITs and bridges."

Yerodin taps his forehead lightly. "Right, of course. I guess I'm a bit out of it today." He stretches and stands. "I'll grab us all some coffee. It's been a long day. Who wants what?"

Everyone places their order — except Zalika, who continues sipping her Maté, and Michael, who raises his green tea with a smile. Amal asks for a cappuccino, while Xuefang goes for a double espresso.

Before Yerodin heads out, the group agrees to build a PIT for the product dimension — primarily to accelerate temporal joins by precomputing them. Amal marks the decision on the whiteboard and circles it. The product Hub and Satellites are joined first to load the PIT.

While Yerodin is away, Michael takes the opportunity to share a story from one of his past projects. He settles into an empty chair.

"I once worked on a project where a report was generated daily from a virtual data mart," he begins. "Since performance wasn't critical, nobody minded that the queries took ten minutes. But for another dashboard —one that had over a thousand accesses per minute— the same setup couldn't keep up."

The others listen closely as Michael continues.

"We ended up using pre-aggregated tables with indexes to meet the performance demands. In one case, we even changed the technology in the access layer to handle the volume of user queries." He takes a sip of tea. "That's one way to solve it — with more computing power or different technology. But another solution was to keep all business logic out of the presentation layer views."

"Oh yes, I've seen that too," Amal says, nodding. She leans back in her chair.

"Exactly," Michael agrees. "From that point forward, no new presentation layer views contained business rules. And this was in a project where some views had hundreds of lines of logic. To bring that back to our concept: we handle those transformations upfront with PITs and bridges, reducing the logic in views to a minimum."

Xuefang taps her pen thoughtfully on the table. "But it might also be a sign of a modeling issue. For instance, if reference data is modeled as a CBC, you could end up with too many links."

Their conversation is briefly interrupted as Yerodin returns, carefully balancing a tray of coffee cups. Everyone reaches for their drinks with a word of thanks.

After a few more minutes of discussion, the team gets back to work, pushing toward the finish line of the data mart.

The following day —the final day of the third HackMatrix— they succeed. The data is ready for Philomena to test. All artifacts are checked into Git and properly documented.

Michael looks around at his team with visible pride. They've accomplished a lot in a short time. Hackathons, it's clear, have become a cornerstone of success for the DMCE team — a format they'll continue to embrace.

The new report

The team can now deliver a data mart for the RelCol report that is both content-accurate and enriched with applied business logic and data validation. Numerous processes that were initially perceived as complex have been implemented for the MVP, providing a foundation for the Data Engine. With this, the team feels confident they can ensure high data quality, sufficient performance, and stability in data delivery.

Philomena is more than satisfied with the progress. After just a few days, she's using only the new report. In all her test scenarios, its contents match those of the previous version.

"There's no longer any reason for me to keep using the existing report. I'd be happy to move the new version to production as it is," she tells Zalika during one of their check-ins.

"After that, we can completely replace the existing report," she continues her thought.

Philomena knows that shutting down the existing reporting is not part of the MVP scope. That can only happen once all the required features are in place and all users of the existing report are able to switch to the new one.

Zalika reflects, "Mhh, yes, but replacing the complete report isn't part of our scope. But wait, it might be possible to work towards that in the short term if we know what else is required to get there."

"Good point," Philomena nods. "Let's sit down and go over it together. We'll take the information model and check if it fully reflects the business requirements for the complete report — both for the work done and the remaining features."

Together, they carefully review the information model to ensure it supports the full replacement of the RelCol report. They analyze both the correctness and completeness of the requirements, identify overlaps, and define what still needs to be done.

They present the updated plan to Michael for input on the next steps.

"You've done a great job working this out," Michael says, taking a sip of his beloved Yabukita White Tea. "Let's go with this plan. We'll just need a few team adjustments since we're also continuing to evolve our Data Engine."

"As soon as everything's aligned," he continues, "we'll move forward with replacing the existing report — as you suggested."

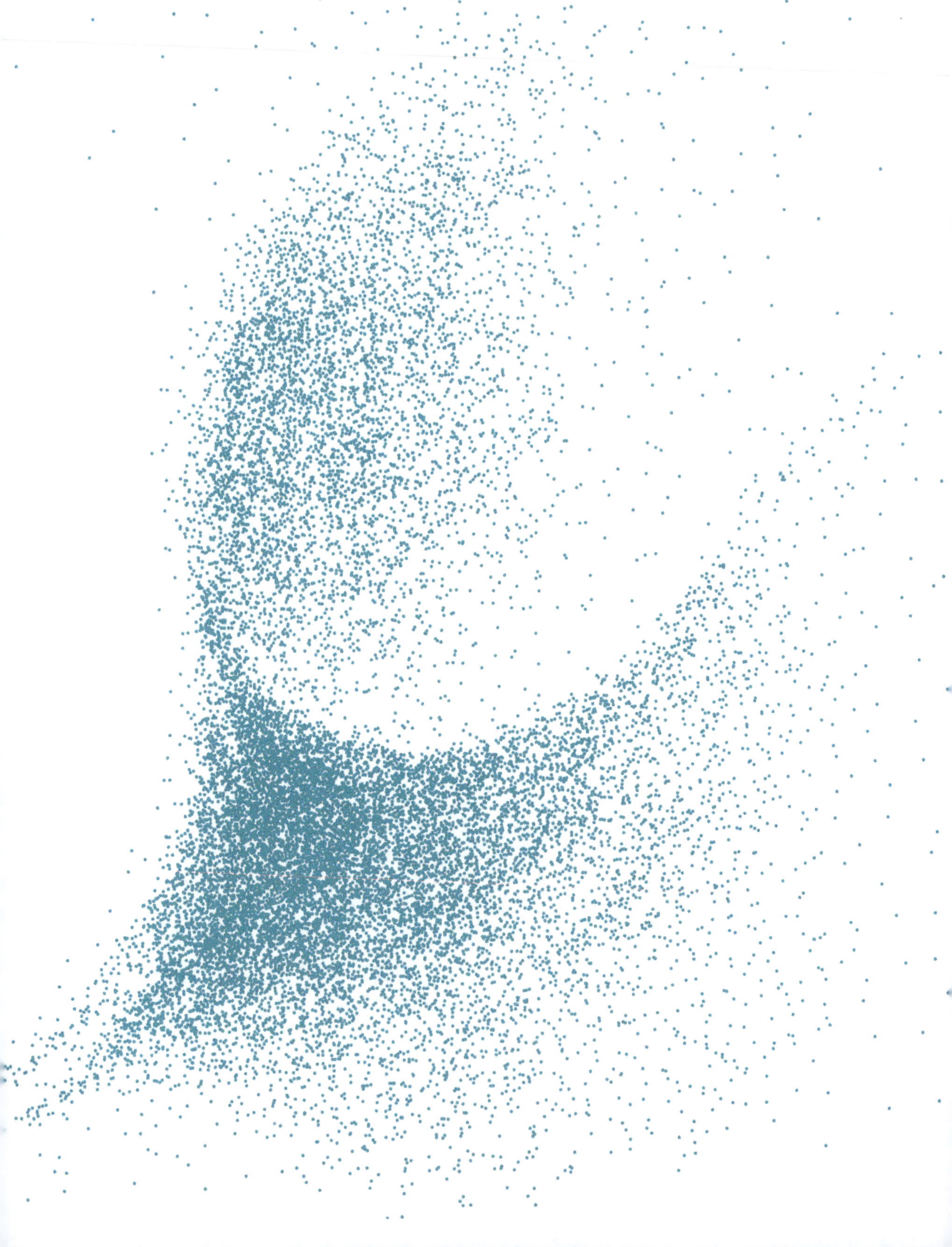

13 Completing the engine

With all architectural layers, areas, and frameworks now in place – from staging and integration to presentation – the final step is to connect the dots and ensure the entire solution runs as a cohesive, fully automated system. This chapter focuses on the final components, and the mindset needed to turn the architecture into a fully operational Data Engine.

The goal of Data Engine Thinking is a system that is fully automated, metadata-driven, and capable of running with minimal –or even no– human intervention. We'll recap how metadata enables even further automation, and what it takes to deliver a fully automated delivery platform.

It's time to start the engine!

Assembling the final pieces of the engine is as much a mindset as it is a technical implementation step. Already, the solution can trigger automated builds based on various events. For example, the monitoring framework might signal high demand in certain business areas or detect a large number of redundant records. The optimizer might determine the best key strategy (hash keys versus natural business keys), recommend table elimination based on usage patterns, or suggest changes to optimize compute and I/O costs.

Of course, manual development efforts promoted through development, testing, and production environments can also trigger deployments.

The true final piece of the puzzle is connecting the information model to the design metadata, enabling changes in the model to automatically generate updated physical structures and corresponding data logistics.

Connecting the information model

With the engine nearly complete, the final step is to fully connect the information model to the design metadata.

This creates a living bridge between business meaning and technical implementation – allowing changes in the information model to automatically flow through to physical structures.

It's the moment where architecture, automation, and agility converge: an adaptable data solution, ready to evolve with the organization's needs.

From this point forward, the solution is no longer static. It listens, learns, and responds to changes – whether those changes are triggered by business demands, technical optimizations, or development lifecycle events.

Objects in the information model are simply more data objects and –following the schema for data solution automation– these data objects can be connected to other data objects using data object mappings.

This is how connections between the operational systems, the information model, and the physical model can be established.

Conventions that govern the conversion of the information model object to the physical model object(s) can be encoded in this data object mapping metadata. For example, the metadata can define which standard columns should be added, when and how objects should be split (such as splitting Satellites), and what naming standards or optimization rules apply.

Other examples include automatically placing sensitive attributes into protected Satellites, defining business key strategies, setting historization types, and applying techniques for managing time-variance in relationships.

In this way, the physical model becomes a direct, automated outcome of the business-driven information model – all governed through structured metadata: data objects and data object mappings.

Changes in metadata are again captured through version control, providing the mechanism to trigger automated builds and deployments.

Connecting the models, step by step

Let's revisit the examples from earlier sections, representing a company that sells products to customers, but using different terms across some areas of the business for what is generally considered a 'branch.'

The information model aligns terms, removes ambiguity, and provides a communication tool between subject matter expertise and technical implementation.

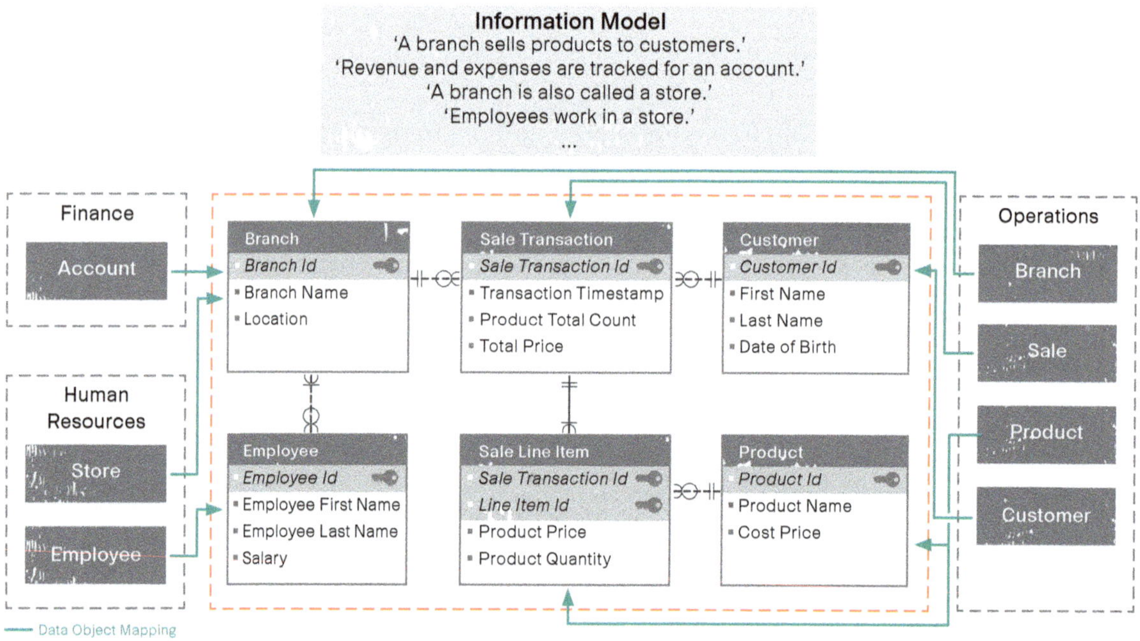

Objects from operational systems are connected in the design through data object mappings, showing how different systems –using different vocabularies– align to the information model. The information model itself is also described in metadata using data objects and their relationships, and can be derived from higher-level modeling approaches such as FCO-IM.

Supporting tooling can be configured, or connectors can be created, to interface these modeling details directly into the schema for data solution automation.

As a result, changes in the verbalizations (for example) can automatically update the design metadata schema.

Deriving the physical model

With the information model connected to operational systems and recorded in design metadata, enough detail is now available to generate the physical model.

This happens iteratively: optimizations are added into the information model to produce a physical representation that aligns with the intent and principles described in this book.

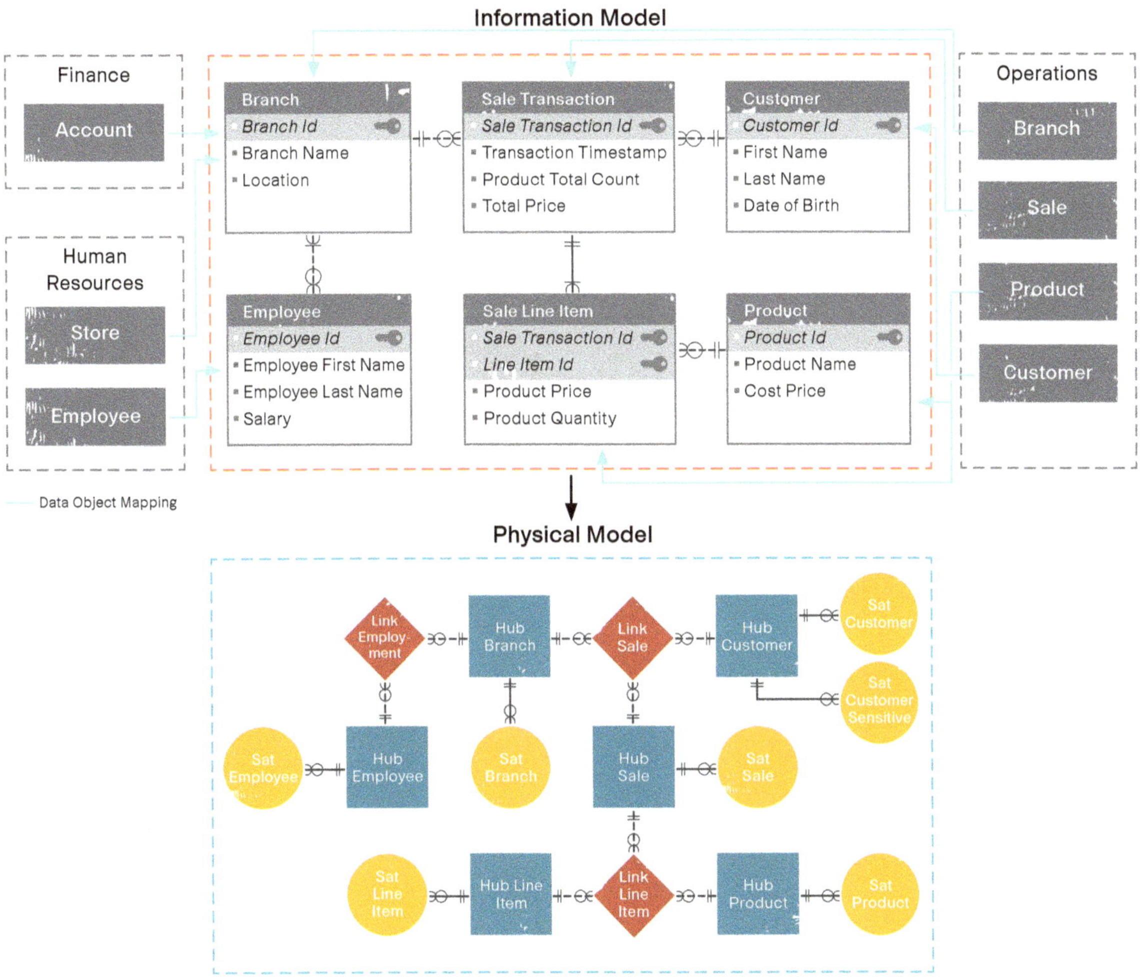

The physical model consists of data objects and their relationships, generated by code generation templates that leverage the information model's metadata.

Properties defined in the information model, such as tags for sensitive data, influence the physical structure. In this example, the customer context details are split into two Satellite objects — one dedicated to store sensitive data.

As part of this, the data object mappings that link the information model to the physical model are preserved – supporting future refactoring and providing lineage tracking over time:

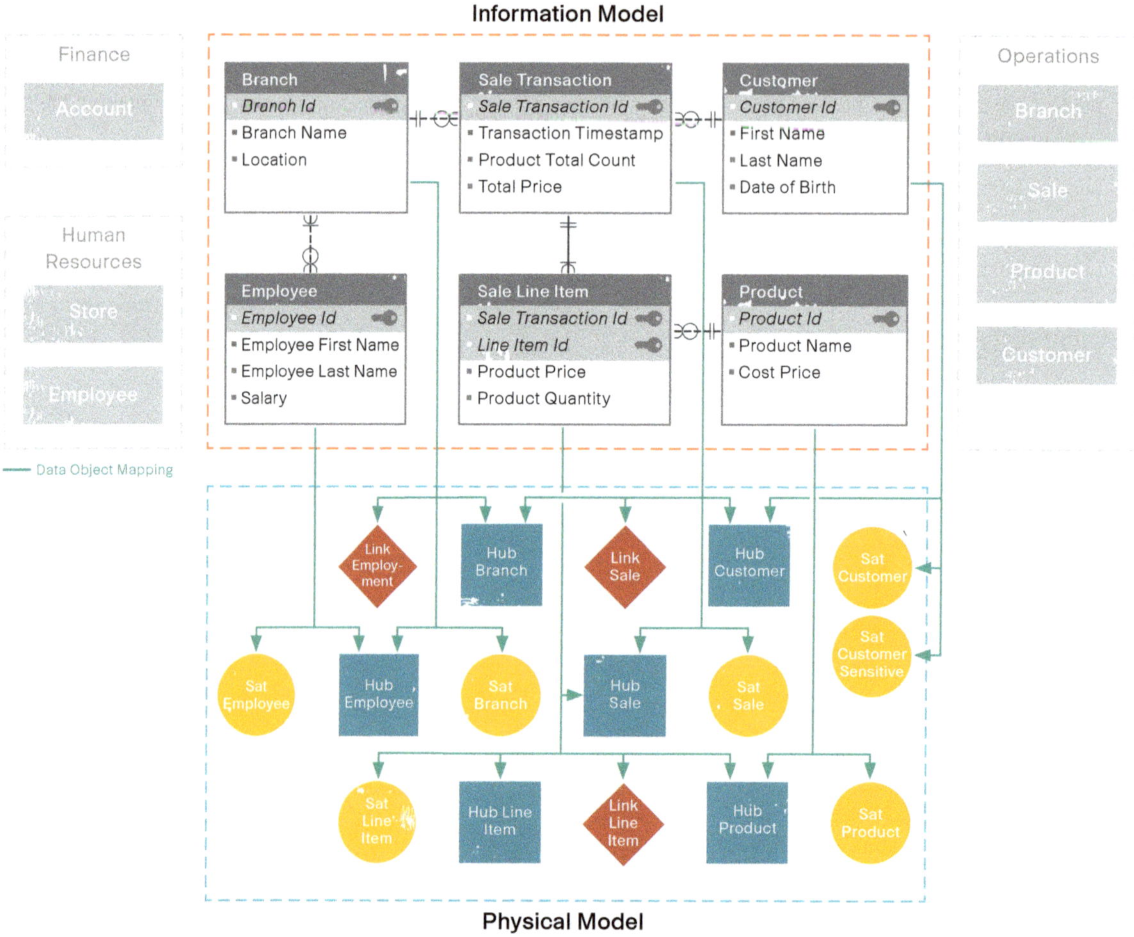

Mapping the physical model to operational data

Now that the relationships from operational systems to the information model are understood, and the physical model has been derived, the final set of data object mappings can be created.

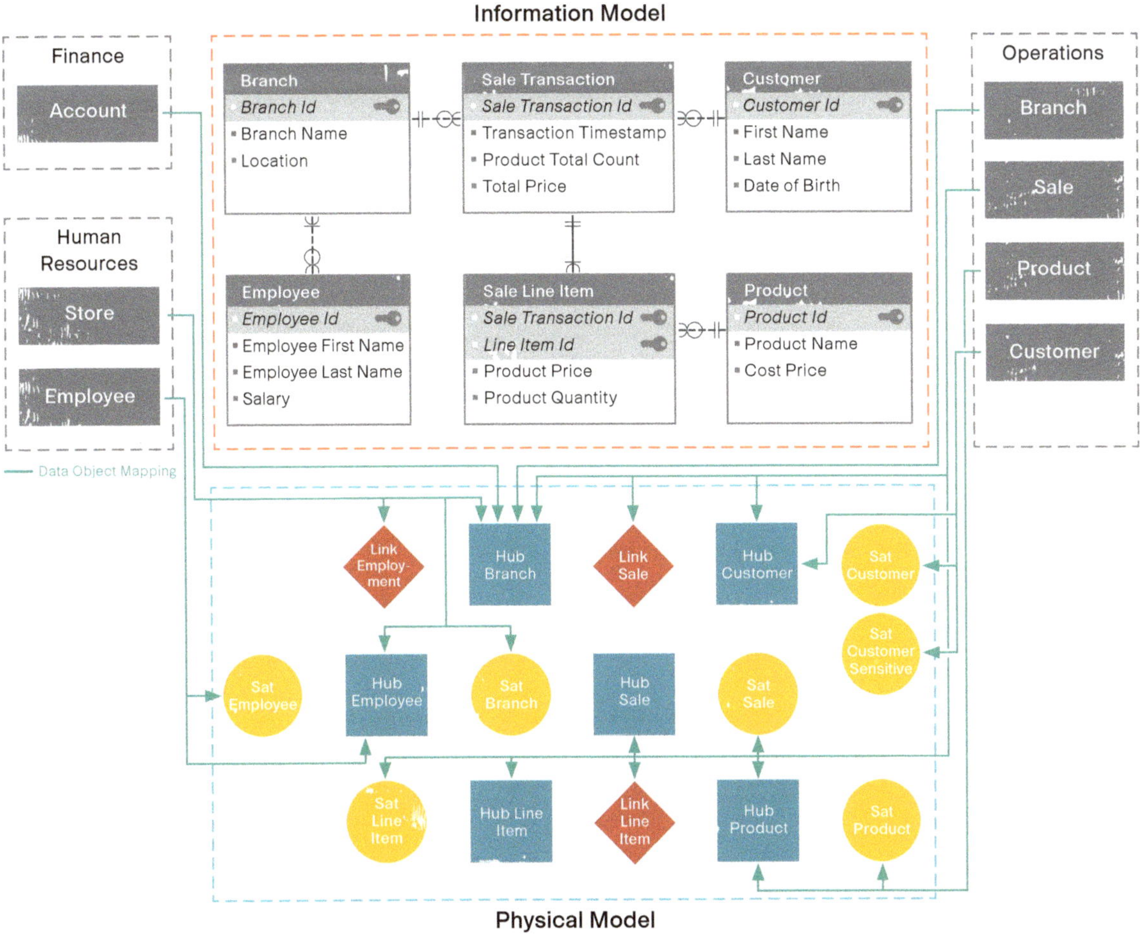

These mappings logically follow from the metadata already captured. They reuse the lineage between operational systems and the information model to connect the physical model directly to the data sources.

These —more technical— mappings are used to generate the data logistics processes, and also include the 'integrity mappings' needed to ensure consistent, independent, and parallel data processing.

You can start to see why automation becomes essential!

As noted earlier, all metadata is version-controlled. Every change can trigger automated builds, and outcomes can be reviewed with subject matter experts quickly — simplifying collaboration and speeding up every iteration of the process.

Beyond DevOps

The Data Engine is designed to shorten the delivery cycle, improve quality, and —most importantly— facilitate communication between all parties involved in data design, integration, and delivery. In short, it helps turn raw data into meaningful information.

In practice, much of this comes down to understanding and applying DevOps principles —which are primarily about aligning working processes— and adapting them to the data domain.

By following the DevOps practices outlined earlier, trust can be built into deployment steps, enabling greater automation and reducing the need for manual intervention. For example, this could mean automating the definition and approval of pull requests, with human approval only required for changes to the information model or when a build is ready for production deployment.

The goal is to gradually replace manual control with trust in automated processes, expanding the testing framework's coverage, and shifting the team's focus toward the information model itself.

Starting the engine

Everything is now ready to go. The metadata is connected to the information model and stored in the repository. Physical model conventions have been codified to facilitate the translation from the logical to the physical layer, and optimization directives are in place.

Changes to the information model trigger automated refactoring builds, awaiting approval for final production deployment. Once approved, changes are applied either by rebuilding specific parts of the solution or by performing an instant switch-over once the updated structures are complete. Meanwhile, the production environment is continuously monitored to detect and report any exceptions, both in terms of usage and to prevent regressions.

We hope —believe— that this approach will free up data specialists to work more closely with the wider organization – helping to implement robust data architecture and governance under a broader data management umbrella. Step by step, the organization moves closer to the utopian vision of a fully integrated data environment, where all systems, processes, and people seamlessly communicate.

The Resurrection
Foundations of the Future
Fast Change Co

14 FastChangeCo — The Resurrection

The Resurrection is drawing to a close.

After a short but highly focused phase, the team has completed the core concepts for the data engine. This time, instead of an offsite, they've gathered in a special workspace. Sylvia has booked a meeting room in a modern conference center—remarkably built around the preserved walls of an ancient building.

The symbolism is striking: sleek, contemporary architecture built atop millennia-old foundations. Flexible rooms that expand and contract automatically contrast with the exposed floor plans of rough stone—solid enough to last centuries, yet inflexible and brittle.

Just like the building in which they meet, the new data engine embodies the contrast between old and new system architectures. The existing data warehouses at FastChangeCo resemble the ancient, rigid walls: robust, yet rigid inflexible and ossified. In contrast, The Resurrection represents a modern, adaptive architecture — as flexible as the dynamic spaces that envelop the old foundations and reinterpret them. Where once there were isolated data silos, a dynamic ecosystem is now taking shape — one that transforms and contextualizes FastChangeCo's historical data assets seamlessly.

The session, which the team calls 'Foundations of the Future,' is defined by a short but focused effort to align their results with the overarching vision and strategy.

Sylvia, attending despite her limited availability as CFO, is captivated. The concepts and methods presented align well with the strategic goals. She is pleased to see that the team has delivered a cohesive, comprehensive framework. Only a few open items remain in the backlog.

She has full confidence in Michael and his team, and feels vindicated in her decision to place her trust in them from the very beginning.

Prototyping the engine

The day after the 'Fundamentals of the Future' meeting, the team is eager to push the engine forward through a hackathon. However, everyone is currently busy with the daily demands of maintaining the existing Data Warehouses – making a traditional hackathon seem unrealistic for the moment.

Michael hesitates before voicing an unconventional idea. His approach is hardly standard at FastChangeCo, but his enthusiasm wins out.

"I'd like to invite you all to my house by the lake – for the weekend. We'll barbecue, hang out, and work on the hackathon while we're there. We used to do this kind of thing all the time in the startup world. What do you say? I've got plenty of stories for around the campfire!"

The team's initial reaction is one of incredulous excitement.

"Did you just invite us to your house by the lake?" Yerodin asks, wide-eyed.

A flurry of reactions follows:

"At the boss's house for the weekend?"

"Stories and barbecues around the campfire!"

"What lake? Where is it?"

"Will there be a compensation?"

"Are there enough rooms and beds?"

Michael watches the buzz with amusement. "Well, what do you think? You will, of course, get the days back as annual leave. I'm confident there will be ample opportunity to take some time off once the MVP is fully up and running and the old report has been replaced."

"Definitely! This is the startup vibe! I'm in!" Zalika exclaims. After a bit more excited discussion, the entire team agrees.

The team spends a focused weekend barbecuing, sharing stories and, of course, prototyping together to develop new capabilities for the engine.

Amal demonstrates the result with pride: "Look – if I change something in the information model, everything is automatically refactored. And when I roll back to an earlier version, everything resets perfectly."

Zalika nods, visibly impressed. "It's amazing how far we've come. And to build this in just one weekend? That's proper startup. I love it."

"A great foundation for the next stage of our data engine," Yerodin says, clearly pleased. "Fantastic team effort."

"We really ought to have a party to celebrate our success – and ourselves," Zalika grins, turning to Michael. "My uncle told me that back in the New Economy days, startups were always throwing parties. I guess they had a lot to celebrate."

Michael chuckles. "Hmm … I think that's a great idea. Have I told you the story about…" And with that, the group gathers around as he launches into another one of his New Economy tales.

Then, suddenly, Michael turns to the team. "So who wants to organize the party?" Zalika and Xuefang immediately raise their hands. He is very happy to give them the task.

Driving home, Michael reflects on the weekend. What I'm most happy about is the success, he thinks to himself. And he's quietly glad he followed his instincts and proposed the weekend hackathon.

Team triumph

The days after the hackathon fly by and the party is just around the corner.

Xuefang and Zalika have transformed the office space into a festive venue. Garlands hang from the ceiling, and drinks are lined up on the tables. The DMCE team has every reason to celebrate: the successful completion of their first MVP, built on the new data solution.

Jeff, Terence, and Diego are also invited and, of course, they've come to join the celebration.

By the window, Yerodin is deep in conversation with Amal. "To be honest," he says, taking a sip of sparkling wine, "I had my doubts at times about whether we could really pull it off."

Amal laughs and gives him a friendly pat on the shoulder. "Never underestimate this team. We can move mountains when we stick together. And we've really grown — both as individuals and as a team."

Not far away, Jeff and Sylvia are chatting.

"It was a challenge," Jeff says, glancing at his beer glass, "and I don't just mean your running meetings. But the teamwork really paid off."

Sylvia nods. "Every single person contributed. We can all be proud of that."

Meanwhile, Terence approaches Michael with a small package of green tea. "For the successful MVP delivery! And guess what? We managed to integrate SPEEDY into the IT landscape. Just in case you ever need SPEEDY."

Michael smiles, clearly pleased, and shakes Terence's hand. "Congratulations!" They clink glasses and toast to both successes.

Across the room, Zalika —maté in hand— and Xuefang take a moment to look around with satisfaction.

"Zalika, we did a great job with the party. Everyone's celebrating and having fun." Xuefang raises her soda and nods toward Philomena, who —as always— is drinking a Repsi. She pulls Zalika into a quick hug.

"It's so great to be welcomed into the team like this," Xuefang says. "It really means a lot to me." They clink their drinks — maté calebasse against soda can.

Laughter and conversation fill the space, wrapped in an atmosphere of success, connection, and well-earned celebration.

Looking forward

The day after the party, Michael sits back and reflects on the journey his team has taken. From those first hesitant steps to the completion of a fully functioning MVP – a path filled with challenges, surprises, and unexpected moments.

The need for a data initiative – that's where it all started. A mandate from FastChangeCo's leadership that, at first, felt like a mountain to climb. A complex challenge – exactly the kind that management had in mind when they hired him.

As an outsider, I brought new ways of thinking into FastChangeCo's BI world. The thought brings a slight smile to his face. How often had the team chuckled at his fresh, unconventional perspectives? And yet, it was precisely those stories and out-of-the-box ideas that helped drive the project's success.

The new data solution —the Data Engine— hasn't just changed the information landscape. It's begun to reshape the company's culture as well. At least within the DMCE department, Michael is certain of that.

He brews a new pot of tea and returns to his thoughts.

The central question he asks himself: have we achieved our vision and strategy?

Definitely, Michael thinks. No more DIN/A3 reports!
A quiet sense of satisfaction flows through him. we've done it:

The Resurrection – the revival of meaningful data!

And yet: what's next?

The age-old debate returns: Build or buy?

FastChangeCo had drawn up extensive requirements, created long wish lists, explored the market – only to conclude that no existing tool fully met their needs. Even Jeff and Terence, enthusiastic as ever about SPEEDY, had to admit there was no perfect fit.

A decision is slowly taking shape: perhaps the answer lies in creating their own tool – something open-source, something they can shape and evolve themselves. After the last hackathon, Michael is more convinced than ever that their existing framework should be developed further into an open-source product.

We are on the right track, we have the patterns and the evidence. We should share it and collaborate. Perhaps I should write a book about it.

The journey continues. The vision is still alive.

Automation. Flexibility. Determinism. Agnosticism. Idempotence.

Continuous development.

These are the keys to success.

"As it turns out, it's super easy," someone once said in a meeting.

Michael smiles.

15
Data Engine Thinking — taking the next step

Ready to put Data Engine Thinking into action?

You've explored the principles — now it's time to bring them to life in your organization. Whether you're just getting started or ready to scale, we're here to help you go further, faster.

As your journey continues, we invite you to connect on https://dataenginethinking.com.

Our website has the latest information about the services we provide, including:

→ Our training schedule
→ Our coaching opportunities, including individual and team-based coaching
→ Talent mentoring
→ Assessments and reviews
→ Consultancy

Let's unlock the full potential of your data together.

Footnotes

1 https://en.wikipedia.org/wiki/Title_case
2 https://www.ansi.org/
3 Larissa T. Moss — Extreme Scoping
4 There are many forms of hybrid modeling techniques, aimed at the physical model design, of which Data Vault is the leading approach at the time of writing
5 A relational database management system (RDBMS), further referred to as 'database'
6 Atomicity, Isolation, Consistency and Durability (ACID). In computer science, ACID is a set of properties of database transactions intended to guarantee data validity despite errors, power failures, and other mishaps. In the context of databases, a sequence of database operations that satisfies the ACID properties is called a transaction — Wikipedia
7 This term is a generic version of 'DataOps,' 'DevOps,' 'MLOps' etc.
8 GOOF — the Giant Operational Organization Functions (another fictitious company)
9 https://en.wikipedia.org/wiki/Data_vault_modeling
10 MOOSE - Mail Order Online Systems Enterprise
11 The Matrix: Watch it if you haven't. Men in Black: Think of the locker scene
12 https://en.wikipedia.org/wiki/JSON
13 The Eisenhower Method: https://en.wikipedia.org/wiki/Time_management#The_Eisenhower_Method
14 Comma Separated Values
15 General Data Protection Regulation — https://gdpr.eu/what-is-gdpr/
16 Atomicity, Consistency, Isolation and Durability, principles that guarantee reliable processing of database transactions
17 As a side-note on using larger data types: the way technical platforms manage these can sometimes vary. In many database platforms there is no penalty on using larger variable data types such as VARCHAR or NVARCHAR. The unused space will not be used. In most cases, the additional bytes required to store variable data types will be worth the flexibility. However, this is not consistent across all technology platforms. If unused space is still stored it may be better to find a balance between disk space and I/O cost and reliability in the back room processing
18 When describing integration layer entities at a conceptual level, we refer to Hans Hultgren's Ensemble Logical Model (ELM) overview
19 A foreign key is a set of attributes in a table that refers to the primary key of another table — Wikipedia
20 We follow Tom Johnston's terminology as described in his book 'Bitemporal Data — Theory and Practice'
21 Ralph Kimball et al, as written in the Data Warehouse Lifecycle Toolkit
22 See for more details 'The Data Warehouse Toolkit 3rd edition, Kimball, Ross
23 Kimball et al
24 Kimball et al
25 Timestamp is a defined temporal term for date and time which may be only date but also can be more atomic until seconds. A time-stamp is a sequence of characters or encoded information identifying when a certain event occurred, usually giving date and time of day, sometimes accurate to a small fraction of a second. [https://en.wikipedia.org/wiki/Timestamp (2021-06-14)] In the book context timestamp is as a term independent from any technical implementation of a domain/datatype like datetime2(7) in MS SQLServer
26 Keep It Short & Simple, or Keep It Simple Stupid — depending on your preference
27 https://www.inf.ethz.ch/personal/wirth/Miscellaneous/IEEE-Annals.pdf
28 The use of DNA to explain design metadata has also been explained as Documentation, Navigation and Administration by Larissa Moss in 'Extreme Scoping.' This is a very good way to look at this, and we wholly subscribe to this view
29 https://en.wikipedia.org/wiki/Git
30 Although technology changes, various data logistics tooling can work this way. For example Azure Data Factory, Informatica, and AbInitio
31 At the time of writing, many freely available libraries are available such as for example Mustache/Handlebars, Scriban, Jinja, Pebble, and many more
32 Using Handlebars notation: https://handlebarsjs.com
33 Examples are Biml from Varigence but also Pebble, Scribn and DBT
34 Further documentation is available at https://git-scm.com/
35 In an inspiring presentation called 'Inventing on Principle', the US computer scientist Bret Victor (http://worrydream.com/) discusses how ideas come into being and how sad it is when these do not manifest in reality, or are missed entirely, due to limitations in our (technical) environment or when things are simply too hard
36 https://en.wikipedia.org/wiki/Endianness
37 Some implementations prefer to retain the Audit Trail Id in the LDA to collect statistics on logistic processes, and the number of records processed.
38 https://en.wikipedia.org/wiki/Unicode#UTF
39 https://learn.microsoft.com/en-us/sql/sql-server/maximum-capacity-specifications-for-sql-server?

view=sql-server-ver16

40 CRC — Cyclic redundancy check. See https://en.wikipedia.org/wiki/Cyclic_redundancy_check and https://crccalc.com/

41 http://tdan.com/data-vault-series-1-data-vault-overview/5054

42 Unified decomposition is a term coined by Hans Hultgren and is often used in the ELM data modeling context

43 The ISBN of Data Engine Thinking (print softcover, 1st edition)

44 At the time of writing, there are two major opinions on 'how to do Data Vault', and how Link-Satellites are modeled is an important consideration here. Our views on this are documented in the 'Time-variance in Links' section

45 Johnston & Weis (2010). Managing time in relational databases: how to design, update and query temporal data. Morgan Kaufmann

46 The Allen Relationships:
https://www.ics.uci.edu/~alspaugh/cls/shr/allen.html
Wikipedia: https://en.wikipedia.org/wiki/Allen's_interval_algebra

47 The Allen Relationships:
https://www.ics.uci.edu/~alspaugh/cls/shr/allen.html
Tom Johnston: Bitemporal data 2014, p. 113

48 Data Definition Language (DDL), the syntax to define database objects such as tables, indices, views etc.

49 The complete procedure is described in: — Fact Oriented Modeling with FCO-IM, 2015, Jan Pieter Zwart, Marco Engelbart, Stijn Hoppenbrouwers — Just the Facts, 2024, Marco Wobben All sentences and the current information model can be found on our website

50 See our website for the MVP example: https://dtng.link/mvp-example

51 https://www.kimballgroup.com/

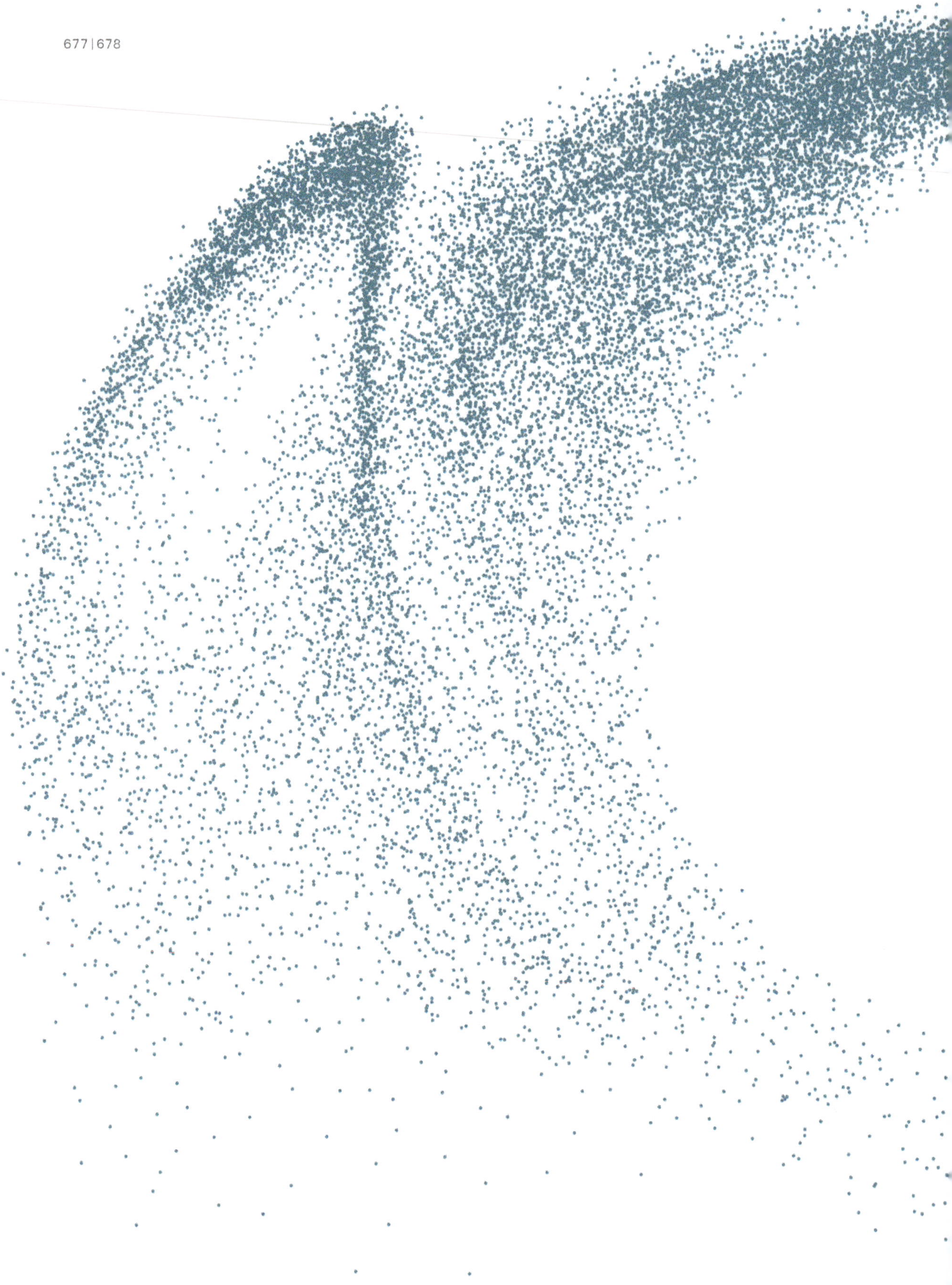

About the Authors

Roelant Vos

Roelant is a globally recognized data expert, speaker, and writer with over 25 years of experience in data management. As a consultant, trainer, developer, software vendor, and corporate decision-maker, he has experienced data management from many angles. His passion for automation and model-driven engineering has been a constant throughout his career.

After beginning his career developing BI solutions, he quickly became fascinated by pushing the boundaries of automation, especially in the data integration space. Having led large-scale data projects worldwide, he remains a firm believer that harnessing patterns, automation, and code generation is the key to making data solutions more efficient, manageable, and, most importantly, adaptable.

Dirk Lerner

Dirk is an experienced independent consultant and managing director of TEDAMOH — the Data Modeling Hub. He is considered a global expert on BI & data architectures, modeling, and is highly regarded for his work on temporal data — including groundbreaking examples on his blog and in his trainings that highlight the many aspects of managing time in data, and how to solve them.

With a 25-year career centered on data modeling, temporal data, and automation, Dirk has consistently applied these disciplines to create flexible, lean, and extendable architectures.

As a pioneer for Data Vault and FCO-IM in Germany Dirk has written various publications, and is a highly acclaimed international speaker at conferences.

www.ingramcontent.com/pod-product-compliance
Lightning Source LLC
Chambersburg PA
CBHW041749220926
51847CB00014B/150
* 9 7 8 3 9 8 2 7 1 8 0 0 2 *